TREASURY

OF

JOB

VOLUME ONE

TREASURY

OF

JOB

VOLUME ONE

WILLIAM HENRY GREEN

JOSEPH CARYL

JAY GREEN

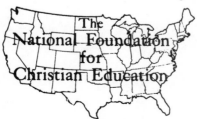

The
National Foundation
for
Christian Education

MARSHALLTON
DELAWARE 19808

PREFACE

The work of Joseph Caryl on this book, entitled, *An Exposition with Practical Observations upon the Book of Job* (printed in London, Volume I in 1647, completed in Volume XII in 1666) has been the most famous exposition of this precious, ever-current Book since it was first printed. It could well be famous merely from the size of it, having comprised no less than 8700 pages in its twelve volumes. But it is in fact most famous for its content, being indeed the most practical and useful of all the commentaries ever penned on this Book. All commentators who have become in any way famous for their work on Job will have to acknowledge their indebtedness to Joseph Caryl. Some have used it profitably, others have abused it shamefully. Some have plagiarized it, shamelessly receiving the credit that is due to Mr. Caryl. But none have offered to reprint it. Admittedly the cost is high, in both money and time needed for such a project. But now you will see it is worth all any man chould choose to invest in the sayings of Mr. Caryl—the master has a masterpiece here which James I. Packer says is of the utmost beauty and satisfaction, one that is gigantic in thought, scope and size — yet Mr. Caryl never wanders off of his canvas (from the article in the new *Encyclopedia of Christianity*, Volume II).

THE CONTENTS AND FORMAT OF THIS EDITION

The reader of these volumes will be greatly assisted if he will attend to the following details regarding the makeup of the work:

1. The treasury section will appear in the third volume only. Patterned after Spurgeon's famous and helpful *Treasury of David* (also published by us), the most useful and profound comments from over forty excellent expositors of this Book have been selected.

2. The first section consists of a sharp, accurate and revealing overview of the scenes and characters of this Book of the Bible, by William Henry Green. This first appeared in the nineteenth century under the title, *The Argument of the Book of Job*. Do not miss this!

3. The exposition is intended to be a practical one, not a critical series of scholarly essays (in which one usually finds more of the thought of the scholar than of the thought of God, as He spoke to us in *The Book of Job*). It is planned to bring satisfaction and spiritual health to those who study it. It certainly reflects the fact that Mr. Caryl was a scholar of the highest calibre. It is doubtful that anyone ever learned more about this Book than he! He also had very few peers in the knowledge of Holy Scripture as a whole. But his design is clearly to create a body of divinity which will benefit the children of God in all the ways God uses such books. Anyone too scholarly for Mr. Caryl's book may suffer great loss.

4. This edition is basically an abridgment of Mr. Caryl's 8700-page exposition. It will contain approximately 1,000,000 words, of which Mr. Caryl's contribution will be approximately 700,000 words. This, we calculate, is some 50% of what is written in the original. The aim and final execution of this abridgment is discussed in the Editor's Preface.

5. All the Scriptures in this edition are italicised, for emphasis and for easy reference.

6. For easy assimilation of the Biblical message, the text quoted in this edition is that of *King James II*, rather than the original Authorized Version. Not only does the Scripture under discussion transfer more readily because it is written in the English of our day, but we believe the translation of Job in the original *King James Version* was not nearly so accurate as it is in this new edition (much of which was influenced by Mr. Caryl's exposition).

Publication plans call for Volume I in 1970, Volume II in 1971 and Volume III in 1972. If the Lord Jesus Christ should not come before it is completed, we trust and pray that He will use this work to reveal far more of Himself to all who read it.

EDITOR'S PREFACE

"Whatsoever you do, do all to the glory of God"—In accomplishing this work, this view has been held strongly, that reverence to God requires all to be done in a way which will give Him the utmost glory. It is Him that we adore, honor and seek to justify. And only uttermost exactitude in gleaning the meaning from His words will give success here. That is our reason for choosing to spend eight years in an effort to bring you this extraordinary exposition of Joseph Caryl. Mr. Caryl preached on this book for 24 years — it is not too much to ask that we spend eight in presenting the best of his work to this generation and to an unpredictable number of generations which may yet come after us.

At first it was the plan to merely abridge the Elizabethan English edition of this work. However, the overriding plan to convey the deepest and most rewarding knowledge of the words of God kept interfering with the original plan. It is true that some would be willing to read this exposition in that old form of English, perhaps even willing to look up words they did not know. It is also true that some will condemn us for putting what they consider to be presumptuous hands on the work of this great author. But eventually it was decided that the work must be in the language of today if it was to get the wide readership that it deserved. Finally, however, it became my conviction that this work would be most helpful in the long run if there were a general restatement of the great truths God revealed to Mr. Caryl, putting them into today's scene more fully, into today's thought patterns at least enough to bring serious consideration of the message Mr. Caryl was conveying.

To implement this final plan, much closer study of the man's message, and of the meaning of the words in the *Book of Job*, became necessary. A study spanning five years was given to this. Then that which follows was conceived and executed for your benefit.

SOME THINGS IN THIS EDITION WHICH REQUIRE YOUR ATTENTION

Because we have rewritten virtually all of Mr. Caryl's sentences, it will be necessary to give you fair warning. Whatever you find good and spiritually beneficial in this book may without doubt be credited to God's gracious Spirit, who revealed so much to Mr. Caryl of a helpful and God-honoring nature. But whatever you may find to be dross, to be of lesser value, that you may be sure comes from the mind of Jay Green. It is regrettable, perhaps, that you must get Jay Green's version of Joseph Caryl. Perhaps it will stimulate someone who strenuously objects to this edition to recreate completely the original edition of Caryl. Until then, however, I can offer you only my own poor efforts, believing that it was God's will that I present this work to you in its present form.

May I point out to you that it was possible for me to have presented this as a new work, as the child of my own brain. There being less than fifty sets of this great work around, it is doubtful that more than a handful would have discerned my original source of material. Doing such a thing has much in the way of precedent, for I could name several works that draw so heavily upon the original writings of the puritan fathers that they could easily be reissued as the work of those great expositors — yet they bear the name of another author. But to me it does not seem right to parade Mr. Caryl's excellencies as my own. It is true I have obliterated the distinction between what is his, and what is mine, for what I consider to be a most important reason, that the reader may absorb the message of God in this Book without stopping to bow to this or that man on the way. But lest any think that this is a means of gaining reputation, I repeat, give all the glory to God for revealing so much of His mind and heart to one Joseph Caryl, a truly great expositor who deserves the utmost of your praise and appreciation. And pray that this poor servant has not interfered with the transfer of God's truths by the methods and words he has used in bringing back this incomparable work of Joseph Caryl, another slave of Jesus Christ, our God and Savior.

May God tenderize your heart and expand your mind as you now study in these volumes in order to grow in grace and in the knowledge of our Lord Jesus Christ.

JAY GREEN, Editor

JOB'S TRIUMPH OVER SATAN

JOB'S TRIUMPH OVER SATAN

CHAPTER I

"There was a man in the land of Uz named Job, and that man was perfect and upright"

The book of Job is one of the most remarkable in the Old Testament. Apart from its inspiration, and considered simply as a literary production, it bears the stamp of uncommon genius. It is occupied with a profound and difficult theme, the mystery of divine providence in the sufferings of good men. This is not treated in the abstract, in simple prose or in a plain didactic method. But an actual case is set vividly before the reader, in which the difficulty appears in its most aggravated form. By an extraordinary accumulation of disasters a man of unexampled piety is suddenly cast down from his prosperity, and reduced to the most pitiable and distressed condition. And then there is delineated in the most masterly manner the impression made on others by the spectacle of these calamities, as well as the inward conflict stirred in the sufferer himself, his bewilderment and sore distress, his alternations of despair and hope, his piteous entreaties for a sympathy which is denied him and his irritation under the unjust suspicions and censures which are cast upon him, his wild and almost passionate complaints against the Providence which crushes him, intermingled with expressions of strong confidence in God which he cannot abandon. This wild tumult in his soul is graphically depicted in its successive stages, until we are brought to the final solution of the whole, and the vindication at once of the Providence of God and of His suffering servant. And all this is set forth in the loftiest style of poetry, abounding in fine imagery and containing passages of deep pathos as well as of rare sublimity and power; while the whole presentation and treatment of the case is managed with consummate skill.

The book of Job well deserves the high encomiums which have been bestowed upon it as a product of the poetic art. And while we humbly receive its inspired lessons, there is no reason why we should be insensible to its other attractions. The Bible is not, indeed, amenable to the laws of criticism, nor to be judged of by ordinary standards of taste. When God speaks to us, we must reverently listen and obey, however homely the medium through which He communicates His will. And yet it adds to the variety of this holy book, and to its adaptation to the needs of all classes of men, and to all the cravings of the human soul, that it addresses itself likewise to the refined taste and the cultivated sense. Like the inexhaustible supplies of Nature in its manifold diversity, the volume of divine revelation gives us not only the massive granite and the ponderous metal, but the sparkling and polished gems of thought; not only the staple articles of food, but the rarer and more palatable delicacies. So that the charms and the embellishments of poetic genius, which invest other subjects with such attractions, are lent likewise to the sacred oracles in the sweet lyrics of David, the impassioned fire of Isaiah, and the marvellous beauty of the book of Job.

The principal personage of this book, and the one about whom the interest chiefly centers, is Job himself, a venerable and patriarchal character, whose fortunes are detailed to us at an important crisis of his life. Some have thought that he was not a real, historical person, and that the narrative of the book is not one of events which actually took place, but that it is rather a fiction or a parable like that of the Prodigal Son or the good Samaritan, and he is designed to represent not some one person to whom all this happened precisely as is here detailed, but a whole class, such as is often met with in real life, or similar character and similar experiences, and the truth of which lies in its general conformity to what repeatedly takes place, and in the correctness of the lessons conveyed. This, however, cannot have been the case. It is related not as a parable, but as a history, instructive throughout, as all the Bible histories are, but still an actual, veritable occurrence. And Job is spoken of in other parts of Scripture as a real person, and in connection with other real persons like Noah and Daniel, and the events of his life are referred to in a manner which implies that they had actually occurred. We can have no doubt, therefore, that, with all the poetic embellishment of the narrative, Job did actually live, and the history took place substantially as it is here related.

That which is in this chapter proposed for consideration in the life of Job is his character and condition when he is first introduced to our notice, his great excellence and piety and his happy, prosperous state, as these are sketched briefly, but strongly, in the opening verses of the first chapter, and again in chap. xxix., where, after his gloomy reverses, Job pathetically recalls the joys of former years.

We commonly think of Job as a sufferer; and the lessons that we most associate with him are those which concern affliction. His great sorrows form indeed the grand crisis of his life; and it is to their exhibition, together with the attendant principles of the divine administration, that this book is chiefly devoted. But the very point of the whole lies in their exceptional character, which requires an explanation. If this were not so, there would be no mystery to be elucidated. The enigma is in the contrast between what Job had to endure and what is in fact the ordinary experience up to the time when he was overtaken by these extraordinary calamities. "Godliness is profitable unto all things, having the promise of the life to come." This was fulfilled in the life of Job up to the time of his heavy trial, which had been one continued course of prosperity and happiness. It seemed as though nothing were left him to desire. As he himself expresses if: "In the days when God preserved me, when his candle shined upon my head,... I washed my steps with butter, and the rock poured me out rivers of oil;... my root was spread out by waters, and the dew lay all night upon my branch." The freshness of a well watered tree, the richness of butter and oil, the brilliancy of God's own light, are the figures which set forth his joyful and prosperous abundance. And, as the tempter sneeringly said, Job had not feared God for nought. God has made an hedge about him and about his house and about all that he had on every side. He had blessed the work of his hands, and his substance was increased in the land.

While, therefore, we go very properly to Job's dark hours to learn the uses of affliction, and all the salutory lessons which accompany it, it behooves us likewise to remember the lesson of all those years which had preceded; vix., that God's blessing attends the righteous. *"He that will love life, and see good days, let him refrain his tongue from evil, and his lips that they speak no guile: let him eschew evil, and do good: let him seek peace, and ensue it. For the eyes of the Lord are righteous, and his ears are open unto their prayers; but the face of the Lord is against them that do evil." (I Pet. iii. 10-12.)*

Let us attend, then, to the piety and to the happy estate of Job, with the view of taking note how these are combined in the ordinary providence of God. It is not said that there are no exceptions. There are such exceptions. There are grave and weighty reasons why there should be. Job himself was a notable exception at one epoch in his life. Nevertheless the ordinary rule remains; and in the number and the mystery of the exceptions we must not forget that it is the rule, a rule verified for the most part even in the general tenor of their lives who constitute the most signal exceptions, a rule which found its evident exemplification in the greater portion of the life of Job himself. Goodness and happiness go hand in hand in the ordinary experiences of this world.

Let us review, in the first instance, the simple description here given of the piety of Job. He is evidently portrayed as a model man. God Himself says of him, "There is none like him in the earth." And in the delineation of Job's piety, notice, first, two negative particulars, two omissions in the narrative, which are highly significant, especially as found in a book belonging to the Old Testament.

The first is that no account is made of ancestry or of connection with the covenant people of God. There is no mention of Job's parentage, no hint of his relationship to Abraham. He was plainly not one of his descendants. Now if what secures the favor of God be a pious ancestry, or a connection with the outward visible Church, it is unaccountable that in the case of Job, held up as a model before all ages and generations, and of whom God gives such a testimony as he does of no other, that these things are not so much as one alluded to, even for the sake of explaining their absence or omission. Evidently it is not outward associations or connections, though of the most sacred kind, that constitute the evidence and pledge of God's favor, but personal character and life. In every nation and in every communion, he that feareth God and worketh righteousness is accepted of Him. The important question is not, Are you a Jew or a Gentile? Are you a member of this or that particular branch of God's visible Church? Nor even, Are you a member of any outward body of professing Christians whatever? but, Have you personally that character which is acceptable to God, and are you leading a life that is pleasing in His sight?

A second omission in the account of Job's piety similarly significant is that it is not described as consisting of ceremonial observances. No mention is made of any round of ritual service, no fasts or purifications or tithes, no rigouous periods of abstinence or self-mortification or ascetic observance, no priestly intervention or sacerdotal absolution, no holy order or men through whom grace was dispensed as its sole appointed channel. The only religious rite referred to is the simple sacrificial worship of patriarchal times, maintained in faith of the sacrifice and the atonement that was to come, and which was afterwards accomplished by the Son of God on Calvary. Job was priest in his own house; his own hands offered the sacrifice, though devoid of the grace of orders, and without priestly consecration, and it was accepted. Job's religion was one of the heart and of the life, not of ritualistic service.

And it is the more striking because this is a model of piety belonging to the Old Testament. It is another illustration of the pains that were taken, even under that restricted and legal economy, to fortify the people against that spirit of bigotry and Phariseeism into which they were so prone to fall, and did fall, and which has in fact been the bane of vital religion in every age. Here was an outstanding and shining example. Job was an eminent saint of God, though his line of descent was not counted from Abraham, and though he did not practise the multiplied rites of the Mosaic ceremonial. Whatever advantages there may be in an outward connection with the people of God or the visible Church, and whatever benefit may arise from outward attendance upon the services of religion,—and certainly neither of these are to be decried or undervalued, when rightly understood and put in their proper place,—that piety which has the approbation of God is something different from them and independent of them.

The general description of Job's piety is given briefly and simply in four particulars: he was perfect and upright, and one that feared God, and eschewed evil. But this statement, brief as it is, is very comprehensive. "He was perfect and upright." Uprightness denotes, in the first place, honesty, straightforwardness, sincerity. There was no double dealing or duplicity, no hypocritical pretence with Job, either towards God or man. He was sincere in his professions and honest in his practice. Uprightness, moreover, means conformity to the standard of right, and this both inwardly and outwardly. We read both of the upright in heart and of the man that is upright in his way. He was a man of integrity, therefore, both in spirit and in life,—a man attentive to his obligations both to God and man, and who punctually discharged them. And, with all, he was perfect,—perfect and upright, perfect in his uprightness. Perfect, not of course in that sense in which, according to the uniform teaching of Scripture, and the universal experience of men, perfection is unattainable in this life. Not that he was absolutely faultless, for there is no man that liveth and sinneth not. Job never claims spotless innocence. He himself says, "I have sinned; what shall I do unto Thee, O Thou Preserver of men?" "How should man be just with God? If he will contend with Him, he cannot answer Him one of a thousand." "If I say, I am perfect, it shall also prove me perverse." But he was perfect in the sense of completeness. His uprightness was not of that partial, limited kind, which restricts itself to certain classes of duties, while neglecting others; or confines itself to special times and occasions, while at others it is laid aside; which is very zealous about some of the commandments, to the disregard of others, tithing it may be the mint, anise, and cummin with scrupulous exactness, while neglecting the weightier matters of the law, or manifesting great devotion on Sabbath days or periods of special religious observance, while the duties of other days are overlooked. A man who can be devout in Church and dishonest in his business, penitently ask God's forgiveness and yet be unforgiving himself, who can profess great love to the Saviour and yet be heartless to Christ's needy poor, this was not the style of Job's piety. He was perfect as well as upright. There was a completeness in his piety, which compassed the whole round of obligation. He studied conformity to the rule of right in all things, at all times, under all circumstances.

And the spring of this perfectness and uprightness, or this complete integrity, was that he feared God. He set the will of God before him as his rule, the glory of God as his end, the approbation of God as his highest reward. In this pious fear of God he walked all the day long. This was his grand motive, overpowering every thing else. This closed his ear against the siren song of temptation. This shut his eyes to every gilded lure of sin. The one thought, "Thou God seest me," was his safeguard and his stimulus. This impelled him to prompt and ready obedience to every divine command. This made him steadfast in his uprightness, and led to his perfectness and completeness in it.

It also led to the sedulous avoidance of its opposite, and thus completed the perfect square by the fourth side, which is the finishing stroke to this description of a well-regulated piety. He "eschewed evil:" he carefully shunned all sin, kept aloof from every thing that was wrong in heart, speech, and behavior. Some eminently good and holy men have great blemishes; they apparently lay out all their strength on the positive side of religion, and neglect its negative; they endeavor strenuously to do right, and forget to strive against doing wrong. And thus they leave the periphery of the Christian character unfinished: the last side, which completes the whole, and gives it symmetry, is never added. A great gap is left unfilled. There was no such lamentable deficiency in the case of Job. "He was perfect and upright, and one that feared God, and eschewed evil."

Besides this general description of Job's pious integrity, two special traits are incidentally mentioned in different parts of the book, by which he was particularly characterized, and which belonged to him in separate walks of life. Not as though these were by any means the only ways in which his piety manifested itself. But they were marked and prominent, and they may serve as illustrations of his habitual piety and consistency in two several spheres; viz., home and abroad, in the intimacies of the domestic circle and in his intercourse with others less nearly related to him. In regard to the former, mention is made of a fact which serves to show Job's pious regard for the spiritual welfare of his children. It was the sacred habit of the family to throw the safeguards of religion around every period of mutual entertainment and social enjoyment. Whenever his children gathered, as they did regularly, at each other's houses on festive occasions, cementing and displaying their fond fraternal affection, it was Job's invariable custom to summon all together afterwards, and sanctify them, and offer burnt offerings according to the number of them all. For Job said, "It may be that my sons have sinned, and cursed God in their hearts." "Cursed God" is too strong an expression for the meaning intended here. It is not blasphemy, or defiance of God, or malignant hatred of His service that he feared. The word is properly a formula of blessing, used in taking leave of friends. It is commonly translated "bless" and is the same that is employed where it is said, *"And Laban kissed his sons and his daughters_ and blessed them_ and departed." (Gen. 31:55) "So Joshua blessed them_ and sent them away" (Josh 22:6);* that is, he took leave of them, he said farewell to them, he bid them adieu. Job was afraid that his sons might have said farewell to God in their hearts; that they might have taken leave of Him; that in their thoughtless hilarity, they might have forgotten God and His presence, and acted as though they were out of His sight. He recalls them to solemn thought and to their sins by the offering of sacrifices according to the number of them all.

Job's piety manifested itself at home in thoughtful care for his children's spiritual good. But it was not limited to his own household. He sought the good of all. And he was especially forward in the relief of the necessitous and the protection of the injured. "When the ear heard me," he says, "then it blessed me; and when the eye saw me, it gave witness to me: because I delivered the loor that cried, and the fatherless, and him that had none to help him. The blessing of him that was ready to perish came upon me: and I caused the widow's heart to sing for joy... I was eyes to the blind, and feet was I to the lame. I was a father to the poor... And I brake the jaws of the wicked, and plucked the spoil out of his teeth."

We are further told that Job's outward lot was as happy as his character was exemplary. God's blessing was in the most marked manner bestowed upon his faithful servant, bringing him the most distinguished prosperity. He was happy in his family, having seven sons and three daughters, who were all settled near each other, and near their paternal home, and lived in the most delightful harmony and fraternal intercourse. He had large possessions: his wealth in flocks and herds is recited, and it is added that he was the greatest of all the men of the East. And he was treated with the utmost deference and respect by all classes, and held in the highest esteem. He says in his retrospect of these happy days: "When I went out to the gate through the city, when I prepared my seat in the street, the young men saw me, and hid themselves: and the aged arose, and stood up. The princes refrained talking, and laid their hand on their mouth... I chose out their way, and sat chief, and dwelt as a king in the army." There seemed to be nothing to be denied in the way of worldly prosperity or earthly joy, beyond what he possessed.

Our thoughts are turned so frequently to the discipline of affliction and the spiritual profit which arises out of it, that we are in some danger, perhaps, of losing sight of the rule in the prominence which is given to the exception. And yet religion has its temporal as well as its eternal rewards. The blessing of God attends the good, even in this present life and in regard to their worldly estate. There are promises of long life and prosperity, as far as it shall serve for God's glory, and their own good, to all those that keep His commandments. "Blessed is every one that feareth the Lord; that walketh in His ways. For thou shalt eat the labor of thine hands: happy shalt thou be, and it shall be well with thee." "Evil doers shall be cut off: but those that wait upon the Lord, they shall inherit the earth." "Verily there is a reward for the righteous: verily he is a God that judgeth in the earth."

It is true that worldly possessions bring a snare. And our Saviour said that it is a hard thing for them that have riches to enter into the kingdom of God. And an apostle adds,

Not many wise men after the flesh, not many mighty, not many noble, are called. So likewise another apostle: Hath not God chosen the poor of this world, rich in faith, and heirs of the kingdom? There is a peril, no doubt, in having a large share of this world's good. The danger is of cleaving to the world unduly, and of setting the affections upon earthly comforts and earthly pleasures,—of being content with an earthly portion and ceasing to strive after or long for one that is heavenly. If the heart is given to the world, and worldly objects, be they what they may, become our end and aim, then we are worldly-minded and are not the servants of God. If any man love the world, the love of the Father is not in him. Ye cannot serve God and Mammon. They that will be rich, *i.e.*, that seek riches as their chief good, and make this their main, controlling object of pursuit, fall into temptation and a snare, and into many foolish and hurtful lusts, which drown men in destruction and perdition. The love of money is a root of all evil. Our Saviour's rule is, seek first the kingdom of God and His righteousness,—first in order of time, first in importance, first in the urgency of desire and in the strenuousness of endeavor,—and all other things shall be added unto you.

If this true order is preserved, then other things may be safely added, and no harm will result. The damage arises from the prevailing disportion to invert this order, to seek, the world first, and then as much of heaven as can be had without too great a sacrifice of worldly interests. Now upon the basis both of Scriptural teaching and of the common experience of men, it may confidently be affirmed that the true way to a happy life, even in this world, is found in the service of God. Our Saviour announced the universal law when he said, "Whosoever will save his life, shall lose it: and whosoever will lose his life for my sake, shall find it." This is a seeming paradox, but it is perpetually verified. He who aims at worldly good fails to attain it. He either is unable to acquire that form of worldly good which he seeks, or, if he gets possession of it, he does not find it what he expected: it proves to be empty and unsubstantial, and does not yield the satisfaction which he anticipated and desired. But he who abandons this world as his object, and aims at God's glory instead, gains that and this world too. It is as in the case of Solomon, who prayed not for riches, nor for long life, but for wisdom. God gave him that he asked: He gave him wisdom, and added long life and riches besides. Selfishness defeats itself: in grasping with eagerness after earthly good, it snatches a painted bubble, which bursts in its hands. Our truest welfare and highest happiness, even if we limit our view to the present life, will be most effectually secured by faithfully serving God and doing His will. It has passed into a proverb that honesty is the best policy. In a like sense and with similar limitations it is equally true that piety is the best policy. He who refuses to defraud his neighbor, not from any principle of integrity, but simply because he will thus in the end enhance his gains, does not deserve the praise of real honesty. And he who adopts the guise of piety to further worldly ends forfeits alike the approbation of God and the esteem of men. Nevertheless goodness has its temporal rewards. Length of days is in Wisdom's right hand, and in her left riches and honor.

That this is so in the general, and in its application to communities and masses of men, is obvious upon its simple statement.

Religion fosters those qualities and habits which tend to worldly prosperity and success and to the promotion of the general good. It encourages industry, thrift, and frugality, and thus lends its aid to accumulation, while on the other hand it represses all those forms of vicious indulgence which lead to profligacy, neglect of proper occupation, and wasteful dissipation. A large part of the extreme poverty and suffering that is found in the world is either directly or indirectly the consequence of criminal or vicious conduct, its natural and inevitable retribution affecting the vicious themselves or those connected with them. And it is not the evils of degraded poverty alone that arise in this way, but miseries that affect wealthier classes, desolating families in high life, withering every joy, and blighting all their possessions. God has set the brand of his disapprobation upon sin by these moral sequences, which he has fixed in the world and by which a penalty has been fastened to transgression. These consequences can only be averted by drying up the sources of the evil; and this religion does.

Another fertile cause of suffering and sorrow in the world, which the prevalence of true religion would obliterate, is the injustice and unkindness of man to his fellow-man. The strong oppress the weak, and they who cannot defend themselves are mercilessly trodden in the dust. Each man becomes the antagonist of his fellow, with rival interests, profiting by his downfall; instead of his brother, co-operating with him, mutually helpful and serviceable to each other. Hence the struggle of injurious competition, none caring in his greed of self-advancement that his neighbor is driven to the wall. Hence those fends of mutually dependent classes; labor and capital seeking each its own advantage, and forcing hard terms upon the other, or coming to open rupture to the injury of both. Hence discords, tumults, wars, with all the sorrows they occasion and the miseries they entail. How would the world blossom like an Eden, if religion held full sway, and its golden rule were enshrined in every heart and acted out in every life!

And religion is the only salt which can preserve from national corruption and decay. The history of the past utters its warning voice, showing how the downfall of nations swiftly follows on the heels of national prosperity, and the seeds of dissolution are involved in the very materials of their greatness and splendor. Accumulation multiplies the opportunity and the facilities of indulgence, and public virtue gives way, amid the glittering prizes held out for its allurement. Recent events have suggested gloomy thoughts to many reflecting minds amongst ourselves. Can virtue and integrity be maintained in our rulers and among our people, amidst the manifold temptations which are now assailing them, and before which many once trusted and confided in have sadly fallen? If honesty and integrity fail us in the centres of authority, if the enactment and administration of law can be tampered with by corrupting influences, and the public conscience becomes itself debauched by the corruption that is coming in like a flood, what must every sane mind anticipate as the inevitable result? In this growing—we fear it must be said rapid—decay of virtue and integrity in legislative halls, in some quarters even in courts of justice, and in leading financial circles, the most portentous evils are opening before us. Can they be arrested? The answer to this question depends upon another. Have we vital Christianity enough among us to check the progress of moral decay? Is there that fear of God and love of truth and right among our countrymen, which will insist on honesty and integrity in the administration of public affairs and in the conduct of moneyed corporations and commercial enterprises. The religion of the gospel is the stronghold of our national safety and of the perpetuity of our institutions. The more thoroughly this gospel shall leaven our people, the stronger we shall be, the firmer will be the pillars of our national prosperity, and the more abundant and widely diffused will be the blessings enjoyed by all our population.

But the temporal blessedness springing from true religion has its application to individuals as well as to communities and masses. Communities are made up of individuals, and what tends to promote the welfare of the whole must in the same ratio be conducive to the good of its constituent members. Upon this there is no need to dwell; but there are other considerations, which should likewise be taken into the account.

Happiness is not so dependent on external circumstances as many suppose. It is far more powerfully affected by men's own character and disposition. It lies not so much in the abundance of outward sources of enjoyment as in the capacity to enjoy. It is not graduated by wealth, or social position, or success in worldly schemes. They who look at the bare outside of things are often grievously mistaken in their judgments. A splendid mansion may be the home of misery and care. And he who reclines on the most luxurious couch may be a stranger to repose. When we speak of the blessing of God accompanying fidelity to His service, we do not mean that the pious man will always be rich, or that he will always attain distinction, or that he will be invariably successful in his worldly schemes. But we say that while in ordinary cases he will not be damaged, but rather furthered, even in outward prosperity, by his religion, his real substantial happiness will be vastly promoted. He will the better enjoy what he does possess, he will draw a livelier and purer satisfaction from it, than if he had not the love of God in his heart and the fear of God before his eyes. If his religion has simply taught him this one lesson, in whatsoever state he is, therewith to be content, it has done much to establish and confirm his earthly happiness. For "godliness with contentment is great gain." It frees him from the dominion of evil passions, envy, jealousy, hatred, and the like, which are a fruitful source of discontent. It relieves him from the galling slavery of those in haste to be rich, with its attendant cares, anxieties, and consuming toil. It leads him to see in his earthly lot the appointment of his Heavenly Father, and thus cures him of all restless endeavors to overleap bounds he cannot pass. It gives him the consciousness of being at peace with his Maker and with all the world. He has the joy which flow from doing right; and every outgoing of unselfish love, every exercise of pure affection, every act of generous kindness to the necessitous to which his religion prompts him, is a new source of pleasure. And all this is additional to the delight of communion with God, the acting of his regenerated faculties, the enjoyment which is inseperably linked with the Christian's duties and privileges and his glorious hopes,—in fine, all that is summed up in that insignificant phrase, "the joy of the Holy Ghost," a joy which is oftentimes unspeakable and full of glory.

If any man on earth should be a happy man, it is he who is truly religious. Looking barely at this present life, and at the sources of gratification which are opened before us here, the good man is most truly blessed. Religion does not foster gloom it is perennial spring of cheerfulness and joy. It does not abridge the enjoyments of life: it multiplies and heightens them. And there is no step that any person can take, more fraught with blessing to himself in this world as well as in the next, than that which he makes choice of God as his portion and his friend, and pledges himself to be His ever-faithful servant.

CHAPTER II

Again there was a day when the sons of God came to present themselves before the Lord, and Satan came also among them to present himself before the Lord. —Job ii. I.

SATAN

We are now introduced to a scene in the invisible world of a most impressive and surprising character. The singular spectacle is presented of the Prince of Darkness appearing in the train of the Most High. He comes not hypocritically in the guise of an angel of light, but in his proper character, with the rest of God's servants, to offer his homage, to receive his commissions, to render his stated account of work done and service performed. This astonishing and unusual representation has led some to entertain the opinion that the Satan of the book of Job is a different being from the Satan of the later Scriptures. Else how could he have his place among the sons of God? How could he come with them at stated times to present himself before the Lord? How could this be said of the enemy of God and the adversary of all goodness? A deeper view of this passage, however, reveals the harmony between the character in which Satan appears here and that which he maintains throughout the rest of the Word of God. He is not a mere spy, traversing the earth and intent upon ferreting out all that he can discover. He is the old spirit of malice and wickedness, aiming to pervert men from the right ways of the Lord, and to destroy all goodness as far as it is in his power. And there is a profound meaning in his appearing here among the sons of God before the Lord. It is designed to express his subordination and subjection to divine control. He cannot act untrammelled and at his own discretion. He is not at liberty to pursue his mischievous designs to whatever extent he may choose. There is a superior restraint to which he is obliged to bow, a superior will that sets limits to his rage, and allows him even within these limits to act out his evil nature only for the sake of some divine end, which he is made to be instrumental in achieving. It is evil in the person of its arch-representative and head, subject to good and constrained to be its minister. It is Satan actually exhibited in the attitude of a servant of God, and made subservient to the discipline and training of his people.

Satan is the enemy of goodness and the archangel, and with the malice and subtlety of a fiend, he is intent on our destruction, and hesitates at nothing by which it can be accomplished. He pursues his mischievous designs with sleepless vigilance and untiring assiduity. Invisible to human eyes, he has all the advantage of secrecy, and taking his victims at unawares. He has his tools and associates in vast numbers of spirits of wickedness, who acknowledge him as their head, and are animated with a rage and cunning similar to his own; and in wicked men who are led captive by him at his will; and even in friendly hands from whom no danger is suspected, and who little think themselves whose commission they are unwittingly fulfilling. He has a control over external nature and over the bodies of men, which we have no means of estimating, but which can only be conjectured from such facts as the disasters he brought upon Job, and the maladies he caused in the time of our Lord. And, more than all, he has direct access to our souls: he can touch in some incomprehensible way the springs of feeling and conduct, and exert an influence over us, which it may well make us shudder to think of.

All this is terrible. It is a dreadful thing to have a constant consciousness of danger, and especially of unknown danger; to apprehend that an implacable and unscrupulous foe is seeking your life, and that he has woven his plot so stealthily that you know not when you are safe, nor whom to trust. But the assassin can only kill the body. Satan is a murderer of souls.

It is an awful thing to be exposed to his treacherous solicitations. To come under his power is perdition. It is to be alienated from God and to incur the sentence of everlasting death. To yield to him in ever so slight a degree is to contract untold guilt, to bring ourselves under the displeasure of God, and put our eternal all in jeopardy. And yet we have no might to stand up against him. Surely, if there is any petition that we offer in all sincerity and with agonizing fervency, that which our blessed Lord has taught us should be so offered, "Lead us not into temptation, but deliver us from the evil one."

And yet these temptations cannot be escaped. It may be said, in a sense which is in no danger of being misunderstood, that by an ordinance of God they belong to this present state. Jesus was tempted of the devil; and the disciple is not above his Lord. The members must be made like their head. Through much tribulation we must enter into the kingdom of God. Fightings and fears beset the passage to the crown. The peril is awful, but success is glorious. "Blessed is the man that endureth temptation: for when he is tried, he shall receive the crown of life."

Before entering strictly upon the development of the teachings of this book, which is the chief design of this little treatise, we may be here permitted to devote a chapter to a preliminary inquiry of no small practical moment. What is the design of God in subjecting his people to this terrible ordeal? What are the disciplinary ends of the temptations of Satan, and how may we best attain them?

And to this we answer: —

I. They should drive us to take refuge in God. One grand aim of the earthly discipline of God's people, in all its parts, is to bring them to a closer acquaintance with Him and dependence upon Him. They are made to learn more and more of His fulness, and to draw from Him larger and richer supplies. All the disclosures of His grace and of His unbounded resources made in His Word are designed to bring them to Himself as to an overflowing fountain, that they may drink the water of life freely. But in order that they may be stimulated to avail themselves of these benefits, and not perish in sight of abundance, an inward appetite is necessary, a hungering and thirsting after God, a craving for those blessings which He has to bestow. And the more imperative and urgent the sense of need which is awakened, the louder will be the cry for help, and the more importunate the application for it.

Here precisely the temptations of the Evil One have their place in God's great scheme of training. Every instinct of self-preservation in a gracious soul should lead it to cry mightily unto God for His delivering aid. Every temptation is attended with an imminence of peril, which should startle us out of our security, and lead us to fly for safety to Him who alone can save. He who has any just sense of his won weakness and frailty, and of the frightful evil of sin, must be incessant in his entreaties that he may be upheld in steadfastness by an almighty arm, and guarded from the assaults of one who succeeded even in enticing angels to their fall, and prevailed over our first parents in all the vigor of their early integrity, and to whom we shall prove an easy prey, unless One, stronger than the strong man armed, interferes for our rescue.

A proper sense of our peril will not only tend to beget the general conviction than in God alone is our help, but will, in addition, lead us to fasten upon those particular assurances and grounds of encouragement which are afforded by Him for just such a crisis as this. The knowledge of the vast power of our spiritual adversary will lead us to take refuge in the omnipotence of God, to place a new value upon this glorious attribute, to avail ourselves of it as a basis of repose and confidence, to make experience in our daily consciousness of what it is to have a God of such infinite resources to supply our pressing need. The almighty power of God is then no longer an abstraction to us, —an intellectual conviction, —but a present practical necessity; not a perfection which we distantly contemplate, but one by which we live and without which we perish. The dire necessity which drives us to the fount of life is, in its results, an incalculable blessing. And the temptation of Satan, which terrifies the soul out of all self-dependence and creature-dependence, and compels it to find refuge in an almighty Saviour, has accomplished a gracious end.

And as with this, so with other perfections of the ever-blessed God, and with the precious promises of His Word, and with the merciful provisions of the covenant of grace, and with the priceless salvation of our Lord Jesus Christ. The tempted soul learns afresh how to prize them, and embrace them, and cling to them, and rest upon them, and live by them. To what can he have recourse for protection against the subtlety and craft of Satan but the infinite wisdom and knowledge of God? How his dread of the rage of Satan enhances to him the value of the love of God! His unseen approaches exalt in our esteem God's gracious omnipresence. His access to our minds and hearts can only be baffled or rendered abortive by the indwelling and illumination of the Holy Ghost. What new delight is awakened by the thought of God's providential control, when we remember that He who has set the seas their bound restrains likewise the malice of Satan, suffers him not to overstep the limits which our Father's love has fixed, and will not allow His people to be tempted above that they are able to bear, or without providing a way of escape for them that they be not overcome thereby! And what completeness is imparted to Christ's redemption, when we see that He triumphed over Satan, bruised the serpent in the dust, and shall bruise him under His people's feet! With what new eagerness will these dreaded temptations compel us to look to the cross, which is the symbol and pledge of victory over the destroyer!

2. The temptations of Satan answer the important purpose of training the believer in the duties and exercises of the Christian warfare. The sacred historian informs us that there was a providential design in leaving a remnant of the Canaanites in the land of Israel, viz., to teach succeeding generations of the people war. There is no teacher like necessity, and no training in the military art comparable to that enforced by actual hostilities.

What emphasis there is in that direction of the apostle, "Put on the whole armor of God, that ye may be able to stand against the wiles of the devil"! It is not a time of peace and security, but of deadly conflict. It will not do to remain defenceless, and no armor that is defective or incomplete will answer in this terrible exigency. The weapons of our adversary will be swift to find it, if there be one weak or unguarded spot from head to foot. And what a school for practice in all the measures of offence and defence is this contest for life or death with such a foe! It is said of a great master in the art of war, that he learned his skill in strategy entirely from the powerful and able leaders with whom he was obliged to cope. The Christian, in his protracted and stubborn contest with the wiliest of all antagonists, cannot fail to make distinguished progress in spiritual generalship, as well as to develop the qualities of a good soldier of Jesus Christ.

Nothing is better adapted to call forth a manly vigor than the necessity of strenuous exertion. The struggles one must make, the endeavors one must put forth to resist temptation and to overcome the evil one, react to the greatest advantage upon Christian character. The circumspection necessary to escape his insidious designs, the vigilance of one who is obliged to be ever on his guard, the fixed determination of one who has set his face like a flint for the celestial city, and who has resolved that he will be true to his God and his Saviour at all hazards, tend to elevate rapidly the standard of the inner life.

And these temptations exhibit grace as well as develop it. It can never be shown either to himself or to others what a man is until he is tried. The constancy of Job and the power of his faith could never have been made to appear so conspicuous, if it had not been for the severity of the test to which he was subjected. This lay not only in the accumulated sorrows by which he was so suddenly overwhelmed, but chiefly in the suggestions of the tempter, who was mercilessly goading him on to give up his confidence in God, and to re-nounce His service. It was these sore temptations, based on the mystery of dispensations which he could not unravel, and backed by a logic which he knew not how to confute. which tortured him almost to despair, and wrung from him those bitter wailings with which the book abounds. And yet in spite of all, out of the midst of the depths we hear him utter in the very face of the tempter his unabated trust in God, "I know that my Redeemer liveth."

3. The temptations of Satan, if properly met, may be made a means of intensifying our hatred of sin. He who has barely escaped the fangs of venomous reptile will ever after enter-tain a deeper abhorrence of it. Sin is in every temptation offered to our choice. But it need only be stripped of its disguises to present it in its repulsive and odious features, and make us shrink with loathing from the contact. The very act of repelling it will cultivate a spir-itual sensitiveness which can less and less endure its hateful presence.

But, in the fourth place, observe that temptation may be an aid to self-knowledge. The germs of evil often lie undeveloped in the heart, and the man himself never suspects their existence until under the influence of some sudden or strong temptation they are brought to light. It is like the searching tests of the assayer exposing the presence of alloy in what might easily have passed for sterling metal. Such mortification enters into the Christian's daily experience, humiliating discoveries of the strength of latent corruption and subdued propensities to evil, appetites which he supposed he had under subjection resuming the mastery in some fatal moment, the feebleness of his resolutions, insincerity in motives, imperfection in his best services. If these discoveries serve to humble him in the dust, and bring him in penitent brokenness of heart to sue for pardoning mercy, and lead him to be more watchful against his besetting sins, the ends of divine grace in suffering him to be overtaken by this temptation will be answered.

It was thus with Job. God himself testified that there was none like him in the earth, a perfect and an upright man, that feared God, and eschewed evil. And yet there was a leaven of corruption in his imperfectly sanctified nature, of which he was not aware, until by the terrible thrusts of Satan it was exposed. Underneath his really sincere and fervent piety there was a taint of self-righteousness, which made him smart as he did under the reproaches of his friends, and which, in the awful darkness of that mysterious dispensation in which he was enshrouded, led him even to the length of justifying himself rather than God. Brought at last to himself, and dismayed at the thought of what he had allowed him-self to utter, he says, "I abhor myself, and repent in dust and ashes." The design of God in this severe but salutary discipline was accomplished. Job had been led to know himself better than he did before, and he was humbled by this knowledge. The evil which before lurked within him unsuspected was detected and renounced.

5. The temptations of Satan afford the occasion to grace to develop itself in forms which otherwise it could not assume. Thus all that is implied in patient continuance in well-doing could have no place under other circumstances than those in which we are. The blessed inhabitants of that upper sphere, where sin and sorrow never enter, know not what it is to drag for ever after them this body of corruption, to be checked and hampered in all their aspirations by a law of sin in their members to maintain their steadfastness

amid surrounding foes, to preserve the flame of piety bright and clear under the deadening influences of this ungodly world, to keep a cheerful hope in the midst of discouragement and ill success, and doubts and fears; or to continue to trust unwaveringly in the Lord, when deprived of the light of His countenance. Now, however God may be glorified and His law honored by the unhesitating obedience rendered by the countless ranks of those who do not understand from their own experience what temptation means, it would appear as though there was something yet more signal and illustrious in that willing obedience which costs many a weary effort and many a painful struggle, —in that loyalty to Jesus which is maintained not amidst the sympathy and applause of those who likewise adore His name, but in the face of derision, obloquy, and persecution; in that unfaltering submission, which can say not merely in the sunlight of the throne, but in the howlings of the pitiless temptest, "Thy will be done." The post of danger is the post of honor, if it be well and bravely defended. Is it no honor, then, which the Lord of all puts upon faithful souls when He sets them in the fore-front of the battle, where the fiery darts of the adversary shower thickly around them, and bids them stand firmly there, and bravely maintain His cause? Might not angels envy them this exalted privilege?

And then, besides, there are forms of pious service which are conditioned by the temptations of Satan directed not upon the actors themselves, but upon others, —those holy Christlike ministrations to the sinful and the suffering, the ingorant and the needy, —those beautiful acts of heaven-born charity which so illustrate and adorn the gospel, and shed a fragrance so pleasing both to God and man, —all this belongs to a world where sin abounds, and Satan has free scope, and can appear nowhere else.

A sixth gracious end, which temptations may be designed to accomplish, is to wean the heart from the love of this present world. It is sheer cowardice or faint-heartedness in a soldier to be for ever whiining about the dangers or hardships of the campaign, and importuning for a release. And it would be reprehensible in the Christian to be indolently sighing for the coming rest, merely to escape the toil of laboring in his Master's service. But this error is far less common than the opposite extreme of clinging unduly to this vain world., and having the affections too firmly rooted here. To counteract this dangerous tendency, measures must be employed to loosen this attachment, by making the world seem desirable, and causing us to sigh for what is purer and better. The weariness induced by the incessant conflict between the flesh and the spirit often weighs heavily upon the soul. It is a hard thing to be for ever crucifying our corrupt nature, to be always struggling against a power which we find it impossible to subdue, endeavoring to keep down principles and propensities which we strive in vain to eradicate or extinguish, and never able with safety to relax our vigilance or to desist from effort. And it is disheartening to find how slow is our progress towards the completed conquest, even if we advance at all; how often the ground which we seemed to have won is wrested from us, and foes that we thought slain rise again to their feet as powerful as before. All this, though it should not lead us to abandon the fight while the enemy is still in the field, would make the news of victory more welcome. It gives sweetness to the thought of a world where there shall be no more sin, and into which temptation cannot enter, where inbred lusts and native corruption shall be removed for ever, and Satan shall at length have ceased to annoy. And this suggests the farther thought: —

7. That the future glory shall be heightened by the temptations of this present time, which have been bravely met and successfully resisted. It is not merely that the coming blessedness shall be an ample compensation for all that tempted souls can now endure, that the flood of joy shall swallow up all thought of present pains, and the light affliction,

which is for a moment, shall be followed by a far more exceeding and eternal weight of glory. But this glory shall, in various ways, be directly enhanced by those temptations, in so far as they have not been criminally yielded to, but in the name of the Master stoutly repelled. And thus what Satan intended for your hurt shall be converted into a source of everlasting profit. The experience of rest shall be heightened by the contrast of the antecedent toil and strife; and the felicity granted to the ransomed soul shall be likewise enhanced in its absolute amount. If the reward, though wholly the gift of grace, is in proportion to the service done or the fidelity shown, duty resolutely performed in the face of temptations of the evil one will surely receive a marked and signal acknowledgment. The training given to the spiritual faculties in the exercises of the Christian warfare, the development and expansion thence resulting to the powers of the soul, bear directly on our capacity for bliss and holiness. They who have attained the highest measure of fitness thus for the enjoyments of heaven shall have the largest experience of its blessedness. And further, those who have been driven by the assaults of the adversary into the closest union with their covenant God, and the most entire dependence upon Him, shall for this reason again partake most freely of those joys which flow from endless communion with the infinite source of all blessedness.

8. And lastly the temptations of Satan redound to the glory of divine grace. It belongs to the magnificence of God's universal government that opposition and hostility, to whatever degree and from whatever quarter, instead of tending to thwart or retard His plans, invariably contribute to further and promote them. Satan forms no exception. This archfiend, with all his legions and the entire kingdom of evil which he instigates and controls, in spite of their gathered forces and formidable numbers, and subtle craft and hellish spite, is absolutely powerless to prevent or to retard the execution of the least of God's designs. An infant in the arms is not more impotent to arrest the movement of the spheres than Satan is to check the fulfilment of God's sovereign decrees.

And this absolute control is rendered more illustrious by the manner of its exercise. It is not by bringing the resources of omnipotence to overpower the devil and his crew, and to chain them in the awful prison-house prepared for them, so that, driven entirely away from the theatre of His operations, they can no longer interfere with or obstruct them. On the contrary, Satan is allowed free range, as the prince of the power of the air. He has installed himself as the god of this world. He is busy with his plans and his combinations. They are laid with consummate skill, and he is working them with tremendous energy. He is laboring to undo the work of God, to defeat the atonement, to destroy souls whom Christ would save. But his machinations shall recoil upon himself. Do what he may, let him rage as he please, let him accomplish his worst, and he is after all only building up what in his blind fury and malice he is endeavoring to tear down. The decrees which he would frustrate embrace himself and all his hateful deeds, as agencies co-operating to their fulfilment. With all his hatred of God and spite against His people, he cannot emancipate himself from that sovereign control, which binds him to God's service. In all his blasphemous designs he is, in spite of himself doing the work of God. In his rebellious efforts to dethrone the Most High, he is actually paying Him submissive homage. In moving heaven and earth to accomplish the perdition of those whom Christ has ransomed, he is actually fitting them for glory. Fiend as he is, full of bitterness and malignity, and intent on every form of mischief, he is constrained to be that which he most abhors, and is furthest from his intentions and desires, helpful and auxiliary to the designs of grace. Like the sons of God who assemble in the presence of the Infinite Majesty to receive the commissions of the King of kings, prompt to do His bidding and to execute His will, Satan is, though most reluctantly, and in a different sense from them, yet as really and as truly, in the case of those who, like Job, steadfastly resist his insidious assaults, a ministering spirit sent forth to minister to them who shall be heirs of salvation.

But the enforced subordination of this spirit of malice and wickedness to the ends of divine mercy and grace is rendered yet more illustrious, both to the praise of God's glory and to Satan's everlasting shame and crushing defeat by another particular in the achievement of this triumph. This is the immediate agency by which his subjugation is effected. The New Testament seer beheld a vision of war in heaven. Michael and his angels fought against the dragon; and the dragon fought, and his angels, and prevailed not. Neither was their place found any more in heaven. And the great dragon was cast out, and his angels were cast out with him. Here, though he was defeated, it was by an antagonist worthy to cope with him. The rival forces fairly matched his own; and, however disastrous his overthrow, there was no dishonor in falling by such hands.

But when, smarting under his defeat in heaven, he went to make war with them which keep the commandments of God, and have the testimony of Jesus Christ, he prepared for himself a most ignominious repulse. He who aspired to be the leader of the host of heaven, and drew a third part of the angels in his fall, assaults the feeble children of men, and utterly fails to compass the ruin of one of them upon whom Jesus has set his love. He can terrify them; he can torture them; he can make them drag on the weary conflict with sin and corruption while life lasts; he can extort from them bitter groans of agonizing distress; he can shower upon them his fiery darts; but he cannot destroy them. The glimmering spark, which divine grace has kindled, he cannot with all the floods of temptation extinguish. Satan cannot by any means harm the feeblest of God's saints, who stands up against him in the name of the Lord. If he have on the armor with which divine grace has furnished him, and use aright the weapons with which he is supplied, and in humble dependence on his Lord abides faithful at his post, he is invincible; and the boastful foe, who came upon him ready to swallow him up, shall be driven back in shame and confusion. Resist the devil, and he will flee from you.

In the rapid view which has been taken of the subject, our attention has been confined to the temptations of Satan, as directed against the individual believer. Our limits will not allow us to extend our view to his assaults upon the kingdom of God in its collective capacity, and see how there, too, he most unwittingly acts under orders from the throne; how, in stirring up opposers to combat the truth of God, he but contributes to clear its statements, to unfold its richness, and render its defences more impregnable; how all his designs upon the Church, whether in provoking against her the hostility of the world, sowing dissensions in her own ranks, or in whatever way he may endeavor her injury, are unable to effect her overthrow. The gates of hell cannot prevail against the Church. The earthquake, which in its violent upheaval threatens to demolish the city of God, but shows how absolutely secure its firm foundations are. He may shake earth and heaven, and the crash will only bring down what he had himself essayed to build with rude untempered mortar, and it will only reveal in its unique stability, and bring to view in its fair proportions, free from every disfiguring addition, the solid, immovable building of God.

And now in this warfare we are engaged. The temptations of Satan are not to be escaped: no sheltered position, no seclusion from the world, no sacredness of occupation, can screen us from them. The only question is, Shall they prove our infinite damage, or shall they be made to recoil harmless and pointless? It is the most awful question which we can be summoned to answer; and yet the decision of this question may be said to have been placed by the infinite grace of God within our own control. If you yield to the tempter, you be-

16

come his helpless prey. If you steadfastly resist him, confiding in the grace of God and the salvation of Jesus, he cannot touch a hair of your head. Temptation and sin, if you bravely resist them, will react to your everlasting welfare: you position is impregnable, the protection is ample, the armament is invincible, the supplies abundant, and the fortress can never be entered by the enemy, unless betrayed into his power by your own treacherous hands.

CHAPTER III

The Lord gave, and the Lord hath taken away; blessed be the name of the Lord.—
Job i. 21.
*Shall we receive good at the hand of God, and shall we not receive evil?—*Job ii. 10.

JOB IN AFFLICTION

We have seen Job in his piety and prosperous estate. We are now to see him in his sad reverses, and to witness his behavior in affliction. A change of circumstances often makes a great change in men themselves, or at least exposes a new and previously unsuspected side of their character, and develops unlooked-for results. Sometimes it brings to light defects that had never been dreamed of in those who were esteemed almost faultless; sometimes it reveals unanticipated excellencies. Emergencies are the making of some men, and destruction of others. The former rise in greatness, and in every noble quality of soul, in proportion to the increasing demands of the occasion. The latter are unable to abide the severity of the test applied to them, and fall before it. How will it be with Job?

A disclosure is made at the outset, to the readers of this book, of things that are concealed from the human actors in it. The veil that hides the unseen world is partially drawn aside, so as to afford us a glimpse of a spiritual agent, who is to give a new turn to events. The arch-enemy of man has had his eye upon Job. True to the instincts of his own vile nature, he has no faith in the reality of goodness. He sees in the piety of Job nothing but a refined form of selfishness. He serves God because it is his interest to do so. God protects and blesses him, and as a matter of course he inclines to the quarter from which the favors come; but if these favors were to cease, the tempter urges, Job's piety would vanish with them. His goodness has its spring in its attendant rewards: withhold the latter, and Job will soon take leave of God and His service, which no longer yields him any advantage.

Satan is allowed to bring to an issue this question which he has raised. He may put Job's piety to the test, and in him he may test the question whether there is such a thing as real piety in the earth, a piety that is not merely self-seeking and actuated by a hope of gain, but which heartily loves the right and cleaves to it, and chooses the service of God though no hope of profit can attach to so doing. Job is on trial, though he knows it not; and unfriendly eyes are eagerly watching for his halting. And he is on trial not merely for himself: the cause of religion is represented in him, the cause of God on earth, though he also is unconscious of the dignity of his position and of the sacredness of the interest which he is set to sustain, and of the fact that the eyes of the Lord of all are turned upon him with approval, and with a lively concern for the favorable issue of the struggle in which he is engaged. Of the spiritual significance of this transaction, Job is profoundly ignorant. He feels the terrible pressure of his heavy sorrows, but he is not aware that they have been sent upon him as a test of character. He knows nothing of Satan's malicious designs, who seeks to prove his piety a pretence. He knows nothing of the sovereign purpose of God, who means to establish its reality and power to the confusion of the tempter.

It is with trembling apprehension that we see such power granted to this unseen adversary, with liberty to use it against the unsuspecting patriarch: "Behold, all that he has is in thy power," "Behold, he is in thine hand." The contest seems fearfully unequal between this arch-fiend and mortal man, however firm his integrity, whatever the sincerity and strength of his piety. It reassures us somewhat, however, when we observe that the tempter is, after all, limited and restrained by Job's almighty Guardian and Friend. The fiend can-

17

not frame and carry out his malevolent designs unchecked. He acts only by sufferance. He must have leave from the Most High, before he can touch Job at all to harm him or lay his hand upon any thing that he has. And, when permission is given, it is within fixed limits, which he may not overstep. When Job's property was put at Satan's disposal, it was with the accompanying restriction: "Only upon himself put not forth thine hand." When Job's own person was further subjected to his power, it was with the added requirement, "But save his life." With all the limitations, however, a tremendous range was conceded to this enemy of all righteousness, and the assault which he makes is a frightful one. Can Job endure the shock?

In order that we may properly appreciate the conduct of Job in his affliction, we must further take into account another consideration. Job went into his trial destitute of many of those firm supports and grounds of consolation, which are now so plentifully supplied to suffering saints. Those revelations had not yet been made, upon which the believer now so firmly rests his hope in times of deep distress. Truths, which are as familiar to us as household words in the gracious disclosures of the gospel, had never yet been clearly set before the minds of men. Perhaps it may be said that the faintest conceptions of them had scarcely dawned on any human consciousness. The king's broad highway through the wilderness of earthly sorrow, along which suffering pilgrims can now pass in comparative safety and comfort, had not then been constructed. Its route had not even been surveyed, not a pathway broken. Job was one of the hardy pioneers to whom this primary task was committed. He had to make his own way, without guide or chart or knowledge of the ground, through the tangled, trackless, howling waste; with no light to relieve the darkness of the night that enveloped him but the lone pole-star of his unshaken trust in God, and this, alas! dimmed often, and obscured by the black, threatening clouds which swept athwart his sky, though ever and anon peering forth afresh; unsheltered, too, from the tempest and the storms, which broke over him without mercy. Prophecies yawned at his feet, swollen streams ran across his route, and there were treacherous bogs in which he might be hopelessly mired. Is it strange if his stout heart quailed at the terrors which surrounded him? It is strange if groans of distress were extorted from him? Yet, in spite of all, he pushed his way through, and the path which he opened has defined the route for many travellers since. There is not a weary sufferer in Christendom who is not indebted to the patriarch of Uz, who has not been helped and aided by his example of fortitude and constancy, and in addition had reason to be grateful for the lessons of comfort and hope transmitted to us from him. He grappled with the mystery of affliction in all its unexplained darkness and diffiway, or which were graciously vouchsafed to him in his trial, have been the heritage of God's people ever since.

Think for a moment what it would be to enocunter crushing sorrows not only without Calvary and Gethsemane and the sympathy of the incarnate Song of God, who is Himself touched with the feeling of our infirmities, for He was in all points tempted like as we are, yet without sin; but to go into trials that offer no bright spot this side the grave, with no clear views of that eternal blessedness, in comparison with which all earthly sorrows, however grievous in themselves, and long continued, are nevertheless light and momentary; without the assurance that present griefs and sufferings shall be overbalanced and outweighed by that far more exceeding and eternal weight of glory, whose absolute amount they shall themselves greatly enhance. What would it be to encounter frowning providences without the distinct understanding that these are nevertheless consistent with the abiding, unchanging love of our heavenly Father? They are not tokens of His displeasure; they are not evidences that He has withdrawn His love or has shut up His tender mercies. On the contrary, whom the Lord loveth He chasteneth. There is a paternal discipline in affliction. It has a gracious design, and will have a salutary result. The rod is in a loving Father's hand: its strokes are not capriciously nor unkindly given, they are administered solely for our good.

Deprive the sufferer of the solace afforded by his knowledge of these precious truths, hide from him the benefit to be derived from affliction, take away his consciousness of the divine love in the midst of it all, and remove from him the assurance of the everlasting reward which shall infinitely more than compensate all that he now endures, and how defenceless would he appear in the presence of heavy griefs! These wellsprings of consolation had not yet been opened. These comforting truths had never found utterance in human speech. Simple and obvious as they now appear to us from frequent repetition, and belonging to the very alphabet of our religion, they had never been distinctly formulated, and no clear conception of them had ever been reached. Job must fight the battle without the aids which his experience as well as later revelations have furnished us. His sorrows came upon him, not for his own sake merely, but for ours. A new lesson was to be given to the world; and Job was to be the medium of instruction. The stream of adversity swells around him, until in danger of sinking he is compelled to struggle with all his might to get upon the sure foundation. Where he finds firm footing, other children of sorrow may safely tread.

The spectacle before us, then, is that of this eminent man of God, chosen to be the leader of the band of sufferers in their mortal conflict with evil and the evil one. He goes into the strife unpractised and unawares. The onset of the foe is fierce and furious. Will even Job be able to stand in the evil day?

The conflict unfolds itself in three successive stages of growing violence, and the demeanor of this holy man is depicted to us in each. In the first, we behold him in one evil day suddenly and irretrievably despoiled of all his possessions. In the morning his sky was without a cloud. He was in the midst of the prosperous abundance which he had long enjoyed, and seemed to have every reason to feel secure of its continuance. It was in fact a day of special festivity and family reunion; and, so far from leading to the anticipation of evil, it was an occasion of more than ordinary joy. Happy in his children, and in his possessions, and in the respect and consideration universally accorded to him, his cup of blessing overflowed. And there was nothing to suggest the likelihood of a coming reverse. And yet, before that day was ended, every thing was gone. To such destitution was he reduced that his condition is aptly likened to that of a newborn child. He came naked into the world; and now. that he had been stripped of all, he shall leave it as naked as he came.

Suddenly, and without a moment's warning, the storm of calamity burst over the head of the doomed patriarch. One messenger of evil chased another with tidings of disaster. One had not ended his tale of loss before another came with a tale more doleful still. His oxen and his asses were driven off by the wild and roving tribe of the Sabeans; his sheep were consumed by fire from heaven; his camels were carried away by plundering bands of Chaldeans; and his servants put to the sword. And, to complete the dismal intelligence of woe, the house in which his children were assembled, and passing the hours in glad hilarity, was overturned by a tornado and fell upon them all, crushing them to death. In one moment of terrible reverse the stricken patriarch is bereaved of his children and despoiled of his property. All is taken from him in an instant; and, of all that he had cherished and delighted in and prized of earthly good, he had nothing left.

If the calamity had been less sweeping and universal, it would not have been so overwhelming. If something had been spared him, if it had been only a part of his property and not the whole which was taken, the loss might still have been considerable, it might have been heavy, it might have involved the greater part of his fortune; still, if he had not lost all, it would have been easier to bear it with equanimity. Or though all his property were taken from him, if those possessions had been left which were dearer far than flocks and herds, those precious domestic treasures which he valued beyond all his wealth,—if his beloved children had been spared, it would have been easier to bear the loss of all beside. It would have been hard to part with one of that cherished circle that he prized so much and loved so fondly; but all, and all at once, this was bereavement and desolation indeed.

If the blows had not fallen so suddenly and in such quick succession; if he could have had some time in which to steady himself for the shock; if there had been some intervals of relief in which he could have summoned all his strength to meet the coming blows, it would have seemed less dreadful, it would not have been so crushing as when the whole dire weight came down upon him at a stroke. By this accumulation of sorrows so suddenly sprung upon Job, the violence of the attack was increased to the utmost, and thus his steadfastness was put to the severest test. Can the tempter drive him thus to give up his integrity and abandon his trust in God?

Under the pressure of sore affliction men are in danger of falling into one or other of two opposite extremes, either of which is inconsistent with fidelity to the Lord's service. The first is that of repining and murmuring at the divine allotment: the other is that of bearing it in a spirit of stoical indifference. The wise man warns us against both. "My son despise not hou the chastening of the Lord, nor faint when thou art, rebuked oft son, despise not thou the chastening of the Lord, nor faint when thou art rebuked of Him." Job avoided both these dangers in that subdued but noble demeanor which has been in all ages since the model of submissive resignation. The stricken patriarch, bowed with grief, adopts the token of the most profound humiliation and sorrow: he rent his mantle, and shaved his head, and fell down upon the ground. Not to sit in sullen silence and brood despondently over the terrible losses which he had sustained: not to complain of the providence of God, which had dealt so hardly with him: no, he prostrates himself in reverential worship; he bows with meek submission to Him who had smitten him: and his only language is that of grateful adoration to the Source of all blessings, who in removing all had but taken away what He Himself had given. Job fell down upon the ground and worshipped; and said, "Naked came I out of my mother's womb, and naked shall I return thither. The Lord gave, and the Lord hath taken away; blessed be the name of the Lord." Can humble, trustful piety reach a sublimer utterance than this? He has been cast down from the height of his prosperity; has suffered the total wreck of his fortune and the loss of all his family; he is weighed to the earth with his crushing sorrows; and yet, with bleeding heart and prostrate form, this venerable man utters not one word of complaint. So far is he from giving up his confidence in the goodness of the Lord, that he strengthens himself in this confidence by the very greatness of the calamity that he has suffered, and draws his argument of praise for the multitude of God's mercies from the very bitterness of the cup that is now pressed to his lips.

The submission of Job is not merely that he yields to what is inevitable; that seeing the stroke of fate has fallen, and its blow cannot be turned aside, and the past cannot be undone, he resigns himself to what is beyond the possibility of repair. Nor does he merely succqmb to Omnipotence, convinced that it is futile to resist what the almighty God has appointed. None can stay His hand, or prevent the execution of His sovereign will. It can be of no avail to oppose himself to Him, and so he subsides in forced acquiescence. Nor is it merely the rectitude of the infinite Ruler before which he falls prostrate, who has a right to do as He will with His own, and who can dispose of his creatures according to His sovereign pleasure. Job meekly bows not before the stroke of inevitable fate, not simply before the resistless energy of almighty power, nor simply before the righteous control of the sovereign Ruler; but before the goodness of the Lord, a sense of which now fills his heart proportioned to the magnitude of the reverse which he has sustained. "The Lord gave, and the Lord hath taken away; blessed be the name of the Lord." The bitterness of his loss is made the measure of the preciousness of the blessings God had given. The severity of his trial consists in parting with what God had bestowed. Every pang that now rends his heart is a fresh proof how gracious God has been. The magnitude of the loss determines the value of the gift, and the depth of his anguish enhances his grateful sense of the goodness of the Giver. The more deeply he mourns the treasures which have been taken away from him, the higher is his appreciation of the gracious kindness of Him who bestowed them. Thus the more profoundly he grieves, the more fervently he still blesses the name of the Lord.

Not that he sees the goodness of God in afflicting him. This was a lesson Job had not yet learned. The benefits and uses of affliction, and the gracious design with which it is sent of God, had not yet been revealed. It was through these trials of Job himself, and the disclosure of His purposes thus given, and the providential issue of His dealings with His servant, that the first rays of light were shed on this dark and mysterious subject. It was partly in order to afford an occasion for giving these lessons to the world, which might lighten the sorrows, and ease the burdens, and mitigate the trials of subsequent sufferers, that these distresses were sent on Job. Thus did he in a measure suffer for our sakes, and by his stripes we are healed; as a forerunner and a type of the great Prince of sufferers, of whom this was true in its strictest and highest sense.

But these lessons, which we have learned from the example of Job and the measures of God's grace with him, as well as from later revelations, were all unknown as yet to the patriarch himself. He knew not that affliction was a means of grace; that there was healing in the bitter draught; that there was mercy in these seeming frowns; that all that he experienced was in fact the chastisement of love. He knew not even that it was a trial and a test of his integrity and pious faith in God; and that the Lord regarded with complacent approbation his steadfast endurance of the test thrust upon him by his great adversary.

And it heightens our conception of Job's sterling piety, and gives us loftier apprehensions of the nobility of his character, and enhances to our view his sublimely meek and submissive demeanor, when we see him confronting the unsolved enigma of this mysteriour dispensation, and deducing from it fresh matter for grateful praise. He not merely confesses that He who gave might justly withdraw His own, so that, whatever his losses, his mouth is stopped from making any complaint. But the withdrawal of the gift makes him sensible of its greatness, and, instead of drawing from him the language of repining, compels him to the utterance of praise,—"Blessed be the name of the Lord."

The first stage of the trial is ended, and the tempter is foiled. The record is, "In all this Job sinned not, nor charged God foolishly."

But the tempter is not yet satisfied, and Job's piety must be put to a yet further proof. He has borne with becoming resignation the loss of all outward possessions, the ruin of his property, the decease of his children; but how if the blow should fall not on what he owns, but upon himself? Satan accordingly meditates a fresh onset, and leave is given him to aggravate the sorrows of Job already so great by an additional disaster. To the calamities previously sent is now added an infliction upon his own person,—a most distressing, offensive, and acute disease, one of the symptoms of which was an eruption of painful ulcers, covering his entire body. He was smitten with sore boils from the sole of his foot to his crown. "And he took him a potsherd to scrape himself withal; and he sat down among the ashes.

Can Job bear up under this new distress? What will be the effect of pain and bodily suffering added to the shock of former sorrows? Now that he is weakened by disease and distracted by torturing anguish in every member of his body, will it be strange if the trustufl submission which he has maintained hitherto gives away? and though he has borne his previous trials with noble fortitude, and he has seen his property swept away, and his children taken from him with tranquil resignation, he should be unable to withstand the pressure of this new calamity, and physical suffering should extort from him murmurs and repining words, and lead him to cherish hard thoughts of God, and give up his trust in His goodness and His gracious providence; and thus the tempter should at length succeed, and Job's piety be put to a test which it could not bear?

The trial proves too much for his wife. Her fortitude forsakes her at this new spectacle of woe. "Dost thou still retain thine integrity?" she says to him: "curse God,"—or rather, take leave of God, abandon his service,—"and die." The wife of Job has often been misjudged, and the meaning of her words misunderstood. She has been censured as though she were destitute of piety, had neither love nor sympathy for her husband, and were lacking, in fact, in common humanity. It has even been hinted that Satan showed his hostility to Job no less in sparing her to be a torment to him than in taking the lives of his children. The representation if frequently made, that, never having sympathized with Job in his piety, she was provoked that he should maintain it still when it had proved so unprofitable and was so poorly rewarded. And she bids him curse God and die, as though she would have him bid defiance to his Maker, from whom he received nothing but unmerited injuries and ill-treatment; as though she would have him upbraid Him with the causeless suffering He had brought upon him, if he perished for it; with the intimation perhaps that he might as well die in the wretched condition in which he then was, it would the sooner end his misery; and possibly also with the hard-hearted suggestion that it was of little concern to her, as he had ceased to be any thing but a burden, of which she was willing to be relieved.

We cannot but look upon this severity of censure as quite undeserved. It is unfair to put the worst construction possible upon the language of Job's wife in this case, and then make her conduct on this occasion the index to her whole life. Such a judgment is altogether misleading, and gives a perverted view of the incident itself which is here recorded, and of the design with which it is introduced. There is no intimation either here, or in the single allusion subsequently made to the wife of Job, xix. 17, that there had been any unhappiness in Job's domestic life; that his wife had been uncongenial to him, a thorn in his side, or any thing other than the worthy partner of such a husband, his joy and solace. united with him in heart and life, approving and sharing his uprightness and pious trust in God. Else in the days of his former prosperity his felicity could not have been as pure and untroubled as it is represented to have been; and when his prosperity again returns there is no intimation that she served in any wise to make his happiness incomplete.

And, so far as appears, she had borne their first terrible trial with a like spirit of meek and submissive resignation to that of Job himself. She had faced adversity as bravely as he. At least we hear of no murmur from her lips any more than from his on that dreadful day of disaster and sudden reverse, when property and children were all swept remorselessly away, and they were left destitute and alone in remediless desolation. She offered no word of protest then, against Job's utterance of pious resignation. So far as appears, her heart went with his. She, too, parted with her wealth and with her children without repining word.

But when her last earthly prop is breaking, and her only surviving solace is perishing before her eyes, and she sees her husband in such misery and suffering, and sinking into death by so frightful a disease, she is well-nigh frantic in her despair; her fortitude gives way; her trust in God, which she had cherished hitherto, passes under a cloud. She feels that it is a cruel dispensation, and He is cruel who has inflicted it. She cannot longer give her adoration to a Being who rewards His faithful worshippers thus; who wantonly sends such dire extremity of woe, and has brought such desolation upon her household and her heart. And she cannot bear to have her husband in his helpless misery continue to bless and to adore the God who is torturing him to death. A God so pitiless and so cruel it were better, to take leave of than to worship; to renounce His service than to serve Him, and be requited thus. It were as well to curse Him as to bless, for in this desperate extremity it can make matters no worse, for death is equally at hand in either case. Since you must die cursing, not blessing, the author of your misery, the source of all our bitter woe.

And thus the loving wife in the frenzy of her anguish has ranged herself unwittingly upon the tempter's side. It is not the first nor only time that fond hearts and friendly hands have unknowingly leagued themselves with the destroyer, and ignorantly done the work of Satan. That Job's wife did what she did under the impulse of her affections, seems to be implied in the connection. Her words are introduced as adding force to the temptation, and affording a fresh exhibition of the firmness of Job's piety. Cold, unfeeling sarcasm and impious taunt from his wife would not have enticed, but rather repelled. Instead of assailing his integrity at a new and tender point, it would have naturally thrown him into an attitude of resistance to the heartless and wicked suggestion.

But the case is altered, if we see in his wife one who tenderly loves him, and whom he fondly loves. She has stood firmly with him hitherto, but now at length her constancy is overcome; and she would persuade him, too, to abandon his piety, which has not availed to save him from this dismal fate, and to give up the service of a God who, with such a disregard of His constant, faithful worship, has so causelessly and cruelly afflicted him. Job has borne all former disasters unmoved. His bodily sufferings even cannot shake his integrity. And now the solicitations of his wife he turns aside. His reply to her suggestion is not harsh and severe, as it is frequently interpreted, but rather the language of pained surprise. It is not a stern censure, but a mild rebuke, though decided in its rejection of her ill-judged counsel. He does not rudely charge her with being herself a foolish woman, whether the meaning be destitute of sense or lacking in true piety. He simply says this was not spoken like herself; it is such a suggestion as he would not have expected from her. She had spoken not with her usual wisdom and pious feeling, but as one of the foolish women speaketh. "What! shall we receive good at the hand of God, and shall we not receive evil?"

Job's trust in the goodness of the Lord does not falter yet. Here was not, as in his former trial, a simple withdrawal of what God had previously given and in which the amount so withdrawn was simply an index to the goodness of Him who had bestowed it. There was now not the mere privation of good, but the positive infliction of evil, of suffering and pain. Job knows not that this suffering encloses a benefit, and is sent with a benevolent design. He cannot, therefore praise God for the suffering itself, and acknowledge in it a token of the divine goodness, as he might have done if the lesson had been taught him which the apostle expressed when he said, "We glory in tribulations also," "I take pleasure in infirmities, in reproaches, in necessities, in persecutions, in distresses for Christ's sake." Job did not yet know that all things work together for good to them that love God. He did not understand that pain and suffering were or could be any thing else but evils. Yet regarding them simply in this light, as evils, and evils received from the hand of God, they did not blind him to the fact of divine goodness and the great preponderance of blessing received from His bountiful hand. The evil does not by any means match the good, much less outweigh it. Shall we forget the immensity of the benefits bestowed because He also sends some suffering? Shall we receive good at the hand of God, and shall we not receive evil?

Job is again victorious, and the tempter is one more foilde. His piety has proved equal to the severity of this fresh test to which it was subjected. "In all this," the record runs, "did not Job sin with his lips."

But Job's trial is not yet ended. He has passed through two stages of it, and has successfully surmounted them. Thus far his piety has b rne the test triumphantly, to the loss of his property and of his children with noble resignation; with his heart wrung with grief, clad in the insignia of mourning and prostrate on the earth, he still blessed the name of the Lord. He bore the further infliction of what was deemed a fatal disease, accompanied by acute bodily suffering, with heroic fortitude; and though his wife herself threw her weight upon the side of temptation, he still held fast his integrity, and submissively received evil as well as good from the hand of the Lord. But the third stage of the temptation is yet before him, and it will test his endurance more severely still. It is the persistence of suffering, its continued pressure through long intervals of time.

Many a citadel is proof against assault, which yet may be obliged to succomb to the slow and steady progress of a siege. Constant dropping wears away rocks. There are limits beyond which human endurance cannot go. The first onset of pain and suffering is not nearly so formidable as its protracted continuance, which wears out the strength and uses up the capacity of resistance. Pain which can be patiently borne for a short time becomes intolerable after a longer period. Sad indeed is the condition of the worn and weary sufferer, whose strength is exhausted, his spirits sunk, his buoyancy gone, all hope fled; unable to calm his irritated nerves or ease his aching limbs, restless and unquiet, finding no repose no comfortable posture and no cessation of pain, just wearing out the tiresome hours as they drag heavily along; through all the tedious night, and through all the day sighing for the night, though the night brings no repose. It is not so much the amount of pain endured at any one moment as its long and wearisome continuance that is so hard to bear. This weary, exhausting round of suffering, with no prospect of relief, is the third stage of Job's heavy trial. The tempter, who had twice failed in his fierce onset, would now wear him out, if possible, and break his strength by continued endurance.

Day after day, week after week, he is still compelled to drag his heavy burden, and he does so in silence. How long we know not. It was some time after his seizure before his friends arrived to comfort him. Doubtless a number of days had passed before they heard of his calamity. A further interval was consumed in concerting an appointment to come. When they arrived, his disease had already so altered his features and form that they lifted up their eyes and knew him not. And after their arrival they sat with him seven days and seven nights before Job uttered a word of lamentation. Through all this protracted period he bore his grief in silence. But at length his sorrows grow beyond his power to suppress them, and he breaks forth in the piteous moanings of intolerable anguish. He has borne the torture with pious fortitude, until at length nature can hold out no more: he can endure it no longer, and he gives vent to the most distressed sighs and groans; but in it all observe that he does not rail against God.

In the most passionate manner he utters his wailing cry. With the most vehement expressions he heaps execrations on the day in which he was born; he wishes that day blotted from existence,—in other words, that it had never been,—so that it could not have inflicted upon him the misery of an intolerable existence. Oh that he had never been born! Oh that when born he had perished, neglected and uncared for, and thus might never have come to know the wretchedness of living! Oh if he had but found in early infancy a grave, which closes over all alike, and sweeps into its all-devouring maw the rich and great, kings and counsellors, the prisoner and the oppressor, the master and his slave, gathering all into that profound and undisturbed repose, which now is denied to him! Oh, how he longs for death! he would clutch at it as the miser grasps his gold, as men dig for hidden treasures. Why is this coveted privilege of death denied him?

Thus poor sufferer bemoans his dismal fate. It is the doleful lament of one who has more laid upon him than he can bear. It is not the utterance of considerate reflection. It is not the expression of deliberate views. The sentences are not to be nicely weighed, and their propriety or impropriety passed upon as though they were spoken in moments of calm repose. They must be judged of from the situation of Job. They are the language of one tortured beyond endurance, who cannot support the anguish that he suffers, and whose life has become an intolerable burden. Allowance must be made for these paroxysms of helpless, hopeless sorrow. His strength was not the strength of stones, nor his flesh of brass. He was incapable himself of weighing what he uttered. It only represents the bitterness of irrepressible woe.

Still, burised as he is, hopeless of good, with but one wish, and this that he might die, Job does not reproach or revile his Maker. The tempter has broken his spirit, and crushed him to the earth; but he has not succeeded yet in wresting from him his integrity or bringing him to forsake his God.

Here we must leave the patriarch for the present. This third, most dreadful stage of his trial is not yet ended. The tempter has not relaxed his hold. He has new instruments of torture to apply to the victim already reduced to so pitiable a condition; and he will use them mercilessly. He sees his advantage in Job's extremity of misery, and he will push it to the bitter end, if so he can wring from him the renunciation of his trust in God. Will he be able to compass his malicious design? The future will reveal. Meanwhile let it be recorded that he has not succeeded yet. In the desperate straits to which he has been driven, Job has not yet renounced the service of the Lord.

And may He whose grace supported Job in all his dreadful trials hitherto grant like grace to us,—grace according to our need, grace to do according to the measure of the task required of us, grace to bear according to the measure of the burden laid upon us, And to His name be praise. Amen.

CHAPTER IV

Now when Job's three friends heard of all this evil that was come upon him, they came every one from his own place; Eliphaz the Temanite, and Bildad the Shuhite, and Zophar the Naamathite: for they had made an appointment together to come to mourn with him, and to comfort him. —Job ii. 11.

JOB'S THREE FRIENDS

Job's sorrows seemed to have reached their last extreme. And now some new personages are introduced upon the scene, who are to be quite conspicuous in the remainder of the book. Three friends meet by appointment at the house of the suffering patriarch, to condole with and to comfort him. The prominence accorded to them from this point onward shows that their visit is no unimportant incident, but that it is a fact of great consequence in the transaction here recorded. A very large space, and indeed the greater portion of the book, is occupied with what they say to Job, which is here reported in detail, and with what he says in reply. We cannot be mistaken in supposing that they have much to do with the case here pending. They are not mere spectators in a scene which deeply affects them as concerning their intimate and lifelong friend. They are themselves actors and participants, and that in a most significant and important way. They appear in the very crisis of Job's trial; in the last and most terrible stage of his sufferings, and when it would seem as though nature could bear no more. They, too, are unwittingly taken into the service of the tempter, who makes use of them to add a fresh aggravation to Job's intolerable woe, which is most artfully contrived to drive him to that result which Satan seeks to compass, to make him do what his cunning and unscrupulous enemy has from the first been aiming to bring about, viz., to renounce the service of the Lord.

The alternate discourses of the friends and of Job are not simply a discussion of the mysterious subject of God's afflictive dispensations. They are not to be sundered from the circumstances in which they are uttered, which preclude an abstract treatment of a general theme. They are occupied with the case of Job, and every word uttered by his friends finds its way to the sufferer's heart. He is wounded by their harshness, stung by their censures, exasperated by their reproaches, and driven into antagonism by their arguments. They are the professed advocates of religious obligation. They represent the cause of God, enforcing His claims on Job and justifying His ways with him, which they do in a spirit that repels him, with assumptions that experience does not sanction, and which his own inner consciousness falsifies. The unfairness, if not disingenuousness, with which they plead God's cause, place him under additional temptation to reject that cause itself. The hopeless variance which they assume or create between God's justice and Job's integrity, for which latter he nevertheless has the testimony of his own conscience, which he cannot surrender or falsify, tends to place before his mind a distorted image of the character of God. God appears to be torturing him for crimes which he has not committed, to be relentlessly pursuing him as an implacable foe, and without justice or reason to be employing His resistless power to crush him to the earth. This is the phantom which his friends are constantly setting before him, this false notion of God as unjust and pitiless toward him; and this his own intolerable sufferings, for which he cannot himself otherwise account, seem to rivet upon him. This phantom, apparently so real, he is incessantly obliged to fight, or it would drive him to absolute despair, and force him to give up his confidence and trust in God, and thus throw him completely into the

26

tempter's snare.

This is the point around which the conflict in Job's soul so fearfully rages, which is depicted in this book in its various phases with such a master hand. This is the very acme and crisis of the temptation. This unwelcome apparition, which his friends are constantly bringing up and dressing out before him, of a God of arbitrary power, whose justice, as they assert it, would be rank injustice, and who seems to be devoid of pity, —this it is which fills him with the deepest anguish. And yet, in the darkness and the mystery of his unexplained sufferings, how is he to rid himself of it? how chase the dreaded spectre away? To admit this conception of God, which both his own helpless misery and the arguments and assertions of his friends appear to force upon him, is to fall inevitably away from God's service. Such a God might be dreaded; but it is impossible that He could be either loved or feared.

Here, then, are Job's three friends, who as the self-constituted advocates of God, and the monitors of Job, concerned about his spiritual good, are busily engaged in letting fly their poisoned arrows and flinging their envenomed darts. And here is Job himself exposed without shield or buckler to their dangerous attacks. Can he sustain the weight of this new burden? Can he hold out against this fresh assault? Can his confidence in God remain unshaken when every prop is removed and the very foundations seem to be swept away? His heart is all laid open before us, down to its lowest depths, in his discourses with his friends. Every thing is faithfully photographed. We see all the tumult of his soul in its conflicting emotions. We see him now sinking, now rising; now almost gone, tottering on the very verge of the precipice, over which to fall would be fatal; now recoiling in the energy of his still unvanquished faith; giving vent to expressions wrung from him in the bitterness of his spirit, which he would not have uttered in calmer moments, until we almost dread to have him open his mouth again, lest he should in his desperation be betrayed into speaking the fatal word to which Satan by all this combination of forces is ceaselessly urging him, and apparently shutting him up; beside himself with intolerable anguish, the terrors of God driving him to distraction, yet through it all he is still ever and anon turning into God and tearfully looking up to Him, his only hope and solace. Can even Job's piety still hold out? Shall the tempter at length succeed?

In order that we may the better understand how and to what extent the friends of Job aggravated his temptations, it will be necessary to pay more particular attention to the persons of these friends, and their conduct and language towards Job. This is the purpose of the present chapter.

The censure which the Lord Himself passes upon Job's friends at the close of the book, and the fact that they misapprehend as they do the cause of Job's sufferings and the purpose of God's dealings with him, has often led to an undue depreciation of their character. Against this we must carefully guard, or we shall weaken the force of the temptation so far as they are concerned, which lies greatly in this,—that such men can take part in it, and that they do this just as they do, and to the extent that they do.

We have reason to believe that these were eminent men, wise men, and good men. They were cherished and familiar friends of Job, such as he would naturally lean upon in a time of trouble, or turn to in perplexity for counsel and advice. They were venerable men, men of age and experience. Eliphaz says to Job, xv. 10: *With us are both the gray-headed and very aged men, much elder than thy father."* We cannot think of Job, with his ten children grown up to manhood and womanhood, as at this time much less than fifty-five or sixty years old. Eliphaz in this statement probably refers to himself, since the precedence is accorded to him among the friends. He in every instance speaks first, and is followed by the others, and may therefore be supposed to be their superior in age. If this be so, and he alludes to himself as "gray-headed and very aged," and "much elder" than Job's father, he must have been at least as old as seventy-five or eighty. And age commanded reverence, more even then, in the patriarchal period, than with us. And it was significant of distinction, when the oldest living ancestor was the chieftain of the clan; when he was the visible lord of his descendants, and the recognized authority looked up to, deferred to, and obeyed in all their families and dependants. It was significant, too, of wisdom gathered by long experience and observation, when intercourse with men, and acquaintance with things rather than knowledge of books, were the chief sources of information.

The region in which Job's friends resided should also be noted, for it was proverbial for the sagacity of its inhabitants; and it is not unlikely that it is for this reason, to suggest that they were men of superior ability, of intellectual acumen, and of extensive acquirements, that the residence of each is particularly mentioned,—Eliphaz the Temanite, Bildad the Shuhite, and Zophar the Naamathite. Teman was famous for its wise men, and their profound, sententious sayings; so was in fact Arabia, or the East, the country to which the other friends likewise belonged. To this well-known reputation of the region the prophet alludes, Jer. xlix. 7: *"Is wisdom no more in Teman? is counsel perished from the prudent? is their wisdom vanished?"* And when the eminent endowments of Solomon were to be exalted by a comparison, the sacred writer says of him, I Kings iv. 30: *"Solomon's wisdom excelled the wisdom of all the children of the east country."*

And that Job's friends were worthy representatives of a land of sages is shown by their speeches here recorded, which are marked by extensive observation and careful reflection, and abound in beautiful and appropriate illustrations drawn from both nature and experience. Their reasoning is fallacious, indeed, because built on false though specious premises; but their arguments are coherent and strongly put. They fail to convince or to confute Job, but it is from no want of skill in advocacy: they prove themselves no mean antagonists, and it requires all his address to parry their blows. What saves him is not his superiority in argument, but that it is a matter of personal consciousness about which they contend. No subtleties and no cogency of demonstration can convict him of offences of which his own conscience pronounces him innocent. They misinterpret the ways of providence, and fail to explain the mystery of Job's sufferings. But this is from no mental incapacity. Job can see no farther into this dark dispensation than they can. He knows that they are mistaken. But he no more understands the real state of the case than they do. The fact is that the enigma is insoluble by the unaided reason of man. God can alone declare the purpose of His afflictive dispensations, and this He had never yet revealed. These distresses of Job were to afford the occasion of shedding the first rays of light upon it. It is no ciscredit to the friends any more than to Job that they did not discern what they had no means of knowing. In what they really were to blame, and to what extent, we shall inquire presently.

They were, moreover, good men, and had at heart a real affection for Job. The whole tenor of their speeches shows that they were concerned both for the honor of God and for the spiritual welfare of Job. They advocate and approve what is good, they reject and condemn the bad. Their discourses sparkle with gems of morality and religious truth. The principles which they propound are mostly just and unexceptionable as general maxims. It is only the application which they make of them to a case that they do not really cover, which is false. They entertain a true friendship for Job; but the mistake under which they are with regard to him and his trials warps their judgment; and, in their desire to reclaim him from imaginary wrong doing, they are themselves guilty of actual though unintended injustice, and treat him with unmerited severity.

The friends of Job, then, as we may conceive, were men of distinction, eminent for wisdom and of approved piety, worthy confidants and intimates of Job, trusted and tried doubtless in the companionship of years. They hear of the great sorrows of their friend, and they show their attachment to him by agreeing to meet at his house to mourn with him and to comfort him. They bring him in actual fact but little comfort, it is true; but this is the design and expectation with which they come.

It is important to observe the change which takes place in the friends themselves in their feelings and attitude towards Job in the progress of the book. This is depicted with admirable art, and is essential to a proper understanding of the whole transaction. To impute to them from the beginning the harsh and ungenerous suspicions which they come entertain and express towards the last, is to mistake their character entirely, to confuse what is perfectly distinct, and to lose sight of that inward revolution in their sentiments respecting Job which is so skilfully drawn and is so true to nature. The longer the friends argue with him without convincing him, the more obdurate and incorrigible he appears to them, and the more severe is the censure which they are disposed to pass upon him.

They come with sympathy and sorrow for him in his griefs. Finding him so changed that they no longer recognize him, they are affected to tears. "They lifted up their voice, and wept; and they rent every one his mantle, and sprinkled dust upon their heads toward heaven. So they sat down with him upon the ground seven days and seven nights, and none spake a word unto him: for they saw that his grief was very great." They could not more tenderly and delicately express their commiseration for him in this terrible sorrows, which it was beyond the power of human helpers to mitigate or to relieve. In all this there was genuine pity and compassion. There is no room for supposing that they entertained any other than the most friendly feelings, or that any ungenerous suspicions had as yet taken possession of their minds as to the reality of Job's piety or the reasons of these extraordinary sufferings which had been sent upon him.

Job first breaks the mournful silence by his outburst of lamentation, extorted by insupportable distress. Eliphaz, probably the eldest and most respected of the three friends, as he is certainly the most dignified and courteous in his style of address, first makes reply. And, as Job answers him, he is successively followed by Bildad and by Zophar. As the interview still proceeds, and Job continues to respond, the friends once more address themselves to him in the same order; and yet again the third time. Only in the third and last series of discourses the third friend, Zophar, fails to speak, for a reason to be stated hereafter. Eliphaz and Bildad accordingly each speak three times, and Zophar twice, Job invariably responding. There is thus a triple series of discourses, in which the growing alienation and distrust of the friends can be plainly traced. They begin with comparative mildness and expressions of regard. But, as the discussion advances, they are astounded and excited by Job's opposition to what they esteem primary principles of religious faith; they are provoked and incensed by his obstinacy, his want of submission to the divine allotment, and by his language, which appears to them to savor of irreverence and impiety; until at length they lose all confidence in his uprightness and sincerity, and believe him to have been secretly guilty of the most atrocious and outrageous crimes.

When Job, unable longer to contain himself under the pressure of his anguish, utters his wail of frantic grief, cursing the day in which he was born, and complaining that life with all its miseries is forced upon him, when he would so gladly be blotted from existence or seek rest in the grave, Eliphaz feels called upon to interpose a remonstrance. He makes an endeavor in this first speech to rouse his friend from this utter despondency, to remind him of the moral reasons of this terrible infliction, and to exhort him to that more complete submission which would be followed by the return of God's favor, and by more than his former prosperity.

He begins in an apologetic and insinuating strain: "If we assay to commune with thee, wilt thou be grieved? but who can withhold himself from speaking?" He then proceeds by bidding Job remember how he had strengthened and comforted others in their affliction; and he ought not now to show weakness himself. As a good and righteous man, he should not despond, but hope in God, who would not suffer the innocent to perish, nor the righteous to be cut off. As to the source of his troubles, he reminds him of the universal sinfulness of men. Mortal man cannot be just in the sight of God, nor man pure before his Maker. Men are sinners; hence their frail and perishable nature. They are crushed before the moth, they are destroyed from morning to evening. Affliction cometh not forth from the dust, neither doth trouble spring out of the ground. They arise from no extraneous sources. But man is born to trouble as the sparks fly upward. He is involved in it by a necessity of his nature: it springs directly out of his inborn sinfulness. Hence he admonishes him to submit his case humbly and trustfully to God, under whose universal and righteous providence the poor hath hope, and iniquity is compelled to stop her mouth "He shall deliver thee in six troubles: yea, in seven there shall on evil touch thee." And he concludes by describing in beautiful and impressive terms the happy consequences of submissively accepting the Lord's correction.

To this plausible and, rhetorically considered, elegant address of Eliphaz, there are two exceptions to be taken. In the first place, it could not but grate harshly on the ears of Job that his friend should expect him to sustain his long-continued and bitter sufferings with equanimity, and that he should appear to reproach him with not himself exhibiting that fortitude now in his own case which he had inculcated in that of others. As though there were no limits to human endurance, and it were possible to bear up under misery like his without a word of complaint. The sobs and groans and lamentations wrung from him by an anguish too severe to be quietly endured is surely a weakness that is not to be too harshly judged. And the appeal to Job's piety, as though this should have quieted his clamor and led him still to maintain a cheerful hope amidst his overwhelming distress, showed a want of consideration for the condition in which he then was. There was in all this a lack of that tenderness and that appreciative sympathy which was a prime requisite in one who would comfort such a mourner as Job.

The second point open to exception in the discourse of Eliphaz in not a matter of feeling, like the preceding, but of principle. It is the manner in which he represents sin and suffering as linked together in God's providential dispensation, as though this afforded an adequate explanation of every case of affliction, Job's included. This point is so skilfully put, that what he actually says can scarcely be objected to: it is only what he implies, by offering this as the solution of the case in hand. He brings no harsh or doubtful charge against Job. He expresses no suspicion, and apparently entertains none, of the depth and reality of his piety. His plea is rather based on the assumption that Job is really what he has ever been supposed to be in uprightness and the devout fear of God.

He lays no accusation upon him but such as is common to all who are sharers of our degenerate nature. All are impure in the sight of God, and all are in consequence born to trouble. Exposure to suffering, and suffering itself, being an inevitable result of that corrupt nature with which we were born, the wise and reasonable course, and the truly pious course, is not to indulge in passionate outcries against the divine orderings, which can only be productive of harm to the sufferer himself (v.2). Rather, it is wise to meekly accept and submit to the sorrows which He sends, who makes sore and binds up, who wounds and His hands make whole. Such submission will surely lead to peace and to salvation.

It is undoubtedly true that where there is no sin there will be no suffering among the subjects of God's moral government. All suffering has sin as its invariable and necessary antecedent. It is also true that the consciousness of sin and ill-desert must forever close the mouth of every sufferer from any well-grounded complaint against the righteousness of God. The holiest and the best are sinners nevertheless. And whatever may be the sufferings they endure in the providence of God, it cannot be said that they are unjustly treated. For, as Zophar states in more developed form to Job, "*God exacts of you less than your iniquities deserve*" (11:6). No man's sufferings in this world are equal to his just deserts.

But, while this is true and incontestable, it does not account for cases of special and extraordinary suffering, and especially such as occur in the experience of good men, such as we have here in Job's case. The general sinfulness of men may account for human sorrows so far as they are uniformly distributed. And a like principle may be applied where they are plainly graduated in proportion to the demerit of the sufferers. But special suffering, not involving special guilt, cannot be accounted for in this way. A sinfulness common to all cannot be the reason why one is singled out rather than another, and made to endure extraordinary sorrows.

The special significance of suffering, therefore, remains unexplained. Its importance as a means of discipline and training, and the far more exceeding reward by which it shall be abundantly compensated, are not once suspected. Eliphaz alleges that man suffers because he is a sinner. He did not know that a man may likewise suffer because he is a saint, that he may thus exhibit more distinctly his godly character, that he may be ripened still more in holiness, and that his final reward may be proportionately increased. To Eliphaz, suffering was ever and only a punishment, a judgment for sin, an infliction of the divine displeasure. He did not know that it might also be a token of love, a means of grace, a blessing in disguise; that whome the Lord loves He chastens, scourging every sin He receives.

The other friends, in their discourses, follow Eliphaz in the principles and method of discussion, only with increased vehemence and more open censure of Job. Their axiom is that God cannot deal unjustly, and therefore suffering must be the fruit of sin. Bildad intimates that Job's children had but suffered the consequences of their own misdeeds, so that this loss which he had experienced was the result of sin, not his own indeed, but theirs. And he puts and 'if' before his affirmation of the piety of Job himself, "*If you are pure and upright, surely He would awake for you and make the dwelling-place of your righteousness blessed*" (8:6). Zophar puts the 'if' before the contrary hypothesis as to Job's character and conduct, implying at least the possibility, "*if iniquity is in your hand, put it far away, and do not let wickedness dwell in your tents. Surely then you shall lift up your face without spot; yea, you shall be steadfast and shall not fear; for you shall forget your misery, and you shall remember it as waters that pass away. And your life shall be clearer than the noonday; though there be no darkness, you shall be as the morning*" (11:14-17). The vividness and beauty of the imagery which they employ, and the force and vigor of their expressions, cannot fail to charm and to impress, however unsatisfactory their treatment of the mystery with which they deal, however unsound or rather one-sided the conclusions to which they come--and however unjust and ungenerous they may be in accusing Job.

When Eliphaz speaks a second time, it is plain that he has undergone a considerable change in his feelings toward Job. He reasserts the fundamental principle common to him with the other friends, of the necessary connection of suffering with sin. But he no longer illustrates or defends it by the consideration of the universal and native sinfulness of the race. It is not of man as *"born to trouble"* that he now speaks, so much as of man *"who drinks iniquity like water."* It is the fate of the ungodly and wicked man that he holds up before Job for his warning. And instead of presupposing Job's integrity, and urging him in consequence to cherish the hope that he should not be utterly cut off, he charges him rather with serious guilt. It is true that he does not charge Job with criminal misdeeds or acts of sin, but with wicked words. In his speeches now uttered in the presence of the friends he has inculpated himself. He has maintained principles and uttered expressions inconsistent with pious reverence for God. *"You do away with fear, and take away prayer before God."* That is to say, Job, you are putting an end to piety and are emptying prayer of its value by the sentiments which you have propounded here. *"For your iniquity teaches your mouth, and you choose the tongue of the crafty. Your own mouth condemns you, and not I; yes, your own lips testify against you"* (15:4-6).

Bildad and Zophar once more follow Eliphaz in the same general strain, holding up before Job the destruction that is certain, sooner or later, to overtake the ungodly. And they intimate plainly that this is the explanation of the dismal things which have befallen him.

Eliphaz in his third discourse makes a further advance. He now, without any ambiguity of language or indirectness of intimation explicitly charges Job with the most atrocious wickedness. He has become more and more estranged from him as the discussion has proceeded. He has become more and more convinced from the language of Job himself that he is destitute of real piety, until at length all his former confidence in Job has utterly vanished, and he not only believes him capable of any amount of wickedness, but he is persuaded that he has actually perpetrated crimes of the most serious character, and that the sorrows by which he has so suddenly and so fearfully been overwhelmed are thus easily accounted for.

It is not now the general sinfulness of human nature which he adduces against him, as in his first discourse. Nor does he merely allege the language of impiety and irreverence to be found in his speeches which he had here uttered in their presence, as in his second discourse. Nor does he content himself with indirect insinuations and implications that his fate was but the customary fate of the wicked, as the other friends had already done. But he goes beyond all this and makes open and direct charges of habitual and gross transgression. *"Is not your wickedness great, and your iniquity without measure? For you have taken a pledge from your brother for nothing, and have stripped the naked of their clothing. You have not given water to the weary to drink, and you have held back bread from the hungry.... You have sent widows away empty, and the arms of the fatherless have been broken. Therefore snares are all around you and sudden fear troubles you"* (22:5-10). A just and all-seeing God has detected the villany and set the brand of His reprobation upon it. Eliphaz thinks that Job is suffering just what might be expected as the righteous reward for the iniquity which he had practiced. His fancied impunity was at an end, and deserved vengeance has overtaken him at last.

What a spectacle this is! And what a lesson we may learn here. This man is one whom GOD has declared to be without equal for piety, a perfect and upright man, one who feared God and turned away from evil. And yet here are good and wise men, men of age and experience, his friends and intimates through many former years, knowing him not merely by reputation but by personal, familiar and long acquaintance, who do not hesitate to cherish the grossest and most unjust suspicions, and actually to charge him with the most vicious type of misconduct. And they do all this without the slightest foundation in actual fact! It is purely their inferences and suppositions which underlie their charges. Yet they lay it upon him as though they had the most undoubted evidence of its reality. Again we say, What a spectacle! what a lesson we may learn here!

These friends of Job, we have admitted, are not to blame for not knowing what could only be known by divine revelation--and we know what had not then been revealed. It does not imply any moral blindness nor any dullness of intellectual perception that they could not discern the true intent of the sufferings of Job, or the divine purpose in permitting them. This was a secret still undisclosed. The mystery of the afflictions of the righteous was now to be unveiled as it had never been before. And the sufferings of Job were to furnish the occasion for the lessons which God was to teach. But this was not to be done until gifted minds, well instructed in the general truths of religion at the time, had grappled with the problem and had shown by the trial the incompetency of unaided reason to solve the riddle, or to dissipate the darkness which overhung the dispensation. The ignorance of Job's friends, and of Job himself, regarding the meaning and design of God's dealings with him, was not reprehensible. This could not have been otherwise, for they could not know.

So far then they are excusable. But what cannot be excused in them is that in the first place they undertook to expound what they did not understand, acting as though they had full knowledge in the case. In so doing, they rested the divine procedure on insufficient reasons, seeking to square it by their own limited notions. If they had confessed the mystery and admitted their ignorance, all would have been well. They would have saved themselves from the errors and mistakes, the gross injustices which they visited upon Job. By acting as they did, they in fact arraigned the providence of God, which they were professedly defending. They prescribed a rule for its administration as the only one compatible with justice, which is not, after all, the method which it actually follows. Suffering is not distributed according to the ratio nor on the principles which they allege to be absolutely demanded by God's essential attributes. By defending His dispensations on grounds which are demonstrably inadequate, and insisting that these are the grounds on which their defence must necessarily be tested, they in fact proclaim that these dispensations are indefensible. And they do their utmost, though unwittingly, to bring them into discredit.

And in the second place, they were inexcusable in another respect. They not only entered a weak and unsuitable plea as the only one upon which the cause of God could be rested or His providence justified, but they likewise undertook to bolster up His cause by a contrived, if not positively immoral method. As Job charges upon them (13:7), they spoke wickedly for God, they talked deceitfully for Him. They accused Job of things which they, by experience or evidence, had no means of knowing to be true--and which, in fact, were not true. They inferred from false premises, and were willing to conduct the defence of the divine government in this way. They were guilty of making rash and reckless assertions as they professed to defend the cause of true religion and piety. They were unjust to Job, not only harboring baseless suspicions, but in venturing upon positive declarations of his guilt in matters of which he was wholly innocent. They were shamefully cruel to their suffering friend, causelessly aggravating his distress, which, professedly, they had come to soothe. And this at a time when he was already weighed down by troubles that should have disarmed malice itself and softened hearts of stone. Nothing in their argument could justify a course like this. And no straits in which the defence of God's righteous government and the claims of religion seemed to be could justify it. If the divine administration could not be honestly and truthfully defended, and without a resort to what is questionable and false, they should have concluded that they were not called of God to be His champions in this particular. They should have admitted the mystery and confessed their ignorance, and waited patiently till the Lord Himself disclosed the impregnable basis on which He chose to have His cause rested. Confiding in Him who does great, unsearchable things, and whose ways are past finding out, they should have trusted that he would make all plain in His own good time, instead of presuming to put forth unholy hands to support the ark of God, and darkening His infinite counsel by words without knowledge.

The gross charges put forth by Eliphaz could not be repeated by Bildad in his speech, which followed, in the face of Job's solemn insistence upon his innocence, and his appeal to the omniscient Judge of all. Accordingly he recedes from them entirely, falling back on the original position of Eliphaz in his opening speech; viz., the universal sinfulness of men, in which Job is of necessity involved. He thus not only impliedly retracts the charges before insinuated or openly made against Job, but concedes his inability to conduct the argument further. He has nothing to add but what had been said and answered long before. The same thing is likewise intimated by the brevity of his speech, which consists of but a few commonplace sentences. And Zophar makes no attempt to speak at all!

The friends accordingly give up their argument with Job. They cannot convince or confute him. They entered their protest against his complaint in his wild outburst of grief. They sought to convict him of the irreverence and impiety of which they thought him guilty, and to bring him back to what they esteemed right views and a proper spirit. Instead of this they threw themselves upon the side of the great adversary. They became the tools and accomplices of Satan in his sore temptation, giving all their weight to the side opposed to God and goodness, embittering Job against a cause which was upheld by such methods; casting discredit upon God's governing providence, so inadequately defending, justifying Him by arguments which were palpably false; tempting Job to renounce the service of God Himself, whom they represented in a light that served only to repel.

The question has now reached its utmost intensity. Can Job withstand the temptation which is brought to bear upon him with all this accumulated force? With his property swept away, his children gone, himself the victim of a loathsome and painful disease, his own wife begging him to abandon the service of a God so cruel as to be the author of all their woes, his agony, both of body and of mind, still growing, without the prospect of release--and now the trusted friends of former years deserting and scorning him, stinging him with their undeserved reproaches, while he himself is totally unable to comprehend the righteousness or the reasons behind these dreadful inflictions--can Job bear it all, still maintaining his unswerving trust in God. The answer is to be found in Job's successive replies to his friends, in which all the workings of his soul in this fearful crisis are so vividly and faithfully portrayed. The examination of these replies are now in order. May He, who alone can, in mercy uphold and comfort all His tried and suffering saints.

CHAPTER V.

My friends scorn me: but mine eye poureth out tears unto God. – Job xvi. 20.

JOB'S CONFLICT

Satan now has his train completely laid; and it would almost seem as though at length he has his victim entirely in his power, and there **was** no escape out of the fatal snare. Job, with all he had, was put at the disposal of the evil one, with the single limitation that he must spare his life. And Satan has used the liberty accorded to him without stint. He has brought the most frightful complication of sorrows and sufferings upon the unsuspecting patriarch, and set every influence at work that he could bring to bear upon him, to overturn his integrity and detach him from the service of God. Can he succeed in his fiendish purpose?

He has crushed the spirits of Job, and quenched his hopes. He has accumulated pain and grief upon him, until, in the depth of his long-continued anguish, existence itself has become an insupportable burden. The weary sufferer, stunned, bewildered, tortured to the last extreme of despair, curses the day that he was born, and longs for nothing so much as to die. It would seem as though nature could hold out no longer. Satan perceives his advantage in this crisis of Job's misery, and presses it relentlessly, through the medium of his friends, who unwittingly range themselves on the tempter's side. These professed ministers of consolation and advocates of piety treat him in a manner which embitters him against them and the cause which they defend. Their pleas for the equity of the divine administration are repugnant to his sense of right, and to the testimony of his own conscience. They represent his aggravated sufferings as a righteous retribution, either for the sinfulness inborn in our common human nature, or for the sin betrayed in his present irreverent and unsubmissive speeches, or for the guilt of some gross criminality now first detected and brought to light. These assumptions Job repels point by point. His sufferings cannot be so explained. What, then, is the inevitable alternative? Is not God unrighteous? is He not treating him as an offender, when He knows him to be innocent? Or is He not at least like an implacable foe, mercilessly and gratuitously inflicting upon him these grievous sorrows? If woe like this be not the award of justice, must it not be injustice or wanton cruelty? and, if God be either unjust or pitiless, how can the sufferer, crushed beneath His arbitrary inflictions, adore or trust Him?

Job's triumph is, in the most absolute and unqualified manner, the triumph of faith over sense. He seems to outward view to have no ground left to stand upon. Satan has apparently shut him up to conclusions respecting the providence of God, which positively exclude worship and piety. It would seem as though every thing conspired to show that God was persecuting him, and treating him as an enemy. Yet from an angry God he can turn nowhere but back to God Himself, in whom he does and must confide, in spite of his apparent hostility. God is still his only refuge, even from the fierceness of His own displeasure. "Though He slay me, yet will I trust in Him."

Job's triumph was not easily gained. He was indeed hardly beset by the adversary. The struggle was desperate, and tested his constancy to the utmost. The contest was not barely one of fortitude, of capacity to endure of power to bear up under calamities and sufferings, and to rise superior to that terrible combination of distresses which was weighing him down. The question to be settled was not whether Job had that heroic firmness, and indomitable self-mastery and self-control, or rather self-sufficiency, which was the Stoic's ideal, and could calmly bear all outward losses, and support undisturbed the most grievous inflictions of pain and sorrow. His trial lay in a totally different plane. The point of it was, whether he would still cleave to God and maintain his trust in Him, when there no longer remained any thing external to attract him to His service, but every thing combined to repel him and drive him from it.

The hand of God was in these dreadful sorrows. Why had He sent them, or permitted them? The Christian can readily answer this question, and can comprehend without difficulty how afflictions are consistent with the divine goodness and love. But the revelations which shed such a cheerful light for us upon this mysterious subject had not then been given. Job was left to confront the difficulty, with no help afforded him for its solution. He was in utter darkness and perplexity, and unable to apprehend the reasons of the dispensation. And the only solution which offered itself, and towards which he was persistently driven by antagonism to the inadmissible position urged upon him by his friends, was not reconcilable with the goodness or justice of God. Hence the tumult of his soul, and the tempest of conflicting emotions which rages within him. Reason and sense urge him in one direction, and the strong recoil of faith drives him back in the other; and thus he is swayed perpetually to and fro, still hoping against hope, ever afresh seeking unto God who had cast him off, unable to release himself from the toils which Satan had so artfully woven around him, yet continuing to struggle, and never submitting to be captured; unable to escape from conclusions to which the logic of his sufferings seemed to constrain him, or to banish the forbidding spectre of an angry God which they perpetually raise before him, and yet holding fast to his inmost convictions, in spite of all that seems to contradict them.

This inward struggle of Job is not made the subject of any formal description; but it is vividly depicted in his successive speeches in reply to his friends. These lay bare all the workings of his soul, and the fearful agitation which was going on within him. They disclose the terrible conflict through which he was passing, in its various phases, until out of the depths of despair he fought his way to solid peace. They show into what distress the tempter plunged him; what gloom and darkness had settled upon his path; to what spiritual straits he was reduced; but how in spite of all he never abandoned his faith in God. He staggered and tottered under the tremendous blows which were given him, and it seemed at times as though he could not recover himself, and must fall. But somehow he always regained his footing, and never lost his balance entirely. The adversary was foiled, notwithstanding all his arts and all the weapons he employed. And the piety of Job, which he sought to undermine or to destroy, sustained the test, and triumphed in the encounter.

Job's opening speech, in which he first breaks silence and pours forth his piteous plaint of woe, is a soliloquy. It is the melancholy wail of insupportable anguish. It is the frantic outburst of grief, which has been held in until it can no longer be repressed, and to which he now gives vent, apparently unconscious that nay one is present, bemoaning himself without the thought of being overheard. The burden of his speech is the misery of this intolerable existence: Oh that I had never lived! Oh that now I might cease to be!

When Eliphaz and the other friends undertake to address him, reproving him for his want of submission, justifying the dispensation under which he suffers, and pointing out what they conceive to be the true method of relief, Job directs his replies partly to them and partly to God. He speaks to his friends with the double aim of exciting their pity and replying to their arguments. What he says to God is likewise of a twofold character: he both wrestles with God, in the way of expostulation for the misery which He has inflicted upon him,.and he affirms his confidence in Him. It is in these addresses to God that his inward agony most fully asserts itself; that the antagonistic emotions with which his soul is rent asunder meet in the sharpest contrast and collision; and he undergoes the greatest and most sudden transitions of feeling.

The progress and the stages of Job's inward strife are very plainly marked. His ineffectual appeals to his friends for the sympathy which they deny him throw him back more and more upon God, as his only source of help. Refused the pity that he craves on earth, he can look nowhere but to Heaven, and is forced to seek his only refuge there. Accordingly, that which overwhelmingly occupies his mind in the first instance is the relation between himself and God. Is God his Enemy, or is He his Friend? Despair and hope struggle for the mastery, and the conflict grows more and more intense until the climax is reached at the central point of the discussion between him and his friends. Corresponding to the three series of speeches addressed to Job by his three friends, who follow each other in the same invariable order, are the three series of his replies severally addressed to them. Throughout the first series of Job's rejoinders, and into the middle of the second the conflict in his soul continues to heighten, until in his second reply to his second friend, Bildad, it attains its acme. Here the opposing principles come to their most intense encounter. His sense of the hostility of God to him reaches its most vivid and vehement expression, but is immediately succeeded and swallowed up by the conviction which overspreads his soul of the certainty of God's friendship and favor, which, though the worst comes to the worst, must and will manifest itself, hereafter if not now, in the world to come, if not in this. With this burst of triumph the temptation is trodden under foot. Satan is vanquished, and Job's inward conflict is substantially over. Faith has gotten the victory. He has gained the assurance that God is his Redeemre, come what may and in spite of all adverse appearances. And with this the whole power of the temptation is broken.

The darkness is not dispersed. The mystery of the dispensation is no nearer its solution. The enigma remains, and is as inexplicable as ever. Why he has been made to suffer or allowed to suffer so terribly he does not know. He has not the faintest idea of the reasons of the infliction. He does not discern how it is to be reconciled with the goodness of God, or His righteousness, or His favor towards himself. But he has laid hold of the fact with the strong grasp of faith. He is assured that God is his Redeemer and his Friend; and his confident trust does not again give way. Notwithstanding the continuance of his sufferings and the difficulties that encumber their explanation, he is now on the solid rock. The floods may dash around him, but they cannot break over him; and he is no longer in peril of being overwhelmed.

Having thus reached comparative peace, and settled the question which chiefly agitated him hitherto,—of his relation to God,—Job next turns his attention more immediately to his controversy with his friends. He has denied the truth of their position before, and stated facts at variance with it; but in his subsequent speeches, viz., the last of the second series and in those of the third series, he refutes their position by reviewing their arguments in detail, and he shows that they have furnished no adequate or satisfactory account whether of God's providence in general or of his sorrows in particular.

Having thus hastily sketched in outline the current of Job's feelings toward God and his attitude toward his firends, we may now return to take a more deliberate survey of his several speeches, with the view of noting more minutely his demeanor at each successive step of his great struggle.

In his first reply to Eliphaz, Job is in the same state of unrelieved despair as in his opening complaint. The poor alleviation even of the sympathy of his friends had been denied him, and he bitterly upbraids them for withholding that pity which was so needful to him in his distressed situation, and would have cost them so little. Eliphaz had reminded him of the infinite greatness of God, and of the feebleness and frailty of sinful man, and urged these as reasons why he should be submissive under his sufferings. To Job's mind these are but an aggravation of his misery and a fresh justification of his complaint. He had but one brief life to live, and this was filled up with weariness and woe. "Therefore," he says, "I will not refrain my mouth; I will speak in the anguish of my spirit; I will complain in the bitterness of my soul." And he converts these into pleas with the Almighty that he would mitigate the severity of his treatment. He was too insignificant and frail, sinner though he was, to deserve or to require such terrible constancy of attention from the infinite God. It was making too much of a creature so trifling and so powerless, that he should be so fearfully visited, and made a mark at which God was always directing His shafts, and never allowed a moment's respite day or night, when he would shortly sleep in the dust and cease to be.

There does not appear to be a single ray of comfort nor a gleam of hope for the stricken sufferer in the present or the future, from man or from God. But from this abyss of darkness and cheerless despondency he struggles constantly upward towards the light. In each successive speech some slight advance is made; there is each time some fresh reaching out towards help or hope. Every address made by his friends shows him more and more plainly that nothing is to be looked for or expected from them: they still persist in refusing to him even that measure of relief or consolation which human sympathy might supply. Cut off from all earthly assistance or even pity, there is no one but God to whom he can have recourse. And here he is torn by conflicting feelings. God is persecuting and afflicting him, and, to all outward appearance, is treating him as an enemy. And still he cannot let go that inward persuasion, which manifests itself at first dimly, and yet grows in clearness and strength as he recurs to it, that God will not altogether withhold his favor from him. Each time that he essays to speak, sense and faith stand in blank antagonism. His sufferings press overwhelmingly upon him with their apparent evidence that God is against him. But Faith comes with its whispers, scarcely audible, and yet refusing to be stifled, that God must nevertheless be on his side.

These suggestions of his unquenched confidence in God are only hypothetical at first. If such an obstacle were only removed, or if such a condition could only exist, then God would surely manifest Himself in his favor. But the obstacle remains, the condition is impossible to be realized; and so he sinks back each time into a state of unrelieved despondency and gloom. But his despair is no longer absolute and total. These suggestions of faith and hope gradually assume a more definite form, and take upon themselves more reality. They gain in strength, and come to a fuller utterance with each successive response he makes to his friends, until at last they grow into a clear and decided conviction which dissipates the clouds of despondency, breaks through the toils which the adversary has thrown around him, and vanquished the temptation completely and forever by the language of triumphant assurance, "I know that my Redeemer liveth."

In the reply to Bildad, the second of the friends, we see the first budding of this rising hope, the first glimmer of the coming dawn. We there find the earliest suggestion of a more favorable issue; but it is a suggestion clogged with an impossible condition, and which cannot be realized in the form in which it presents itself to his mind. If he could but speak with God on equal terms, if God would lay aside His infinite majesty and divest Himself of His awful terrors, then he would present his case before Him and it would be acceptably heard, and he would be vindicated by his Judge. But how is such a hearing to be obtained? "He is not a man, as I am, that I should answer him, and we should come together in judgment. Neither is there any days-man betwixt us, that might lay his hand upon us both." He nevertheless pours forth his expostulation with God pleading with Him for His righteousness' sake and for His past mercies, upon which he fondly dwells, not to destroy him. "I will say unto God, Do not condemn me. Is it good unto Thee that Thou shouldest oppress, that Thou shouldest despise the work of Thine hands, and shine upon the counsel of the wicked?"

When Zophar, the last of the friends, speaks, it is in the same strain with those who had preceded him, only with greater harshness and impetuosity. If Job had entertained a lingering expectation of pity or even justice from at least one of his friends, this is now gone. And he retorts in terms of bitter and indignant rebuke for their arrogant conceit in adducing the familiar common-places of God's rectitude and justice, as though they were an adequate solution of the mysteries of His providence. These rest on totally different and as yet unexplained grounds. They were undertaking to vindicate God's providence in a manner which would not be sanctioned by God Himself. They were justifying the dealings of God by false and unfounded assumptions. They were in fact impugning the righteousness of God, which they professed to defend, for they suspended its defence on the assumption that He invariably acted on principles, upon which He did not even ordinarily act in His administration of human affairs, and upon which Job knew from his own inward consciousness He was not acting in the present instance. He was confident, therefore, that God would declare in his favor and not in theirs. He was sure of a vindication, if his case could only come before God. And his mind recurs again to the same twofold obstruction as before; and the hypothesis of its removal, though doubtful and distant, does not seem so absolutely impossible as before. "Only do not two things unto me. Withdraw Thine hand far from me: and let not Thy dread make me afraid. Then call Thou, and I will answer: or let me speak, and answer Thou me."

But the sense of his misery returns upon him, and of his life almost at an end, cut off admist his hopeless sufferings; and what possibility remains of a divine vindication?

"There is hope of a tree, if it be cut down, that it will sprout again, and that the tender branch thereof will not cease. But man dieth, and wasteth away: yea, man giveth up the ghost, and where is he? As the waters fail from the sea, and the flood decayeth and drieth up: so man lieth down, and riseth not: till the heavens be no more, they shall not awake, nor be raised out of their sleep." Oh if it were otherwise! If death were but a temporary suspension of his earthly life! If he could go down to the grave for a season, until God's favor were restored to him, and then could return to the land of the living and come back to his former abode, he would patiently bear all that was laid upon him now. "Oh that Thou wouldest hide me in the grave, that Thou wouldest keep me secret until Thy wrath be past, that Thou wouldest appoint me a set time, and remember me! If man could die and then live again, all the days of my appointed time would I wait till my change come," my restoration from death to life.

Job is trembling here on the verge of a hope full of immortality, which is soon to assume its proper form before his mind and to swell to its just dimensions. But it is as yet only inadequately conceived by him. A conscious state of existence beyond the grave was part of the faith of the early patriarchs, who looked forward to being "gathered to their fathers." But the future state was then revealed only in the most dim and shadowy outline. It was to them an unseen and unknown world; no bright and joyous anticipations were connected with it, no clear disclosures had yet been made regarding it. The bare fact of its reality was almost all that was known. The veil was about to be lifted to the wrestling soul of Job further than it had ever been raised to human eyes before. The lesson of his immortality was one of special value for his present need. And he is here darkly and vaguely feeling after it, and reaching out towards it. In all his speeches hitherto the grave has been the end of all that he expected or hoped for,—not, we may assume, the end of being and conscious spiritual existence, but of life in any desirable sense. He had no anticipations of good in the grave or beyond it, no thought of blessedness in another state, which could outweigh or alleviate his present sorrows. All his notions of the future were negative. He conceived of it simply as a state of privation of all earthly good. He had no idea of the positive blessings belonging to it, of its bliss and glory and beatific vision of God. He looked downward to Sheol, the land of ghosts and shades, not upward to heaven, the abode of glorified spirits in the immediate presence of God Himself.

The mists that shrouded the future would were never taken completely away until Jesus Christ abolished death, and brought life and immortality to light through the gospel. The apostles and disciples of Christ stand in an entirely different attitude to the future world, and hold a different language respecting it from the saints of God, who preceded his coming. The consciousness that to die is gain, the desire to depart as far better than to abide in the flesh, belongs wholly to the New Testament: it has no parallel in the Old. Nevertheless, preliminary lessons of great value were already given under the former dispensation. And one of the first gleams of heavenly light sent to irradiate the darkness of the grave is found in this book of Job. It is born of an assurance graciously vouchsafed to his soul as he struggles with his terrible temptation.

In all that he has said hitherto of death, it has been spoken of as terminating every hope and every joyful prospect. *"As the cloud is consumed and vanisheth away: so he that goeth down to the grave shall come up no more. He shall return no more to his house, neither shall his place know him any more"* (vii, 9, 10). *"I go whence I shall not return, even to the land of darkness, and the shadow of death; a land of darkness, as darkness itself; and of the shadow of death, without any order, and where the light is as darkness"* (x. 21, 22). But in the speech to Zophar upon which we are now remarking, he ventures the hypothetical suggestion of a return again to life from the dead. If that were only possible, it would relieve the gloom of this dark dispensation under which he is suffering. It would allay the strife, which now rages in his soul between his conviction that God will declare on his behalf, and the outward appearance as though God were his foe. It would open the way to a reconciliation between these seeming contradictions. It would afford an opportunity for the divine favor, of which he was inwardly assured, still to manifest itself to him. In the precise form in which this vague suggestion has arisen in his mind, it cannot again be renewed. And with this impossibility he relapses again into his former state of cheerless despondency. But the germ of hope is there, which will soon unfold itself in a more practicable form to the assured conviction of God's favor manifested to him in a future life.

The temptation is now approaching its crisis; and Job's inward conflict is becoming more and more intense. In his next two speeches he says little almost nothing, to his friends. He merely in a few words at the beginning gives vent to his impatience at their unfeeling speeches, and begs them to desist and torture him no longer. He makes no reply to their arguments, but turns from them to God and pours forth all the agitation of his soul before Him. Despair and hope in his bosom, and the struggle is a fearful one indeed. His agony and inward distress are at their highest point, and are reflected in the vehemence and even passionate character of his expressions. He is bowed down by the sense of God's anger as apparently shown in these terrible inflictions. "He teareth me in His wrath, who hateth me: He gnasheth upon me with His teeth; . . . I was at ease, but He hath broken me asunder: He hath also taken me by my neck, and shaken me to pieces and set me up for His mark. His archers compass me round about. He cleaveth my reins asunder, and doth not spare; He poureth out my gall upon the ground. He breaketh me with breach upon breach, He runneth upon me like a giant. . . . My face is foul with weeping, and on my eyelids is the shadow of death."

And all this, as his inward consciousness of integrity and his total inability to comprehend why God should have treated him thus, prompt him to exclaim, "Not for any injustice in mine hands: also my prayer is pure." Such violent treatment, which he has no consciousness of having deserved, dealing with him as though he were a gross offender, which he was not, and carrying the infliction even to the point of destroying his life, extorts from him the passionate outcry as from the victim of atrocious injury: "O earth, cover not thou my blood, and let my cry have no place." I must die, but it is unrighteous murder. Let the earth refuse to drink in my blood thus unjustly shed, so that it may remain forever exposed, a constant witness to the terrible wrong perpetrated upon me; and let my death-cry never be hushed to silence, but resound forever in testimony of the cruel violence under which I suffer. I die, unable longer to sustain these dreadful inflictions which God is bringing upon me; but I die, protesting against the injustice and the outrage.

Has Satan then gained his end, and has Job at length fallen into the snare? In the frightful darkness, which has to outward view obscured the evidence of God's rectitude, has Job given up his sense of that rectitude? Is his confidence in God's eternal justice gone? Then has he indeed been driven to that renunciation of God's service to which Satan has relentlessly endeavoring to force him.

But no! In all this agony and darkness and inexplicable mystery, Job cannot let go his ineradicable trust in God. Brought, as it might seem that he was, almost to the point of abandoning it, the strength of that trust only becomes more conspicuous from the strain to which it has been subjected. By its powerful recoil it carries him suddenly back from the verge of the abyss to the immovable foundation. The faith that seemed to be vanishing, if it had not already vanished, rises unexpectedly superior over all the tumult of his soul, and all depressing circumstances. From his frantic outcry against the injustice that is slaying him, he passes to the instant expression of his unabated trust in God. "Also now, behold, my witness is in heaven, and my record is on high. My friends scorn me: but mine eye poureth out tears unto God." Only the infinite exaltation of the Most High still interposes its impassable obstruction, and places him at such a remove that his case cannot be adequately brought before God to be rectified. And yet he pleads with God, who alone will or can, to be his surety and take his part. All others have deserted him. All others misunderstand his character and misinterpret his condition. God is his only refuge. But, under the returning sense of his misery and approaching end, he sinks once more at the close of his speech into a cheerless and despondent frame.

But the victory for which he has been struggling is now near at hand. The elements of hope, which have been gathering in his soul, have attained a consistency, which will make them superior in the strife. And his trust in God is preparing to assert itself invincibly, though deprived of all external supports and in the face of all opposition from outward sense.

The more particular examination of the language of his triumph will occupy another chapter.

Now unto Him that kept Job from falling, and who is able likewise to keep us from falling, and to present us faultless before the presence of His glory with exceeding joy, to the only wise God our Saviour be glory and majesty, dominion and power, both now and ever. Amen.

*For I know that my Redeemer lives; and that He shall stand at the latter day upon the earth; and though after my skin worms destroy this body yet in my flesh shall I see God: whom I shall see for myself; and my eyes shall see, and not another; though my reins are consumed within me--*Job 19:25-27

JOB'S TRIUMPH OVER SATAN

Job's triumphant assertion of his unshaken confidence in God, which he reaches near the close of the nineteenth chapter, is deservedly ranked as the most important passage in all his discourses. In some respects it is one of the most signal passages in the entire Old Testament, not so much in the positive amount of revelation which it contains as in the intrepid spirit of an unconquerable piety which it discloses. It exalts the patriarch of Uz to a level with the patriarch of Ur, the acknowledged father of the faithful, and marks Job as no less conspicuously an example and a pattern of faith than Abraham--the one as distinguished and heroic in his constancy in suffering as the other in his unswerving obedience.

The central position of this noble utterance in the discourses of Job has been before referred to. And that it is the turning-point in his discussions with his friends, the culmination and the close of his sore inward conflict, the full and complete outcoming of a trust which has been gradually gathering strength in the fact of the most formidable opposition, and struggling to find expression, it is indeed the crowning victory over Satan's fiercest and most subtle temptation. It is faith planting itself firmly on the unseen, when not one single external ground of support remains. The flukes of his anchor have taken hold of the immovable Rock of Ages, and the rage of the tempest and the dashing waves and the heaving sea cannot tear his vessel from its moorings. Held by the strong grasp of the invisible, which is no less real, solid and abiding because it is out of sight, he can safely defy all that is visible and on the surface, the mutable and the transient--even Satan's most furious assaults have no power to dislodge him or unsettle his sure and well-grounded persuasion.

The suffering patriarch is, to all human appearance, and in his own estimation, sinking rapidly to the grave under an accumulation of disasters, which seem to exhaust Satan's fiendish ingenuity of torture, and which appear to betoken the divine displeasure. His friends charge that God is bearing testimony against his aggravated criminality. Conscious of his integrity, and yet confounded by these apparent evidences of God's hostility to him, he piteously pleads with God no longer to treat him as a criminal, since he does not deserve to be so treated. Rather he asks that God's heavy hand be removed, that He bear witness to his innocence and uprightness. But his cries are unanswered. He cannot get his case before the supreme Judge of all so as to obtain the hearing and the adjudication to which he makes his appeal. The Most High does not in any way interfere to take his part, or to redress the wrongs which His servant is enduring, or to correct the grievous and unjust imputations which offer themselves as so direct an inference from God's own dealings with him. The heavens are silent. The situation remains unchanged. The sufferings of Job are unabated. His friends continue to taunt him with this plain evidence of guilt.

43

We have observed the growing intensity of Job's inward struggle, and the strife is not yet allayed. He repels the insinuations of his friends. He rejects their conclusion, for it is contradicted by his own consciousness. But he cannot break the logic of their argument. As a consequence he is tossed by conflicting emotions. He seems to be shut up to the conclusion that God is unrighteously oppressing him, afflicting him without cause, or punishing him for crimes which he has not committed. And if God is unrighteous, then He is not a God to be worshiped and confided in. If he admits this, he has fallen before the temptation--and Satan has gained the victory. But how can Job escape it? The facts stare him sternly in the face. And even if he were disposed to shut his eyes to them, his friends with officious pertinacity are forever obtruding them upon him with their inevitable deductions.

It is a time of outspoken frankness, in which the convictions of his soul utter themselves without reserve and without disguise. He cannot shelter himself behind conventional phrases which may have a religious sound, though emptied of their meaning and not expressive of his real and honest faith. He is not in a mood to save appearances by the gloss of pious professions. He dare not deceive himself and others even by uncandidly smoothing over difficulties in the divine administration, and persuading himself that he has explained what he has simply evaded. His whole soul is opened before us down to its inmost depths, and his most secret imaginings. He is engaged in a contest for life or death, in which every thing is involved, and no mere pretense or flimsy material can avail him. He must have truth on which he can rest with unshaken conviction. He cannot save even piety by shallow pretext or insincere profession.

In the unshrinking truthfulness with which he utters his inmost feelings, we are startled sometimes by the boldness and seeming irreverence with which he arraigns the rectitude of the divine proceedings. But it is not the daring recklessness of presumptuous speculation intruding on the unrevealed. Nor is it the profane utterance of the impious transgressor blaspheming his Maker. It is the transparent sincerity of the tempted soul, driven almost to distraction by suggestions which are forced upon him, and which he cannot shut out. They are not cherished thoughts on which he loves to dwell, and to which he gladly reverts. They are like frightful spectral illusions from which he shrinks away, but which continue nevertheless to glare upon him until by the surpassing energy of faith the dreadful spell is broken, and the temptation vanquished.

In his former speeches Job has been struggling desperately with the idea perpetually thrust upon him by his friends, and forcing itself upon him from all that he endured, that God was his enemy. Germs of hope have arisen within him, but they have not been sufficient to lift the burden off his heart. In the beginning of this speech he is still oppressed by these evident tokens of God's antagonism. But the argument of guilt deduced from it by his friends he warmly repels. It is not true, as they urge, that he deserves what he suffers. It is not true that this is a display of divine justice! No, it is injustice! He says, "If you will magnify yourselves against me and plead my reproach against me, then know now that God has not overthrown me." Literally he is saying, "God has not perverted, distorted, or wronged me." It is the very word that Bildad had used in a former address, in his pious indignation at the sentiments of Job, "Does God pervert judgment? Or does the Almighty pervert justice? (8:3). And it is the same that Elihu uses subsequently in his rebuke of Job's rash and impatient utterances, "*Yes, surely God will not do wickedly, neither will the Almighty pervert judgment*" (34:12).

But such perversion Job boldly affirms to exist in his own case. In his conscious integrity he denies the righteousness of any infliction which charges that upon him of which he is not guilty. He denies the justice of executing sentence upon him for crimes of which he was free. If God, in sending these sufferings upon him, has marked him out as a criminal, as his friends allege, then He has perverted justice, He has done him wrong. He adds, "*Behold, I cry out, Violence! But I am not heard. I cry aloud, but there is no justice*" (19:7). He is the innocent victim of most cruel treatment. He is the defenceless subject of ruffianly violence, who screams for help against pitiless and inhuman outrage, who calls for justice against the most grievous oppression and wrong. But his cries are uttered in vain. No help is given him. There is no relaxation of the extreme of injury inflicted. And he proceeds with his harrowing recital of these causeless and gratuitous inflictions: "*He has fenced up my way so that I cannot pass, and He has set darkness in my paths. He has stripped me of my glory, and has taken the crown from my head. He has destroyed me on every side, and I am gone, and He has uprooted my hope like a tree. He has also kindled His wrath against me, and unto Himself He counts me as one of His enemies. His troops come together and raise up their way against me, and camp around my tent*" (19:8-12). My brothers, acquaintances, kinsfolk, familiar friends, my servants, and my very wife--everyone I have loved has turned against me. "*My bone clings to my skin and to my flesh, and I have escaped with the skin of my teeth. Have pity upon me, have pity upon me, O my friends! For the hand of God has touched me. Why do you, like God, persecute me and why are you not satisfied with my flesh?*" Why will you too join in this relentless persecution which God has initiated against me, and which can only be compared to ravenous and savage beasts of prey tearing and gnawing my flesh with a greed that cannot be satisfied?

Against such cruelty and injustice on the part of both God and man he enters his earnest protest, and he would have his words put on permanent record. Outcast alike from God and man, he makes his appeal to the rocks. Let the enduring rock be his monumental witness. Let there be carved there, in letters that shall not fade, the inscription of his innocence. Though God and man combine to condemn him, let his own statements of his integrity be engraved with an iron pen, and be filled in with lead in the rock forever. And thus may the everlasting rocks, in legible inscriptions never to be effaced, bear testimony on his behalf. And may the justice that he vainly craves elsewhere find at least its indelible record there.

It is customary to understand Job here as saying that he would have the words which immediately follow engraved in the rock. He would have that golden sentence, "*I know that my Redeemer lives, etc.*" stand on perpetual record, his legacy to future ages, his testimony through all time that, forsaken as he seemed to be by God and man, he never gave up his confident trust in God his Saviour. In his last and darkest hours he still held fast his unwavering assurance that God was his Redeemer and Friend, and though his body perished and crumbled into dust, he would still with his own eyes see God, who would appear on his behalf. And if any prefer so to interpret the patriarch's wish, we make no serious objection. These words are certainly worthy of being recorded on the solid rock. No grander monumental inscription can be found. Job could not have a worthier epitaph upon his rock-hewn tomb. In no way could a more exalted testimony be rendered to his steadfast piety than by preserving this outburst of triumphant faith, uttered under such circumstances. These words stand out conspicuously upon the speeches of Job, as the noblest, the loftiest, the most characteristic that he ever uttered, and the most aptly significant of the power of his faith, and the reality of his pious trust in God. So that, if any prefer to regard these as the words which Job desired to be carved on the rock, we make no serious objection.

Yet it seems to us that those interpreters have more accurately divined Job's own meaning, who think that he would have in lasting record on the rock, not the particular statement about to be made, but the things he said, the protestations of his innocence which had appeared in his former speeches over and over. So that this desire to have his words inscribed upon the rock is not so much an introduction to what follows, anticipating and preparing for the exultant announcement he is about to make, as rather the conclusion of what precedes. It does not represent his rising consciousness of triumph, but rather his lowest depth of desolation and hopeless despair, joined with his inward consciousness of integrity that demands some recognition. Bereft of every helper, human and divine, and crushed beneath an unrighteous sentence, his appeals to God unheard, and his friends joining in the merciless persecution, he asks that the rocks may take up his dying declaration, and that his words may be indelibly written there, so that the imperishable stone may speak his innocence of these false charges, and testify of the wrong that has been done him, after his own voice is gone. And so his appeal to the rocks to transmit his defence to all coming time will be parallel to his passionate apostrophe to the earth in his last speech, *"O earth, do not cover my blood, and let my cry have no place"* (16:18). It is the outcry of one hopelessly overwhelmed by unjust imputations and wrongful treatment, one to whom his integrity is dearer than his life, and one who insists that what is true and right shall have the assertion to which it is entitled. Here is one who cannot but believe after all that eternal justice shall find a response somewhere and at some time. What is right and just must be.

This view of these words is confirmed by the form of Job's triumphant declaration which follows. This is not a separate, disconnected sentence, as though it were framed to be inscribed by itself upon the rock. But it is intimately linked with what precedes, as though it had been intended not to stand alone, but to form part of a continuous context, beginning as it does with a conjunction. *"For I know,"* or, more exactly rendered, *"And I know that my Redeemer lives."* A monumental inscription could not begin with 'and.' This necessarily marks a connection with some thought either expressed or implied in what precedes. And this connection or continuation, while it would be wholly lacking in an isolated legend on the rocks, is readily traceable upon the explanation adopted above.

Perishing under groundless accusations of whose falsity he is profoundly conscious, but which he has no means of adequately refuting--God apparently testifying against him by the sufferings which He sends--his friends open-mouthed and loud in their reproaches and censures--deserted by all, and despairing of relief from any quarter--he utters as his last wish --even while the grave is opening before him--that this amount of justice may be done him, to place his statement of innocence on record in the rock. And as he utters the wish, the certainty that justice must and will be done flashes with strong conviction on his soul, "I have asked a record on the rock; and all the while I know that my Redeemer lives. I need no monument of stone to vindicate me, no inscription engraved with an iron pen and filled in with letters of molten lead. I have an ever-living and almighty Redeemer, who will rescue me from wrong and defend me against calumny, One who will certainly reveal Himself to me as my Friend. Therefore I will with implicit confidence entrust my cause to Him.

There cannot be a moment's doubt as to the identity of the Redeemer Job is trusting to rescue him. It is the same of whom he spoke in his last speech, *"My witness is in heaven, and my record is on high"* (16:19). This is the One he had begged to be his surety when all others refused to espouse his cause. Again and again he had expressed his strong assurance that if his cause could but be brought before Him then the sentence would be in his favor. Now all doubts have vanished. Every condition that had previously clogged his hopes is removed. The Lord has undertaken for him. The Lord has engaged upon his side. The Lord will defend him against all injury and wrong. God, who seems to be persecuting him with such relentless hostility is not his enemy--He is his Redeemer.

It is commonly supposed, and with reason, that in this word 'redeemer' there lies an allusion to an institution dating from the simple and as yet but partially regulated society of patriarchal times, and which was subsequently admitted with some restrictions and modifications into the Mosaic code. It was the office of the next of kin to espouse the cause of his injured or impoverished relative. He was to redeem his property, restore it to him if he, in any way, forfeited it or had been obliged to sell it. He was to defend him against injury and wrong, especially, he was to avenge his blood if he had been unrighteously slain. Now God has assumed the part of the next kinsman in relation to Job. He shall redress his wrongs and avenge his injuries. He shall deliver him out of the bondage of his sorrows (which very figure appears later in this book, when the Lord is said to have *"turned the captivity of Job."* The frequency with which the title of Redeemer is applied to God in the Old Testament makes still plainer its application here. Jacob speaks of the divine Angel that redeemed him from all evil (Gen. 48:16). Moses sings of the people that God has redeemed (Exod. 15:13). David invokes the Lord, his strength and his redeemer (Ps. 19:14). With Isaiah, it is a favorite name: The Redeemer, the Lord of hosts, who is first and who is last.

When Job expresses his assurance that his Redeemer lives, he means not merely that he now exists (as opposed to the idea that there is no one now existing who can appreciate his case and understand his real character, and who is willing to avow Himself his friend). It is not that Job believes he must wait until some future generation in a distant age shall read with unprejudiced eye his words sculptured in the rock in order to have an advocate and friend. Nor is it simply meant that He possesses a conscious existence in contrast with the lifeless, insensate rock; so that Job is not limited to the mute testimony carved upon the motionless, unconscious stone. He has a living witness and defender. Nor is it simply existence in its highest style that is here affirmed, as though he claimed that his Redeemer was the ever-living one, to whom life is essential and inherent, the self-existent and eternal. But life involves active agency in the character maintained, or in the sphere to which it belongs--as when the Lord is styled the living God in contrast with the dead and lifeless idols, who are of no service to their worshippers. The living God is a God who has power to save and to destroy, and who exerts His power as the occasion demands. A living Redeemer is one who is more than a nullity or a name. He is one who will act with real substantial effect.

The rest of Job's triumphant testimony, as it appears in the King James Version, would lead us to suppose that Job expected his vindication to be postponed until the end of the world and the general resurrection. It runs: *"For I know* that *my Redeemer lives, and* that *He shall stand at the latter* day *upon the earth, and* though *after my skin* worms *destroy this* body, *yet in my flesh shall I see God."*

Our translators have here followed older versions. And without designing to warp the meaning of Job or to change the purport of his words, they have been unconsciously guided in the sense which they have assigned to his expressions by their knowledge of doctrines subsequently revealed with a clearness greater than that with which they had been made known in the time of Job, or with which they are here presented to his own mind.

Job is speaking under strong excitement, and in the language of lofty poetry. He uses no superfluous words. He simply indicates his meaning in the most concise manner, without rounding out his periods or using those connectives and significant particles which would be demanded in perspicuous prose. So his sentences are abrupt and elliptical, and exactness of translation is difficult. The embarrassment of the English translators is shown by the unusual number of words supplied--and these are of no small importance to the meaning. There are a few grammatical questions in the original passage which it is difficult to settle with absolute certainty, but which, however determined, do not materially affect the general sense. Without laying any stress upon these, therefore, we propose the following rendering as sufficiently accurate for our present purpose: *"And I know my Redeemer lives, and last on earth shall He arise; and after my skin, which has been destroyed thus, and out of my flesh shall I see God."*

He does not say that his Redeemer shall stand upon the earth or make His appearance on it, but that He shall arise, address Himself to action. He shall no longer sit still, as though He were not concerned or were disposed to take no part in what was happening. He shall arise and participate actively. As when the suffering Psalmists so often call upon God to arise: *"Arise, O Lord! Save me, O my God!"* (3:7). *"Arise, O Lord! Let not man prevail!"* (9:19). *"Arise for our help, and redeem us for Thy mercies' sake"* (44:16).

My Redeemer shall arise last--which may mean simply, He shall arise at last, or hereafter. Or the strict force of the words may be retained. Job and his friends had been contending first. He shall arise last, enter latest on the scene, with the implication that He shall take the matter entirely in His own hands and settle it in His own way. And still further, for this too lies in the proper meaning of the word, this shall be the final settlement of this much disputed case. He is the last, and none shall come after Him to derange or alter what He has done. It is a word that looks to all futurity and stretches to the utmost limit of time that the subject spoken of admits, reaching out to a boundless eternity even. For it is the term applied to the unending duration of God Himself, who is both first and last.

He shall arise last on earth, here spoken of as the scene of the conflict and the trials which He is to terminate and rectify. Or, as the words may mean, and some able interpreters with a measure of plausibility understand them to mean, 'over the dust.' The dust, that is, into which my body has meanwhile mouldered away. Upon which rendering there would be a distinct assertion of what was already, perhaps involved in the term 'last,' and what is more fully brought out in the words that follow, that this intervention of his great Redeemer shall occur after he is dead. It will not take place until his body shall have been committed to the grave and mouldered back to dust.

But whether this meaning be expressed in this particular phrase or not, it is made distinctly prominent in what follows, *"And after my skin, which has been destroyed thus, and out of my flesh shall I see God."* He looks to a period after the destruction, the complete disintegration of his skin. And when he himself, the living part, the vital spirit, shall be separated from his flesh, his decaying and lifeless body--that will be the time he looks to. The just sense of these expressions compels us to regard Job as contemplating the time after he shall be dead, and affirming that then his Redeemer God shall manifest Himself to his disembodied spirit.

Another interpretation which has been put upon this verse, and upon this whole passage, conceives Job to be here looking forward not to a future state, but to the restoration of God's favor, and his own deliverance out of all his troubles in this present life. This is not wholly a modern view, nor has it been confined to unbelieving interpreters. On the contrary, it was adopted by some of the most eminent of the Christian Fathers, and has been ably advocated both in ancient and in recent times. The decisive objections to it are:

1. It does not give their fair meaning to the expressions just recited, which must denote something more than a skin damaged and a body emaciated by disease. It is something posterior to the total destruction and dissolution of the body that is referred to.

2. This is further evident from the constant tenor of Job's language elsewhere. He regards himself as on the verge of the grave, which is already claiming him as its own (16:1) Every temporal prospect has vanished. He invariably repels the idea of any improvement of his condition in this world as plainly impossible, and as though the very suggestion of it were an insult to his understanding. He cannot, therefore, himself anticipate what he uniformly pronounces irrational and absurd.

3. The same thing appears from the general drift of his argument with his friends, both prior to this passage and subsequent to it. His friends affirm that men are rewarded or punished in this life according to their characters. Job steadfastly denies it. If he here utters his expectation that God will interfere to reward his piety in the present life, he completely abandons his own position and adopts theirs.

4. His desire to have his protestation of his innocence recorded in ineffaceable characters upon the rock becomes ridiculous, if he cherished the assurance that the strife between him and his friends would be settled in his favor by God's intervention in his own lifetime.

5. This passage forms the grand climax in the utterances of Job's faith and pious trust, to which he has from the first been slowly but steadily rising. He has put the hypothesis before of a life beyond the grave, though under the impossible condition of a return to this earthly life from the silence and the darkness of the tomb, when God's favor should be restored to him once more, and He should again have a desire and a loving regard for the work of His own hands. In another place he had uttered his outcry of atrocious murder, appealing to the earth not to cover his blood unjustly shed, and he had found the witness to his integrity in Heaven. He now takes one step in advance, and faith reaches its clearest and fullest expression, and confident assurance takes the place of a fitful, trembling hope. The hypothetical life beyond the grave becomes a real vision of God by his disembodied spirit. The witness to his integrity on high, to whom he had appealed to become his surety, but without any positive response, becomes his Redeemer, the avenger of his innocent blood, vindicating him, appearing as his champion, and, as he in the verses next ensu-

ing warns his friends, punishing them that have done him wrong.

6. It very materially lowers the evidence and the power of Job's faith, if we suppose him to be referring to the present life. The victory which he here gains, and which assures his triumph over Satan's temptation--over every possible temptation--is the victory of faith over outward sense. If any possible hope were left him in this world, the triumph would be less conspicuous and complete. It is only when we see him shut up absolutely to the unseen, and see that with his trust in God he ventures boldly into it, not groping blindly or bewildered as in the dark, not hesitating as in uncertainty or perplexity, not shrinking as from possible danger or mistake, but confident as if treading on solid ground, and amid positive and ascertained realities, that we discern the true heroism of a faith like that of Job, and its unconquerable energy. In his own esteem he is sinking into the grave with every indication surrounding him of God's relentless hostility. Every possibility of a return to God's favor in this life is, to his mind, utterly shut out. And yet so fixed is he in his inward persuasion of the real friendship and redeeming grace of God to him, he bursts the boundaries of time, passes the limits of the visible and the tangible, and knows that the manifest tokens of the divine love, which are denied him here, will be granted to him there. What can shake the trust or destroy the peace of that man who rests his certain hope on the immutable attributes of God? Satan and the world may vent their rage and ply their arts against him in vain. He is proof against every assault, for his steadfast trust is founded upon the eternal rock, and this is a foundation which never can be shaken.

It is no real objection to the view which has been taken of this passage, that in the subsequent course of the history God actually did interfere for the delivery of His servant and the restoration of his prosperity in the present life. What was in the secret purpose and plan of God must be carefully distinguished from Job's situation as it appeared to his own mind. It was the fact of his being left so entirely in the dark, and without the slightest clue as to the design or issue of his sufferings, that created all the mystery of the dispensation, and laid such demands on his faith, and established such a searching test of the reality and power of his adherence to God's service. God did indeed remove Job's sorrows, renewing to him the open pledges of His favor in this life. He thus rewarded His servant's faith, contrary to and beyond all expectation. Job never dreamed of such a result, as all his speeches show, nor once conceived it possible.

Nor is there any force in the objection that Job has in his previous speeches uniformly spoken of death as the end of every activity and hope, and has never let fall a syllable from which it could be inferred that he believed in the reality and certainty of a future state. The conclusion has hence been drawn that this cannot have been an article of his faith, and that he could not therefore have referred to it in the passage now under consideration. But this is to overlook entirely the progress in Job's own mind, which is delineated in such a vigorous and masterly manner in the course of his speeches. We see Job in the beginning involved in all the mist and obscurity which overhung the future state in the patriarchal age, when no clear and unambiguous revelations had been made upon this subject. The continued conscious existence of the soul was known, but all was vague and shadowy in regard to that other life. Job is, by the intensity of the struggle in which he was engaged, driven step by step into clearer views of this subject than he possessed before. We can watch his gradual advances toward it, his uncertain reachings out after it. And here we see him grasping it with all the fulness of assured conviction, as the only way out of inextricable darkness and despair, the inevitable deduction of a most indubitable axiom, the only resting place of his unwavering trust in the immutable grace of God, which nothing can wrest from him. Of God's unchanging favor he is inwardly and most thoroughly persuaded. There is no room remaining for that favor to display itself to him in this world.And the imperative necessity of his holiest and firmest convictions compels him to the declaration, I know that God will manifest His favor to me, though it be after my body has decayed and my spirit has forsaken this tenement of clay.

Nor is there any greater weight in the additional objection that Job makes no further use of this great truth in his controversy with his friends. He never refers to it subsequently, whether to console himself under the rigors of his own hard lot, or to shed light on the e-nigmas of Providence in the unequal distribution of good and evil, or to refute the con-stantly repeated tenet of his friends of a retribution in the present life. A doctrine of such vast importance in its bearings on the subject under discussion could not, it is alleged, flash up in one single passage and then never be alluded to again. The fact that it is not brought up and insisted upon elsewhere is held to warrant the inference that it is not really here.

But this is to mistake entirely the part which this doctrine plays in the book of Job. It is not offered as a solution of the enigmas of divine Providence. It is not even presented as the basis of consolation for the tempted and afflicted. The comfort of the sorrowing rests on a deeper ground than this, as is subsequently unfolded in the speech of Elihu, and by the Lord Himself, to whom it is reserved to present in its true light a subject which has on-ly been growing more and more perplexed under the reasonings and discussions of Job and his three friends. The doctrine of immortality comes in solely to still Job's inward conflict, and bring him to a settled conviction that there is peace between his soul and God, which no outward and temporal troubles can destroy. This it effectually does. Job's inward agit-ation ceases from this moment. He is no longer distracted by the sense of God's hostility and wrath. His outward situation is unchanged, and the problem of his sufferings is as myst-erious as ever. But he has attained to inward peace. He knows that his Redeemer lives, and that, after his worn and suffering body shall be resolved into dust, the clouds shall break away, which now obstruct his vision of the face of God. The lesson of immortality has ac-complished its end. It need not, therefore, be repeated. And that it is not applied to mat-ters with which in the plan and purpose of this book it has nothing to do, is surely no ar-gument against its appearance here, where its introduction was essential.

But in what relation, it may be further asked, does this passage stand to the doctrine of the Messiah and of a corporeal resurrection? Is Job's Redeemer ours? Is his faith the same in which the people of God now rejoice in the completed victory over death and the grave? In germ and substance it was, but, as it lay before his consciousness, not in the same dev-eloped form. God was his Redeemer: Christ, who was in the beginning with God and was God, is ours. When Job appeals to his Redeemer, he does so without even remotely appre-hending that He is the second person of the Godhead. For he knew nothing of the distinc-tion of persons in the divine Being, and of the doctrine of the Trinity as unfolded in the New Testament. But he addresses Him in a character, and solicits the fulfillment of an of-fice which distinctively belongs to God the Son. He is, and has been in every age, the Re-deemer out of every distress, the Guardian and Protector of His people, and their Deliver-er both from temporal distress and from that everlasting woe of which the former is the figure and the type. It is He to whom the saints of God are indebted for that joyful prospect of the vision of God beyond the grave, to which Job looked forward. So that the doctrine of Christ is here approached from its divine side, not as Abraham's son, but as God's.

And then perhaps it may not be without its deeper significance and its divinely intended meaning that the term Redeemer had the association linked with it, both in patriarchal and Mosaic usage, of the next of kin. Is there not here possibly a shadowing forth of more than Job himself intended or imagined when he used the word? an index pointing to that divine Redeemer, who is after all our nearest Kinsman, and who allied Himself to us in the bonds of our common humanity, bone of our bone, and flesh of our flesh, that He might have a kinsman's right to espouse our cause, to vindicate us from the accusations of the law, and free us from the sentence of death written in our members, and open to us life and immortality with the beatific vision of God? So that as Abraham saw Christ's day, it may likewise be said of Job that he rejoiced to see Christ's day, and he saw it and was glad. Only it was the seed of Abraham to whom the father of the faithful looked forward. It was his divine Redeemer that gladdened the believing soul of the man of Uz.

The human aspect of Christ's work, so far as it is foreshown in the book of Job, is chiefly set forth by Job himself, in his own person, as the type of the man of sorrows, forsaken and persecuted by his friends, and abandoned apparently by God, and yet for whom the cross was the passage way to the crown, and suffering to a glorious reward, and the fruit of the travail of whose soul abounded to the blessing of others, as Job's intercession also brought healing to his three friends, and he has been a helper to the distressed from his own day to this.

The resurrection of the body was probably not present to Job's thoughts, certainly not in the form of a general and simultaneous rising from the dead. And yet it is so linked, seminally at least, with our continued spiritual existence, and it is so natural and even necessary for us to transfer our ideas of being, drawn from the present state, to the great hereafter, that it may perhaps be truly said that the germs of the doctrine of the resurrection may likewise be detected here. Job says, *"Whom I shall see for myself, and my eyes shall behold, and not another"*--so natural was it to transfer the thought of those corporeal organs along with this personal identity, upon which he insists, even while speaking of himself as disembodied. We shall not here revive the curious and profitless speculations to which these words have given rise, nor shall we involve ourselves in any discussion as to whether Job means eyes of the soul or eyes of the body. It is enough that we find here suggested the intimacy of the link which binds the two parts of our nature together, and the powerful association which almost inevitably carries us forward from the continued life of the soul to the restored life of the body. And then, when we add to this the ambiguity of certain expressions here employed, and which may not have been wholly unintended (shall we say?) by the Spirit of truth, so that they yield themselves readily to the setting forth of the doctrine of the resurrection, as shown in our own English translation and in various other versions, ancient and modern, it will appear that this passage has not been without important bearings, at least, upon the history of the belief in this great, and cardinal doctrine of the gospel of the Son of God, if not upon its actual disclosure in the course of divine revelation.

CHAPTER VII

"How then do you comfort me in vain, since in your answers there remains transgression?"
--Job 21:34

JOB REFUTES HIS FRIENDS

The crisis of the temptation is past, but Job's perplexity is not yet removed. He refuses to be driven from his constant trust in God by all the influences that Satan has arrayed against him. Amidst all the seeming evidences of God's hostility, he maintains his confidence in him as his Redeemer. He who is afflicting him now will effect his deliverance hereafter. But the time of this deliverance has not yet come. He is walking in darkness, trusting in the Lord. The storm of calamity continues without abatement, and the mystery of his sorrows is still unsolved.

Until now Job has spoken principally to God. It was with Him that he had to do, rather than with his friends. That which has been chiefly agitating him, and which was in fact the mainspring of the temptation, was the question of his personal relation to his Maker. When his friends affirmed and reiterated, as they did in every speech they made, the doctrine of a providential retribution, that it was the wicked who suffered under God's righteous rule and in proportion to their wickedness, Job made immediate application of this, as they designed that he should, to his own case. He had, indeed, more than once declared the falsity of the general principle, *"He destroys the perfect and the wicked. If the whip kills suddenly, He will mock at the calamity of the innocent. The earth is given into the hand of the wicked; He covers the faces of its judges"* (9:22-24). *"The tents of robbers are at peace, and those who provoke God are sure, in whatever God brings into their hands"* (12:6).

But this was only incidental to the main current of his thoughts. He was in no mood for an abstract discussion. The personal question involved in it swallowed up every other consideration. It concerned what was dearer to him than life. It affected the very foundation of his trust in God. It was not simply that he had a tender regard for his reputation, and that he could not bear to have a cloud brought over his good name. He who had borne the loss of property and children, and endured the sufferings inflicted on his own person with such noble resignation, could also have submitted with equanimity to unjust censures and false reproaches. That was not the tenderest and most vital point. The estimation in which he was held by his fellow-men was not his chief treasure. But his conscious integrity was an inalienable possession. This he could not part with. And if what his friends said was true, and the rectitude of Him who ruled the world seemed to give it sanction, then God was punishing him for crimes which he was conscious that he had never committed. He was, indeed, in a most pitiable dilemma. If he denied the position of his friends, then the plain inference was that God was unjust. If he assented to it, then God was unjust. And, in either case, how could he serve a God who was unjust, and was withal so pitiless and cruel?

Satan at last seemed to have driven him into a position from which there was no escape. How can he do otherwise than renounce the service of God? What basis remains for that confidence and reverential homage which is essential to true worship? Satan has completely enveloped him with his deadly snare, and it would appear as though there were no alternative. Job must fall before his adversary.

We have traced the fierce and weary conflict to its final issue. We have watched him in his

53

inward strife, in his piteous moans, his expostulations with God, his vain appeals to Him to declare Himself on his side. We have seen him driven to and fro in his tumultuous agitation, until, forced to the very edge of the precipice, and apparently about to fall hopelessly and helplessly into the awful chasm that yawned beneath him, he cleared it by one energetic act of faith, reaching forth into the unseen, holding himself up without any visible support.

The personal question is now settled, and his intense inward agitation has subsided. He is in a much calmer and more tranquit state of mind. He has gained that unshaken conviction of the rectitude and goodness of God, which enables him to claim Him as his Redeemer in spite of all adverse appearances. This source of his disquiet is put to rest. The power of the temptation is broken. Satan cannot detach him from the service of God, since he holds fast to his faith in Him, in spite of all the suggestions of sense and of reason.

Job is safe from falling. But outward sense and human reason still present a problem, which baffles him completely. He holds fast to his confidence in God, but he is bewildered nevertheless. The solution of his friends is no solution. According to their principles, indeed, there is no enigma in Providence. They see nothing but the evident and uniform reign of justice. Job shows, on the contrary, that this is not the case. He takes issue with them in regard to their fundamental principle and exposes its falsity. It is not, as they allege, a fact of uniform experience that the righteous are rewarded and the wicked suffer. This is the point to which he addresses himself in his remaining speeches.

It is, as he says, a most distressing truth, one that fills him with painful emotions at every contemplation of it, and at which they might well stand aghast themselves. The administration of this world is not conducted on such evident principles of equity as they have maintained. *"Turn unto me and be amazed, and lay your hand upon your mouth. Even when I remember I am afraid, and trembling takes hold on my flesh"* (21:5,6). So far from just retribution overtaking the guilty, bad men are often signally prospered. *"Why do the wicked live, become old; yes, become mighty in power? Their seed is established in their sight with them, and their offspring before their eyes. Their houses are safe from fear; neither is the rod of God upon them. Their bull breeds and does not fail; their cow calves, and does not cast her calf. They send forth their little ones like a flock, and their children dance. They take the timbrel and harp, and rejoice at the sound of the organ. They spend their days in wealth and go down in a moment to the grave."* Their mery, joyous prosperity continues to the very last. Experiencing no reverses and no unusual calamity, with no check upon their good fortune, and no term of suffering that could be regarded as a penalty for their misdeeds, they go down peacefully and quietly to the grave. Their life is filled up with pleasure, arid with every form of earthly good to its very close. And the natural consequence follows. In their arrogant and impious presumption they refuse all subjection to the Most High. *"Therefore they say to God, Depart from us; for we do not desire the knowledge of your ways. What is the Almighty, that we should serve him? And what profit should we have if we pray to him?"*

Bildad had said, *"The light of the wicked shall be put out;"* and, *"destruction shall be at his side"* (18:5,12). Job asks in reply, How often is this the case? It is by no means the invariable rule. *"How often is the candle of the wicked put out, and their trouble comes upon them! He shares out pains in His anger; they are as stubble before the wind, and as chaff that the storm steals away."* (21:17,18).

But, interpose the friends, the retribution is sure to come. It is only delayed awhile. *"God lays up his iniquity for his children"* (5:4; 18:18; 20:10). This, Job retorts is no retribution at all in any proper sense. *"Let Him reward him,"* (that is, the sinner himself, in his own person) *that he may know it. Let his eyes see his destruction, and let him drink of the wrath of the Almighty. For what pleasure does he have in his house after him, when the number of his months is cut off in the midst?"* How is he affected by what happens to his children after he is dead and gone? They were presuming to *"teach God knowledge"* by thus prescribing a law for His government of the world, and might justly fear that sentence with which He rewards the proud. On the other hand, he alleges that in actual fact there was no discrimination exercised in the fortunes allotted to men. No reason could be assigned why some men never have trouble, and others never have anything else. *"You say, Where is the house of the prince? and where are the dwelling-places of the wicked?"* (implying that they have disappeared, or that their ruins only remain as monuments of God's righteous vengeance--but this is not so:) *"Have you not asked those that go by the way? and do you not know their tokens, that the wicked is spared in the day of destruction? they are brought off in the day of wrath."* They are often screened from calamities that befall better men. And when they die, instead of being followed by execrations or regarded as malefactors, cut off by the just sentence of Heaven, they are buried with every mark of distinction, attendant crowds doing honor to their memory and perpetuating their pernicious example.

Astounded by this audacious attack upon their stronghold, this plump denial of what they have all along been asserting as an incontrovertible axiom, and the foundation of their whole argument, the friends are obliged to modify materially their method of attack. Eliphas, who speaks next, comes to the rescue of the principle by a furious onslaught on Job himself. Their oft-repeated maxim itself, in its broad universality, cannot again be affirmed in the face of what has just been said. But he is more than ever convinced that it exposes the real secret of all Job's troubles. Whether it can be established as a general rule or not, whether it is applicable to all other cases or not, it unquestionably holds true in this instance. He therefore restricts himself no longer to covert insinuations or indirect suggestions, but makes positive and explicit charges of enormous wickedness, and assigns this as the undoubted reason of these terrible inflictions. God could have no motive for dealing with Job otherwise than with impartial justice. He must have been guilty, therefore, of atrocious crimes, the righteous penalty for which he is now enduring.

The whole matter is thus brought to a simple issue. Is Job a gross transgressor, or is he not? The charge is open and unambiguous. Job promptly takes up the challenge and meets the charge with an equally explicit denial. God has indeed hidden Himself in the mystery of these inexplicable sorrows, which continue to press upon him with the same dire weight as before. He is withdrawn beyond the reach of outward sense. But concealed as He is from sight, impossible as it is to penetrate to His secret seat to urge his plea, and to obtain the removal of these distresses under which he now groans, Job yet makes to Him his confident appeal: *"He knows the way that I take; when He has tried me, I shall come forth as gold. My foot has held fast to His steps; I have kept His way, and have not fallen away. Neither have I gone back from the commandment of His lips; I have counted the words of His mouth more than my necessary food"* (23:10-12). And, as he proceeds to say, the world is full of just such enigmas, of open wickedness that is allowed to go unpunished, and of grievous wrongs that are not redressed.

As the charges brought against Job are wholly destitute of proof, being mere inferences from a principle (which has been shown to be unverified by the actual experience of the world,) Bildad cannot again repeat them in the face of Job's solemn asseveration of his innocence and his appeal to the Searcher of hearts. There is consequently nothing for him to do, if he would maintain the show of an argument, but to fall back upon the sinfulness inherent in human nature. No man can be pure in the sight of the infinite God. This point had been made by Eliphaz at the very outset of the discussion, and it had been sufficiently answered long since. Bildad, sensible of the weakness of his position, makes no attempt to illustrate or enforce it, and, after a few feebly uttered sentences, relapses into silence. The friends withdraw discomfited from the contest.

Job cannot refrain from taunting them with the completeness of their failure in an argument which they have been conducting with so much pretension. He then seizes the opportunity to guard his language against misconception. In saying what he had done regarding the inequalities of divine providence, he had neither meant to reflect upon the glorious nature of God, nor to deny the existence of moral retributions. He accordingly affirms the exalted majesty of God in as lofty terms as his friends themselves could employ. And though he continues to insist on his own integrity, notwithstanding the afflictions sent upon him, he freely admits the reality of God's providential government, and that punishment does overtake the ungodly. Nevertheless there is a mystery enveloping the divine administration which is quite impenetrable to the human understanding.

This thought of the impossibility of men's arriving at any comprehension of the divine plan in the administration of the universe, by their own unaided powers, is illustrated with great beauty. An apt figure is taken from the art of mining. Men can discover the precious and useful metals, though they are hidden deep under ground. They will descend into the bowels of the earth and push their shafts remote from the habitation of men. Regardless of the obstructions that block their way, and of the gathering streams that hinder their progress, and of the obscurity which reigns in these dark abysses, they cut a passage through the rocks to the treasures which they seek. But there is a greater treasure, by far, which cannot be obtained in this way--a treasure that gold or silver cannot equal, and which vastly exceeds in worth the most valued of jewels and precious stones. This can never be discovered by the searching or by the ingenuity of men. Where shall wisdom be found? Where is the place of understanding? It is hidden from the eyes of all living. Even the world of the departed does not possess it. They have heard the fame of it, but they are not able to grasp it. There is but one Being in the universe who does possess a perfect comprehension of God's grand plan, and that is He who adjusted all things with infinite precision; Him who is guiding all to His own preordained results. And He who is infinite in knowledge has disclosed to man wherein true practical wisdom lies--*"God understands the way of it, and He knows the place of it. For He looks to the ends of the earth, and sees under the whole heaven; making a weight for the winds, and measuring out the waters by measure. When He made a decree for the rain, and a way for the lightning to thunder; then did He see it and declare it; He prepared it, yea, and searched it out. And to man He said, Behold, the fear of the Lord, that is wisdom! And to depart from evil is understanding!"* (28:23ff)

The providence of God is not conducted upon such a palpable rule, and one so perfectly simple and susceptible of easy application, as the friends have maintained. The dealings of the infinite God are not regulated on a principle so obvious as to be level to the humblest understanding. On the contrary, they are enveloped in the profoundest mystery. It is impossible to lift the veil which obscures His designs, or to penetrate the reasons which govern the divine proceedings. This is not because there is no reason in them. The impossibility of discovering the divine order does not arise from the absence of any real order in the universe. The world is not under the dominion of chance, swinging to and fro at random without intelligent oversight. a ship without chart or compass or rudder, tossed by the waves and driven by the winds. Nor is it under the blind sway of inexorable 'fate.' Nor has it been surrendered to the mere control of physical laws, working out their fixed and uniform sequences with a relentless disregard for anything but inherent material properties, which with undeviating precision pursue each their own affinities, without owning a superintending control or a subordination to high moral aims. Nor is the Ruler of the universe a capricious tyrant whose absolute power is directed by mere arbitrary will, without wise forethought or well-considered purpose.

Infinite wisdom reigns through the universe. He who adjusted the physical forces of external nature with such admirable precision, who balanced their action with such delicate nicety, that perfect equilibrium is maintained and no derangement ensues in the onward movement of all this complicated machinery through successive ages. He who established and perpetuates this universal harmony in all material things, giving their weight to the winds and their measure to the waters, orders with equal wisdom the multitudinous affairs of men. There is a divine method. There is an infinite plan. And it is one that is worthy of the supreme Intelligence. It bears throughout the stamp of consummate wisdom. But it is past finding out.

We cannot attain to a comprehension of all the wisdom of God. We cannot see how its several parts cohere with each other, or how they consist with the perfections of Him who designed it and who is conducting it. There is much that, to human view, seems to be at variance with a well-ordered administration. There is much that we cannot account for, much that we cannot understand. There are many things in the management of the world that completely baffle every attempt to unriddle them. We cannot see why they are, nor why God permits them, nor how He can consistently permit them. With our limited understandings and our restricted range of observation, we cannot pretend to fathom the bottomless deep, nor measure what has no bound. We cannot, even by the most prolonged search or the most elaborate investigation, attain to a thorough understanding of God's infinite designs. But the keenest insight and the most indefatigable application of the human faculties fail to discover the Wisdom that rules in all. The secret that resolves all mysteries, harmonizes all strifes, reconciles all contradictions, and reduces this seemingly inextricable confusion to perfect symmetry and order is hidden in the God's mind alone.

Man can never aspire to a comprehension of the absolute wisdom, but the Most High has mercifully revealed to man all that is necessary for his practical guidance. He may not presume to know how God governs the world, or what rules He prescribes for His own procedure, but he has been sufficiently taught how to direct his own conduct and how to govern his own life. He cannot solve the mysteries of Providence, but he may solve what is of more immediate moment to him, all questions of personal duty. He cannot tell the end, which is subserved by everything which God permits or brings to pass, but he does not need to be in doubt as to how he may accomplish the true end of his own being, how he can secure his own highest welfare. *"The fear of the Lord, that is wisdom; and to depart from evil is understanding"* (28:28).

Job pauses here, as he had done once before, waiting to see if his friends had more to say. Whether on account of his obstinate persistence in his own views they think that it will be of no use to argue further, or whether they begin themselves to suspect the unsoundness of their position, and to perceive that there is more of mystery in the case of their suffering friend than they had imagined--they at any rate say nothing. Job then proceeds to state at length the unsolved enigma of his sorrows. His friends have shed no light upon this distressing dispensation, and he can get none himself. He dwells upon his former happy condition, then recites the dismal reverse which he has experienced. Finally he solemnly affirms his innocence of any crime which could account for his being treated in this way.

The words of Job are here ended. He stands face to face with a mystery that is thus far wholly unexplained. He has no theory, and can imagine none upon which his present sorrows can be accounted for. His friends undertook to silence his complaint, but he has instead silenced them. He holds fast to his faith in God, but he does so notwithstanding the fact that he cannot rid himself of troubled questionings that have arisen in his soul. Nor can he align his faith with the facts which he can neither escape nor explain away, those which seem to be directly contrary with the divine attributes. He gloomily says, *"Therefore I am troubled at His presence; when I look, I am afraid of Him. For God makes my heart soft, and the Almighty troubles me;"* expressing the uneasy apprehensions that mingle inside him as he thinks of God. There is an unrest in his soul which he cannot compose. Satan has not been able to destroy him, but he has plunged him into darkness and distress, out of which he cannot find his way. His trust in God continues, however. He still confides in his Redeemer, who after his skin is destroyed and his flesh has mouldered back to dust, will reveal Himself to his disembodied spirit. But will God allow his servant to go on in darkness to the end, bearing his heavy burden, and hoping against hope? Must Job die under

CHAPTER VIII

"Then the wrath of Elihu the son of Barachel the Buzite..was kindled. His wrath was kindled against Job, because he had justified himself rather than God. Also his wrath was kindled against his three friends, because they had found no answer and had condemned Job. ...And Elihu answered..."--Job 32:2,3.

ELIHU

The three friends of Job cannot answer him, and yet it is plain that he ought to be answered. He has silenced his friends, showing that the principle which they have so confidently urged will not explain the mystery of God's dealings in general, nor solve the enigma of his own case. But he has not brought the question to any satisfactory issue. The friends undertook to justify God's providential dealings. The failure of their argument apparently leaves the divine proceedings open to censure and without any adequate vindication. They aimed to show Job that he had no right to complain of the sufferings which God had sent upon him or permitted to befall him. But they were not successful, for Job has triumphantly maintained his ground in his controversy with his friends. But there is danger that he will entertain the impression, or that the impression may be made on others, that he is likewise right in his controversy with the providence of God. This dangerous impression needs to be corrected, both for his own sake and for the sake of those to whose instruction his great trial, and the book that records it, was designed to contribute.

In the vehemence of his opposition to his friends, in the intensity of his inward struggles, Job has been betrayed into expressions which cannot be approved, those in which he seems to arraign the equity of the divine administration. Great consideration is required in judging of these expressions, and in estimating their real meaning. Allowance must be made for the circumstances in which they were uttered. Words wrung from him in the bitterness of his heart, and in the tumult of his feelings under the terrible pressure of his sorrows and the exasperating treatment of his friends, are not to be regarded as though they had been spoken in calmer moments. But if Job had gone no further astray than this, that in his desperation and intolerable distress he had occasionally let slip what he subsequently regretted, and what did not express his real state of mind, no correction might have been needed.

The fact, however, is that Job was involved in an irreconcilable conflict with himself. He was in a dilemma from which he could not by his own skill or power be extricated. On the one side he was conscious of his own integrity. He knew from the testimony of his own conscience that he was not a gross and wicked offender. But how, then, can he maintain his confidence in the justice and rectitude of God in His providential government? A God who lets the wicked triumph and who afflicts the just, how can He be a righteous and a holy God? Job cannot put these two things together, though he holds them both and will not abandon either. And yet, in the honest frankness of his soul, he does not and cannot shut his eyes to the fact that they do seem to clash. Being guileless, he says what he feels.

His controversy with God's providence is not therefore limited to a few passionate outbursts, which in moments of reflection he would gladly recall. But it is forced upon him by an inward necessity which he cannot escape. He still holds to his own integrity, but he also holds with an unslackened grasp to his confidence in God's righteousness. The right-

59

eousness of God shall shine forth radiantly hereafter, but why is it so strangely obscured now? This Job cannot answer. And, though his trust abides in God's ultimate justice, it is after all a trust in a God who has hidden himself.

A glimpse into one design, at least, of this infliction has been given to the readers of the book at the beginning, in what is said there of the agency of Satan in bringing it about. Satan fiendishly plots the ruin of Job, laying snares which he confidently boasts will overthrow this godly man, bringing him to renounce the service of his Maker. The Lord permits the tempter to try his arts to the full. The result is his complete defeat. For Job holds fast his trust in God and succeeds in trampling the temptation under foot. And so it will always be whenever the malice of evil spirits and the rage of wicked men are allowed to assail the saints of God. God's martyrs, suffering for their attachment to their blessed Lord, will adhere to Him in spite of all that can be turned against them--they will be true in order to illustrate the reality of godliness--they will glorify God out of the midst of the fires.

But what did the Lord intend by permitting Satan to bury Job under affliction? This has not yet been stated. There was, of course, a design. It cannot have been to gratify Satan, nor did God need such a test to satisfy Himself of the reality of Job's faith. Nor can we suppose that God would have allowed such overwhelming distresses to befall His faithful servant merely to convince Satan that his malicious suggestion was false. God must have had a purpose which directly affected Job himself. God would not have made Job suffer as a mere spectacle for others, when there was no end to be answered affecting himself. God must have intended some good toward Job in permitting him to suffer as he did.

Some inkling of the divine purpose may be gathered from what has taken place thus far. We have already seen how triumphantly Job bore the severe and searching test applied to him. We may be sure that the desperate struggle through which he passed has developed and strengthened his faith. Job has learned to maintain his faith under new and most difficult circumstances. He has risen to a loftier exercise of faith than ever before. With no external props and aids, and in the face of all the suggestions of outward sense, he was obliged to maintain himself by the simple putting forth of faith in the unseen God. His faith could not but gather strength and clearness by the effort. When he learned to say with such confidence, *"I know that my Redeemer lives,"* in spite of all that had conspired to kill his hopes and quench his trust, there was a positive and decided spiritual gain. He was lifted to a higher spiritual sphere by all that had gone before.

And associated with or growing out of this new elevation and increase of Job's faith is the fresh enlargement of his spiritual perceptions, his keener insight into religious truth. In groping eagerly about for something to lean upon, for something to support his soul in this time of deep distress, he grasps the firm pillar of his immortality and puts it into a connection previously unknown or unthought of with his present needs. A new element of truth is won in the struggle, a new ground for the tempted to stand upon, a wellspring of consolation to thirsty, fainting souls.

Still, though we may gather something by inference respecting the design of God in this mysterious and clouded providence, we feel the need of some authoritative disclosure of this design. We feel this need likewise and particularly for Job's sake, and for those who are to be instructed by his example, that the question raised between him and his friends should be at rest, that the truth should be distinctly stated which they have both vainly tried to discover, that the antagonistic principles in Job's soul should be composed, and that the righteousness of God should find a satisfactory vindication.

The solution of the perplexed problem is given partly by Elihu and partly by God Himself. Elihu, who here appears for the first time, and whose descent is somewhat particularly described, and his motive for speaking as well, first addresses Job in a series of chapters. He pauses at intervals apparently for the sake of giving Job an opportunity to reply. Job, however, says nothing. Then the Lord speaks to Job out of the whirlwind and finally brings the whole matter to an end by restoring Job to more than his former prosperity.

No portion of this book has proved more embarrassing than the discourse of Elihu. And there is not such a great diversity of views in regard to any other portion. From early times, there has been a wide divergence of opinion as to the part God assigned Elihu--or why he is introduced at all. There has been confusion as to what relation Elihu's answers have to the mystery of Job's affliction, or what the relation of his speech is to that by the Lord. The perplexity is increased by the difficulty on the one hand of harmonizing what Elihu says with the lessons to be drawn from the discourse of the Lord; and on the other hand, of discriminating in a clear and satisfactory manner between the sentiments propounded by Elihu and those which had been previously advanced by Job's three friends.

Many have concluded that the lessons taught by Elihu and the Lord are hopelessly at variance, while the doctrine of Elihu and the three friends are identical. Consequently, they say, Elihu contributes nothing toward the true and proper settlement of the question at issue. His solution of the enigmas of Providence is alleged to be substantially that of Eliphaz and his associates, and accordingly open to the same condemnation--and they are set aside by the subsequent decision rendered by the Lord Himself, which is alone to be accepted as the true solution. On this hypothesis Job does not reply to Elihu because he really advances nothing new. And the Lord makes no allusion to him because he is a mere intruder who has said nothing deserving of special regard. Moreover, they say, Elihu is involved in the censure passed upon the friends, whose tenets he had simply repeated.

Among those who hold this view there is still a diversity of judgment as to the ability displayed by Elihu in the presentation of his argument. Some say he is a shallow pretender, a vain upstart intruding his opinions unsolicited, whereas wiser and better men had already exhausted that side of the question. Others concede that his several points are put with skill and cogency. They consider him the exponent of human reason, representing the highest results attainable without immediate divine revelation. God alone, they say, can give the correct answer where the wisest and most sagacious of men are incompetent to discover the truth. Elihu's failure then makes it necessary for the Lord himself to intervene.

However, surely it is highly improbable that so much space in the divine Word would be devoted to Elihu if he really contributes nothing, only repeating what Job's friends had said before. This view then paved the way for another, which says the speech of Elihu is not a part of the original book, but a later addition. Some then say this mars the symmetry of the book; others say it adds fresh and valuable thoughts.

The difficulties which have been felt with regard to Elihu will disappear, and the hypotheses above will vanish upon a more careful study of the speech, together with close attention to the language with which he is introduced. It is plain the writer of the book does not regard him as siding with the friends. He represents him as equally displeased with both contending parties: *"His wrath was kindled against Job because he had justified himself rather than God. Also his wrath was kindled against his three friends because they had found no answer and had condemned Job"* (32:2,3). Elihu then steps forth as an arbiter, putting the question at issue upon entirely new ground. He does agree with the friends in some of their positions, which as general statements were quite correct. But his fundamental teaching is totally different from theirs.

Elihu is not spoken of in the beginning of the book, when the arrival of the three friends is mentioned, because there was no occasion for speaking of him then. He only engages in the dispute because the three friends have failed to find a satisfactory answer to Job. To speak of him in the outset would have been to anticipate their incapacity to deal with the subject before they had made the attempt. Job does not answer Elihu because he is convinced of the truth of what he says, and therefore he has nothing to reply.

The Lord makes no allusion to Elihu because he was not one of the parties to the strife which was to be adjusted. He was not one of the contestants, but an arbiter whose decision was preliminary to the Lord's. The infinite God could not in dignity place Himself on a level with his dependent creature by entering into an argument with him in justification of His own sovereign acts. Therefore, as far as there was any occasion for arguing the case with Job to correct his misapprehensions, or to vindicate the divine proceedings, this was committed to Elihu, who could meet Job as an equal. This course was also really best for Job. There was no divine terror to appall him, no effulgence of the infinite majesty to overwhelm him. Job could stand on a par with Elihu, God's messenger, and could make reply without irreverence if the considerations presented did not convince him. Elihu's arguments were convincing, therefore Job yielded to his arguments and did not reply. He tacitly confesses the justice of all that Elihu says. His false views are corrected and his misconceptions of God's providences and plan in sending affliction upon him are removed. The way is thus prepared for the Lord to appear, and by the simple majesty of His divine perfections to make the needed impression on the heart of Job. The awe-struck patriarch bows at once in submissive penitence, for he has learned from Elihu to see in God no longer the impersonation of arbitrary power yielded for his destruction, but the God of grace, in whose hand even the rod of affliction was a means of blessing.

It appears that Elihu had been present during the discussion, though not spoken of before. He had said nothing, maintaining a respectful silence. This suggests the probability of the presence of others likewise. The fame of the patriarch's sorrows had gone far and wide. And as all his relatives and acquaintances came to him after his restoration, so doubtless they did while his sorrows lasted. Eliphaz, Bildad and Zophar were the spokesmen to whom the the rest deferred as their superiors in age and in reputed wisdom. But the friends had shown themselves unable to still Job's complaint or to answer his arguments. They vindicated God's providence by discrediting Job's character. So far it might appear as though Job's complaint were justified. Upon the principles of his friends, God was treating him as though he were guilty of offences which he had not committed. The mystery of God's providence was still unsolved. Elihu had waited, expecting the three friends to bring out the true moral reasons of the distresses that befall good men like Job, and to show the harmony of the perfections of God with His providential government. When they failed, he was irresistibly impelled to speak. If, as surmised, he was kin to Ram, and Ram is the same as Aram, Elihu came from a different region, and this may be significant.

Eliphaz and Teman were names perpetuated in the territory of Edom (Gen. 36:10). And the Shuhite recalls the children of Keturah (Gen. 25:2). All belonged to a region renowned for the wisdom and sagacity of its inhabitants. But Elihu comes, it may be, from a territory with associations of a different sort. When Balak was in straits and felt the need of a higher than human help, he sent to Aram for one who heard the words of God and knew the knowledge of the Most High (Num. 23:7, 24:16). It was from Aram that Abraham came; and the epithet 'the Buzite' reminds us of Buz in the family of Nahor, Abraham's brother (Gen. 22:21). It is not impossible that there may lie in these names the suggestion of a land of immediate divine revelation, as opposed to the land of the highest earthly wisdom. The representatives of the land of sages first confront the enigma, but they are baffled: the resources of human reason are inadequate to the task. Then Elihu comes as the messenger of God. He is but a youth, with no pretensions to superior sagacity, and without the age that ordinarily brings wisdom--but the inspiration of the Almighty had given him understanding (32:8). And he unravels the mystery which the wise could not rightly expound. The wisdom of man is at an utter loss, for God alone is competent to relieve the difficulty, *"God thrusts him down, not man"* (32:13).

Elihu begins with an apology for speaking, which may seem repetitious. But this arises from the diffidence of youth and inexperience in the presence of the aged and wise. Yet he felt constrained to declare the truth which had not thus far been uttered, to return the proper answer to Job. He promises that he shall be perfectly impartial, without respect of persons and without flattery. He proposes to put the matter on an entirely new basis, one altogether different from that on which it had been placed by the friends, (32:14).

That which chiefly distressed Job was that God seemed to be treating him as an enemy. He had dwelt most pathetically on this and had recited his dreadful sorrows as so many evidences of the fierceness of God's anger and the bitterness of His hostility. It is to this error that Elihu first addresses himself. He says, Affliction is not a token of God's displeasure but one of the measures of His grace. It is not sent in wrath, but with a kind and merciful design. It is one of the ways in which God draws men from sin and promotes their welfare.

God employs two principal methods in detaching men from wrong, in establishing them in what is pure and good; viz., His word and His providence. God's word is described in terms appropriate to the period when Job lived, prior to a written revelation, and allusive to one of the most usual forms in which immediate divine communications were then made (33:15, etc.), *"In a dream, in a vision of the night, when deep sleep falls upon men, in slumberings upon the bed; then He opens the ears of men and seals their instruction, that He may withdraw man from his purpose and hide pride from man."* By these sacred instructions He saves him from sin and from its punishment, *"He keeps back his soul from the pit, and his life from perishing by the sword."* He goes on to say that God uses affliction for the same gracious end. He sends sickness and suffering to recall men to the path of uprightness. And then if the sufferer recognizes this merciful intent of his sorrows, and yields himself up to it, his pains will be removed. Their whole design will be accomplished.

This is an entirely new doctrine and exhibits the matter under a totally different aspect. The friends have seen in suffering nothing but the punishment of sin, and the displeasure of God against it. Job sees it as an arbitrary infliction, irrespective of men's deserts. But the idea of a gracious purpose in earthly distresses, the idea that they show God's goodness and love, that they are meant to accomplish a kindly end, had not dawned upon any of them. Eliphaz did in his first speech approach it, using expressions akin to Elihu's, so that a hasty and superficial examination might pronounce their teachings identical. Eliphaz is saying that the man God corrects is blessed, and he tells Job not to despise the chastening of the Almighty (5:17), *"for He makes sore, and binds up; He wounds, and His hands do make whole."* This looks to the possibility of good results following upon affliction, which may so far counterbalance the evil that he may be pronounced happy who endures it. And God who now sends sorrow may hereafter send joy. Suffering is to Eliphaz in its proper nature punitive, and it represents God's displeasure against sin. Suffering to Elihu is a curative, and it represents God's affectionate concern for the true welfare of the sufferer. The two ideas are as far apart as the poles. On the one view, God in afflicting a man regards him as a sinner, and treats him as such: his sufferings are tantamount to a sentence of condemnation. On the other, God regards rather his capacity for goodness and seeks his purification and improvement. The development of the doctrine of the friends led directly to their gross and unfounded charges of hypocrisy and guilt. Elihu's teaching is perfectly consistent with Job's true character as affirmed by God Himself. And it quite disarms Job by showing that he has been neither unkindly nor unjustly treated. God is not treating him as a foe or a criminal, but He is showing a solicitous regard for his highest good.

The suggestion of Elihu as to the divine purpose in suffering also adds to that which is stated in the opening of the book as the occasion of the sorrows of Job. But it is not inconsistent with it, nor is it excluded by it. Though it was permitted at the instigation of Satan, who sought Job's hurt, it does not follow that the Lord had no plan of His own. Undoubtedly one design of God was to exhibit the reality of Job's faith, and its adequacy to bear the test, terrible as it was, which Satan proposed. But nothing obliges us to believe that God's merciful purpose was simply commensurate with the mischeivous intention of Satan, or that it was limited to the defeating of the harm concocted against Job. Why may He not likewise have had positive designs of good, which Satan's malice was by overruling grace to be made the instrument of effecting? Elihu declares this to be God's plan. And we have already seen good coming to Job out of this seeming evil. Job has been purified and, besides being instructed, his faith is strengthened. Therefore the teaching of Elihu doesn't conflict with the rest of the book, it finds in it ample justification and support. It was the purpose of God from the first to bless Job by means of this trial. And although this purpose has not been previously announced, it is already gradually working itself out.

Job was not told that he was being put on trial, for it was not the truth he needed. But now that he has successfully borne the test, he needs to know why he was afflicted--not so far as Satan was concerned, but its end for himself. He needs to know that it was sent out of God's love, and that it enclosed a real benefit. It was necessary that he should understand this in order that he might be thoroughly released from Satan's snare, and so that he might receive the full profit that was in store for him.

Elihu's doctrine of suffering is not hampered by the rigid and inflexible rule of exact retributive justice maintained by the friends. Nor does it conflict with the general facts of Providence or with the consciousness of Job. Job's arguments against the friends do not lie against it. In fact, Job has no disposition to argue against this view. It gives a satisfactory account of the inequalities of human condition. The unbending rule of strict justice would have required a uniform and precise correspondence of men's fortunes with their characters. There could be no deviation, though there might be temporary delays. The divine retribution might be postponed, but it must never fail to be ultimately meted out to all, in the true proportion of their merits and demerits.

But a gracious purpose is from its very nature free. It cannot be bound by any rule but the disposition and will of Him who exercises it. The only limitation upon a providence so conducted is God's good pleasure. None can prescribe in advance where He shall send joy or sorrow. He may by His goodness lead men to repentance. He may use chastisement to wean them from the love of this world or to turn their hearts from sin. The method He uses in each particular instance depends solely upon His sovereign will. This allows all the free variety found in the actual experience of men, while at the same time it neither divorces the world from God nor represents His dealings as capricious and arbitrary. He governs in all the affairs of men, and He does so in a manner worthy of Himself. There is a method in all that occurs, and a purpose and a divine intelligence. Providence is harmonized with the infinite rectitude and the universal moral government. It becomes in fact the expression, the visible manifestation of God's holiness as well as of His grace. For it is directed with the view of reclaiming men from sin and training them in holiness and virtue. It is not graduated by any formal mechanical rule of correspondence with men's deserts, but it is wisely adapted, nevertheless, to their multiform needs by Him whose resources are endless and whose understanding is without a bound.

This doctrine likewise supplies the hitherto undiscovered key to the enigma of Job's sufferings. No reflection is cast on his integrity or on the genuineness of his faith. His afflictions are neither an indication of the Lord's displeasure nor of His wanton hostility. A gracious God is by this severity of discipline purging away the dross which still adhered to His faithful servant, and refining the gold to a higher measure of purity.

Accordingly, when Elihu pauses in his discourse (33:32) to give Job an opportunity for reply, he makes none. He has nothing to say in opposition to what he has heard. It has wrought conviction in his soul. It has composed the strife which previously agitated him. It has reconciled the conflicting opposites. It harmonizes his convictions respecting God with what has until now been inexplicable in His providence. It makes all plain in his own case, where before it has been dark and impenetrable. God has not been impeaching his integrity by these terrible sufferings which He has inflicted or permitted. God has not been charging upon him a guilt of which the testimony of his own conscience acquits him. Nor has He been treating him with causeless and gratuitous severity. There is no hostile intent on the part of God: all has been done in kindness and in love. The truth evidences itself to him by its adaptation to all the exigencies of the case in hand. It finds a prompt echo in Job's heart and he bows in mute acquiescence to the force of what has been said. Elihu has not only gained his ear, but his heart. And the solution of the mystery which has so baffled and perplexed him begins to open before him.

Having established this main position, Elihu proceeds to comment on some of Job's ill-considered and hasty utterances, which had fallen from him in the heat of his controversy with his friends. They were incessantly representing God's justice as being hopelessly at war with the idea of the integrity of Job. Not seeing, in the desperate gloom that enveloped him, how this conclusion was to be escaped, Job boldly admits it, and in the thorough consciousness of his own rectitude is driven to affirm that God has done him wrong. But now that this antagonism has been done away by the new principle which Elihu has announced, Job is no longer under any temptation to dispute the righteousness of God's providential administration. Elihu accordingly holds up before him some of his most extravagant statements, pointing out their absurdity and impropriety. When Job said, *"God has taken away my judgment,"* (27:2) he was consorting with wicked men and loosening the foundations of God's universal government by claiming God has despoiled him of his rights. Shall not the Judge of all the earth do right? It is repugnant to every notion of right to charge the supreme and all-perfect Ruler with injustice. If a conflict arise between God and His creatures, whom He can be under no possible temptation to injure, the overwhelming presumption is that He is right and they are wrong, whether they can see it to be so or not! *"Surely it is right to be said to God, I have borne chastisement, I will not be wicked; that which I see not, teach Thou me, if I have done iniquity, I will do it no more"* (34:31,32). And he adds, *"Do you think this to be right, that you said, My righteousness is more than God's?"* (35:2).

Job had invariably resented such language from his friends. Their appeals to God's righteousness always exasperated him, for the necessary implication from it, as presented by them was that he was a guilty man who deserved all that he suffered. He was indignant at these unjust imputations and indirect reproaches. But in the mouth of Elihu there is no covert censure, no aspersions or insinuations. The simple truth of the perfection of the ever-blessed God stands alone before him in its innate majesty, free from all distortions or false conclusions. Job cannot oppose what is so self-evident. He bows in silent agreement.

Having corrected Job's errors and reproved the rash speeches into which he had been betrayed, Elihu reverts again to his fundamental principle of the design of suffering, making special application of it to the case of Job, basing it upon a faithful admonition (36). He repeats, Afflictions are sent upon the righteous for their good, and this experience is alive with solemn responsibility to the afflicted themselves. If they recognize the gracious purpose of God in their sorrows and heed the lesson they involve, then the design of this painful dispensation will be accomplished--and it will be itself removed. If, on the contrary, they disregard the voice of love and warning which speaks to them in these distresses, they will incur the divine displeasure and bring God's judgment on themselves in the form of still heavier sorrows than they have yet experienced. So, Elihu tells Job, it will be with him. He might have found deliverance already if he had profited sufficiently by the teachings of his sad calamities and had learned from them to be more diligent in avoiding sin-- and had learned to cleave more unreservedly to the service of the Lord.

Elihu has now fulfilled the task assigned to him. He was charged with removing misapprehensions from Job's mind, and correcting the mistakes into which he had fallen. But it was not given to him to extricate Job entirely out of Satan's snare, and to accomplish for him the full and blessed effects of his trial. This work the Lord reserved for Himself, to be performed by Him in His own person. Elihu is but His messenger sent before His face to prepare His way before Him. And now even while he is speaking the rumbling is heard of distant thunder (37:2). Heavy masses of cloud begin to darken the sky, and the advancing tempest betokens the Lord's approach. Elihu points to these insignia of the divine Majesty as they steadily draw near, and his own voice is hushed in awe. All are mute in solemn expectation. It is the LORD who comes.

CHAPTER IX

"Then the LORD answered Job out of the whirlwind, and said, Who is this that darkens counsel by words without knowledge?"--Job 38:1,2

THE LORD

We have now come to what is beyond all comparison the most sublime portion of this wonderful book. All the discourses until now, whether of Job or of the other speakers, have been well conceived and admirably expressed. They present their profound and earnest thoughts with singular beauty and force. They glow with elegant and appropriate imagery. And they body forth in vividly graphic language the inward excitement and changing emotions of those by whom they are uttered. All had been well and ably spoken. But now when the Lord himself speaks to Job, His discourse is fitly marked by a grandeur and a majesty altogether unmatched before, and which is worthy of the divine Being.

It might upon the first view of the case appear as though the discourse of the Lord had no particular relevance to the circumstances in which it was uttered. And the question might be asked, What do these appeals to the magnificence of the works of God in nature have to do with the solution of the enigma to which this book is devoted? How do they contribute to the explanation of the mystery that is involved in the sufferings of good men? The fact is, this discourse is not directed to the clearing up of that mystery at all. It is not God's plan to offer a vindication of His dealings with men in general, or a justification of His providence towards Job. He has no intention of placing Himself at the bar of His creatures and erecting them into judges of His conduct. He is not amenable to them, and He does not recognize their right to be cnesors of Him and of His ways. The righteousness of His providence does not depend upon their perceiving or admitting it. The Lord does not here stand on the defensive, nor allow it to appear as though He were in any need of being relieved from the accusations of Job. It is of little interest to Him whether feeble worms approve of His dealings or confess His dispensations to be right. He puts himself in a totally different attitude and moves upon quite another plane. He is the sovereign Lord of all, accountable to no being but Himself. He does not appear to vindicate Himself, but rather to rescue Job.

Job has been exposed to the fierce assaults of Satan and has successfully withstood them. The tempter employed all his power and all his craft to bring Job to forsake the service of God, but he remained firm in his steadfastness nevertheless. The reality and the strength of Job's faith were conspicuously established from the moment he uttered his memorable statement, *"I know that My Redeemer lives."* His heroic trust in God was not destroyed by the direst calamities, nor even by the wrathful frowns that seemed to darken the face of God. Job was fully vindicated against Satan's baseless slander.

But the affair was not to be terminated there. It was not the divine purpose that the trial should end with this merely negative result. Nor was it enough that he should simply receive the profit which had already accrued to him from the struggle through which he had just passed. The Lord had still larger designs of good in store for His faithful servant. The true vindication of God's providence lies in the event. It must not be judged by the confus-

67

ed and tangled threads which it seems to present to the beholder while in the process of being wrought, but by the completed pattern when all shall be finished. The Lord has been in no haste to justify Himself by a premature disclosure of His plans. He has suffered things to move regularly forward and to take their appointed course. But now the time has arrived for His own intervention to bring the matter to its intended end.

Satan had been allowed to bring a double evil on Job, in his outward circumstances, then in his spiritual state. He had inflicted severe external losses and sufferings, and he had involved him in a sore inward conflict. Job had fought this latter through victoriously, so far as it was possible for him to do from his previous standpoint in spiritual knowledge. He had risen to the sublime assurance that God was his Redeemer and friend, and always would be. No floods of temptation could destroy this conviction, no fierceness of Satan's assault could wrest it from him. Still the cloud and the mystery remained. A disturbing element had been introduced into the patriarch's inward experience, to which he could indeed so far bid defiance as to hold fast to this faith in God in spite of it--but nevertheless it was producing disquiet and distress within him. He could not restore that unruffled state of calm repose which marked his condition before his trials came. But his disturbance was not to last.

It had been a valuable discipline to Job in two respects. He had been instructed and also strengthened by the intensity of the struggle which had been forced upon him. And he had in addition been prepared to receive a further spiritual lesson: he had been made sensible of a need which he did not previously know to exist- a need for instruction and succor requiring a heavenly gift. He was now in a state of readiness to welcome a new communication from God. Satan meant to tear him away from God. But he instead opened the way for larger and fuller impartations of divine knowledge and grace. He had but prepared the way of the Lord, who was now to come to Job with a nearness and fulness never before manifested to him.

The sore discipline of Job had run its course. It had brought its full effect in preparing Job to receive the blessing which God had intended all along to be the issue of his severe trials. In answer to Satan's two challenges: the outward and temporal, the inward and spiritual, God now comes to give him benefits, both outward benefits and inward benefits.

First, the Lord produces an effect on the heart of Job. He makes such a manifestation of Himself to the sufferer's soul as brings him to the deepest humiliation and contrition for all his rash and impatient utterances, and all the improper reflections he had cast upon God for His providential dealings. He had already found peace with his Maker so far as his personal relation to God was concerned. Now he is entirely acquiescent in all the Lord's dealings--he repents of his murmurings, he surrenders his wayward resistance to the divine orderings, his will is henceforth coincident with the divine will and completely swallowed up in it. And he is amazed at himself and filled with self-abhorrence that it ever could have been otherwise with him. Then the Lord restores Job's outward estate and raises it to a higher measure of prosperity than before. The whole matter is thus brought to its final issue: Job's faith is elevated, and his welfare and happiness are promoted. The latter is recorded in the historical paragraph which concludes the book. The former is accomplished by the Lord's discourse, which does not do its work, however, by means of arguments addressed to the solution of the enigma that has occupied the minds of Job and of his friends. This discourse contains a solution only in so far as it is effective in bringing about that result, which is itself the explanation of this mysterious providence.

The meaning of the Lord's discourse here in its relation to Job and to the problem of the afflictions of the righteous has been variously misconceived and misstated. As it is chiefly occupied with appeals to the works of God in nature, which display in such a striking manner the omnipotence of the Most High in its contrast with the impotence of man, it has been thought that the main idea advanced is the infinite exaltation and power of God. His sway is irresistible. It is vain to think of opposing omnipotence. And the lesson thence deduced is supposed to be that of unconditional resignation to the will of the Infinite Sovereign. Since God is almighty, His orderings must be submitted to. The creature must yield unresistingly to what the Creator decrees. It is worse than useless to repine or murmur. Man must bow with meek submission to any allotment, coming from such a Source.

But submission to the inevitable is stoicism, or fatalism, not scriptural resignation. We have to do not with overwhelming force, but with our heavenly Father, who demands our love as well as our willing obedience. We should submit to Him, not by constraint, but with a ready mind. We may be compelled to yield subjection to irresistible power, but it will not satisfy the reason nor the sense of right. It was this, in fact, which lent its chief aggravation to the temptation of Job. His unaccountable sufferings, the baseless reasonings of his three friends, and everything in his whole situation conspired to set the Lord before him in the aspect of a Being of absolute and arbitrary power, who was using His omnipotence to torture and destroy him without any ground or reason. Such an almighty tyrant on the throne of the universe would indeed inspire terror, but he could not awaken confidence or love. He might break down all open opposition and stamp out the very semblance of it, but He could not compel the adoration of the heart. Job, prostrate and bleeding, protested with what he supposed to be his dying breath against the cruel wrong which he thought was being done to him. Violence, when it is inescapable, is only the more dreaded and detested on that account. God is more than almighty power, or Job would not have humbled himself before Him in cordial homage and submissive self-abasement. He fell prostrate before an inward constraint which was very different from outward compulsion.

Again it has been supposed that the burden of the Lord's discourse here is God's infinite wisdom as displayed in His works, which so far transcends our faculties, baffling the most adventurous efforts of the human understanding. These appeals to the incomprehensible marvels which everywhere abound in the world are intended, it is said, to suggest the existence of marvels equally incomprehensible in God's providence. There is a mystery in all His ways, in nature, and in the affairs of men, which no human intelligence is able to penetrate. It must be accepted as a product of the infinite reason without insisting upon knowing how or why. It is not given to man to fathom what it belongs only to the divine understanding to comprehend. The ways of God are inscrutable. Man should adore where he cannot understand, and submit without question to allotments. It would be arrogant to suppose that God's decrees could be made level to man's feeble comprehension.

There is a partial truth in this view as in the preceding. God is infinitely wise and infinitely powerful. and both of these attributes of God supply considerations which enter into and enforce godly resignation. But the lesson of the book of Job in these its most solemn utterances from the mouth of God himself is something more than that there is nothing that we can know; that the mystery of the sufferings of good men must remain unexplained because no explanation is possible. This would not be to set at rest troubled questionings and anxious inquiries into the principles of the divine administration, and its consistency with God's unspeakable perfections. It would rather tend to repel all inquiry as profitless and leading to no certain or safe result, even if it is not positively profane, and a pernicious treading on forbidden ground, a prying into what it is not allowable to know. Instead, then, of shedding any light upon this mysterious subject, the only teaching of this book would be that we must remain content with a darkness that can never, from the nature of the case, be dispelled. Instead of adding to our knowledge, it would declare that further knowledge was unattainable.

And if this were the case, why should the Lord have revealed himself to Job at all in so august a manner? In what respect was Job helped or instructed by the manifestation of God to him. if it had no other intent than that just stated? If the discourse of the Lord, with all its rare sublimity, does not carry him beyond the point which he had already reached himself, what was the need of any immediate divine intervention? Job was profoundly sensible of the mystery of God's providence. And he had confessed it to be quite impenetrable. The wisdom that could fathom it, he had said, was *"hidden from the eyes of all living,"* and was possessed by God alone. Again, the highest wisdom to which man could attain was the fear of the Lord (28:20-28). Job had learned to adhere to his pious fear of God, though he could not comprehend His ways; to avouch the Lord to be his Redeemer, though His providence remained an incomprehensible mystery. The lesson of the Lord's discourse must be something beyond what Job had himself already attained to.

There are two things which may supply the key to what this lesson really is. The first is the preliminary speech of Elihu, by which that of the Lord is immediately preceded. The Lord's discourse is not to be torn from that of Elihu, which was the preparation for it, which was followed by it without any pause and so to be merged into it, and which was taken for granted by it. Elihu was sent with the theoretical, as the Lord supplies the practical, solution of this great problem. He was commissioned to make the needed explanations to Job, to rectify his mistakes and point out to him wherein he had erred. His task was to disabuse his mind of every false impression and prepare him for the coming of the Lord, so that upon His appearance he might instantly recognize Him in His true character, and feel toward Him as he should. To Job's mind his sufferings had been hostile treatment on the part of God. He could look upon them in no other light than as tokens of God's displeasure. God was dealing with him in anger. He was indeed able notwithstanding to affirm that God was his Redeemer. But Elihu opens up to him a new view of the case. He shows him that this imagined hostility is not really such. God has not been dealing hardly and cruelly with him, but has been accomplishing the purposes of His grace on Job's behalf.

This alters the whole aspect of the matter. The face of God seems no more to wear a forbidding aspect. What he had thought to be the terrible seizure of a mortal foe is the powerful grasp of a friend. What he had imagined to be the deadly thrust of hostile weapons proves to be the skillful incision of the great Physician who wounds only that He may heal. The chief source of Job's agitation and distress is gone. The seeming contradiction has vanished between the actual and the ideal, between what he experienced and what he might have expected, between the God of the present and of the future, between the God who afflicts and the God who saves. God is his redeemer, not merely out of existing sorrows, or in spite of them, but in them and through them and by means of them. Faith is no longer reduced to such straits that it can barely maintain itself by looking away from the present and holding fast to the unseen future. It has a visible and tangible basis in the present itself. In these very trials which had threatened to sweep away his trust in God, that trust now finds a new and firm support--for he sees in them the clear signs of God's love.

The cloud has disappeared which for a time had hidden the bright shining of his Father's face. And now when God manifests Himself to Job, there is nothing to obscure his sense of the divine favor and loving-kindness. The distorted image of God has passed away completely and forever. Unspeakable love is restored to its true place among the perfections of the Most High. His might and greatness do not stand alone, for He is also infinite in His love. It is sufficient to point out any indication of the Lord's presence or of the grandeur of His being, to bring all the divine attributes full-orbed before the mind of Job. He sees the Lord no longer through a false medium which shuts out half His glory, but as He truly is.

The same thing appears from the effect which the Lord's discourse produces upon Job. It gives him a new and more distinct apprehension of God, a more vivid and powerful impression of His glorious nature. It was not the perception of one attribute isolated from the rest, or exalted above the rest, which led him to exclaim, *"I have heard of Thee by the hearing of the ear, but now my eye sees Thee"* (42:5). All his previous conceptions of God were faint and distant compared with the intimate and thorough conviction of His exalted being which now possessed his soul. It was as that which is learned by distant report compared with that which stands revealed with the clearness and evidence of eyesight. This points to no partial, imperfect, one-sided view of God, in which certain attributes are made prominent at the expense of others, some being hidden altogether, but to a complete and true perception of God in His real character. Job's impatient utterances under the pressure of his afflictions were due to a defective apprehension of the glorious character of God. Now that he sees God as He truly is, he is abashed and confounded that he ever could have spoken as he did or indulged such feelings as he then had.

The Lord's discourse was spoken with the aim of producing this effect upon Job and of bringing him to this humbled and repentant state of mind. The important fact, and that which is really influential in the case, is that God now manifests Himself to the soul of Job. This discourse is simply an accompaniment or a medium of this manifestation. It opens up to Job and brings home to him in the most impressive manner the greatness and the perfection of that Being with whom he has to do. The whole address is but the unfolding of the thought, I am the infinite and all-perfect God. And this truth is set before his mind by a series of appeals to the grandeur of God's works, by which His perfections are so strikingly displayed in contrast with the utter insignificance of man. Job is made to feel at once who it is that is speaking to him, and how completely he had stepped out of his province and of what incredible arrogance and presumption he had been guilty in venturing to pass his judgment upon the doings of the Most High.

"Then the Lord answered Job out of the whirlwind." The clouds, to which Elihu had pointed as covering the light, had grown darker and more threatening, until they overspread blotted out the day. The lightning, the thunder and the tempest in which the Lord had veiled His awful majesty had been steadily approaching and filled all hearts with dread. And now from the bosom of the rushing storm comes forth a voice, the voice of Jehovah, in unapproachable sublimity, speaking to Job: *"Who is this that darkens counsel by words without knowledge?"* Who and what is he who has been daring to obscure the wise orderings of My gracious and holy providence by the ignorant and empty reflections he has cast upon them? What is his ability, and what his claims to act as the censor of the divine pro-

ceedings? *"Now gird up your loins like a man; for I will ask of you, and you shall answer Me. Where were you when I laid the foundations of the earth? Tell if you have understanding! Who has laid the measures of it, if you know? Or who has stretched the line upon it? Upon what are foundations of it fastened, or who laid its cornerstone, when the morning stars sang together and all the sons of God shouted for joy? Or who shut up the sea with doors, when it broke forth as if it had come out of the womb? When I made the cloud its robe, and the thick darkness a swaddling band for it, and set My limit to it, and set bars and doors, and said, You shall come this far and no further; and here the pride of your waves shall stop? Have you commanded the morning since your days, and caused the dawn to know its place?"* (38:3-12).

The Lord further continues His appeal to the marvels of the sea, of death and the unseen world, of light and darkness, of the snow and rain, the ice and cold, of the stars, of the various celestial changes with their terrestrial effects, of the soul of man, of the instincts, habits, and adaptations of various orders of the animate creation; and concludes with the pointed interrogation, *"Shall he who contends with the Almighty teach Him? He who reproves God, let him answer it"* (40:2).

Awestruck and abashed at his own littleness and at the absurd pretensions involved in his rash and inconsiderate complaints, Job answered the Lord, *"Behold, I am vile; what shall I answer Thee? I will lay my hand upon my mouth. Once I have spoken, but I will not answer; yea, twice, but I will go no further"* (40:4,5).

The Lord then speaks once more to Job with the view of deepening the impression already made, and of showing still further of what vain conceit of his own powers Job had been guilty, and what unheard-of assumptions were involved in the language he had allowed himself to use. Was he prepared to assume the government of the world, and to take it out of the hands of the Most High, whose administration he had ventured to judge? God challenges him to show a power or execute deeds of judgment which would warrant these bold pretensions. *"Will you also set aside My judgment? Will you condemn Me so that you may be righteous? Have you an arm like God? Or can you thunder with a voice like Him? Adorn yourself now with majesty and honor; and dress yourself with glory and beauty. Cast abroad the rage of your wrath; and behold everyone who is proud and humble him. Look on everyone who is proud, and bring him low; and tread down the wicked in their place. Hide them in the dust together; and bind their faces in secret. Then I also will confess to you that your own right hand can save you"* (40:8-14).

So far indeed is he from being able to measure himself with God that he cannot even cope with His creatures, as he is reminded by a reference to two formidable animals, behemoth and leviathan--probably the hippopotamus and the crocodile. The full impression intended has by this time been made on Job, and he falls prostrate before the infinite God in self-abasement and self-reproach. Convicted of his fault, he makes instant confession, *"I have spoken what I did not understand; things too wonderful for me, which I did not know. I have heard of Thee by the hearing of the ear; but now my eye sees Thee. Therefore I despise myself and repent in dust and ashes"* (42:3, 5).

Job has now reached an elevation far above his former self. The depth of his humiliation is really the summit of his exaltation in piety, and in the fear and love of God. That Job now looks down upon himself as he does, shows how he has been raised above what he was before. He has made a great advance beyond the fervor of that moment when, in the darkest period of his struggle, his faith looked out with more than eagle glance into the unseen, and by one mighty effort rose superior to every temptation based upon the visible and the temporal, affirming God to be his redeemer in the face of everything outward which seemed to forbid all hope. The faith, to which he has now attained, would not only have gained the mastery in this frightful contest, but would have trampled Satan's temptation under foot without a conflict.

The faith, which shone out so conspicuously in that triumphant exclamation, was nevertheless defective, or the struggle would not have been so fierce, nor the triumph so hard to gain. He trusted in God, who was afflicting him, so far as steadfastly to believe and to declare that God would certainly hereafter, in the world to come, if not in this, lay aside His seeming hostility and reveal Himself as his friend. He trusted in God in spite of these afflictions, confident that He would deliver him out of them and would then be his God. But his trust in God was not such as to persuade him that in afflicting him He was still acting as his gracious God and redeemer. He was so far under the dominion of sense that there was still a region which faith had not completely subdued to itself. The opposition between God's present treatment of him and His loving regard for him still remained in his mind, and he did not have that implicit trust in God which could dissolve it. He had a faith which could resolutely turn its back upon the mountain of difficulty, but not one which could say to it, Be removed! Be cast into the depths of the sea and sunk out of sight! Or, Be dissolved in the ocean of divine love! There was still to him an apparent contradiction here, which his faith could disregard but not annul--a present breach between God and himself, which his faith could bridge over but not close up.

Now, however, he has learned to exercise a more perfect trust in God. He now confides in Him more thoroughly than before. He can now trust God in everything, and believe that He does all things well. He has gained such a view of God and of the perfections of His being, that he now believes that the Most High cannot do anything that is out of harmony with His perfections. All that He does must be right and wise and good. Job's faith may not enable him to fathom the mysteries of God, or to solve the riddles of His providence, but he knows that God is all-perfect and all-glorious. And he has that confidence in Him which assures him that these things must be so. If He has sent affliction, this is not even a temporary interruption of His favor and love, though these are sure to shine forth again hereafter clear and full. Nor is it enough to say that affliction is capable of being reconciled with the divine love. It is itself a fruit of that love. God is equally loving and gracious when He sends affliction and when He sends prosperous abundance.

Job's afflictions have not abated yet. His terrible losses are still as great as they were, and his bodily sufferings are as grievous. But the cloud is gone. He has lost all disposition to murmur or repine. He is amazed at himself that he could ever have done so. Since the Lord has disclosed Himself to him, such a sense of the divine perfections has filled his soul as forms the basis of an absolutely unlimited confidence. The temptation is not vanquished, it simply disappears. It is not overcome by a tremendous effort; the huge mountain just sinks down to a level plain. Though the sea roared before and was troubled, he walked in the midst of its waves unharmed and dry-shod. But now his faith has gained in strength until it has been able to bid the sea become dry land. The billows have ceased their tempestuous roll, and there is no more sea.

Job has now come to the end of the third temptation, which is the last and most fearful stage of the temptation. The struggle has been tremendous. It has been a long and a wearisome conflict, one desperately contested. But there is a glorious issue. The forces of his adversary are not merely driven back, not merely routed and put to an ignominious and disordered flight--they are positively annihilated! The victory is complete and final! Job's resignation and humility in the first and second stages of his affliction were sublime. How much more sublime are they now. When his property and his children were all swept away, Job still blessed the name of the Lord, mindful of the fact that the Lord had given what He now took away. Then when his own person was visited with a dreadful and seemingly incurable malady, he meekly received the evil at the hands of the Lord, still mindful of the good which He had previously bestowed. His constant trust in God rooted itself each time in the past, in the abundance of former mercies, his grateful sense of which was not effaced by all the severity of his present trials. He put his trials in the scales over against the benefits which the Lord had so bounteously conferred upon him. The bounty largely outweighed the afflictions.

Nevertheless each infliction of hurt and loss was an opposing weight, acting with whatever force it possessed in a contrary direction from God's mercies, and to that extent detracted from his sense of the goodness and love of God. This laid him open to the temptation of Satan. And it created the possibility that if weight enough could be accumulated on the side of affliction, it might at length create an equipoise, finally turning the scales the other way. And if this takes place, Job has fallen--Satan has gained the victory. During the most terrible period of his sorrows, when Satan seemed to have summoned every influence possible to depress the scale, Job was indeed hard-pressed by his wily and unscrupulous foe, and was put to the greatest straits. It was as much as he could do, by straining his God-given strength to the utmost, to maintain the balance on the right side. It was only by the strenuous efforts of a faith that took hold of the unseen, brought to its aid the world of the future, and laid its grasp upon the immutable attributes of God Himself, thus pinning the scale down to the everlasting Rock, that he could keep the balance on the side of God against a pressure too great for nature to sustain.

So there was, to some extent, a foundation for Satan's malignant sneer when he asked if Job feared God for nothing. The enemy had detected a crevice in the structure of Job's faith, into which he hoped to drive a wedge that could .tear it asunder and bring it down crumbling into ruins. Job's sense of God's goodness rested on the benefits received from Him, instead of the divine goodness being itself the fixed foundation, and everything received from the hand of God being for that reason counted a benefit. He judged of God by his own partial and defective notion of His dealings, instead of judging of those dealings by his knowledge of God. Job had, in the fierce conflict which Satan had waged against him, been driven by sheer necessity to base his faith on the immovable Foundation, notwithstanding the darkness and confusion of mind which still rested on the mysterious subject of his sufferings. But now God's messenger of instruction, Elihu, had pointed out to him the gracious ends of affliction, and the Lord had revealed Himself to him in the true glory of His nature, the previously existing flaw in Job's faith is closed up. The perfections of God have now become his first postulate, self-evidented and independent of any support to be derived from His particular dealings with him.

Heaven and earth may pass away, but the perfections of God abide, incapable of mutation or decay. This is the one invariable, fixed point, the basis of all certainty and of all correct judgments. It is, in mathematical phrase, the origin to which everything is to be referred, and from which everything is to be estimated. God must ever act like God. Whatever He does must be consistent with His glorious attributes, must be in face the outflow of those attributes. The orderings of Providence have their spring in the perfections of the ever-blessed God. Sense cannot discern this. But faith affirms it, and persistently adheres to it.

This is the lesson which Job has now learned. So he retracts all his murmuring words, and all that he has said which reproached his Maker.He abhors himself for having uttered them and repents in dust and ashes. He would nto now ask that question, Shall we receive good at the hand of God and shall we not receive evil? There is no evil, there can be no evil from the hand of the Lord. Evil is good when it comes from Him. He no longer puts the benefits received from God in one scale and the afflictions in the other. But afflictions are now put into the same scale with the benefits--for they, too, are benefits when God sends them. Therefore, instead of tending to create a counter-poise, they but add their weight to that of obligation previously existing. The nerve of Satan's temptation is now cut completely. Every weight goes from now on into the scale of God's goodness, and there is no possibility of disturbing the existing preponderance. He who has learned to place his sole and undivided trust in God, and to estimate all things by the standard of His perfection, is beyond the reach of any serious attempt to detach him from the Lord's service. To such a faith Job has risen under the felt power of God's immediate presence. He is now in a perfectly impregnable position, and Satan can assail him no longer. His spiritual deliverance is complete.

The Lord's purpose in permitting these dreadful sorrows is at length fully accomplished. There is no further occasion, therefore, for their continuance. Accordingly, the Lord now interferes for their removal. And first he pronounces in Job's favor and against his friends, *"the Lord said to Eliphaz the Temanite, My wrath is kindled against you and against your two friends. For you have not spoken of Me what is right, as My servant Job has"* (42:7). They had really brought God's providence into disrepute by their supposed defense of it. By covering up and ignoring its enigmas and seeming contradictions, they had cast more discredit upon it than Job by honestly holding them up to the light. Their denial of its apparent inequalities was more untrue and more dishonoring to the divine administration, as it is in fact conducted, than Job's bold affirmation of them. Even his most startling utterances wrung from him in his bewilderment and sore perplexity were less reprehensible than the false statements and false inferences of the three friends. In saying that God was treating Job as a gross offender, they indirectly charge Him with injustice and cruelty to a faithful servant of His. Job's impatient outcries under his sore distress were less offensive to God than these unwarrantable misrepresentations. And now the humbled and penitent Job has retracted all that he had rashly spoken, and everything is forgiven and forgotten but his present noble confession. Stricken as he was in the dust, bleeding at every pore, he had yet placed God upon the throne and had submitted without a murmur to His holy will.

The friends of Job, who had thought him an outcast from God's favor, can only be restored to that favor themselves through the intercession of their much-maligned and injured friend. Job, of course, does not withhold this intercession. He bears no malice toward them, and no resentment for all their ill-treatment. The bitterness that had sometimes broken out in his former speeches is entirely gone. He forgives them as God had forgiven him. And with this renewed evidence of the profit which he had derived from his afflictions, Job's captivity is turned and his former prosperity is renewed and doubled.

Job is now entirely extricated from Satan's snare, and released from his burden of woe. And the riddle is at length solved. The explanation of the sufferings of God's dear children may be embraced in the following particulars. They afford to all gainsayers a plain test of their integrity. The very intensity of the struggle develops their faith and other graces, leading them on to clearer views of heavenly truth. These sorrows are sent on the part of God with a gracious design, and afford the occasion of His revealing Himself to chastened souls with new fullness and power, in consequence of which they are brought nearer to Him than ever before, and their happiness and welfare are proportionately promoted.

To this the Apostle James adds his voice, *"Behold! We count those who endure happy. You have heard of the patience of Job, and you have seen the end of the Lord--that the Lord is full of pity and of tender mercy"* (James 5:11).

CHAPTER X

"Blessed are they that mourn! For they shall be comforted."--Matthew 5:4

THE PLACE OF THE BOOK OF JOB IN THE PLAN OF HOLY SCRIPTURE

Having made our way through the book of Job, it behoves us not only to form the right estimate of the book itself, but also to learn where God intended to lead us. Germs of truth are planted here, truths which God intended to expand in the Scriptures subsequently. The lines of thought which are started here lead on to far-reaching consequences. The sorrows of Job stand like the smitten rock of the desert at the head-waters of the stream of consolation. This precious tide flows on with ever-deepening current, gathering fresh tributaries as it flows, and bearing more abundant blessings on its bosom, until it comes out into the boundless, unfathomable ocean of divine grace and love, within view of which we are led to the gospel of Jesus Christ.

No book of the Bible stands apart by itself. None can be fully understood when studied separately and in its isolation. It is part of God's gradually unfolded revelation. Every book of the Bible belongs to a well-ordered system. It is a link in a chain. It is a member of an organism. It is what is is, not for itself alone, but has been shaped with reference to the position that it is to occupy and the function it has to perform in the plan of the whole. The history of Job is one among a gread body of signal facts illustrative of God's ways with men, one of many intended to reveal His plan of grace. The book of Job is one of a long series of inspired writings through which it has pleased God to make known His will and to reveal Himself. What precise part does it take in the successive disclosures of the truth of God? How does it advance upon what had been made known before? How does it prepare for what was to follow? What educating power lay in the truths which it lodged in the minds and hearts of men, and of what further consequences were they fruitful? And how do its teaching stand related to the completed revelation of the gospel?

It would be impossible to treat such a theme as this exhaustively within the narrow limits to which we must confine ourselves. And the attempt to do so under any circumstances might savor of arrogance and presumption. It will be sufficient, we trust, to venture a few observations by way of suggestion.

In logical order as in actual fact the law precedes the gospel. It is so in the experience of the race of man as a whole, in that of the chosen people, and in that of individual men. The covenant of works goes before the covenant of grace. The sentence upon our transgressing first parents before the promise of Him who should bruise the serpent's head. The commandments given by Moses must go before the grace and truth that came through Jesus Christ. The conviction of sin must come before the apprehension of saving mercy. Unless the lesson of the just desert of sin and of the inflexible righteousness of God has been first learned, the necessity and value of the offer of salvation cannot be understood. The doctrine of retribution is a necessary prerequisite to that of delivering grace. God must be seen as a Lawgiver and a Judge before He can be known as a Redeemer.

In a general sense, the Old Testament may be said to contain the law, and the New Testament the gospel. They are so contrasted by the apostle in respect to their tendencies on the whole, as the letter that kills and the spirit that gives life (2 Cor. 3:6). The foundations were laid broad and deep, strongly cemented by ages of the continued inculcation of God's essential righteousness. What is the Old Testament in its grand divisions but the Law proclaimed at Sinai, confirmed by the providential retributions of the History, devoutly meditated upon and practiced by the Psalmists and other inspired poets, and expanded and enforced by the added revelations of the Prophets? When the law had thus been wrought by all these concurrent methods into the minds and hearts and lives of men, then and not before was there an adequate basis on which to rear a superstructure that should match it in amplitude and in solidity, the revelation of God's immeasurable grace.

While, however, the two Testaments are predominantly what has now been described in general, they are not exclusively so. The statement, though correct in the main, is not exhaustive. The gospel was already witnessed by the Law and the Prophets (Romans 3:21); and the faith of Christ re-enacts and establishes the Law (Romans 3:31). Coupled with the revelation of God's justice under the Old Testament, there was a co-ordinate disclosure of His grace. For grace was set forth with growing clearness and fullness from the beginning to the end. Every advance in the presentation of the one was attended or followed by a corresponding advance in the knowledge of the other. Judgment and mercy are concomitants, as well as mutual opposites--or rather counterparts, being reverse sides of the excellence of God. Acts or declarations confirmatory of one serve consequently to illustrate and enforce the other. And the two series of progressive and related lessons move along together side by side throughout the whole of the former dispensation.

While, however, the gospel was already substantially preached before Christ came, this was prevailingly done in a legal form and under legal aspects. The pardon of sin, for instance, and reconciliation with God, were accomplished by sacrifices. It is true that these prefigured the atonement of the Son of God and derived from it all their present efficacy. Nevertheless they were a ceremonial institution, enacted in the law, to be performed by the offerer himself, and making up a part of his righteousness in view of the law. Mercy came to him indeed as unmerited grace to an offender, and yet under the form of an acceptance or justification procured by a performance of his own, or an act in whose performance he took part. The mercy that cancels sin did not drop out of sight, but it could not stand forth so conspicuously and in its own proper simplicity as now, when the typical sacrifice has been merged into and superseded by the great reality, and our entire pardon and justifying righteousness are seen to be worked out by another in our stead.

And so long as the free grace of the gospel was not yet exhibited in its fullness, it was also impossible that the law itself, to which the former dispensation was mainly devoted, should attain its complete expression. Dark and threatening as Sinai was, the law never appeared in such majesty, was never enforced by such sanctions, never exerted such a constraining power on men's hearts, and the exceeding breadth of the commandment was never so laid open as in the transaction on Calvary.

We must now inquire into the particular function assigned to the book of Job in unfolding this blended revelation of law and gospel. One obvious characteristic belonging to it in common with the other poetical books, and in which it stands in marked contrast with the rest of the Old Testament, is that it is occupied with what is individual and personal. The books of Moses contain God's covenant with Israel as a nation. The historical books record His dealings with the people as such. The books of the prophets make known His will to Israel and concerning Israel as the people of God. These set forth the general principles and methods of God's administration. The promises and threatenings concern the entire body of the people, or some considerable section of them, and individuals share the fortunes of the mass. If prosperous abundance is sent upon an obedient people, the wicked among them participate in the abundance. If a nation of transgressors is led into captivity, the calamity involves the righteous along with the rest. But Job stands alone and by himself. He is dealt with as an individual, not as one of a certain race or nation. Particularly, he is not dealt with as one of a covenant nation, for he did not belong to such. In his history we see the righteousness of God in its relations not to Israel, but to a single man.

The Psalms record the devout meditations and aspirations of pious souls, taking as their theme God's attributes, His word or His works. The Song of Solomon, which celebrates the divine institution of marriage, forms a striking parallel to the forty-fifth psalm. Lamentations is properly an appendix to the book of Jeremiah. Leaving these out of view for the present, the three poetical books are occupied with the righteousness of God as verified in the experience of men. Proverbs exhibits this verification as a fact of ordinary observation. On the whole, and as a general rule, and agreeable to the native tendencies of things, virtue is rewarded and vice is punished. But general rules have their exceptions. And to the common order of Providence as exhibited in Proverbs there are two apparent exceptions. These are so serious in their character, yet of so frequent occurrence, that they simply demand attention. There may be prosperity without piety, and there may be piety without prosperity! The first of these is treated in the book of Ecclesiastes. It presents the case of a man of the rarest wisdom, and with every facility that abundant wealth and royal station could supply, who set himself with deliberate purpose to extract gratification from all earthly sources--but he concluded that everything was vanity. And after the baffling experiments of a lifetime, he at length came to the conclusion that the only way to secure real enjoyment and true personal welfare was through the fear of God and the keeping of His commandments.

The other exception furnishes its theme to the book of Job. This deals with the case of piety without prosperity, or the righteousness of God as exercised toward faithful sufferers. Its lessons all grow out of this theme, or cluster about it. It is here, therefore, that we are to look for that unfolding of doctrine which belongs to it in the system of the Old Testament. The righteousness of God in its more general and obvious manifestations is assumed as the starting-point. This is taken for granted as well as understood and agreed on between Job and his friends at the outset. But a crisis occurs in Job's spiritual history in which the opinions that they have hitherto entertained are not adequate. A state of affairs arises at variance with their defective notions of the divine righteousness. In the struggle that now ensues, new light is imparted and more accurate conceptions are reached. The righteousness of God had been inadequately understood in two respects, belonging severally to the two poles of Old Testament truth (or, the two phases of Old Testament instruction) the law and the gospel. The question that agitates the soul of Job is that of his personal relationship to God. Is he the object of God's displeasure, or will God accomplish his salvation? But in fact he knew neither the extent of the divine displeasure nor the greatness of God's salvation. The righteousness of God condemned more in him than he suspected; while that which he looked upon as a sentence of condemnation was a measure of God's grace.

The new impressions which Job gains of the extent and spirituality of the law of God appears from his altered language respecting himself. His oft-repeated assertions of his righteousness, which were even carried to the extent of chiding with God as having done him wrong in sending afflictions upon him which he had not deserved, are superseded by penitent confession and self-abhorrence, *"I abhor myself, and repent in dust and ashes."* The change was wrought in his mind by the instruction received from Elihu, coupled with the manifestation of God as personal instructor. Elihu took the stumbling-block out of his way which had led to his previous false conclusions, by showing him that in inflicting extraordinary sufferings upon him God was not thereby charging him with unusual guilt. This cause of offense being removed, Job could listen with unprejudiced ear to Elihu's interpretation, that there was a deeper and more spiritual view of the nature of sin, as not merely consisting in actual transgressions such as the friends had linked with God's judgments, but as represented likewise in pride of heart and evil purpose (33:17). With his thoughts thus turned inward, Job finds reasons for the strokes of divine chastisement which he had not previously recognized, so he cannot regard himself with the same complacency as before.

But pious men under the Old Testament nowhere reach the platform of the New in this respect, and it was impossible that they should, because the facts on which the Christian doctrine of the law and of sin is based had not then been made known. This ought to be borne in mind in estimating the language of these ancient saints. We see them maintain their own righteousness in the view of God, when we would look rather for an humble confession of utter unworthiness. They plead with God to save them for His righteousness' sake, when we would expect to hear them beg instead for unmerited mercy. And we find it hard to enter into their feelings. We can scarcely acquit them of irreverence, or comprehend how such good men can speak as they do.

It will afford us a partial explanation of the matter if we see that these assertions of their own goodness are mostly made in opposition to implied or open charges of criminality of which they are guiltless. The Psalmists were often like Job the objects of unjust aspersions and slanders. And they were entitled to declare their innocence of what had been falsely alleged against them. But they do not limit themselves to the claim of being pure from that which has been wrongfully attributed to them, nor to the claim of an integrity that should shield them from the censure of men, but while with the same breath confessing their sinfulness they lay claim to an uprightness of such breadth and purity that it can maintain itself at the bar of God.

It is also true that in making their appeals to God's righteousness they include under this term His faithfulness as well as His justice. They intend by the righteousness of God that attribute in virtue of which He does right, not merely in view of their deserts, but in view of His own gracious engagements. They remember His covenant and His promises. And the righteousness of God assures them that He will keep that word which He mercifully gave.

But with all these explanations and abatements we cannot but feel how differently the apostle Paul is accustomed to speak of himself, and what a different estimate he puts on his own deservings--*"Not by works of righteousness which we have done, but according to His mercy He saved us."--"I am carnal, sold under sin....The good that I would, I do not; but the evil which I would not, that I do....O wretched man that I am! Who shall deliver me from the body of this death?"* (Titus 3:5; Romans 7:14-25). Such an experience belongs to the New Testament exclusively. There is repentance in the Old Testament, and there are confessions of sin. There are deep views of its greatness and vileness and enormity. There are prayers for forgiveness. There are fervent breathings after greater conformity to the will of God. All the roots of the apostolic experience are there, but they are never quickened into the same intensity of life, they never reach the same expansion, they never gain that ascendency and complete mastery of the soul which shapes all its thinking and feeling. Such excellencies as these are what makes a constant attitude of helpless unworthiness before God. Why did they not have them? Because they had never learned the lesson of the cross of Christ. The vastness of the provision first gave an idea of the greatness of the need. The sinfulness of sin was never so plainly seen as in the light of the infinite merit of the atonement which was required to efface it. And the utter worthlessness of our own righteousness first became manifest from the fact that men are justified without any worthiness or deservings of their own. Instead, they are justified by simple trust in the righteousness of Another. The full knowledge of this humbling and abasing truth altered the whole complexion of piety. It changed the very basis of men's standing in the sight of God. Or, at least, it enabled them to see where they really did stand, more distinctly than was possible before. It swept the gathered sand and rubbish from the rock, precluding the possibility that they would imagine they could heap these together and add to the security of their hope. But this, while it banished forever all thought of any claim of merit or righteousness in the sight of God, gave a new and impregnable basis of confidence before Him, --a confidence which no craft of Satan and no storms of affliction could disturb.

It is, however, on the side of the gospel that the lessons of the book of Job chiefly lie. These are all in the direction of the more complete revelations which would subsequently be made, though they do not surpass the knowledge of God's grace which was intended for that time, nor do they ever anticipate in its fullness what was reserved for a brighter future. Piety was still *"the fear of the Lord"* (28:28). The love of God had not yet been made perfect (1 John 4:16,18).

In these unfoldings of gospel truth we are not to expect any direct presentation of the person of the Messiah. He is not in the Old Testament invoked in individual straits or in present necessities. He is ever exhibited rather as the Hope of Israel and the Saviour of the world. His coming was to introduce an era of peace and holiness and bliss. He was held forth as the one by whom Judah would be saved from degeneracy and defection, from the calamities which threatened or overwhelmed them, from the growing power of their adversaries. His reign was to benefit all nations, for they would flock to the mountain of the Lord, beating their swords into ploughshares and learning war no more. But it was not so clear to them that this same Saviour was the present deliverer of each one of His people in his own individual distress. So suffering saints in the time of their trouble are not seen calling on the name of the Messiah for help and rescue, but they call upon the name of Jehovah, unaware that they are directing their petitions to the same Person whose appearance among men shall introduce the anticipated glories of the future.

But addressing Jehovah as they do in the capacity of their covenanted Redeemer, asking of Him the help which He alone can supply, making Him the sole ground of their confidence as well as of all their affection and desire, it is in fact the Son of God to whom they make their appeal. All the knowledge they gain of this divine Saviour, all the homage they learn to pay to Him, all the trust they repose in Him, is a direct preparation for the doctrine of Christ. They did not know at the time that this line of instruction would converge on that other line which taught them of the Son of David and the King of Israel. The point of junction was first visibly reached when the Word was made flesh. Then the divine Redeemer and the expected Saviour were consciously identified as the Lord from Heaven to whom each struggling soul had looked for succor, and the son of Abraham in whom all the families of the earth were to be blessed. He it was that baffled Satan's wiles and rescued Job from his snare, for He was the Seed of the woman who was to crush the serpent's head and restore the fallen race of man (Genesis 3:15).

Additional elements of Messianic instruction are found in the typical character of Job and that of Elihu. They are each representative of a class which finds its highest example in Christ. Whether the type was discerned to be such by the writer of this book and his original readers, it would be difficult to determine. But it supplies an exemplar conformed to the model of Him who was afterwards to be revealed. It presents a character which would be better understood and appreciated when realized in Christ. And the idea to which it gives rise is certainly linked with the expected Saviour in other parts of the Old Testament in a way which shows that this connection was known to the inspired penmen themselves.

As we suggested before, Job makes a good type of the Man of sorrows in his sore afflictions. This resemblance to Christ is not casual or accidental. It is a principle of divine administration that His children are made perfect through sufferings. So it was with Job. So it has been in every age. There is a difference in circumstances and in application, but the principle is always the same. God's own Son when revealed in human flesh learned obedience by the things that He suffered (Heb. 5:8). This uniform method of God's grace is especially dwelt upon by the Psalmists, and its highest application is deduced or foreseen by them. On the basis of their own experience of trial, with its resulting benefits to them, and and through them to others, they repeatedly portray the righteous man oppressed by calamities. The picture which they draw is mostly a general one such as has its counterpart in any one of a multitude of God's faithful servants who have passed through deep waters and eventually found safety in delivering grace. But sometimes, as in Psalm 22, the picture is an ideal one. The human characteristics are preserved, but the excellencies are heightened until they have become faultless; imperfections are removed until absolute sinlessness is reached; suffering is followed by unbounded exaltation and glory; and the blessed results of the sorrows swell to proportions that admit no limitations. The picture is plainly human, and yet it transcends all ordinary human experience. It can have but one realization: the Holy Sufferer is the incarnate Son of God.

Elihu is himself such a "messenger" as he describes (33:23), an interpreter, *"One among a thousand, to show man what is right toward God."* He had been selected from all others and sent by God to expound to Job the divine will and purpose in this dispensation, and to make known to Job his duty. And this was the result which he had foreshown, *"then He is gracious to him and says, Deliver him from going down to the pit, for I have found a ransom."* Elihu acts the part of an instructor who is the instrument of salvation to his suffering and needy friend, He fulfills in a lower sense the very function of the great Teacher and Prophet, in response to whose prevalent vindication the same reply is given, *"Deliver Him from going down to the pit: I have found a ransom."* Only the ransom is then no longer limited to the figurative sense in which Elihu uses it. The great Teacher has provided a ransom in the strict and proper sense for the release of His people, now and forever.

As the book of Job circles about the conflict in which this man of God was engaged, its lessons mainly concern the foe with whom he had to contend on the one hand, and the supports and encouragements given to him on the other. His real adversary was not God, as his friends alleged, and as he sometimes understood it, but Satan was his foe. And here a new view is opened into the darkness. The great foe to human peace and goodness is here for the first time in Scripture disclosed in his proper person and character. The serpent had tempted Eve, yet the narrative of the Fall requires the assumption of a spiritual agent concerned in the transaction, though his agency is only vaguely inferred. Here in Job, however, he is explicitly named as Satan. His spiritual nature, his malignity, his great power, his subtlety, his untiring assiduity of evil are exposed. Yet he is also shown to be limited, restrained, overruled, and under God's direction so that good may be brought out of the evil he devises. This is an important advance toward the full New Testament revelation on this subject, in which a disclosure is made not merely of a single adversary, but of the whole hierarcy of evil, and of a heightened assurance of victory over foes already vanquished by the Captain of our salvation.

We see in Job how his afflictions were a test of the sincerity and strength of his pious fear, and how his confidence in God's righteousness carried him successfully through; how he clung to his belief, in spite of all outward appearances, that God was faithful and would not desert His servant, and how at length he learned that affliction might be converted into a benefit. Of course there is a striking difference between the demeanor of the apostles and followers of Christ under calamity and that of the saints of God in the Old Testament. The moans and complaints of desertion which are so often heard from faithful men of old in times of sore distress grow directly out of the legal aspect under which they contemplated the character of God. How different it would have been if Job and the others had read, as we do, *"He who did not spare His own Son, but delivered Him up for us all, how shall*

He not with Him also freely give us all things?" "Who shall separate us from the love of Christ? Shall tribulation, or distress, or persecution, or famine, or nakedness, or peril, or sword?...No, in all these things we are more than conquerors through Him who loved us. For I am persuaded that neither death, nor life, nor angels, nor principalities, nor powers, nor things present, nor things to come, nor height, nor depth, nor any other creature shall be able to separate us from the love of God which is in Christ Jesus our Lord." (See Rom. 8:32-39). Surely in this consciousness Job would have gloried in tribulation, assured that he would be kept from real harm by his Heavenly Father, looking unto Jesus and rejoicing to be conformed to Him who endured the cross, despising the suffering and shame. Knowing that the love of God is sending the affliction, is carefully supervising the instruments of affliction, and is intending to deliver you a better person and a more godly character from the affliction certainly changes your attitude toward the affliction.

Again, how differently would the saints of old, such as Job, have felt if they could have know of the heavenly inheritance, that far more exceeding and eternal weight of glory ·with which the sufferings of this present time are not worthy to be compared. Job was brought in his conflict into contact with the doctrine of immortality, but he only attained a limited conception of this blessed truth. He was not able to draw from it that abundant comfort which it is adapted to supply. His confidence that God would not forever withhold His favor from him, coupled with the fact that there was no room left for that favor to display itself in the present life, had driven him to the conclusion that it must be granted to him in the world to come. He laid hold of his immortality to steady himself in the absence of any earthly hope. It never occurred to him to prefer it to every earthly hope, even if this latter had been possessed in the fullest measure. Life without God's favor and blessing would not indeed have been an object of desire to him any more than to the Psalmist, who exclaims, *"Whom have I in Heaven but Thee? And there is none upon earth that I desire besides Thee"* (Ps. 73:25). But life with God's favor was his chief inheritance and his portion. The idea had not presented itself to his mind that the boundless hereafter with the blessing of God's everlasting presence was a more desirable portion than this brief life could be with the same divine presence and blessing here. He had faith that God would vindicate His servant and appear upon his side in the future state. But he did not have the full conception of a life with God, a life free from sin and every form of sorrow, a glory and bliss eternal. It was not until the divine Saviour had Himself appeared, and the magnitude of redemption and its unending results had in consequence been disclosed, that men could say with the apostle Paul that though to live was Christ, yet to die was gain.

The sense of immortality to which Job attained was likewise echoed by the Psalmists, who speak upon occasion of the future life, but in ambiguous and doubtful phrase, which leaves it uncertain how clear their conceptions may have been. The prophets reached the same result by a somewhat different route. God's covenant faithfulness to Israel secured His people as a whole in all perpetuity against death and destruction. Or if their fortunes were so broken that they seemed dead and buried, He would accomplish their resurrection. And this deliverance from death and from all the evils resulting from the Fall, which was guaranteed to the body as a whole, was secured likewise to its constituent members.

But these flashes of assurance which we find in the Old Testament are as nothing compared with the clear and steady light shed on the future life in the New Testament. And this fullness of revelation has revolutionized the whole idea and aim of life. The believer has learned to regard the transient present as of small account in comparison with the eternity that lies before him, to set his affections on things above, not on things on the earth, to lay up his treasure in Heaven, to look not at the things which are seen and which are temporal, but to look at the things which are not seen and which are eternal. With such a blissful portion in prospect, what are all the light, momentary sorrows we suffer now?

TREASURY

OF

JOB

VOLUME ONE

A TREASURY OF JOB

THE EXPOSITION BY JOSEPH CARYL (1602-1673)
(AS ABRIDGED, PARAPHRASED, EXTENDED AND AMENDED BY JAY GREEN)

"There was a man in the land of Uz, whose name was Job. And this man was perfect and upright, and one who feared God and turned aside from evil"—Job 1:1 (KJV II).

This first chapter may be divided into three parts, (1) a description of Job in his prosperous estate—verses one through five; (2) Job's original affliction—verses six through nineteen; (3) Job's bearing and behavior as he achieved victory through faith—verses 20 through 22.

1. Job was prosperous in three ways: in his person; in his possession; in his holy life.
Two physical facts and four spiritual facts are given us in regard to this man. First, God tells us that he lived in the land of Uz; secondly, that his name was Job. More importantly, (3) he was perfect; (4) upright; (5) one who feared God; (6) one who turned from evil.
Those who write of great men usually give us some description of their persons before they set down their undertakings or achievements (as you see in 1 Samuel 17:4-7, where the great giant, Goliath, is described). So here the Holy Spirit by the penman of this book is giving us the description of the divine hero's person, and the abilities of his spirit, before he records a glorious combat — not a combat with flesh and blood alone, but with principalities and powers. This is a wrestling with mighty and strong temptations besides. So then we have the height and stature of the combatant. We see what were his weapons, where he lived, what his name was.

"There was"—This refers us either to the truth of the story or to the time of the story. There was such a man, that is certain. There was such a man, but the time is uncertain. The time is given only indefinitely. There was such a man, but when he lived is not precisely set down. The Scripture often keeps exact account of years, but sometimes, as here, leaves the time indefinite. Some have undertaken to discover the precise time when Job lived, but I do not want to be so accurate, because the Spirit of God has left the exact time unrecorded. This much we may safely say, that Job lived between the times of Abraham and Moses, and nearer Moses than Abraham. For this, I believe there is evidence: First, Job offered sacrifices at that time in his own country. After the giving of the Law, all were forbidden to do this, both Jews and proselytes. Any who were acquainted with God's ways knew that they must worship by sacrifice only before the Tabernacle.
Secondly, in all this book there is not the least mention of anything which concerned those great and glorious passages of God's providence towards the people of Israel, either in their deliverance from Egypt or in their journey through the wilderness of Canaan. There is hardly a book of Scripture which was written after the Exodus which does not mention or refer to some passages concerning God's wonderful dispensation of mercy to Israel then.
As to Job's genealogy, there are several opinions as to his family line: (1) that he descended from Nahor, the brother of Abraham (Gen. 22:21); (2) that he was in the line of Esau, and that Moses called him Jobab (Gen. 36:33); (3) that he was kin to Abraham by his second wife Keturah (Gen. 25, where it is said Abraham sent her many sons into the East country); that Midian was his father, and that Job was descended from Him.
Since there is none but conjectural grounds, nothing definite can be said.

"a man"—Job is not called a man in the sense that he was barely more than a rational animal; nor to distinguish him as to sex. But he is called man by way of excellency; that is to say, he was a man among men. There are three words for man in original Scripture: (1) man is called *Adam*—it was the proper name of the first man, and it became the common

1

name of all men since--so man is named for the dust of which he was made (Adam, from *Adamah*). (2) Man is called *Enosh*. And he is called so in regard to his infirmities, his weaknesses, his sorrows, which he has contracted by his sin. Since the Fall, earthy man and the whole groaning creation has been moistened with tears and mixed with troubles. (3) Man is called *Ish*. The excellency of man's being; the heat, courage, and spirit that flames in a man is set forth in this word. This man Job is *Ish*, an excellent, worthy man--a man of an extraordinary spirit, a man fitted to honor God and govern men. (For example, see Ps. 49 and Isaiah 2:9, where men are divided into high and low, great and lowly, by being called on the one hand, sons of Ish, and on the other, sons of Adam.)

Job was an *Ish* man, a man who was great, probably a man in authority, perhaps a judge. Some even carry it to the point of making him a king. Only the first is certain (see 29:7).

"In the land of Uz"--This Uz may be taken for the name of a man. There are three called Uz in Scripture (see Gen. 10:23;22:21;36:28). The land of Uz was clearly on the borders of the Chaldeans, the Arabians, and the Sabeans. Uz and Edom are mentioned together in Lamentations 4:21. Uz must be located in the vicinity of these four people. As for the inhabitants of Uz, it is apparent they were a profane people. The descendents of Esau are considered so throughout Scripture. It was among such people as these that Job lived and governed. Here he exercised those precious graces and practiced those excellent duties, displaying holiness toward God and justice toward men

GOD HAS HIS SERVANTS IN ALL PLACES, EVEN IN THE WORST PLACES

There never was any air so bad that a servant of God might not breath in it. Here God had a choice man placed in the land of Uz, a Bethel in Bethaven (a house of God in a land of wickedness). Lot lived in Sodom, Joseph in Egypt, David in Gath. There were saints in the household of that most wicked Caesar, Nero. Babylon held many of God's people, but let them not make such places their refuge, much less their choice.

It is a great honor to be good and to do good among those that are evil. You shall be recorded in God's book for it. That is why God tells us Job lived in Uz, that we may know that he was good in spite of the evil examples around him. Though he lived among those who were scoffers and wicked, yet Job was holy. As regarding love and affection, it is said that men love those that love them. But only Christians may love a man who hates him. So in regard to living and conversing, as of loving and affecting, we may say that it is most wicked indeed to be perverse among those that are good--it is a great aggravation of sin to be unholy in the presence and sight of those that are holy. But how much more excellent is it, how much more glorious, to be good among those that are perverse--to worship God among idolators, to fear God among those who have no fear of God before their eyes. To be perfect among hypocrites and upright among the unjust is an honor and commendation for Job.

Grace will preserve itself in the midst of the greatest opposition. Grace is a fire which has no water to quench it. True grace will keep itself sound and clean among those who are unclean, it will overcome and master all evil that is about it. God has put His mighty power into grace, so that if it possesses the heart, then not all the wickedness in the world; no not even the devils can dispossess it. As all the water in the salty sea cannot make the fish salty, so all the wickedness and filthiness in the world cannot defile true grace.

"And that man was perfect and upright"--Job was perfect. Of course, he did not have a legal perfection, such as the Roman Catholics and others claim a man may attain. Job himself said, *"If I say I am perfect, it shall also prove me preverse"* (9:20). And he freely acknowledges that he has sinned (7:20). This perfection, then, is not an absolute perfection. To clear the word, there is a twofold perfection ascribed to the saints in this life: a per-

fection of justification, and a perfection of sanctification. The perfection of justification is a complete perfection: the saints are complete in Christ, they are perfectly justified, not one sin is left uncovered; therefore, there is no guilt that has not been washed away in the blood of Christ--His righteousness is enough to cover all our nakedness and deformities. In this respect all the saints are perfect, for *"by one offering Christ has perfected forever those that are sanctified"* (Heb. 10:14). Job was perfect in this way.

As to perfection of sanctification, or holiness, it has to be either with the beginnings of perfection, or with the desires after perfection. Even in this life the saints have a perfect beginning of holiness, because they have begun to be sanctified in every part, being wholly sanctified, in soul and body and spirit (1 Thess. 5:23). Though every part may not be wholly sanctified, yet all parts are included in the beginnings of sanctification — and this is a perfection. When the work of sanctification is begun in all parts, it is a perfect work.

Likewise, the saints are perfect in regard to their desires and intentions. Perfect holiness is the aim of the saints on earth, and it is the reward of the saints in Heaven.As God accepts the will for the deed (1 Cor. 8:12), so He expresses the deed by the will. God interprets him to be a perfect man whose heart yearns to be perfect. God calls that person perfect whose desires are to have all his imperfections cured. This is a second way Job was perfect.

A third way is this, Job was perfect comparatively, comparing him with those who were either openly wicked, or those who were openly holy. In either company, by comparison, Job must be counted perfect.

Again, the perfection here spoken of may be the perfection of sincerity. Job was sincere, he was sound of heart. He did not act a part, he did not personate true religion, but he was truly godly. He was not guilded, he was gold (as some interpret the word). Some say, Job was a simple man (not simple as put for weak and foolish, but simple-hearted, in contrast with a double-minded man). Job was single in purpose and in mind, not one who had *"a heart and a heart."* He was not a compound, speaking one thing and meaning another, but he meant what he spoke, and he spoke his mind.

"and upright"--the former word which was translated *"perfect"* is often translated upright in other texts. But when we have both these words together, as here, we must distinguish the sense. It is not a tautology, a renewing of the thought in other words. Therefore, the former word being taken for inward soundness, simplicity and sincerity, this latter word must be taken for outward justice, righteousness and equity. Job was a perfect man in his plain-heartedness and he was also plain in his dealings. The one refers to the integrity of his spirit, the other to the honesty of his ways, "his heart was plain, and his dealings were square." In chapters 29 and 31 of this book, Job expresses fully his uprightness. When Job bought and sold, bargained, promised, or covenanted, he was perfectly upright. He gave everyone his due, whether as a magistrate or no. He never spared nor smote in order to serve his own ends. He did not either justify the wicked or condemn the godly. He was not biased by affection or interests, he was not carried away by his own hopes or fears. This is uprightness, and the prophet tells us, *"the way of the just is uprightness,"* that is a way of saying that the just are upright in their ways and in their hearts. For this reason, God tells us, *"He that is upright in the way is hateful to the wicked."* Uprightness, then, refers to the way a man deals with men, In this, there are two ways to be upright: upright in words, and upright in works (*"He who walks uprightly and works righteousness, and speaks the truth in his heart; who does not backbite with his tongue"*--Psalm 15:2,3).

"one who fears God"—the fear of God is taken in two ways: the natural, inward worship of God which causes a man to lovingly obey the whole will of God; the external, instituted worship if God which requires that a man worship God according to directions given by

God. Job is a man who feared God both ways, both inwardly and outwardly. He loved and revered Him (*"let us have grace, by which we may serve God acceptably with reverence and godly fear"*—Heb. 12:28). Job also performed that worship to God which He directed —fearing God and worshiping God are the same. Fearing God includes both the affection of a worshiper and the duty or act of worshiping. And it must not be that fear which is commanded or devised by men (Matthew 15:9; Isaiah 29:14).

"and turns away from evil"—Evil, here, is taken for sin. Before sin came into the world, there was no evil in the world. But when sin came, it brought all other evils in with it. Sin has in it the whole nature of evil, and all the degrees of evil, and from it proceeds all evil effects. Sickness and death and Hell are called evil; how much more evil is that from which these originated! Furthermore, evil is here put indefinitely. Job not only turned away from this evil or that evil, but every evil without exception and without intermission. Again, we are to take evil here as he himself afterward expounds it in his practice. Not only did he hate evil and turn positively away from the acts of it, but he also carefully avoided all the occasions, the appearances, the provocations and the incentives of or unto evil. An insight into his way of thinking and doing is seen in that one instance, *"I made a covenant with my eyes, why then should I think upon a virgin?"*

Job not only turned away from evil, turning aside as he saw it looming in the distance, he also diligently labored to preserve the life and grace which made him able to do so. As the proverb goes, That man has both his money and his wits about him who suspects and provides against thieves. There is more to saying a man eschews evil than merely to say that he did not commit evil. Not only did Job's hand and tongue not meddle with evil, but his heart despised it, and his spiritual stomach was nauseated by it. The Hebrew word here translated, "turned aside from" signifies a turning aside with abhorrency. As there is a great deal of difference between the doing of good things, and a delight in doing good, so a man may be one that does not commit this and this sin, seemingly doing no harm to anyone, yet that man may love the very sins he does not commit. Such a one is not a man who hates and turns aside from evil. Job's heart rose up in indignation against any kind of evil.

GRACE AND GRACES

When God describes one of His excellent men, He sets forth first the grace He has given him. So here, Job is said to be a man who was perfect, upright, loving God, hating evil. If God has given a man grace, than he has the best and choicest of all that which God can give. God has given us His Son, His Spirit, and the graces of His Spirit--these are the finest of the flower, the honey out of the rock of mercy. Though you may not have Job's children, or his riches, if you have his graces, you have all. Any who are perfect and upright, who find in their hearts the love of God and the desire to worship Him reverently, may count themselves blessed indeed. Why should they be discontented in any condition, or envious of the condition of any other, when they clearly have the one thing needful?

Where one grace is, there is every grace. Grace is poured into the soul in all its parts. Be assured, there is somewhat of every grace laid into the soul of every believer. We do not see that one man has one grace and another man another grace, but every man of God has every grace. Not all have this grace or that grace in the same height or degree. Some are obviously blessed with more of this grace than of that one. Yet everyone who has any grace at all certainly has every grace in some degree, for all graces go together.

SINCERITY

It is sincerity that especially commends us to God. Just as surely as Job's graces are preferred before his riches, so sincerity is the crown upon all his other graces. It is sincerity that makes us acceptable and pleasing to God in the acts of our heart and of our hands.

Take a man who is ever so just, one who worships God in all His ordinances, one who evidently avoids the paths of evil, but in all this the man is insincere--all is lost, he is abominable in the sight of God. Some look upon sincerity as a distinct grace (for my own part I believe sincerity is not properly a distinct grace, but the perfection of every grace). It is without doubt that which commends a man to God. Without sincerity, all our good-deed fulfillments are but empty sounds, *"as sounding brass and tinkling cymbals"* (1 Cor. 13).

It is not all you can do, or all you can say, or all you can suffer, or all you can sacrifice that can make you perfect in the esteem of God without sincerity. Add sincerity to the least duty performed and it gives you the denomination of perfect. God accepts the least offering from one that is sincere, and He counts it as a rich present, as He pronounces the one offering to be perfect. But He will refuse the greatest riches, the most magnificent and mightiest efforts, from one who is insincere.

FEARING GOD AND TURNING ASIDE FROM EVIL

Holy fear keeps the heart and life clean. For a holy fear is full of love toward God. Love causes the lover to take thought beforehand lest he displease the one he loves. Fear of God carries with it such love, but added to love is a deep and ever-present reverence. Holy fear stands at the gate, examining all who come, stopping all unclean and unfit thoughts and affections from entering our minds and hearts. *"The fear of the Lord is to depart from evil," "to hate evil"* (Proverbs 3:7 and 8:13).

But godly persons do not only forbear to sin, they hate sin. It is not only that they have their hands tied so that they are prevented from sinning, but they have their hearts fixed so that he sets himself against all inward and outward forms of sin (Ps. 112:7). And he is against all sin, his opposition is universal—it was not just this sin or that sin Job hated, hatred is against the kind, so Job hated every kind of sin and all kinds of sin. Not one sin did he hide under his tongue. Furthermore, godly persons do not merely avoid the acts of sin, they carefully avoid all occasions of evil (1 Thess. 5:22; Proverbs 4:15).

CHAPTER 1, VERSE 2

"and there were born to him seven sons and three daughters"--Job 1:2

This verse contains the first part of Job's outward happiness, the blessing of children. The Scripture is plain in denoting children as a blessing and heritage which the Lord gives for our happiness (Ps. 127:3). Job was given ten children, seven sons and three daughters-- both numbers of perfection. The word translated 'son' means to build, for the children are means of building up their father's house. Or it may be because they are built and framed out of their parents. Jacob reflects truly God's views as to children when he said to Esau, *"These are the children which God has graciously given your servant"* (Genesis 33:5).

When a description is made of Job's goods, the best is put first. First, his spiritual blessings are set down, then comes the best of outward blessings, his children. It is better to have a child with his precious soul given to us, than to have the whole world full of possessions. And many there are who would give all their possessions just to have one child. But Job was given ten children, and unlike many in our day, he counted each new one a blessing. And while it is true that each new child may in some way require some attention from the father, none of the ten, nor all ten children hindered Job from doing his duty toward man and toward God. This sincere love and attention to what is right is undoubtedly a cause of Job's prosperity. Not only was he able to feed and clothe his children, but a host of others.

CHAPTER 1, VERSE 3

"His possessions also were seven thousand sheep and three thousand camels, and five hundred yoke of oxen, and five hundred she-asses, and a very great household--so that this man

was the greatest of all the men of the east"--Job 1:3

The Holy Spirit now proceeds to show us the kind and extent of Job's outward blessings. He owned several kinds of stock, such as sheep, camels, oxen, and asses. And the numbers of each were extraordinary in Job's day--enough of each and all kinds to make him a substantial man. Though riches are but external and temporary, a man is usually called substantial when he has gained enough substance to sustain himself without the help of his fellows. Others do not need to prop him up. He subsists from his own possessions.

"possessions"--The Hebrew word which we translate possessions or substance is a word a man may use indifferently as to the kind of possession owned. But since the Hebrew economy was an economy based on various kinds of stock, this word is used most often of the animals held in possession.

"7000 sheep"--Sheep were used for both meat and clothing. Seven thousand sheep were enough to feed and clothe a great many people. And in Job's day the total population per square mile was so small that these same sheep could feed and clothe a large percentage of the total population of the area. This made Job a great man, a noted man in all eyes.

"3000 camels"--The Hebrew word *Gamel* has the basic meaning of recompence. No one can be certain as to why it is used of the camel, but in the Middle East the camel may surely be said to give abundant recompence to his master for his keeping. They were, and still are, the chief beast of burden, as well as the main means of transportation in Job's day. A herd of camels of this size was probably unknown to any other man within reach of Uz.

"500 yoke of oxen"--Oxen were the work animals for cultivating the ground.

"500 she-asses"--These were used for local travel and burden-bearing.

IF JOB WAS SO RICH, WHY DID HE NOT HAVE GOLD, SILVER AND JEWELS?

God's inventory of Job's possessions does not mention gold, silver or jewels. Nevertheless, it is certain that Job had these also. In chapter 32, he says, *"If I have made gold my hope, or have said to the fine gold, you are my confidence."* It would not have been right for him to deny that gold was his hope in this sense if he did not own gold in abundance. As for jewels, we are told that God had men give Job jewels, double all that he owned before (in chapter 42, *"everyone an earring of gold."*) We know from Abraham's story that a rich man in those days had gold, silver and jewels in abundance (Gen. 13:2; 24:35,53).

But here Job's estate is reckoned all in cattle, with no mention of gold, silver and jewels, and precious stones? First, animals were the center of the economy in those days. Just as we count a man rich by his money, his rents and revenues, in our day, so then riches were counted in the number of animals a man owned. The owners of these were sure to be able to buy all the jewels and rich appointments he desired. Secondly, gold and jewels are but dead substance. Cattle in their own nature are more excellent than gold and silver, for they have life. The lowest creature that has life is better than the best without life. Job's estate was in natural and living riches, not in artificial or dead riches. The ancients called money *pecunia* (which comes *a pecude,* from cattle) because they stamped the form of a sheep or ox on the money they used, For these were the riches that a man sought, or had.

"and a very great household"--the original indicated that a great number of servants attended the herds that Job owned, cultivated the ground for food, and managing his house. No numbers are given here, but obviously the wealth of the man demanded multitudes of servants (and it is possible that the numbers of the animals were only symbolic, with perhaps myriads of others owned by Job not counted before our eyes, but covered therein).

"So that this man was the greatest of all the men in the east"--He was greatest in riches, in power, in honor, in grace (which is the greatest of all riches). Of all the men of the east,

there were none greater nor richer than Job. Since the east country was no doubt a very large country, and since this area had very many rich men at all times, it is evident that Job was truly great. And the Holy Spirit tells us that he not only was one of the richest men, but that he was the greatest and the richest of all men in that country.

The question may be asked, why does the Holy Spirit spend so many words and become so accurate in telling us of Job's outward estate. There are three reasons for this.

1. He is described to be a man of very great estate so that the greatness of the affliction might appear afterward. A man's loss must be measured against what he lost. What he lost depends entirely upon what he had. If a man only has little, and he suffers loss of that little, then his affliction cannot be truly great. For a man's affliction to be great, his loss must be great also. If a man abounds in possessions, then loses all, obviously his loss is great. Besides the actual loss of goods or riches, there is a loss of enjoyment and privilege which also would be very great.

2. The greatness of Job's estate is set forth for us that we might know the greatness of his patience. It does not take much patience for a man who is poor to bear becoming a little poorer. But for a man to have nothing at all after he has had all things, yes, even the greatest of things, this indeed would require much patience. Job was a man who had not only riches and possessions, but servants and the homage of all his friends and neighbors. It would be hard to lose all your possessions, but when you lose those who serve you all is much harder. The hardest of all losses for many, however, is the loss of the respect and reverence of friends and neighbors. In Job's case, it was not only the loss of fair weather friends, but also the loss of many that he had considered to be dear friends.

3. The listing of all of Job's possessions was given as a testimony so that those who read the story of Job might realize that he not only was rich in money and goods, but he also was rich in grace and holiness. He was a man of extraordinary strength of grace. Why? Because in the loss of all things, he still held to his integrity. He kept up his spirit in the way of holiness in spite of the fact that he was lifted up with abundance, and he also kept up his spirit in the way of holiness when all his things were taken away. To be very great and very good at the same time is proof that a man is good indeed. It is rare for a man to be great and good, rich and holy at the same time. Usually riches not only fatten the body but fatten the pride of man. Riches are most often a way to wither the soul. Possessing many things in this world oftentimes eats out all care for heaven. Therefore Job was truly one of a myriad, being at once great in riches and rich in goodness.

In Proverbs 30 we read of Agur praying to the Lord as follows, "Give me neither poverty nor riches" (Proverbs 30:8). It is indeed a great temptation to have great riches, for most rich men have a tendency to kick against the Lord. Likewise the poor kick against the Lord, blaming Him for what they do not have. It is difficult either way to give the Lord His just due. But Job was full of grace when he was rich, few men desiring to dispute this. When we became poor, however, then was his grace truly displayed. This was proof that the grace which he appeared to have he truly had. So Job, the greatest man in the east, was given both the greatest of riches and the greatest of poverty, all in a shocking few days. That which Agur prayed that he would not have, Job had, and this quite suddenly and unexpectedly. Yet in all of these things he did not sin against the Lord.

OBSERVATIONS

1. Plain and honest dealing are no hindrance to the gaining or the preserving of an estate. Honest dealing is not a bar to getting that which this world has to offer. There is a cursed proverb amongst most of us which, it is feared, some walk by. This says, that he who deals honestly with others will die a beggar. Job gives the lie to this devilish saying, for he was an honest man, a man who dealt carefully with men lest he fail to do his duty to them and lest he should fail to do his duty to God. In doing so, and in becoming exceedingly rich,

the greatest of all the men in his area, he proved that honesty and fair dealing is the safest way to riches. It is true that most men who are rich have a wound in their conscience. Many of them as they gather many goods fail to realize that the way they gather them causes them to lose all the benefits of being rich. What advantage is it to a man who loads his ships by trading on forbidden coasts when by doing so he makes shipwreck of his soul? A man who builds his estate by sin will lay up iniquity for his children.

All these things of course are being said about riches in this world. He who is rich in Heaven, in the grace, in the many treasures of the world to come shall not be guilty of any sin in the getting of them. That is to say, it is impossible to get the riches of grace by way of sin. That is why we are to seek those things which are from above, those things which have to do with the pleasing of God. He who does this is the richest of all, and he who does this shall have a pure conscience to comfort and encourage him.

2. The Scriptures tell us that, *"Godliness has the promises of this life as well as of that which is to come"* (1 Tim. 4:8). Job was a God-fearing man, yet he was a rich man. Job was a faithful man, one who believed the promises of God. It is true that we are told that there was not many rich, not many mighty, not many hornorable, and not many great ones who are called. However, it does not say in the Scriptures that there are not any called, etc. The faithful are children of the King, and it should not be thought unusual, let alone impossible, for a child of the King to be rich both in the riches of this world and in the riches of the world which is to come.

3. Time spent in holy duties is no loss. Job not only spent some time, much time, nor nearly all of his time in the service of God. Job never failed, no not for a minute, in his desire to give the utmost glory to God. This meant that God was served by Job continually. Now most any man you ask upon the earth will tell you that you cannot serve God continually and still enrichen yourself. Here is Job to give the lie to such a story. The fact is that Job grew continually rich just as he served God continually. The time he spent in the service of God did not rob his purse nor impoverish his family. Job was able to maintain both his calling and his business; all of his particular calling in relationship to men, whether as a witness for God and his goodness, or as a support and help to his fellow men, as both went together. There was no hindrance to Job's work among men because of his work for God.

There are those who seem to think that the time spent in spiritual duties is a time of waste. They think that it is only the weak who crawl off into the corners and offer up their prayers to God. Those who are strong and who are running well need not depend upon God nor suspend very much of their efforts in prayer to Him. But most men of God have found, as did Martin Luther, that when they are the busiest, that is the time they must pray the most. Whatever the spiritual duty, it will not only be time well spent, but it will tool up and oil the machinery which God has given us for our benefit, both physical and spiritual.

4. Lastly, there is the very frequent blasphemy in the world which professes that a man goes backward in his estate according to the amount of time that he spends in holy duties. Therefore they say when he has lost his estate that it was because he spent too much time hearing sermons and paying attention to godly duties. Actually, the reason why many men who are apparently holy men lose their estates is because they do too little, not too much. Many times the body may be exercised often, but the spirit works only seldom. That is why a man who professes to be godly may well provoke God to blast his outward estate. It is seldom that a man is found who truly believes that if he seeks first the kingdom of God and His righteousness, then all things shall be added to him. Many who have become rich through the blessings of God find their minds unable to concentrate on things of God, but rather that they are taken over and over again with those things which belong to this

5. That a man may lose his estate and still retain his godliness is also proven by Job. In fact we see that a man may lose his estate for reasons other than failure either toward man or toward God. It may simply be because it is the will of God and for the working of God's plan. God gets much glory in upholding a man when he has lost all but Jesus Christ. A man who does not know God will never believe it, but when Job was made poor, thereby he was made rich. And we who do believe God shall also become rich if we see the lessons which God has given to us in this book of Job.

CHAPTER I, VERSE 4

"And his sons went and feasted in their houses, each one on his day. And they sent and called their three sisters to eat and to drink with them" -- Job 1:4.

This first implies Job's riches in outward things, that is, in his possessions of many children. But not only did Job have many children, he had children who were cheerful and ready to associate with one another. It is a blessing to have children who are unanimous in their family devotion. These had one mind, they met together in love, though they were ten in number they were of one heart and of one spirit. They were feasting in their own houses, indicating they did not go to places of doubtful reputation, but met together in their own private houses and family. In this way they might celebrate in security, both in their bodies and in their souls. Also the frequency of their feasting would indicate that they enjoyed the company of one another. It is not known how often they met, whether every day, every week, or on some special days, but it is known that they met rather often in unity.

The fact that the sisters were invited indicates the extraordinary oneness of mind. It was not usual for brothers to invite sisters in Job's day. In fact women were not as socially prominent in that day as they now are.

It is a great blessing for a father to have children who love one another, children who enjoy the company of the others. It is a great sorrow to have children who are torn by divisions amongst themselves. It withers the comfort that a parent has to see his children absolutely at war with one another. The blessing of unity among children is not one which is common to this world, Adam did not have this blessing, for one of his sons murdered another. Abraham did not have this blessing for Ishmael mocked Isaac. Jacob did not have this blessing for it was seldom that his twelve sons ever agreed upon anything. Then when they did agree, it was to see Joseph into slavery. David did not have this blessing, for one of his sons murdered another, who had raped one of his sisters. Also one of his sons actually tried to take the crown from off of his own head. It is easy to see in reading Scripture, which is honest about the lives of men, that it is a true blessing to have many children and to have them at one with one another.

IS FEASTING SINFUL

Some have asked, were the children of Job sinning because they were feasting. No, one may feast to the glory of God. The Christians in the early churches had their love feasts. In a feast there are two things, extraordinary provision, and extraordinary company. Both of these are lawful. God has given us the things of this world not only to meet our absolute needs, but also for our delight. The fact that God has provided us with more than we need for our bare necessities is proof that he intends for us to have moderate delight. Abraham made a great feast at the weaning of Isaac. Isaac made a feast for Abimelech and Phicol. The Lord Jesus Himself attended a feast in Cana.

Because feasting is so often abused and turned into wantonness, it is generally thought that feasting must be wicked. A child of God is right to attend feasts which are truly given for the glory of God. However, since it is so easy to abuse feasting, it is only right that some warning be given to all of us who are apt to attend feasts.

1. Feasting is sinful when he who provides the feast is lavish and spends more than he

ought. Feasting which is at the expense of a man's friends, his creditors, or his family is certainly a sin.

2. A feast may well be sinful when the rich feast the rich. The usual reason for the rich feasting the rich is for the purpose of showing off their own riches. It is very difficult for the glory of God to be served when the rich are entertaining other rich people. However those who feast the poor may find it easier to do so to the glory of God. Certainly when the rich feast the rich and let the poor starve this is very sinful.

3. There may be sin in feasting when too much care is lavished upon the appointments. Though we may feast for our delight, it is not right to feast for our lust. Those who make their belly their God are soon known by their effort to obtain all kinds of expensive and foreign foods for the mere serving of lust. When vanity dictates the food that is to be served at a feast, there may be a choking amongst the guests similar to the choking of the Israelites on the Quails.

4. Feasting is sinful when there is excess or intemperance. Those who eat too much are just as guilty of sin as those who drink too much. A man who eats excessively may well turn himself into a beast. It is better for us to put a knife to our throat then that we should offend God.

5. Feasting may be sinful when it is too frequent. Feasts are not for every day. When we spend too much of our time whether day or night in feasting, then we are apt to be guilty of the same sins as those who do immoral things. We shall have to give account for our idle words, and we will have to give account for our idle time. Men oftentimes complain that they have spent too much money in feasting, but it is rare that any have admitted that he has spent too much time in feasting. Nevertheless, there is a danger in feasting away the time that should be spent in other duties toward God.

6. Feasting is sinful when it is at the wrong time. The apostle James tells us that there is a time when our laughing should be turned into mourning. A time of mourning is not a time of feasting. The Israelites in the days of the prophets were guilty of this great sin. They feasted and played the viol when they should have been mourning and afflicting themselves before God. In days like these, when our nation is headed toward hell, it is not good for us to be feasting our time away. It is very sinful to have our hearts grounded in the things of this world when we can hear the voice of God threatening us with the removal of all these things we have come to cherish.

CHAPTER I, VERSE 5

"And when they had gone around the days of their feasting, Job sent and sanctified them, and he rose up early in the morning and offered burnt sacrifices according to the number of them all. For Job said, It may be that my sons have sinned and cursed God in their hearts. So Job did always"—Job 1:5.

Before we had seen the grace of Job in his heart, now we see the grace of Job in his life. A holy practice will make our grace visible. There are three things which we can see in this verse, (1) Job sent and sanctified them; (2) he offered burnt offering according to the number of them all; (3) he was concerned lest his sons had sinned against God in their hearts; (4) Job was constant in his holy practice, he did not serve God in fits and starts, and he did not love his children in that way either. He continually was concerned with both God and his children, lest their relationship to him should have suffered.

"Job sent and sanctified them"—How could Job sanctify his sons and daughters? A parent may provide for his children, but can he provide grace also? Can a parent put holiness in the hearts of his children? Is not sanctification the proper work of the Holy Spirit of God? Some say that Job sent up prayers to God in order to sanctify his children. Prayer does sanctify, that is, it sanctifies a holy heart. Many times God may use your prayer for the sanctification of another heart. Secondly, some say that he sent them to the place that

was appointed for sacrifice where he intended to sanctify them. But, thirdly, I rather think that he sent a message to them commanding them to prepare themselves for the holy duty of offering the burnt offering. They were to purify themselves and be ready to meet their God at the place of sacrifice.

To sanctify, in the Scripture, can mean the infusion of a holy habit. Or, it can mean the preparation of the soul for holy duties. Now when it is said that Job sent and sanctified them, it is not meant that he was able to infuse in their souls any holiness. It was not in his power to make them gracious. That, indeed, is the work of the Holy Spirit of God. But Job was able to send to his children to command them to prepare themselves. He advised them and warned them that they should purify themselves and be ready for this holy duty. This preparation to holy duties is often called sanctifying. In Genesis 35:2 Jacob ordered His children to put away the strange gods and be clean—that is, sanctify yourselves. In Exodus 19:20 God tells Moses to go to the people and sanctify them today and tomorrow. He was to prepare the people for the sacrifice that was to come. So we hear that Job is sanctifying his children by sending to them and warning them to be prepared for the time of the burnt offering, which he in his day was to offer for his family. For in the days of the patriarchs, the father, the head of the family was the one who offered up sacrifices for all the rest of the family.

It may be noted that Job did not call them away from their feast, but when each one had had their feast, then Job sent to them to sanctify themselves. He has allowed them to take this moderate refreshing and recreation with one another. Though they were in their own houses and at their disposal, being grown men and women, there were a host of duties still due from the father to the children, and from the children to their father. One thing is shown here, that Job's love for his children caused him to send to them to have them sanctify themselves.

PARENTS MUST NOT CAST OFF THE CARE OF THEIR CHILDREN

There are those who think that they have a duty to put their children through school, to give them some few instructions in their early years, and then they need not trouble themselves any further. This is the way of animals, not of men. Parents should not only love their children in their early years, but for all the years of their lives. Love is strong as death, and a parent's love will not permit the shirking of duties which are for the everlasting benefit of the children. Job felt a responsibility for the spiritual wellbeing of his children. Therefore, he both prepared a sacrifice and beforehand warned them of the need for sanctification before they appeared at the sacrifice.

CHILDREN MUST NOT CAST OFF LOVE AND OBEDIENCE TO PARENTS

Even though children have been brought up carefully to a responsible, intelligent adulthood, and have been blessed with mates and children of their own, they still owe reverence and obedience (as well as love) to the lawful commands, counsels and directions of their parents. The fact that virtually everyone in this day has rejected this truthful reflection of the teaching of the Scriptures about the duties of children will not change God's mind when He sits in judgment over those who have despised and disobeyed the parent who lovingly kept the precepts of God before the faces of the children.

Job's children obeyed. Not one of the ten accused Job of interfering with their lives. Not one murmured, but all willingly prepared themselves for the sacrifice.

A PARENT'S MAIN AND SPECIAL CARE SHOULD BE SPIRITUAL

Job did not send a messenger to ask if each one were in good health. He did not ask of their physical or financial welfare. His main concern was with their spiritual health. The fact that most parents look after the physical welfare of their children and leave them comfortable on the road to hell did not deter Job from showing his concern for the souls of his children. His greatest joy would come when he heard that his children walked in the truth. Being a holy child of God himself, his love could only be fully proven by a full and complete dedication of himself and his energies for the sanctification of his beloved children. Just as a wicked man is not happy or satisfied until he sees his children being formed in his own wicked image, so a holy man yearns to see his children formed in the image of Christ Jesus. There is no such thing as a wicked man who is satisfied to have the whole world holy if they will but leave him alone. Likewise, there is no such thing as a holy man who is satisfied to leave men alone to go to hell as long as he knows that he himself is destined for the bosom of Christ.

"and rose up early in the morning"--Job's love for God and love for his children brought him out of bed early in the morning. This expression, *"in the morning,"* is a Hebrew word denoting diligence and care. It is not enough to rise in the morning. If you are to show the greatest care and concern for God and for others, you must rise in the first of the morning and show your diligent care. It is our duty to dedicate the first of every day to God. Imitate David, who said, *"You shall hear my voice in the morning. I will direct my prayer to You in the morning"* (Ps. 5:3). The morning is a great friend of our graces. That is why mornings are so fruitful to those who pray then.

"and offered burnt offerings according to the number of them all"--Job did not lump together all of his children, but individually he offered up prayers and sacrifices for them.

There are different kinds of offerings mentioned in the Bible. There are burnt-offerings, trespass-offerings, sin-offerings and peace-offerings. In all the offerings but the first above, some portion of the sacrifice was reserved for others. But the burnt-offering was to be completely consumed (in the New Testament, the word is translated by the Greek word meaning holocaust--signifying the fact that the offering was to be totally consumed). The word in Hebrew has the meaning of lifting up, of elevation, of ascension. The burnt-offering in being wholly consumed was totally lifted up to God, and to Him alone. Not only did the smoke of the sacrifice ascend upwards toward God, but the sweet smell of the incense put upon the altar would go up with it. Then the priest would lift up the sacrifice on the altar and hold it toward Heaven. Finally the people would lift up their hands and their eyes, and spiritually their souls and spirits toward God in Heaven also. The final fulfillment of the type was of course in the sacrifice of Christ and His ascension into Heaven to present His blood before God for the cleansing of His people.

That the holy men of the Old Testament saw these things in their true spiritual setting may be seen in the expressions recorded for us, such as David saying, *"Let my prayer be set forth before You as incense, and the lifting up of my hands as the evening sacrifice"* (Ps. 141:2). Prayer is the lifting up of the soul, an elevation of the spirit to God. Isaiah was told to instruct Hezekiah to *"lift up his prayer for the remnant that are left"* (2 Kings 19:4). And Jeremiah laments against prayers that are unanswered with this pictorial language, *"You have covered Yourself with a cloud so that our prayer should not pass through"* (Lam. 3:44).

As to the fact that it was Job himself who offered the sacrifice, instead of a priest, it is to be remembered that this offering was before the giving of the Law and the establishment of the Levitical priesthood. Distinguish the times and the Scriptures will agree. The father or the eldest of the family was a priest to the whole family in the patriarchal days.

Some will have this worship of Job to be will worship and not divinely-appointed worship. It was divinely appointed, though not written. The law of sacrificing was given from the very beginning. God never allowed a single day in which men should contrive their form of service toward Him. He early condemned Cain for attempting to substitute his own form of sacrifice for the divinely-ordered sacrifice. A sacrifice of whatever nature is abominable to God unless it is an obedient sacrifice, *"obedience is better than sacrifice"* in God's eyes, but obedient sacrifices are even better. The law of sacrifice, then, was one established by God from the beginning. And it had been passed down from heart to heart, from hand to hand for centuries from the father to the children.

"For Job said, It may be that my sons have sinned and cursed God in their hearts. So Job did always"--Holy duties are always grounded upon reason. There must be a reason why we pray, for to pray out of custom and formality would be a despising of God. So Job must have a reason for his sacrifice — he feared that his children had sinned, that they were in need of a sacrifice at which they would faithfully repent of their sins and lift up their hearts to God to see His forgiveness, cleansing and refitting them for service to Him.

But why does it say that Job said, *"It may be"*? Did he not realize that every man is a sinner, and that continually? Without question, Job was fully aware of the universal corruption of man. His many statements while disputing with his friends are evidence of this. Man's thoughts, imaginations and notions are only evil continually (Gen. 6:5). There is an uncleanness which cleaves to us, which never leaves us, which even the saints of God have to plague them (as indicated in Paul's words, *"O wretched man that I am! Who shall deliver me from the body of this death? I thank God through Jesus Christ our Lord!"*--Rom. 7:24).

To sin is sometimes put for these common and daily infirmities. Just as surely as a man who washes his hands before he goes to work in the morning may be sure that his hands will need washing when he comes home, so may we sinners be certain that we need to repent and to be renewed daily because of the sin of our nature. Every man has a fountain of uncleanness in him, and there will always be some sin, some filthiness bubbling and boiling up, if not actually flowing forth for all to see.

To sin is also put for some special act of sin, that which in Scripture is called a fall or a fault, *"If anyone is overtaken with a fault, you that are spiritual restore him"* (Gal. 6:1).

There are three degrees of sinning:

1. Daily infirmities, weaknesses caused by inward corruption, are sins.

2. Wilful sins, those in which the sinner delights in acting contrary to God. Those that are born of God cannot sin in this way (1 John 3:9).

3. Faults, or falls. Even the greatest and most noted of saints have fallen into scandalous sins. Yet the apostle John writes, *"Little children, I write to you that you sin not."* That is to say, though you have your daily infirmities, yet you must avoid falling into scandalous sins. He who says he has no sin is a liar. But for those who fall into sin, there is an Advocate. Job, even though he was without the clear revelation of the written word, was aware of the inherent corruption of his children. But he says, *"It may be"* because he has in mind the possibility that they may have fallen into some form of sin which is above and beyond the sins of infirmity. This very use of the words, *"may be"* may indicate that the children of Job were in his eyes considered to be godly persons. However, if they do indicate instead a suspicion on his part, let it be known that it is not a breach of Christian charity to suspect others of sin, provided we intend and strongly desire their good. It is true that we may not press charges against others merely because we suspect they may be guilty of some sin unknown to us. But it is not uncharitable to pray for anyone, whatever his relationship to us, desiring that his sins and failings may be pardoned by God. Job in the right spirit was turning his suspicion of sin into prayer and supplication for the pardon of sin. It is true he had no actual report of any sinful behavior on the part of any of his children. But he loves them enough that he prays and always labors for them, that they might have a complete reconciliation with God, that their relationship to Him may not be poisoned and made ineffectual.

"and cursed God in their hearts"–Interpreters are much divided about the sense of these words. Only four of the interpretations will be set out here.

1. Some observe that the Hebrew word here translated 'cursed' not only means 'to bless,' but also to bow the knee, e.g. Solomon *"kneeled down upon his knees"* (2 Chron. 6:13),– the same word there is translated *"kneeled down upon his knees"* and here is translated 'cursed', Furthermore, sometimes *Elohim* is applied to angels, sometimes to idols or false gods *("Now I know that the Lord is greater than all gods"*–it is the same word). Again, that which is here translated 'in their hearts' can also mean the middle or center of a thing. From all these possible uses of the single terms, these interpreters read this phrase as follows: *"It may be my sons have sinned, bowing down to the false gods that are in their midst."* Feasting and false worship, sensuality and idolatry go together, as when Moses came back into camp and found the golden calf – they had filled themselves, then they had turned to other gods. Yet nothing we know of Job's children could cause us to suspect them of degenerating into such idolatry.

2. Others take the word *barach* in its proper sense of blessing. They say the words read, *"It may be that my sons have sinned and rejoiced and blessed God."* Instead of being humbled for their sin, they have blessed God in their sin. Just as a thief may thank God for giving him the opportunity to steal much, so these claim that Job's sons have done ill in their feasting, yet they have been lifted up in their hearts and have blessed God for the plentiful provisions which occasioned their sin. Such were those in Zech. 11:4: those that were supposed to be feeding God's flock were instead destroying them, yet they held themselves not guilty. These are their very words, as reported by God Himself, *"Blessed be the Lord, for I am rich."* This also is a possible interpretation, and a very clear one. Again, it is not right to think of Job's children as being so great in wickedness as to bless God in their sins, unless God Himself should tell us that such a thing is so.

3. Jerome Zanchius has an exposition which would be an excellent one if the words in the original would but bear it. He says we should read, *"It may be my sons have sinned and have not blessed God in their hearts."* It would be an excellent and clear sense to understand Job's concern as one that suspected his sons of not blessing God enough in their hearts. But the original will not bear it. Though Zanchius makes up a rule, that where a negative is in the former part of an affirmation, then a negative is to be understood in the latter part. He cites several instances. But here we find no negative particle in the former part of the verse. Therefore, how can we understand a negative in the latter part?

4. Most interpreters, both ancient and modern, expound the word here as 'cursed.' The original does not allow for different interpretations, so after this preferred sense is cleared it will be left up to you to judge which is God's intended meaning in this place.

The word for 'blessed' may be translated 'cursed' either by an antiphrasis (the speaking of one thing in a sense opposite to the proper meaning,) or because of fear. In I Kings 21:13, Naboth was charged with a capital offence, that of 'blessing' God and the king. He was stoned to death because actually he was charged with 'cursing' God and the king. So here, not wishing to put the words 'cursed' and 'God' together, they have used the word for 'blessed.' *"It may be that my sons have sinned and have cursed God in their hearts."*

How could Job suspect his sons of such a thing, the cursing of God in their hearts? First, there need not have been an open reproach cast upon the name of God, no malicious or virulent blaspheming of God is necessary in order for men to be guilty of cursing God in their hearts. For to curse God in your heart, you need only have irreverent, unfit and unholy thoughts of God. Any thought which is unbecoming to the glory and majesty of so great a God is equivalent to a despising and cursing of God. And who does not know how quickly such thoughts can arise within one's heart while feasting and conversing. Job is being set forth to us as one who is concerned lest his sons have failed to give God His due, thus cursing God in their hearts. Even if they had offered thanks to God at the feast, but had done so in a light, half-hearted manner, as a mere formality, they would have been guilty of cursing God.

WE SHOULD BE VERY DILIGENT ABOUT KEEPING OUR HEARTS

If you allow your heart to become disorderly, you may be guilty of cursing God. Not only should you be careful to keep your heart stayed upon God when you are praying, or when you are hearing His word, but you must also remember to keep your heart when you are feasting, when you are about your daily chores or business. The sins of the heart are very dangerous sins, for God looks upon the heart and gives sentence accordingly.

A man's heart is open only to God. None may say positively what is on the heart of another. Sometimes men express what is in their hearts through their mouths, sometimes in their actions, *"for out of the abundance of the heart the mouth speaks,"* and the hand works. But unless a man gives witness against himself, we may not judge a man to have sinned in his heart. So here Job can only suspect what may have happened in the hearts of his sons.

"So Job did always"--again Job's constancy is held forth for us to see. *"All the days,"* the original says, Job went on praying, sacrificing, loving and trying to be of help to his children, both physically and spiritually. Not that he actually did sacrifice daily for his children, but he continually, perpetually, without end, was unceasingly praying and working for the good of his children. Knowing that a man will sin the same sins over and over, Job both prayed and sacrificed again and again. Renewed sins must have renewed repentance. Until a man is glorified, he may not leave off repenting and lifting up his heart to God in faith, seeking His cleansing and rehabilitation for holy duties. As long as we have these many sins to eat holes in the bottoms of our souls, we must have the pump of repentance to cast out sin and make ready for renewed grace within.

Now the introductory sketch of Job's character and his possessions, with his careful obedience and his concern for his children, has been completed. We have seen God draw Job's portrait in a few lines. He has put in the dignity and sincerity of Job's person. He has shown us his prosperous surroundings. He has made plain Job's holiness, his piety. Here is a man who has no peer upon the earth, set up by God as His champion. All is now ready for the trying of his faith, that he may be seen to come forth from the furnace of affliction, with a purity and a glory which he never could have had without such a trial.

CHAPTER 1, VERSE 6

"Now there was a day when the sons of God came to present themselves before the Lord. And Satan also came among them."--Job 1:6

Before Job is tried, before he triumphs, before he is crowned a champion, God would have us to know that all of these were not due to accident or chance, not attributable to Job's natural strength, nor to Satan's inability to triumph over his relatively weaker foe. That we may see this, we are taken behind the scenes, being allowed to see that God has planned this test, that He is in control of it at every point, and that it is His power and faithfulness which brings Job through with flying colors. We see Job's affliction described in four ways: (1) by its cause; (2) by its instruments; (3) by its manner; (4) by its time.

From the sixth to the twelfth verses, the causes of Job's affliction are revealed to us:

1. The efficient causes are two; the first being the Supreme Cause, the great First Cause, God. He is the one who is ordering and disposing the affliction of Job. The second cause is subordinate to the first, Satan is the efficient subordinate cause. He is efficient in at least three ways: (1) in temptation; (2) in slandering; (3) in finding cruel instruments to use in attempting to subvert Job and overthrow his faith in God.

16

2. There are material causes of Job's affliction. When God said, *"all that he has is in your power,"* He is allowing Satan to use Job's outward estate in a way which might be thought certain to overthrow his faith. Everything precious to Job, apart from his person and his soul were given into the hand of Satan. But God lays down a negative, forbidding Satan to put forth his hand upon Job's person. Thus He has determined how far the affliction may go, giving to Satan according to his first accusation enough leeway to prove Job's reverence for God, that it had nothing to do with his possessions.

3. There is a final cause of Job's affliction. That is stated as a dispute between God and Satan, with God challenging Satan to observe Job, that he is perfect and upright, that there is none like him on the earth—with Satan contending that Job fears God only because He has blessed him above all other men on the earth. The determination of this question is the final cause of Job's affliction: he must be afflicted in order to prove that God's estimate of Job is the correct one.

All of this is of course set forth to us in an anthropopathy (as if God had the passions and desire for vindication that a man has). God oftentimes expresses Himself in His actions and dispensations as if He were a man, or like a man. So He is setting up a scene for us, as if He were a great King sitting on His throne, having His servants around Him, and having His subjects and commissioners come before Him for review and for assignments. He does this as a condescension to our understandings. It is not to be thought that God does in fact have certain days when He calls together the good and the evil angels. God is not in need of any reports from them, nor would Satan actually be permitted in the presence of a pure and holy God (who cannot look upon sin). Nor would God receive an accusation from Satan, much less a slander of one of His beloved sons. But God speaks in this way that we may get some correct views of His government of the world, of His providential dealings with His creatures. The actual scene did not take place, but the teaching which we get from this pictured encounter between God and Satan is true, and it is important that we realize from this portion of Scripture that God is showing us His supreme right and power to direct all His creatures, even this one who rebelled and was thrown out of God's presence for his sin.

If God did not give us this glimpse of His providential dealings, then some might imagine that Satan was in his own power able to afflict and to hold captive whomever he would, even God's chosen children. So here we have God represented as if He sat on a throne and ordered all things from there. A similar representation is seen in 1 Kings 22:19, where the prophet Micaiah said he saw, *"The Lord sitting upon His throne, and all the host of Heaven standing by Him."* Of course, God never called together a synod of spirits, that one lying spirit might present himself to God as a willing instrument to deceive Ahab. The reason for the scene is to affirm to us that all things, all efficient causes, are subordinate to God, the great First Cause of all. With these precautions, then, we may proceed to see what it is that God intended for us to learn from the following verses.

"Now there was a day when the sons of God"--Although the posterity of Seth (who were the visible church at that time) are called the sons of God, it seems certain that here those called the sons of God are the good angels (see Job 38:7). To any who may say that the apostle worded Heb. 1:5 so as to exclude this meaning, there is this answer. The angels are not the sons of God in the same way that the Son of God is His son. For He was a Son by eternal generation, they only as temporal creatures. They are not begotten of God, but created by God. But the angels may be called sons of God in three respects: (1) Because they are mighty in power, like God in dignity, they may fairly be called the sons of God; (2) Because they willingly, readily, cheerfully serve God, giving to Him a filial and sonlike obedience, they may be fairly called the sons of God; (3) Because God gives them the

privilege of being His companions, His attendants, His executors, they may be fairly called sons.

"came to present themselves before the Lord"--Not that the angels are at any time out of the presence of God, for Christ is express in saying, *"the angels always behold the face of My Father"* (Matt. 18:10). They are said to come and present themselves much in the same way that we are said to draw near to God. God is everywhere, He is omnipresent, and in fact we are never out of His presence. But it helps our understanding to think of ourselves going to present ourselves before Him, and to think of the angels doing the same. Gabriel, even when he was standing in front of Zachariah, said that he was standing in the presence of God. Likewise are we always in His presence, and it behooves us to remember it.

"and Satan came also among them"--Satan, the chief of the evil angels, is given the name of adversary (when it is said that *"The Lord stirred up an adversary against"* Solomon, the original actually says that He *"stirred up a Satan against"* Solomon). But how can it be said that Satan came among the sons of God? Note that it is not said that Satan presented himself before God, for never would he present himself to do good service for God. In fact, as was noted before, the evil angels would not be permitted to come among the pure angels, much less to see God, but here we see him as a spirit, one who has lost his excellency but not his nature. Being a spirit, he may of course pass here and there, go up and down as he is permitted by God.

The obedient angels are called here the sons of God. Satan is called the adversary. Yet in the first creation, Satan was a beautiful, pure and altogether excellent angel. What happened? Satan had decided to serve himself and his own interests rather than God and His interests. From this we learn that every creature, however excellent and pure in his creation, must be sustained and empowered moment by moment in order to remain so. For when a creature is left to himself, he will quickly undo himself. This is evident from the life of Satan and of Adam, both of them having come from the hand of God pure, holy, just and good. How much more, then, should we realize that there is no trusting in any estate, no resting upon any excellencies, outside of Christ. He alone is our wisdom and righteousness, our sanctification and redemption (1 Cor. 1:30). Therefore let us remember that if we are to boast, if we are to glory, then we must glory in the Lord Jesus Christ.

How quickly did this pure angel lose his designation as a son of God! How quickly did he earn his present title, 'adversary!' Then it is plain that we are no sooner sinners than we are satans—adversaries to God and to all goodness. As much as we oppose God, that much of the devil do we have in us. Christ did not hesitate to call Peter, a chief apostle, Satan, saying, *"Get behind Me, Satan."* And when Elymas opposed the godly teachings of Paul, he likewise was given the designation of adversary, *"O child of the devil, enemy of all goodness"* (See Matt. 16:23 and Acts 13:10).

If, then, the opposing of God's will, the attempt to thwart the progress of God's truth, is to assume the work of Satan, then how many in our day bear plainly the mark of the devil in their brazen foreheads! O how many visible, walking satans do we have among us, men and women who oppose our peace, our liberty, our Gospel and our Christ! Nothing that is good, that is godly, that is honoring to God, will get past these destroyers. Even the smallest act by the most insignificant person will be challenged and smashed if it is suspected of giving any service whatever to God. If ever there were a time when Satan has been let loose on the world, that time must be now. For he works mightily and openly in the hearts and spirits, in the hands and tongues of the children of disobedience, What, then, shall we who are the children of obedience do? Why we shall obey that command which says, *"Resist the devil!"* (James 4:7). If Satan and his myriads of followers resist the truth, the giving of glory to God, the telling of the good news about Jesus Christ, then they are our enemies as well as God's. If they seem too powerful for you to resist, remember these two things: (1) Their power is puny compared to God's power, yet they do not hesitate to resist the almighty God—therefore, the power of the enemy is not sufficient excuse for us when we acquiesce in his evil designs; (2) God's promise is express to us in this situation, saying, *"Resist the devil, and he will flee from you"* (James 4:7)—whatever power he and his companions may have, imagine it to be as great as you may, he and they will turn tail and run under the hail of God's words when you hurl them at them.

Just as it is the height of wickedness not only to do evil but to oppose good, so it is the height of holiness not only to do good but to oppose evil. Are you holy as Christ is holy? Then you will be like Him, who was a friend and patron of goodness and an enemy of all forms of evil. If He has many challengers, then let us see that He also has many champions. Do not only love the truth, but maintain the truth. Keep it flowing out, keep it free from adulteration, keep it clearly on top of all evil imaginations and sayings. To be an adversary to Satan is the work of a Christian, and it is glorious work which will have unspeakable rewards from our Lord and Savior, who will judge us either faithful or unfaithful before the judgment seat of Christ.

"And the Lord said to Satan, Where do you come from? Then Satan answered the Lord and said, From going to and fro in the earth, and from walking up and down in it."

God is said to speak as men are said to speak, but God does not speak as men speak. He is said to have a mouth and a voice, but it is only in a figure. The Lord God does not form words by certain organs or speak them with tongue and mouth. If there is indeed a sound, as there was when He spoke from Heaven, saying, *"This is My beloved Son, etc.,"* God is forming and creating a voice in the air. By far the most instances when God is said to speak to men refer to God manifesting and declaring Himself to the spirits of men, revealing within them that which He desires them to know. So when God speaks to angels, or to devils, as here, it is not to be understood that he formed and spoke audible words. Instead, understand that God is making known to the creature what is His will and mind at this point in His administration of the world. In this instance, the devil is having revealed to him only so much of God's mind and will as will serve the purpose of God. Satan responds to God's question in the same way, but with this difference, that God knows all that is in Satan's mind and heart both now and always.

In asking Satan this question, the Lord is not seeking information, as if He had been asleep, or as if He were sometimes ignorant of the whereabouts of some creature. Rather, there are four ways in which questions in Scripture may be understood.

(1) A question in Scripture may be for the purpose of pulling a confession from the one asked. Satan may well confess to what he has been doing, however reluctantly. Adam in the Garden, after he sinned, was aked the question, *"Where are You?"* This, and subsequent questions were for the purpose of securing a confession from Adam. Likewise, in the case of Cain, an opportunity to confess was given when God asked the question, *"Where is your brother Abel?"* So with Elisha and Gehazi, who knew perfectly well where Gehazi had been, and what he had done. So the Lord asks questions for a purpose, even when He knows the answers—both the true answer as to where and what we may be or do, and the lying answer that we by nature are so prone to give Him instead of the true answer.

(2) A question may be asked as an indication of the dislike God has for a person's recent activity. When Hiram asked Solomon, *"What cities are these, etc.,"* he knew what they were. But he was not pleased with them and was in this way rebuking Solomon. When God said in Hosea 4:8, *"they have made kings and I did not know it,"* He is showing His displeasure, not His ignorance. We often do such interrogations, asking our children as to the events which have been reported to us, that we may show our abhorrence of their acts.

(3) God's question may be for the purpose of chiding Satan for the wickednesses which he had been committing. Certainly He was chiding Jonah when He asked, *"Do you do well to be angry for the gourd?"* So He may be showing His reprehesion to Satan here.

(4) God may ask a question as a means of setting up a series of providential actions, for

His ultimate glory. So here, as God prepares to gain much glory by sustaining Job's faith in the face of all Satan's wiles, power and malignance, He asks His first question of Satan in order to set up the framework for the forthcoming test between Satan and Job.

"Then Satan answered the Lord and said, From going to and fro in the earth, and from walking up and down in it"—verse 7c. If, as it is said in Jude 6, the fallen angels are *"reserved in everlasting chains under darkness unto the judgment of the great Day,"* how can Satan here say that he has been going to and fro in the earth? The answer is this, that the devil does indeed go to and fro in the earth, but he is in chains when he goes. In fact, he is in double chains: (1) He is in a chain of justice, being under the wrath of God; (2) He is in a chain of providence, being under the eye of God and under His constant direction — he can go no further than God permits him, God letting out and lengthening his chain whenever God's purpose is served by doing so.

But if Satan is under the wrath of God and in a chain of justice, how can he be allowed to plot and execute the temptation, subversion and overthrow of souls? Especially, how can he be allowed to disturb and contort the churches of God throughout the world? How can Satan take his mind off his torment and emerge from the horrible darkness of his misery long enough to be concerned with the other creatures in the world? To answer this, it must be noted that Satan is under the wrath of God, but he is not under the fullness of wrath which shall be His portion soon. He is discontented, but not so much as he will be. When the demons said to Christ, *"Have you come to torment us before our time?"* they were showing that they recognize that the time soon will come when they will be filled with torment, such torment as will make their present torment seem like pleasure. It is the very misery he is in, the suffering under the portion of God's wrath which has fallen upon him already, that causes Satan and his demons to hate God and His children, and to determine to destroy all who were or are in the image of God. There is no Savior provided for angels who have fallen, only One for men who have fallen. This puts a fearful edge on the vengeance of the demons, for they by creation are a higher order than we.

Satan's claims as to his activities are framed in a way as to indicate his feeling that he is a king who has been reviewing his troops and viewing his subjects. He is Beelzebub, the chief of the demons, the prince of the power of the air, one who takes men captive at his will. Actually, of course, Satan does not walk. He does undoubtedly compass the earth, going to and fro in the manner of spirits. But it is not to be thought that he is both here and there. He is a creature, and he can only be in one place at a time. He is ubiquitous only in the imaginations of men. In fact, only God can be omnipresent, everywhere at the same time. It is his commanding of myriads of demons all over the world which makes it seem that Satan is everywhere—they are all little satans, who are of one mind with Satan, their chief and instructor in evil ways. In this we see that Satan does not spend his time in going to and fro as a sightseer, but rather he goes about to direct the work of destruction which all demons work upon men.

1. Satan is searching diligently for ways to implement his power, as is indicated in the original Hebrew word here. He is spying on us, observing and considering what he may do to us. The same word is used in Daniel 12:4, where it is said that, *"many shall run to and fro, and knowledge shall be increased."* Obviously, knowledge shall not be increased if the many spend all their time running to and fro in the usual sense. No, but what is being put forth is this, that many shall go up and down to observe, to search, to learn the wisdom of God—then knowledge shall be increased.

2. Satan shows his restlessness. He is a disturbed person, one who is never quiet or satisfied—*"there is no peace for the wicked."* A soul out of favor with God has no place to go for rest and peace, for there is no true rest or peace apart from that which is in God. Just as Cain was a fugitive and a vagabond, so is Satan one that is incessantly compassing the earth in discontent and misery. To depart from the living God is to exile oneself to a restless compassing of the earth, without hope, encouragement or comfort for the rest of time and all of eternity yet to come.

3. For those who have concluded that there is a kind of fiendish pleasure afforded to Satan when he is able to ruin a man, it should be remembered that Satan's lost, undone and condemned condition will allow him no pleasure of any sort—not even a fiendish rejoicing. And while he may be said in a way to delight in seduction and destruction, it is with him as it is with us when we have wreaked vengeance upon another—there is immediately forthcoming further condemnation and misery, so as to swallow up all that pleasure which we had imagined would come to us when we had been able to do our evil will. But no doubt it is with him as it is with all who are not restrained by the Holy Spirit, he will immediately deceive himself and imagine within himself that the next effort to destroy will not only bring success but also pleasure and delight. His example in this should give all men pause, for if Satan can for thousands of years be deceived by himself, completely without profit, then so may we spend a short lifetime as fools opposing God.

Satan, it may be noted, does not reveal his evil designs. He makes it appear as if he were but a wise and harmless tourist, going to and fro in the earth. But God tells us that *"he walks about like a roaring lion, seeking whom he may devour."* Unless we resist him, being steadfast in the faith, it may be that we shall lose an arm or a leg to him before our Shepherd rescues us. Thank God for this, that the *"Shepherd and Bishop of our souls"* is even more diligent and more intelligent in His inquiries and searches than Satan. For it is He who works in us to watch, to put on the whole armor of God, that we may stand fast against the wiles and machinations of Satan, his demons, and his willing helpers among men.

There is comfort in the knowledge that Satan is confined to the earth and its environs. He is cast out of Heaven, and he cannot go there again to disturb our eternal rest when we come there. In short, we have him to resist only during this short span of life, and there is a day fast approaching when we shall no longer need to watch him lest he devour us.

CHAPTER I, VERSE 8

"And the Lord said to Satan, Have you set your heart against My servant Job, because there is none like him in the earth, a perfect and upright man, one who fears God and turns away from evil?--Job 1:8

The Septuagint puts it, *"Have you attended with your mind upon My servant Job."* To put a thing upon the heart is to have serious and special regard to it. So here, it is as if God said to Satan, 'I am sure that in your travels and wanderings about the world you could not but choose to take notice of Job. He is one of my jewels, one of my darlings, a special man among all the sons of men. He is such a spectacular man as may justly draw all eyes and hearts toward him.' Just as surely as the eyes of the Lord are upon the righteous, and as surely as His heart is concerned with them, so are the eyes and heart of Satan upon the righteous. He takes it to heart when he finds a man championing the truth, and this man Job was incessant and untiring in his resistance to the devil.

As a part of this question, as to whether Satan had been considering and taking to heart the life and person of Job, it may be that God is asking Satan if he has been beating his brains in an effort to discover a way to subvert Job. Have you had a tilt with Job? Have you been outwitted by Job? Have you found him a tough piece of spirituallity? Have you been testing and probing around in an effort to find his weakness?

Satan, like all creatures, is likely to pay attention to those who are the most noble and eminent foes. If one can defeat those who are considered champions, then it becomes an easy matter to destroy lesser foes. So Satan sets his strongest engines, his hottest assaults against those men whose lives are a living sacrifice, transformed and renewed in holiness day by day. Yes, and he troubles his heart about them too, for he loves to be feared, he cannot stand to be shunted aside by anyone. There are those who are easily taken captive at the will of Satan (2 Tim. 2:26), who run when he whistles, but these he despises and he in no way sets his heart and mind on them. The ones that interest him are those who are walking in wisdom toward those on the outside, redeeming the time, letting the word dwell in them richly, admonishing and teaching all to obey God, singing psalms in their hearts. Such strongholds of grace anger Satan. He will not rest until he has used all his wiles to bring about an act or a course of sin. Just as there is joy in Heaven when one sinner is converted, so there is merry laughter in Satan's dominion when one saint is subverted. The legions of darkness will be encamped around the godly man, and the more godly the man, the more satans there will be opposing him.

"My servant Job"—note the title which God gives to Job. A true servant is one who is at the beck and call of another. They are living instruments of another's will. Such a servant was Job, and such a servant we ought to be unto God.

Job was a servant distinguished by the fact that he was God's servant, *"My servant."* He was not the servant of Satan, nor of any other creature. He was not his own servant, being bought with a price and belonging to another, God. There are those who serve their own bellies, their own lusts and pleasures (Rom. 16:18). but Job was not such a servant. And it is notable that God by saying *"My"* is sparking Satan's opposition by making it plain that Job served God instead of Satan. God's elect people are His servants simply because He chose them as such. They are His because He has bought and purchased them (1 Cor. 6:19). They are servants of God by covenant. And they are God's by obligation, for He has given them His beloved and only-begotten Son, and with Him all things else.

It is a great honor to be God's servant. It is a privilege and a cause for joy that God should choose you for the important work which He has to do on earth. You have great reason to glory and rejoice when you think of God as your God, your Lord, and as your Master.

When God speaks of His people by name, there are usually to follow some experiences in which will show His special care of them, His extraordinary love for them. It is only His sheep He calls by name (John 10:3), and they follow Him wherever He may lead. It is certain that God mentions by name those who have found grace in His sight in a special way, such as Christ (Isa. 49:1) and Moses (Ex. 33:12). Therefore, Job is such a person, one loved by God in a special way. God know the names of all men, but it is only His chosen vessels which He tells us He knows by name—*"Yet You have said, 'I know you by name'"*God knew the names of all men, but the name, Moses, was written down in His Book of Life. If your name is written there, it is because God has called you by name. Therefore you should rejoice, for it is nothing if you own the whole world, or if the evil spirits obey your voice, but it is an unspeakable ecstasy to know that your name is written in Heaven (Luke 10:20). The names of emperors, rulers, the potentates and powers of the world, are not written in the Book of Life. Nor are the principalities and powers of the air. But everlasting remembrance of the acts of faith of the least of all saints is a fact which Satan cannot erase, not even dim. Therefore, rejoice! Again I say, rejoice!

"because there is none like him in the earth"—not here, as in verse 3, where it is said that Job was the greatest of all the men of the East. It is but Job's temporal possessions which are in view there, but here his considerable spiritual qualities are being pointedly drawn across the envious mind of Satan. What could whet his vengeful appetite more than this, to know that God Himself has chosen Job as the champion who will challenge Satan? And of all the words which God could have chosen to describe Job, these words, *"there is none like him in the earth,"* present Satan with the greatest challenge, for this is the highest praise a man can have. Just as surely as God says many times that there is none, no other God like Him, so here God is saying there is no other man who compares to Job as a man.

There is a comparison here, not only a comparison with other men, but a comparison with other saints. As to Job's qualities, they excelled all men's qualities except those who were God's children. All the saints have the same qualities, and none have more than another. However, not all the saints are equal in their conformity to the image of Jesus, the holiness which causes a man to yearn to be fully, completely and continually in the will of God. All are made partakers of divine nature, if they are made the children of God. As Christ was, so are we who have been blessed by being made heirs and partakers of His life. In some measure, all the saints have that mind which was in Christ Jesus. But not all are equal to Him, nor equal to each other, in the exercise of those graces and qualities given to them. Just as wicked men are all alike, all being capable of the blackest and most degrading of vicious acts, yet not all do actually equal each other in their commission of such acts—so with the saints, some excel others in the exercise of their graces. At this particular time on earth, Job excelled all others in the graces which distinguish a true son of God.

It is common in Scripture for God to use this type of expression of a man with the purpose of making known some particular excellency. So it was said of Solomon that there was none like him (See 2 Kings 18:5) among the kings of Judah. Solomon was noted for his trust in the Lord, and for his wisdom among men. But in another generation, Hezekiah also gets this name, that there was none like him among the kings of Judah. In his case, the commendation is for his thoroughness in cleansing the land of idolatry. Later, Josiah also gets the name of being a none-such king among the kings of Judah, because he turned to the Lord with all his heart and soul and might (2 Kings 23:25). So it may well be a wise consideration if we limit Job's superiority over other saints to his own generation. Yet in the doing of this, it must not be thought that Job also only excelled in one or two or three of the graces of God. It is true that he has the name for being the most patient of men (James 5:11), but it will be seen in this man's recorded trials that he excelled in grace after grace after grace. There was none like Job in the earth, he was a perfect man, an upright man, an humble man, a good man who was loaded down with the good fruits of the Spirit of God—he was full of love, joy, peace, hope, gentleness, longsuffering, goodness, faith, meekness, temperance; all the graces which God gives were abundantly displayed in this man Job.

From this we learn that God has servants of all statures and degrees. Also we see that a man may be so advanced in the exercise of his graces as to excel all others, yet he must not presume upon this blessed state. Such a man is just as dependant upon God, just as much at God's beck and call as any other—yea, he is apt to be more busily employed in God's work of convincing the world that God is glorious. To do this, Job was called upon to sacrifice everything that he owned; and he was nearly called upon to agree to the complete obliteration of himself from God's work in the world. Futhermore, we see that a man who is given much grace does not complacently content himself with that measure of grace. Job continued to add to his stock of graces until the day came when God could say, *"there is none like him in the earth."*

Learn from this also that God keeps a close watch upon all of us, being able at any given time to state exactly what progress we have made in grace and knowledge. What would He say about you today? Is there none like you? ARE YOU ONE WHO IS PERFECT AND UPRIGHT? One who turns away from evil, one who fears and reverences God? Do not fear, God will give you a testimony up to and including your utmost worth. Not a one of your graces, not the least of your goodnesses, not a single one of your obediences, not any act of faith will be concealed. Nothing you have believed, thought or done for Him can ever be forgotten, for He desires to advertise them all, keeping His book of remembrances day by day (Mal. 3:16). However, it must not be forgotten that He is the keeper of the Book, and any praise which you may put forth for yourself is a usurpation of His office. Not only should you *"let the mouth of another praise you,"* but it is best to wait until God Himself is the one who does so. He who falls into the error of the Corinthian satans will always be ashamed. It is not wise to compare ourselves with others and then to commend ourselves for excelling them. Rather, it is God who shall actually judge what is and what is not excellence. The things that men commend about themselves may well earn them many torments when God's judgment is made known. The wages or rewards of this life are for the most part to be paid at the time of the Judgment, and afterwards. Even the wicked do not yet know the extent of their rewards, their punishments. Neither can the saints conceive of the final disposition which God will make of their thoughts and acts on this earth. Therefore, leave it to God to speak well of us. Then the slander and persecution of the world will be a matter of laughter, and there will be neither tears nor fears any more.

CHAPTER I, VERSE 9

"Then Satan answered the Lord and said, Does Job fear God for nothing"--Job 1:9

What Satan cannot contradict, he will misinterpret. He cannot deny that Job is God's servant, therefore he will have it that Job's motives are base and his sincerity a bribe. Does Job fear God for nothing? Is his service merely the way he earns his extraordinary blessings? Fear is of course worth nothing unless it is based on respect and love. If Satan can prove to his own satisfaction that Job's fear is a pretended one, then he shall happily conclude that his estimate of Job is a better one than that given by God.

But what is it that Satan actually is saying of Job? (1) Some, who translate it, Does Job fear God in vain, say that Satan is accusing Job of serving God for the riches He gives. (2) If, as may be the true meaning of the words, Job is fearing God without cause (See Ps. 35:7, where the word is so translated), then Satan is saying that God has given Job cause enough to be a pretended servant. There is reason enough to serve when one has houses and flocks and servants, not to mention ten children and the praise of his fellows. (3) If the word be translated "freely," then Satan is saying that Job looks upon his obedience as labor, a labor which deserves these extraordinary rewards which God has given him. It seems to Satan to be ridiculous that any man would give such unremitting and intelligent service to God merely out of respect and love.

So, in total, it would appear that Satan is answering the Lord like this: 'Do you ask if I have considered Job? Yes, and I acknowledge that he is very diligent and zealous in all that you have commanded him. Nor is it any wonder that he is so, since You have bribed him with heaps of benefits far in excess of the actual service he has rendered. You may indeed get many servants with payments like these. It is no marvel that Job is willing to do whatever you command, for you give him everything he desires. When you are neglecting all other men and lavishing goods and praise on this man, is it not clear that he is no more than a hired servant, one who fears you for all these things?'

There are three lies that Satan tells with that one short question, Does Job fear God for nothing:

1. Satan is saying that riches will make any man serve God. That a man may be holy is no wonder, when it is seen that he has been given abundance to cause him to be so. Of all his lies, this one is perhaps most often disproven in the Holy Scripture. "You did not serve the Lord your God with joyfulness and with gladness of heart for the abundance of all things" (Deut. 28:47). Abundance does not draw the heart to God. Nothing in this world can change the deceitful and desperately wicked heart of man and cause it to do service for God. Not even the most grievous affliction will turn a man's heart to God—and a man will do more to be rid of affliction than he will do merely to earn riches. This lie of Satan's is a deliberate one, one which Satan himself knows to be such. For if what he says is true, then it could be retorted to him, Why then did you not continue to serve God? Who was more blessed than you were when you were in Heaven. Were you not the anointed cherub? the leader of excellent angels? What could God have given Job that you did not then have? Right in the midst of all abundance, when you were holding the greatest of riches, you rebelled and refused to serve God. Riches and abundance are not enough to keep a creature serving God, how much less do they cause a person to leave off doing those things that please himself in order to start serving God.

2. The second lie Satan tells here is this, that God has no servants who obey Him and magnify Him because they love Him. In fact, Satan implies that it takes an extraordinary amount of rewards to cause anyone to serve God at all. He would have us believe that God is such an undesirable Master that we must be allured to do so at double cost to Him. The truth is quite different, of course, for God's servants follow Him for Himself. Not only the majesty and riches of God attract them, but His excellent person, His loveliness in all the ways that attract us, His sweetness and kindness and gentleness, His generosity and His constant care, His forgiveness and mercy—all these multiply our love toward Him according to the measure we experience them. God does indeed make us promises. But He does not bargain with any of us. His promises become precious only after He has blessed us with grace on top of grace. We serve Him because we love Him. We obey Him freely because of that love. And, of course, we love Him because He first loved us (1 John 4:19).

24

It is Satan that tries to bargain with us for our service. Witness how he tries to bribe Christ with the whole world, *"all these things will I give you if you will fall down and worship me"* (Matt. 4:9). If Jesus would but once bow down to Satan, then Satan promises to give him the whole world. That is how much he wishes that he were God, for he cannot but envy God for the love and willing obedience He receives from us.

3. The third lie of Satan is this, that there is no gain in godliness, that godliness has no delight in itself. Because all that Satan has to give are the things of this world, he must insist that it is the things of this world which give anything its value. Godliness must not be worth anything unless it earns the godly person some of the things of this world. Job must not be allowed to desire to please God simply because he loves to please God. He must be seeking his own advantage, his own glory among men, else he would not accept all these constraints on his will and all these limitations on his lusts.

If Satan were right, then God would never have said these words to David, *"I anointed you king over Israel, and I delivered you out of the hand of Saul. And I gave you your master's house and your master's wives into your bosom, and gave you the house of Israel and Judah. And if that was too little, I would have given to you such and such things besides. Why have you despised the commandments of the Lord, to do evil in His sight?"*(2 Sam. 12:7-9). If David had been serving God for the riches and possessions he had, then he would never have risked them with this kind of act. But things which caused David to repent and to melt back into the bosom of God were entirely different from the things of this world, *"Against You, You only, have I sinned and done this evil in Your sight."* It was not the loss of the things of this world that broke him up, but it was the loss of the loving presence of God. It was the lovingkindness and tender mercies of God which were to blot out his transgressions, not this and that bundle of riches—*"Create in me a clean heart, O God, and renew a right spirit within me...restore unto me the joy of Your salvation and uphold me with a willing spirit..."* (Psalm 51). You can see that he is panting after the things of God, those things which are not seen, which are not made with hands. What in the world could ever solace and restore a man who has lost the joy of God's presence?

Actually it is lawful for us to look to the rewards promised us as an encouragement to persevere in our duty. It is said of the Lord Jesus Christ Himself that He endured the cross, despising the shame, for the joy that was set before Him (Heb. 12:2). Expecting benefits from the hand of God is sinful only when we make those benefits the main cause for our obedience. When we do anything God commands for our own sakes, whatever may be the reward we think we shall receive, it creates a stink in God's nostrils and He will not accept it. As Christ rebuked those in John 6 by saying, *"You seek Me not because you saw the miracles, but because you ate the loaves and were filled."* Those who accept God's mark merely for the cattle and substance they imagine they will get, they make themselves mere Shechemites, and they court their destruction as well. Such are Satan's servants, not the servants of God.

In the serving of God, take these directions: Set God's glory as your goal; set your desire for Heaven and rest on the right hand; set the fear of Hell and the avoiding of misery on the left hand; then set your desire for the outward comforts of this world loosely on your footstool. There may be times when the things of this world are used as encouragements to us in our service, but they must never be the reason for our doing any thing. It may be a lovely child, a pleasing experience, an adoring wife, a certain situation may be encouragements to us to be holy. But if so, they are only the medium through which we see the bounty and goodness of God. If we fix and terminate any of our desires on these things, instead of on God, then we shall suffer much loss. And not the least of the losses would be this, our integrity when we would answer Satan's calumnies against us, denying that we serve God for the things that He gives us, rather than for Himself.

CHAPTER 1, VERSE 10

"Have You not made a hedge around him, and around his house, and around all that he has on every side? You have blessed the work of his hands, and his possessions have increased in the land"--Job 1:10).

Satan desires permission to prove that Job serves God for gain, so he charges that in three specific ways God is bribing Job to serve Him with extraordinary benefits:

1. You have made a hedge around him, and around his house, and around all that he has.

2. You have not only protected Job from being spoiled and harmed, but You have given Him your blessing and benediction.

3. You have made certain that these two would not fail to buy Job's service by adding a third, the multiplication of his substance day after day.

GOD PROTECTS THOSE THAT ARE HIS

1. As to the first point, God has indeed made a hedge around Job, and around all of those that belong to Him. God has said, *"The Lord knows those who are His"* (2 Tim. 2:19) – that is, He knows them in the way of love. These that He loves are delivered out of all their troubles. But those who are not His are willing captives of Satan until that day when they shall hear the Judge speak that woeful sentence, *"I never knew you! Depart from Me!"* (Matt. 7:23). Those He has foreknown, having loved them from the beginning with an everlasting love, He shall love them to the end, predestinating them to be conformed to the image of His Son (Romans 8:29,30; Jer. 31:5). In order to protect those He loves, God has made a hedge around them. It is one of the ways He comforts and encourages us.

"You have made a hedge around him"–It is a metaphor often used of the Lord. Fields with hedges and towns with walls were considered to be safe: *"For I, says the Lord, will be to her a wall of fire all around"* (Zech. 2:5). He speaks of Jerusalem there, but He is spiritually speaking of us. In this place, God is the immediate hedge, as is so often pictured in the Psalms, *"You are my rock and my fortress, my deliverer, my strength, my buckler, the horn of my salvation and my high tower"* (Psalm 18:2).

Sometimes God uses His creatures to protect those who fear Him: *"The angel of the Lord camps around those who fear Him and delivers them"*–*"You shall not need to fight in this battle. Set yourselves and stand and see the salvation of the Lord"* (Psalm 34:7; 2 Chron. 20:17). There God worked marvelously to keep even a drop of the blood of His people from falling to the ground.

What kind of hedge did Job have? Job had all the kinds of protection that God so graciously gives. He was protected in his body, from all forms of disease and wasting so common to sinful human bodies. He was protected in his soul, from lusts that war against the soul, from temptations that were too heavy to bear, etc. Furthermore, there was a hedge around his household and family. There are cases when God will not forbear to bring judgment for sin even if *"Noah, Daniel and Job were in it, they would deliver only their own souls"* (Ezekiel 14:14). But it is more common for God to protect the families of the ones He has set His love upon. Satan, then, resented not only the protection given Job, but also that which was given to his family.

This wall of protection even extended to Job's possessions, *"and around all that he has on every side,"* meaning his cattle, etc. This full circle of protection extended on every side and to everything connected with Job. O truly He is a God to be loved and praised who takes such pleasure in His people as to fence them in with His power and wisdom!

Satan, frustrated and defeated by God's wall around His servant, shows his anger. For the question often expresses passion and anger in the Old Testament. But even in his anger, and even though he is the father of lies, the old devil tells the truth here. Yes, he sometimes tells the truth – whenever it seems to be to his advantage, he will do so. He is willing to speak well of God on the one side if he thinks he can tear down more on the other side. When Satan speaks the truth, you can be sure that the truth hurts. For though he may have the truth in his mouth, he always has deceit in his heart. If he extols the power of God, it is to impress us with the false notion that God will use that power to withhold good from us. In the case before us, Satan is acknowledging God's sovereignty, but he is implying that this sovereignty destroys Job's independence and increases his hypocrisy.

But why must a wall be erected around God's people? Is there need for protection when there is no enemy? The facts are plain. God's own are surrounded by danger because the whole world lies in wickedness and we are the objects of its hatred. They scoff at us, as if we were idiots who do not deserve their attention. Yet who is more envied and spited than the child of God? Do we not need this wall of protection? Yes, for God does not spend His strength where it is not needed. No city fortifies its walls unless there is danger. God does not fortify us without cause. If Job was safe from Satan and his followers, why then did Satan try to take down this wall? And what happened to Job when God took it down? Only God stands between each one of us and the worst that Satan can do to us.

"You have blessed the work of his hands,"—The original word means to bow (it is not the word for happy). There are three ways of blessing, varied by those being blessed:

1. Man blesses man. Jacob blessed Pharaoh — that is, Jacob bowed to him and acknowledged God's authority was residing in Pharaoh at that time. But Jacob also blessed his sons before he died; that is, being close to God via special revelation, he passed on blessed information which he had gotten from God's Spirit. Man also blesses man when he wishes him well. True love is this, to pray that God will bless the souls of our loved ones with a conformity to the Lord Jesus Christ, causing them to have that mind which was in Him. If you would bless someone, then, pray that this shall happen to them.

2. Man blesses God. He does homage to Him. He not only genuflects, but he bows down in absolute prostration to the mysterious, august, majestic Ruler of all the earth. Man blesses God when he praises Him, when he offers up a prayer of thanksgiving—*"Bless the Lord, O my soul, and forget not all His benefits"* (Ps. 103:2). The cup of communion is truly the *"cup of blessing"* because it is our taking pains to give thanks to our Lord Jesus for the unspeakable benefits which God the Spirit conveys to us by the blood of Christ.

3. God blesses man. God condescends to bless man. God bows down graciously to give believers the love and benefits purchased for them by their Savior. But first, it was an unspeakable condescension for Him to give His only-begotten Son that we may have life and happiness in Him. When God blesses, when God bends down to wish man well, then immediate operation follows. Only with God is the wish the command. When man blesses, he merely desires the well-being of another. He cannot put it into immediate effect. He must wait upon a higher power to effect the blessing. Not so with God, as Satan here grudgingly acknowledges, for God desired to fashion Job into a man among men, one who would witness of the power and wisdom of God for millenniums to come, and He immediately put into operation His plan to bless Job. The power and wisdom of God were so greatly multiplied by His permission to Satan to do all that he could do to thwart the will of God that God is going to use these foolish attempts of Satan to ruin Job as evident proof that He can bless in the face of any and all opposition — from Satan or anyone else.

"the work of his hands"—that is, all that Job ever did. In Isaiah 53:10, it is written, *"that the pleasure of the Lord shall prosper in His hand,"* yet the will of God was not done by the very hands of Christ, but by all that He did with both body and soul. As judge and minister, master and friend, all that Job undertook was blessed by God. And Satan complains at this use of superior power, for it tends to embarrass the demons when God says, *"You shall be blessed when you come in, and you shall be blessed when you go out"* (Deut. 28:6).

"and his possessions have increased in the land"—The word translated *"increased"* is a word which means much more. It is such an increase as breaks all bounds, an increase in such abundance as cannot be any longer contained in the same place. In short, Satan is complaining that everything Job owns is multiplying and superabounding. Possessions had flowed in upon Job like a flood from a broken dam (for the word properly carries the meaning of breaking through—as when it was used to name Pharez, when he broke through his mother's womb). Yet for all of this Job did not sin against God. The rich fool sinned a-

gainst God (Luke 12:13-20), not because he intended to pull down all his barns and to build bigger ones, which Job probably had done many times, but because he presumed that he was independent of God and was in control over his own life and destiny. Job never made such a fool mistake. He clearly saw that it was God who provided and controlled.

FOUR THINGS IN REGARD TO THE BLESSING OF THE LORD

1. All success in obtaining the possessions of this world is due to the direct provision of the Lord. Even Satan admits it when he says, *"You have blessed, etc."*

It is said of Joseph, *"whatever he did, the Lord made it to prosper"* (Gen. 39:23). Peter and his friends fished all night without catching a single fish, but when the Lord appeared the blessing came with Him. They then caught such a multitude of fish that it was difficult for them to pull them in (Luke 5). Were they not good fishermen before Jesus came? Yes, but the ordering of all things belongs to the Lord. Every creature obeys Him willingly, except sinful man (who obey Him unwillingly), God working in them to will and to do of His pleasure (Phil. 2:13). Not only the cattle on a thousand hills belong to God, but all things are His. And He gives them to whomever He pleases (and withholds them from whomever He pleases). Yet what truth is more often made out to be an uncertainty? Men promise themselves wealth as a reward for their labor, fame as a reward for their intelligence in applying their talents, and health as a reward for their care. Professing themselves to be wise, they become fools in allowing themselves to be deceived by Satan's lie, that they are the masters of their own destiny, that they may successfully make their own way.

In this regard, Satan's lies are quoted as Biblical truths by the majority of sinners on the face of the earth. Who has not heard these typical lies, (1) God helps those who help themselves; (2) The strong take it from the weak, and the wise take it from the strong; (3) We may do evil that good may come. Not only are those statements missing from the Bible, they tell exactly the opposite of God's truth, for, (1) God hates those who help themselves —and He often thwarts their efforts to prove themselves successful in providing their own needs, thus denying Him the glory—*"When the Lord shall stretch out His hand, both he who helps shall fall, and he who is helped shall fall down, and they shall all fail together"* (Isa. 31:3); (2) It is God who takes it from the strong and gives it to the weak, who takes it from the wise and gives it to those who are fools for Christ's sake—*"My grace is sufficient for you, for My strength is made perfect in weakness"* (2 Cor. 12:9); (3) God shall punish all evildoers, both those who do so ignorantly and those who do so willfully (even though they excuse themselves and expect a reward because they believe they can bring good out of their evil seeds. Only God is good and only God can do good. God is of purer eyes than to look upon evil, much less would He be able to do evil that good may come. It is even more impossible that He could call anything good which He Himself had not originated, decreed and finally worked out in the person who performs the good deed.

No one can justify nor prove his conceited notion that it is his own talent, intellect, skill, dexterity and strength that brings him his possessions—*"For who makes you to differ from another? And what do you have which you did not receive? But now if you did receive it, why do you boast as if you did not receive it?"* (1 Cor. 4:7). When all else fails, men give credit to a heathen god, Luck. But Job knew, and all God's children know in their hearts, that God is all the 'luck' a man may have, that there is no such thing as 'luck' or 'fate' which can bring anyone a blessing. All is by God's provision and decree alone.

2. We find that the Lord is usually pleased to bless those who are industrious—*"the hand of the hard worker brings riches"* (Prov. 10:4b). Yet the balance to this also appears, *"The blessing of the Lord itself makes men rich"* (Prov. 10:22). The riches of this world are not necessarily blessings, though men most times count them so. Those who get riches in such a way may well find that *"the rust of their gold and silver will eat their flesh like fire"* (see James 5:3). They will prove to be a curse, not a blessing from God.

3. Everyone should be busy with hands and heart and head. The Master said, *"I must be about My Father's business."* Should we do less than He? There are many who seem to think that they are being holy because they zealously worship, pray and witness on occasion, that they may be holy and also may count a portion of their time as their own, to do with it as they please. Nothing could be further from the picture of a true saint as we see

God draw it in the Scriptures. Look at Job here, at David in the Psalms, at Paul in the Epistles. To be holy is nothing more, nothing less than to continually and without intermittance to do only and all the will of God. Only God may please Himself and yet be holy. No creature has the right to please himself at any time unless in doing so he is primarily pleasing the Lord God. In other words, if it pleases you to please God, then you may be holy as you receive pleasure. Paul wrote, by God the Holy Spirit, *"if I were still pleasing men, I would not be the servant of Christ"* (Gal. 1:10). Do you think this still leaves you room to do your own will? Not unless you think that you are better, more privileged than Jesus Christ, *"For even Christ did not please Himself..."* – *"I have come down out of Heaven, not to do My own will, but the will of Him who sent Me"* (Rom. 15:3; John 6:38). In what moment did He ever say, This is My minute and I will do with it as I please? If He had ever had such a moment, He would have sinned. Therefore, no such moment ever occurred in the life of our Lord. As our incomparable Example, He commands that we be holy in the same way He was holy while He walked this earth (1 Peter 1:15,16). If it is your delight always to do the will of your Father, then you will be blessed in the same way Jesus was blessed. That is to say, then you will accomplish all that you try to do for the glory to God.

4. When God decides to bless, it is certain that we shall be blessed. Just as surely as the fact that all power in Heaven and in earth belong to Him, that certain it is that we shall be blessed. Let fools give credit to riches, to influence, to governments, to charms and heathen gods. It is because he has said in his heart that there is no God that he is driven to the expedient of devising superstitions which will deceive him during his short testing time on earth. But let us be believing, not unbelieving. Let us say at least as much as an unbeliever could say, *"Behold! He has blessed, and I cannot reverse it"* (Numbers 23:20—Balaam).

What then? If God is our wall of protection, if God is the One who blessed the labor of our hands, is the One who increases and multiplies our goods and our services according to His good pleasure, then shame on every one of us who wears a long face! There is no room for both faith in God and an attitude of defeat. We cannot both profess Christ and present to the world an obvious attitude of unconcern about being conformed to His image. Are you truly in Christ Jesus, or are you no more than a pious hypocrite? If you know Him, you know that you can draw near with a true heart in full assurance of faith. For if we hold fast the confession of our Hope, then we will lift up our hands and set our feeble knees in motion, making straight paths of holy testimony to the power and goodness of God as we eagerly pursue after the Lord Jesus. He will bless us with grace on top of grace. And as he multiplies our spiritual substance and lays up treasures above for us, Satan may have good reason to complain that God is leaving him no room to practice his devil's wile.

"But put forth your hand now and touch all that he has, and he will curse You to Your face"—Job 1:11.

Satan, seeing that his own conclusions are closing him in, hastens to seek to set God against Job, at the time making a nasty accusation against him. He feels he must move with speed if he is to accomplish his devilish design. He knows God well enough to anticipate that Job may be turned over to him. Yet do not miss the fact that he does not have the knowledge of God which his age, experience and superior intelligence would seem to make certain. In all the centuries since Satan was thrown out of Heaven, he has learned little:

1. Satan is far from omniscient. Many revere the old serpent for his wisdom, yet he is a fool, relatively speaking. He is indeed superior to man. He does indeed have wisdom of a sort. But he does not possess the knowledge of God which even the least of the saints embrace. You would think that an intelligent being would learn not to join battle again and again with One who had defeated him in every single encounter millions and millions of times. If Satan had any true wisdom, he would know that his trial of Job would without doubt vindicate God's judgment of Job's character.

2. Malice insures its own defeat. Neither guile, craftiness nor wiliness can give the victory to a malicious mind. Satan is so full of hate and evil design toward God and Job that he cannot reap the benefit of an intelligence that is far superior to Job's (but not to God's).

3. Unbelief cannot conceive of the goodness of God and of the happy state of God's o-bedient servants. Unbelievers deceive themselves deliberately as a defense against the truth that is always beating at the doors and peeking in at the windows of their minds. They are seeking always to find proof that everyone is made in their own image, that God is not at all, or else that God is no more than a superman. God clearly exposes this as evil, *"You give your mouth to evil and your tongue frames deceit...you thought that I was One like yourself,. .Now think of this, you who forget God, lest I tear you in pieces and there be none to deliver you"* (Psalm 50:21,22). On the other hand, God clears believers of this satanic weakness, saying of those that obey Him that they *"have not received the spirit of the world, but (they) have received the Spirit which is from God, so that we might know the things given to (them) by God.. But the natural (unbelieving) one does not receive the things of the Spirit of God, for they are foolishness to him. Neither can he know them, because they are spiritually understood. But the spiritual (believing) one understands all things, and he is judged by no one"* (1 Cor. 2:12-15). Unbelieving devils and men cannot believe God because their inward rottenness corrupts their minds and souls.

"But put forth Your hand now"—To a hypocrite, there are no persons who are not hypocrites. They are always certain that there is a selfish reason behind the acts of everyone. So it is with the evil 'angel of light,' he is certain that Job is a hypocrite who serves God for gain. Therefore he suggests that God will find Job to be a false lover, that all it will take is the subtraction of some of Job's possessions to prove him to be a mercenary hypocrite.

To put forth or send forth the hand in Scripture is either a signification of help or harm. There is a putting forth of God's hand to deliver, to heal (Ps. 144:7; Acts 4:30). But usually the putting forth or stretching forth of God's hand is for affliction or punishment. In Isaiah, for instance, several times God depicts Himself stretching forth His hand to punish, *"He has stretched forth His hand against them and has stricken them"*—*"His anger is not turned away, but His hand is stretched out still"* (Isaiah 5:25; 9:21). It is in this sense that Satan uses the word, saying, Let Job feel the weight of Your hand, let him but be afflicted and You will find that instead of blessing You, he will blaspheme You.

"Your hand"—The hand of God in Scripture signifies the purpose of God, the Spirit of God. God accomplishes His purposes with His hand, *"They have done whatever Your hand and Your counsel determined before to be done"* (Acts 4:28). Sometimes, especially in the prophets, the hand of the Lord is the Spirit, *"The hand of the Lord was upon me"* (Ezekiel 37:1). That is, the Spirit of the Lord was upon him. Again, *"The hand of the Lord was upon Elijah"* (1 Kings 18). That is, the power of the Spirit of God was upon him, giving him strength to run before Ahab's chariot and to arrive before him. *"The hand of the Lord is not shortened"* (Isaiah 59:1). That is, the power of the Spirit of God is never hindered so that it cannot save. We see God's hand, then, acting in three ways:

1. God's hand protects, so that there is *"no one who is able to pluck them out of My Father's hand"* (John 10:28). God has His sheep in His hand. He will protect them from all harm, both from inside agents and outside agents. He puts a hedge around them, and He puts His Spirit within them to protect them against all forces which would hurt them. Satan must have a double leave before he can do anything to God's children. He must first have permission from God, then he must have permission from us — although our permission may be by an omission of our duty toward God or toward men, we should be thankful that God's permission is given with full intent and complete realization of the consequences. Except he is given express permission from God to touch us, no demon can do us the least harm, for he lacks the power to break through God's hedge. As an example of the complete control that God maintains over the demons, note that they had to ask

Christ if they could enter the swine (Luke 8:32). Satan was forced to ask God for permission to sift Peter, *"Satan has claimed you for himself, in order to sift you as wheat."* He did not sail in with great power and seize Peter, but he had to ask God for permission to do it. Then Christ says, *"But I have prayed for you, that your faith will not fail—and when you have turned back, etc."* It was not possible for Satan to cause Peter's faith to fail. And it was such a certainty that Peter would turn back to God's service that Christ takes it for granted and gives him instruction as to what he is to do then. What a great comfort it is to the saints to know that their great, their most subtle and most watchful enemy cannot hurt them without God's leave!

By God's order, the Devil must also have our assent before he can assault us, in the ordinary course of our lives. That is to say, we are promised that he will flee from us if we resist him (James 4:7), and if we subject our lives to God as we ought, then he will not be able to assault us. This is what makes Job's case such an extraordinary one. This is a case where Satan is permitted to assault Job with devastating blows even though Job has not either by sins of omission or sins of commission brought such damage upon himself. Because it was an especially unique case in those patriarchal days, Job's friends are certain that he must surely have committed the whole catalog of secret sins to bring such misery and loss upon himself. The believer normally suffers assault from Satan, however, when the old serpent comes and finds something within us which he can use against us. For a comparison, note that God gave Satan permission to tempt Christ, but he failed because there was nothing in Him to give Satan a handhold. Peter blamed Ananias for allowing Satan to fill his heart with deception (Acts 5:3). He did not rebuke Satan, but Ananias. The only way we can be certain that we are not taken captive by the Devil is this, that we resist him by following God's scriptural directions.

2. God's hand corrects, *"His hand was heavy upon me"* (Psalm 32:4). *"For whom the Lord loves, He corrects. And He whips every son whom He receives"* (Hebrews 12:6). That is, He uses His hand of power to teach, to instruct—for the basic meaning of that word which is so often translated *"afflict"* is this, 'to teach.'

3. God's hand revenges. There are vessels of mercy and there are vessels of wrath (Rom. 9:21-23). For the vessels of wrath there is a destroying hand, a punishing hand. To them, God is surely a consuming fire, and it is a most fearful thing for them to fall into His hands (Hebrews 10:31). *"Vengeance is Mine, I will repay,"* says the Lord. And this avenging hand is awesome indeed when the time comes for God to teach His enemies that they invited everlasting destruction when they despised mercy.

In this place, when Satan asks God to put forth His hand he does not mean for God to stretch out His hand to protect Job or to correct Job. He wants Job to be severely smitten. And it is his suggestion that this should be an immediate handling of Job by God Himself. For there are times when a man is visited with severe trials and punishments, when God without the use of any other creature destroys from the outside, or tears down on the inside of a man. That which we call evil may come immediately from God, as may be drawn from Isaiah 45:7, *"I make peace, and I create evil."* Now a creation must be out of nothing. If this is true, that God creates evil, then it must be immediately from God without the possibility of any other agent originating it. But the evil which God is said here to create is not that evil which God cannot look upon. It is not that which God looks upon as evil. Therefore it cannot be thought that God is here saying that He authors sin. Evil to God is sin. Or, to make it more plain, a thing is evil when it does not please God. Sin is evil only because sin is the pleasing of self, of someone other than God. Whatever does not please God is evil. God calls that evil which does not please Him. And it is the same with men. A man considers all things to be evil when those things do not please him. Anything that happens to thwart the plans or pleasures of a man is considered by him to be an evil thing, an evil happening. Therefore he calls it evil. It is in this sense that God uses the word here. When He says that He creates evil, He is saying that He brings to pass those things that men call evil, things which are highly displeasing to men. Satan is here asking God to do such things in Job's life. He obviously believes that if evil things happen to Job, then Job will prove to be evil, that he will curse God.

"now"—The original word can be translated, *"a little," "please,"* or, *"now."* The sense in our translation is this, that God should not even wait a little, but that He should immediately set His hand against Job. He would not give God a minute's respite. He must not stop to consider this thing, but He must do it now. Sinful devils and men are in haste to shed blood, their feet are swift to shed blood and they want God's hand to be equally quick to deal blows to His followers. When he wants God to perform something that pleases him, tomorrow is too late for the Devil. But when we are called to give ourselves up to God, then tomorrow is soon enough—even next year is time enough for repentance, etc. Sin and destruction should be done now, today, but there will be time enough to do good when you are old, says Satan.

"and touch all that he has"—To touch is sometimes put for a very heavy affliction; at other times only for a small and light affliction. When Job says, *"for the hand of God has touched me"* (19:21), he is describing the most severe affliction a saint may have. And when David said, *"all the day long I have been plagued,"* (the word is actually the same,) he is saying, *"all the day long I have been touched"* (Psalm 73:14). Then sometimes the word is put for a very light touch, as in Genesis 26:19, when Abimelech denies that any of his people had touched Isaac or done him the least harm. When God says, *"touch not My anointed,"* He is saying that none should do them the least bit of harm. Here it could be that Satan is saying, You say that Job is perfect and an upright servant, so that there is none like him in the earth? Then put forth your hand and smite him but a little blow. You will see that he is a hypocrite when He curses You.

Why would Satan say such a thing? Is he not speaking from experience? Has he not seen myriads of professing Christians fall apart from just a light touch of affliction? Even the closest-living hypocrite dwells in a house of cards—he will ruin all his years of posing as a child of God when someone only touches his dignity, or wounds his pride. Sometimes all they have to do is to brush up against a true saint, to receive a prick or two from the word of God, and the rottenness of their hearts springs out—they may at any moment break out into a blasphemous cursing of God. There may be some tares which will remain among the wheat until death, but there are others that are apples of Sodom, beautiful to behold in their outward profession, but ready to fall to ashes when they are touched by God's hand. The difference between a Judas-like hypocrite and a true saint is that life which God infuses into His new creatures. They may look alike, they may act so much alike that they themselves do not know that there is a difference between them—just as all the apostles failed to recognize Judas as a hypocrite. For did they not all begin to ask the Lord Jesus, *"Lord, is it I?"* And did not Peter signal to John to ask Him which one of them was so wicked as to be His betrayer? There had been an unspeakably deep difference between Judas and the others, the difference between a live saint and a dead hypocrite, but this did not become evident until both Judas and Peter had been turned over to Satan. Jesus dipped the morsel of bread in the dish with Judas, *"then Satan entered into him."* There was not an iota of the life of God in Judas, therefore he slavishly fell to doing Satan's will. But with Peter it was different. For though he was even brought to the point where he cursed and denied knowing Jesus, the life of God was in him, and his faith did not fail! Satan is in effect himself cursing God now. He yearns to prove that Job is really a child of Satan (John 8:44) instead of one full of the life of God. If he is asking God to put forth

His hand in severity, handing out destruction and misery to Job, as we think he does, then it is because he wants Job to learn to hate God with the same malicious hate which he has for Him. Satan is saying that either God is ignorant and cannot read the heart of Job, or that God is a liar and misrepresenting what Job is. Is it any wonder then that he thinks Job is an unholy and insincere man, one who fears God for what he can get out of it? The Scripture tells us whom we are to believe in this dispute, *"Let God be true and every man a liar,"* or, *"every one else a liar."* Of Satan, it is written, Satan is *"a liar,"* *"the father of lies"* (See Romans 3:4, John 8:44).

"Now...touch all that he has"—It is written that men are swift to shed blood, to do evil, etc., but how much more is this true of Satan. He cannot wait for God to lay hands upon Job, pretending that he knows Job will be unmasked as a hypocrite with cursing in his heart. These further things may be extracted from this verse:

1. God can and sometimes does destroy a man and his estate with but a light touch, only a flick of the finger sending him careening off the stage of life. If God could speak the world into existence, with its almost unbelievable order and profundity, could He not destroy it just as quickly and as easily? If in but a relative moment He touched the earth and destroyed whole lands, made mountains and dug seas, can He not in a moment touch a man and all that he has and cause him to turn to ashes?

2. Malice is not satisfied with anything but total victory. Satan cannot wait to see Job destroyed, for as long as Job continues in his life of service and obedience he is damaging the reputation of the old devil (who prides himself on being king of this world, the one who passes out the blessings of prosperity). If it is true that only a light touch would expose Job, then why does Satan not merely ask that half of Job's goods be taken, or that one of his sons be killed? No, but all he has must be taken—he must be stripped of all he owns and all he loves. Here is but a foretaste of the history of the church. In the Reformation, God's servants heard these same accusations. There were threatenings, then fines, then imprisonment, then whippings, then the rack, then burning at the stake. Why? Malice is not satisfied with anything but a total blotting out, an erasing and effacing of the image of God from the faces and lives of His truly upright and sincere servants.

"Touch all that he has now, and he will curse You to Your face"—literally in the original it is, *"Touch all that he has now, if he does not curse You to Your face."* A proper rendering might be, *"see if he does not curse You to Your face."* Most versions translate it, *"he will curse You to Your face."* In any case, Satan is saying, Job will curse You as soon as he sees that he will lose all he has gained by serving You.

"he will curse You"—it is the same word translated curse in verse 5. Again we say that the primary meaning of the word is *"to bless."* Thomas Aquinas translates it here, reading it in the past perfect tense, saying in effect, *"If You afflict him you shall find that all his former religion was nothing but mere outside formality, that he served You only from the teeth outward; that is, he did not worship You because he loved You or delighted in You, but he blessed You because You first blessed him, etc."* There are those who draw near to God with their lips when their hearts are far from Him. This is certainly Satan's opinion of Job, but the tense here is certainly future. This means that Satan believes that Job will curse God, not that he has blessed God in the past.

"to Your face"—Job has been cursing You in his heart, Satan infers, but now he will curse You to Your face. If You take away all that a man gains from You, many will cease to pretend that you are a friend. All experience tells us of those who hide hatred and malice and envy and unprovoked bitterness in their hearts, yet who declare undying love and devotion to those who are watering their gardens and showering them with blessings. These may be known to talk about their benefactors behind their backs, but never to their faces. Only the love of God shed abroad in the hearts of men by the Holy Spirit can cause us to both speak well of God behind His back (so to speak) as well as before His face.

WHAT DOES IT MEAN TO CURSE GOD?

Satan claims that out of the abundance of his heart Job will blaspheme and curse God, and that to His very face. But what would Job have to do in order to be guilty of cursing God? Must he spit forth evil words like excrement? Must he use the foul curse words that men use to curse one another? No, it is not necessary for a man to do so in order to curse God. God has His own definitions, as in Mal. 3:14, *"Your words have been hard against Me, says the Lord."* But what were these strong words that they used? They themselves ask, *"What have we spoken against You?"* The answer, *"You have said, It is vain to serve God; and, What profit is it that we have kept His ordinance and that we have walked mournfully before the Lord of hosts?"* It is said there that they called the proud happy, that they exalted those who worked wickedness, and that those who tempted God were thought to have escaped. Yet they said, What have we spoken against You. What was this but a cursing of God to His face, thinking that He was of no earthly use to them, believing that those who had not served God were happier and wiser than those who had loved and served Him?

Be careful that you do not fall into the sin of the Psalmist who first wrote, *"I have made my heart pure in vain"* (Ps. 73:13). It is a cursing to say that your friendship with God is of no value. Let a servant of a dictator or an emperor say to him to his face that it is of no value to have his favor, and you will find that servant either imprisoned or beheaded. What do you think of persons who think that you are not worth their time or attention? Would you not rather have someone curse you than to despise you. So God is cursed when you and I despise Him, think lightly of His opinion, are careless of His power, boldly deny the value of His love. God and God only, is worthy of our love for Himself alone. It is nothing more than sin for you to ask that you have both God and something else. Those who are not satisfied with Jesus alone, who make Christianity out to be Jesus plus baptism, or Jesus plus good works, or Jesus plus anything at all, are the kind of false professors who will hear Him say, *"I never knew you, Depart from Me, cursed ones."*

AFFLICTION IS THE ACID TEST OF OUR SINCERITY

Satan, not being omniscient, cannot read the hearts of men with any exactitude. He can and does guess at their state, using his centuries of experience and his intimate knowledge of the evil nature of mankind. He has learned how to test the sincerity of a man's profession. But he can never be sure as to the genuineness of that profession until the test is over. Else why did he even tempt the Lord Jesus Christ? The demons knew Him well enough to ask Him if He came to torment them before their time (Matt. 8:30). Did not the Prince of demons know? Yet he presumes to shoot Him down out of His heavenly glory with various temptations which would not appeal to anyone who was pure, holy and full of God's word? Satan does not know. But he will sift and test everyone God will turn over to him. And he has found that affliction is the most successful test he can give a man.

Affliction is always for the glory of God. Whether you are afflicted in order to melt away your dross, as Peter; or whether you are being punished for your sins, as Herod; God gets glory for Himself. He proves that He both rules and overrules, that He directs all our steps:

1. If it is a child of God that is afflicted, God is glorified. When God throws His own children into the fires of affliction, He sits alertly by the fire, tenderly tending and nursing them. He watches carefully that nothing but dross is taken from them. He polishes and shines them even before they leave the fire, purifying them for their future good and for His glory (See Mal. 3:3; Luke 22:31; Jas. 1:2-4; 1 Peter 1:7). Once the earthliness has been removed from His jewels, the image of God shines forth brightly for all to see.

2. Affliction is a great discoverer. It unmasks and reveals us. If we are fine gold, then we are revealed as gold. If we are hypocrites, then our rottenness is exposed to view. If we are evil, then as our form appears in the light we are seen to have a conformity to Satan. After God pulls back the veil to reveal us to ourselves, God can and does reward us. If we are fine gold, we discover again that we are so only because we are one with Jesus Christ. It's the partaking of the divine nature and holiness that makes us fit for reward, not our nature.

34

3. Pain, loss and discomfort are not the only ways that our all-wise God can afflict. There are times when God afflicts a man with prosperity, with fullness of bread. Certainly He uses prosperity as a test, often giving us over to Satan to prove that a true child of God will not trade his God for his gold, or for power, or for fame.

Satan now knows that Job will not fall prey to prosperity, for even now he is the greatest man in the East. He also knows that riches and religion can go handsomely together until a choice between them must be made (See Luke 18:18). Satan, seeing that Job did not sin for all of his possessions, now reasons that he will surely sin without them. Given Satan's basic unbelief, this is a logical assumption. If it is true that no one loves God for Himself, that no man could do so, then Job could be such a person. Then to remove those things which are causing him to be a perfect servant would cause a collapse of his desire toward God. When zeal is kindled only with the beams of worldly hopes, then that zeal becomes extinct when the worldly hopes fail. Will a man persist without hope? But Satan's premise is wrong, for Job's hope was that Blessed Hope, Jesus Christ. That Hope never fails—a man who once has hope in Christ can never lose that hope forever.

"And the Lord said to Satan, Behold! All that he has is in your power, Only do not put forth your hand upon him. So Satan went forth from the presence of the Lord"—Job 1:12.

God gives Satan a commission, *"Behold! All that he has is in your power;"* and also a limitation on that commission, *"only do not put forth your hand upon him."* Lastly, we see that Satan does not lose any time in acting upon this permission.

"Behold! All that he has is in your power"—it is literally, *"All is in your hand."* God had refused Satan's challenge that He put forth His hand upon Job. Instead He put Job's possessions into the hand of Satan. Why? If a man wanted to take vengeance upon an enemy, would he trust that work to someone who loved his enemy? If he did so, would he not be apt to complain that true vengeance was never taken? God does not intend to leave Satan any ground for cheapening Job's triumph over this trial, so he allows Satan to conduct the test. Job's possessions, including his children, are given over into Satan's power. Could not Satan have used this permission and this power to thwart the will of God? No, certainly not! For just as all power comes from God, so all authority in Heaven and earth is given from God. And God always limits the power and the authority that He gives. It is written, *"The Father loves the Son and has given all things into His hand"*—yet Jesus did not have the right to do anything beyond the will and decree of God, for it is also written, *"I must work the works of Him who sent Me," "I always do the will of My Father."*

Job himself is not here put into Satan's hand, but only all things that he owns and cherishes in his outward life. Satan, like Herod, Pilate, the heathen, and the people of Israel, could do no more than what God's hand and counsel had before determined to be done (See Acts 4:28).

Satan had claimed that Job served God for gain. God now says to Satan. All that he has is in your hand, prove to Me that Job only serves Me for the things that he owns. When you have removed all, you will see that Job is a perfect and upright man, My servant, one who fears God and turns away from evil.

1. Note that Satan was given that which he asked. Perhaps this made him gleeful anticipating much glory to himself as he triumphs over this inferior man. But we shall see in the outcome of this that we are not always being blessed simply because we are given all that we asked. God gave the Israelites quail for their meat, after they had lusted for it in an inordinate and sinful way. But even while the quail was between their teeth, the pestilence began. Paul prayed earnestly that God might take away the thorn in his flesh, but God did not do it then, or later. Those who despised God got what they asked. He who loved God did not get what he asked. The first got what they deserved, fear, disease and death. Paul got more than he deserved, more than he asked, God's sufficient grace.

2. Observe here the impotence of Satan. He had no power to act against Job without the express permission of God—*"Resist the devil and he will flee from you"* (James 1:7). Why?

Because you are then opposing Satan's power with God's power. What can Satan do? We see it here, he can do as much as God gives him permission to do, and no more. You will soon see that he does not attempt to touch Job's person until God gives him a further commission to do so (2:6). The demons cannot even so much as enter into swine without Christ's express permission. Why then do you fear that they will plague you? If you have sinned in your heart and have despised God, then you may reasonably expect some visitation from Satan (to shake you and winnow you). Otherwise, you are safe in the hand of God, who will protect you by keeping Satan from practicing his malicious acts upon you. And when God does turn you over to Satan, as He did Peter, it is for the purpose of perfecting you, of purifying you, of drawing you closer to Him. Then shout with an unspeakable joy when you fall into different kinds of temptations (James 1:2-4), for God is using the whole universe to make you perfect and whole, sound in spirit, pleasing to Himself.

IS IT POSSIBLE FOR GOD'S WILL AND SATAN'S WILL TO BE DONE AT ONCE?

God is light. Satan is hellish darkness. God wills that Job shall be tried by Satan. Satan desires that Job shall be given into his hand. Yet there is an infinite distance between them in the willing of it. The will of Satan was sinful, but the power given to him was just. Why? Because Satan's will was from himself, and the power was from a pure and holy God. Satan had no power to do mischief but what God gave to him—and God would not give him the evil will to do mischief, yet He did give him the power. A similar view is given to us in the case where the lying spirit went forth to deceive Ahab, in order that the will of God might be done. Ahab was under condemnation to die, execution was at God's disposal (as with all men who are outside of Christ), and the time had come for him to die. Ahab hated God and His prophets, but he was always willing to believe a lie. The spirit was sent forth from God, but he lied from himself. God knew that he would lie to Ahab, but God did not tell him to lie, nor did he lie because God influenced him to do so. The spirit knew how to lie, and he desired desperately to lie to Ahab. Ahab desired desperately to be lied to. God justly sent the lying spirit to Ahab, but both Ahab and the lying spirit were unjust from within themselves. God's will was done. Ahab's desire was answered. The lying spirit was given what he asked.

In the case before us, Satan desires to destroy Job and to embarrass God. God wills that good shall come to Job, that he shall come forth from the affliction purified. God permits Satan to think that Job will curse Him, though witnessing plainly to him that Job is not such a person at all. Then God permits Satan to do his utmost against Job's possessions, and he sweeps them all away with the fullness of destructive force given to him. He employs the utmost of his satanic intelligence to destroy Job's possessions in a way that will shock him and be most apt to cause him to curse God. Yet for all this, God's will for Job was done, and not a whit more. All of Satan's malice, power and intelligence can do no more than to fulfill God's holy will toward Job. Even when Satan gets his will, he is also doing the will of God—not willingly, but very effectively.

Is Job being used as a pawn between these powerful adversaries? By no means. Job is being permitted the role of a spiritual knight in shining armor—the whole armor of God. In his trials he is strengthened and comforted, so much so that onlookers cannot but see that he is God's favorite. And when they see that God makes a better man in the midst of the fires of affliction, they are encouraged to consider Jesus Christ, the Author and Finisher of faith. It is faith that overcomes the world, the flesh and the devil. And faith becomes strong according to what it has overcome and resisted (like an oak tree that has been in many storms). Job's faith was immeasureably strengthened in this first test. And he also became aware of his integrity in a way that never occurred to him before.

"God is faithful, who will not allow you to be tempted above what you are able" to bear(1 Cor. 10:13). If Satan were indeed left to himself, he would grind you to dust and distribute you. But God does not allow him to do more than to lick you on the outside. And He only permits Satan to do this so that you may shine with God's glory.

"And Satan went forth from the presence of the Lord"—With his chain shortened so that he cannot reach any further than Job's possessions, Satan hurries out to do all that was in his authority to do. He does not go forth from God's presence in a way that would violate Psalm 139:7, for none may go out from God's presence in that sense. Literally, the meaning is, *"Satan went out from the face of the Lord."* The face of the Lord may be taken in several ways in Scripture:

1. The face of the Lord is taken for His essential glory (Exodus 33).
2. The face of the Lord is put for the favor and love of God (Daniel 7:19).
3. It is sometimes put for the anger and wrath of God, because anger as well as love may be seen in the face (Lam. 4:16, *"The anger (face) of the Lord has divided them."*)
4. The worship of God is connected with the face of God, because in the obeying of His ordinances and in the worship of Him we find God is revealed to us. Those keeping the Law *"appeared before God."*
5. It is put for God's omnipresence, for He is everywhere at once.

Obviously Satan did not go forth from God's omnipresence. Nor is Satan permitted to view God's essential glory. Certainly he is not permitted to see the face of God shining with favor and love. He would not come before God's face to willingly worship Him. Nor can it be said that God is pictured here as in wrath, so Satan is not going from His face in that sense. What then? This going forth from the presence or face of the Lord is spoken according to the manner of men. It is an accommodation to our limited understandings. It is only meant to convey to us that Satan now is no longer speaking to God, that he is not permitted any more charges against Job, that he is now sent forth to do what God had before determined to be done. It is the picture of a servant, an unwilling one, who has been given permission to go and do something he has asked. In this case, he leaves quickly and gladly, for this is something he very much wants to do.

"And there was a day when his sons and his daughters were eating and drinking wine in their oldest brother's house"—Job 1:13.

As Job's afflictions are now to begin, it would be well to note six things about these afflictions: (1) The time of the afflictions—it was a certain Day, (2) The instruments of the afflictions—Satan, his chosen servants, and natural forces such as wind and fire, (3) The matter of his afflictions—his outward estate and loved ones only, (4) The variety of his afflictions—not just in one thing, or two, or many, but in all things that he owned and loved (5) The suddenness of his afflictions—they all came upon him in one day, (6) The continuance of his afflictions without cessation—before one sad tale was told, another began. All of these things were factors in applying force and shock to Job in order to get him to curse God.

"There was a day"—There is a time for every purpose, for God, for Satan, and for man. Not just any day would serve Satan's purpose to subvert Job's faith. There is an emphasis in the Hebrew original here, this is a special day, a day among days. But what day was it? It was a special day in these ways: (1) It was a feasting day. Not every day was a day for feasting; (2) It was an extraordinary feasting day, not just any feasting day. For it is said that they were eating and *"drinking wine."* In Job 1:4, it is not said that they were doing so. In Scripture, a banquet of wine is more than just a banquet where wine is served (see Esther 5:6). When wine is mentioned as being part of a feast, it is a special feast. When the spouse would set forth the wonderful fullness of spiritual delights which she had from Christ, we read, *"He brought me into the banqueting house,"* it is in the Hebrew, *"He brought me into the house of wine."* (3) They were feasting in the oldest brother's house. This, then, was a further revelation that this day was an extraordinary one. Satan picks the day when he may make the most of his opportunity—a very special day of gladness.

There was no other day on which Satan could have shaken Job from his heavenly moorings more than on this day. The mercies of God are more dear to us when they come to us at a time of especial need. There are times when our obedience to God is rewarding the more because of the particular circumstances that prevail against us at that time. Again, our sins are greatly aggravated by the time and season when they are committed. To sin on a day when we have been clearly warned against that sin would make our sin greater. In these days of apostacy, of hypocrisy, it is no time to receive money and fancy clothing (see Kings 5:26). It is a time to let our laughter be turned into mourning (James 4:9).

Satan knows that afflictions at one time will be more bitter, more destructive of our well being than at another time. Solomon tells us that it is too much for us to sing songs to those who are heavy in heart. It is too much for the spirit to bear at such a time. How much more different is it to bear sorrow upon a day of rejoicing. Such is this day in Job's life. All was well with his Job, with his children. Then suddenly Satan strikes. For he well knows that afflictions press most when they are least expected. He strives to carry a man from one extremity to another in the shortest possible time—for this is the greatest of all extremity. To make a day of a man's greatest rejoicing to be the day of his deepest sorrows, this is a killing sorrow indeed—it is enough to unhinge most men.

If Satan is careful to choose this day, or that day, to make certain of success in doing evil, then much more ought we to watch for this day, or that opportunity to do good. This is a day when the sons of Belial will not abide Christ's yoke, they are conspiring to break it from the necks of all. Then let us join together this day to defeat their purpose by the telling of the good news about Jesus Christ. If we are silent, it may be that God will save His people through other instruments than us. But we shall bear the blame nevertheless unless we are alertly siezing every opportunity to salt down the world with the Gospel.

Our best days may well turn out to be our worst days. This was as beautiful a day, one as comfortable as any day ever began in Job's family—yet all was darkness and sorrow and bitterness before nightfall. Ungodly men should take heed to this, for as it was in the days of Noah, and of Lot, all the world may come to an end suddenly. For ungodly men, the sun often sets at noon. When they have concluded that all is well, judgment mixed with wrath is often standing at the door. Godly men should pay close attention also to Job's story – all their outward comforts, all they own in this world may disappear on any given day. Even though they are using them all to the glory of God (1 Cor. 10:13), yet it may be the day that they are to lose them. Therefore, we are to rejoice as if we rejoiced not in the creature, to eat as ,if we did not eat, to buy as if we did not own anything (1 Cor. 7:30). For the world, and all the things of the world, are passing away. Those who cling to them with a death-clutch may pass away with them. It does not matter how much your world is adorned, how much of the world you have gathered into your possession— all may be blasted, may be pulled down and disappear in a day. Possessions can take wings and fly away at the very time you are making doors and locks, bolts and bars to keep them in.

"And there came a messenger to Job and said, The oxen were plowing, and the asses feeding beside them"—Job. 1:14.

The Jewish Rabbins and a few of the Fathers would have us believe that these messengers were demons. But this opinion has little likeness to the truth, being just another of the strange tales of those unstable men. We shall see later that these were Job's servants.

"the oxen were plowing, and the asses were feeding beside them"—The messenger tells this so that it may be seen that they were all hard at work, that the asses were being cared for. This sad loss did not come through the negligence of his servants. All the care and diligence in the world cannot make outward things safe.

"And the Sabeans swooped down and took them away. Yea, they have killed the servants with the edge of the sword. And I only have escaped alone to tell you"—Job. 1:15.

The Sabeans came down with such sudden violence that they are pictured here as coming in like a storm upon Job's oxen, asses and servants. These were a violent people, inhabitants of *Arabia felix*. They are famous only for the robberies and plunders which they visited on their neighbors. How did they happen to come at this time to swoop down on Job's possessions? Satan had used them as his tools to assault Job. But how could he prevail upon them to do his evil work? Satan leads wicked men captive to his will (2 Tim. 2:26). While they conceive themselves to be conquerors, triumphantly preforming their own wills, they are all the while working for Satan. But can he force men to be his instruments? No, Satan cannot force or compel men against their wills, but he is the prince of the power of the air, he works in the children of disobedience powerfully (Eph. 2:1-3). He cannot overpower them and compel them to work, yet he can bring them to do his will:

1. He finds out the temper and disposition of the one he desires to serve him. He has developed a great deal of skill in doing so. He knows that these Sabeans are a people who love to plunder, so he knows what is in other men also.

2. He lays his bait of temptation so as to please a man's inclinations and desires. If a man lusts for riches then that will be the bait. If he lusts for fame, that will be the bait.

3. Satan can put into the mind of men notions and motions to do evil. He not only can present a certain oportunity to sin, but he can put it into the heart of a man to betray Christ and God (as he did with Judas—John 13:2). He is a spirit and has access to our spirits in order to make his filthy suggestions to them (as he did to Christ in the wilderness). *"Why has Satan filled your heart,"* Peter said to Ananias.

So here Satan has filled the heart of the Sabeans with the desire to rob and murder Job's servants. And, more, he is able to irritate and to provoke the hearts of those who do not immediately fall in with his purposes. Satan was able to provoke David to number the people (1 Chron. 21:1). He did not only inject the thought into David, but he provoked him, never letting him alone, not letting up until his solicitation had been acted upon. Yet all Satan's servants are volunteers, he cannot commandeer an army from either the ungodly or the godly. Of course, some come into his service easier than others. He needs not prod some into running to do his will because they are already running to do so. Just as the Assyrians were doing the will of God gladly (Isa. 10) because they strongly desired to destroy the Israelites and to seize their country, so do Satan's helpers in every age gladly fulfill his will.

Satan could have destroyed all of Job's estate by his own mighty power. The wicked angels are principalities and powers—they can do many things without using men for their instruments. Why then does Satan here use man? It is because he loves to draw men into sinning against God. He can do his work alone, yet he desires to have men join him in it. He is imitating God, who can do all things without the help of man, but who chooses to use men to fulfill His purposes as a means of showing His power and glory. Satan does indeed do mischief to Job either way he chooses, but by using the Sabeans and other men he does evil to both Job and to those he uses as instruments. He not only desires to make Job miserable and the Sabeans miserable, but he wants to make sure they do not serve God in anything they do. Sin separates between God and the creature. Therefore, Satan seeks to make men sin. The Lord Jesus said that there was nothing in Him which Satan could use in tempting Him. But all men have much sin and corruption for Satan to rake in. The Sabeans loved to rob and plunder, so Satan shows them where they can do so.

"they have killed the servants with the edge of the sword"—It was a great affliction to lose his oxen and asses, but this loss of his servants was a far greater sorrow to Job. The mouth of the sword had devoured his servants, with only one to come and tell the sad tale. *"And I only have escaped alone to tell you"*—The man is both horrified and amazed that he is the only one to escape the mouth of the sword. Satan had seen to it that this one was left to come and trouble Job. It was intended to increase the weight of sorrow, to be certain that the man's tale would start Job's wounds to flowing, that one was left. And no other one would do, for it must be Job's own trusted servant to tell the story. Rumors are too uncertain to cause shock in a man like Job. Truly the tender mercies of Satan are cruel, for he spared one man that he might destroy another.

"While he was still speaking, there also came another and said, the fire of God has fallen from the heavens and has burned up the sheep and the servants, and has destroyed them. And I only have escaped alone to tell you"—Job 1:16.

Afflictions seldom go alone, they more often come one in the neck of the other. Job was still laboring under the heavy blow just delivered to him by the first servant when this one brings still a sadder story. Satan has been careful not to give him the least breathing spell. As wave overtakes wave in the sea, evil often treads upon the heel of another. With demonish glee, Satan sets out to overwhelm Job's spirit.

"The fire of God has fallen"—Why is it here called the fire of *"God"*? Some say it is because the fire was sent from God (as in Gen. 19:24, *"the Lord rained fire and brimstone"* upon Sodom. In many places fire comes down out of the heavens as judgment from God). But here it is called *"the fire of God"* for another reason. This is not a fire sent from God in the usual sense, for it is Satan who kindled it, who had been given the power and authority to bring it down on Job's helpers. But it may be called *"the fire of God"* because of the strange wonder of this fire, it was an extraordinary fire. It is usual to use the name of God (*El, Elohim,* or *Jehovah*) as an epithet, as a descriptive word to heighten the excellence or rareness of things. For example, we find the phrase often, *"a man of God."* The Hebrews call one a man of God only if he is an extraordinary man, a man of an excellent spirit, a holy man. In Psalm 80:10, that which is called *"beautiful cedars"* is in the original actually *"the cedars of God."* That which is called a most *"vehement flame"* is actually *"a flame of Jehovahh."* This, then is called a fire of God because it is an extraordinally vehement flame. The Hebrews call all wonder and excellencies the things of God because all the glory and goodness that is in a created thing is but a footstep, a print or a drop of that excellency and glory and power that is in God. It is peculiarly fitting that God's name should be stamped upon all excellent things in the creation, for He is the cause of all our creature-excellence.

It is presumed that this fire which fell down from the heavens was a massive flash or sheet of lightening. The Devil, being the prince of power in the air (Eph. 2:1) can do mighty things in the air when God sets him loose to do so. He can raise storms, with fearful rolls of thunder and lightning. If man with his skill can do wonderful things, how much more might we expect from the angels! He performs signs and lying wonders which we may not conceive (2 Thess. 2:9), so it may be that such a marvel as this is well within his power.

"and has burned up the sheep and the servants, and has destroyed them"—Literally, it burned them and ate them up. After the devouring sword above comes this devouring fire to eat up Job's sheep and another group of his servants. Not that they were necessarily consumed, for the same word is used of Nadab and Abihu, yet they were not burned to ashes (for they were carried out and buried in their garments).

It is interesting that Satan chose to burn up these sheep and servants, instead of having a group of plunderers swoop down upon them. No doubt the reason is this, that there would be more sting in his affliction for Job because fire coming down from the heavens might persuade Job that God had become his enemy. When we suffer from men and devils we moan to God and seek solace in Him. No doubt Job did this when the first messenger was reporting his calamity. Now, however, with Satan whispering in his ear that God was the one bringing disaster upon him, where can he go with his complaint? So did Satan try to undermine Job's faith. As it happened, Job did still go to God, proof that he had an extraordinary skill and strength in spiritual matters.

One of the chief designs of Satan is to provoke a servant of God to think ill of God. He tries to persuade them that God is their enemy. He tries to arouse suspicion in us that the love and good will of God is for someone else, and that it is for His selfish purposes. And those afflictions which appear to be directly from God are most grevious ones. Even if God only withdraws His comforts from us, our souls sink. How much more do we faint when the wrath of God appears to be upon us. But we do not let Satan persuade us to quit praying, then Christ will come and intercede for us, casting Satan down to defeat again. *"While he was still speaking, there also came another and said, The Chaldeans made out three bands and swooped down upon the camels, and they have carried them away; yea and have killed the servants with the edge of the sword. And I only have escaped alone to tell you"*—Job 1:17.

The main difference between this affliction and the first affliction is in the people Satan used. The Chaldeans are painted in Scripture as *"that bitter and hasty nation which shall march through the breadth of the land to possess the homes that are not theirs. They are terrible and fearful...Their horses are swifter than the leopards and are more fierce than the evening wolves. And their horsemen shall spread themselves...They shall all come for violence..."* (Hab. 1:6-9). They were sent against the Israelites as God's judgment for hypocrisy. In this place, they are sent upon Job's possessions and servants by Satan in an effort to breach Job's faith. In both cases it is the wicked who seemingly prosper. Habakkuk is scandalized by this fact, asking of God, *"You are of purer eyes than to behold evil and cannot look upon iniquity—why then do You look upon those who deal deceitfully; Why do You hold Your tongue when the wicked devours him who is more righteous than he?"* If ever you set out to plead with God about such things, be certain to arm yourself with Jeremiah's argument, *"You are righteous, O Lord"* (12:1) before you open your mouth. It is a rare thing for God to make a good man his rod to scourge another of His children. Usually He uses the worst of men as His rod, His sword, to afflict His people. And they may be compared with the basest things in life, being mere scouring pads to shine up the gold in us.

"While he was still speaking, there also came another and said, Your sons and your daughters were eating and drinking wine in their oldest brother's house. And, behold, a great wind came from the wilderness and struck the four corners of the house, and it fell upon the young men, and they are dead. And I only have escaped alone to tell you"—Job 1:18,19

This fourth affliction is the worst by far. Satan has waited until Job is beaten down by blow after blow, now he delivers what he considers to be the death blow to Job's faith. If he had sent word about the death of his children first, then word of the other losses would have been as nothing to Job. But as Job's estate melted away and he became distressed at each report, there was reason to believe that the loss of his children would leave him amazed, dispirited and open for evil suggestion. A man's children are an extension of himself, and in those days the loss of even one son was counted matter for consternation. By bereaving Job of all his sons, Satan has all but disemboweled Job. That he should also at the same time lose all his many daughters was a further shock. An affliction is lesser or greater according to the impact it produces, the sorrow it spreads upon us. Truly, then, this was a great affliction for Job, one that smothered him in sorrow.

That all the children were taken away suddenly and unexpectedly further heightened the affliction. One can prepare in some measure for an expected death—though how one might prepare for the death of all ten of his children might be questioned. But when such news is delivered amidst joy and a sense of wellbeing, on the heels of other disasters which are seldom visited upon anyone, there is certainly a crushing weight added to the father. And there is something further in the fact that their death was a violent one. It stirs the senses and quickens the loss when we see in our imagination the violent blows falling on the heads of our loved ones. Then, too, there is always a suspicion in the public mind that those who die extraordinarily violent deaths are greater sinners than others (as Paul with the viper hanging from his arm).

Lastly, they were taken away when they were feasting and drinking wine. If Job (verse 5) felt constrained to offer up sacrifices lest his children had sinned and cursed God in their hearts, while they were alive—how much more might he have been saddened by such a thought after they had been suddenly stricken with death during their feasting. What if they had died without reconciliation to God? Did David lament over Absolom? How much more could Job lament over the death of all ten of his children.

The people of God should be stirred up by this sad but informative family history. When afflictions seem greatest, more may be behind. Let your ties to Christ be strengthened; let your prayers be without ceasing, for then as Satan increases the ferocity of his attacks you will also see Christ increase and multiply His assistance—you will be given strength and faith to bear up under all the blows, however violent, however unexpected they may be.

"Your sons and your daughters, etc. "—this verse is covered under verse 13.

"and behold, a great wind came from the wilderness"—When you see a *"behold"* in the Scriptures, you may expect something which warrants your complete attention. It is God's word for, *"Listen!"* or, *"Watch!"* or *"Beware!"* Great things, sudden and unexpected, things, rare things which are properly cause for wonder and admiration, these are nearly always prefaced with a *"Behold!"* This, then, being the greatest of the afflictions upon Job, there is an *Ecce* to center your attention upon what follows, for it is most important that you do not miss it.

"a great wind"—Not only a strong wind, but an extraordinarily great wind. *"came from the wilderness"*— or literally, from beyond the wilderness. Winds come from various quarters of the globe. In various localities, there can be some predictions made about the winds that come from this or that quarter. It was an east wind, a burning, cutting wind that set upon Jonah and made him want to faint and die. This wind is from beyond the wilderness, presumably the wilderness of Edom; or, perhaps it was the Arabian desert.

As with the fire from the heavens, this could have been from God or from Satan. Ordinarily the winds are in God's control, *He gathers the wind in his fists and sends it which way He pleases"* (Prov. 30:4). But at present the winds are given into the hand of Satan; or, at least this particular wind was so given. And it was a terrible wind, a great wind.

"and struck the four corners of the house"—The Hebrew word is the same used in verse 11, where Satan says, *"touch all that he has."* Here it is, *"and touch the four corners."* How could a wind coming from one quarter smite all four corners of the house? It is an extraordinary, a fare wind, one that is brought to our attention with a *"behold!"* Could it not have been a whirlwind, a tornado? Perhaps, but it may have simply been a wind to accomplish Satan's purpose, one which has no counterpart in our everyday world.

"and it fell upon the young men, and they are dead"—But what of the three daughters? They are not named, but they are also involved. It is not unusual for both sexes to be included when only the superior sex is mentioned. Later we are told all Job's children died.

"Then Job arose and tore his robe, and shaved his head, and fell down upon the ground and worshiped. An he said I came naked out of my mother's womb, and naked shall I return there. The Lord gave, and the Lord has taken away. Blessed be the name of the Lord. In all this Job did not sin, nor charge God foolishly"—Job 1:20-22.

These three verses make up the third division of the first chapter. We have seen Job's character described, with a list of his possessions. We have seen afflictions, with a full revelation of the causes. We have seen the instruments and the manner of afflictions. Now we will see whether God or Satan is right in telling the character and purposes of Job:

1. We have in these three verses Job's carriage and behaviour, then God's testimony as to how he behaved. We are told what Job did, then what Job said.

A. Job arose; he tore his robe; he shaved his head; he fell down on the ground; and he worshiped God.

B. Job said, I came from my mother's womb naked; I shall return naked; The Lord gave; The Lord has taken away; Blessed be the name of the Lord.

C. God gives His testimony that Job had not sinned in his heart, or by his mouth. He could well challenge Satan to bring forth a single thought or word which could be in any construed to be a cursing of God.

"Then Job arose and tore his robe"—Nothing of Job's actions or words are recorded in regard to the three great afflictions which hit him first. But this last blow was so terrible, so soul-disturbing as to move him into action and words. He arose. Not that he necessarily was sitting or lying down before, but in Scripture one may arise when he is doing a thing speedily, or when he does a thing immediately (when Joab arose and went to Absolom,

the meaning is plainly that he rose up quickly and immediately went to see why Absolom had set fire to his fields). Secondly, to arise in Scripture is sometimes put for the courage, constance and strength of those who go about a business. These do a thing with spirit and determination. So here, Job arose and tore his robe, with spirit and determination seizing upon God's for his strength, he shows he was not drowned in the sorrows which had flooded in upon him. When Eli heard that the Ark of God was taken, he had no more spirit in him, he fell down backwards and broke his neck. When Nabel heard of the danger he was in from speaking nasty words to David's men, *"his heart died within him, and he became like a stone."* But when Job heard all that Satan had brought upon him, his spirit was still in him and he arose to prepare himself for the worship of God. Then he fell down and worshiped Him.

"and tore his robe"—There are two cases when the robe is torn in Scripture: (1) when there is extreme sorrow; (2) when there is extreme indignation.

(1) There may be sorrow because of affliction, and there may be sorrow because of repentance. In great funerals, in cases of mourning, it was usual for the Hebrews to tear their garments (and it was not unknown to other nations, either) Also in cases of repentance, there was usually a tearing of the clothes (when Joshua humbled himself because of the defeat at Ai, *"he tore his clothes and fell to the earth"*—Joshua 7:6). Josiah tore his garments when he realized how far the nation had departed from the rule and word of God (2 Chron. 34: 20).

(2) Hezekiah is an example of a Hebrew king tearing his garments because of indignation, (1 Kings 19:1). Indignation is anger and sorrow boiled up to the height. It is the extract of both of them. It is especially stirred when one who loves the Lord sees or hears blasphemy of blatant wickedness directed against his beloved God. Paul and Silas tore their clothes when they saw and heard the people of Lystra prepare to sacrifice to mere men.

As for Job, he may have torn his garments for any of these reasons. His sorrow was very great indeed. This can very well be seen by the fact that he was so hurt and so much humiliated under that hand of God, with repentance for his many sins welling up within his breast-for though he had not sinned in these particular matters, he knows that no human being is clean and pure from sin at any time.Lastly, he certainly is filled with indignation at the blasphemies which Satan must have been suggesting to him in trying to break down his faith. Surely, if Satan desired Job to curse God, then there is little reason to doubt that Satan accompanied every messenger of doom and solicited Job to think evil thoughts of God for allowing these calamities.

"and shaved his head"—The shaving of the head has different significations at different times in the Scripture. This instance in Job was prior to the giving of the Law, and there was certainly no law against the shaving of the head in times of grief. Even after the giving of the Law, there were numerous instances when the prophets called for the shaving of the head, *"In that day the Lord God of Hosts called to weeping and to mourning and to baldness,"* that is, to the shaving of the head (Isa. 22:12). Both Job's tearing of his robe and his shaving of his head, then, are expressions of his great sorrow.

WHEN GOD AFFLICTS US WE SHOULD FEEL IT—WE SHOULD BE HUMBLED

There are two extremes to avoid during a time of affliction: (1) despising the affliction; (2) fainting at the affliction. Both are mentioned in one verse, *"my son do not despise the chastening of the Lord, nor faint when you are rebuked by Him"* (Heb. 12:5).

(1) We despise the chastening of the Lord when we do our utmost to keep our afflictions from affecting us. If we are losing our state, then we must not act as if it did not matter. If our children die, we must not act as if no great affliction had been visited upon us. When God lays His heavy hand upon us, dare we to act as if it were not there? Job did no such thing, but he arose and tore his robe, displaying his sorrow and repentance, readying himself to worship God, to kiss the hand that was afflicting him.

(2) Some go to the other extreme, they do not despise and take lightly their affliction.

but they faint under it. When a child dies, the spirit within the parent dies too. When their worldly hopes are dashed, they either become suicidal or go clear out of their minds. Job walks in the middle of these two dangers. He does not carelessly despise the chastening of the Lord, neither does he unbelievingly faint. He rises up and tears his robe, making it known that he did not faint under the stroke, and also that he felt the stroke. He did not attempt to make of himself a stock or a stone, nor was he trying to attain a Stoical apathy. He faces up to his sad state with Christian fortitude and magnanimity. James teaches us to rejoice in many tribulations, but that does not mean that we are to slight them, much less to make sport of them. Rejoicing is the direct result of a holy satisfaction which we feel toward God in all His dealings with us. Despising arises from an unholy contempt, or at best from a stupid insensibleness which does not recognize how God is dealing with the despiser. There is no virtue in bearing what we do not feel. *"and fell down upon the ground and worshiped"*—To fall upon the ground prior to worship is an acceptable gesture of worship, whether one is in sorrow or is in a state of rejoicing. The wise men were rejoicing when they fell down to worship Christ. There are other acceptable worship-gestures, such as standing, sitting and walking. Solomon stood before the altar of the Lord (1 K. 8:22); David sat before the Lord and prayed (2 Sam. 2:18); and Isaac walked as he prayed (the original word means to pray, not just to meditate)—Gen. 24:63. But usually the Hebrews fell to the ground to worship God, and in N.T. worship we have followed this pattern.

To worship is to give to anyone the honor that is due to him. We worship God when we give Him the love, reverence, service and honor which is due to Him; *"Give to the Lord the honor due to His name"* (Ps. 29:2). There is an internal worship of God, and there is an external worship. We worship God internally when we love Him, fear Him, rest in Him in hope and confidence. You may be sure that Job worshiped God by putting forth love and holy fear, acting in his heart to feel dependence upon God, placing complete faith and trust in Him. Thoughts like these may well have come from Job's heart, 'Lord, I will not depart from You or deal false with You even though all this has come upon me. I know that You are the same today as you were yesterday, true, holy, gracious, merciful, loving, kind, all-sufficient and ever-present. Lord, here I lie before You with a yearning to have You love me more, to have You fill me with reverence toward You. Lord, I trust You. Lord, I know You are my portion forever. Though there would never be anything more for me than what I have in You, O God, I would be content; yea, I would rejoice. You are enough; You are more than enough for me; You are my all in all, come what may.'

External worship is the serving of God according to His own express. He has instituted a form of worship, He has written in a book, and it is up to us to see that we study His directions so that we may worship Him in spirit and in truth and in the exact way that He has commanded. Job worshipped God acceptably when he fell to the ground and worshiped; by praying to Him, and by acknowledging His rights.

Job showed his sorrow by his acts. Yet we must not forget that he did not sorrow as do those who have no hope. He gives his respect to his departed children, but he reserves the best part of himself for His everlasting Father. His body fell to the earth, but his heart was raised up to Heaven. His afflictions had separated him from all that he owned on this earth, but they drew him close to God and all that he had for everlasting possessions in the world to come. He turned all his afflictions into prayers and praises. God strikes, Job prays. God afflicts, Job worships. Grace makes every condition work for God, just as surely as God makes all things work together for good to those who are the called.

"And he said, I came naked out of my mother's womb"—As Job opened his mouth, no doubt Satan is there looking for the opportunity to snatch a word out of his mouth and prove that Job had cursed God. Even as he fell to the ground, after having torn his robe, and shaving his head, Satan and others might have thought that he was but enraged and maddened, distracted or drunked because of sorrow. But now he opens his mouth and issues gracious words, not only rational and intelligible words, but words which have the very stamp of God upon them. Every word gave God glory, yet every word seemed espec-

ially tailored to give the lie to Satan's slanders. How crushing it must have been when Job blessed God—not cursed, but blessed— *"Blessed be the name of the Lord."*

Job is speaking here of his bodily nakedness, for he was far from naked spiritually, being more richly clothed upon with spiritual ornaments and dress than ever before. But it is not only the lack of clothing of which Job speaks, but the lack of all bodily comforts as well.

"and naked shall I return there"—The only difficult word is the word *"there."* Where? Certainly he does not contemplate returning to his mother's womb. Some say it means the grave, or return to God. There is a possibility that adverbs of place, as this is, not only signify place, but also a state, a condition in which one may be. So when Job says, *"naked shall I return there"* he may mean, I was naked before, so I shall return to such a state of nakedness again.

Yet it may be that Job refers to the womb of the earth, that is, the grave. Taking the womb of his mother properly and the womb of the earth (the earth is the common parent of us all) improperly, Job shall return to that womb naked again. The earth then will be a-gain pregnant with mankind, and one day shall bring forth mankind again. For the whole creation groans now, waiting for the redemption. And resurrection is called a birth in Acts 13:33, where Paul refers Psalm 2:7 to the resurrection of Christ;

A GODLY MAN FINDS ARGUMENTS TO JUSTIFY GOD IN ALL HIS DEALINGS

Job could not have found a better or stronger argument for acquitting God than this one, that he still has as much as he brought into this world. What harm had been done to me, he says, I still have all I had in the beginning. Wicked men are not so, for they will fall to studying out a way to blame God for their troubles (as did Adam and Eve). But godly men labor to clear God, as did David, *"I will confess my sin...Against You, You only, have I sinned and done this evil in Your sight; that You might be justified when You speak and be clear when You judge"* (Ps. 51:3,4). He is not seeking to lay the blame on God. He is seeking to take the blame off of God and onto himself. So Job here sees things in God's light, that God gives where nothing is due, that God sometimes takes off what He gave, and that there is no possibility that we shall have less in the end than we had at the very beginning. If he had nothing but the clothes on his back, he had more than he had in the beginning. The clear knowledge of what we were, and of what we shall be at death makes a godly man content, and godliness with contentment is great gain.

"The Lord gave, and the Lord has taken away"—Job mounts another argument for the justice of God in His severe dealings with his possessions. Job is not merely admitting his frailty, his inability to help himself. He is acknowledging God's sovereignty, that he knows *"every good and perfect gift is from above"* (James 1:17). The Lord gave—it was a gift, a gift is undeserved, not earned. Not only the gifts of grace, the fruits of the Spirit, but also every gift of the things of this world are undeserved by any of us. We have nothing that we have not received as a free gift. Now God had given Job such and such things, houses, cattle, servants and many children—all gifts, all undeserved. Job does not say that he earned them, or that he was rewarded with them. God gave them.

"The Lord gave"—It is proof of Job's honesty. If he had gotten riches by stealing, by oppressing and grinding the faces of the poor, by deceit or by fraud, then he could not have said, The Lord gave. The Lord does not give in any such way, except it be a judgment on the one receiving goods in this way. Unlawful acts are under the eye of God's providence, but they are not under the influence of His blessing. Wicked men may thrive, but they are never blessed. Any prosperity they have is but a curse upon them.

These words, *"The Lord gave"* will cut off four monstrous lusts, two of which afflict the rich, and two of which mostly afflict the poor. The rich swell with pride. The rich fill with contempt. The poor, on the other hand are filled with discontent. And they are assaulted by envy.

As to the pride of the rich, they are warned, *"Charge those that are rich, that they be not high-minded nor to have hope in the fickleness of riches. But let them hope in the living God"* (1 Tim. 6:17). Paul's argument holds for temporal things also, *"If you have received it, why do you boast?"* (1 Cor. 4:7). If your estates are of God, where is there room for any pride? God cannot be imagined to be under any obligation to you, else it would be no gift. And if your estates are gotten by dishonesty, then they are the gift of Satan—surely that would be no reason for pride. As for contempt, those who despise others, for whatever reason, also despise God. Once they admit that it is God that gives, they also admit that God may just as well have made the other person rich and talented, etc. How can a man be contemptuous of another man, when that other man could just as well tomorrow exchange places with him? God builds up. God tears down. God makes rich, and poor.

The poor often are endangered by the lust of discontent. If they would but remember that it is the Lord who gives, they would find themselves content. If it is God in His wisdom who has determined your portion, how can you imagine yourself to be better able to determine your share. Everything in this world is in a precarious balance. God is the One who holds these things in balance. Would you upset the balance by grasping for the things that you are not supposed to have? You shall fall, but God will not give you a whit more than He has wisely decreed for you to have. As for envy, remember the Lord's own words, *"Is it not lawful for me to do what I wish in that which is mine? Is your eye evil because I am good?"* (Matt. 20:15). If all were taught well that it is God that gives, this evil malignancy of envy would soon be dispelled. If it is the Lord who gives all, then we should be studying how we may repay somewhat to Him—not how we may snatch from others what God has given them. In fact, they own nothing, and you own nothing. All belongs to God. He has loaned out this and that to you. You have the loan of this, another has the loan of that. In God's wisdom, this is how it ought to be. In your thankfulness for the things you are allowed to use, be diligent to look for ways to give God His glory, His service.

"And the Lord has taken away"—Sabeans took the oxen and asses; fire took the sheep; Chaldeans took the camels; Satan's windstorm took the children; but Job sees through it all, that it is the Lord who has taken away. The thievery belonged to men, the wickedness to men and Satan, but the ultimate glory belonged to God. For God has men and devils, fire and wind, everything in His hand, to dispose of as He will. Job knew that if there was evil in the city, the Lord surely has disposed it to be so (Amos 3:6). He looked beyond the created things and sent his heart flying up to Heaven to get an explanation of things as they had fallen out. Note that Job is not angry with God, or with Satan, or with those cruel men who murdered his servants. He puts his trust in God and waits for Him to do whatever He will for the future. Not knowing the mind of God, not knowing what God must do in order to bring about all His purposes, Job humbly bows, like David when he said, *"I opened not my mouth because You were the One who did it."*

"Blessed be the name of the Lord"—With these words, God's judgment of Job is completely and unquestionably vindicated. The name of God is in Scripture taken for God Himself, *"according to Your name, so is Your praise"* (Ps. 48:10). The name of God is also put for the attributes of God. Thirdly, the name of God is put for His ordinances or worship. Again, the name of God is that reverence, esteem and honor which angels and men give to God.

We bless God when we praise Him for His goodness, greatness, mercy, faithfulness, etc. God is blessed when we have great and glorious thoughts of Him, when we inwardly fear and love Him. So, we bless with the tongue, and with the heart. When the tongue blesses without the heart, it is but a tinkling cymbal. When the heart blesses without the tongue, it is giving forth music to God, but not to men. Job blesses God in both ways. For it would not have been enough for Job merely to bear his affliction in silence, or even with grace. He must bless God for sending these afflictions to him, for this is the highest form of grace. If we bless God in our afflictions, then our afflictions shall indeed be a blessing to us. It is a signal that the time has come for the goodness which has been hidden in back of the afflictions to come forth and make the heart of the troubled one glad. Pour out for yourselves the oil of gladness by pouring out of your heart blessings upon the name of God.

"In all this Job did not sin, nor charge God foolishly"– This is God speaking of Job, giving testimony which cannot be overturned, that Job has passed his severe test without sin. But is it possible for a man to be entirely free from sin in any action, or course of actions? Because the Roman Catholics try to use this verse and a few others to build a false doctrine, that a man may be kept from all sin while in this life, we answer:

1. Job affirms himself that it is impossible to act without sin, saying, *"Who can bring a clean thing out of that which is unclean? No one!"* (14:4), and in another place says, *"The stars are not pure in His sight, how much less man, who is a maggot...a worm?"* (25:5,6).

Sinful actions are of two kinds: (1) some are sinful in the thing that is done, such as stealing, lying, etc.; (2) others are sinful in the way they are done–a good work may be done only in the way that God prescribes, for the same act done in another way will be displeasing to God, therefore sinful. A regenerate person may follow a course of actions, doing many things, none of which are sinful things. The divine nature, of which we partake, being guarded and nurtured by the Holy Spirit of God hovering over us, will insure that we for the most part of our lives will be choosing out activities which have the approval of God. But, at the same time, it is positive that the works of regenerate persons have some defilement in them–yes, even their best works will have sin in them to some degree. There is a great deal of difference, however, between a sinful action and sin in an action. In Ex. 28:38, we see this distinction pictured for us. The High Priest there is said to *"bear the iniquity of the holy things."* They were holy things, yet there was iniquity in them. They were holy things by definition, in the matter of them. But in the manner of performing them, there was sin.

When it is said that *"in all this Job did not sin,"* we are to understand that Job did not do any sinful act in all this time of trial. Job did not complain, he did not charge God with blame, he did not mourn inordinately, he did not wish he still had his possessions, etc. It is not said that no sinful notions ever entered into Job's head, or that there were no sinful thoughts not connected with these trials, but that in these things he did not sin.

Again, it should be noted that Scripture often gives an overall judgment of a life, or of a character. David is said to have been a man after God's own heart, except in the matter of Uriah the Hittite (1 Kings 15:5), that he did not turn aside from anything the Lord commanded except in that matter. Yet the Scriptures note for us David's inordinate grief over Absalom, David's lie to Achish, etc. On balance, David's life was a holy life, one given to God to use as He would–so he is given this character, that he was holy, a man according to God's own heart, etc. So here Job is said not to have sinned, in the way the Apostle writes, *"little children, sin not"* (1 John 2:1). That is, do not sin as wicked men do, who choose out nothing but sinful acts to perform. Job avoided all forms of sin, did not sin against God though his whole world was snatched out of his hand. It is not said that there was no defilement to be found, because that is not what is being taught here.

"or charged God foolishly"–Literally, he did not give God any folly. This word translated *"foolishly,"* or, *"folly,"* is a word which means nothing that is unduly disposed. Job did not accuse God of disposing things in a wrong way. It also means that Job did not accuse God of any kind of disorder. There was no madness, no lack of order, no unseemliness, no unsavory aspect to the acts of God in dealing with Job and his possessions. But if Satan's estimate of Job had been correct, Job would have been mouthing all kinds of charges against God by now. You have heard such mad and foolish words from some, no doubt: 'What have I done that I should deserve this? Is this the thanks I get for serving God night and day, sacrificing my time, my money and my talents to bring glory to Him? Does He seek to discourage me from working for Him? Will not others despise Him because of what He does to a good servant like me? Is there any justice in a God who makes the innocent suffer? If someone had to lose all he had, why couldn't it have been some swearer or adulterer? Is this the way God protects His servants from men and Satan? Then how can it be said that He is all-powerful and omniscient?' etc. Men do not lack blasphemies to hurl at God's head. But Job did not charge God with such folly. If he had, he would have cursed!

Some things may be learned from these words:

1. Impatience under God's hand, murmuring at ill-happenings which God brings across our paths, is a charging of God with foolishness and disproportionate distribution of His favors. If you do not realize that complaints have a charge in them, try making a complaint to someone you love and then listen. You will hear them deny the charge you are making against them. It is only by living quietly and willingly under the chastening hand of God that we give Him praise and honor and glory.

2. One of the highest acts of grace is to be composed in thoughts and word while under great afflictions. It is a real evidence of God's inworking power when His children evidence their complete trust in His management of the world. Rare are those who attain this true serenity, this full faith.

3. When we have done truly well, God Himself will give testimony. And God's testimony will be a fair one. It is true that when we have done all, we have but done what we ought to have done—we are still to be considered unprofitable servants. Yet, by the goodness of God, in the purpose of God, there is a ready acknowledgment of all our obedient acts. It would be possible, even right, for God to shut up our good deeds until the day of judgment. But here it pleases Him to bedeck Job with His garland of praises, giving him public notice so as to endear him and advertise him to all generations from then until now. Who then could blow his own trumpet and get such a long-lasting effect? If you are a hypocrite, then well might you need to blow your own horn. But if your acts are truly worthy of praise, then who gives praise better than God Himself?

Now that Job has come through these first severe trials without wound and without any touch of sin, Satan is beside himself because of his defeat and frustration by Job. So his engines are set at work to find out a way to still prove that he was right in charging Job with self-serving instead of God-serving love. A wicked mind will never believe that there is any other kind, *"Unto the pure, all things are pure. But to the defiled and unbelieving, nothing is pure—but both their mind and conscience are defiled"* (Titus 1:15).

"Again there was a day when the sons of God came to present themselves before the Lord. And Satan also came among them to present himself before the Lord."—Job 2:1

As the prophet Ezekiel in his vision was shown one abomination, then was led forward and was shown another and another; or, as the angel proclaimed in the Revelation, *"one woe is past, and another woe is at hand,"* so it is in the history of Job's sorrows. Having seen his first afflictions, now we shall behold greater afflictions than these. Having watched him in one woeful day of catastrophe, now we must watch greater woes than these.

In this second chapter, we see in Job's second great trial the following: (1) the occasion; (2) the causes; (3) the manner, or, the way it happened; (4) the consequents.

(1) The occasion was when Satan was again summoned before God, where God questions him regarding Job's successful defense of God's word and power in sustaining faith. Satan replied with slander, and put forth a proposition designed to entrap God into giving Job to him under better circumstances than those that prevailed before.

(2) The causes of this affliction again were two, God and Satan. God permitted this second trial by Satan for purposes of His own glory and for Job's well-being in the future. Satan lashed out in vengeance against Job, inflicting all the pain and misery he was permitted by this second commission.

(3) This time Satan was permitted to strike Job's body, and he proceeded to do so with the most troublesome disease and the most debilitating circumstances he could devise with his trained, wicked mind.

(4) The result was that Job's wife immediately fell victim to Satan's assault, counseling Job to curse God and die. Secondly, Job's severe illness brought his three friends to comfort him.

"Again there was a day"—Since most of the matter in the first three verses here were covered in the exposition of the first chapter, only a little inquiry as to what day this might be, plus the time that may have expired between these two days, remains.

The Jewish doctors would have us believe that this was the first day in the year, that God had a day of audit each year, a day when He convened the angels to report. This is a gross and groundless assumption. Others fix this as the last day of the week, the Sabbath day. These say that this was a solemn assembly called for the worship of the Lord (presenting themselves before the Lord—worshiping before the Lord. Some even affirm that throughout the Old Testament the *"sons of God"* are always angels, and that in Genesis 6 the angels, either good or bad, took on bodies and begot giants. This is a conceit of the evil imagination mentioned in Genesis 6:5, a monstrous idea which belongs among the fables of men. On the other hand, Chrysostom claims that angels are never called *"sons of God,"* which is the other extreme.

We may safely walk in the middle of these two extremes. Both angels and men are called *"sons of God."* See verse six of chapter one for instances of angels being so called. As for men, they are called sons of God for their power, or for their greatness. In Gen. 6:2, those called sons of God may have been so called because of greatness and power. But, secondly, they may have been so called because of their piety and holiness, by which they resembled God. They were serving God as sons serving the father. There was a sonship purchased by Christ, *"in the fullness of time...God sent forth His Son...so that we might receive sonship"* (Gal. 4:5). Those in the Old Testament were sons, as we are, though not in the same fullness and abundance of grace. In Scripture a thing is spoken of as newly done when it is more fully done (John 7:39). The Holy Spirit is said not to be given at that time because He had not been so plentifully given. In Heb. 9:8, we hear that the way into Heaven had not been opened because it was then more clearly opened. So we are said to receive the sonship when Christ came in the flesh because then our sonship was more apparent—yet is was just as real before.

So then according to this interpretation, the sense of these words may be that the servants of God (the faithful of that age and place) came together on the Sabbath day to worship God. And Satan, who lies in wait for the opportunity to oppose and resist us, to interrupt and disturb us when we appear before the Lord to worship, came among them also. This is but an opinion, but one which may answer to the facts revealed here in Scripture. It seems that the providence of God toward man is more in evidence here than a disconnected teaching regarding a congregation of the angels.

As to how much time may have passed between the first afflictions of Job and this set, we are not given any hint. It may be assumed that there was sufficient time for Job to fully recover his spirits and to be without excuse under the second onslaught. Just as the Devil *"departed from Him for a season"* when he had failed to tempt Christ, so it may be assumed he also went off here to lick his wounds.

"And the Lord said to Satan, Where do you come from? And Satan answered the Lord and said, From going to and fro in the earth, and walking up and down in it"—Job 2:2. A full exposition of this verse may be found under Job 1:7.

"And the Lord said to Satan, Have you set your heart to My servant Job, that there is none like him in the earth, a perfect and upright man, one who fears God and turns away from evil? And still he is keeping hold of his integrity, although you moved Me against him without cause"—Job 2:3.

That Satan may see that he has gained nothing by his first slanderous, then vicious assault upon Job, God repeats word for word His estimate of Job at this later date. However, He adds a further commendation, that Job has kept hold of his integrity. God calls to the attention of Satan, and to us, that Job has gained considerably from his first tribulations. Before he was a holy man, but now he is not only a holy man, but one who has been tried and approved as a soldier for the King. There has been combat, and the experience has brought a glorious additon to Job's character—integrity.

THOSE THAT HONOR GOD SHALL BE HONORED BY GOD

No one can lose anything by suffering for God, *"But even as you share in the sufferings of Christ, rejoice that also in the revealing of His glory you may be beside yourself with joy"* (1 Pet. 4:13). Once Job had suffered in order to glorify God, his old characterization will not serve any longer. He must now have this improvement of his gracious character made known. If we speak only a word for God, it shall be read back again, *"Those that feared the Lord spoke often to one another, and the Lord listened and heard it. And a book of remembrance was written before Him"* (Mal. 3:16). Not only is it recorded, but God is not like Ahasuerus, who forgot the service done him by Mordecai. Nothing done for God will be buried in dead files, everything we do shall be recompenced. When a soldier does well in battle, it is common for him to have a medal—here Job gets a greater honor, a new title is given him: Man of Integrity.

"And still he is keeping hold of his integrity"—Not only was Job such a man in the past, but he is even more so now. Time has not changed him for the worse. Afflictions have not changed him for the worse, but for the better. Then he was rich in this world's goods; now he is rich in treasures in another world. Job was a perfect man before, but now he has learned by suffering, he has been perfected, *"But may the God of all grace Himself make you perfect after you have suffered a little while"* (1 Pet. 5:10); *"But let patience have its perfect work, so that you may be perfect and complete"* (James 1:4). When all was light and gay in Job's life, he blessed God. Now that darkness has set in and has persisted, he still blesses God.

Our language is not comprehensive enough to express the meaning of the one Hebrew word which we translate *"keeping hold."* There is an implication of strength in holding, plus a firm and unyielding clinging. Furthermore, there is the implication of a growing strength, a faster hold resulting in a prevailing power (the same word is used when it is said that *"the king's word prevailed against Joab"* —2 Sam. 24:4). Job is growing stronger and stronger in his integrity, while his sinful propensities are growing weaker and weaker.

"his integrity"—Literally the word means all or any of these: sincerity, perfection, or

integrity. Now he is holding faster to these than he formerly could in his prosperous condition. If Satan found him a pestilent fellow before, a sincere man who stuck out like a sore thumb in Satan's world, now he looks upon Job as he kept hold of his sincerity, his perfection, his integrity, and growing stronger as he did so. He always devises his wiliest temptations for such men as this. It was not his oxen, his servants or even his children that Satan desired most to pull away from Job. It was his integrity that he yearned to undermine. Yet the very thing that Satan sought most to destroy is the thing which Job is said here to be holding faster and faster. Unless he could be separated from his integrity, there would be no malicious rejoicing among the denizens of Hell.

WHATEVER A GODLY MAN MAY LOSE, HE WILL HOLD TIGHT TO HIS GRACES

Let his worldly possessions go, let his freedom go, yes, even his children if it must be, but a godly man cannot let go of his God and Savior. And in order to hold fast to Christ, a Christian must hold fast to his integrity. Only a fool will sin in order to hold on to anything in this world. It is never necessary to sin in order to hold on to anything good. If it is good for you to have your children about you, then God will never call upon you to sin in order to keep them. But remember this, God is the One who decides what is good. You cannot possibly know what is good, either for your children, or for you. Once He decides to providentially separate you from your children, or from anything in this world that is dear to you, you may not keep hold of them—no matter how many sins you commit, no matter how you compromise or surrender your integrity, God's will shall be done and you will gain nothing by trying to delay or thwart it. The just can live only from faith to faith. His graces are his life, eternal life, the kind of life which he may not give to or for another. A godly man's only hope is in this one thing, that he may hold fast his integrity. Even in the heaviest storm of affliction, in the lowest slough of despondency, in the miriest pit of sin (as David in the matter of Uriah and Bathsheba), taking a stronger and stronger hold on one's integrity is the only hope you have of escaping with your eternal life.

Integrity is a Christian's weapon. Job lays hold upon his integrity and uses it as a sword to cut Satan's cords away, that he may sail back into godly waters. The Hebrew here may be fairly translated, *"he is prevailing in his integrity."* In the war with Satan, there are always and continually battles. As in a war between nations, one that lasts a century, there are times when one wins a battle, other times the other; sometimes, however, one begins to prevail and gets stronger and stronger until he wins the war. In this war with Satan, it is integrity which prevails. Our graces grow stronger and stronger, and we find that we truly are *"more than conquerors through Christ."*

"although you moved Me against him to destroy him without cause"—Literally, there is more than a bare motion, a bare persuasion here. This is a vehement instigation, a forceful argument which is urged more and more. Just as Jezebel *"stirred up"* Ahab to work wickedness (it is the same word as here), so Satan presented incitements to God in order to get Job turned over to him for destruction. But will God be moved by Satan? I answer:

1. The words of the saints in prayer are said to move God. Some, mistaking the efficacy of prayer, have thought that prayer is a means of persuading God to give things which were not before intended. These think that by their much speaking they can persuade God, or by words of wisdom and reasonable argument they can move Him to give what He before had refused to give. Such people are implying that God's mind may be changed. They are simply showing their ignorance of God. And since these things about God are a matter of record in the Bible, they are showing their ignorance of the Bible. Oftentimes it is a willful ignorance, an ignorance to make them more confortable in their sins.

God has said, *"I am the Lord, I change not!"* (Mal. 3:6). If God may be moved by your prayers, your arguments, then there is no such thing as a changeless God, as eternal decrees, as purposes fulfilled before the foundation of the world. If God ever changed, if even one new thought were to occur to Him, then He would no longer be God (or, it would prove that He was not God in the first place). For if God changes for the worse, He will no longer be God, for He will no longer be perfect. A god that is not perfect is not God at all. If, on the other hand, God were to change for the better, it would be proof positive that He was not perfect—for if He were perfect, He could not be better, and He would not be able to change for the better.

God is said to move, or to do this or that after we pray because He has decreed to move, or to do this or that at that very time, after we pray. It is all in God's purpose from eternity: (1) that you pray; (2) that you pray certain words in a certain manner, from a certain frame of heart; (3) that you are in Christ Jesus at the time, and that Christ intercede for you; (4) that He would at that time give to you such and such mercies—or, such and such chastisement for praying amiss. What a blasphemous pride seizes upon those who think themselves so skillful or so pure as to persuade even the everlasting God to act on their behalf. And as for those who think that God is obligated to move for them if they should follow the proper ritual and say the prescribed words. Satan has a field day with these self-deceiving hypocrites. Let them read the history of the Jews. They will see that God again and again rebukes them for such desperately wicked thoughts. See Isaiah 1:10-18, where God says, *"When you spread forth your hands, I will hide My eyes from you; yea when you make many prayers, I will not hear."*

God had a purpose from all eternity to try Job. He also decreed the way and the means. He even foredetermined that Satan would be the instigator, that Satan would come and ask God for permission, even thinking himself able to persuade God to give it. All things which come to pass, according to God's eternal purpose must come to pass in the exact time and order as God desires it—it is the only way He can administer this world, the only way He can control all forces and cause them to work together for the good of the saints, for the punishment of the wicked. Let those who do not understand such things make it a matter of prayerful study, for there is much in the Scriptures which may be understood by the poorest intellect, *"If anyone wants to practice His will, he shall know of the teaching"* (John 7:17). What is not written is not meant to be understood by us, at least not until we sit at the feet of the Lord Jesus Christ in Heaven.

This is another case, then, of God speaking of Himself as if He were a man like us, one who could be moved by incitement and persuasion. The truths to be conveyed to us in this whole picture are these: (1) Satan is an earnest solicitor of evil against God's people; (2) God intends to uphold His people against Satan, even when he is allowed to do his utmost damage to them.

(1) Without ceasing, Satan seeks to provoke God against the godly. Bending his wits and straining to reach the heights of insinuation, the old serpent petitions to have them put into his hands. And this notwithstanding his failure to do anything but improve them in every cause since the world began. If the Devil himself is so earnest and so zealous against us, is it not a shame to us if we are not equally earnest and zealous against him? If he is always moving against our fellowsaints, should we not always be looking for opportunity to encourage them and strengthen them against Satan? God has words to urge us to such duties, *"For Zion's sake I will not hold my peace"* (Isa. 62:1); *"give Him no rest until He makes Jerusalem in the earth"* (Isa. 62:6,7). Let your prayers of importunity be laid against God's door, for fervent prayer of a saint for another is mightily effectual.

"to destroy him"—Literally, to devour him, or to swallow him up. This is Satan's work, *"Be careful, watch! because your enemy, the Devil, walks around like a roaring lion, seeking whom He may swallow up"* (1 Pet. 5:8). When the seven lean ears ate up the seven full ears (Gen. 41:4), and when the rod of Moses swallowed up the rods of the magicians (Ex. 7:12), this same word is used. All the while Satan was claiming that he wanted Job but touched, he was actually wanting to destroy him, to devour him, to swallow him up.

"without cause"—Literally, for nothing. Satan is seeking to have God destroy Job for no reason at all. Job has not given any cause why Satan should devour him. Indeed the holiness and goodness of Job caused Satan grief and trouble, but it was not because Job was doing anything which was worthy of destruction. Or, the meaning may be this, that Satan

had given no sufficient cause for God to move against Job. That which Satan urged against Job, that Job served God for nought, was something he dreamed up out of his own brain. God will not have Satan's suspicions confirmed in any way, calling them entirely, *"without cause."* Again, the meaning may be this, that after all you said, after all you did, after all Job suffered, Satan, you have only proved that you are moving me against Job without a cause.

If you refer the words, *"without cause,"* to God, then let it be said that God does not do anything without a cause. The all-wise God does all things by weight and measure, with good reason. The least thing He does is based upon greater reason than the most important deeds of men. God's reasons for permitting Satan to test Job are many, among them being His desire to magnify His grace, His power, His love for His people. At the same time, He is showing Himself mighty and wise to strengthen Job's faith, to uphold him against the most violent onslaughts, to perfect him in patience and other graces right under the very nose of the Devil; yea, right in the midst of his powerful blows.

It should not be missed here that there is an answer in this verse to the later accusations of Job's friends. A man's afflictions may indeed come upon him, to the very uttermost of suffering, without a cause—that is, without the cause being in the sufferer, in the way of sin. There is of course sin enough in all of us to warrant the severest misery at any time. Yet it is not to be presumed that suffering and affliction are meted out in exact proportion to the sinfulness of the sufferer. It is here with Job, as it was with him in John 9, the happenings were against Job so *"that the works of God might be made manifest."*

Note this, that it is God who sums up for us, that we may not fail to be cleared from any guilt, that no one may be allowed to maintain malicious accusations against us. God does sometimes allow others in this life to add up the actions of the saints and come to a wrong conclusion. But at the Judgment, it will be found that God was keeping His own books, and He will announce the true sum of our attainments.

"And Satan answered the Lord and said, Skin for skin—yea, all that a man has he will give for his life"—Job 2:4.

Yes, says Satan, I have considered Job, and I have concluded that the only reason he is still holding onto his integrity is that you have kept me from putting him to the true test: For a man will give up everything in order to save his life. Here again we see why he is called the Tempter, the Accuser, The Slanderer, and The Father of Lies. He again boldly, calls into question God's conclusions, and he again slanders Job by inferring he is only a painted hypocrite.

We see here that malice is often steeped in wit. Satan uses a proverb, *"skin for skin, etc."* There is no admission that he was wrong before, when he was saying that Job served God for his riches, for his comfort, for his blessed life. But now his slander is changed, Job not any longer having these things, he now says that Job is serving God, for his breath, fearing for his life.

"Skin for skin"—The many interpretations of this obviously proverbial saying are enough to warn us that the meaning is obscure. Some of the interpretations are, (1) A man will venture the skin of one member of his body to save that of another. For instance, he will put up his arm to protect his head, willing to lose skin from the one to prevent the greater danger to the other. Thus, *"skin for skin, a man will give all he has for his life."* (2) In the days of the patriarchs, the economy was based largely on animals, and the skins of these were important sources of wealth. These interpreters believe that this *"skin for skin"* refers to the willingness of the ancient owners to give all their estate for their lives. (3) Then others think that because some early money was cut out of skins, this may be the reason for the proverb here. (4) The original may be rendered, *"skin upon skin,"* and if so, then the meaning may be that though a man had skin on top of skin, he would give them all to save his life. (5) Another possibly rendering would be, *"skin within skin,"* thus possibly referring to the two layers of skin every man has, inferring that he would give both his skins in order to save his life. (6) The copulative particle here may sometimes be rendered, *"so"* and in that case the reading would be, *"As a man will give skin for skin, so a man will part*

with all he has for his life" (See Proverbs 25:3, 25 for particles translated *"so").*

Whatever may be the actual meaning of *"skin for skin,"* it is certain that the teaching is this, that a man will barter anything for his life, risk anything for his life—life is precious and worth the sacrifice of anything and all things. From this we should learn to value our lives. If Satan thinks it important to rob you of your life, then you may be certain that it is of great value in the service of God. If a living dog is better than a dead lion, how much more is it so that a living saint is better than a dead hypocrite—not that all are better at acting like Christians than the hypocrites, but that all have become partakers of the divine nature and thus are capable of giving the greatest glory to God every day of their lives. And if your life is of great value because it gives opportunity to serve God, how much value must your soul have! Your life is but a vapor that appears for a little while, then vanishes away. Therefore we must not save our lives at the costs of our souls—What if you gain the whole world and save your life as well, but lose your own souls? Just as nature teaches us to value our lives above the world, so grace teaches us to value our souls above our lives.

"a man will give all he has for his life"—The Lord Jesus proved that there is something more precious than life when He gave His life a ransom for the souls of His people. He spent His whole life in the service of others, preparing a prefectly righteous life to give, then He gave that life that we might have Life, that abundant life, that everlasting life which the godly have as a gift from Him.

"Put forth Your hand now and touch his bone and his flesh, and he will curse You to Your face"—Job 2:5.

In 1:11 we have discussed the meaning of *"put forth Your hand,"* also the meaning of *"touch."* Here we have a different object suggested by Satan, who asks God to touch the bone and the flesh of Job this time. The bone and the flesh make up the whole body, so we know that Satan is asking for such a sore affliction as will sink into Job's very bones and marrow, one that will destroy the wellbeing of his entire body. Although the bone itself has no feeling, everyone know that some of the greatest pain a body can feel can come from pain in the bones, or around the bones.

"he will curse You to Your face"—this has been expounded in 1:11 also, but will have less force here because his first prediction of Job cursing God did not come true. There is in this expression, however, the implication that Satan may be blamed and proven to be wrong if Job does not in fact curse God after his bone and flesh are destroyed.

Again it would be wise to recognize that Satan does not give up, even when there is no reason to expect success, he keeps on trying to do evil. So ought we to feel in the doing of good, even when it seems we are not having any success. Note that when he could not prevail over Job by lesser means, he chooses out still greater means, promising himself success all the while. If we do not grow stronger and stronger in grace as he increases the assault upon our souls, then will we be inviting much misery into our lives.

There was wisdom in Satan's choice of Job's body for his next assault. Pain in the body will often unhinge or disturb the mind. Paul called his fleshly infirmity (whatever it was, no one knows) his *"temptation in my flesh"* (Gal. 4:14). If a man is afflicted sorely in his body, it is best for him to pray (James 5:13). When the fourth vial was poured out on the inhabitants of the earth, they blasphemed the name of God—it is possible for men to be brought to cursing God by miseries in their bodies.

*"And the Lord said to Satan, Behold! he is in your hand—but save his life"*Job 2:6.

The most fearsome thing for a man is to fall into the hands of the living God. Next to this, surely, is the falling of men into the hands of Satan. He did not get that name, Destroyer, for nothing. He has smitten bodies for dozens of centuries, millions upon millions of men have felt his sorceries. Again, here, God gives over to Satan power and authority to afflict Job, thus avoiding suspicion that the greatest of torture was withheld. Do not think that this excruciating trial of body, soul and spirit which Satan lets loose now upon Job is less than Satan could do. He has done his very utmost—there is no fine point of tribulation which Satan could devise which is not let loose on Job. Yet, for all that, the

Lord God could have troubled Job far more in a moment than Satan managed in days and days — simply by withdrawing the assurance of His presence, by ceasing to sustain Job's faith, God could have brought an unspeakable misery upon Job far greater than anything Satan could do. Yet it will be seen that Job's afflictions are cleverly designed, that they exceed what men alone could have planned and executed.

Satan again has his commission, but here is the chain, the limitation: *"save his life!"*—It may be needful for us to be turned over to Satan to sift, but God never gives us into his hand without a plain and clear limit to what he can do: 'Satan, you may do this. But you may not do that.' In this case, Satan may touch and destroy Job's body, but he cannot take his life.

Actually the word translated life here is the word for the soul. The soul is often put for life, it being the spring and fountain of life—as soon as the soul departs, our life goes too. Both the Hebrew and the Greek word for soul have their names from breathing or respiring. When breath ceases, life ceases. And when our soul leaves, our last breath has been drawn, *"the Lord...breathed into his nostrils the breath of life, and he became a living soul"* (Genesis 2:7).

How strange, on the face of it, that Satan should be warned to save Job's life. Has he become a savior? His name is Destroyer, shall we then send to the wolf to save the sheep? Only negatively is he a savior here, for he is but saving Job's life because he has no permission to take it. And let no one doubt it, God would not have put a chain on Satan to save Job's life if there was no danger of Job losing his life. Satan certainly would have loved to see Job dead. Why? Because that is the only way he can be sure that Job will no longer be a source of embarrassment to him in his kingdom, this world. If Job were dead, it would not be necessary to go to so much trouble to try to defeat his spiritual strength. Again, as the Pharisees sought to kill Lazarus, because he was living proof of Christ's power to give life, so Satan would love to see Job dead. Job is living, breathing proof that a man is able to resist the onslaughts of Satan. Besides, with Job dead, the old Devil might succeed in lying to many men, perhaps in many cases succeeding in persuading them that Job did not actually defeat the wiles of Satan — was he not now dead?

Why save Job's life? Because God intended to make him a monument of mercy as well as a monument of suffering. The whole world has heard of the patience of Job, because God said to Satan, *"save his life!"* The courage and ever-growing faith of Job have been the greatest source of encouragement to myriads of saints since that day. Will a man say, How can I be expected to wrestle with principalities and powers? Then let him look at Job, he will see proof that a man may do so and come forth from the battle ten times better.

"save his life"—For once the Talmudists may be right, when they say that the grief of Job in his manifold temptations, the pain and the vexation of them all, was not so great for Job as was Job's triumph a torment to Satan. How much torture it must have been to Satan! How much more must it be today that he has this book of Job still sticking in his gut, twisting and wrenching pain from him every time someone reads of his defeat.

WHY DOES GOD ALLOW MEN AND DEVILS TO DEFILE OR PAIN OUR BODIES?

"he is in your hand"—Do with him as you please. To the finite mind, it seems strange that God should give devils free rein to inflict pain and degradation upon the bodies of His children (which are called temples of the Holy Spirit in one place). That He does is not only apparent from our text, but from many other Scriptures, and from experience in the world of men, *"others were tortured...underwent mockings and whippings—and ever more, of chains and of being in prison—they were stoned, they were cut apart with saws, they were tempted and were slain with the sword. They wandered about...being in want afflicted, tormented"* Who? The saints of God were so treated (Heb. 11:35-38). And in New Testament days even worse things were done to those godly men who pulled down the power of the Roman Catholic empire by speaking and living the Gospel — for those devilish priests and their helpers invented the most hellish instruments ever to be in this world, that they might boil the saints in hot oil, melt their flesh from their bones in fires, pull their bones apart all over their bodies and yet leave them alive, put them on the rack

and the wheel and in boxes that slowly bled them to death. What? Should the precious blood of the saints be spilled by the fiendish servants of Satan? Yes, for every drop of blood drowned a multitude of sinners, and the whole world was turned upside down by those martyrs who spoke their faith as they were tortured. Why did God allow it? First learn from God's word that though the lives of the saints are precious in the eyes of God, He is committed only to the preservation of their souls. The purposes of God must stand. His glory is the most important thing in His eye. Our bodies, our lives are but means of bringing glory to God. When pain and torment in our bodies will serve to bring God glory, and will bring more grace to our souls, then God willingly brings us into circumstances which will bring us into pain and torment. Sometimes he does this by giving us into the hand of Satan, as here. Sometimes it is a giving of us into the hands of men. Sometimes He immediately smites us a blow, that we may learn our manners in dealing with Him. In all three cases, however, it is the everlasting love of God which lines the sorrows we receive, so that we may rejoice even while we are tormented.

"save his life"—Lastly, note that our lives are in the hand of God. They are not in the power of Satan, nor in the power of any man or group of men. Daniel told Belshazzar, There is a God *"in whose hand your breath is."* Belshazzar's life was taken that night by the conquering Medes, but his life was in the hand of God, who gave permission for those men to take it. There are times when God does not say to Satan, *"save his life."* There are times when men are given into the lives of other men. But there are some times when God is very explicit in his instructions to men, as with Laban, *"Take heed that you speak to Jacob neither good nor evil"*—yet Laban had said, *"it is in the power of my hand to do you hurt"* (Gen. 31:29). There is a time to be born, and there is a time to die. Both are in the hand of God. What a comfort to us in life, to know that we shall not be put to death by accident, that no amount of 'bad luck,' or other superstition can take our lives from us. Then it is also a great comfort to us in death, to realize that now is the time that God has chosen for us to be melted into His bosom Shall a man wail and cry when he knows that he has been chosen by God to be His companion, and that now is the time to enter His presence. Take careful note of this, that God did not say, *"save His life,"* when they crucified Jesus Christ. There was a time when Jesus was to die for the glory of God, that He might return into the bosom of God. Such a time also comes to us, though our death may not procure grace and glory, as His did.

"So Satan went forth from the presence of the Lord and struck Job with sore boils from the sole of his foot to the top of his head"—Job 2:7.

Again Satan takes off quickly to execute his plans upon Job. See 1:12 for exposition.

"and struck Job with sore boils"—Angels can smite mightily and quickly, as when Herod was smitten and the worms ate him before he could get down off the platform (Acts 12:23). The Devil asked God to *"touch,"* but when he is given into Satan's hand, he *"smites."* Deceit was in his heart even when he was talking to God—he cannot cease from sin. Here we see (1) that Satan struck quickly, and, (2) he struck Job with all his might:

(1) This disease did not grow on Job by degrees. He broke out with sore boils from the top of his head to the sole of his foot, suddenly.

(2) This was no light blow, but a vehement stroke, intended to bring Job to the very door of death. A sudden, heavy blow was intended to bring distemper of the mind as well as of the body; and, it became a disease, it was intended to look like a blow from God Himself. This being a rare disease, and a loathsome disease, a non-communicable disease, it is possible that Job did indeed think that it was a visitation upon him from the hand of God. Certainly, he never once attributes it to Satan.

How could Satan be said to strike Job. Angels do not have hands, and in this case there was no man used as an intermediate agent to inflict the wounds. We cannot say how an angel can smite. It is a secret not revealed to us. But we certainly know that angels do have the power to strike, and that most mightily—for example, it was an angel which struck and killed one hundred and eighty five thousand Assyrian soldiers in one night (Isa. 37:36).

"with boils"—Literally, an ulser, a burning or inflamed ulcer. The idea of heat, of a hot ulcer is also included. It is as if Satan had kindled a fire in Job's bowels, and all over his body at the same time. Just what kind of sore, boil or ulcer it cannot be said for certain. But we do know that this same word was used to describe the plague which God brought upon the Egyptians and magicians—this was God smiting on this occasion—there *"shall be a boil breaking forth with sores upon man and upon beast. And the magicians could not stand before Moses because of the boils"* (Ex. 9:9,11). It is a pain to have even one hot ulcer upon the skin, but to have one's body covered from head to toe with them—that is the worst and most tormenting disease that Satan could think of. The pain was intensive, and extensive. Yes, it is one of the most frightening descriptions that God ever gave in His word, *"From the sole of the foot even to the head there is no soundness in it; but wounds and bruises, and putrefying sores; they have not been closed, nor bound up, nor soothed with oil"* (Isa. 1:6).

One part of Job's body was left free from these ulcers—his tongue. Satan left his tongue free from malady that Job might use it to curse God.

"And he took a broken piece of pottery to scrape himself with. And he sat down among the ashes"—Job 2:8.

There were four aggravations to Job's affliction:

1. He could get no one to dress his sores. He had to do it himself. Neither his wife, nor his servants nor his friends would come near him. They hated the very odor of his breath.

2. He had no salves and no instruments to relieve his hurt. The only tool he had was a poor one, a broken piece of pottery. No fine linen, no oil, only a hard piece of pottery as his surgical tool.

3. It may be that his body was so loathsome that he even hated to touch his own body. He may have found his diseases so foul as to turn his own stomach.

4. He had no bed, no pillows, nor even a roof over his head while he is distempered and in severe pain.

"he sat down among the ashes"—Either he sat down in the ashes voluntarily, or he sat there out of necessity. Some think he sat in the ashes as an act of humiliation and abasement. Repenting in dust and ashes is a common happening in the Old Testament (Jonah 3:6). As to the possibility he sat in the ashes out of necessity, it may be that he did so out of poverty and want, or, more likely, his disease was so loathsome that none could stand to be in the same house with him, there being such an odor to it.

Either way it is understood, Job suffered sorrow and humiliation, and it was a great aggravation of his grief. Disease is the result of sin, for before sin there was no sickness. A realization that this is so, and how quickly the seeds of destruction that are in us can be used of Satan to smite us, surely will bring us to a state of great thanksgiving for our usual good health. What a blessing is a body so healthy as to allow us full swing in the service of the Lord. Job had nothing but pain from the top of his head to the sole of his feet, yet here are you without even a twinge of pain from top to bottom—give thanks to God.

Learn, too, the blessing of God in leaving you with wife and children, servants and good friends. Job only had that One who will never leave nor forsake His children. And He is enough. Yet, ordinarily, God gives us these others, that we may have more comfort while in the body. Still yet, Job had more grace—and more grace is better than more comfort.

"Then his wife said to him, Do you still hold to your integrity? Curse God and die!"—Job 2:9.

Another crushing blow falls—Job's wife weighs in on the side of Satan, tearing Job's soul with a wrench no other soul on earth could have given him. Now the answer comes to that nagging question at the back of our mind ever since we read of the first afflictions of Job— why were the possessions and servants and children of Job all swept away, but not Job's wife? Because she was outside of Satan's commission? No, but because Satan was saving her to use as an instrument to tear down Job's resistance to evil! A man may concede that others may fail him, his servants or friends or even his children, but the one person he is certain will stand by his side and help him is his wife. Is she not one flesh with him? The history of the world, and in Scripture, is replete with instances of a good wife standing with her husband against all the world. But now, when Job needs her most, more than any other time in his life, where is she? Standing over him, not beside him, and she is telling him to curse God and die. Of course she is not the first woman to be used of the old serpent to undo her husband: (1) There was Eve, who listened to the old serpent and persuaded her husband to take his advice; (2) There was Jezebel, who persuaded Ahab to work wickedness such as had never been seen in Israel before that time. There are others. Satan is most careful to choose the best instruments to smite us with, and the choice of Job's wife was a stroke of genius. For the nearer the person, the dearer the person is to us, the more likely are we to take counsel with them. And when treachery is done to us, the pain, the sorrow, the grief is greater according to our regard for the person doing it. If it is an enemy who has done it, we feel no pain or wretchedness. But if it is a friend, the pain is very great—how much greater then, how unspeakably shocking it is when the traitor is the one who lies in his bosom, the woman he loves with a fierce and undying love! How devastating it is when she who is supposed to comfort him when he is traitorously wounded proves to be one of those who delivers blows to his spirit! Then who will comfort? Who will bind the wound? Who will share the pain? How ingenious of Satan to use the wife!

"Do you still hold to your integrity?"—This thing was not done in a corner. Job's wife realizes that he is still holding fast to his integrity. But she has concluded that it is futile, that it is foolishness to keep on holding to his integrity, that he should go on and die and get it over with. It is obvious that Job's wife had come to the end of her patience, though Job himself still had not done so. And it should be mentioned that the same losses that had been suffered by Job were also suffered by his wife. She had lost all that she had owned, possessions and servants and children. She had come thus far, with great loss, at her husband's side. Now she steps over on the other side, suddenly deserting him. Before she no doubt had been a tower of strength to him. Now she quickly turns adversary.

It is not very likely that these are all the words Job's wife said to him. It would be unusual in such a case for her only to give the poison in such bare words as these. Rather are we to think that this is probably her conclusion, and that Job's answer is only the antidote, not his whole answer to her. For instance, the *Septuagint* brings to us the claim that Job's wife said all of the following: 'How long will you hold out, saying, Behold, I wait while expecting the hope of my salvation? For consider, your remembrance is blotted out from the earth, even your sons and your daughters, the pains and travail of my womb, whom I brought forth in vain. You yourself sit here in the rottenness of worms, abiding all night in the open air. I, poor handmaid, wander from place to place, from house to house, looking when the sun will set that I may take a little repose from the pains and sorrows which now oppress me; but utter some word against the Lord and die.'

As to these words, what they mean, see the exposition of the third verse of this chapter. But it is necessary that we note the difference in the speakers, and the difference in the intention of the speakers of those words. God speaks them in honor to Job. Job's wife speaks them in contempt. There is approval in God's speech. There is disapproval in the words of Job's wife. From this we learn:

1. Those things which commend us most to God usually make us most contemptible in the sight of the world. *"for that which is highly praised among men is a hateful thing before God"* (Luke 16:15). Job's wife scorns him for the very thing God has but recently prized very highly—his integrity. She, like all men by nature, is averse to spiritual qualities. Therefore she perversely criticizes Job for counting spiritual health far more important than anything else in his life. But God's commendation meant more to Job, and means more to us, all of us who are in Christ Jesus.

2. Satan is able to persuade most men that the profession of holiness is vain and unprofitable. Those blinded fools say it later in this book, Who is the Lord, that we should serve

Him. For those who live for their bellies, who worship the figments of their own imagination, who count the opinions of men more important than the Lord's well done, it is no wonder that Satan persuades them to believe what they already naturally have concluded. But that those who name the name of Christ upon themselves should listen to the wicked lies and scurrilous scoffs of the old Devil, this is a shame, a disgrace, a dishonor to Christ. His insinuations having failed to work with Job (such as, Job, be wise, take a little counsel at the last, Do not hold on to something that will get you nothing—you have nothing for your pains, for all your playing at holy living these many years—give up this foolish notion that you will serve yourself best by holding on to your integrity, then you shall see that comfort and gain shall come quickly to you,) Satan found Job's wife with open, itching ears. Now she is doing, or trying to do, Satan's dirty work for him.

Having no use for such things as the love of God, holiness, praying, the promises of God and the satisfaction which saints get from simply pleasing God, Satan waxes fervent indeed when he tackles one of us. The lust of the flesh, the lust of the eye, and the pride of life are the downfall of Christians altogether too often, and it is these that Satan uses to stumble them: What ease do you have, where can you go, what can you eat and drink? This holiness is just God's way of cheating you out of the best things in life. Don't do this, Don't do that; you can't have this, you mustn't own that lest some bluenose will think ill of you. Where are your gains from this foolishness? Where are your victories? What have you got that others do not have? This is the language of Satan, who cannot see any advantages in denying oneself anything at all. Of course, those who know God, who believe that He is a rewarder of them that diligently seek Him, will answer: It is far better to die praying than to conquer blaspheming, or gain by lying, or experience ease by cheating. Try those satanic lures on the hypocrite, who secretly wishes that he could have the best of two worlds, but you are wasting your time dropping your line in holy waters. It is true that there is no such thing as a ton of grace, a houseful of patience and longsuffering, etc. A godly man neither weighs nor measures those things he treasures most from God. For it is harvest time for him, that he might gather the fruit which he will take with him to the world which is soon to come—he will live from this fruit, relish it and fatten off it in a way too marvelous for any time-serving worldling to ever conceive. It is not unusual for a man to deny what he cannot conceive and has never experienced. Yet one who has been blessed with a blissful satisfaction in the things of God cannot be persuaded that there is nothing worthwhile in such an experience. If we refuse to allow the flesh to lord it over us, Satan will find no handholds on us. to turn us around and drown us in the cares of this world again.

Notice carefully what Job's wife concludes. All that she can think of in the way of sage advice is this: *"curse God and die."* That is her improvement on holding to integrity!

"curse God and die"—Again the word means *"to bless,"* and some here take them in this good sense. Some claim that Job's wife is advising him to bless God, to humbly seek His face and praise Him, then he may die happily, being released from this miserably painful world Beza is one who strongly excuses Job's wife, though he grants that she has been deceived by Satan, and is at work for him. He claims she has been watching Job's silence and that she suspects that he is standing too much on his integrity, that he had too good an opinion of himself and his holiness, that he suffered from a partially seared conscience and therefore she advises him to bless God, humbling himself before Him, thus preparing himself to die in a holy manner. Beza could not believe that a wife that had been in the family of Job for so long, had been his companion, should be so full of the Devil, so in tune with him, so willing to do his work. There are some objections to this interpretation (1) If Job's wife were to give good counsel to him, she would be foiling Satan's design. For this would lighten Job's load, giving him another person to lean upon—for even though she was wrong, it would have made Job feel better that his wife loved him and wanted to make his burden lighter. (2) Job reproves his wife strongly, which he would not have done if she had meant well, and if her advise was from a good heart.

"curse God and die"—Some see Job's wife as jeering at her husband because he has been so precise in his religious duties, and had been so nice in holding on to his integrity. "See what you have got for your pains, being so intent on being holier than anyone else!' It is possible, say they, that she is showing Job that words will not help him now, that there is no charm he can grasp to ward off death, therefore he may as well curse God and die. The same scorning, scoffing result could be true even if she is saying, *"Bless God and die"* —Go ahead and pray, take your fill of blessing God, bless him as long as you can, but you shall die anyhow.

The meaning most suitable to the context is that which lies on the fact of our translation —*"curse God and die."* This thread is of the same spinning with the former, it carries the secret plot of Satan forward, on his own principles. Coming from Job's wife, these words are unspeakably more devastating than they would be coming out of the foul mouth of Satan. But could Job curse God and die? There are those who claim this is a suggestion of suicide—God is plaguing you, He has judged you and found you lacking, so curse Him and die. Some would have the advice to be this, that Job should curse God in the hope that He would slay Job and thus relieve him of his misery.

To those who claim that Job would not have such a bad wife, that she could not imagine such wicked thoughts, much less have the boldness to offer such ungodly advice—A good man may have a very bad wife. A husband cannot infuse holiness into his wife. Marriage and companionship will not give a woman a new heart (except that spiritual marriage with Christ). A person out of Christ is capable of doing anything—there are none good, no not one (Rom. 3:10-12).

It has been said that Job's wife may have said these things and yet have been a holy woman. One ancient expositor said, 'these are the Devil's words, not the woman's words.' But this is not so merely because he thinks it so. The woman spoke the words. The question is, What kind of woman was she? She could have been one of God's children. Did not Peter so speak the mind of the Devil that Christ rebuked him, *"Get behind Me, Satan"*? (Matt. 16:23). Do you find these words of Job's wife to be scandalous? Those of Peter were also scandalous, *"you are a scandal to Me,"* Jesus said. Did not David, a man after God's own heart, do Satan's work more than once (in numbering the army, in ordering Uriah put in a spot where he would be killed, etc.)? The woman could have fallen prey to Satan's evil suggestions, may have become his foil for the short time needed to give this bad counsel. It could be that the text might somewhat absolve her, for when Job rebuked her he said only that she was acting like a foolish woman. He did not say, You wicked woman, you abominable wretch! Is he not saying to her, You are not like yourself, you speak foolishness like other woman. (Mr. Caryl leaves it like this, giving the impression that he regarded Job's wife as a good woman who had been temporarily led astray by Satan, in order to deliver a crushing blow against Job. See the treasury section in Volume III for a refutation of this view—Jay Green).

"curse God and die"—there are these further things to be observed from these words:

1. Satan is a physician of evil intent when he suggests that we can make a gain by committing one evil in order to shake off another. Job was grievously diseased, but Satan's cure is worse than the disease. The least evil is sin, says he, for it is foolish for you to suffer like this, especially when you did nothing to deserve it. Go ahead, curse God and die.

2. It is sinful to wish ourselves dead, whatever may be our condition in this life. We may, as Job does later, submissively seek death at God's hand, He being willing. To live is an act of nature. To be willing to live because God wills it, no matter what our life is like, is an act of grace—it is more than the flesh can manage. Just as we ought to be willing to die for God's glory, that His will may be done, so ought we also be willing to live, for the same reason. Paul desired to be dissolved and to be with Christ, but he was willing to live until Christ wrote, *"It is finished,"* to his life. As for illness, some of the most God-glorifying lives ever lived were those of persons too ill to take part in the normal activities of life (Richard Baxter wrote *The Saints' Everlasting Rest* on what he thought was his deathbed;

John Owen wrote most of his seven million words of divinity and exposition while he was quite ill, over many years; William Cowper was ill during most of his adult life; etc.) It is sinful to wish for death absolutely, as if we could petulantly seize from God's hands His perogative of assigning certain days to us. And if it is sinful to wish for death, how much more sinful is it to seize our own throats and try to pull down our house of clay, whether God be willing or not.

3. Satan lies again when he would have us believe that death is a door that leads to ease; that death is an end to our troubles. This of course contradicts the entire teaching of the Scripture on the subject of life after death. Death to the ungodly is but the beginning of real troubles, and if they but knew what lay beyond death, they would take more care to preserve their lives. How sad to see some launch themselves right into Hell by suicide!

4. The devils begged Jesus not to start their torment a day early (Matt. 8:29), yet they busy themselves to persuade men that they should be willing to die—and the times they pick are the worst possible times for a man to die. They would not want you to die until and unless it was the worst time. So here, Satan has chosen this time for Job to die, but first he must have Job curse God — it is the reason for all of Job's afflictions.

"But he said to her, You speak as one of the foolish women speaks. What? Shall we receive good at the hand of God, and shall we not receive evil? In all this Job did not sin with his lips"—Job 2:10.

Job first reproves his wife, then he refutes her claim that it is best to curse God now.

"You speak as one of the foolish women speaks"—Here is a firm rejection, a reproving of his wife's counsel, Literally, it is, *"as one of the foolish ones,"* women not being in the text here. The word *"foolish,"* comes from *nabal,* which signifies properly a thing fallen off, such as dried leaves or withered fruit. It is by a metaphor that it is applied to a person who has lost his wisdom, or had no goodness, or sap—a sapless person. It is also applied to a vile person, one base and low, one with a withered, fallen spirit that has sunk below any holy resolution. This *"foolish"* one has had his judgment faded, has had his holy principles corrupted. The *"fool"* has said in his heart, There is no God—it is this word, only here it is in the feminine. Surely Job's wife is speaking like a heathen woman here, one who has substituted an idol for God. The heathen are foolish, they can be heard to curse their gods, rail at their 'fate,' wrangle with 'fortune,' etc. When their gods abuse them, they abuse their gods. This is a fools game, a sure sign of a person without heavenly wisdom.

Job here becomes passionate and warm in his response. It is the first instance of his holy zeal. When it is his own suffering, he can bear it without heat. But when God is dishonored, and that by his own wife, he passionately rebukes her. And passion becomes the cause of God in cases like this. Christ was meek and humble, but when the Pharisees lied against the truth and robbed God of His glory, Christ waxed warm, rebuked them as *"a generation of vipers, painted graves, blind guides, an adulterous generation, and, children of the Devil."* (It is right and proper to be angry in such cases. Most modern translations have removed it, but the proper reading of Matthew 5:22 is, *"He that is angry with his brother WITHOUT A CAUSE shall be in danger of the Judgment"*—But, the opposite teaching is implied, he that is angry with his brother, having a good cause, is NOT in danger of the Judgment. If you remove the one Greek word translated *"without a cause,"* you will have this, *"he that is angry...is in danger of the Judgment."* Translations that read like this do not reflect the true original, they could not do so, for if this were truly the Scripture, then Christ Jesus would be in danger of the Judgment because of His anger displayed many times. Christ could not possibly be in danger of the Judgment, for any cause, because only a sinner can be in danger of the Judgment. Christ never sinned, not when He was angry, or at any time—and He was never in danger of the Judgment. The textual critics are patently wrong—even wrong in spirit for being willing to make Christ a sinner in danger of the Judgment rather than to admit that their 'research' had failed somewhere.

Job does not call his wife a fool, but says that she speaks as one. It may be that love has mitigated or softened his reproof. Or, it could be that he is using a similtude to make an assertion.

These further observations might be made from this reproof to Job's wife:

1. Job does not fall out with the whole female sex. He compares his wife to one of the foolish women, but does not say that all women are foolish.

2. He does not fall out with marriage, though at the time he could look at the present state of his marriage and become dissatisfied. Instead, his love continues to operate.

3. He is not angry with God for giving him this wife, any more than he is angry with God for sending him these afflictions. Some wish that God had never providentially provided them with the wife of their bosom—but these are guilty of as much sin as any their wives may have committed. Job rejects his wife's counsel as foolish, and he reasonably refutes what she said, but he does not reject her from being his wife. This was a blessing God in mercy was giving to him, for the day was to come when Job and his wife were once more to be in a state of bliss together. In fact, they had ten more children after all of this.

4. God's outward dealings with a man may not be judged by his circumstances or condition. It is a foolish spirit that concludes an afflicted man an enemy of God.

5. To do wickedly, or to speak wickedly, is foolish. Sin is the greatest folly in the world. Sin is a declining from the rule of right reason, both from spiritual reason and from natural reason. Those who have rejected the word of the Lord have lost their wisdom (Jer. 8:9). True wisdom is to walk by a right rule, to a right end. While we sin, lust in some degree is the ruler, and self is the end. In both which we join hands with foolishness and are the companion of fools.

"Shall we receive good at the hand of God, and shall we not receive evil?"—The emphasis in the original is this, Shall we receive good with hand and heart at the hands of God, and shall we not in the very same manner receive evil? For the word *cabal* signifies the receiving of a thing with the hand and with the heart—that is, to receive gladly and thankfully, to kiss the hand that gives, whether good or evil. Also included in the word would be a reverence and veneration for the giver. That is why the Jews call the teachings which are received, venerated and transmitted from hand to hand *Caballa*. We receive good things cheerfully, thankfully, reverently, and kiss the hand that gives them. So ought we to receive those things which we count evil, for the same Person is giving them—He is still the same merciful, kind, gentle and loving God who gives to us from a good and faithful heart. It is impossible for you to get your good from God, and your evil things from another source—that is the heathen approach, many gods, each one fashioned according to our own minds.

"Shall we receive good"—What kind of good is meant here? Some would have it the good which we receive in the next life, in the sense of the apostle Paul's assertion, *"I reckon that the sufferings of this present time are not worthy to be compared to the glory which shall be revealed"* (Rom. 8:18). But the comparison in this place is better if we understand the good things of this life, outward comforts, prosperity, etc.

What kind of evil is meant here? The evil here comprehends those things which we call evil. Afflictions and discomforts are not according to our mind—they do not please us, so we count them as evil. Whatever pleases God, God calls good. Whatever displeases Him, He calls evil. With Him, this is proper and right—He is the Master of all, Ruler and Creator of the universe—He alone has the right to please Himself, and to demand that everyone of His creatures please Him. When Adam sinned, it was because he wanted to be as God. When Adam sinned, all sinned in him. Now all men by nature desire to usurp the place and rights of God. They love and serve themselves, they idolize themselves. That is why they claim the right to determine what is good and what is evil. Whatever pleases them, they call good. Whatever displeases them, they call evil. As it is in fact with God, so they imagine it is so with them. Godly men prove themselves to be godly (godly=like God) by exercising their new nature to think the thoughts of God after Him. Godly men learn to agree with God as to what is good, and as to what is evil. Here, however, Job is talking about good and evil as men see them. So he says, *"shall we receive those things which we call good from God, and shall we not gladly and cheerfully also receive those things which we call evil?"*

There is a lot of reason in this question of Job's. It is reasonable to believe that if we refuse to accept all that God gives us, the good with that which we count evil, then He may well stop giving us any good at all. Why should He allow us to decide what He will give us? We are condemned sinners, under sentence of death for our traitorous deeds toward God, waiting only for the day of execution. What right do we have to demand that He call the same things good that we do, and the same things evil that we do? Is that not demanding the right to be God? Should His mind be according to our mind? Such perverseness could exist only in sinful man and rebellious demons. Reproofs from men of reason carry a lot more conviction. Some reprove with rage and not with reason, some with passion and not wisdom. Job mixes reason with his passion, he gives his wife an argument and a rebuke.

How can evil come from the hand of God. He says it plainly, *"I make peace and create evil"* (Isa. 45:7). Man-made gods may be distinguished from the true God in this way: the man-made god only gives man what man wants to have—It is still another god, a cruel god who keeps man from having what he wants; whereas the true God gives man what He has purposed for him to have, and it is the same true God who withholds from man what he does not want him to have—this true God also gives to many many things which man does not want, causes things to happen in ways displeasing to man. It is the only way to run a world. Good of every kind, and all kinds of penal evil come from God. In a world full of evil appetites, each man demanding that he have the prerogatives of God, it would be impossible for any man to get only what he wanted—that which he calls good. Furthermore, it would be totally incongruous for a good God to reward sinners with good only. Even regenerated sinners cannot expect unalloyed and uninterrupted good until they are in another world. Even though an evil happening (a displeasing or discomforting happening,) comes from the hand of men, God's word teaches us to remember that He is the great first cause. Just as surely as He sent the Assyrians to shave Israel, and Satan to sift Peter, that surely He sends us this or that circumstances. And though he persists in defending himself against his three misguided friends, Job always acknowledges what he has said here, that it is God's right to send evil happenings, that we should kiss His hand when He does send them.

How shall we receive evil? Not as if it were proper evil, not as if God were forcing us to sin. May God forgive anyone for thinking such a thought. Will not the Lord of glory do right? God is sovereign; He is the ruler. He is Just. He can do no wrong. If we believe that He is truly God, we believe these things about Him. And if we believe these things about Him, then when He sends us bitter medicine to take we shall receive it as if He were the Great Physician. A man who dashes the medicine out of the hand of the physician is a fool. If we trust the doctor, we take our medicine and believe that he gives it for our good. If we trust our God, we cheerfully, gladly, thankfully and reverently receive from His hand all that is bitter and all that is sweet, with much that is bittersweet. To murmur and complain is to show our utter distrust of God, or to pretend that we could do better in choosing what is best for us—a blasphemous thought! When afflictions are seen as coming from a loving hand of God, they are as Moses's serpent—a rod to correct, a staff to comfort and heal us; To illustrate this, Scripture gives us these three examples:

1. David fled from Saul to prevent Saul from murdering him. He soon meets with Saul's son, Jonathan, and said to him, *"If there is any iniquity in me, kill me yourself"* (1 Sam. 20:8). He would rather die at the hand of Jonathan than at the hand of Saul?

2. Elijah fled from Jezabel, crying, *"she seeks my life, to take it away"* (1 Kings 19:4). He ran all day and night to escape being killed by her, coming finally to sit down under a juniper tree. And what did he do there? He requested that God kill him. But, Elijah, if you

were so willing to die, why did you flee from Jezebel? She would have given you your wish for death soon enough. But Elijah preferred to die at the hand of God.

3. Christ saw it as it truly is, saying, *"The cup which My Father has given Me, shall I not drink it?"* (John 18:11). It did not matter what was in the cup — God was giving it!

The love of man may turn to hatred. A friend may become unfaithful. When this happens, it is bitter and grievous indeed. But when God strikes His friends, He is still their friend. When He afflicts, it is in faithfulness (Ps. 119:75). He is good to us when He sends us evil. That is why David chose to fall into the hands of the Lord and not into man's hands.

The evil that we receive from God's hand is a backdrop so that we can appreciate His goodness and mercy. It gives us balance and the ability to judge good and evil. And if we are thinking straight, we will conclude with Ezra, that *"our God has punished us less than our iniquities,"* and with Jacob, *"Lord we are not worthy of the least of Your mercies"* (Ezra 9:13; Genesis 32:10).

There are those who cannot seem to remember past mercies and past benefits. They are apt to say to God, What have you done for me lately? These are called fools by a heathen philosopher. For says he, those who think there is no benefit in benefits nor blessing in blessings, except they be present, is a fool. And he who is of the opinion that he has a right to complain when free gifts cease, is but an unthankful fool. If we cannot remember our good things, do not credit them as worthy of receiving a few evil things, then we are apt to find that we have only evil things coming into out lives until the day we become more thankful for past favors from God.

"In all this Job did not sin with his lips"—Again, this second time, God gives testimony that Job did not sin. Even when he was confronted with the treachery, or failure, of his wife, his trusted and beloved helpmeet, he still did not sin, let alone curse God. The Holy Spirit has given the victory to Job. Satan is foiled, his plot fails, the weapons of his warfare are all broken and successless. All his fiery darts have been either quenched or beaten back upon himself. Job stands like a house build upon a Rock. His arms have been held up by everlasting arms.

These words refer to the trial just passed. Job did afterward fail and sin with his lips; so he confesses, *"I have spoken what I did not understand"* (42:3). But this far, at least, he has not sinned with his lips. Nor are the Roman Catholics right in pretending that Job in his heart sinned, but not with his lips. This is not according to Scripture, which says, *"for out of the abundance of the heart the mouth speaks."* These words above argue the opposite, that his heart was free from sin because no sin issued from Job's lips.

The greatest of all victories in this life is not to sin. God applauds this victory. Anyone who comes out of a heavy temptation untouched by sin shall be counted among Christ's worthy. To govern the tongue, particularly, under great affliction is a high act of grace. Moses was a holy man, a meek man, but *"he spoke unadvisedly with his lips."* David was so aware of the danger of sinning with his tongue that he resolved, *"I will take heed to my ways, that I do not sin with my tongue."* He who sins not with his lips is called by James *"a perfect man,"* (James 3:3-9). But Job did not sin with his lips in these first two severe trials, the kind of temptations that threw many other men.

"Now when Job's three friends heard of all this evil that had come upon him, they each one came from his own place—Eliphaz the Temanite, and Bildad the Shuhite, and Zophar the Naamathite. For they had met together to come to mourn with him and to comfort him"—Job 2:11.

These next three verses continue Job's trial, with the third and heaviest part of Job's second affliction now beginning.

These three friends of Job, Eliphaz, Bildad, and Zophar, each came from afar because they had heard of his plight. And they had made an agreement among themselves to come. Their reasons for coming are two: to commune with him, to mourn with him; to comfort him. They say that his grief was very great indeed, and they silently wept beside him.

"Now when Job's three friends heard of all this evil"—Job's troubles had been advertized far and wide, even into foreign countries. For none of Job's three friends were from Job's area. So closely watched are men of God, that any fall of theirs is quickly reported to the whole world. This is especially true of their sins, and almost as true when afflictions come upon them. There is nothing that is more talked of, than the trouble that befalls godly men. When the three friends heard of this evil, they came to Job. When trouble comes to saintly men, the wicked come out of curiosity, and to rejoice over them. When other godly men hear, they come to weep with those that weep, or mourn with those who mourn; and to offer whatever godly advice they find needed, God willing.

"each one came from his own place"—Place here could mean a country, a city, or a region. Most believe here that these came not only from the place where they lived, but also from the place where they governed. The Jewish doctors, who specialize more in fables than in truth, tell us that these men were kings. The *Septuagint* agrees. Beza says it is another fable. The Scripture is not explicit. Whether they were kings or subject, whether they came from their homes or their palaces, it is clear that they were great men, eminent persons in their country. The disputes that follow testify that they were men of great wisdom and learning, as well as understanding, according to the progress of knowledge up to their time.

We have their names, and the name of their country (or, perhaps, of their family).

"Eliphaz the Temanite"—In Gen. 16:11, Esau fathered Eliphaz, his chief son and eldest in the family; then Eliphaz fathered Teman. This Teman is supposed to be the father or the ancestor of Eliphaz. In this case he is called *"Temanite"* because it was his family name. Or, Teman means in Hebrew, The South, or, The Southern Country. In this case he is called *"Temanite"* because of the country he came from. Teman was a place for we read, *"Is wisdom no more in Teman"* (Jer. 49:7). Teman was in Edom or Idumea. It was a place known for its profession of wisdom and learning. So either we may take the word *"Temanite"* from the stock from which Eliphaz sprung, or the place where he lived. The Hebrews refer it to his family, his pedigree. The *Chaldee Paraphrase* says it is his country.

"Bildad the Shuhite"—All that can be found for his pedigree is that there is a Shuah among the children of Abraham, by his second wife Keturah (Gen. 25:1). The Shuhites would come from Shuah. Therefore it is possible that Bildad was from this family line.

"Zophar the Naamathite"—There is even less certainty in tracing the line of Zophar. It is presumed by some that Zepho, a grandchild to Esau by Eliphaz, would be a possible ancestor. The best conjecture as to Naamathite takes it from Naamah, the name of a city which Joshua mentions (Joshua 15:41).

"For they had met together"—It is apparent that they had agreed to come together; it was not an accidental or coincidental meeting. The Hebrew word carries the meaning of a solemn pact. The same word is used for congregating together for worship. Origen's attempt to make this meeting of the friends a miracle is defeated by the explicit meaning of the text—it was a covenant and agreement between the three.

"to mourn with him and to comfort him"—Literally, the word for mourn here is a word which means *"to move."* Cain's judgment, that he should be a fugitive and vagabond is this, that he should be, *"Nod,"* that is, a mover from place to place. Later, it is said that he lived *"in the land of Nod."* The explanation? His conscience quaked continually, because of the guilt that was upon him for murdering Abel—so the very earth seemed to be quaking under him, wherever he might be. Now this meaning may be translated into *"mourning"* by a metaphor (one which is used many places, e.g. Nahum 3:6, *"bemoan"* Isaiah 51:119, *"sorry"*).This word meaning *"to move"* may be properly translated *"to mourn"* because a person in mourning will run, go or move from place to place, or because when a person is in mourning, others will move from place to place in order to comfort them (as we see in the case of Job and his friends). Again, it could be this, that sorrows and

mourning cause the people to express themselves by movements of the body—we lift our hands to Heaven, we rub or shake the head, we stroke or beat upon our breasts. This same word is also used at times for the trepidation or trembling of the heart which come along with our troubles, those convulsions of the spirit, that fearful motion within us (e.g. *"the hearts of the people were moved, as the trees of the wood are moved with the wind"*—Isa. 7:2).

"to comfort him"—Another word meaning *"to mourn"* is used here. This word is usually referring to mournings of repentance. There is a sorrow that goes with repentance. True comfort does not arrive before true repentance. Joy often comes out of sorrow, so the same word is applied to both. Worldly joy and sorrow are contrary to one another. But godly joy and sorrow are inseparable causes of one another—they mutually affect and help one another.

OUR DUTY TO DISTRESSED PERSONS

1. It is an act of true friendship to mourn with and comfort those that are in affliction. This is what seals a man as a true friend, that he will leave off those things which are interesting him in his own life, in order to step into his friend's shoes and mourn with him. Many friends will come and rejoice with you. They will feast with you. But how many will share the sour episodes of your life? Will they not drop off when they must weep with you? But it is different with a friend indeed, *"a friend loves at all times, and a brother is born for adversity"* (Prov. 17:11). Whether they are afflicted by God directly, or by men as the immediate instruments, a true brother mourns and comforts. Christ commends the ones who acted thus, *"You are those who have continued with Me in My temptation"* (Luke 22:18). Some friends come and sing with you in the summer, but when winter is bringing discomfort then they seek a more comfortable climate. You can't get rid of this kind any other way than by falling into affliction and mourning. Then they cannot be held, there is not a way to make them stay.

2. Not only is it an act of friendship to mourn with and comfort the afflicted, but it is a duty. Some think they owe their friends nothing, that they go to comfort them out of the kindness of their hearts, and for no other reason. It is good to be loving and kind, but it is possible for you to neglect to weep with those you do not love, those you feel no kindness toward—if you go only for these reasons. No, rather look upon it as a duty. If you go for the sake of love and kindness, let it be that you love Christ, and that for His sake you will comfort those that mourn and weep. He Himself noted it as a test of true love toward Him, *"I was sick, and you visited Me"* (Matt. 25:36). But Christ Himself was never sick—sickness comes from sin. Truly He bore our sicknesses by compassion and by compensation, but it is as if we were going to visit Christ Himself. *"True religion and undefiled before God the Father is this,"* What? *"to visit the fatherless and the widows in their affliction"* (James 1:27). Of course all afflicted persons are covered under those two examples, the fatherless and the widows. This is pure religion, to obey Christ and visit His afflicted ones. 3. As soon as you hear of others suffering, you should be strongly moved, and you ought to go and mourn with them, to comfort them. Our text says, *"as soon as they heard."* etc. Many times we hear rumors, or gossip. We are altogether too quick to censure as soon as we hear something ill of another. But when we hear a rumor that such and such a one is sick, are we as quick to rush to their side for the purpose of comforting them? *"Remember those that are in bonds, as if you were a slave alongside them;"*"Bear one another's burdens;" "Rejoice with those that rejoice, and weep with those that weep;" "All of you be of one mind, having compassion for one another"* (Heb. 13:3; Gal. 6:2; Rom. 12:5; 1 Pet. 3:8). There was a time when Paul stood alone, none stood with him. There was a time when David needed a friend, *"I looked for some to take pity, but there was none; and for comforters, but I found none"* (Ps. 69:20). It is sinful not to take pity, not to comfort one who is under the afflicting hand of God. How sinful is it to add

to his sorrows and woe. There were those who gave Christ gall and vinegar while He was on the Cross.

"they came"—They were not sent for, no one asked them to come. It is not necessary for us to wait for an invitation to come and comfort one in affliction. It is good manners to be an uninvited guest in a house of mourning. It is also good to contact other friends and to make arrangements to meet them there. When Job's friends came, they came that they might mourn with him, but in such a way as to bring him comfort. It is not right to add sorrow to sorrow, to be always drowning the afflicted in his own sorrows—they must be useful in bringing him to the end of sorrows. To help the afflicted rest themselves upon God is the end of all true friendship. These three friends of Job had good intentions in coming, but alas! they failed in their mission. Instead of comforting him, they afflicted Job to the point that he cried out, *"you are all miserable comforters."* From this, some are of the opinion that these are false friends who came with prejudiced and embittered spirits in order to distress Job. But God has absolved them of this, when He tells us that they met together for the purpose of mourning with him and to comfort him.

"And when they lifted up their eyes afar off, and did not know him, they lifted up their voice and wept. And each one tore his robe, and they sprinkled dust upon their heads toward Heaven"—Job 2:12.

While these could possibly be the acts of a hypocrite, we know from the preceding verse that they are true acts of compassion.

"And when they had lifted up their eyes"—To lift up the eye is a frequent Scripture phrase for seeing. Man has a special nerve in the eye which actuates muscles that turn the eye upward. The same word is used for lifting up the voice in other places.

"afar off"—It seems, from this, that Job was outside. But it could be that these saw Job at some distance within his house.

"they did not know him"—We need not take it absolutely, as if his disease had so disfigured him that he could not be known by his friends. Often in Scripture that which is put as an absolute negative is intended for a weak affirmative (*"When Christ came, He came to His own, and His own did not receive Him"*—here is an absolute negative, yet, *"as many as received Him, to them He gave authority to become the sons of God"*—the first absolute negative is denied by the following affirmative statement that some did receive Him—see John 1:11). In Hosea 9:6, it is said, *"they shall bear no fruit,"* yet we see just below *"yea, though they bring fruit, yet will I slay the beloved fruit of their womb."* They may bring forth a few, but I will destroy them. So here, it may be that *"they did not know him"* actually affirms that they did know him, but that he could hardly be distinguished as the old friend they had known for so long.

They were amazed, astonished. What a spectacle Job presented: his entire body covered with ugly, seeping sores, his face disfigured by pain and sorrow; his form wasted away; and no doubt his former bold demeanor had changed to one of dejection. The like picture is given of Christ, after He had borne our sorrows and sicknesses to the point of exhaustion, *"His visage was marred more than any man, and His form more than the sons of men"* (Isa. 52:14). When Satan is given leave to afflict to the uttermost, you may be sure those afflictions will be severe enough to blast the beauty and change the form of the one afflicted. Even the mind and soul will suffer disfiguration, and the image of God further defaced, if the person afflicted is not a child of God with His hedge around him. In Job's case, his soul was beautified by all this—no sickness can wear out the marks by which Christ knows us—but his friends could not see anything but his sad face and form.

"they lifted up their eyes and wept"—We read of the *"valley of Baca,"* the valley of weeping, for so the word means. They lifted up their voice and wept—it was a violent weeping, a vehement wailing. They eased their minds with sorrow, as the phrase indicates. David's sorrow was increased while he remained silent (Ps. 39). Great sorrow is expressed by the

figure of a woman in travail. Crying out expresses pain, yet it may lessen pain.

"And each one tore his robe, and they sprinkled dust upon their heads toward Heaven"
—Now they performed ceremonial acts, the first of which is the tearing of the mantle, or robe. Then they sprinkled dust on their heads toward Heaven. There are two ways of sprinkling dust. There is the taking of the dust and sprinkling it on the head. Then there is the taking of it up and throwing the dust into the air, from where it falls down on the head. This act was to signify that all things were full of sorrowful confusion, the earth and the air were mingled. Heaven was clouded and darkened. Further, the sprinkling of dust on the head was a memento of mortality—they put dust on the head to make them remember that man himself is but dust.

"So they sat down with him upon the ground seven days and seven nights. And no one spoke a word to him, for they saw that his grief was very great"—Job 2:13.
Here is another ceremonial act, the throwing of themselves down on the ground beside Job—for you will remember that Job fell to the ground (1:21). This is an act to show humility. It is best to lay ourselves as low as we can when God is laying us low. It is possible for the body to lie groveling on the earth when the spirit is nestling among the stars — in pride, as Lucifer (Isa. 14:1.). However, it is an act of humiliation, a proper position for mourning, to be on the ground. And Job's friends surely proved their sincerity when they remained there beside him seven days and nights. The time seems almost incredible. How could they sit there that long? Is it not amazing that Job himself, a sick, debilitated man, conclude that these sat there continuously, without rest, for seven days and nights. There are instances in Scripture when a part is put for the whole: *"The disciples were continually in the Temple"* (Luke 24:53). *"Anna the Prophetess did not depart from the Temple, but served God night and day"* (Luke 2:37). These were not there without intermission. They were there nearly all the time. Paul testifies to the Ephesians that for three years *"he did not cease to warn everyone, night and day"* (Acts. 2:31). Did he do this without any intermission? That would have indeed been a long sermon. So we may understand it here, that they sat down with Job those seven days and nights, nearly all the time. As for Origen's notion that they were here without intermission, without sleep, without food, for all that time, and therefore this was another miracle— there is no Scripture to warrant this.
The number seven could be understood indefinitely, a certain time being put for an uncertain time. *"She that has borne seven is languishing"*—that is, she who has borne many children. *"Give a portion to seven"*—this is, to many. It could be that this means that the three friends sat there many days and nights. However, if it is taken for precisely seven days and nights, then it refers to the ceremony of mourning for the dead. It is a custom to be in mourning for seven days for the dead. Job's friends may have considered him practically dead, thus their mourning for seven days, (see Gen. 50:10; 1 Sam 31:13).

"And no one spoke a word to him"—Here is the last of the ceremonial acts. It was proper in great mournings to be silent *("the elders...sit upon the ground and keep silence"*—see Lam. 2:10). Again, it is not necessarily so that they never spoke a word. It is said that Isaiah walked naked for three years, yet it cannot be conceived that he walked stark naked for so long a time. He is said to walk naked, because he had not on his usual clothes, but only perhaps his undergarments. So they here may have spoken but little, thus expressed as though they said nothing at all. Nor is it necessary that they should have said something. It is possible to be so long without speaking. At least, and this is the point, they did not open their mouths in disputation during this time.

"for they saw that his grief was very great"—The original word here denotes a very intensive grief, a deep sorrow. Even without the expression *"very great,"* the grief could have been translated so. The word will express all kinds of sorrows, of body and of mind. But we see here the growth of the impression of grief on the friends: they saw his grief; they

saw his grief was great; they say his grief was very great. This winds up their sorrow and pity to the greater height. There is a growing realization of the seriousness of the situation oftentimes when we have time to sit and consider what it all means. These kept silence, and as they silently observed, they meditated upon Job's problems—*"they saw that his grief was very great."*

It is fitting in cases of overwhelming sorrows to keep silence and to observe, then meditate upon the situation of the person we have come to comfort. The afflicted one may be of a mind not to attend to words. Perhaps there must be a oneness of mind established by the combination of silence, observation, and meditation. No wise physician quickly gives medicine in the midst of a fit. There must be a settling down, a contemplation and analysis, a diagnosis, then the preparation of the patient for the medicine. A talkative comforter may well be another disease to a sick man. Untimely counsel may be a torture to the patient. It is not only a point of prudence to know what to advise a distressed friend, but to know when to do so. *"There is a time to keep silence, and there is a time to speak."* *"It is a day of trouble,"* said Isaiah, and, *"Look away from me; I will weep bitterly; do not labor to comfort me..."* (Eccl. 3:7; Isa. 22:4). When a man is resolved to mourn, let him be. Your advice may anger him, but it will not help him. Sorrow must be given time to make way for comfort. So these friends are being wise, prudent and friendly when they resolve to wait silently until there is some subsiding of Job's overwhelming grief.

CHAPTER III

"After this Job opened his mouth and cursed his day"—Job 3:1.

The astonishing silence is broken. Job, the man who had not sinned with his lips under crushing blow after crushing blow has opened his mouth to curse his day. The reason for this amazing speech from Job seems to be the same as the reason for his friend's silence: the greatness of his grief had overwhelmed him to the point where it must have some vent. After this Job opened his mouth. Twice before Job had opened his mouth, both times in the midst of great sorrow and disappointment—both times he has spoken gracious words, words so glorifying to God, so pure, that it is said he did not sin with his lips. This time he did not justify his God, nor bless his God. This time he cursed, not as Satan wanted him to curse, but nevertheless he for the first time is affected so much he is not in complete control of his tongue (*"no one among men is able to tame his tongue—it is an evil that cannot be controlled, full of deadly poisen"*—James 3:8).

The argument, the subject of this whole chapter is contained in this first verse. Three particular things need our attention in this chapter: (1) What is it that Job is cursing, and how does he do it?; (2) The reason Job cursed; (3) Job's attempt to justify his cursing.

"After this"—After what? After the greatest afflictions Satan could devise and execute had been brought down upon Job's body and mind, after his wife deserted him, after his grief had multiplied and his sickness had progressed, then his friends came and sat silently beside him for many days. After this, his sorrows having boiled to the very height, they perhaps now begin to remit a bit, so that he could breathe and give vent to his feelings. For great sorrow may oppress both the spirit and the tongue. *"I am so troubled that I cannot speak"* (Ps. 77:4). Hannah prayed, her lips moved by her heart, but no sound was heard (2 Sam. 1:12).

"Job opened his mouth"—To open the mouth and speak is more than merely to speak. To open the mouth and speak signifies a speaking with a clear and loud voice. Also there is an elegancy in such a speech. When Christ says, *"you are bought with a price,"* it is an unnecessary thing to say, *"with a price,"* everything being bought with a price. But this is added by the Holy Spirit so that we might know that Christ paid the uttermost price. He gave all He could possibly give, Himself. So here Job opened his mouth and cursed loudly and clearly, a great curse, the uttermost curse he could utter against his day. But it also is true that to open the mouth and speak signifies a speech made after mature deliberation. A fool has no door to his mouth, but a wise man has bolts and bars on his mouth, and he usually does not open it without some previous deliberation. So there is more here than bare words. Job opened his mouth to speak boldly and confidently, freely and deliberately cursing his day. He passionarely cursed his day, but as you shall see as the chapter unfolds, he also spoke as one who had carefully considered the words he would utter, and their order.

"and cursed his day"—This word here is not the same word for curse that was in the first two chapters (which meant in its native sense, to bless). This word is derived from a root which signifies a thing that is light, movable or unsettled. By a metaphor, it is used for any thing which we despise, any person which we consider contemptible and beneath our notice. As a contrast, the word in Hebrew meaning to honor is a word which means heavy. Because we usually curse or blaspheme those we despise and take lightly, this is the word used here. Hagar despised Sarah (it is the same word used here). To curse in this manner, also carries with it the wishing of ill. As Job explains his curse in the several parts of it, you will see that he wishes all evil to his day. A curse carries in it all kinds of evil.

"his day"—What day? His birthday, for he thought that if he had never been born, so this unbearable trouble would never have come upon him. He wishes upon his day all the evil that a day may have. But can a man really curse his birthday? or a person or thing?

69

Blessings and cursings are in the hand of God. But there is a ministerial curse or blessing in the hand of man. He may not magisterially, as a judge, bless or curse any thing or person. Balaam was boasting when he claimed that he could bless and curse whom he would. If men are given foresight or insight into God's foredetermined judgments (as Peter in the case of Ananias and Sapphira—Acts 5), it is as He said in the Gospels in regard to binding and loosing, *"whatever you may bind on earth shall come to pass, having been already bound in Heaven"*—Matt. 16:19. Whatever a man may curse, if the curse does seem to take effect, it is because that curse was already issued in Heaven before the world began. If judicial curses were in the power of men, what a miserable world would we have! As often as Balak sent for Balaam to curse Israel, how could any godly man or men have stood if ungodly men could put a curse upon them? No, if men curse, and if God permits them to curse us, then remember what David said about Shimei as he cursed, *"Let him curse, because the Lord has said to him, Curse David"* (2 Sam. 16:10). When God pronounces a curse, it shall be a curse. When man pronounces a curse, it shall not become one unless God concur in it.

But is it lawful to curse created things, such as Job's birthday? The apostles tells us to *"bless and curse not"* (Rom. 12:4). But in some cases, when we are acting as ministers for God, it is our duty to curse. In other cases, when man curses for his own sake, it is a sin. A man may curse as Jacob did when he placed a curse upon Levi and Simeon's anger (Gen. 49:7). He may curse the plots and counsels of wicked men; we may curse the enemies of Christ. David did this many times in the Psalms, but it must be considered if these imprecations were not prophetical of the Messiah. But I believe a man may curse if he will observe two rules: (1) He must aim his curse at the destruction of sin, not of the sinner; (2) He is to have God's justice in mind when he desires the punishment of a seemingly incorrigible sinner. It is a weakness to curse anything passionately, as Job did here. It is a wicked and gross impiety to curse any thing or person maliciously.

But can a day be cursed? When a thing has neither life nor reason, it cannot properly be cursed. That is, a day or a thing is not morally evil, neither are the lower animals, therefore they are not liable to a curse, which is a penal evil. But a thing may be cursed for the sake of man. The earth was cursed for Adam's sake (Gen. 3:17). Christ cursed the fig-tree to teach man the duty of fruitlessness to the glory of God, or the power of faith. God cursed the serpent because of the sin of man. It was both an admonishment to man and a punishment to man. The whole creation is cursed because of man's sin, and it groans until the day of redemption arrives (Romans 8:21-23). Things may be cursed in reference to the suffering of man upon them, as David cursed Mount Gilboa (2 Sam. 1:21).

As David cursed a place, so Job curses a time—the day in which his sufferings began. But Jeremiah also cursed his birthday, *"Cursed be the day in which I was born, let not the day in which my mother bore me be blessed"* (Jer. 20:14). He even cursed the man who reported his birth. Why so bitter a curse? Because his days were to see labor and sorrow and consumed with shame. It was in reference to himself. If he had cursed the thing or the person of the work of God, it would have been a great sin. Job is being weak, he is allowing his grief and emotions to overweigh his reason. If he is sinning, it would be difficult to measure the degree of his sin. The degree of sin depends on the intention of the sinner.

"And Job spoke and said, Let the day perish in which I was born, and the night in which it was said, A man-child is conceived"—Job 3:2,3.

Literally, Job answered and said. And with these words, the style of composition changes from prose to poetry. The passions of the man have reached the point where we must have poetry as his medium of expression. Poetry is most suitable for the expression of emotional matter. That is why the Psalms are written in poetry, and the Song of Solomon, as well as the Lamentations, the triumphant joy of Deborah, etc. Love, joy, sorrow, fear, hope, anger, zeal, and all the passions are wound up in the highest strains by the Spirit of God in the poetical eloquence of holy prophets and psalmists. He has chosen this form to present the grief and passion of this deeply affected, because heavily afflicted, man, Job.

For a full discussion of Hebrew poetry, its differences from other poetry, etc. see the treasure section in Volume III.

"Let the day perish in which I was born"—A thing is said to perish when it is annihilated and returns to nothing. It also is true that when a man is said to perish, it is a becoming miserable. When a beasts perishes, he is not. When a man perishes, he is, but he is not happy. He does not lose his being, but his wellbeing. Again, to perish is to be impaired, to lose dignity and respect. Here, *"let the day perish"* may be taken in this sense. Let not that day be solemnized, let it not be remembered as an important day. A day which has been counted important would be said to perish if it were no longer counted to be so. In ancient days men celebrated the birthdays of kings and other important men. But when these died, and others assumed their places of dignity, those other birthdays perished, new ones took their places. The Scriptures, however, do not ever tell of a good man celebrating his birthday. The day we were born is not a day of remembrance, for we were conceived in iniquity and born in sin (Ps. 51). Only the birthday of grace is worthy to be rejoiced in. Not only in this day of grace, but in that future day of glory we will receive because of the day we became new creatures in Christ Jesus. Eternity, which is the day of glory, is one continued triumph for our birthday in grace. Lastly, *"let that day perish"* may be understood in this way: Let it be lost, let it not be counted in the calendar any more. When the Nazarite did in some way fail to obey the Law of his separation, his days were then lost, that is, they perished. Job then is saying, Let the joy and solemnity of my birthday be laid aside; let it be celebrated no more; let it be blotted out of memory.

"And the night in which it was said, a man-child is conceived"—In Hebrew, the night is pictured as the one saying it. It could be that Job is also wishing that the night he was conceived also may be blotted out, or perish. But the word translated *"conceived"* may also be translated *"born"* in which case it is still his birthday which is meant. In this case, he is cursing both the day and the night, lest he miss that portion of the day when he was born. From here he starts opening boxes of curses for portions of both day and night.

HOW CAN JOB BE NOTED FOR PATIENCE WHEN HE IS SO IMPATIENT HERE?

Some have had difficulty reconciling Job's reputation, as presented by God in the first two chapters, with his explosive emotions as displayed in this chapter. Does he not here appear to be a mirror of impatience, the pattern of an unquiet and uncomposed spirit? Instead of submission and humility, he seems here to lack prudence, grace, reason, and good nature. His madness and distraction, they say, break the bounds of modesty and of moderation and prove that he fails completely as an example to us. But let us see.

There are some who are so impatient with Job's impatience, that are so passionate about Job's passion that they are not in the proper frame of mind to understand this chapter. Most of the Jews accuse Job of either blaspheming, or bordering on blasphemy. Some even accuse him of being superstitious to the point of depending upon astrological observations and assigning of days to them. This is utter nonsense, censure straight out of the bias of the individual writers, or out of their overworked imaginations.

Others, on the other hand, excuse Job completely, many commending him in this act of cursing his day. They say this curse is an argument of his holiness these expostulations, are a part of his patience. They attempt to convince that Job ought to express his suffering to show his sensitivity, showing that he is a patient Christian, not a Stoic or a stone. They contend he spoke this with exact judgment, according to the law of soundest reason. They claim he spoke not out of impotent anger against his day, but out of perfect love to God. As if he had said, I wish I had never been born, rather than I should be an ocassion for any to think hard of God. If he was beside himself, they say, it was for God's sake.

No doubt Job loved God, and he loved Him exceedingly all this while, but whether we should completely absolve Job of guilt is doubtful. Are not these words included in his confessions (42:3)? If he had spoken only out of love, he needn't confess and withdraw

Then he would not have had reason to say, *"I despise myself, and repent in dust and ashes"* (42:6). We therefore take the middle road, that Job is not to be accused of being either profane or blasphemous, but that he is not to be commended for his complaint. Surely, Job discovered and revealed much frailty and infirmity here. His passion and sistemper in this complaint and curse are not according to godliness. Yet, for all of this, he was a patient man, the very mirror of patience, and this we will prove:

1. His suffering was great, his wound was very deep and deadly, his burden was too heavy for any one to bear. When the sufferings of Christ, which are not to be compared to those of man for the greatness of them, caused Him to complain this His *"soul was exceedingly sorrowful even unto death"* (Matt. 27:38), was He not there showing that there is a point at which human frailty will assert itself, where the highest manhood will not hold back the words of complaint? Yet in Christ's words were no impatience. His cry, *"My God, My God, why have You forsaken Me"* was a passionate complaint, but without any impatience at all. Those who cry out and complain when they are but lightly touched do indeed show a sinful impatience. For a man to emit a groan when he is overwhelmed with sorrow does bespeak frailty and weakness, but it does not prove that he is not a patient man. Grace does not take away sense, it does not give a man a heart of stone, but a heart of flesh—grace heightens a man's senses. If you could feel what Job had felt under these satanic blows to his body and soul, you would see how much the man endured, you would see how little impatience there was in him. Who gave him the name of being patient? God! When? Hundreds of years later (James 5). How can you deny God's final judgment?

2. Not only was his affliction great, but they were multiplied, they increased by leaps and bounds. A man who is cut in a thousand places knows that it is worse than being cut with one grievous wound. Many pebbles added one by one will prove to be a heavy burden indeed. Job's afflictions came upon him suddenly, like an army, and he was completely surrounded with them. He was borne down with them, they continued to pile up on him at a fearful rate. He could have borne some of them—he did. He could have borne many of them—he did. But was there no limit to his patience and grace? Yes, he complained.

3. Not only were his afflictions great, and many, but they continued days on end. The conjectures as to the actual time are endless, ranging from many weeks to many years. A man may bear up under a heavy assault for a spurt, for a short while, but if repeated assaults continue over a long period of time, his strength will give out. Day and night, as he tells us later, night and day there was no rest to this sick and weary man. *"I am made to possess months of vanity, and weary nights are appointed to me"* (7:3).

4. Yes, Job complained, and there were a number of these complaints. But what of his acts of submission and meekness? Did they not far outnumber and outweigh those other failures. Of course many acts of evil cannot be balanced by any number of good acts. But here we are talking about acts of complaint. You say they prove him to be an ungodly man? But this cannot be, for his acts of patience, humility, faith, hope and love certify him as a true child of God.

5. Lastly, his complainings were bitter, but he was given grace to recover from them. He did emit some impatient speeches, but he was not overcome by impatience. He recalls all that he spoke in this manner, and he repents of each instanse. You do not denominate a man a liar because he has told some lies, all of which he repented of. Nor do you call Job an impatient man because he made some impatient speeches, which he repented of. A man may be a conqueror, though he has slipped many times and received many wounds in the battle. Job has his ups and downs, his wounds and his slips, but in the end Gód upheld him as the conqueror of Satan himself!

EVEN THE HOLIEST OF MEN DO NOT REMAIN ALWAYS IN A HOLY FRAME

Job in the third chapter does not seem to be the same man as the Job of chapters one and two. First he blessed, now he curses. The best man in his best estate is an imperfect man. At some times we are more imperfect than at others. Faith is never very strong, but there are times when it is stronger than at others. Our love to Christ is never very hot, but there are times when it is colder than at others. A man may in the same circumstances fail one time, and conquer the next, or vice versa. A Christian's life is progressive, they go from faith to faith—there is always growth. Yet, considering each step of the way, there are a great many stops and declinings in his life. There are sicknesses and times of weakness in spiritual health, just as there are in physical health. Look at Abraham when he lied; at Isaac when he lied; at Jacob when he deceived his father; at David in the matter of Bathsheba; at Moses when he spoke unadvisedly. All saints fail at times, though they be Peters or Marks. Only He from whom comes down every good and perfect gift is wholly and completely *"without variableness or shadow of turning"* (James 1:17).

Job is the man we are observing now, but look at how many other godly men complained under great pressure: David (Ps. 77:2); Heman (Ps. 88:3); Hezekiah (Isa. 38:14), etc. Jeremiah in the place mentioned above said many of the same words as Job here, yet we do not find God censuring him for them. And in the case of Jeremiah, there may have been a strain of impatience beyond that of Job. He that understands what man is made of, how sinful his nature is, how weak and frail he is, will have much compassion and will not be questioning whether or not a man is sincere, merely because he groans under his burden.

SATAN HAS FAILED THIS TIME TOO, THOUGH JOB HAS NOW CURSED

Job opened his mouth and cursed, but he only cursed his day—not his God. Satan with his utmost power and wit, with his strongest temptations and assaults, can never fully attain his ends upon the children of God. He has done his worst, he has spent his malice on him, but he could only make Job curse his day. This was far from victory for Satan. The gates of Hell cannot prevail against those who are founded upon the rock Jesus Christ!

GOD IS GRACIOUS TO FORGET OUR FAILINGS WHEN GREATLY TEMPTED

When God comes to question with Job in the end, we do not hear a word or hint about this hot speech of Job in this chapter. His distempered speeches and bitter complaints are not remembered against him. Instead, God takes notice of what Job has spoken that is right (42:7), but not a word about what he had spoken ill. If there was iniquity in his bitter speeches, they could not be found, for God had pardoned them. Although we shall give account of every idle word at the day of judgment, and shall be either justified or condemned for them (Matt. 12:36,37), not all words of complaint are idle words. Job's words had error in them, but were they idle? Even when his tongue slipped, his heart was right. He repented, and thus was forgiven, for his errors. Then, God, as is His way, blotted them out of His book forever. If God has been gracious to forget Rahab's lie (James 2:15), and Samson's dealings with Delilah (Heb. 11:31), why not Job's complaints under affliction? God has compassion, He pities us in our weakness and frailty. Christ came and was tried and suffered so that He might have compassion on us.

"Let that day be darkness! Let not God look upon it from above, neither let the light shine upon it"—Job 3:4.

Job begins to affix a curse to each part of the day he was born. He says, Let that day, the day between sunrise and sunset, be darkness. He wishes the day blotted out, for a day that is darkness would not be a day at all. Darkness is nothing else but a privation of light, it is not positive in nature. This is Job's meaning here, Let that day be deprived of its light, then it will perish.

"Let not God look upon it from above"—This is a more grievous curse. The word for God is a singular word, *Eloah*, meaning Almighty. *"look upon it"*—the word sometimes means to inquire after, or to take account of in an exact and judicious manner. Or, it can mean, to have a care for a thing or person. Job says, Let not God take any account of my birthday, nor have any care over it.

"neither let the light shine upon it"—Light in the Scripture expresses all good, as darkness is all evil. Jesus Christ, the most transcendent blessing of all, is called light, *"the Light of the world."* Job desires all blessing, all good, all light removed from his birthday.

"Let darkness and the shadow of death claim it. Let a cloud dwell upon it; Let the blackness of the day terrify it"—Job 3:5.

That which is translated *"the shadow of death"* may be translated *"the image of death."* And because the shadow of a body gives us the image of a body, the outline and general form of the body shadowed, the Hebrews by a metonymy call an image a shadow. Job is not content to say, Let darkness stain it, or claim it, but he adds the degree of darkness he desires—the worst kind of darkness, that darkness which is the image of death. Let my day be buried in the grave. Job heaps up words, all alike in sound and in sense, all concurring to make up one sense. Such amplifications in Scripture are vehement declarations, *"He confessed and denied not, but confessed, etc."* (John 1:20).

That which is translated claim or stain, is a word which signifies properly to redeem a thing, either by price or by power. In this sense, he is saying, O that darkness and the shadow of death might redeem it, reclaim it, rescue it from the light. If *"stain"* is preferred, it gives the sense of polluting the day, of obscuring it that it might not be known.

"Let a cloud dwell upon it"—The heavy condensation in a cloud intercepts and shuts out the light. Clouds and darkness go together, with a cloudy night being the darkest of nights. Job is drawing in every obliterating agent he can think of, to blot out his birthday.

"Let the blackness of the day terrify it"—Job passions are filtering out one by one in the form of imaginative poetry, all now concerned with blanking out the memory of his day. Blackness is more than darkness, so he adds blackness, as in that phrase used by Jude, *"the blackness of darkness forever"* (Jude 13).

"terrify the day"—The day is of course not capable of fears, but Job intends that the blackness of darkness shall make it a terrible day; as some say, It was a black day. Such a day, when no light comes forth at all, is indeed a terrifying day.

"As for the night, let darkness seize upon it! Let it not rejoice among the days of the year. Let it not come into the number of the months"—Job 3:6.

Job has finished with the daylight portion of his day, now he takes up cursing the night. He begins to load down that night with as many evils as he can think of. The first is that darkness might seize upon it. Obviously night is not night without darkness, but there are degrees of darkness, and every darkness is not proper to the night. The word here used for darkness signifies an extraordinary thick darkness, a darkness that is joined with a tempest. Let the thickest, stormiest of darknesses seize upon that night!

"Let it not rejoice among the days of the year"—Night is a part of any 24-hour day. Now Job would have the night deprived of its chief privilege, that of being part of the day. The night has no glory except it have union with the day.

"And let it not come into the number of the months"—Literally, the number of the moons. The same Hebrew word signifies month and moon (and the Greek word also.) The reason is that they counted their months by their moons. Just as a night disjoined from a day is useless, so a night severed from its month would be nothing at all.

"Lo, let that night be silent; let no joyful voice come in it"—Job 3:7.

If the night were severed from the day, and from its month, then it would be solitary and voiceless. Silent nights, without converse with friends or loved one, are blasted nights.

"let no joyful voice come in it"—It was a sad night to Job in his present frame of heart and mind, so he curses this night that it might have nothing joyful in it, not so much as a cheery voice.

"Let those curse it who curse the day, who are ready to stir up Leviathan"—Job 3:8.

Now that Job has cursed the day of his birth, he is wishing for others to curse it also. Let those who come to mourn with him also curse his day. There is much variety in the translation and interpretation of this verse. That which is translated *"curse"* is also translated *"enlightening"*—and that which is translated *"Leviathan"* is also translated *"mourning," "dragon,"* and *"whale."* Junius concluded that it was the stars which were to curse the day; and the wind was the Leviathan which was raised against it. Stars enlighten the dark part of the day, and wind stirs up the waters, bringing the giant sea animals to the water's top.

Rather, the meaning is most likely this, that those who fish for the giant sea animals find the night advantageous for their purpose, and they curse the day because it ends the advantage they have. Whale fishermen fish by day, but Leviathan is not necessarily a whale. That some fish by night is proven by Peter's remarks (Luke 5:5).

But if the meaning is keyed to the translation, *"stir up Leviathan,"* then it may be that it is a day of no success that is being cursed, rather than merely the light of day. Who is more adept at cursing than the usual profane fisherman?

There is another meaning, which says that those who curse the day are mourners. There were in ancient days in the East those who were hired mourners, who made both a profession and a profit of mourning. These were skilled in lamentation. And many among them would often be heard mixing execrations with their lamentations — curses with their tears: 'O for the day!; Alas that such a day ever came!' etc.

"who are ready" —It is more than an immediate preparing for a thing, for it includes in it a studying of the thing so as to be best ready to do it.

"stir up" —A word meaning properly to awaken out of sleep, to cause to arise.

"Leviathan" —The Hebrew doctors most often translate it *"mourning"* or, *"sorrow."* It is their opinion that this is the plainest meaning of the word. The word from which this is translated is *lavah,* that is, joined or associated. The word for society or fellowship came from this word. With this word for society, *leviath,* the pronoun added, we come to the word, Leviathan, which has the meaning, "their society" or, "their company." This in turn may indicate a certain company, a company of mourners. How? Because the company of mourners was usually a huge company, and they usually made great effort to arouse each other.

There are many other opinions, but this is enough to show that there is no certain meaning known beyond this, that Job desires that this curse be the greatest and most severe of curses, and his figurative language sought to display this passion of his.

"Let the stars of its twilight be dark; let it look for light, but have none; neither let it see the dawning of the day" —Job 3:9.

This is the last part of Job's curse on the night. Some comforts of the night are natural, others not so natural. Job in the former verses wishes away the comforts which are not always common to night (such as joy). In this verse, he removes the natural comforts of the night: starlight and the dawning of the day.

The stars are a comfort because they serve for light in the absence of the sun. They also serve as a promise that there shall be a sunrise and glorious, warm sunlight soon. If these stars are dark, then the night is robbed of its comfort. By *"twilight"* is meant the beginning of the night, the evening when the stars appear (although the same word signifies the twilight of the morning also). In this time the stars are resplendent in their beauty and size. These being those stars which give the most comfort and light, he wants them to be darkened most of all.

"let it look for light, but have none" - Let that night long for the light, expect the light, and let it be disappointed.

"neither let it see the dawning of the day" —Literally, *"let it not see the eyelids of the morning."* Those first peeps of light, when the sun peeps over the horizon, when rays or streams of light begin to bring comfort and hope out of the darkness, Job would have them never come.

"because it did not shut up the doors of my mother's womb, nor hide sorrow from my eyes" —Job 3:10.

Job has finished his cursing of his birthday, and now he will give us his reasons for doing so. He says, I am cursing my day, both the night and the daytime of it, because they did not shut up my mother's womb and hinder me from coming out of it. Indeed, there is more passion than reason in this. Effects are produced in time, but time does not produce effects. Days and nights cannot hinder any happening. But actually Job is cursing the day, not because it did not shut up his mother's womb, but because such a day was.

Literally the words read, *"because it did not shut up my belly,"* which we believe to signify the belly of his mother, or his mother's womb. Now only God can shut up a woman's womb, as He did all the wombs of the house of Abimelech (Gen. 20:18). And only God can bring forth a child from the womb, *"Lord, You are the One who took me from my mother's womb"* (Ps. 22:9). The physician or the midwife may assist, but it is God who opens the womb and brings forth the child. Therefore, Job's accusation against the day and night was without reason.

"nor hide sorrow from my eyes"—Sorrow here is more properly labor, or weariness. By the hiding of sorrow from his eyes, he is picturing the sorrow which has come from his weary labor for his lifetime. These, he says, were not hidden from him by the day and the night of his birth. That which is seen often affects the heart; yea, afflicts the heart.

"Why did I not give up the spirit when I came out of the belly?"—Job 3:11.

Before Job has spoken against his conception and his birth. Now he begins to wish he had died, that his cradle had been his grave. If I had to be born, why did I not die. Contrary to the shallow divinity of some, there are some of whom it may be said, *"it would have been good for that man if he had not been born"* (Matt. 26:24). But for Job, a special favorite of the Almighty God, it is the grossest ingratitude to take the attitude that it would have been good if he had never been born, or that he should have died then.

"why did I not give up the spirit"—It is but one word of the Hebrew which expresses the five English words, *"I give up the spirit."* A godly man gladly gives up his spirit, saying, *"Even so, come quickly, Lord Jesus."* Though he die a violent death, he does not die violently. But an ungodly man dies violently, though he die in quiet surroundings, for he will never give up his spirit—it must be wrenched from him (*"today shall your soul be required of you"*—Luke 12:20).

"Why did the knees go before me? or why the breasts, that I should suck?"—Job 3:12.

Now Job progresses to the point where he was lifted from the womb, set upon the knees of the midwife and cleansed. Why did they not let me die before this? Why did they bind me and clothe me?

"or why the breasts, that I should suck"—The next step is to complain that the breast of his mother was ever presented to him, to sustain his life. If these things had never been done, he implies, then I would have never seen this sorrow. There were in those days unnatural mothers who abandoned their babies at birth.

"For now I should have lain still and been quiet; I should have slept. Then I would have been at rest"—Job 3:13.

He is enlarging upon his former statement. He imagines that he would have been still and quiet, sleeping and at rest, if he had been abandoned at birth. He in the next verses tries to prove this point. Needless to say, there is a poetic blindness here, for Job is considering death strictly from the outward viewpoint. There is an appearance of quiet, of sleeping and rest in death. But he is not addressing the true spiritual state of things, that eternal existence that begins even before that body assumes a position of quiet repose. *"Blessed are the dead who die in the Lord from this time on. Yes, says the Spirit, that they may rest from their labors"* (Rev. 14:13). The saints shall rest, they shall be quiet and peaceful —but if these be scarcely saved, what of the ungodly? Shall they have rest and quiet? Not at all, not for a moment!

"I should have lain still"—Job uses four words to multiply his thought, *"still," "quiet," "slept,"* and *"rest."* Sleep is a short death, but death is a long sleep, *"Many of those that sleep in the dust of the earth shall awake, some to everlasting life, some to everlasting con-*

tempt" (Dan. 12:2). Rest is more than sleep, for many men sleep and do not rest. But the combination of rest and sleep is a perfect sleep. But again, *"there is no rest for the wicked,"* and all these fine words have not a whit of comfort for them. The tranquility of the grave is so commonly accepted as truth, especially to troubled souls unable to manage the shredded fabric of their lives, that many commit self-murder to gain it. But it is an allusion, a conspirational idea which all sinners are apt to teach as true. Can clay feel love and hope? Can clay have faith? No more can clay be still and quiet and sleep and rest! Only the soul of man is capable of these things.

Those that die in the Lord are indeed blessed with rest. They rest from the labor and travail of this world. They rest from the trouble, oppression and tumults of this world. They rest from the passions, sorrows and griefs of this world. And best of all, they rest from sin in the new world. There is a full discussion of how man is born unto trouble in the fifth chapter, but for now let it be noted that there is no perfect rest in this world of sin and tears. It was for that reason that Christ wept over Lazarus. He did not weep because Lazarus was dead. He wept because He knew that He was going to bring Lazarus back to life again and that Lazarus would then have to suffer the disquiet of this world for a long time.

IS IT SINFUL TO WISH THAT THE THINGS THAT ARE SHOULD NOT HAVE BEEN?

Some have questioned whether it was lawful for Job to wish or desire these things that already had been providentially acted out in his life. Are we not bound to rest satisfied with the present and already past dispensations of God. Should we not be content with things as they are? The answer is no. It is not sinful to wish or desire something that is to be different. In fact, some things which are so ought to be so distasteful to our spirits that we would wish them not to be so. It would be a sin not to wish them never to have been so. Anything that is at present in our life, or which has happened in our past, which robs God of His glory, which provokes God, which is hurtful to God's children, should be a matter of repentance to us, and we should wish that they had never been. God frames a wish of this sort, to show us the way we should feel, *"O that My people had listened to Me and Israel had walked in My ways!"* (Ps. 81:13). Of course, with God, He is accommodating Himself to our way of thinking and doing. What? Could God not have caused them to listen and to walk in His ways? But it is very commendable to wish that a course of action had been followed which had been in strict obedience to God's word.

However, it is most abominable to wish that things were otherwise than they are simply because they do not please us. Merely wanting to change what God does is a foolish sin. When our wills rise up against the will of God, when we cannot be contented to be what God has willed us to be, to suffer what God has chosen for us to suffer, it is a shame and a disgrace to our Christian profession. How much more sinful is it when we undertake to give God counsel, informing Him of a better way to govern the world, so that it will be more to our liking!

There are two ways permitted to us in presenting our wishes for change, or to bewail our circumstances:

1. If we must question God's providential dealings with us, first we must be in a frame of mind and heart which adores God, His justice and His unsearchable wisdom especially. The prophet pleaded with God about His administration, but first he humbly premises, *"Righteous are You, O Lord, when I plead with You"* (Jer. 12:11). When we ask God a question, let us be sure that there is not the least jealousy or suspicion of his righteousness or of his wise judgments.

2. We may sit down and bewail the state of things. This is what Job is doing. But this is a tight, thin rope to walk, and even the most agile saint is apt to fall off on the side of sin. The bounds and rules are these: (1) Do not complain of any creature that is involved; (2) Be careful that your complaints do not come from your tender feelings, your delicate spirit, or an unwillingness to lie under the cross because it spoils your fleshly pleasure or dignity. If we bewail our cross, we should be working our hearts to a willing and cheerful sufferance of the cross. Though a man does not love that which he bears, yet let him love to

bear. It is a high strain in spirituality in bearing burdens when a Christian can say, I do not love that which I suffer, yet I love to suffer. To love to bear, and to suffer is proof of a high affection for Christ, and an humble subjection to His majestic will. Learn to say with the apostle Paul, *"I rejoice in my sufferings;" "I take pleasure in reproaches, in necessities, in persecutions, in distresses for Christ's sake"* (Col. 1:24; 2 Cor. 12:10). Can you glory in tribulations? God forbid that you should glory in anything else but the cross of Christ. (Gal. 6:14). (3) Do not allow your complaints to arise out of distrust and unbelief. Such complaints are provocations to God (see Ps. 95:8) for a case in point). Mix faith with your tears and believe that God is good, that God is good to us, whatever our condition. Believe in an all-sufficient God, one both able and willing to deliver you—then you may wish that you might have a change in things as they are.

Futhermore, a man may desire a thing which God does not desire (in His secret will). It is not lawful to desire a thing which is forbidden by the word, which is obviously contrary to God's revealing will. But, for instance, you could pray for the removal of a thorn in the flesh. It would be lawful. But God may say to you, My grace is sufficient to you.

You may on the other hand sin when you ask a thing that God wills. It may be the will of God that your father may die. But it would be a sin for you to desire it.

"with kings and wise men of the earth, who built ruins for themselves"—Job 3:14.

The word here denotes a ruler who rules by law, as opposed to tyrants that rule arbitrarily. Job is talking of these great kings and counselors sleeping in the grave, though they had been so busy, had built so much, all now was in ruins and they themselves in the grave. Think of Babylon buried under story after story of sand, great Babylon which had been a famous beauty spot, one which caused Nebuchadnezzar to boast so loudly in the face of God—that is the picture here. Though some say that it refers to the ornate and monumental buildings built for tombs of the great, and Job is saying that he could be just as quiet and restful as any of them.

"or with princes who had gold, who filled their houses with silver."—Job 3:15.

The word for prince means one who is chief, the head, the first. Gold and silver had they, for princes need treasure (Eccl. 2:8). But they need not necessarily fill their houses with it. But it may be here that Job is referring to the fact that all their gold and silver went down into the grave with them, for the word translated *"houses"* can be translated graves. It was not unusual for a prince to bury all his treasure with him. But the most precious of all that they own they completely ignore and forsake—their souls. How often does the grave prove that princes and wise men are fools, for they carefully provide for their bodies to rest, but they carelessly refuse to look after a resting place for their souls.

"Or as a hidden untimely birth I would not have been, like infants who never saw light"—Job 3:16.

Job now goes to the other extreme. He had said that if he had died very early, he would have been equal in death with kings and counselors. Now he compares with infants that never knew the light of day. The word translated *"untimely birth"* signifies to fall down or off, as a piece of fruit falls off before it is ripe. It is also the word for any dead carcass. The Greek and the Latin words for a dead body have the same meaning of falling off. The words here are *"hidden untimely birth,"* hidden because the abortive birth is usually not one that is attended by many, if any.

"I would not have been"—Though he lived as a fetus, an untimely birth robs the infant of being, in the usual sense of being in this world, and having life in this world. Those that are dead are referred to in Scripture as not being, *"because they were not"* (Jer. 31:15).

"like infants who never saw light"—This clause may be an exposition of the former. Yet all infants that never see the light are not untimely births. An untimely birth is one that occurs before the normal period of pregnancy expires. Some infants are still-born when they arrive at the usual hour. So Job has another comparison here, different in that the first phrase describes an abortive birth, a miscarriage, and this a normal but still-born one.

"There the wicked cease from troubling, and there the weary are at rest"—Job 3:17

Job's passionate claim that he would have had rest and quiet if he had been put into an early grave continues. He had spoken of the rest of death for the mighty ones, then for the infants who never spent a restless day in this world. Now he speaks of the wicked, saying that they and the weary are alike put to rest, as kings and infants are. That is, all have a rest so far as outward bodily troubles are concerned.

True rest and wickedness never meet. The word for wicked here is one which signifies a high degree of wickedness—these are men who have actively sought out wickedness to do. They could not sleep while there was mischief to be done. They were vexed, tormented with the urge and the lusts to do evil. Yet these too are equal in the rest of the grave; they cease from troubling so far as this life is concerned. Their raging comes to a silent end as they lie still in the grace.

"and there the weary are at rest"—Just those wearied by the wicked may be meant here, and these too are relieved and put to rest in the grave alongside their tormentors. But it is probably true that this group described as "the weary" also denotes the wicked. Wicked men trouble others to the point of extreme weariness, but they also become weary in the doing of it. How wearing it must be on the spirit to always be driven by evil lusts to oppress others.

"There the prisoners are at ease together; they hear not the voice of the slave driver"—Job 3:18.

Another group, the prisoners are brought in. These may be slaves, or they may be men imprisoned for a crime. But they are this only while alive, when they go down to the grave. they become equal in death to all other classes of men.

"they hear not the voice of the slave driver"—Taskmasters are usually given the character of being cruel and loud in their oppression. But the grave brings relief from their cruelty. Wounding words will never again slash their souls with pain and misery, when they meet with kings and taskmasters in the grave.

"The small and the great are there, and the slave is free from his master"—Job 3:19.

Small and great refer to their stature in the civil life of this world, not to their physical measurements. Masters have a seeming greatness, towering over their slaves while in this world. But they shrivel and shrink until they are equal to the small when they hit the end. Death seizes upon all sorts and degrees of men. The great put off repentance until they may have savored some fruits from their riches. The small put off repentance until they are great, wanting what they consider the extra advantages of being a bit crooked in gaining riches. But when death comes, as it does all too suddenly upon most, both land in the very same ditch together. All distinctions and degrees end at the mouth of the grave. There is only one distinction that will outlive death. Death cannot take it away. It is the distinction between holiness and unholiness, clean and unclean, faith and unbelief. Not only do these distinctions remain after death, they remain forever and forever.

"Why is light given to him who is in misery, and life to the bitter in soul?"—Job 3:20.

Job begins here to justify his cursing of his day. He has wished his day had not come; then that he had died when he entered this world. Now he begins to argue that he ought to be cut off from life because his life is miserable and bitter. Show me a reason, he says, why my life should be prolonged, who must live in misery, when I would die willingly. He is trying to establish that there is no reason why a man that lives in misery should be denied the right to die. At the twenty-fourth verse he will try to prove this assumption.

"Why is light given"—You may say *"why"* when you doubt the reason for a thing. You may say *"why"* when you mourn over a thing (Why? O why did this have to happen?). You may say *"why"* when you are complaining, as Job is doing here. As for the light, it is presumed by some that knowledge is meant here. Why am I enlightened with the knowledge of my misery? If I did not understand the sadness of my condition, I would not be

so miserable. But in this case the question is this, Why am I given light to see my misery? Why does my life continue so that I might be miserable and bitter? Actually, the expression, *"in misery"* means more than a mere miserableness. Just as to be in the spirit denotes an especially high state of spirituality, so being in misery marks out a very high state of misery.

"and life to the bitter of soul"—Life departs when the soul and body part. Job asks, Why is my life still in me that I might be bitter in my soul? While my soul was sweet, it was a pleasure to have it in my body. But now that my soul is bitter, why must I continue to be in bitterness with it. Bitterness of soul is a deep intrinsical or inward sorrow. To have soul trouble is the very soul of trouble. There can be no bitterness equal to bitterness of the soul.

Job's whys are common to man, for when one sees no reason for a thing, cannot understand the reason for a thing, he begins to conclude that there can be no reason at all. Job in his darkened condition cannot see the reason why he must live in his present state. But there is a reason, and we are privilege to know it.

In fact, there are many reasons why a man might be asked to live a life in misery. What if God were to appear and ask you to live a miserable and bitter life? Would that not be reason enough to do so? It may be that the life of nature must be continued, and that in great misery, so that the life of grace may be made to abound. Some learn obedience by suffering, some learn humility, some learn to rejoice exceedingly in God, some learn that nothing in this world is important but God Himself. There are those who are patterns for other Christians. Some are towers of strength to encourage others. Some cannot develop empathy with the suffering of others, and they cannot help them until they feel the same. In every case where a Christian becomes bitter and miserable, He shall discover the power and the love of God. For He can make bitter souls sweet, miserable lives joyful.

It is a trouble to possess good things when we cannot enjoy them. Job is not really wanting to rid himself of light and life because they themselves make him miserable. But it is his misery which makes him want to be rid of light and life. He cannot enjoy these great and wonderful possessions, so he will be rid of them. None of the good things in this life would change his misery into happiness. Only the things of grace could do so.

"To those who long for death, but it comes not; and dig for it more than for hidden treasures?"—Job 3:21.

So bitter is he at soul that he longs for death; yea, he will even dig for it as if it were hidden treasure. There is bitterness in the death of the body, but some are so bitter of soul that they count the very bitterness of death as sweetness. The word translated *"longing"* signifies a very vehement desire. He hotly lusts after death. He violently pursues death, in a headlong rush to seize it. Two words come from this root, one for the palate of the mouth and the other for a fishhook. Thus the original word carries in it this picture of Job hungrily desiring death, his mouth waters for it; and of death as a bait which he will greedily swallow down. Also clear is the exceeding intensiveness of such a longing after death.

"and dig for it more than for hidden treasures"—A covetous man has one of the strongest lusts that a man can have. The lust for gold has caused men to trade even their lives for it. A man may long for something, but it is another degree of desire that comes upon him when he starts to pursue it and dig for it.

IS IT LAWFUL TO LONG AFTER DEATH?

Death in itself is in no way desirable. We cannot desire that which is an enemy, a destructive force to us (not if we are in our right minds). If any should desire death as death, or under the notion of death, they would be seeking to find out an enemy, *"the last enemy to be destroyed is death"* (1 Cor. 15). Many have desired death, but it is not death they truly want. Let us consider what could make the desire of death lawful:

1. If we desire death in order to be free from sin, it is a holy desire.
2. If we long to have more full communion with Christ, it is lawful to desire death.

However, again it is needful to remember that even in these things, we ought to say, *"God willing."* As the Apostle did when he desired to be dissolved and to be with the Lord Jesus Christ. And he proved the subjection of his own will to that of Christ by acknowledging that it was the will of God to remain here for the sake of the saints.

To long for death as a cure for our troubles in this life; to seek the grave as a place of rest for our fleshly man, this is a great sin. Those who think that life is not worth living unless it is cushioned with outward comforts are right—their life is not worth a thing. How cheaply do we hold life if we become weary of it when we have a period of adverse circumstances. Jonah belongs in this class, for because he was embarrassed, because his pride was hurt, he was ready to give up his life. If life consists only of the plaudits of men, of the feeling that we are ten feet tall and ought not to be crossed, then it is indeed easy to give up such an empty and dissatisfying caricature of life. Why not seek unto God by prayer, that He would remove the evil circumstances which are so vexing to us. What if He does not open the door of the grave and let us in? Does it mean that He is not your loving friend? If you want to really live, if you want to get completely free from tormenting doubts and troubling circumstances, if you want to slay fear and laugh at oppression, remember that it is faith that overcomes the world. It is the world that lies in wickedness, that abounds with torment and trouble, fear and oppression, Only believe, and the world can never again crease your skull with anxiety or fear. But I will confess that there is a mystery in this, that there are secrets which a Christian must know and apply if he is to effectively escape from the world's claws:

1. If you want to cease seeking after death as a solution to your problems, and if you really want to live in all the fullness and abundance of contentment which can be had this side of Glory, then first you must get your thinking straight—that is, you must begin to think spiritually, the way God teaches you to think in the Bible, The first step in this is to resolve that you shall not seek a single thing to be added to your life. It is normal for men to say, If only I had this, or that, then I would be happy. Not so! The way to happiness is by subtraction, not by addition. You are not happy with what you have now, so how can the addition of this or that, or ever so much make you happy? Things will not do it, no, nor any person or persons in the world. But if you subtract from your desires one of the things you do not have, then you will be a little happier. Suppose you desire a pretty house, and you have suspended your happiness on getting that house—you will not be happy until you get it. If God says no, then you will continue to be unhappy. But, suppose on the other hand that you subtract your desire for that house, you decide you will not suspend your happiness on a house — you will be a lot happier. Now apply this principle, keep subtracting from your desires all the things which you do not now have. Continue subtracting until you are down to those things you own now. Then you will find that your desires match what you have—you are content because you have all you want.

But if you want to reach the highest heights, then keep on subtracting, even those things which you now own, in your imagination take them all away, one by one, until you have nothing—that is, until you have nothing left but Christ. Now do this slowly and deliberately —consider whether or not you can live without Christ. If you cannot bear to subtract Christ from your life, or even the thought of it, you are truly a saint. Now think! What is it that you must have to be happy? You have Christ, What more do you need for happiness? If you say even one thing is necessary in order for you to be happy, that is one thing more than Christ, then examine yourself carefully to see if you are truly in the faith. If Christ satisfied you completely, then what are these things that you are subtracting? They are but sticks and stones. O there is neither mineral, vegetable or animal that a true Christian needs in order to rise above all that this world can offer or threaten.

2. If you want to be content, whatever state you may be in, then learn the ABC's of Christianity. Learn them by saying them over and over until you have them in the heart:

A. I am nothing.
B. I deserve nothing.
C. I can do nothing.
D. I am worse than nothing.
E. If I perish, nothing will be lost.

Add to those Christ, and, (A) you will be some one that God has loved from everlasting —Jer. 31:3; (B) you will receive all things, *"He who did not withhold His own Son, but surrendered Him for us all, shall He not also freely give us all things with Him?"*—Rom. 8:32; (C) you can do all things, *"I can do all things through Christ who strengthens me"*—Phil. 4:13; (D) your sins will be blotted out and you will be one of God's jewels—Isa. 44:22 and Mal. 3:16; (E) you shall not perish, but have everlasting life—John 3:16.

"to those who rejoice exceedingly, and are glad, when they can find the grave"—Job 3:22.

Having said that they long for death and are willing to dig for it as for hidden treasure, he now supposes that they find death and rejoice that they have found the grave. Some connect this verse with the last, taking this as the sense: They long for death, they dig for it as if it were hidden treasure, rejoicing exceedingly as they did, but they merely find the grave—not what they thought they would find, no true treasure. This could be the meaning.

Death is dreadful, The grave is a place of darkness. Most would not long for it, and it is certain they would not rejoice to find it. But there are some who will rejoice when they find whatever it is that they have longed for—even death and the grave. So strong are the desires of some, they will be pleased to gain them however hurtful they may be in themselves. Sometimes to be relieved of an impending evil causes joy, though the present may have a present evil in it. Joy is an affection of the mind which arises when the mind believes it has found something good. It may be a foolish joy, one which will appear to be foolish when the next world has come, yet there may be rejoicing now.

"Why is light given to a man whose way is hidden, whom God has hedged in?"—Job 3:23.

Job began in the twentieth verse to ask why a life that is miserable is continued. Why could not those who will to die be permitted to do so? Now he continues to question, saying here: *"Why is light given, etc"*—the same words which he used in verse 20. In this verse, however, he does not repeat the part about misery, but tells of a man whose way is hid, whom God has hedged in. Actually the first four words are not in the original. They are supplied by the translator because they are obviously appropriate to a continuation of the argument, to refresh the reader's mind as to what begins the question.

"to a man whose way is hid"—This is a metaphorical way, not a way in which one travels from place to place. The way of a man is his purpose, or intention (e.g. This is the way he planned it). A man's way may also be his course, the way he walks in this life. A man walks before God both inwardly and outwardly. Man in his inward parts converses with God and behaves himself in a certain way with God. When God commanded Abraham to *"walk before Me and be perfect,"* He was referring to his inward behavior, walking before God in a perfect way. Job knew that a man's way could not be hidden from God, so this is not the meaning here. As for a man's outward way, the word abounds with commandments to walk in a godly way. These are not hidden, else they would not qualify. Job does not mean this outward way either.

This is Job's complaint, that the way that God has marked out for a man was hidden from him. He could neither understand nor interpret what God was doing, yet he knew that God's actions were determining the way that Job was going to go. (1) He could not see the cause of his affliction, God had hidden it from him. Elihu advised him in this regard, *"Surely it is right to be said to God, I have borne chastisement...that which I see not, teach me"* (34:31,32). (2) He could not see what was going to be the end of these frightening ways of God in afflicting him without seeming cause. 'I cannot see ahead, I am so enveloped in darkness and pain—why am I being taken this way, and why is my way hidden from me?'

"whom God has hedged in"—Satan complained that God had a hedge around Job. Now it is Job's complaint about a hedge God has placed around him. But it is not the same hedge. The hedge Satan hated was a hedge of mercy, of blessings, favor and protection. Job's hedge here is one of thorny troubles and pricking sorrows. The hedge Satan envied was a hedge of roses, so high that no evil could break through and annoy Job. This one of Job's anticipation as Job appears to be coming apart under this severe trial, but if God were not assisting by hiding from Job the reason, etc., the old lion would not be roaring so loudly now. Job did not have the benefit of New Testament comforts, for if he had this verse Affliction and darkness usually go together. It is not unusual for an afflicted man's way to be hidden from him. The way he got himself into it often is hidden; the way to get out of affliction is most often hidden; and the way to act while under it may be hidden. This of course increases the depth and pressures of an affliction when the reason is unknown, the way out is not seen, and the way to act is not clear. The Devil is leaning forward in anticipation as Job appears to be coming appart under this severe trial, but if God were not assisting by hiding from Job the reason, etc., the old lion would not be roaring so loudly now. Job did not have the benefit of New Testament comforts, for if he had this verse inscribed for him, he would have been well on the way to recovery by now—*"God is faithful, who will not allow you to be tempted above what you are able, but with the temptation He will make a way of escape, so that you are able to bear it"* (1 Cor. 10:13). As Job peers out of the darkness, he sees God making a fence around him, instead of making a way to escape.

"For my sighing comes before I eat, and my groanings are poured out like the waters"—Job 3:24.

In this verse, Job leaves the third person and takes up the first person, saying I, not *"him who is in misery,"* or, *"a man whose way is hidden."* Now it is *"I eat,"* and, *"my groanings."* Literally it is, *"Before the face of my bread, my sighings come."* This is a most emphatic construction, denoting a continuance of his sorrows without intermission. He has ashes with his bread and tears with his drink.

"my groanings are poured out like the waters"—Here we have extremity pictured. It is a great affliction that brings forth complaint, a greater affliction that brings tears and mourning. But the greatest affliction is that which leaves a man no more spirit than will roar forth in groanings and moanings. Job is a man of stature, stamina, spirit and courage. But here he sighs and roars, alternately wilts and groans. It is as if he were altogether melted into sorrow, *"poured out like the waters."*

"For the thing which I greatly feared has come upon me, and that which I was afraid of has come to me"—Job 3.25.

The word translated *"for"* is not used for cause. It is rather used for affirmation and certainty. For now I know that what I feared has come upon me — this is the sense.

"the thing which I greatly feared"—Literally, *"I feared a fear, and it has come upon me."* This use of *"feared"* and *"fear"* together doubles or multiplies the greatness of the fear. Job is acknowledging that he has before had misgivings in his spirit, a terrifying apprehension that some black day would come when he was hedged in and could not get out. Once again, the question arises, was it lawful for Job to have such fears? We are commanded not to be anxious in anything (Phil. 4:6), and Christ rebuked the disciples because they were afraid in a storm—was it right for Job to fear even when he was basking in the sunshine of God's blessings?

There are different kinds of fear: (1) There is a cautionary fear, the taking of thought beforehand to prevent the coming of trouble; (2) There is a fear which is opposed to pre-sumption and carnal security, *"do not be high-minded, but fear"* (Rom. 11:20); (3) There is a fear that makes us provide for an evil day; (4)There is a fear which keeps us from do-ing things which displease or provoke God; (5) There is a fear that our hearts will harden that our graces will fade; and many more fears might also be mentioned.

Job's fear was a fear of wisdom and caution, not one of torment and vexation. He fear-ed presumption, an evil day that might find him unprepared, any occasion which would arbitrarily seize upon him and his good suddenly — no such fears were consistent with his faith, for perfect love casts out fear.

If we consider Job, how unmovable he was in the face of those great afflictions which flooded suddenly into his life, how he successfully wrestled with all those distresses, then we shall see the value of taking thought beforehand as to what might come upon us. By a holy fear Job had set himself for the blows that rained down upon him.

"I was not in safety, nor did I have rest, Nor was I quiet; yet trouble comes"—Job 3:26.
Job adds to and expounds the former verse. It is not that he was not safe behind the hedge of God, but that he is claiming he did not fall into a false sense of security, a carnal dependence upon his fame and fortune, his friends and forces. He did not count himself safe because of these. Nebuchadnezzar said, *"I was at rest in my house"* (Dan. 4:4), it is the same word used here. The king thought himself safe enough in the very midst of his splendid house and secure kingdom. Job denies that any such pride ever took hold of him.

"neither did I have rest, nor was I quiet"—He did not reach a certain height and then take his ease. He did not rest upon his laurels. He did not rest in his own wisdom and ab-ilities. He never placed any happiness in things, nor hopes upon creature. Compare Job with the fool rich man of Luke 12, you will see the difference between resting in riches and attainments, and not resting in them. He did not quietly cease to seek to God, count-ing himself to have already attained.

"yet trouble comes"—All these ways Job had sought to avoid trouble: He had a holy fear and prepared beforehand for trouble—this is the best way to avoid trouble. He did not seem presumptuous, had not rested in anything or anyone but God Himself. He did not get his peace and quiet from contemplating his greatness or his skill. It is usual for a man of this sort to avoid many troubles that other men fall into. Yet trouble came. He has proven the truth of these claims, for he did not set his heart upon riches—when they were taken away, he was not cast down, He did not rest his happiness upon family—however happy they may have made him—for when they were suddenly removed, he did not sin nor act as if his props had been pulled from under him. He enjoyed these, as God's bless-ings should be enjoyed, while he had them. But when God removed them, he did not curse God and die.

Job is troubled by his trouble. He is saying to himself, 'If I had been counting myself se-cure because of what I was or had, if I had given myself up to the contentments of the flesh, of if I had trusted in any man for safety, then I would not have wondered when calamity came upon me. But this is a riddle that I cannot explain, that when my heart was in no way set upon my estate, yet my estate fell. When I did not rest in the creature, I met with no end of troubles in the creature.' This is not God's usual manner and Job knows it. God often pulls comforts away from those who are glued to their comforts. When any shall say, *"peace and safety, then sudden destruction shall come upon them"* (1 Thess. 5:3). He that desires to save his life shall lose it. So it usually is with a man's possessions. But when the contrary is true, you may not rest in that either. You cannot say that because you trust and rest in Him, no trouble shall come. He does what He pleases, and sometimes His purposes call for trouble in a holy life!

CHAPTER IV

"Then Eliphaz the Temanite answered:"—Job 4:1.

Job's three friends have been silent all this while, perhaps divided between compassion, and indignation. They could pity his sad condition, but they thought it only right to be angry on God's behalf. Therefore their zeal kindled and their hearts waxed hot. They were mute, but they were musing — the fire being fed by Job's impassioned words. At last, now, they can hold their tongues no longer. A hot dispute follows, bitter words becoming more bitter as each man spoke. Eliphaz begins, the others follow. Finally God Himself must appear to moderate the dispute and to make judgment between them.

THE PRINCIPLES OF JOB'S FRIENDS

Now it is that the discussion of that great mystery and profound doctrine, the providence of God in the distribution of the good things and the evil things of this life. The question is, can God be just and good while He distributes the good things of this world to those who are evil, and the evil things of this world to those who are good? This is touched upon in many books of the Bible, but only in Job is it given a complete discussion. There are six persons who speak to the question: Eliphaz, Job, Bildad, Zophar, Elihu and God.

There are many threads of the same color and substance mixed and interwoven by the disputants throughout the discussion. The three friends agree in setting up Job as their mark, yet they take different standings and perhaps different levels, varying from each other in some things.

However, there are four principles on which all three friends agree. In three of these principles Job agrees with them. On the fourth principle, Job utterly disagrees, and his answers are mostly in refutation of this false principle.

These are the three principles on which Job and his three friends agree:

1. That all the afflictions and calamities which befall man are seen and known by God.

2. That God is the author and efficient cause, the orderer and disposer of all those afflictions and calamities.

3. That God is unquestionably sovereign over all. He does no wrong, nor can he do any injury to his creatures, whatever affliction he lays upon them, or however long they last.

All fully insist upon all these principles, speaking very glorious things of the power, wisdom, justice, holiness and sovereignty of the Lord. Job is clearly the champion in praising God's attributes.

The fourth principle is grounded upon the two following assumptions:

A. That whoever is good and does good shall receive a present good reward, in the same measure as the good he has done; and, say, Job's three friends, but not Job, that whoever is wicked and does wickedly shall be punished in the present, in the same measure as the evil that he has done.

B. That if at any time a wicked man flourishes in outward prosperity, his prosperity will be short-lived and will end in visible judgments during this life. Contrariwise, that if at any time a godly man be cast down in adversity, his affliction will be very short and he shall be recovered and rewarded with visible blessings in this life.

4. Building on the above assumptions, the fourth principle of Job's friends is this, that whoever is greatly afflicted and is held under the pressure of his affliction for a long time is to be numbered with the wicked, even though there is no other evidence or witness to prove this to be so.

THE ERRORS OF JOB'S FRIENDS

1. The three friends never considered the true state of affairs, that God may afflict without any evident cause at all. They constantly insisted the opposite, that God never afflicted

85

without definite cause, that the cause of all afflictions was sin. Job did not know the true state of affairs either, being as much in the dark as his friends. But he insisted without faltering that it must be so that God would afflict without evident cause, because there was no evident cause to be found in his inward or outward life.

2. The friends presented God from one side only: His abhorrence of sin and His punishment of sin.

3. They presented God as arbitrary, indefensible on any other grounds, and imputed all afflictive acts to God's power, while obscuring and even denying God's never-failing mercy and goodness.

4. They ignored God's promise never to leave or forsake His own, and the consequent effectual working of God within the sufferer to bring forth faith and repentance as the fruit of the Spirit's afflictive teaching.

5. Instead of using God's providence as evidence of His love, and as ground for hope they used it deceitfully, as a razor to shave off Job's righteousness, as an instrument to kill Job's conscious conviction that he had done no more wrong than those who were not severely afflicted.

6.They played the hypocrite in pretending to understand Job's affliction, being willing to condemn him for it, to prescribe for it, even though they were actually not in possession of either the external facts or the internal motives which affected Job's situation.

7. They spoke wickedly for God. They made plain charges of the most flagrant wickedness against Job, based not upon facts or divinely revealed principles, but upon mere inference from false premises. They were unjust to Job, not only in harboring baseless suspicions, but in making rash and reckless assertions of his guilt.

8. They spoke wickedly for Satan, being shamefully cruel in assaulting a suffering and distracted friend, causelessly aggravating his distress by trying to rob him of his true and comforting views of God, and to substitute in their place a God who was pitiless, unjust, and an inexorable adversary who intended to crush him unless he admitted to a degree of guilt which Job knew to be absolutely untrue.

9. The friends had no real conception of the special significance of suffering. They did not realize that God uses suffering as a test of character, as a means of discipline, as a teaching device to train His children in godliness. It was of course unrevealed at this time that a man may suffer not only because he is a sinner, but because he is a saint. It never occured to them that suffering might be a proof of God's love, a means of grace, a blessing in disguise—the very proof of sonship being chastening and scourging. These things are divinely revealed, and the book of Job was chosen by God to reveal much of the teaching which He gives us on the subject of patience in suffering. The presumptuous friends could have admitted their ignorance, they could have joined their friend in praying for divine guidance in discovering the truth in regard to these matters.

10. These men were proud, presuming immediately that they were more pure and more innocent than Job. That they so easily and so readily made this conclusion, merely because Job was suffering affliction, while they themselves were not being afflicted, proves that they were far more overly righteous than Job. Suffering the ravages of pride, they assumed such a high position as to make them inerrant in their judgment of Job's trouble and his character. They fell from this into destructive mercilessness, the unfeeling vindictiveness which accompanies pride. They did not hesitate to set up their own standards, then arraign Job before the tribunal of their own judgment. They should have arraigned him before God, leaving to God the judging and disposing of the charges. No! but they must not only judges, but also the prosecutor; yes, even the right to be Job's defense attorney

was arrogated to themselves.

Job's friends were like Job's messengers. The messengers came one on top of another carrying evil tidings, inflicting wounds by the bad news that they brought him. The friends are now going to stand up one after another, tumbling over one another in their haste to wound him with harsh censures, hard thoughts, evil insinuations and a falsified God. They are playing Satan's game to the hilt, however unwittingly. They put more pressure on Job than all that has gone before, and they work hard to subvert him in order to wring from him a confession of hypocrisy. In this way Satan devised his plan, hoping to drive Job from his integrity and thus to cause him to curse and desert God.

ELIPHAZ

Eliphaz speaks first, evidently being the eldest of the three and thus taking precedence over them—it being presumed that the eldest was the wisest. Apparently, Eliphaz was old enough to be Job's father (Job 15:10). He seemingly set out to rouse Job from the sad state of despondency which is settling in upon him. To do this he seeks to expose the moral reasons for this terrible infliction, and to exhort Job to an humble and complete submission to God's ruling hand. The return of God's favor and his former prosperity is then held out as the incentive for such submission.

Eliphaz makes two serious mistakes, imperceptive and blundering assumptions which crucify Job's spirit, not his fleshly passions:

1. Both Eliphaz and Job sat there in the dust, both had wept silently for many days and night. But there was a difference, Eliphaz was suffering no pain. From his coarse handling of Job, it could not even be said that he suffered vicariously for his friend. Eliphaz had suffered no losses of property, servants or children. Eliphaz did not have the jeering words of his wife dinning in his ears, saying, *"curse God and die."* Lastly, Eliphaz did not have an old and close friend sitting at his elbow assuring him that he had no reason for complaint, that he only had to flick a switch inside himself and begin confessing his sin in order to regain all he had lost or suffered. In short, it ill-becomes anyone to talk to a suffering friend as if the extent of his suffering should not have any serious bearing on the way he acted. Job could not be expected to bear up bravely, not to break during all the days and nights that he was being assaulted with every kind of satanic blow a man can suffer. Eliphaz can testify that man is born unto trouble, yet he seems to have little consultation within himself as to the last serious trouble that had flooded through his door. Else would he not have been more compassionate and understanding? Who, besides Job, ever bore such indignities, pains, losses and shocks without spraying sins in every direction? Certainly, Job spoke unadvisedly in his past speech — but who wouldn't under such rare circumstances? Job answered Eliphaz well when he told him, *"pity is due from friends."* Not accusation, not insinuation, nor false assumptions, but pity is the duty of Eliphaz.

2. As to the principle involved, Eliphaz simply does not know what he is talking about. It is a lesson everyone should mark well, that you can say a multitude of things, each one true in some sense, yet completely miss the truth when the whole discourse is applied to a given situation. Eliphaz artfully and skillfully paints many truths upon his canvas, so that it would seem that you could object to none of it fairly. Yet beneath his low-keyed presentation of Job's case as he sees it, there is this false conclusion that Job's suffering is equal to his sin, and God is punishing him in exact measure for those sins, *"The ones who plow iniquity and sow wickedness reap the same"* (4:8). He presents God's providential dispensations of affliction as strictly punitive. Of course, all men are sinners, and there is no suffering without sin as the precedent cause. But a clear picture of where Eliphaz is wrong can be seen if you will consider this, that just as Job was a sinner by nature, so was Eliphaz — why then was he not suffering severely with the kind of afflictions that were crushing Job? Eliphaz answers this with the false principle we are discussing, by saying it is evident that Job has committed unseen and especially wicked sins, else he would not be suffering these extraordinary afflictions. If asked, Eliphaz would say he had not sinned so.

For proof of his convictions as to Job's sins, though undeveloped at the time of this speech, see Job 22:5,6 where he says, *"Is not your wickedness great, and your inquity without measure?"* He goes on to accuse Job of the most heinous sins a man may commit. Righteousness was upholding Job, self-righteousness was strangling Eliphaz. He had been blessed with a life that was at least relatively free from affliction. To what effect? That he might lord it over those who were afflicted? That he might assume himself to be more pure than those who were tortured with anguish and piercing sorrows? What fools are those who think themselves God's favorites because they never suffer! (See chapter 21 for Job's answer.) How ungrateful they are to God, when they smear their proud accusations all over His suffering servants, and arrogate to themselves the position of God's champion saints. How unscriptural, for invariably the champions of God regard themselves as the *"chief of sinners,"* rather than the ultimate in sainthood.

"If we try a word with you, will you be grieved? But who can withhold himself from speaking?"—Job 4:2.

The first argument of Eliphaz begins here. He intends to prove that Job is guilty of hypocrisy, though it does not yet appear that he is willing to denominate him a hypocrite. He is arguing that a man's religion is emptied of all force if in his teaching he teaches others to have patience under affliction, but he himself shows impatience under affliction. Then he applies this to Job, concluding that Job has proven to be hypocritical because he has just broken out into these passionate complaints. God judged Job patient, Eliphaz did not.

"If we try a word with you, will you be grieved?"—Here is an effort to convince Job that the following words are out of friendship and good will, that no harm is meant to him. The idea is this, that heartfelt interest compels this old friend to speak thus.

The word for try here properly means to tempt, either for good or evil. A man who is tempted is tried, or tested, that it may be seen what kind of man he is. Eliphaz is suggesting that some words will be said that will try Job's case, that he may be proven out, and that good may come of it. Seriousness is also inherent in this expression.

"will you be grieved?"—A weariness which may end in positive action, perhaps in rage, or in fainting, this is the meaning of the word *"grieved"* here. The question is, Will you withhold yourself from falling into a fit of passion such as you were just in? I must in good conscience try to help you.

"But who can withhold himself from speaking?"—Why this is a wonderful thing, that Eliphaz is so agitated by one short passionate outburst from Job, and that he cannot bear it. He must speak out immediately—and, note it, at much greater length. Yet he has taken the attitude that Job ought to have kept his mouth shut, even though the sufferings of Job are far more full of necessity, there is a much greater need for Job to vent his feelings. Eliphaz felt no pain from Job's pain, at least he could sit and say nothing as he watched Job suffer for days on end. But Job's outcry from his pain gives Eliphaz such a pain that he cannot forbear to speak!

The word, *"withhold,"* denotes a locking up, so that nothing can get out. It is used of fire, which was shut up in Jeremiah's bones and could not get out (Jer. 20:9). What a low boiling point Eliphaz had, compared to the fires that ate at Job's vitals for a time far longer, and raging to far greater intensity before Job broke forth into a scream of anguish.

It was right for Eliphaz to give a friendly rebuke to Job. Reproof is a bitter pill, so it also was right that it should be wrapped in a coating of love and trust, but with meekness also being a prime ingredient—*"if a man is overtaken in some fault, you, the spiritual ones, restore such a one in a spirit of meekness"* (Galations 6:1). Just as a surgeon sets a broken bone, using comforting words and a soft hand to make the very painful operation as easy as possible, so ought we to use holy skill and scriptural words in the repairing of any spiritual damage which we may see in a fellow saint, and which we are called on to repair.

It is not easy to bear reproof. It takes a lot of spiritual wisdom to give it, and it takes perhaps even more to receive it. Reprovers are disqualified if they have no love in their bosoms. Love in him who is being rebuked is even more important, for it is natural for men to hate and to lay a trap for him who gives warning in the gate. If you want to be known as a man who belongs among the spiritual giants in God's family, first you must prove that you can be reproved without raging or fainting. There are times when it is our duty to reprove men, whether they are troubled or not. If God is dishonored by what another professing saint is doing or saying, he is in danger and we should say scriptural words to snatch him out of the fire, before he becomes too spotted from the flesh (Jude 25).

"Behold you have instructed many, and you have made the weak hands strong"—Job 4:3. Behold, as has been said, is a word to call immediate attention to what follows. It can be used as a word of derision, being intended to set up a jeer. But here it is to arrest the mind (Listen!). There are four acts of love which Job is being credited with here and in the following verses: (1) teaching the ignorant; (2) encouraging the weak; (3) supporting those who are apt to fall; and, (4) comforting those who are ready to faint.

"You have instructed many"—This word for *"instruct"* can be translated by *"correct," "chasten," "afflict,"* and, *"teach."* Not only did Job correct and teach his own family,. but many others far and wide. He loved all, so he instructed all.

"you have made the weak hands strong"—These are hands that are remiss, hands that hang down. Negligent, lax, or idle hands could be so described, as well. The grieved, the dejected were among those that Job stood ready to strengthen, for they were in his heart. This word for *"weak"* is also translated, *"dead,"* because all strength has departed from the dead. Even the giants in Scripture get their names from this word, in that the sight of a giant brings on dread and drains men of their spirit and strength. Some have strong heads, but they have idle or slothful hands—they are weak. Some are vigorous with strength, but fear will make them weak (Isa. 35:3). Some who are of good natural strength will become weak through irresolution—they are between two opinions, they know not which way to turn—a double-minded man is not dependable in any of his ways, for he is weak (James 1:7). Then there is a weakness of hands which comes from grief and sorrow, those that are mentioned in Heb. 12:12, *"lift up the hands which hang down and the feeble knees."*

"Your words have upheld him who was falling, and you have made strong the feeble knees"—Job 4:4. Job was the kind of man who supported and helped up those who were falling, admittedly the kind of man that would be needed in this very situation. Why was Eliphaz not doing for Job what he says here that Job had done for others? The word, *"falling,"* pictures one who stumbles or strikes his foot against a thing and begins to fall. There are three types of falling in Scripture:
1. There is a falling into sin, for that man who was overtaken in a fault in Gal. 6:1 was stumbling or tripping and falling into sin. We all often fall into sin.
2. There is a falling into affliction, into troubling circumstances, *"the just man falls seven times, and rises up again"* (Prov. 24:16). He often falls into afflictive corrections.
3. There is a falling under trouble. So it is here in Job. These have fallen because the griefs and sorrows are stumbling them. They are not able to take strong steps to help themselves. Some fall easily, they cannot maintain an upright position even under a light affliction. To these, and to all, Job extended his hand, and his shoulder. He was willing to be their staff; yea, the very ligaments in their loins and knees. He was practiced in setting props under tottering souls, using holy skills and holy words to do so. The art appears to be unknown to Job's friends, and how much more is it so in our day!

"and you have made strong the feeble knees"—The Hebrew word for a knees signifies (in the root) to bless or to pray, because in these we ususally bow the knee. The word translat ed *"feeble knees"* here is actually, *"bowed knees."* A knee that buckles under us and bows is a feeble knee. Hands hanging down indicate despair in some degree; feeble knees develop from an expected evil, usually. Not only did Job uphold those who were in present trouble, but also those who fearfully were expecting blows to rain about their heads. Those who know God are very ready to communicate the knowledge of God to others, *"Then I will teach transgressors Your ways, and sinners shall be converted to You"* (Ps. 51:13). If some physical support was needed, Job gave it (see chapter 29). But then, as now, the greatest support and comfort, the most effective defuser of rumors, or even truly impending doom is the word of God. Love to man is this, that you desire his utmost good. It is not that all the good things, so called, of this life may be given to him, but that one thing needful be give him—the grace and knowledge of Jesus Christ.

Job was the greatest of all the men in the East. Yet he counted it no waste of time, nor any loss, to lean down and support those who were weak. Most generally, it is easier to get blood out of a turnip than to get help from a rich man. But those who are rich in grace will not hesitate to use any riches in this world's goods when a fellow saint needs help.

"But now it has come upon you, and you faint. It touches you, and you are troubled" —Job 4:4.

There are as many advisors in the world as there are troubles. It pays to be careful as to the ones you tell your troubles to, for an avalanche of advice is bound to come your way Now it is being suggested to us that Job is such a one, a person who is great for giving advice, but when the same thing happens in his life, he faints and falls out. It's not true.

"and you faint"—This is an extraordinary fainting, one which makes the loved ones a fraid that the fainting person is going to expire, or go out of his mind. The word is some times translated *"grieved,"* and sometimes even *"mad"* or *"furious."* (*"the land of Egypt fainted because of the famine"*—that is, they were maddened, crazy from hunger). Eliphaz is saying that Job has given such wise advice before, but now he has lost his senses, he has fainted under his trials.

"It touches you"—The Devil wanted Job touched. Now Eliphaz says he has been, and that in the severest of blows, multiplied and leaping one upon another.

"and you are troubled"—Here is another word with great emphasis, denoting a vehement and amazed trouble (the kind of amazement that set upon Saul as he was stricken by the words of the apparition of Samuel).

Eliphaz is butting Job. When a man commends you highly, for however many sentences then starts the next sentence with a *"But,"* you are about to be stabbed! Those who speak sweet words to you as they draw out their secret daggers (as Joab did when he killed poor Amasa,) then they suffer from the leprosy of sin—avoid them assiduously. If you cannot praise a man without adding a *"but,"* then you are either playing the hypocrite, or you are about to gossip. Would you like for men to butt you like this, 'But he is a hypocrite or, 'But he is a gossip?'

It is good to commend a man for the good that he has done, especially when he is deject ed and disarmed by grief or fright. The apostle Paul followed this policy regularly, as in Hebrews 6:10, *"For God is not unrighteous to forget your work and labor of love, etc."* The words of Eliphaz would have been good words indeed if he had not made the wrong application of them. For in drawing the comparision between the past and the present, he completely lost sight of anything in Job's condition which would cause his present com plaints. By discarding, ignoring, and even obscuring the reasons for Job's behavior, he can more easily deceive himself into thinking that Job is a hypocrite for the present.

"Is not your fear your hope? Is not your hope the uprightness of your ways?"—Job 4:6

God tells us that Job was a God-fearing man. Reverential fear is essential to godliness The fear of God is not only the beginning of wisdom, but it is the proof of godliness. It most proper that we who are but dust and ashes should have fear for a majestic, glorious and infinitely higher Being than ourselves. God condescends to be loved by us. He even calls for our love as a Friend, as a Father, but what is love without respect? And to whom can we give the kind of reverence that we give to God? A man who loves his wife will be fearful lest he displease his wife (1 Cor. 7:33), and vice versa. A man who loves God will be no less careful lest He displease the One he loves. Job professed to have this fear in his heart and life. Eliphaz is asking him, What has become of it? He jeers, Where is it now? You say you hope in God, but now you are troubled and terrified and thrown into such consternation that you are mouthing all these rash expressions about God and His providence. Even if Eliphaz has still some confidence in Job's true piety, he is shocking him by questioning whether or not Job has lost confidence in his Fear, that is, his God.

Confidence is more than faith. Just as patience is hope lengthened, so confidence is faith strengthened. A soul who believes is blessed, but a soul who believes and confides in his God moment by moment has a working faith that puts him into a higher region of grace and comfort. Assurance is the highest degree of faith, and confidence is the highest degree of assurance. Confidence has in it a cheerful abiding trust; courage to cast our carnal fears, and despondency; boldness to attack and cast aside all cowardice; a glorying in God which bubbles up beyond and around any crushing blow.

"Is not your hope the uprightness of your ways?"—Shades of Satan! Here Eliphaz is making the same charge against Job, that he serves himself, that he trusts in himself and not in God. God said that Job was an upright man. Eliphaz suggests that Job is trusting in his uprightness, not in his God. The hope here is a strong intention of both body and mind to wait for and confidently expect something. So Eliphaz chides Job with this, Where is that unremitting hope that you have always displayed? Did you not expect to always be blessed with increase upon increase, with comfort on top of comfort, with health and wealth and friends, because of what you considered yourself to be? Did your Fear, your Confidence, your Hope, and all those glistening honors and sterling characteristics all disappear with your goods and your health?

This question is the very question to ask a hypocrite. For a mere pretender to godliness does make his works his confidence. He has hope only in himself. He plays the role of a godly man merely for the gain that is in it. There are a host of people today whose aims are refined, whose morals are constrained, whose dealings are outwardly honest, because they are holy for holiness' sake, religious for religion's sake—that is, they want the name and the fame of being holy and religious. These usually wilt when persecution comes, or in the fire of affliction. Eliphaz is really asking Job, Are you not really a hypocrite? Or, at least, Haven't you been acting the hypocrite? There is such a thing as a hypocrite that does not realize that their graces are false until they are brought to great trials. They run with other hypocrites, allowing their standards to be the rule of their faith, thinking that their works are equal to any. Some are active hypocrites, intentionally acting a part, deliberately deceiving others by a religious mask over their filthy faces. Others are passive hypocrites who are miserably deceived by the collusions of Satan and their own treacherous nature.

Of course it is true that true and holy fear will preserve the soul and keep it in the will of God. Holy fear is as a golden bridle to the soul, turning it this way or that way as the Lord directs. Love is strong as death, but when love fails to keep you from the raging wave of corruption which will spring up from your fleshly nature, then fear will come in and shore up the walls of your faith. This is not a slavish fear we speak of, but a holy respect for God, a reverent desire to do everything to please Him that we are able to do. *"The fear of the Lord is to depart from evil"* (Prov. 16:6). The fear of the Lord is also a strong hope and a fountain of life (Prov. 14:26, 27). Therefore, in affliction, sorrow, and even the flooding of grief, our Fear gives us hope, and we will not ordinarily break over into passionate complaints that do the Lord no honor. But Job's trouble is no ordinary disaster, nor a single calamity—he showed his holy strength against such things as these.

DID JOB'S FAILING BY COMPLAINING PROVE THAT HE WAS FALSE BEFORE?

May a man decline from what he was before, fail to meet the challenges of sin and Satan as strongly as before, and still be counted a truly godly man? Well, of course he may. Did not Abraham, Isaac, Moses and David all have their periods of declension? Then they did not only not deserve to be followed, but they were rebuked for their actions. Indeed, if one could lose an ounce of grace, which is the freely bestowed favor of God, one might cease to be godly. But true grace is everlasting, true holiness endures as long as God.

1. Job was perturbed and broke out into complaints, but it was a sudden failing, not a resolved and considered course of action. An unexpected storm hurried his spirit so violently that he was not master of his own actions. His passions got the bridle on their necks, and were away so fast that he was not able to stop or allay them.

2. These things came from solid causes, there was a reason for him to be perturbed. The heated, misshapen words which poured from him were issued from the pain in his flesh, not from the perverseness of his spirit. He did not intend to place himself crosswise to God, but he was cross with himself and his life.

3. His graces were hidden behind the cloud of passions, they were not dissipated or hamstrung. They were not acting in their usual strength, but the habits of grace still managed to show through. If his grace had been completely lost, he would have cursed his God.

4. If everyone who falls into sin also falls from grace, then who has any grace? He that says he does not sin is a liar and the truth is not in him. Neither can it be argued that because the sin is great, therefore the person sinning has no grace. After (not just before) David had committed the series of horrible sins attached to the matter of Bathsheba and Uriah, God called David a man after His own heart (except in that matter). True grace does not work uniformly; though it is ever the same in itself, it is not always the same in its effects. True grace cannot be killed, it is alive always, and it will always be acting in some degree of strength—but its level of action may fall off until it is not immediately discerned. Job was loud and distasteful in his emotional crackup, but an examination of all the things he did not say will convince you that his graces were restraining him at every breath.

"Remember, I pray you, who ever perished who was innocent? Or where were the righteous cut off?"—Job 4:7.

Now Eliphaz proceeds to his second argument, in which he further spatters the innocency of Job, in the hope of convincing him of hypocrisy. His argument is this: Innocent persons do not perish, and righteous men are never cut off. But you are perishing, and you are cut off; therefore, Job, you are not innocent nor righteous. He challenges Job to give a single instance to the contrary; Show me a man who perished and was innocent.

"Remember, I pray you"—He suggests gentleness, as he asks Job to take serious thought as to the questions he is going to ask. He is inviting Job to search the records of his mind and try to refute the clear implications of his questions. Memory is a God-given blessing, when it is stored with the wisdom and knowledge that God teaches us. Our memory, like all our other faculties, was blighted and all but destroyed by our falling into sin in Adam. What formerly was a memory bank which could catalog all the body of knowledge in the world now became a weak and unreliable faculty for remembering—and, sadly, now the memory more readily and usually remembers evil things and happenings than it does the things and happenings that are God-honoring. Nevertheless, as with all other faculties and abilities, we are totally responsible to God to do all the things we could before we sinned in Adam, and therefore to remember everything God ever taught us by word or by experience. It is a sin to forget what we ought to remember, and we all ought to remember that.

"who ever perished who was innocent?"—The word translated *"perished"* is a word which has various connotations. It can mean an utter perishing, as with the beast that dies. It can mean to die, to have the soul and body disunited—see Job 34:15. It can mean the debilitating losses which come from severe afflictions. It can mean eternal misery (John 3:16).

The word translated *"innocent"* here means *"empty."* It is applied to innocent persons because such persons are emptied of malice and wickedness, their hearts are swept and cleansed, purged and washed. Every man's heart by nature is brimful of wickedness (see Rom. 1:29; Gen. 6:5). A converted person is emptied of that throng of sinful thoughts and multitude of profane urges which are natural. Of course, some evil thoughts remain. But comparatively he is empty of wickedness.

"or where were the righteous cut off?"—*"There is none righteous, no, not one"* (Rom. 3:11), but righteous here does not mean that there are persons who are righteous in a legal sense; that is, any who had never broken the law of God. But these are called righteous in the Gospel sense, because they are regenerated, because they are intentionally righteous, because they are righteous by imputation. We have righteousness by justification in the Lord Jesus Christ, and by sanctification from Him. He is the Lord our righteousness. With these meanings in mind, consider the following in regard to this verse:

1. Take perishing or cutting off as annihilation, a returning to nothing: in this sense, none shall ever perish, neither the guilty or the innocent can ever be annihilated. As everlasting as God is, so everlasting is every soul—whether for punishment or for reward.

2. Take perishing as dying: Then everyone shall perish, both the guilty and the innocent. Yes, God has made the exception of Enoch and of Elijah, perhaps, but for the rest, *"it is appointed to all men once to die."*

3. Take perishing as the suffering of loss, either from the world temporally, or from the hand of God immediately, or mediately through the hand of man. Both righteous and unrighteous may perish in this way; both the innocent and the guilty. Suffering is not only not confined to the wicked, there are notable cases (of which Job is one) where the righteous have suffered far more than any wicked man this side of hell. David wrote of the prosperity of the wicked, and of himself said, *"All the day long I have been plagued, and I am chastened every morning"* (Ps. 73:12). He gets his whipping for breakfast, and the bread of sorrow with the water of adversity all day long. Noah and Lot would be opposite examples, where it was the ungodly that perished while the righteous were saved.

However, it is not to be imagined that both the righteous and the wicked perish in the same way. There is a difference in their sufferings. God sometimes sends the very same affliction upon a wicked man, and upon a righteous man (illness, imprisonment, etc.). But the wicked man is being punished, while the righteous man is being chastened. The one is being hardened in his sin, the other is being sifted and tenderized, so as to sin no more, or not so much. When love is mixed into the cup of sorrow, there is a difference. When wrath is mixed into a cup of sorrow, there is a galling, misery-producing effect. The children of God are under wrath until they are saved by grace. But after that, there is never any wrath poured into their cups. There is much that pains, much that crushes, much every way that God deems necessary for the purifying of His saints. But as for the wicked, he perishes in a different way, without hope, without comfort, without any ameliorating agent.

4. Take perishing as eternal destruction: Eliphaz is right, the innocent never perished eternally; the righteous were never cut off from eternal life, from God, *"I give to them eternal life, and they shall never perish"* (John 10:28).

5. If perishing is taken for a present destruction, a present cutting off from the favor of God, then Eliphaz is right again. No righteous one ever was cut off from the favor of his God; no innocent man ever perished during this lifetime in this sense. The apostle wrote, *"We are in trouble on every side, but we are not distressed; we are perplexed, but not in despair; we are persecuted, but not forsaken; we are cast down, but not destroyed"* (2 Cor. 4:8,9). David said, *"I have been young, and now am old, yet have I not seen the righteous forsaken"* (Ps. 37:25).

It is this last sense in which Eliphaz uses the words, *"perish,"* and, *"cut off."* He seems to be sure that Job's ill-conceived speech has proven him to be among those that have been forsaken by God. Look at him, Job is a forlorn sight, full of rotting sores, bereft of his children, abandoned by his wife, stripped of his possessions, and with one foot in the grave.

Surely no such person could dare to claim that God was like him. The assumption, the application of the doctrine, these are untrue. The statement is true, that the righteous do not perish in this sense. The statement is false, the inference is false, that Job has perished. It was not possible for Eliphaz to know the true state of affairs, he lacked the facts.

WHY DID THE OLD TESTAMENT SAINTS MISREAD PROVIDENTIAL AFFLICTIONS

David, Jeremiah, Habakkuk, a multitude of the saints in the Old Testament dispensation stumbled over this matter of God's providential distribution of suffering and loss. The reason is this, that in those times God had made some special temporal promises to His people. Obedience was often rewarded with temporal rewards (see Deut. 28; Levit. 27, etc.). It was not God's plan to reveal all the glorious mysteries of the Messianic promise at once. In that age, God often carried them on by outward and temporal promises. Therefore, it was assumed oftentimes that a troubled person, an afflicted one, was guilty of breaking God's laws. Now, of course, we have more precious promises, and a revealed Lord Jesus, and the result of all this Light is that the things of this world are eclipsed by that exceeding glory which we see in His face. Never in the Old Testament do you see the saints promised persecution, warned that they shall have trouble in the world, or commanded to be prepared to take up the Cross. Much less could you find any references to a glorying in infirmities, or persecutions, or afflictions—as you see in Paul. There was not so much as a single written page of Scripture in Job's day. How, then, can you feel so superior to the men, such as Eliphaz, who misread God's providential dealings? Do you not still do it in a day when you not only have every single page of the Scripture to pore over, but have as well a great body of literature to explain to you what every jot and tittle of it means?

"As I have seen, the ones who plow iniquity and sow wickedness reap the same"—Job 4:8. Eliphaz, feeling that he is on absolutely unassailable ground, gives Job no opportunity to answer. He goes on to rip Job's back with an unmistakable inference that he has been plowing iniquity and reaping his just reward for it.

"Even as I have seen"—Not the seeing of a thing with a fleeting glance, but with a critical examination. God saw the light, that it was good—it was after close observation.

"the ones who plow iniquity"—The word translated *"plow"* is a word to denote an act by a skilled worker who uses a tool to accomplish the act. It can be translated, *"engrave,"* or, *"devise."* The farmer engraves the soil with his plow. The ones mentioned here are those that engrave thoughts of iniquity upon their brains, who devise wicked schemes, who artfully contrive means to transgress God's law. The idea of secrecy is certainly included in this word, and especially in this place in Job. Now not every sinner could be called one who plowed iniquity, or a worker of iniquity. This belongs to those who have attained a nefarious skill, a black art, the ability to craft new methods of affronting God.

"and sow wickedness reap the same"—The metaphor is continued, now we have wickedness being sown and reaped. Again, Eliphaz makes a true statement, that those who devise wickedness and sow it shall most certainly reap the same. The New Testament statement of this principle is this, *"For he that sows to his own flesh, from the flesh he shall reap everlasting misery"* (Gal. 6:8). In James you have the progression: *"But each one is tempted when he is drawn away and seduced by his own lust. Then when lust has conceived, it gives birth to sin. And when it is fully finished, sin brings forth death"* (James 1:14). A man lusts; he plows and devises a way to plant it, he sows it and reaps sin. Sin grows until it brings the man death. Death is separation from God. A coward may die a thousand, but a wicked man dies a myriad of these deaths—he lusts and plows and sows and reaps and nourishes each sin until it separates him a little more from God. There is a day, and it arrives very early for some, when they cannot cease from plowing iniquity and sowing wickedness.

The wickedness he reaps in perverseness. Wicked persons labor and toil at their trade until they are completely contrary to God, perverse in all their ways.

"reap the same"—When you sow, you do not get the same body that you sow, but you get the same kind. Sowing wickedness will get a fine crop of wickedness, though it is not the very same wickedness that was marked down in God's book when you sowed it. The fruits of wickedness are called wickedness (Jer. 4:18). The curses, the wrath, the punishments, the sufferings, all these fruits of wickedness become wickedness again in the lives of the sinner. A man who suffers under God's curse will curse God; under God's wrath, will be wrathful against God, etc. *"the same"* here means the same in degree. If he sows much, he will reap much iniquity. There is direct proportion of sins to punishments—it is not possible to get a sentence commuted by God. He did not even spare His own beloved Son, but caused Him to suffer in proportion to all the sins of the elect.

IT IS NOT EASY TO BE A WICKED MAN

A man who plows does not do easy work. To plow iniquity is even harder work than the plowing of the soil. The sons of Belial (men who will not bear the yoke of Christ) are the men who pull Satan's plow, gladly accepting his yoke, expecting to be richly rewarded by him. They tug and sweat, devise and experiment, to find some new way to flout God's laws. But they are the victims of their own skill, they are punished by God for their artful work by receiving from Him complete success in their endeavors. They sow wickedness, and lo and behold, wickedness comes up in abundance and they are inundated by it. They clap their hands in glee and resolve to plant another crop. Like madmen who work hard for deceitful masters, being promised heaps of money for it, being paid in counterfeit coin and rejoicing exceedingly when they get paid. The wicked, however, has a day of reckoning when he shall find the hardest part of all, the everlasting misery which is the true coin which he is earning.

For Eliphaz to apply these terms in their fullest sense to Job is an utter miscarriage of justice. Job in no sense of the word ever devised any iniquity, nor sowed any wickedness. However much may be said to condemn his words in his impassioned speech, not a word could properly be called iniquitous, and not a thought wicked. It was obviously not an artful speech, one that had been studied and carefully tailored to be an affront to God (as would be the case in an iniquitous speech), nor was there any inference or reference to the poor man laboring and toiling to beget even a smidgin of wickedness.

"By the blast of God they perish, and by the breath of His nostrils they are destroyed"—Job 4:9.

Now Eliphaz tells of the judgment of God against those who act wickedly. God blasts their hopes and sends them skittering across the face of the earth by a mighty tempest of wrath. This blast is an utterly consuming force, and God here is *Eloah*, the Almighty God.

"And by the breath of His nostrils"—It is a repeating of the same thing, only with this difference, that this phrase shows us how much the anger and wrath of God is involved. An angry God breathes hot, sending out a stream of destruction more potent than the fire and brimstone that destroyed Sodom and Gomorrah. Nostrils are put for wrath, both of God and man in many places in Scripture (Psalm 95:11; Exod. 34:6; Proverbs 14:17).

There may be a hint here from Eliphaz as to the manner in which Job's children were blasted out of this world, a mighty blast of wind having stricken all four corners of the house at once. He would import this to the wrath of God. God has told us differently.

GOD CAN EASILY DESTROY WICKED MEN

Though to themselves and others they appear as great ones, towering mountains of that which passes for strength on this earth, God can with but a blast of His breath destroy and consume them. *"They are as chaff that the wind scatters or drives away"* (Psalm 1:4). The plots and counsels of the wicked cause God no pain, no sweating, no toil to defeat. When God sent to Hezekiah to assure him that He would deliver him from Sennacherib, He did also tell him how He would do it, *"Behold, I will send a blast upon him"* (2 Kings 19:7). But what a blast it was! 185,000 men of war were blasted out of this world!

Also to be noted about this blast is this, that not a breath of wind was felt. Not one visible sign, not one thing that could be experienced by the senses, yet all of a sudden there lay 185,000 corpses. How fearful is the Lord God Almighty! The Spirit of God breathes where He desires..., but you do not know where He comes from not where He goes (the true reading of John 3:7).

"The roar of the lion,, and the voice of the fierce lion, and the teeth of the young lions are broken"—Job 4:10.

For examples, Eliphaz chooses the strongest of animals (from a destructive viewpoint) and various ages of lions. There are five words in these two verses which signify lion, but with a difference in each:

1. The lion is a symbol of power, and he is pictured here as roaring, renting or tearing all within his reach. Some derive the word a bit differently, giving the meaning of a lion that sees all, that is watchful and intent upon his prey.

2. The second is a primitive, sometimes signifying a leopard, sometimes a lioness. We render it a fierce lion, because nothing is quite as fierce as a she-lion with cubs.

3. The third is a young lion, such as roared upon Samson (Judges 14:5), having strength and agility, with perhaps more persistence.

4. The fourth is a grown lion, a mature animal, which is perishing from hunger, one who is not able to hunt as formerly.

5. The fifth is a lion in his greatest strength and fierceness, at the very peak of his ability to hunt and destroy.

Now all of these are to shadow out to us mighty strong and powerful men, plowers of wickedness in various degrees of ability and strength. The lion is a king among beasts, and in Scripture signifies one in authority oftentimes (as David, and Christ as the lion of the tribe of Judah). Some think that the apostle Paul meant the emperor Nero when he said, *"I was delivered out of the mouth of the lion"* (2 Tim. 4:17). The lion has similarity to kings, particularly those that are tyrants, in the following ways: In pride, stateliness, independence, courage, fierceness, strength, subtlety, cruelty, ability to frighten and in greediness.

But the blast of God, the power of His Spirit in wrath, will silence the roar of the lion, will smother the voice of the fierce lion, and will break the teeth of the young lions. Eliphaz would have Job frightened by all this, especially since he believes Job has already felt the blast of God's breath in the removal of his possessions and children.

"the strong lion perishes for lack of prey, and the strong lion's cubs are scattered abroad"—Job 4:11.

Lions are strong, and they have plentiful power in providing for their hunger. Yet God consumes them, even the strongest and most resourceful of men are unable to provide for themselves when God sets His hand against them, *"The lions shall lack and suffer hunger, but those that fear the Lord shall not lack any good thing"* (Ps. 34:10). Let not the fierce rulers of this world think that they shall feast on the saints. God shall see that they do not fall prey to the oppressors of this world, and even more, He shall provide for them richly.

"and the strong Lion's cubs are scattered abroad"—Not only the wicked men of the world will be destroyed, but their families of them also. He that whelps another wicked one is not going to establish his name upon the earth by him, for God shall blast him also.

Of course, this is the common operation of God. He does not destroy all lions at any one time. If He wanted a world without wicked men, He would have long ago blasted them all out of this world. And as to Job in this scene, again he does not fall into the category at all—God is not going to blast Job nor destroy him, for Job is God's chosen vessel to defeat Satan.

"Now a thing was secretly brought to me, and my ear received a little of it"—Job 4:12.

Eliphaz begins here with his third argument, in which he labors to convict Job for his impatient complainings. In the seventeenth verse he puts it together, *"Shall man who dies be more just than God? Shall a man be more pure than his Maker?''*

Job is being accused, this time it is said that he is making himself more just and pure than his Maker. Eliphaz takes his argument first from divine authority, then from reason. From divine authority, he gives us the twelfth through the sixteenth verses. This is it, that it is a truth which God in Heaven immediately declares to his servant in a vision, even to Eliphaz, that he who contends with God is very sinful. Therefore, it is to be received as a truth.

The argument against Job goes this way, Anyone who complains of God, as if He had done him wrong, makes himself more just than God. But Job has made such a complaint, as if God had done him wrong in giving him a life full of afflictions. Therefore, Job is making himself more just than God, for he intimates that God has dealt unjustly with him.

"Now a thing was secretly brought to me,"—There is a division of opinion as to the authenticity of this vision reported by Eliphaz. Many think that the vision is a fiction, a fraud which Eliphaz has invented in order to make his argument good. They sometimes take it as a delusion sent by Satan in order to apply pressure to Job. Of course, there have been many who have pretended visions from God, and the centuries will not end before such false claims stop. The false prophets Zedekiah, Hananiah, are examples. Whenever a professed wise man wants to fasten something on the people, he dreams up an imaginary vision. However, it is quite possible that this was a true vision that Eliphaz had:

1. When a thing is done as God does it, it is some argument that God has done it. The manner of the vision here is in accord with other true visions. Of course, this reason alone cannot determine the matter.

2. Eliphaz was a godly man. The friends were right in their affections, though they failed in their actions and became deceived by their own false premises. They did not speak that which was right in regard to Job, but that does not mean that they told lies about visions that never happened.

3. What Eliphaz said he saw is a great and holy truth of God. Man's lies and false pretentions do not usually state God's truth and no more. Those who boast of revelations and special light from Heaven almost invariably are setting up their own fancies and delusions — not seeking to establish God's revealed truth.

So then, this of Eliphaz appears to be a true vision. It confirms a truth, and it does not in any way gain credit for any invention of man, nor for any illusion of Satan.

The word translated *"thing"* actually means a word. This word was brought to Eliphaz secretly. God sometimes speaks aloud, and sometimes He speaks a word inwardly. The usual method is for us to have the truth infused into us, born in us. Our hearts by nature are not like a blank piece of paper, but they are like blotted and blurred paper, with not a bit of God's truth standing out upon them. Instead, they are written all over with corrupt principles and self-righteous, self-deifying inscriptions. Now the Holy Spirit comes in and bleaches these out, then He writes down His own golden rules of holy truth and heavenly wisdom. It is the finger of God that writes the principles of grace on our hearts.

"and my ear received a little of it"—He received but a little, but all that he received was complete and right, not distorted by deletions or missing parts. He had not the capacity to understand all the Heavenly vision, but what he understood was right. Though a man be ever so ignorant of the truths of God, if he be a godly man, he will get a little of all the truths that are told in his ear.

"In thoughts from the visions of the night, when deep sleep falls upon men"—Job 4:13.

The word was secretly brought to Eliphaz in his thoughts, in a vision in the night. The original signifies properly the boughs of a tree. Thoughts are called boughs or branches because thoughts grow from the mind, sprout and shoot up from the mind as branches do from the stock of a tree. Also, the boughs of a tree are many, thick, interwoven, etc.—such are the thoughts of a man. But the word means not only a bough, but the topmost bough of a tree. These were the highest thoughts which appeared to Eliphaz in the visions.

"from the visions of the night"—Visions were a special way of divine revelation in olden

days. God at various times and in different ways spoke to our fathers by the Prophets (Heb. 1:1). Among these ways were these four, (1) prophecy, which included visions, sometimes in a trance, or in ecstacy; (2) immediate inspiration of the Holy Spirit, with no visible apparitions or any change in the penman; (3) the use of Urim and Thummin, the casting of the lot with God determined the outcome. Now these three ways of divine revelation ceased in the second Temple, the Jews claim. They add a fourth way of revelation, a voice from the heavens.

A very illustrious text is that in Numbers 12:6-8, *"If there is a prophet among you, I the Lord will make Myself known to him in a vision, and will speak to him in a dream. My servant Moses is not so, who is faithful in all My house, with him I will speak mouth to mouth, even clearly, and not in dark speeches. And he shall behold the likeness of the Lord."* The first way of holy revelation mentioned there is by vision. The second is by dreams (and even the heathen received such dreams, as Pharaoh and Nebuchadnezzar, and the Magi, then Joseph, etc.). The last method is a speaking directly to the penman, clearly and distinctly revealing what is to be written as God's inerrant word. Some of these direct revelations were given through angels (Gal. 3:19), and some immediately from the Lord, as with Moses. In the earlier days, visions were a principal means of revealing God's mind, and a few differences might be noted in those visions: (1) Sometimes a vision is put for any ordinary revelation of the will of God to either His prophets or ministers (Prov. 29:18); (2) Most of the time there was an extraordinary working of God to manifest His mind to His prophets, with visible representations often made before the eyes of their mind or the eyes in their head (*"In the old days in Israel, when a man went to inquire of God, he spoke in this way—Come and let us go to the seer—for a prophet was in the old days called a seer* —1 Samuel 9:9). There were open visions, and there were visions in private (1 Sam. 3:1). The vision that came to Abraham told him to look up to Heaven with his eyes (Gen. 15:1), but he was not in a trance. Balaam, the false prophet, however was in a trance (Num. 24:16). In the New Testament, Peter was in a trance (Acts 10:8), Paul saw visions and revelations, not even knowing if he was in the body or out of it (2 Corinthians 12:1).

Some visions were presented in bare words, others were clothed in types and figures (in the shapes of animals, of trees and stones, combination men and animals, etc.). Lastly, there were visions of the day and visions of the night (Daniel 2:19). But usually the nighttime was the time for visions.

How thankful we should be that we get our revelations from the word of God, without error, without dependence on memory, with the opportunity to study them again and again, and to compare them with Him *"who is the shining splendor of His glory, and the express image of His Person"* (Heb. 1:3). Their light was darkness, in the old days, at best a shadow of the good things to come. Their visions were but obscurities, and their revelations were nothing compared to ours—*"that which was made glorious had no glory, because of the glory which is far greater"* (2 Corinthians 3:10).

This vision of Eliphaz was remarkable in that it fell upon him while he was in a deep sleep which was brought on by labor and travail. He, being dead on his feet, fell into an extraordinarily heavy sleep. But God is able to work against nature, and gave His message even to a man in a lethargy. Imperfections of the body are no impediment to God. It is more important to be withdrawn from human society in order to commune with God, than it is to be thus and thus alert or sensitive. Isaac went out into the field to *"meditate,"* it is the word for praying. It is good to leave the company of this world and seek out God.

"Fear came upon me, and trembling, which made all my bones shake"—Job 4:14.

The appearances of angels caused fear, how much more the appearance of a likeness of God Himself (Judg. 6:22). Eliphaz was made afraid by his vision, and he trembled. This is that fear which is natural, a passionate fear. The foundation of natural fear is usually the feeling of guilt, the recognition that sin is crouching at the door. This natural dread of God's execution of His judgment upon us is heightened by any sudden appearance of God in our lives or affairs. Fear met Eliphaz, it surprised him, and he trembled.

"and trembling"—fear and trembling go together (Ps. 2:11). *"Work out your salvation with fear and trembling"* (Phil. 2:12). Even the devils tremble when they know God (Jas. 2:19).

"which made all my bones shake"—Literally, the multitude of my bones to shake. This in Hebrew usage means all his bones. The word for shake is of the same root as the one for fear. His trembling was so severe because his fear was so great, and it shook all his bones.

"Then a spirit passed before my face; the hair of my flesh stood up"—Job 4:15.
Some, not keeping step with the context, have mistaken this for a great wind. But it is the Spirit who has rushed upon Eliphaz here, though the word for passing here signifies a motion as is of the heavens, or of the winds (as of the living creature in Ezekiel).

"the hair of my flesh stood up"—The hair stands up in time of fear, the blood rushes to the heart and the members of the body become cold. The skin in which the hair is rooted is pressed together, and the hair either stands up or gives the impression of doing so.

It is not unusual for so much reaction to hit a man, even a man God highly recommends, when he receives a vision from God. Daniel, for instance, wrote, *"There remained no strength in me, for my beauty was turned in me into a deathly paleness"* (Dan. 10:8). See how Habakkik and Zechariah and Mary reacted. John fell at Christ's feet as dead.

Here a truth revealed to Eliphaz has set him to shaking, fearing and trembling. How much more fear do you think will come upon those who stand before Him when He is about to *"take vengeance on all those that have not obeyed the gospel of truth"* (2 Thess. 1:8). No terror has yet been known which will begin to compare with the terror of that Day.

"It stood still, but I could not tell the form of it. An image was before my eyes; there was silence; then I heard a voice,"—Job 4:16.
The form adopted by the Spirit for this presentation of truth was in motion, then it stood still, but even then he could not make out the form of it. The form was not distinct, but the voice was.

"it stood still"—To stand, in Scripture, imports not always a settled posture of the body. It is sometimes taken in a larger sense, to note our presence in any place, whatever our posture. Still the posture of the form was such that Eliphaz could see it was still, and this fixed position plus the silence that followed permitted him to be readied to receive the message.

"but I could not tell the form of it"—It could be that God held back his senses, as was the case with the men on the road to Emmaus (John 20), or it could be that there was an obscurity that kept him from discerning the form of it.

"An image was before my eyes"—This word for image is either used for a visible image, or for an image seen only in the mind. The word is used when the Hebrews were forbidden to make a visible image of God; and also when it was said that Moses would behold the likeness of the Lord—the first there was an image to the eyes, the second an image to the mind.

"there was a silence; then I heard a voice"—There is variation in the translations, but the idea of silence and then a voice, or a silent voice, is clear. A voice that is barely audible can be called a silent or gentle voice. A voice heard only within us could be a silent voice. Elijah heard a voice that was subtle, fine, slender, silent, a sweet ravishing whisper (1 Kings 19:12). What is heard more clearly, what is attended to more closely than a whisper?

The interpretation to be preferred, however, is that there was silence, then a voice came. When God has shaken us, terrified us, and caused us to tremble, we ought to listen carefully for a message from Him. If you hear nothing, then take Eli's advice and say to the Lord, *"Speak, Lord, for Your servant is listening."*

"Shall man who dies be more just than God? Shall a man be more pure than his Maker?"—Job 4:17.
This is the kernel, the statement of the argument which Eliphaz is pushing—this is what Eliphaz says he heard when that voice in the vision spoke to him. He has his main proposi-

tion stated now, and he has claimed as his ground the revelation of God in a vision. His following words will be offered in proof of the proposition.

"Shall man who dies be more just than God?"—Man is mortal, not only subject to death, but sentenced to death by an inexorable decree and an incorruptible Judge. Literally, the word means merely man, or, mere man, a man who is weak and frail. It is *enosh*—a poor, sick, weak, dying creature. It is the picture of a sinful man who suffers all the crippling effects of sin in body and mind, including the final certainty of death.

Now, asks Eliphaz, reporting the vision, Shall this dying creature be more just than God? Shall this blob of corruption called man be justified rather than God? Put the Almighty God together in the balance with such a man, and shall not God be the weightier one in the eyes of Justice? Even if you took man in his best estate, strong and powerful and holy, would not the same result be certain? *"Shall man be more pure than his Maker?"*—there it is man at his best. There are these two oppositions in this verse, God compared to man in his worst light, then in his best light. A threefold sense may be made out:

1. There is no real comparison to be made between God and man. No man can honestly and purely compare himself with God. A mortal man ought not to try to compare himself with the immortal God. What equality can there be between Him who has always existed and him who is but of yesterday? The God that cannot die is not only higher than man who dies, but He is of an entirely different kind. Shall we compare sticks and stones with man. Shall we credit a computer with some kind of equality with man? Shall a rat be given some status in the presence of a man? Even much less can man be given any comparative position with God.

2. Shall a dying man be more just than God? God is the Judge of all the world, and shall He not do right? But is there a man who is so incorrupt as to be trusted as a judge of all the world? If there were such a man (and there never has been, except Jesus Himself), still no one but a fool would prefer to take his case to a man instead of to the supremely just God. Eliphaz is telling Job that God will be just, and that no man is more just in determining guilt. Though the Lord Jesus Christ shall sit as the final Judge, as God the judge of all, yet He refused to judge any while He was in the flesh and walked the face of the earth. (See John 8:11, where He said to the adulterous woman, *"Neither do I judge you"*—the proper translation, rather than using the word *"condemn"*).

3. Thirdly, if a man should be so bold, or so foolish, as to present a complaint against the incorruptible Judge, Almighty God, the great Arbitrator and Determiner of the causes and cases of men, then shall he be found just rather than God? Shall anyone justify the man in his complaint against God? Shall the man be found innocent, the Judge guilty? Let it not be said! *"Who shall lay anything to the charge of God's elect"*—much less lay anything to the charge of God—*"it is God that justifies!"* (Rom. 8:33) Only God can justify a man in moral matters. The purpose of Eliphaz is to bring Job to the point reached by David, *"For I confess my transgressions; and my sin is ever before me. Against You, You only, have I sinned, and done this evil in Your sight—that You may be justified when You speak and clear when You judge"* (Ps. 51:3,4). Whether you consider yourself a weak and dying man, Job, or a strong and mighty man, one pure and holy and just and good, you must admit that you cannot compare yourself with God, you are not going to be justified when you measure yourself up against Him, nor lodge a complaint against Him.

By nature a man will not only count himself to be better than other men, but he does not hesitate to compare himself with God Himself. The pride of man joins with his continually evil imaginations, and he elevates himself in that imagination to a level with God, or even above God. It is not so unusual as some think, for a man to say plainly, If God's will clashes with my will, then He has no right to thwart my will. Not only did man believe Satan when he promised him that he would be as God, but he still believes that lie, deceiving himself deliberately that he may temporarily enjoy what he imagines are the pleasures of sin. Do you think it was only Lucifer who said, *"I will ascend into Heaven, I will exalt my throne above the stars of God...I will be like the Most High"* (Isa. 14:13)? Men do it!

"Shall a man be more pure than his Maker?"—A finite creature may be a pure creature, God creates a creature pure. But the purity of the creature comes from the purity of His Maker—he can remain pure only so long as His Maker keeps him that way. In short, the purity of the creature is an unstable purity, one not inherent in the creature, and one not possible to keep without the forthputting of energy from God. Note the purity of God is infinite. There are no limits to His purity, and it is inherent in His nature. A man may be a man and yet be impure. God cannot be God unless He is infinitely pure—it is His essence and being. Purity is not a quality of God, something added, something subtractable—as it is with man. If you could subtract an iota from God's purity, you could destroy God. Let the pot contend with the Potter so much as his sin will drive him, but there isn't the slightest doubt that there will be a Day when all things are revealed, to the impure and to the pure alike, and in that Day it will be seen that only God is pure in the ultimate. Even *"the heavens are not clean in His sight; how much more hateful and filthy is man, who drinks iniquity like water"* (Job 15:15,16).

Eliphaz assumes, is quite convinced, that Job has complained that God has done him an injury by bringing him to birth, then nurtured him. He is trying to convict Job of the impiety of his complaints. *"The Lord is righteous in all His ways and holy in all His works"* (Ps. 145:17), and Eliphaz is laboring to convince Job that he has just spoken words which contradict such well known truths as this.

HOW CAN A JUST GOD MEASURE OUT THE VERY SAME PORTION TO ALL MEN?

If God is so just, if He always does that which is right and equitable, then how can He measure out to the righteous the exact portion of trouble and affliction that He gives to the wicked? As Abraham pleaded with God, *"Shall the righteous be slain or perish with the wicked? Far be it from You to act in this way. Shall not the Judge of all the earth do right?"* (Gen. 18:25). Yet, when famine comes, both the righteous and the wicked perish. When war comes, likewise. When storms and pestilence destroy, usually there are no discernible differences between the ungodly and the godly (excepting in God's witness to the Egyptians before delivering the Hebrews, where else will you find it on a large scale?)

What is justice? Who determines what is just? Will you judge God and tell Him what is just? Justice is the giving of everyone his due. God is the One who decides what is due to each one (*"There is but one Lawgiver"*). God tells us in the prophecy of Isaiah, *"Say to the righteous that it shall be well within him. For they shall eat of the fruit of their doings. Woe to the wicked! It shall go evil with him. For the reward of his hands shall be given him"* (Isa. 3:10,11). Now when God metes out to each seemingly the same providential evils, how can He make good on these promises? If you were appointed to do it, it could not be done—you would never be able to manage God's providence. But God is able, He can do that which we count impossible, which is in fact impossible to anyone but Him.

God is just to trouble the righteous, because the afflictions of the righteous are good for them. God has promised that it shall be well with the righteous. Therefore, when he is troubled, it is well with him. Contrariwise, when a wicked man prospers, it is ill with him. In fact, it is never worse with them in all of this life than when they prosper, *"the prosperity of fools shall destroy them"* (Prov. 1:32). The rich delicacies in their mouths are as swords in their bellies. Thus, it is just for God to prosper the wicked — as much so as if He stuck a sword in them. When they have no judgments upon their wickedness visible to the eye, then they are being scourged, and they will proceed to make themselves miserable.

A godly man prospers when he is suffering under different kinds of affliction, *"count it all joy when you fall into different kinds of temptations, knowing that the proving of your faith works patience...that you may be perfect and complete, lacking in nothing"*—James 1:2-4. Now a man that is perfect, complete and lacks nothing is prospering! Though they have nothing, they possess all things (2 Cor. 6:10). Not a soul on earth can do them any harm; no, not even Satan himself is able to do anything more than to shine up their graces and rob them of their impurities, for God makes *"all things work together for good to those who love God, to those who are the called according to His purpose"* (Rom. 8:28).

A. Their troubles are their trials. Troubles try their graces, purify them, strengthen them, and exercise them. At the same time it shows up their corruptions, by spiritual surgery burns out their rottenness, and leaves them happier, healthier and closer to God. What is unjust about this blessed treatment? They are tried, purged and made white (Dan. 11:33). Is gold made worse by purification? Is a spotted garment harmed by cleansing? If a man is unable, or even unwilling, to wash the filth off his outside, and to purge the filth from his insides, does the one who cleanses him do him good or ill? If that One be God, you may be sure that it is both just and good.

B. Afflictions are the agents of humility. Pride is such a hardy weed that it will grow in any soil, but it also grows in the best soil. A man who has the weeds pulled out of his garden has been greatly helped. A godly man who has had his pride pulled down, even if it is pulled down about his ears, has been greatly blessed. What can a good man lose by being abased? What did God's people ever gain by pride? They do not gain, they always lose by pride—and what is it that they lose that is not due to pride? Only their corruptions. God gives grace to the humble, but He resists the proud. If one of the saints by his pride makes himself ten feet tall, then he is standing among the proud ones. This makes him a target for God's arrows, and they shall stick fast in him until He has bled out all this pride. But if a man is meek and lowly, looking up to God for blessing and direction, he is no target for God's Spirit. He shall be exalted. He shall exult. He shall know, even as he is known!

C. Suffering under afflictions brings the saints nearer to God, "it is good for me to draw near to God" (Ps. 73:28). What if we are violently driven upon the breast of God? Is it not because we were acting against our best interests by staying away from God? Is it not just for God to do us good by taking the whip to quicken our pace to His loving embrace? Do you claim you want to go to Heaven? Why do you want to go there? Is it not because you want to be near to God? (If it is not, then you had best examine yourself, whether you are in the faith.) Then why do you cast aspersions upon the divine justice when He takes steps to bring you near to Himself in this life, and sets your feet in the path toward Heaven in order that you might be nearer to Him in the eternal life to come? It is written, "he that would live godly shall suffer persecution." You have been told that if you stand near to God, then you are going to have to suffer for the privilege—"if they have persecuted Me, they shall persecute you." Yet the place near to God is the place of blessing. Will you not go there to get your blessing simply because you know that you will suffer persecution if you go? Shame on you for even flinching. Follow your Master, who said, "the cup which the Father has given Me, should I not drink it?" (John 18:10). Draw near to God, and He will draw near to you (James 4:8).

God also measures out exact justice to the wicked:

A. The prosperity of the wicked serves the providence of God. Nebuchadnezzar's case. will illustrate. God said, "I will send him against a hypocritical nation," it was God's errand, but see what follows, "when the Lord has done His whole work upon Mount Zion and on Jerusalem, I will punish the fruit of the proud heart of the king" (Isa. 10:6,12). He thought he was prospered by his own strong right arm, by his military skill, but as soon as he had accomplished all that God sent him to do, he was razed to the ground and put out to eat grass. Was that not justice? First against the Jews, then against the proud king.

B. The prosperity of the wicked tests them in much the same way that the righteous are tested by afflictions. By these temptations the wicked are shown how vile they are. Look at Hazael when Elisha went to anoint him king over Syria. Elisha told him that he would dash the children of Israel against the wall, and rip up their women with child. And what did Hazael say?—"What, is your servant a dog, that he should do this great thing?" Never did he imagine at the time that he had such abominations in his heart. But when he murdered his master and assumed the kingdom (which God had sent Elisha to give to him), he proved to be cruel and rotten to the core. By laying the reins upon Hazael's neck, God sentenced him to be eaten up by his rotten lusts—just as surely as Herod was eaten up by worms when he permitted men to worship him. Was not God just in both these cases? Is it not also justice for God to unleash these beastly men upon those hypocrites who named the name of God upon them, but whose every thought and action dishonored and despised Him? But what if these prosperous, wicked men use their riches to oppress the poor? Those who are poor in spirit will be enrichened and will lay up much treasure above while they are being oppressed. If a man says to one who is starving, Be filled but does not give him any help, that man is being cruel and unjust—provided he has the means to feed him. But if the One who looks upon the starving one (a rare case, but a possible one), He will make him happy, He will do him good, He will comfort him, He will deliver him—but all according to the plans and purposes of God before the foundation of the world. If He allows a saint to starve to death (not a normal occurrence in God's providence,) what is the harm? He shall be with Christ in paradise, and like Lazarus shall look down on the rich men in Hell in but a short time.

C. God hardens the hearts of the wicked when He prospers them, or when He afflicts them. It is not necessary for Him to always afflict in order to judicially punish them with a hard heart. A hardened heart brings a man to the hottest spot in this world, to the place of wrath, and such a one is within one step of hellfire. Every thought such a one has is another log on the fires of Hell, his every act adds fuel to the flames which shall make him miserable and more miserable and more miserable as eternity unfolds. Their gold shall burn them; their honor shall drip acid in their faces; their pleasure shall be a multiplying source of sin which will add to their punishment without end.

If you seek to gingerly and carefully inquire into the justice of God, desiring that He shall have more glory from you because of it, then do this:

1. Look at all God's dealings. Take up a viewpoint which is next to God, so that you may see things as He sees them. Read His word to learn how He thinks, what He has declared, what He has illustrated, and what He has warned. Look at each life, if you must, but be sure you look at every life, at all lives, at all the dealings of God from the beginning of the world—then, and this is most important, go back and join Him in His eternal counsels, see Him make His decrees, watch for His purposes, find out what it is He set out to do. You will find that there is an exactitude in His meting out of justice which will amaze you. It would not seem possible that He could decree so many contrary acts, both good and evil, yet keep Himself pure and just, above it all, directing every step of every man for every moment of every year, for all the centuries back to Adam. Never in all that time has there been a step taken without His direction. Never has there been a single injustice done to any man, wicked or righteous. Follow after Him, beginning in eternity and coming forward, see if you can find a single man who has a valid complaint about God's justice.

2. Remember that if you feel the urge to complain that God's dealings have at any time been unjust, then you are making yourself more just and more pure than your Maker. If you fall into this satanic trap, this fleshly pit, then fall to repenting and praying, and assure your God that you never intended to arraign Him before the bar of your sinful heart.

Therefore, Eliphaz again presents a true argument, one that is good for us to study. And, alas! he also once again makes an unjust application of the truth to the case of Job. Job's complaints were bitter; his pains cried out, but not his prejudice. He never lost his high and holy thoughts of God. It is true that if you complain of what God has done in your life, you are secretly saying that you could have done better than God if you were God. This is a great sin, yet one that is common to all every day. If you are under the unbearable pains that Job was under, if your whole life has been blasted and you have lost all, if you are being accused of being a hypocrite when you are not, then be sure that you make any complaint you have to God. Do not complain of God to men. But complain to God, praying that you may be given grace to bear his blows, that you may be given comfort to hold out until His purposes are complete. Job was indeed upon dangerous ground, a little more and he could have been making himself more just than his God, more pure than his Maker. But God Himself absolved him of the charge of Eliphaz here, for God is on record as saying to Eliphaz, *"you have not spoken of Me what is right, as Job has."*

"Behold! He puts no trust in His servants, and His angels He charges with folly!"—Job 4:18.

Not content to show that mortal man is neither just nor pure in comparison with God, Eliphas now turns to the angels for a further comparison. He states that God puts no reliance upon the angels, and they that cannot be trusted by God cannot be justified by God. It is a matter of wonder, but He does not trust angels—thus He uses the word, Behold!

"He puts no trust in His servants"—*"Are they not all ministering spirits"* (Heb. 1:14). The angels are servants of God, and servants of the saints in that capacity. Now the angels are pure creatures, at least the angels mentioned here. Why does God not trust them? It is because they are creatures, and a creature cannot be trusted—there is an instability which goes with being a creature. Creatures cannot stand in and of themselves. They must be held up by Another. So it is not possible for God to rely upon them. Instead they must rely on and trust God. The basic meaning of the word translated *"trust"* is a confiding in, or giving credit to the persons named. Christ would not confide in or trust Himself to certain men, because He knew what was in man (John 2:23). God will not confide in or trust Himself to the good angels, because He knows what is in angels, excellent creatures though they may be. That an angel may not be trusted simply because he is an angel, because he is pure and holy, can be proven by the fact that myriads of angels violated God's will and fell into everlasting darkness. Now if God had committed Himself to them, if He had suspended any part of His everlasting decrees upon their remaining pure and holy and true servants, then all would have been lost with Satan and his horde of untrustworthy angels.

"and His angels He charges with folly!"—Some read it, He judged no clear light to be in His angels; others, neither has He put light in His angels. The many translations are occasioned by the fact that the Hebrew word may signify "shine forth with a resplendent brightness." In a metaphor, it is translated to be famous, or to be praised — because a man is in a sense decked out with light and brightness when he is famous and praiseworthy. By the figure antiphrasis (or contrary speaking) the word means to boast and brag vainly, foolishly. It is the highest foolishness to extol ourselves and to publish our own works. The word has also come to mean mad, vain, foolish—and, in the abstract, madness and folly.

If we read, He put light into His messengers, then we would get this meaning: That God had put the light of excellent knowledge into the angels, yet He could not trust them. If we read it as madness or folly, vain boasting or vanity, taking the original in the figurative sense, then we see God charging that the angels were vain, light and foolish creatures. Now it is well known that the Scripture holds angels up as excellent, intelligent creatures who are diligent in the service of God. How then can God carry out this act, of charging them with lightness and vanity? Shall we restrict it to the evil angels? Or, to good and bad?

Many translators restrain it to the evil angels, the apostate angels. It would be easy to see why God would put no trust in them, why He would charge them with foolishness, even madness. But there would be no need for the text if this is all that God meant. It would not fit the context to bring in the evil angels here. Of course their trustworthiness and purity could not be compared to God's. They could be charged with a lot more than folly.

This brings us back to the consideration of the angels as creatures. They were not foolish in comparison to men, but in comparison to God—utterly foolish, light and untrustworthy. Angels by their very excellency and spiritual natures are subject to the error of pride. It is undoubtedly true that the fallen angels faltered through pride. God cannot trust those that are left, lest they too fall through pride. Therefore, He upholds them, keeps them back from the very breath of error. He energizes them toward good constantly. Now if they were in Christ, under His headship, partakers of His nature, credited with His constancy, etc., then perhaps it might be said in a sense that they had some trustworthiness.

See it as God sees it. When we examine carefully the pure angels, would we find them to be light and foolish? No, but God sees imperfection where we cannot. Yes, even the perfect (by comparison) angels cannot see the imperfections in themselves that God can see. Therefore, do not depend upon your own observations in judging your own reliability. Look to God's word for guidance in making judgments of yourself, of angels and of men.

Lastly, note that God has no need of the creatures, not even the most excellent angels, in upholding the world, and in administering His affairs. He is totally sufficient, totally independent. God and any creature are not more than God alone. He does not need us. It is us that need Him. Whatever there may be in us that may be called excellent, good or pure comes from God. If He was not, we would not be. If He was not good and pure, then we could have nothing of these in ourselves. He has given to you, to me, to others, to myriads and myriads, for centuries and centuries, and yet He has not diminished at all. If this is so, then He does not need any of us. If He can make another incalculable multitude and give each of them all the excellencies that abide in Him, and be not a whit diminished, then He certainly does not need us and any imagined purity and trustworthiness we think we have.

"How much less in those who live in houses of clay, whose foundation is in the dust, who are crushed before the moth?"—Job 4:19.

First, there was a comparison of man with God. Then a comparison of angels with God. Now we have a comparison of angels with men. The argument is this, that if God cannot put any trust in His angels, but must charge them with vanity and foolishness, then how much do you think He can put any confidence in us?

An angel is a spiritual creature, of spiritual substances. Man is a material substance. Men are mortal, they die. Angels are immortal, they do not die.

"How much less in those who live in houses of clay"—The Hebrew may be rendered, *"How much less,"* or, *"How much more."* Translating it, *"How much less,"* it refers to the last verse and draws a comparison of man with the angels. If we say, *"How much more,"* then it means this, that God charges His angels with folly, and charges man with much more. As for *"houses of clay,"* the apostle calls our bodies this, *"our earthly house"* (2 Cor. 5:1) and again, an *"earthen vessel"* (2 Cor. 4:7). Being but dying men, made of dust, we preach eternal life—but all the while we have death in our faces, though the word of life be in our mouths. We are made of clay, not natural and unrefined clay, but clay wrought upon by God to make for us a goodly building—*"we are fearfully and wonderfully made."* This artful construction is reason enough for us to be said to live in houses—for houses are skillfully planned and constructed. The body may also be called a house, because it houses the soul. *"God formed man out of the dust of the earth, and then he breathed into him the breath of life, and man became a living soul"* (Gen. 2:7).

"whose foundation is in the dust"—These words aggravate the weakness of man's condition. Suppose man were formed out of the dust and were but clay, yet had a strong foundation that would support and strengthen him. Then might man claim a little strength to stand. But when the building is weak and the foundation is also weak, then how that building will totter! To be made of light, unstable, moveable flakes of dust—and slimy dust at that—leaves one so insubstantial that God could not rely upon us. We are of the earth, we are therefore earthy. This means we cannot be trusted, for before long we will return to dust. Give God the glory, He has marvelously worked to make this dust beautiful and intelligent. It points up the difference between a real Creator and a mere artisan.

Again, if the body is but dust, why do we spend some large part of our short lives in the painting and polishing of it? Why adorn and decorate a pile of dust, however artfully it is dressed in pink clay and enameled white teeth? Should we not spend that time upon the soul, that magnificent creation which shall live forever? If the angels can be charged with folly, how much more a fool is a man who spends his time feeding, pleasuring and decorating that which is mere dust, that which is certain to return to dust, in but a moment! Yet at the same time he is in possession of a real jewel, a soul that is capable of living eternally with God. Why not face up to the fact that the soul is the man? The body is not the man. If it were, then the man would perish with the body, just as it is with the beasts. The body can be eased and comforted, etc., but it cannot be blessed. Only the soul can be blessed.

"who are crushed before the moth?"—Or, *"who are consumed as a moth is."* As we read it, there may be a threefold interpretation: (1) before the moth, that is, before in time, or

sooner than the moth. How quickly a moth may be crushed! Man may be crushed before the moth is; (2) Before the moth, let it be as much as in the presence of the moth. A man may think he is able to stand out against a powerful adversary, even God Himself, but he is not even able to stand out against a moth (if God were to arm them against him); (3) Man is crushed and torn, vexed and worn out by a thousand miseries and troubles which assail his life, before the moth (or the worm) starts to eat on him.

The general sense is to show man's frailty. *"Lo, they shall grow old like a garment, the moth shall consume them"* (Isa. 50:9); *"do not fear the reproach of men, neither be afraid of their revilings. For the moth shall eat them like a garment"* (Isa. 51:6,7).

"They are destroyed from morning till evening; they perish forever without anyone caring" —Job 4:20.

We may understand the former verse of natural death and this of casual and violent death. Destruction and perishing import violence.

"They are destroyed"—that is, they are subject or liable to destruction. That phrase, *"from morning to evening,"* notes the whole day. They are destroyed continually, or, all the day long (*"For Your sake we are killed all the day long"*—Rom. 8:36). Man is as fragile as a moth, he is destroyable every moment. There is not an hour of the day when he is not in danger of a violent death.

"they perish forever without anyone caring"—To perish here is but to die (*"the righteous perish, and no one lays it to heart"*—Isa. 57:1). But does a man die forever? Is there no resurrection? Shall not soul and body be reunited? Forever is sometimes put for an infinite time, and sometimes for an indefinite time, *"they may dwell in Jerusalem forever"*—that is, perpetually, continually, from now on, an indefinite time. The word is used in this way innumerable times in the Old Testament. In this place, forever means until the end of life. It is the utmost term of time, but does not signify eternity. They perish forever, that is, they shall not live in this world any more. Once he has perished, he shall not return anymore to that place—he is gone forever. A cat is said to have nine lives, but it is certain that a man has only one. When he dies, there will be no more times for him to die—it is forever.

"without anyone caring"—Literally, *"laying it to heart."* This is not an exclusive negative, as if there were none at all that cared. There are few, a handful that care. Among the living you will find only a person now and then who take any thought about the lives of others. We must see a friend gasping and dying before we take any note that he has been declining toward the grave. Some will think of death for a moment while mourning with the bereaved or attending the funeral, but even then it is formality and ritual and rote to too many. As they dragged Amasa out of the highway where he lay wallowing in his blood after Joab murdered him, so that the others would not think upon death, so are we in every instance when we are given an excuse not to stare our mortality in the face. But the thoughtful consideration of death is a good medicine for an evil heart.

"Does not the loftiness which is in them go away? They die, even without wisdom"—Job 4:21.

This verse prevents an objection which might be made, that a man is wronged and his honor taken from him when he is looked upon as a heap of dust, a lump of clay. Yes, he has excellencies, being put a little lower than the angels, having dominion over the earth, being the chief creature in the inferior world, but all of these things go with him when he returns to the dust. The word translated *"loftiness"* or *"excellency"* signifies primarily a residue, a remainder: (1) their friends and loved ones are left; (2) their possessions are also left, including their posterity. There is both a quantitive remainder, or overplus, and a qualitative remainder (the same word is used of Reuben, *"the excellency of dignity"*). Whatever is best in him, this must be left behind.

But some understand the soul, that it leaves the house of clay when it dies and returns to dust. It does not appear to be the meaning, but that would be an excellent meaning. The import here is this, that the beauty and strength of the body, the wit and knowledge and skill of the mind, the riches and honor and authority of the life, all go out when a man dies. *"All flesh is grass, and all the goodliness of it are as the flower of the field"* (Isaiah 40:6). Man in his best estate is altogether vanity. He brought nothing into this world, and it is certain that he does not take anything out of it.

"They die, even without wisdom"—You may look like an angel, and speak like no other man ever spoke, and your mind may have comprehended the entire body of knowledge in this world, but it all goes when you die. The only thing that will last, the only wisdom that will abide, is that which you have obtained by your union with Christ Jesus. That is why Paul urged us to strive for *"the excellency of the knowledge of Christ Jesus our Lord, for whom we ought to suffer the loss of all things, and count them but dung, that we may win Christ"* (Phil. 3:8). Abner was no fool, but he died like a fool. You may have wisdom, but you shall die like the unwise.

It is possible to take the meaning in this way, that you die without preparation for death, Men devise and scheme in a multitude of ways, but seldom do they fit themselves out for death. They are dying before they understand what it is to live, or even why they live. It is in this way that the non-understanding man is like the beasts that perish (Ps. 49:20). It is a great part of wisdom to plan for a departure from this world to another world of infinitely more importance, and of a duration not comprehensible to man. May God grant to us all that great wisdom—how to die—and that we may be found ready when the day comes.

Eliphaz has now finished his third argument against Job, plainly laying at his door the accusation that Job's outbursts of ill-considered complaints have made him guilty of challenging God's justice and purity. He believes that Job has accused God of wronging him by bringing upon him these endless afflictions. Eliphaz is wrong. It must be remembered that he does not have Job's words all written out before him, as we do. He is speaking as from memory. He is going by impressions which he has received from Job's boiling words. It is easy to be wrong in such cases. Remember, if you will, how many times you have in sincerity misreported the import of another's words. So wrapped up are we in our own interests, so intent are we in establishing certain truths which we consider to be of overriding importance, we often miss a word or a phrase or even a whole paragraph which will put the entire speech in perspective for us. Presuming Job to be guilty of hypocrisy, this man, aged and wise though he may be, has failed to consider either the background of the complaints of Job, or the present condition of the man, or the well-proven and admitted holy life of the man. No one brings a man to the bar of justice for remarks he makes when he is out of his head with pain or distraction. Even for a serious injury to another, a man is usually acquitted if it is believed that he had been unable to put his thoughts in order enough to know what he was doing at the time (depending on the reason for it, of course). The judgments of Eliphaz are fortunately not the judgments of God. You would not know that there was any difference between the composure of Eliphaz and that of Job, for it is certain that Eliphaz has not admitted any difference at all.

CHAPTER V

"Call now—is there anyone who will answer you? And to which of the saints will you turn?"
—Job 5:1.

The first five verses of this chapter contain the fourth argument by which Eliphaz continues to convince Job of sinful hypocrisy. This he does two ways: (1) by comparing Job to the saints—he finds him unlike them; (2) by comparing Job to the wicked—he finds him like them. If this be so, then Job is a hypocrite.

Eliphaz argues first that a man is not just and holy if he fails to be like just and holy men. He contends that Job in his affliction is altogether unlike holy and just men. Therefore he concludes that Job is neither holy nor just.

"Call now—is there anyone who will answer you?" Eliphaz is saying that there is none among the saints like Job; that none of the few who had suffered as he is suffering were like Job in bearing their troubles.

"For wrath kills the foolish man, etc." Then in the second thru the fifth verses Eliphaz argues that Job is a hypocrite because he is like the wicked—in two ways: (1) Job is like the wicked in his manner of suffering; (2) in the matter of his suffering. This is the argument of Eliphaz:

If a man behaves like a fool, like a wicked man, when he is in trouble, then that man is either openly wicked or grossly hypocritical. But Job is behaving like a foolish or a wicked man in his troubles. Therefore Job must be wicked.

Eliphaz is saying in verses 2-5 that Job pines, rages, and vexes himself under his suffering in the same way that the foolish and silly ones, the sinful and wicked, respond to suffering. Then he says that Job is proven a hypocrite because his sufferings are the same visited upon wicked and ungodly men when God pours forth judgments upon them. This argument, as to the matter of Job's suffering, follows:

Wicked men flourish for a while, then sudden destruction comes upon them, their children, and their whole estates. But Job, after flourishing a while, has had his health, his children and all his estate suddenly swallowed up and devoured. Therefore, concludes Eliphaz, Job must be a wicked man, a true hypocrite.

Eliphaz contends that God has dealt with Job as an enemy, therefore Job cannot be God's friend. Now we will consider the words and open their sense:

"Call now— is there anyone who will answer you; And to which of the saints will you turn?" (verse 1).

THE PARAPHRASE: *"Call over the catalog of all the saints who ever were and look to see if there are any whose condition or actions will answer in proportion to yours. Turn your eye upon all the holy ones and see if God has dealt with any in the matter or manner of your affliction. Or have any complained to God as you are doing? Job, you stand alone among the saints. Or, go to the fools and the profane, for among them you may perhaps see your pattern; among them you may read the record of your own impatience and miscarriage."*

(For Mr. Caryl's discussion of the foolish notions of the Jews and Papists on this verse, see pages 169-171 of the original folio edition.)

"Call now," or, *"I beg you to call".*

What we translate as *"now"* sometimes is a particle of insulting, but most usually of persuading or entreating. Abraham said, *"I beg of you, say that you are my sister"* (Gen. 12). Then the word *kara* which we translate *"call,"* means first to cry aloud in proclamation: *"Cry aloud...lift up your voice like a trumpet"* (Isa. 58:1). But secondly, it is used by way of prayer, *"call upon Me in the day of trouble"* (Ps. 50:15). But more properly, it means to call in the sense of denominating or naming, *"Do not call me Naomi, call me Mara"* (Ruth 1:20). So here it means to call over the names of all the saints to see if they are all here. As the steward calls each one when he pays the wages of the laborers, paying them one by one (Matt. 20). So we may understand that in this place Eliphaz is telling Job to

108

call over the names of all the saints and to ask each one if they ever had such afflictions as Job has, or any under affliction ever behaved as Job is now behaving.

"is there anyone who will answer you"—the word which we render *"answer"* not only signifies answering to a question, but also answering by actions as well as by words. Then this *"call now to the saints"* means to call up each one and see if there are any like Job in their spirit, in their condition, in their actions; are there any to whom Job can parallel himself. No, says Eliphaz to Job, but you are more like a heathen who does not know God, than you are like the saints in your complaining. And since the mouth speaks from the abundance of the heart, these words show your heart to abound in sin and empty of grace.

"And to which of the saints will you turn?"—vs. 1c

One has said that these words allude to the kind of situation that exists between the painter and his subject. For the painter must frequently turn his eyes upon his subject to see if what he is drawing is like what he has painted on the canvas. And each stroke or two brings another necessity to refer back to the subject, lest he get too far from his prototype. So here it is suggested that we must turn our eyes upon the saints of old in order to see if we are conforming to their approved images. Eliphaz asks Job, to which of the saints will you turn, to look upon and to assure yourself of conformity to the will of God.

The word translated *"turn"* does not simply mean to look about or to turn the eye, but it means to turn the eye with the intention to make a discovery—it is a curious and detailed observation with the determination to find out something. David's prayer, *"Turn unto me and have mercy upon me, for I am very low"* (Ps. 25:16)—in which he pleads for God to find out what charity or mercy should supply. David wanted God to turn His eye upon him to discover what he needed.

So then Job is being asked to which of the saints will he look upon to find out a pattern which resembles his own. It is in itself good advice that Eliphaz gives.

IT IS PROFITABLE FOR US TO LOOK TO THE EXAMPLE OF THE SAINTS

God has not only given us His word for a rule, but He has given us examples as a rule to walk by. First, He has given us His own example: *"Be holy as I am holy,"* for He is the highest pattern of holiness. Secondly, He has given us His Son, for *"He that says he rests in Him ought also to walk in the same way as He walked"* (1 John 2:6). For it is by *"looking to Jesus, the Author and Finisher of our faith"* (Heb. 12:2) that we are able to follow His pattern, which fulfills the will of God. Thirdly, the examples of the saints are also commended to our imitation: *"For as many things as were written before for our learning,"* and that is why the Holy Spirit has set so many pens to work to write the lives of the saints. The sufferings and troubles of the saints are full of practical divinity, as James writes (5:10), My brothers the prophets are *"for an example of suffering evils, and of patience."* That is why the multitude of saints in Hebrews are a *"cloud of witnesses"* to us, for they shower down hope and comfort to us. They suffered joyfully the spoiling of their goods. They lived by faith in the midst of a thousand deaths—do the same in your life. When you are out of course, proud, highminded, earthly, covetous, turn to the saints and correct your practice, for you will learn none of these things from them. A man has reason to suspect he has done evil when he cannot find an example that ever did the thing he is doing, or any who ever repented of doing such a thing.

When God forsakes a man, the saints also forsake him. They love whom He loves and they hate anyone He hates. If you are out of the will of God, doing those things which are ungodly, you will get no help by turning to the saints for a pattern. So Eliphaz tells Job that he is unlike the saints in his suffering and in his reaction to his sufferings, therefore he must surely be a hypocrite.

"For wrath kills the foolish man, and envy slays the silly one"—Job 5:2.

Secondly, Eliphaz has concluded Job to be like the wicked. And he instances in two sinful persons, the foolish man, and, the silly man. As there is a special worm or pest that destroys certain trees, so there are certain lusts that eat out the hearts of certain men, destroying them with a fearful and unrelenting wasting away. Rashness and intemperance inflame and destroy young men. Ambition etches its ugly pattern on the lives of those who desire to be gods. Covetousness tyrannizes and saps and demoralizes robbers and thieves, whether they be 'respectable' or 'wanted'! So here God tell us that *"wrath kills the foolish man."*

"the foolish man." He is a fool who does not have wisdom to direct himself. And he is twice a fool if he will not follow the wisdom of those who are truly wise. Here we have a fool, but not such a fool as the one who had no knowledge. This fool in our text is one who has knowledge but does not make use of the knowledge he has. This ia a man who is hasty, inconsiderate, rushing headlong toward destruction without fear or wit. Such a foolishness is evil, and the original word for *"foolish"* here is the same to a letter in sound with the English word *"evil."* It seems that Eliphaz has carefully chosen the word to hint to Job that he considers him to be intemperate, ungoverned, rash and wrathful in the things which he has uttered. This marks him out to be an evil man, one like the wicked who curse God.

"For wrath kills"—Wrath may be taken here either for the wrath of God or of man. It is true that the wrath of God kills foolish men. But the context would seem to indicate that it is the wrath of man that is meant here. A man's wrath is like a knife at his throat. The word here means indignation, overriding anger. Properly, wrath is an inveterate anger. Anger is a short fury, and wrath is a persistent fury which grows wilder and hotter. When a man is determined in his anger, when his spirit becomes steeped and soaked in anger, then it is wrath. This word here, however, denotes a fervent heat and distemper which breaks forth presently; an extreme vexation which frets and disquiets us. (He shall gnash with his teeth—it is the word here—and melt away—there is the heat of it). But how could wrath kill a foolish man? His wrath is known to kill others, but is his wrath going to kill him? Wrath is said to kill a man first because it thrusts him headlong upon such things as will be the death of him. He runs wilfully upon his own death by doing dangerous things that he would never do if he were not in wrath. It may be his act will be unlawful, and he will be killed judicially. Secondly, wrath may be said to kill a man because his wrath is so vexatious to him, that it makes his life a continual death to him, and at last he becomes so worn out and wasted that he dies. Or, it may be that his wrath will bring on a stroke in the head or the heart which will suddenly snatch him away from life.

"and envy slays the silly one."—There is not much difference between the foolish and the silly ones. But the Holy Spirit uses a different word here, with the root word meaning to entice or allure (which in Gen. 9:27 is taken in a good sense). And because men are often deceived by persuasion, the word sometimes also means to deceive or beguile. From this the word in the text is derived, which we translate, *"the silly one,"* or, *"the simple one."* A man who is easily enticed, deceived or persuaded by another is known to us as a silly, simple man. (Yet, the word is used in a good sense too, *"the Lord preserves the simple"*—Ps. 116:6). Most of the time in Scripture, this word is put for one who is without sense and reason, an incompetent, one easily led into evil. Now it is not hard to understand how envy would slay such an one as this, for he is already half out of his wits. A silly one looking upon desirable things which others have may well afflict himself with envy, and if it does not kill him, he is like one dead anyhow.

Now the reason Eliphaz speaks of these two, the foolish and the silly ones, and has them dying by their wrath and envy, is because he has misconceived Job's troubled and muddy complaints to be impure and filthy springs which proceed from wrath and envy. He thinks that Job is proudly angry and displeased, even enraged at God for reducing him to such straits as he is in. He believes that Job is eaten up with envy because others were still in good health and weath. If Eliphaz were right in his application, then Job would indeed be foolish and silly. But, again, Eliphaz has his truths right and his application to Job wrong. To be angry and discontented with God on account of His providence is more destructive to us than the judgments themselves. God's judgments on His own afflict us, but our wrath will destroy us. When a man is angry and resists God's strokes, then that man strikes the blow deeply within himself. But if he is humble when God strikes, the blow becomes a kiss and a comfort. But Job did not have wrath toward God, or envy toward his friends.

"I have seen the foolish taking root, but suddenly I cursed his dwelling-place"—Job 5:3.

The argument proceeds, with Eliphaz saying in the next three verses: 'Foolish men do flourish a while, but then they come to a certain and sudden destruction. Both they and their children and their estates being crushed and swallowed up. But you, Job, fit this description, for you flourished for a while, yet now sudden destruction has come upon your children and on your estate, everything of yours is consumed and swallowed up. Therefore, you must be foolish and silly, etc.' To him, Job has met all the conditions.

"I have seen the foolish taking root—Before he reported a vision, now he reports his personal experience. Experience should certainly result in a multitude of truths being made sure to you in your mind and heart. God's promises should become real through experience. God's threatenings should take on size and weight through your experience. But experience misread can be the trigger that sets off a sad series of shocks. The word here for foolish is the same as the one above. Fools, like weeds, take root easily. All wicked men are fools, and nothing is more common than for them to promise themselves that today and tomorrow will be just like yesterday, they will buy and sell and profit, etc. until they have reached a ripe old age. They take root in their outward prosperity (as shadowed forth in Nebuchadnezzar's vision—Dan. 4:4). Jeremiah was scandalized at the prosperity of fools, *"You have planted them; yea, thay have taken root, they grow; yea, they bring forth fruit"* (Jer. 12:2). God not only plants some of them, He permits them to take root and grow. This gives much glory to God for His patience with men, these being His enemies. It is also a glorious thing that He is able to put into their heart to do His will (Rev. 17:17) in their role of providing for the saints, and in proving them.

Eliphaz would picture it as a common truth that such men endure but a little while, and that they are always pulled up by the roots and given their just due in this life. All the friends work this theme in and out of their discourses. Job does not answer them, for he is understandably interested in getting at the bottom of his trouble. That these things are not his trouble, he well knows by his own experience. Finally, however, he answers this kind of misstatement of the true state of affairs, in chapter 21, and he simply devastates the argument of Eliphaz here, and of the other friends in other places. For a full exposition of the claims here that the wicked are always punished in this life, that they have no hope of enduring to the end, see the exposition of chapter 21.

"and suddenly I cursed his dwelling-place"—The word here for curse is one which comes from a root word meaning to strike through or to pierce. The word should not be translated, *"abominated,"* or, *"abhorred."* He wished evil to fall upon the foolish, and pronounced evil to come upon him. It is possible for God to give his people predictions which will be carried out (as in David's Psalms, where they are not maledictions, but predictions). It is possible for God to set a man over other men, over nations and kingdoms. *"to root out, to pull down, and to destroy, etc."* (Jer. 1:10). How could one mere man do such things? By denouncing the destroying judgments which God has already proceeding toward them. The truth is, there was never any nation or kingdom rooted up by the sword in these later days, that was not first rooted up by the word of God. We have no reason, however, to credit Eliphaz with any power to curse, to predict, or to pull down. He says he did it, and that he has seen it—and no doubt that is true. But was it because of his curse? Was it not because *"the curse of the Lord is in the house of the wicked"* (Prov. 3:33).

"his dwelling-place"—This word pictures a quiet, settled, peaceable and beautiful habitation. What a shock it must be to one living in such seeming security to suddenly find his life, family and estate swept away! He either had never considered it, or had completely despised the teaching of Scripture that God hates the wicked everyday. Now he sees it.

"His children are far from safety, and they are crushed in the gate, neither is there any to deliver them"—Job 5:4.

These words describe the result of the curse. The master of the family is the tree, his children are the branches, his leaves are his riches and honor. If indeed it were the curse of God which was pronounced by Eliphaz, then it can be seen that creatures cannot stand before the curse of God. How quickly the fig-tree withered under Christ's curse—so it is with the wicked and their families when God's curse comes upon them.

"His children are far from safety"—Or, *were far from safety."* Having shown the curse was laid against the root, now he shows it being applied to the branches. The word translated safety is the word for salvation. However, if it were so translated here, it would mean only that his children were far from being saved (from the results of the curse). The phrase imports extreme danger. If a man is far from light, he is in extreme darkness.

"And they are crushed in the gate"—It pictures a public destruction, for the gate was a public place. It indicates a crushing resulting from judgment. The gate was the place of judgment, because that was a convenient, accommodating place for both strangers and local citizens to meet before the judge. A further reason, was that the judgment given was then more easily made public.

"neither is there any to deliver them"—No one had the power to stay their judgment. No advocate stepped up to plead their cases. No mediation and no alleviation occurred. It is a scandal to some that God should destroy both the wicked and their children in one fell swoop of judgment (as happened to Korah, Dathan and Abiram and their entire families; yea, their entire households—Numb. 16:27-33). Such a misconstruction, yes, charge against God's justice is not new, the Jews spit it in His face, *"The fathers have eaten sour grapes, and the children's teeth are set on edge"* (Ezek. 18:2). They thought themselves free from the sins of their fathers, and they judged that God was punishing them unjustly for those sins. The very fact that they had the unholy boldness to make such a charge against a holy God proved that they had sins enough of their own to warrant His judgments against them. This is the explanation, if God's dealings must be explained: All have sinned; there is none that is good, none that does good, and none that seek after God; everyone is under the sentence of death and misery from the day that Adam sinned. Therefore, when we are born, we are under condemnation—that is, we are sentenced to die. God is the executioner as well as the Judge who issued the sentence. The only thing that is not known to anyone alive is this, the date of his execution. Now, there is but one exception to this condemnation, and that is the promise of eternal life given in the gospel to all who are made alive in Christ Jesus. Anyone who is not in Him, who has received God's word, may expect their eternal destruction any minute of any day. Now when God in a day destroys both the wicked father and the wicked children (all who believe not the Son ARE wicked), it is but the righteous Judge executing His sentence. There is nothing unjust in executing one who is fairly tried, found guilty, and sentenced to death. To any who will persist in questioning, the justice of God in such instances, we refer them to Romans 9:20, *"Yes, rather, O man, who are you that answers against God?...Or, does not the potter have authority over the clay?...what if God, minded to show wrath and to make His power known, endured with much longsuffering the vessels of wrath fitted for destruction?"*

"Their harvest the hungry eats, and takes it even out of the thorns; and the robber swallows up their wealth"—Job 5:5.

By his harvest, we are to understand not only the return of that which he had sown, but all the goods or provisions which he had gathered or laid up for his security. This man's harvest was eaten up, whether he got it by industry or injury, by sweat or by deceit. The word *"devours"* might be a better word to show the completeness of the loss. Great labor usually attends a harvest, for there must first be a sowing, a cultivating, and then the harvest. What a great disappointment, then, to have it suddenly devoured by God's judgment!

If a man enjoys *"the good of all his labor, it is the gift of God"* (Eccl. 3:13). Job himself speaks to this point, *"if any blot has held fast to my hands, then let me sow, and let another eat; and let my harvests be rooted out"* (31:7,8).

"the hungry eats"—there is quite some difference in opinion as to who the hungry are in this text. Some say it is the Devil, and he is indeed one who goes about and devours. But he does not devour harvests, but souls. He devoured Job's gains in order to rob Job of his soul, not what he possessed. Others understand the hungry one to mean the heir of the foolish man who took root above. It certainly is not unusual for the heir to come along and waste the substance of the father (the prodigal son did it while his father still lived). Some think that the hungry are the poor, those oppressed by the foolish rich. They are made hungry and lean by the depredations of the Nimrods of the world. The Septuagint lends its voice to this, reading, *"the just shall eat up the harvest of this rich worldling."* It is not unheard of, that God should give the riches gathered by oppressors to His poor saints, and Job speaks to this point also, *"Though he heap up silver like the dust, and provide clothing like the clay, he may prepare it, but the just shall put it on"* (27:16,17). Again, the hungry may be any who are low and poor, whom God stirs up and sends in judgment as His teeth, to consume and destroy the portion of the earth's fat ones. It is true that there are persecutors who eat up God's people like bread, but there are occasions when God turns the tables, and it is His people who devour the wicked.

"and takes it even out of the thorns"—Again, there is difficulty in coming at the meaning. Some say, *"which he had gotten through the thorns,"* others, *"he shall fetch it out of the weapons."* The word can be made to mean weapons. A worldly man may get his riches by vexing, pricking methods. Some say the men who eat up his harvest are *"men of thorns,"* or men coming out of the thorns. But this is not easily made out of the original. Taking it to mean this, that the hungry eats *"and takes it even out of the thorns,"* it is an indication that these hungry ones will go through the greatest difficulty to devour the harvest of the fools. For as a man is said to take a thing out of the fire, or out of the mouth of the lion, it means that he will do it at great peril. So here, these hungry ones will go to great risks to eat up the harvest of the foolish ones. A hedge of thorns will not keep out God's avengers. But a hedge woven by God's grace around His godly ones will hold.

"and the robber swallows up their wealth"—This is an extenuation of what goes before. The prediction is doubled, like Pharoah's dream, to denote certainty. *"The robber,"* or, *"the thirsty,"* as some translate, shall swallow up their wealth. Their substance, whether vegetable, mineral or animal, shall not escape the robber. It shall be exhausted, which is the true meaning of the word for *"swallow up."* Now Job was described as a man of very great substance, but the substance mentioned here is different. In the first chapter, it was cattle that made up the principle part of his substance. This word covers any and all kinds of wealth. And there is the emphasis of strength, of activity which normally bring wealth. The word can also mean an army (Ps. 33:16, *"the multitude of an army"*), The robber shall come and swallow up, completely exhaust his army. This description is of a total desolation brought upon the estate and family of the foolish man. And make no mistake about it, Eliphaz regards Job as this fool, this silly one, and the recent events as the fulfilling of what he is saying here. He has seen this, and that, and as he now sees it, God has undoubtedly treated Job the same way and in the same destructive measures as He treats rich fools and wicked men. Therefore, though it has escaped his eye, he is certain that Job is such a man. The finest reputations cannot withstand the ill opinions of hasty judges. A man who is willing to blacken the name of another without the aid of evidence gathered and presented to an impartial judge is a man to be avoided. Much cruelty has been perpetrated upon good men by those who insist that their experiences and their principles are the only guides that are necessary for the determining of good and evil. And, alas! none are so quick to prosecute the saints than another who has knowledge of the word of God, but who knows it only in part, and only in a perverted way. That is, they have their own consciousness and experience, then they squeeze, twist and conform the Bible to their liking.

"For affliction does not come forth from the dust, neither does trouble spring up out of the ground"—Job 5:6.

Eliphaz has spent all his time thus far in reproving Job, seeking to convict him of secret sins, or of gross hypocrisy. Now he begins to give counsel and exhortation, directing and advising Job what it is right for him to do, what would be the result if he did do the right thing. The sum of his exhortation is that all the causes for his distemper and ill-manners would be eliminated if he would but seek unto God, beg His favor and believingly commit himself and his cause to God. This from the sixth through the sixteenth verse. Then at the seventeenth verse, he concentrates on begetting humility and submission under the correcting hand of God. The eighth verse contains the main exhortation for Job to seek to God. He strengthens this with two arguments, (1) that the efficient cause of his affliction is God, that the meritorious cause of his trouble in himself, and, (2) that all is being done not only by the power of God, but also by the wisdom and goodness of God. To put it into a paraphrase, it would read like this:

'Who would not seek to a God who is of infinite power, able to deliver? Who would not seek to a God and commit his cause to Him who is gracious, pitiful, merciful, and ready to deliver? Who would not seek to a God who is of infinite wisdom to find out ways and means of deliverance, even though a man's condition may seem to him altogether desperate and beyond remedy.'

1. God is the efficient cause, therefore He is to be supplicated to remove both the secondary causes and the effect of our afflictions. We must commit our cause to Him who is the great First Cause.

This text does not prove the major proposition, that God is the great First Cause of all providential happenings, but it does set out to prove the minor assumption, that God is the efficient cause, the Sender of afflictions. To prove this, Job's friend simply removes all other possible efficient causes. There must be some efficient cause of affliction. Yet it is not at all possible to assign afflictions to any other efficient cause but God. For while some afflictions might be assigned to this or that cause, one that we can see is plainly a factor in causing the trouble we are having, yet there are others which are not assignable to anyone else but God working directly upon the afflicted person. Those that we see are inflicted by visible causes may be assigned to God by simply viewing them as secondary causes—God's instruments in laying on the affliction. But some that are not seen to have a visible cause, how can we assume them to be from some mysterious and unknown source? To deny that God is behind all causation is simply to deny God—and only the wicked says in his heart that *"there is no God"* (Ps. 10:4).

"For affliction does not come forth from the dust,"—Our eyes teach us, we cannot but see plainly that all men are full of trouble—we are no sooner born than we are afflicted. These afflictions come from somewhere. They do not frame, form or fashion themselves. If they do not come forth of themselves, then where on earth, or in Heaven do they come from? We must find an efficient cause either among the creatures, or in the Creator. It is certain that they do not come up out of the dust. That is, they do not come from the creatures, as creatures and as lone causes. Then they must come down from Heaven, from the hand of God Himself, the One who disposes all things according to the good pleasure of His own will (Isa. 46:10; Dan. 4:35; Eph. 1:5,9; Phil. 2:13; Rev. 4:11).

When a thing is lost, we have a way of saying, It surely has not melted into the ground. It must be some place. So, with afflictions, they do not spring up out of the dust—that would not explain their origin or their action. They must come from somewhere. And it is from God that they come. God is the Efficient Cause of all affliction.

2. Man is the meritorious cause of all his afflictions. If sufferings are due to sin, and if sin is due to the man himself, and if this suffering is inflicted on man by God for sin, then it is both right and wise for man to seek to God for deliverance from his suffering. There is no remedy to be had anywhere else. This argument develops from the exposition of the text, not appearing upon the fact of the text.

"for affliction"—The Hebrew particle may be taken three ways, and translators have divided themselves among these three ways: (1) It can be taken causally, in which case it reads, *"for affliction, etc.;"* (2) It may be taken adversatively, as in the A.V. *"although affliction, etc.;"* (3) it may be taken affirmatively, *"Certainly affliction, etc."* The sense is good and plain when either of the three possible translations are used. But there may be some obscuration of the meaning in using the adversative, although.

"affliction"—It is important to take note of the fact that the word by which affliction is here expressed bears a double signification in Scripture. It is used to denote iniquity of all sorts (especially the sin of idolatry-see Hosea 4:15); and it is used to portray sorrow, trouble, calamity or misery of any sort.

1. Surely iniquity does not come forth from the dust. Sin alters the nature of man, so it is no marvel that it alters the names of things—in Hosea 10:15, and often in the Old Testament, this word is added in order to set out the worst of men, *"the workers of iniquity."* The soil where iniquity grows, the shop where sin is manufactured, is in man's heart-*"The heart is deceitful above all things, and desperately wicked; who can know it?"* (Jer. 17:9); *"Keep your heart with all diligence; for out of it are the issues of life"* (Prov. 4:23); *"How can you, being evil, speak good things? For the mouth speaks out of the overflowing of the heart"* (Matt. 12:34,35); *"For out of the heart come forth evil thoughts, murders, adulteries, fornications, thefts, lies, blasphemies. These things are they which defile a man,"* (Matt. 15:19). Eliphaz takes us to the wellhead of our sinful natures, to the original sin of our appointed head and representative, and to the fact that we all sinned in Adam.

2. The word is translated in many places as sorrow, trouble, calamity and all sorts of misery, because sin is the cause, the very mother of sorrow, affliction and death (death= separation from God, the Fountain of true life)—*"when lust has conceived, it brings forth sin. And when it is finished, sin brings forth death"* (see James 1:13-15). The mother, sin, and the daughter, affliction, are called by the same name. We translated both by the cause *"For iniquity does not come forth from the dust,"* and also by the effect, *"Surely affliction does not come forth from the dust."* And, if we are to fully understand what God has written for us here, we must take in both meanings of the original word. If the effect is mentioned, the cause is supposed. If the cause is mentioned, then the effect is also supposed.

It is a universal proverb, that iniquity or affliction does not come forth from the dust. You do not need to confine yourself to Christian circles, or Jewish writings, to read the sorrowful and sinful condition of mankind—the acknowledgment of this is as universal as the universality of sin in every representative of the human race. But not only is the statement here proverbial, so is the form of speaking. For when the heathen wanted to deny that chance was behind a happening, they would say it in this way, 'This did not come forth from the ground.' So a man whose parentage is not known, who cannot tell whence he came, has been called, 'a son of the earth'—importing that his origin could not be determined. Those who originally cannot be assigned are usually assigned to the common original, or, the parent of us all, the earth. In the text here, Eliphaz may well have originated this form of speaking, there being no certainty that any before him ever spoke in this way. But, be that as it may, it is certain that Eliphaz here intends to convey to us that is was nothing so fallacious as luck, or a mysterious and untraceable fortune, which caused afflictions. It was not the heathen god, luck, but the only true God, the Creator and Disposer of us all, who brought trouble down about our deserving ears.

"from the dust"—There is a twofold opposition here. First, as opposed to God, and secondly, as opposed to ourselves. As opposed to God, *"Affliction does not come forth from the dust,"* it comes from the wisdom and power of God working as the efficient cause to implement His decrees, those eternal plans which were made for His own good pleasure.

Secondly, as opposed to ourselves, afflictions do not jump upon us from out of the dust—without a cause—they come to us because we merit them. It is not because of the dust, or because of other creatures, but because of ourselves that we are afflicted. Every man has within himself the ground which produces our troubles; the source of our miseries is is us—the fountain of sinful life bubbles out our sorrows and our sufferings.

"neither does trouble spring up out of the ground"—This is but a doubling of the first part of the verse. The word translated trouble properly means toilsome labor, or laborious toil—which is not an essential part of man's life, but is the fruit of his sin. This adverse addition to our lives fell out of our proud decision to eat of the tree of good and evil. It did not come up out of the ground, it came forth from the heart of man, for *"out of the heart come the issues of life."* The allusion is of course to those plants which grow up out of the earth, which grow wild and seed themselves centuries on end. These experience no troubling pain, for painful labor does not come out of the ground. Nor, in fact, do they simply grow by and of themselves—they do not grow by the agency of men, it is true, but there is a Hand that both plants and waters them.

Since the next verse affords a summation of the point, only an observation or two need be given here in regard to these two phrases:

1. The material cause of sin is in ourselves. We bring forth the fruit at our tongues and from the end of our fingers, because the root is in our hearts. Our sins come from the dirt and filth of our own corruptions—that is the soil they grow in.

2. The meritorious cause of man's suffering is from his sin.

As iniquity springs from ourselves, so we may resolve that misery and suffering springs from our sin. True it is that God in these afflictions upon Job, and in many cases before and since, lays out to His dear children suffering and miserable affliction beyond that given to others. But never has anyone, Job included, suffered more than his iniquities deserved. The world often, with God's permission, inflicts suffering and mounts severe persecutions of all varieties upon the righteous. To these, the Christian might easily paraphrase, 'We have done many good works among you, for which of these do you stone us?' But, it is nevertheless true that even those who suffer for righteousness sake (1 Pet. 2:20) are still suffering because they are sinners. The iniquity of any man is in itself a sufficient meritorious cause of all afflictions. In short, if man had never sinned, man would never have suffered. If a man ever suffers, it is because of sin. We did not say, it is because of 'his' sin, because there once was a Man who suffered for the sins of others although He Himself never sinned. Still, if none of God's chosen had ever sinned, then this Man would not have suffered either. Leaving Him inside the human race, but outside the sin that permeates every other human being that ever lived, it may be truly said that man weaves a spider's web of sin out of his own bowels. Then, alas! He becomes entangled in that web, and the trouble that wraps around him is that which he has twisted with his own fingers.

3. Every man naturally seeks the reason for his sorrows and afflictions outside himself. The sinful nature of man will not permit him to admit that it is his guilt that brings affliction upon him (as in Gen. 3:14-17). It may be this is the reason Eliphaz makes these particular statements here, realizing that a man needs help in order to recognize and admit that he is the cause of his own trouble in that he is a sinner. Why blame the day when you were born? There is something closer you can fix your eye upon, even your birth-sin. Do not persist, friend Job, in the natural idea that all good comes from within yourself, but all evil comes from some other source.

"but man is born to trouble, as the sparks fly upward"—Job 5:7.

The word translated trouble is the same as is in the verse above. It is most often tranlated *"labor,"* but it is also translated in the A.V. as *"mischeif," "perverseness," "sorrow," "pain," "travail," "iniquity," "misery,"* and *"toil."* From this, you will see the breadth of the word, and the inferences which may be fairly drawn from the word. All these are the fruit of sin—without sin, none of these would ever have been coupled with mankind. Man is born in sin (Ps. 51:5), and he is born to sin—that is, he is born with a corrupted nature which is prone and ready to sin. This being true, man is born to trouble, because sin and trouble are inseparable companions. Man has a right to troubles, they are his inheritance, and his due. Man has a talent, a fitness, a skill for falling into trouble. If a man is born to a thing, he needs little instruction, little cultivating in order to accomplish it. There is an innate talent in this man or that for certain accomplishments. All men, every son of Adam, has an inborn talent for getting himself into trouble. His understanding, his will, his affections all are finely tuned for sin, and he needs no more instruction than a tadpole needs to begin swimming. The latter part of the verse clears this fully:

"as the sparks fly upward"—Sparks have a principle within them which causes them to fly upward. They ascend, they need no directing—if a spark comes from the fire, you will be certain that it will not fly downward; it knows only one way to go, upward! Man, too, needs no directions as to how to sin, how to involve himself in toilsome trouble. There is only one way he knows to go—just as surely as the sparks fly upward, that surely will man go downward into sin. If there is a spark of life in a man, he will sin. Except the Holy Spirit of God brood upon a man and beget from him those spiritually good affections and motions of the heart, then you may be sure that the first thing he will do when he is born is sin—and the last thing he will do before he dies is sin. It is that certain that man is born to troubling sin, or sinful trouble. Sin and sorrow and suffering are not his art, they are his nature. If he never saw nor heard of another human being from the time he left the womb until the day he died, he would have no life of comfort, but a life of trouble. To discover the mysteries of iniquity is no impossibility to any member of the human race. Rather, they are certain to find out early, quickly how to make themselves miserable.

The copulative, *"as,"* may be rendered, *"and (the sparks fly upward);"* that is, both the trouble of man and the ascending of sparks are natural. But the word is usually translated as a comparative (Job 34:3; Mark 9:49, etc.). When both this and that are alike, then the comparative is quick and powerful to convey the sense to us.

"sparks"—The Hebrew is, *"the sons of the coal."* Sparks are children of the fire, and it is the better part of wisdom to translate this word in this way. As for the Vulgate, and others who translate, *"birds,"* *"vultures,"* *"angels,"* *"angry passions,"* etc. none of these can be properly said to fly upwards by a law of necessity—see the Treasury of this verse (Volume III, this edition).

ALL SINS AND SORROWS; ALL SUFFERING AND MISERY ARE IN MAN'S NATURE

1. As the sparks *"make high their flight,"* reaching an indeterminable height before they are extinguished, so man soars rashly and rapidly into the heights of sin. However high he may rise, say in the fames and fortunes possible in this world, he shall find there nothing more, and nothing less, than a cup full of sorrow. His bread shall be afflictive, his waters shall be adverse. If he becomes skillful in the arts of sin, so that he has no peer in the securing of the things that he lusts after, then he shall receive double for his wicked deeds, according to his works (*"In the cup which she mixed, mix to her twice as much. As much as she glorified herself and lived in luxury, so much torment and sadness give to her. Because she says in her heart, I sit as a queen, and I am not a widow—and, I will in no way see sorrow—because of this her plagues shall come in one day, death and sorrow and hungering"*—Rev. 18:5-7).

2. It is true that a man never formally commits or brings forth every sin possible to mankind, and it is equally true that a man does not taste of every cup of sorrow, nor endure every affliction possible. Yet, virtually and radically every man has within him every sin possible to mankind—that is to say, every possible sin can be formed and shaped out of the nature of any man. There is no sin that a man could be certain he would not do, if the restraining hand of the Holy Spirit were to be lifted and he be freed to do any sin. Likewise, a man has every affliction, all sorrows within him, so that the justice of God may at any moment form out of him, dreadfully shape from him afflictions for his sins which he never dreamed existed. Just as the sparks remain in the fire, or in the flint, until they are smitten or blown out, so sins lie secretly in our hearts until temptation brings them out.

3. Although sin is burdensome to man, it is no labor for him to sin. As easily as the sparks fly upward, so does man sin. By God's grace, the same may be said of a holy man, or nearly so—that holy duties are not a burden to a godly man, for through grace He does them naturally, he being a partaker of the divine nature. The possibilities and impossibilities of a regenerate man are directly opposite to those of a natural man—"*if anyone is in Christ, he is a new creation, the old things have passed away. Behold! All things have become new!*" (2 Cor. 5:17). The new creature cannot practice sin; the old man cannot do anything else but practice sin. The new man can do nothing against the truth; the old man is always doing things against the truth (1 John 2:20; 2 Cor. 13:8). A godly man is a heavenly spark, he has been set on fire with holy love and he ever ascends upward toward God.

"*Truly I would seek unto God, and unto God I would commit my cause*"—Job 5:8.

There are some translators who think that Eliphaz here is exulting over Job, and some expositors agree. These believe that Eliphaz is assuming a holier-than-thou attitude, as did the Pharisee who thanked God that he was not like the publican (who was at the time humbly beating his breast and confessing his sins unto salvation). There is little doubt that Eliphaz feels superior to Job at this point, due to the fact that he is not under any providential afflictions. But most expositors believe that Eliphaz speaks these words in a sweet and meek spirit, giving Job the best instruction that he knows. For Eliphaz has found by experience that "*man is born unto trouble as the sparks fly upward*," and that when a man is in trouble, there is but one Person who can help and will help. Therefore, it is to God that he points him, advising that he humbly present himself before God and lay his words before Him. The paraphrase then would run like this:

'Since these things are so, since these are undoubted truths (that afflictions do not come from the dust, but come from ourselves and our own sins;) and since it is your circumstance now that you are under great afflictions and troubles, I assure you that if I were in your condition, dear Job, I would no longer stand here complaining against my day, cursing the creatures, distempering my head and disquieting my heart with these passions—but I would go and address myself to God, I would apply to Heaven, I would seek for remedy there, for earth cannot help us.'

"*I would seek unto God*"—The word here carries the meaning of a diligent search, a persistent and determined inquiry. This is a laboring and singlehearted continuing in prayer to the Most High God who dwells with those who are of a contrite and humble spirit. Why does Eliphaz say that he would go to God when he was sorely troubled?

1. He first looks for God to reveal to him how to conduct himself under this affliction.

2. He then looks for God's power and grace to work in him to act like a child of God, a prince of the Kingdom, should act when he is being instructed or disciplined.

3. Next, he looks for God to reveal to him what it is he lacks. If he needs more contriteness, the brokenness that is needed to repent, purity, etc., then he wants God to make this known to him (as David did, "*Search me, O God, and know my heart. Try me, and know my thoughts, and see if any wicked way is in me, and lead me in the way everlasting*"—Ps. 139:23,24).

4. This sense of lacking something will make one restless and unsatisfied, therefore the seeking to God will be more than an approach to a Ruler to make known a request. The need here is troubling, and the prayer will be with strong desire (as was David's when he said, "*I will not give rest to my eyes nor sleep to my eyelids until I find a place for the Lord*"—Ps. 132:4).

5. This seeking will be one in which the penitent and suffering petitioner will labor with all his strength, with all his intelligence, to find God and to interest Him in giving immediate relief. A lazy spirit will find no rest in God. Spiritually lazy people are lukewarm abominations in the sight of God. Presenting oneself before the almighty King of kings is a serious business ("*our God is a consuming fire*"—Heb. 12:30) and it is best not to be a bit slovenly in your appearance or careless in your approach. He teaches importunity in prayer, and He may require it of you before He will lift the cloud of troubles that beset you.

"I would seek unto God, and unto God I would commit my cause"—In the first clause, the word for God is *el*, and in the latter clause, it is *elohim*. Both names denote the power of God, but finely, *el* denotes the power or strength to act and execute; whereas, *elohim* denotes the power or authority to judge and determine. So we have, *"Truly I would go to el* (the strong God,) *and I would commit my cause to elohim* (the almighty God of judgment)"*.*—for the weak and afflicted need strength, and the guilty need judgment.

"I would commit my cause unto God"—Literally, *"to God I would put my words."* We have here a presenting of oneself before God, a placing before Him such words as will call forth from Him the help which we need in our affliction, *"If any of you lack wisdom, let him ask of God, who gives to all liberally, etc."* (James 4:5). Never is wisdom more needed than when one is under severe affliction, and we are told under those conditions to ask God for such wisdom. We are encouraged to do so, for He tells us that He gives liberally, that He also gives again and again without reproaching us for our frequent prayers. Prayer, of course, is a putting of our thoughts and feelings into words. In our deepest distresses, it may be that the best we can manage are but groans, which the Holy Spirit then interprets to God for us (Rom. 8:26). The sense, then, is clear. This appealing to God with the words which are fitting to our need, and to His majesty, is actually a committing of our cause to Him. If the trial is beyond our control, we can no longer trust in ourselves, in a skill or a trait of character which we have developed. Now will we commit our cause to another person, one who does not have control over both the persecuted and the persecutor? This leaves but one Person to whom we can turn with confidence. It is to our shame that we wait and turn to Him last, after we have exhausted all our own resources, plus those of our relatives and friends.

This committing of ourselves and our cause to God, of course, carries with it the determination to accept His judgment as to what we need, what is best for us, what shall be done to us. If He shall reply, *"My grace is sufficient for you,"* then let the afflicted one learn to say with the apostle Paul, *"therefore I will rather glory in my weaknesses, so that the power of Christ may rest in me...I take pleasure, then, in infirmities, in insults, in dire needs, in persecutions, in distresses for Christ—for when I am weak, then I am strong"* (2 Cor. 12:9).

The good advice of Eliphaz had but one flaw. It is not one which affects us, for it certainly is our duty to listen to holy brethren giving us scriptural advice. And since there is nearly always the same elements in an afflictive circumstance, it is always well to seek to God for help and remedy, for deliverance, and forgiveness, and to leave our well-being and welfare entirely up to Him from that point until the day He has set for a change in our circumstances. Furthermore, it was the duty of Eliphaz to give advice, even to reprove his brother for any fault which was evident to him. For to love another child of God, or an enemy either, is to desire that that person be in perfect harmony with God and to be exactly in His will. Since sin separates between a man and God, it is our duty, it is the finest expression of love, for us to reprove him for his evident sin and seek to nudge him back into the satisfying embrace of God, *"let him know that he who brings a sinner from the error of his way shall save a soul from death and shall cover a multitude of sins"* (James 5:20).

Eliphaz, however, made a very common mistake — we should say, he committed a sin against a friend, a sin that is common day in and day out. He gave good advice, but it wasn't the right advice at the right time to the right person. He did not bother to get the facts. This sin which he charged upon Job would have caused Job no distress, if only the original sin of his nature had been intended. Job readily admits to being a thoroughly corrupt sinner by nature, in more than one place. But Eliphaz has without investigation, and in complete contrariness to the open facts in his possession, unquestionably condemned Job —and this merely because of a false principle which he held in common with most men— believing that he who is much afflicted is in the same measure guilty of sin. This was not a revealed truth, either then or now. It was a philosophical hypothesis, and as is usual with the figments of men's imaginations, it was wrong and it was sinful. He had no right to distress this holy man with inferences of guilt without having both the Scripture and the facts straight. The only evidence that he had in his possession was the distraught condition of Job, and the impassioned but misguided speech he had just made. Any other evidence he may have had would have been hearsay evidence, or presumptive evidence—neither of which should be admissible in the condemnation of our holy brothers.

So Eliphaz was wrong in presuming Job to be a hypocrite, to be guilty of unrevealed sins of such magnitude as to cause him to be in his present misery and distress. But he was right in assuming that Job was such a sinner as was described in the past two verses: there is no pain without sin, no affliction without God sending it. To these he added in the clay of his own conclusion, that if God afflicted us for sin, then He surely must afflict us in direct proportion to our guilt, And that is what the book of Job is all about. Yes, the wickedness of man on earth is very great, and *"every imagination of the thoughts of his heart is only evil continually"* (Gen. 6:5). There are no exceptions, There are no intermissions. We are all wicked, all only evil, and that continually. The word translated *"imagination"* is a word pregnant with meaning: every image that is formed in the mind of man is evil. By his inborn, sinful nature, every work, every concept and idea, every fancy or opinion of man is evil. Every device, every invention, every purpose of man is naturally formed for the purpose of pleasing himself. The fact that he is using his God-given faculties for his own pleasure instead of for the glory of God makes them all evil. Instead of loving God with all his heart and mind and soul, he has become a lover of himself rather than a lover of God. Therefore, he is unceasingly conceiving notions and ideas which are wickedly intended to serve his own glory—they are rebellious, lawless and ungodly. Desiring to be as God, he became a god unto himself — but only to himself, for all the others are also gods, in their own evil imaginations.

Yes, Job was born such a man. But he was reborn a totally different man, a new creation of God. Though we are so by nature, there is Hope, and that Hope is Jesus Christ, who lived guilelessly, sinlessly, and unselfishly in this world for a lifetime of continual service to God, of unremitting love and total submission to the will and pleasure of God. Having such a life to give, He gave it, that whoever would believe on Him might have everlasting life. It is to this one that we must commit our cause, our great *"God and Savior, Jesus Christ, who gave Himself for us so that He might redeem us from all iniquity and purify to Himself a peculiar people, zealous of good works"* (Titus 2:13). Job had laid hold on this Hope, although in his day there was but a shadow of the Gospel to be believed. Not only did he not have the New Testament revelation of Jesus Christ, but he did not so much as have the first five books of the written revelation to guide him into the arms of Christ. Yet you will see him totally and completely rest himself in God, you will see him finally follow the advice of Eliphaz here, after his three friends have tried him and almost tripped him into a fall into Satan's plan.

"who does things great and beyond search; marvelous things without number"—Job 5:9.

Eliphaz now seeks to establish his point, that God is infinite in power, wisdom and in goodness. This he does by enumerating many different effects and works, all which call for much power, wisdom and goodness. Here he refers to these as, *"things great and beyond search; marvelous things without number."* Next he will name some of these, some natural, some administrative. Why does Eliphaz both contend that God's works are great and also enforce his argument with accurate and extensive descriptions?

1. He desires to claim that all things are providential disposings from God, directly so.

2. He intends to humble Job, in that he seems overbold in making extravagant speeches in regard to his affliction. Elihu, then God Himself uses this method to finally humble Job.

3. It may be that Eliphaz intends to support Job, to comfort him in his afflictions by reminding him that God is such a wise, great and good God. It is normally very wise to consider God in Himself, and in His works: who He is, what He does—in our extremities, such a view of God may lift the spirits in the saddest and cloudiest day of our afflictions.

4. Very likely, also, there is purposed here the rebuke of Job for being so willing to curiuosly probe into the reason for God's dealing with him in such a severe way. Job was

troubled because he could not see the bottom of God's dealings with him. He could not see what the cause was, why he was being afflicted, or what issues and outlets he could expect to open up for his deliverance. To this spirit of inquiry, Eliphaz replies, God is great and His ways are unsearchable. He cannot be measured in His dealings by the line of your human understanding, and your arithmetic is not going to add up His accounts.

"who does great things"—He does not say it in the past tense, but in the present. The acts of God are present acts, continued from the past, continuing into the future, from everlasting to everlasting. Just as in His nature and essence God always has been, and always shall be, yet He gives Himself this name, *"I AM,"*—so all the acts of God are 'present' acts. Time is a creature. There is no time with God but God's time — which is not actually time at all. It is amazingly clear from Scripture that He regards all as being one present act: Note the present tense in John 5:17, *"My Father works until now, and I work."* Not a word about the past, both Jesus and the Father working now, always in the eternal now.

The word which we translate *"does"* is a word with more emphasis and meaning than the ordinary doing of a thing. In strictness and propriety, the Hebrew signifies a thing exactly, perfectly and completely accomplished. To illustrate, look at Isaiah 43:7, where God desires to magnify the abundant increase He intends to give to His people, *"bring...everyone who is called by My name; for I have created him for My glory, I have formed him; yea, I have made him."* There is a grading up observable here, created, formed, made. He created, brought them from a nothingness to a being. Not only that, but He formed them, that is, He designed them, proportioned them and polished them. Lastly, we have the word in our text, *"I have made him;"* that is, I have exactly put upon him the perfections of nature, the perfections of grace, the impressions of my special love and favor, and I have lifted him up to the top of all mankind—for so some render the word, *"yea, I have magnified him."* God has exalted His people, made them high pinnacles of perfections.

"great things"—Some men with a great deal of pains do nothing. Others with a great deal of art do a thing which is no more than nothing, a trifle or a toy—at most some really worthless or inferior work takes up their time, skill and study. But when God goes to work, you may be certain He shall produce a noble and great work. He who is great may be expected to do great things. With men, a man may be great merely in the opinions of other men. But with God, He is great because He is doing great things, marvelous things without number. If a man does a work, then another man may search it out and understand it; it does not really deserve the adjectives, wonderful and marvelous—for what is the wonder if a man did it, and what is the marvel if a man did it? Neither can a man do so many great things that they cannot be counted by men. Therefore, it is only God's works that can be truly called great, wonderful, marvelous and innumerable. Men are great only by comparison with other men—in comparison with angels, or with God, they are insignificant and incompetent, virtually impotent. There are no truly great men, so there are no great things done by men. Contrariwise, there are no little things done by God, because the smallest of things accomplished by God are great, being done by One who is truly great. And as in an often-used exhortation in Scripture, it is by their fruits or works that you may know the worker. God's greatness is stamped indelibly and unmistakably upon everything He does. From the smallest, inperceivable atom comes forth an undeniable picture of God's greatness, for it is unbelievably perfected, balanced, and employed; having buried within itself the power of God in such unspeakably quantity as to defy description or understanding by the best minds of men (being hampered by sin, as well as by finitude). For greatness, as is the theme of the last chapters of the book of Job, take the universe as a whole, or any of its parts—they are all the extraordinary works of God, easily discernible as His alone.

God does great things, and they are called great because of both quantity and quality. Since all things were created by Him, and nothing came into being without Him (John 1), there is little doubt about the quantity being great—as great a quantity as there is, that is the quantity that He has produced. But God did not produce a mass, an unformed world full of unfinished objects. Not only did He produce perfection in things, but in living creatures as well. And the qualities that He gave to angels and to men are truly great. Then, the work of redemption: what a truly great, wonderful, marvelous, unsearchable work is that! That a man created upright, but completely corrupted into a poisonous mist, a God-dishonoring bit of rotten clay, should be recreated is the grandest proof of God's greatness which we now have. For it is great to create. No man can create. For true creation is a making of something out of nothing. God made man out of the dust, but first He made the dust out of nothing—all the elements of the dust were so created. But it is far greater to recreate a corrupted being. For in redemption there is a double creation: (1) First, the sinner must be made alive—for he is worse than nothing, he is a minus, a rotten negative—dead in trespasses and sins; (2) then he must be perfected in holiness, righteousness and true knowledge. As much creative power went into either of these two creative acts as went into the resurrection of Christ, and in setting Him at God's right hand, above all rule and authority and power and lordship; as much power as it took to put all things under His feet and to make Him the Head over all things to the church (Eph. 1:19-22).

And if it is proper to God to do only great things, then how much more is it our duty to expect great things of Him. If we dishonor Him and despise Him, then we may expect great response from Him. If we honor Him and keep our minds stayed upon Him, then we may expect to have our cups running over with joy, contentment, satisfaction, peace, and all the fruits of the Spirit of God.

"and beyond search"—The import is that here is One who is both so immense and so inscrutable as to be beyond any finite understanding. However much we may search into and discover the workings of either things or living creatures, there is so much greatness of God displayed in them that they could still be called beyond our understanding. If our thoughts rise to the highest attainable plane, still His thoughts shall be higher than ours. Likewise, though we may discover the maximum attainable knowledge about anything or anyone, we shall still lack the knowledge that the Originator and Creator has. Just as one may completely search out, weigh and even catalog every component part of a building, yet not be able to know what the architect had in mind when he planned it—how many and of what sort he decided not to build, why to choose this and reject that, etc.—so it is not possible for the creature to discover even by a most diligent search all that was in the mind of the Creator, nor even what is in the created thing or being.

Some works of God are not to be inquired into—there are things which belong to God and are not for us to know, *"the secret things belong to the Lord our God, but those things which are revealed belong to us"* (Deut. 29:29). Paul heard words which it was not lawful for him to repeat (2 Cor. 12:4). There are some things the creature may not ask of God, *"Yes, rather, O man, who are you that answers against God? Shall the thing formed say to Him who formed it, Why did you make me this way?"* (Rom. 9:20). It would be the better part of wisdom for men to inquire into their own secret ways than into the secrets which God has withheld from us. And the obvious must be said also, it would be well with man if he had a curiosity about the things God has revealed in His word to equal the curiosity he has about things he is not supposed to inquire into!

There are some works of God which He desires us to inquire into. Besides the written record, the Bible, there are innumerable creations which are open to our inquiry. Some of these are open and plain, easy to study out Others are difficult to understand, as Peter remarked about some of Paul's writings; yet we are to try to understand. We must search and labor to understand the things of God so that we might the better understand God. But if we are to understand and know Him, first we must reach a level of humility and contrition for sin which will give us the vantagepoint to observe heavenly things. Then it is imperative that we search the things of God which are open for our inspection with submission to the mind of God. We must not search and study for our own satisfaction only. We must search with the desire to know and to honor God, not to humor ot to honor ourselves. Then our searches will make us more holy, more acceptable, more useful to Him.

Of course, the counsels of God are beyond our search. They are none of our business! Will not the God and Judge of all the earth do right? Yes, and He will also move in a circle of thought and performance which has an exactitude and just balance which is beyond the judgment of man. Even if He should reveal these thoughts and operations to your view, you would neither recognize nor comprehend them. An ant could understand the workings of a computer better than you could understand the workings of God's mind. This means, of course, that His providential dealings with you and with every other person (men and angels) are not within your ability or permissability. He decides what to dispense, what to direct, what to permit, what to perform, what to restrain—and who! It is your part to accept these dispensations of God, whatever they are, and to be content with them — perfectly content, and to regard them with reverence, respect and affection. You are duty-bound, and it is the better part of wisdom, to love everything that God does. A life of faith presupposes the following of God, the trusting of God, the obeying of God without the knowledge of all that God is doing or asking.

"marvelous things"—There is a difference between things that are beyond search and things which are marvelous. Unsearchable things are hidden, they cannot be found. Marvelous things are plainly seen, but their causes cannot be found. The original word is derived from a root which means separated, disjointed, not divided. Marvelous things are expressed by that word because marvels, or wonders, are separated or removed from us—and this by at least three degrees: (1) They are not coherent to us, we cannot reason our way to their causes; (2) they do not make sense to us—that is why unbelievers are so adamant in rejecting miracles. Miracles and marvels are performed before our very eyes, because they are intended to authenticate the truth of God and to confirm faith—or to convict unbelievers of their wickedness in throwing off God's truth. Search the Scriptures and it will become evident to you that the working of miracles was always given in order to do one of these two things. And by this you evaluate the lying claims of the Romanists, who claim that they perform miracles (such as, their supposed miracle of transsubstantiation, in which they claim to turn bread into Christ). They tell big tales, but they can show no miracle—and, more importantly, they can show no reason for the miracle or marvel—that it either authenticates the written word (which is the only truth, all the truth which we are now concerned with), or that it convicts unbelievers of their obstinacy in regard to the truth. A marvel is plain to the senses, but they do not make sense to us because the working of the wonder is not seen or known by us. (3) Marvels are beyond our ability, we cannot (like the Egyptian magicians of Pharaoh) imitate them, much less perform them. So long as God was pleased to allow it, the Egyptian sorcerers seemed to perform every miracle God was working by Moses. But the day came when He proved that the devils are not able to imitate God in all that He does. Their religions and their miracles are but an appearance of God's

There are three things of near alliance in the Hebrew: signs, miracles and marvels. They may be distinguished in this way: (1) A sign is the representation of a thing present, one before us; (2) A miracle shows forth somewhat that is future, or yet to come; (3) A marvel is any act of providence, secret or separate from us in the manner of doing or producing it, which we cannot trace to the causative source. A marvel is but a heightening and/or sublimating of nature, but a miracle is a crossing or contradiction of nature; a work altogether above nature.

Therefore, here we are to understand that God does marvelous things. These are not the miracles of God—He would be just as great if there had never been a miracle, but He performs miracles for His own purposes, not the least of which is to show us that He is not a man as we are, but is able to work either within, without or above natural laws. Such natural wonders as God's creation of the sun, the suspending of the earth in the universe in exactly the place, at precisely the distance, with the rotative speed, etc. which would permit it to sustain life—these are marvelous things, things which we discover but do not truly understand the workings of. Marvels are of God, only He does marvelous things.

SINCE GOD WORKS MARVELS IN OUR LIVES, OUR LIVES SHOULD BE SO

Since God works extraordinary things for us, then let us not allow others to think that our lives are ordinary lives. Let our repentance be the kind that changes our lives. Let our works have that godly stamp which will convince others that we can be no other than true children of God. If our zeal and our courage are not marvelous, then how can we say that we are in His image? Look at the apostles, who carried themselves with such magnanimous heroism in the work of spreading the good news about Jesus Christ that even the High-priest and the Sanhedrin *"marveled"* at them, and knew that they had been with Jesus. Let our love and our thankfulness be a wonder to all those who see us love, who see us give thanks to God by our dedicated lives and words. One of God's greatest marvels is the working of faith in a man, for it is not in the nature of fallen man to trust in God. Now if you claim this marvelous faith, then see to it that you do not fail to impress the unbeliev-ers with the constant, never-failing exercise of that faith. They, too, must marvel when they see you turn your back on your own seeming advantage and take the side of God. Is there any other kind of man than a Christian man who will gladly sacrifice all he has and all that the future in this world appears to promise him, merely because of a command of God in His Book?

"without number"—that is, innumerable things that are marvelous; until there is no more numbers to count. This can mean three things, (1) that these marvelous things He does are innumerable—that is, of course, infinite to the same measure that God is infinite. If God were not infinite, then His marvelous acts could not be infinite. He is, and they are! (2) No man lives who can count so high, by his own act, or by the combined genious and devices of all men together. It is in this sense that God calls angels innumerable; the stars innum-erable—they cannot be counted by man. But of course God can and does count them - all in this sense, that He knows their exact number and intricate makeup from eternity past until all eternity future. Since God never forgets, there is no need for Him ever to count or sum up. (3) Often things are called innumerable simply because they are of a very great number. Just as that which is very high is said to be as high as Heaven (*"cities walked up to Heaven"*—Deut. 1:28), so here it may simply mean that God's marvelous works are so very many as to be without number in the sight and comprehension of man.

God does marvelous things without number. He always has, He is and He always will be doing things which will cause us to wonder and to marvel, so as to give Him the utmost praise. The hand of God is not shortened today, nor has He been running low in His bag of marvels because the ages have passed again and again. Nor will His hand be shortened when this world has melted with a fervent heat and has passed away. God will be God, in eternity, as well as now. If you believe that He is a marvelous God, a wonderful God, then you surely must believe that such a God will always be doing His marvelous wonders for your instruction and delight.

O, my friends, do not let us be guilty of the sin of the fool Israelite, who imagined in his wicked conceit that he was limiting the Holy One of Israel (Ps. 78:41). Men yearn to be so independent that they could not be limited by anyone—from the day Adam was smitten with the desire to be God-like, those born in Adam's image have been scheming and devising some semblance of independence which will permit them to claim that they are not in need of the help of anyone. And, they smirk, the One they need the least is the God of the Christians. Yet these same spiritually ugly people are eating their hearts out day after day because it is all too evident that God blows them here or there, like a leaf they swing to and fro in God's time and to God's tune. Is it any wonder, then, that they become provoked when we ask them a time or two to perform a wonder or a marvel for us, that we may believe that they are truly so great as they would have us think? But, my beloved Christian friends, you need not fear that you will provoke God by asking of Him a wonder, or many marvels, or even so many impossible things as we cannot number. Our God cannot be wearied. If there would be one thing which would weary Him, it would be our unbelief—the notion that we cannot really expect Him to do marvelous things for us. (See Isa. 7:13). His mercies are marvels without mercy. Grace tumbles over grace for us.

Lastly, remember this, that if God never gets tired of doing marvelous things, so many that we cannot count them, then we should be ashamed that we get tired of doing things for Him. The things we do for Him are not marvelous, they are but marvelous in the sight of unbelievers. To us, they are the ordinary workings of grace in a new creature. And if the things that God does for us are without number, if He does not count them as He is doing them, saying, 'this is now the ten thousandth favor I have done for this one, he only has thus and thus many more to go,' then let us also stop this wicked counting of the few things that we do for Him. We are supposed to count our blessings, but we are never given any excuse for counting our good deeds. The fact is, you could no more count your good deeds than you could spirit yourself around the world like an angel. Only God is good, and only God's estimate of good deeds will count. It is true that you may know that anything which you are commanded to do in God's word is good, and if you obey that command in faith, it is a good deed. But, then, who will determine if you did the deed in faith, or for some benefit that you thought you would derive? The very thing Satan charged against Job will also be charged against you, Are you serving God for the pleasing of Him, or for gain? Only God is able to sort out those deeds which are true, and those which you only believe to be true. The depths of sin in man are impossible for a man to plumb by himself So let us leave off this proud practice of counting up our good deeds. After you have done all, you are still going to be an unprofitable servant (Luke 17:10)—so why not pile your heart and mind, your soul and your strength into one concerted, lifelong effort to do all for the glory of God. If you do, there will be no counting of anything but blessings—for nothing but blessings will be coming your way.

"who gives rain upon the earth and sends waters upon the field"—Job. 5:10.

God, then, is to be sought because He does marvelous things without number, and among these is this one, that He forms every raindrop that waters the earth, and He sends the rain down at this time and that time that we may be sustained on the earth. And of course we may easily see that all those things which He sends for our sustenance are called to our minds by this one small instance of His care. It would be monstrous not to allow your mind to race through the other innumerable things that He marvelously provides for you. Those blessings and benefits which He showers down on every man every day of his natural life (Ps. 103:2) could be forgotten only by a man of great and insufferable conceit.

"rain upon the face of the earth"—The Jewish writers do not miss the mark here, when they say that rain is a husband to the earth, making the earth bring forth plentifully as a mother of mankind.

"and sends waters upon the field"—There should be a distinction made between these waters. There is the rain in the first clause, and then there are the waters in the second — these waters are the rivers and streams which irrigate the earth, as noted by the Psalmist, *"He caused waters to run down like rivers"* (Ps. 78:16). The word is of the dual number in the Hebrew, so that some apply it to two sorts of waters: the waters above, and the waters beneath. In Psalm 104:3, we read of the upper waters, *"He lays the beams of His upper rooms in the waters; He makes the clouds His chariots."* In Genesis 1:9, it is the inferior or lower waters mentioned, *"The Lord said, Let the waters under the heavens be gathered together unto one place, and let the dry land appear."* And in verse 7, they were both put together, *"And God made the expanse, and divided the waters which were under the expanse from the waters which were above the expanse."*

"upon the fields"—The word properly means any place that is out of doors, and does not mean fields in the sense of the place where plants grow. It is because these places are outside, therefore open to receive the waters, that this word is used here. Therefore, it takes in all sorts of places, all kinds of fields, those tilled, those untilled, etc.

Considering all of this, that God is the One who forms and sends the rain, who sustains all men upon the face of the earth, then let us smite hip and thigh the false teaching that 'Mother Nature' does this or that for men. This insidious lie has a modicum of truth, perhaps enough to fool a small child, but that grown men should propagate it—that is wickedness! And such a wickedness that men will hardly admit to, that they have lied to children—for it is to children that this lie is most often directed. Listen to the words of God, *"But the Lord is the true God, He is the living God, and the everlasting King. At His wrath the earth shall tremble, and the nations shall not be able to stand His fury. Thus you shall say to them* (that set up false gods, giving them credit for giving bread and water to men, such as 'Mother Nature'), *The gods who have not made the heavens and the earth, they shall perish from the earth and from under these heavens. He has made the earth by His power; He has established the world by His wisdom and has stretched out the heavens by His judgment. When He utters His voice, there is a noise of many waters in the heavens. He causes the vapors to go up from the ends of the earth. He makes lightnings with rain, and brings forth the wind out of His treasures. Every man is like an animal in knowledge... The Portion of Jacob is not like them; for He is the Maker of all things"* (Jer. 10:10-16). Do you believe the Scriptures? I know that you believe, and believing, you will never allow anyone to tell lies in your presence about the source of all our good gifts, God.

"to set upon high those who are low, so that those who mourn may be lifted up to safety" —Job. 5:11.

These words were no doubt spoken to encourage Job to hope in God for a restoration to his place of distinction. If he would but commit his cause to God, then He who sets on high those that are low will no doubt work. The word has in the fabric of it an allusion to kings and judges, those who sit in high places. However, the word may be used to denote those that are low in their own eyes, as well as those that are low only in the opinions of others.

Again, God is the great First Cause, therefore it is not to be thought that men rise up to high places by their own talent, skill, worthiness, birth, or crookedness. Advancement to positions high in the opinions of men, as well as positions of trust, such as judgeships, is from the Lord, *"For lifting up comes neither from the east, nor from the west, nor from the south. But God is the judge; He puts down one and sets up another"* (Ps. 75:6,7). If a man is advanced to a high position by another man, does that appointment not come from God? It comes from God, who puts it into the heart of the king, or person in authority, to advance this one or that one, *"The king's heart is in the hand of the Lord as the rivers of water—He turns it wherever He will"* (Prov. 21:1). Whether you give your credit to men, to skill, or to 'luck,' you shall answer for all of these forms of unbelief, and that day of reckoning will be dreadful indeed if you do not have Jesus Christ to stand for you!

"so that those who mourn may be lifted up to safety"—The Hebrew word signifies to be black, dark or obscured. The reason this word is borrowed to picture mourning or sorrow is because there is a blackness, a darkness of habit and of face when these are our feelings. The face is obscured when clouds of sorrow bring tears streaming down it.

Now, if the mourners will seek God's face, if they will commit their cause to Him, then, *"they may be lifted up to safety."* It is a high place, a place beyond the reach of danger, beyond the reach of an adversary. It is a lifting up unto God, who is *"a strong Tower."* James gives us the same encouragement, *"Be sorrowful and mourn and weep. Let your laughter be turned to mourning and your joy to shame. Humble yourselves before the Lord, and He shall exalt you (lift you up)"*—James 4:9,10. To humble yourself is to make yourself low, in the sense that Jesus was *"meek and lowly."* This is the posture which is prescribed by God, if you are desirous of being exalted, *"He has put down the mighty from their seats, and has exalted the humble and meek"* (Ps. 147:6).

"lifted up to safety"—When men are threatened with injury, they look for strongholds. When men fear oppression, they seek the shield and umbrella of one able to ward off the oppressor. When the saints of God are threatened, they humbly beseech the Lord to lift them up into His arms, to hide them under His wings—in short, to lift them up to safety. He says, *"I dwell...with him who is of a contrite and humble spirit"* (Isa. 57:15), and the Lord said that if you are going to rob a man's house, you must first throw down the

strong man who owns the house—therefore, if anyone thinks himself to be something, one able to oppress God's humble children, then let him know that he must first overthrow the High and Lofty One, He who dwells in eternity! In this verse, there meet two things which are very precious to men: (1) exaltation; (2) safety. Who can count the times that an earthy earthling has rolled riches and titles together into a mountain which he thought to be impregnable? Yet, in a day, as with Belshazzar, it all melted away. But when God is the one who lifts you up on high, and if God is the one who makes you safe, you need not fear any melting or destroying force. When the wicked man is set up high, he is not safe, "Surely, You set them in slippery places," (Ps. 73:18)—he is talking of men of high position. But when He sets His own people up on high, they shall not slip nor slide (unless they take off on a course of sin).

This is a marvelous thing, a thing of wonder, that God lifts up the poor mourners of the earth, and lifts them up high, to safety, to dwell with Him. They have no strength. They have no way to climb to such a position. They have many enemies who would dearly love to keep them down. Yet, the only One who could thwart their enmity comes graciously to their rescue, He lifts them up to safety.

"He brings to nothing the plots of the crafty, so that their hands cannot do wisely"—Job 5:12.

Seek unto God, commit your cause to Him, and you need not worry about the plots of the crafty, they shall be stricken with foolishness, they shall be paralyzed with doubt (see how God protected David from the wisdom of Ahithophel—2 Sam. 17). Here is another of God's wonderful works, that He easily and effectively defeats the craftiest enemies we have, including that great enemy, Satan. This book of Job gives us much comfort, as we are given a good look into the behind-the-scenes working of God to uphold and lift up His people, while defeating and making foolish the actions of Satan. This very verse is quoted by the apostle Paul, "For the wisdom of this world is foolishness with God. For it has been written, He takes the wise in their own wickedness" (1 Cor. 3:19).

"He brings to nothing"—It can be rendered, "He breaks into pieces the purposes of the subtle." They form their plots, they turn them round and round on the lathe of their minds, they temper and harden them in their passions, until they have an instrument of torture for the people of God—then He breaks in and tears them into pieces. These plots, devices, schemes are such as require a great deal of study, a meditative planning. Art and cunning must be used to make this kind of plot, therefore it is appropriate that this word be linked with the crafty. There are those who make it their trade to devise plots for the overthrow of everything that is good, anything that has the sweet smell of God about it. The crafty man is one who is nimble and speedy, subtle and sly—he is able to turn and wind about, he may vary his actions a thousand ways, and his thoughts ten thousand ways. A crafty man is one who may have more understanding than his neighbor, but he always has less conscience. He may have a great wit, but his conscience is so little that it never gets in his light. He measures his actions not by what he ought to do, but by what he wants to do. Alas! All this energy and wit, all this overcharging of his engines, only to meet certain defeat, "These six things the Lord hates; yea, seven are hateful to Him,....a heart that thinks of wicked plans;" "a man's heart devises his way, but the Lord directs his steps;" "There is no wisdom, nor understanding, nor counsel against the Lord" (Proverbs 6:16,18; 16:9; 21:30). God hates the crafty man who is devising plots against His people, and He defeats him by directing the steps of others so as to avoid the snare of the sly one, or else He directs the plans of the crafty man so that he fails to ensnare the godly man.

"their hands cannot do wisely"—It is not enough to work out a plan in your head, however wise it may be. You must also have skillful hands and feet to put the plan into action. The crafty have both. But God is able to throw a fearsome wrench into the working of both the head and the feet. The word translated, "do wisely" comes from a word which means "being," or, as some critics say, it is a negative word meaning "not being." In this case, it is well used here because wickedness is a nothing, as well as being good for nothing, Things which lack true wisdom, the reasoning of God, are as if they were not—or, at least, they will shortly cease to be. Now when the wicked plot against gods of this world, they may well be allowed to prevail for a lifetime. But when they try to ensnare the godly, it is already the beginning of the end for them—their hands will not be able to perform the wickedness which they have carefully worked out in their heads. *"They are wise to do evil"* (Jer. 4:22)—that is their character; whereas, the character of the servants of God are men who are *"simple concerning evil."* Yet though they be as Elymas, who was full of subtlety and mischief, real children of the devil, they shall not be able to defeat the Paul's or the lowliest and slighted of mankind, as Onesimus the slave.

"He takes the wise in their own craftiness; and the counsel of the wily is carried headlong" —Job 5:13.

Not only does God disappoint and bring to nothing the plots of the crafty, hindering the skillful hand so that it cannot do its dirty work, but He even takes them in their own craftiness. It is a great sorrow to a wicked man when he cannot do the mischief when he has so carefully worked out in his mind, but it is a devastating calamity indeed when he finds that God is causing his counsels to recoil and to promote his own ruin. These Judases would rather die than to see their mischief come back upon their own heads. Such a calamity happened to the murderers of Jesus Christ, they decided to kill Christ, they plotted it carefully, executed it beautifully. But what happened. The very success of their plan resulted in the destruction of the Sanhedrin, and all of their beloved Jerusalem. And what of Christ? He rose above them, sat down at the right hand of God, and began to direct the thoughts and steps of all, those who plotted His death, and those who were saved by His death, so that the crafty were taken in their own craftiness, while the humble were blessed in their lowliness.

The Greek word which Paul uses in quoting this verse is a word which has much more depth of meaning than the Hebrew word here. It means that this one has a fitness for all purposes, a dexterity to serve any turn, however sinister or evil it may be. This man can be on any side, for any purpose, according to his desire of the moment. Now a godly man only has one work that he can do—that is, one work of a kind. Every work he does as a godly man has a stamp of goodness, or godliness, or justice, or holiness upon it. But these crafty ones cannot be so easily cataloged and programmed. They may appear in many disguises, working at all kinds of work, with a pervasive odor of evil about them, but defying any categorization. This matters not to God, He takes them in their own craftiness.

"He takes"—it is a word which means to take by force. It also is used of taking by skill or stratagem. God works both ways to cause the crafty to fall into their own traps. Imagine the stupidity of the wise who think themselves able to match wits with the All-wise. He made them, yet they think that they can outthink and outwit Him? Not really! It is a case where their goodness ran out of their teeth when they ate the forbidden apple in the Garden of Eden, and ever since they have not believed that there is anyone who deserves the name of GOD, except themselves. This word is used in those places where there is a taking of a fort by siege, for when God besieges and batters at the crafty, they cave in. A godly man may partake of this forceful power of God to take the crafty, if God so will, and may also see them fall into their own snare. But if this happens, it is God that is doing it, and the man is but remembering what he is taught in the Scriptures, *"the weapons of our warfare are not carnal, but they are mighty through God to the casting down of strongholds"* (2 Cor. 10:4,5). The word may also imply the taking and binding of a man in bonds or in chains, *"His own iniquities shall take the wicked himself, and he shall be held with the cords of his sins"* (Prov. 5:22). If the wicked make chains for the godly, it may be that God will chain them with their own chains. If they set traps, He may well impound them there. If he flees, then God will take him in mid-flight. If he hides, then God will uncover him in his filth and drown him in his own vomit. None can slip out of His hand.

"in their own craftiness"—The preposition, *"in,"* may be understood instrumentally; it is then as much as if it were translated, *"by,"*—*"He takes them by their own craftiness."* The word is translated this way in Gen. 32:10 and Heb. 1:1. The crafty are taken by the very instruments they devise.

No wisdom or craftiness of man can stand before the wisdom and power of God. He not only is able to take them in their foolishness, but in their wisdom. He does not wait until they become weak and ineffectual, but He takes them captive at His will, when they are at their strongest and wisest point. Men usually catch each other when a mistake is made when there appears some error in planning. But God catches men with their own errorless planning, the devices which have been carefully constructed from the most deliberate and sober debates and consultations. For, *"the foolishness of God is wiser than men"* (1 Cor. 1:25). If the wisdom of men cannot match the foolishness of God, then our hope of defeating the wisdom of God is obviously no more than evil imagination. If it were not so, would they not stop falling into their own traps, stumbling over their own devices? It is the part of wisdom to learn from ones mistakes. After God has beaten us with our own weapons, wounded us with our own inventions, destroyed us with the things we had set up for our safety—what claim to wisdom do we have when we continue to imagine that we shall be able to find something which will protect us from Him?

God is greatly magnified by the fact that He is able to take men in and by their own wisdom! He does not trouble Himself to devise something new to combat a new invention of men, but whatever way they go, He goes—for He is able to take them by force, even in the strongest of their fortified positions. It argues for strength to the uttermost, unspeakable power, for one to be able to defy an earth full of evilly wise men to do what they can against Him, and to promise that force shall be met with force, craftiness destroyed by wisdom, etc. You must recognize God's ability to do as He pleases when you see that He has never lost a battle, let alone a war, to any man or devil since the Creation! Think of Satan again, who has been the idea-factory of men for centuries, manufacturing and devising lies for them to tell, inventions for them to use against God. When has this craftiest of all the creatures been able to paint SUCCESS across any single page of his history? If you want to see the misery and the frustration of Satan's life of playing the adversary against God, observe closely the contest which we have been privileged to witness in this book of Job. The entire scene is set by Satan, the instruments of torture especially selected by him, the timing is left entirely up to him. There is only one character which was not chosen by Satan—and, in effect, he also chose Job as the leading character. For it was Satan that challenged God the second time, after having lost in his attempt to prove God wrong about Job in the first contest. Now, having all this advantage, being given both opportunity and time to do that which men always think is easiest for the Devil to do—to defeat a mere man, one who had nothing to use as a weapon besides the word of God and the faith that it begets—Satan is going to fail so miserably that he is not even on the scene when the final outcome of the trial arrives. Job, a poor man with a completely debilitated body, without a friend on earth, in the end prevails against everyone but God, having nothing to hold him up but his faith. The sorrow of Satan was aggravated again, for it is a great sorrow to be taken in your own craftiness. That a man should defeat him is enough to put Satan out of his wits. Yet it has always been so. Each time he carefully constructs a plan, God has pulled him down—and with this humiliation, often by the cords of mere man.

"and the counsel of the wily is carried headlong"—Not only their devices are defeated, but their counsels also fail. A man may use craft on the spur of the moment, but counsel implies debate and close consideration, with the best of wisdom emerging from these. A man's best weapon is his reason, and counsel is the extract of reason. These reasonings of men, even when their heads are put together, are carried headlong into oblivion or utter destruction by a God who is too much for all the heads of men. Of course, it should be noted that these mentioned here are wily, a difference in word to draw out the kind of men God is easily working His will upon. The Holy Spirit uses a variety of words, but the men He describes are all the same. There is not enough variety in the words of all the

languages of mankind to picture or express the variety of wickedness that is in the heart of even one man!

This word translated *"wily"* has a root which means to wrest or turn a thing. Often there is a translation which brings to mind the wrestling of a man with another, or with God. It is interesting to note that Napthali got his name from this same root word, and it was because Rachel named him. For when she thought that she had triumphed over Leah, Rachel said, *"With the wrestlings of God I have wrestled with my sister, and I have prevailed"* (Gen. 30:8). With great and vehement wrestlings, perhaps in prayer, more likely by might and slight (as when she would use Jacob's love for her as a weapon against Leah), Rachel counted herself a victor in her contest with Leah. Again, the Hebrew word for an extraordinarily cunning wrestler is this word here, but with a doubling of the last syllable. And it is doubled because the man is doubly skilled in wrestling. And it also is used to express one that is double-skilled, double-witted, crafty enough for two or three (but not honest enough for one). See Psalm 18:26, where the word is applied to the Lord Himself. If men think that their winding and turning, their trickery and evil wit will be greater than any that ever was, then God will show Himself able to meet their challenge by wholly confining Himself to the same pattern of intricate (but holy) wiliness. If they want to go down into the labyrinths of human wisdom, then He will go down into the labyrinths of divine wisdom, and His sacred craft shall prove to be far too much for them—they shall be carried headlong.

"are carried headlong"—Not only are the counsels of the wise turned backward (Isa. 44:25), but they are also carried headlong. Whether He drives them backward or forward, God is able to take them in their own craftiness. He can cast them back into the teeth of destruction, or He can throw them headlong into destruction—either way, do what they may, they shall be destroyed in God's time and in God's way. Let the enemies of God be forewarned, You may be closest to destruction when all your plans are quickly succeeding, for God may be using your wisest counsels as a means of carrying you headlong into Hell.

"They meet with darkness in the daytime, and grope in the noonday as in the night"—Job. 5:14.

In setting the lowly on high, God brings down the exalted ones to nothingness (vs. 11). He spoils their plots, hinders their hands, entraps them with their own traps, and drives to distraction and distruction with their counsels. Now we see that He makes their light to be darkness, their perception to be blindness. It is a further aggravation to wicked men that they cannot prevail, nor can they even see what is hindering them from success. In the daytime of their greatest glory, when they think their sun is at its height, they become clouded over and meet with the darkness of sorrow—they suddenly are reduced to groping in the darkness of their own inky counsels.

We are to understand here that they have become ignorant of those things which are in fact plain and clear to all others. This is a puzzling visitation upon them, that those things which were as clear as the light should suddenly become impenetrable and indiscernible. God often so sends a spirit of giddiness and blindness upon the counsels of His enemies.

"They meet with darkness in the daytime"—there is a double light needed for seeing a thing. There must first be an external light, then there must be an internal light. There is the eye on the inside, but the eye cannot see without light from the outside. Yea, even the eye on the inside must be enlightened, for a blind eye cannot see anything. So here, the wily may see everything plain and clear, so far as their plans are concerned the sun is shining upon every facet. But their understandings are darkened and they cannot make out what God is doing, because they have invited Satan to rob them of their light, *"in whom the god of this world has blinded the minds of the ones who do not believe, so that the brightness of the Gospel of the glory of Christ...should not dawn upon them:"* (2 Cor. 4:3,4).

"they grope in the noonday as in the night"—It is the description of one who is blind. When a man cannot see, he must use his hands as his eyes—he gropes. Samson asked the

'little lad to place his hands on the pillars that held up the stadium, *"that I may feel the pillars"*—it was a substitute for seeing.

It is a sore judgment not to be able to see when it is light. And for those who consider themselves to be eagle-eyed in the discerning of things which make for them to be unable to see through to the cause of their troubles, it is a far greater, more griping judgment. It is terrifying to have God's judgment upon you by removing the light you see by, but it is even more distressing to have the light but be unable to see by it. When the darkness that is in us is so great that we cannot see by the bright light of God's truth that is all around us, then fears within and fears without are bound to multiply, *"This is the condemnation, that the Light has come into the world, and men loved the darkness rather than the Light —for their works were evil"* (John 3:19). The light hurt the eyes of their ugly souls, so they preferred the darkness. There is no light in them, nor will there be until the Daystar arises in their hearts (Isa. 8:20).

It is always strange to note that the plainest things are obscure to the wisest and most intelligent of men. Men of acute and sagacious understandings prove as dull as beetles when they are asked to perceive God's workings and God's judgments. The eagle is known for his ability to see for miles and miles, yet in the dark he is surpassed by owls and bats—the men who have the most ability to see in the dark and evil regions most traveled by men are not to be admired as the greatest of men. The glory of the Lord Jesus Christ would be evident to anyone, if that one would but be willing to trade his black heart for one that could love God. But God has permitted Satan to blind those who have decided that they prefer the darkness and evil to the Light and good. That this was God's decision may be seen from those congratulatory words of Christ, *"I thank You, O Father, Lord of Heaven and earth, because You hid these things from the sophisticated and cunning and revealed them to babes. Even so, Father, for so it seemed good in Your sight"* (Matt. 11:25, 26). Sometimes it is good in God's sight to make the prudent and the wise, the cunning and sophisticated blind, while at the same time giving wisdom and discernment to babies in the faith. These men of evil are so wise in their own conceits that they cannot conceive the things of God. The babes are so humble in their own eyes that they are able to think God's thoughts after Him, and by doing so, they can see into the most complex spiritual matters. And as it is in these spiritual matters, so often God makes it come out in merely civil matters. Many times the foolish overcome the wise because they foresee the evil consequences of certain acts.

"But He saves the poor from the sword, from their mouth, and from the hand of the mighty"—Job 5:15.

So many times in Scripture we see God giving encouragement to the poor immediately after He mentions judgment and wrath falling on the wicked. Because God's little ones all count themselves worthy of such judgments, being tender in the matter of sin, there is often a reminder of mercy and grace and love for those who are poor in spirit.

"He saves the poor"—These are those who are God's poor. Some are poor because they have labored for the Devil, thay have put their wages in a bag full of holes. The only time the Devil's servants will get their full pay is when they die, they will get death as full wages for their sins. The wicked poor are no more under God's protection than wicked oppressors or wicked rich men are. The question is this, are they God's children, *"The Lord knows those that are His"* (2 Tim. 2:19). If they are His, then they are not truly poor. They may lack the wealth of this world, but God provides their needs. They may lack the friends and influences which are considered so important in this world, but they have a Friend that is closer than a brother—He has influence the world has never dreamed of. The Hebrew word for poor here is a word which comes from a root signifying desire. Poor men are commonly rich in desires; they are full of sensible wants, they are never lacking in earnest wishings. Those that are most empty of enjoyment are the most full of hopes and longing. In line with this, those who are poor of spirit are those who are blessed with holy desires and longings after those spiritual riches which can be gotten only from

Jesus Christ. They are ever craving and seeking after the fullness of grace which He has promised them (grace on top of grace—John 1:16).

"from the sword, from their mouth"—The latter phrase is added to explain the former, in the opinion of some interpreters. That is, God saves them from the evil that will be the fruit of their lips, their untameable tongue. Now the mouth can indeed be a killing instrument, it may devour as much as the sword. Some of the swords of the mouth are even double-edged, such as slander and false-witnessing. By these a man may have his reputation murdered.

But the clearest meaning of the original is to read these three phrases as three distinct evils from which the Lord will save His own. He saves His poor from the slaying sword, from the slandering tongue, and from the oppressing hand. In these three ways crafty men seek to use their power to destroy God's poor. First, they try to kill them. If this does not meet with success, then they slander them and try to nullify their witness. Lastly, they will enslave and oppress the poor if they can neither kill them nor nullify their witness. But let them try as they will, they shall never conquer with malice that grace which God gives His saints, nor can they overmatch the mercy of God in delivering His people from their troubles when their education in the crucible is ended.

"from the hand of the mighty"—The nimrods of this world, those who wield the power in those areas assigned them by the Prince, Satan, think themselves able to do what they desire with the poor. They act as if they own them. But they do not, and especially they do not own God's poor. Nor may they act as if they own them, though they do not. No man, whatever his powers and position, may do any more to God's children than God has decreed. When they reach out to devour them with the sword, they shall be saved from the sword, unless it is time for them to go and be with the Lord. When the oppressor sharpens his tongue and dips it in poison in order to inflict the greatest wounds with his lies, slanders, defamations and false accusations, they shall not cause the slightest discomfort to God's children except there be a necessity of trial by these means in order to conform him to the image of Christ Jesus. And if they decide to seize property of the servants of God, to take away all their liberties and privileges, God shall see that they retain every stick of furniture and all stocks in trade which He has assigned to them for the moment; they shall have not one liberty nor one privilege taken from them without His consent and express desire. It pleases God to prevent His people from falling into the hurts that come from money and wealth, privilege and unrestricted opportunity to sin. Therefore, it is usually true that those He has chosen are from the poor, rather than from the rich. And since they are poor in this world's goods, they are comparatively easy to oppress in the eyes of the rich. But even when God permits them to rob the poor of their goods, they are given the grace to prefer the world to come to this one. They see that they have treasures beyond the reach of the longest arm of greed. So these are happy, while those mighty ones wallow in their misery. This makes the mighty jealous, and they seek even more to hurt. But God saves them from the sword, from the mouth, and from the mighty hand.

"So the poor have hope, and iniquity shuts her mouth"—Job 5:16.

Eliphaz now concludes this section of his address, the encouragements for Job to seek to God and to commit his cause to Him. The conclusion of the whole matter, he says, is this, that the poor have hope. Because the enemies of the poor, whether they are inanimate or animate, are all under the control of God. Since He is the one who is able to perfectly control all the forces which are apt to threaten the poor, they have hope in Him.

The original word for *"poor"* here is different from that in the foregoing verse. This word has the basic meaning of *"exhausted,"* or, *"drawn dry."* Here it denotes the fact that the poor are empty of comforts. Poor persons are exhausted persons; their strength is exhausted; their estates are exhausted; their friends and credit in the world are exhausted. It is a metaphor taken from rivers, which may be drawn dry (Isa. 19:6; 33:21). When Cyprus took Babylon, even the mighty Euphrates River was drawn dry, so that his army might walk into the city. The river was impoverished by the pumping out of its water—it became a poor river. Delilah had her name from this same root—a very interesting allusion to all those lascivious and lust-inducing women who drain dry the men who will allow themselves to be tempted by them. These will not desist until they have extracted the last bit of strength. And there are seemingly unending troops of Samson-type men who are willing to become poor for the sake of the bitter ashes of an affair with a voluptuous woman. These, in turn, are but a type of those who are a far greater number indeed, the ones who are lured by other lusts, knowing full well that these lusts war against their souls.

"The poor have hope"—The word for hope is one which pictures a strong and earnest expectation. The poor man who observes the wonders which God does in the world cannot be without hope, though for the moment he possesses nothing. If he is without strength, then he can join with the apostle Paul and say, *"When I am weak, then I am strong"* (2 Cor. 12:10).

This hope of the poor may be taken two ways: (1) for the object, or the thing hoped for; (2) for the act or grace of hope.

(1) God has taken the wise in their own craftiness; He has disappointed the devices of the crafty. He has delivered the poor from the sword, from wicked tongues, and from the hand of the mighty. Now the poor has the thing which he hopes for, the thing he prays for, the thing for which he has been seeking and waiting upon God. He has been saved and thus is made partaker of his hope, by those glorious administrations of the justice of his God, the God of mercy.

In this sense of hope for deliverance in this world, God's poor may hope for good even in the worst of times. Then when the deliverance comes, they have what they looked for. If it was light, they got light. If it was strength, it was supplied. Their God is never gone, and He is the One who supplies all their needs (Phil. 4:19).

(2) The poor have the grace of hope, those gracious actings of God which give us hope. God is our hope. We have seen Him doing all these wonderful things, restraining the wicked while correcting His children, showing Himself strong on our behalf at the same time He is building our character. The experiences we have of God's power and mercy, when He saves us out of our troubles, is an experience that breeds and nourishes hope in our breasts. Then when future trouble comes, we will believe, *"so that we might not trust in ourselves, but in God who raises the dead. For He delivered us from so great a death, and still does deliver us, in whom we have hope that He also will yet deliver us"* (2 Cor. 1:9,10).

Eliphaz carefully avoided saying that the poor have liberty, peace, riches, prosperity and the praise of men—no, what they have because of the wondrous workings of God is hope. What good is liberty, if there is no hope that liberty will produce any happiness? What good is peace, when peace is bought with the enmity and hatefulness of ungodliness? What good is prosperity, if that prosperity is perishing and disintegrating before your very eyes? And as for the praise of men, remember this, that whatever is high in the esteem of men is low in the esteem of God—better to be loved of God and hated by all men, than vice versa. If your thinking is straight, you will realize that there are no men who have less hope than those who promise themselves liberty, peace, riches, etc. without God.

THERE IS A TRUE HOPE, AND THERE IS A FALSE HOPE

There are four ways to know if your hope is a true hope:

1. True hope climbs above human reason, not looking with carnal eyes, but looking with the eye of faith.

2. True hope is patient, for if the hope is true, there will be such confidence as will make us patiently wait for our hope to be fulfilled.

3. True hope sighs and longs for the thing hoped for. We are grieved by the absence of Christ, and we groan and sigh as we wait for the adoption, the redemption, etc.

4. True hope rejoices while patiently waiting for the Lord Jesus to appear, *"Whom we have not seen, and yet we love Him and believe in Him, and rejoice with joy unspeakable and glorious, receiving the end of faith, which is salvation"* (1 Peter 1:8).

Any hope which is not based in Jesus Christ is a false hope, *"at that time you were without Christ...having no hope"* (Eph. 2:12). Only Christ can deliver the ungodly from their guilt and condemnation—if they do not hope in Him for this reason, their hope is false, *"For what is the hope of the ungodly, though he has increased, when God takes away his soul?"* (Job 27:8).

True hope may be known by its effects upon the life and thought of its possessor:

1. True hope purifies and purges the heart and life, *"My beloved, now we are children of God, and it does not yet appear what we shall be. But we know that when he shall appear we shall be like Him—for we shall see Him as He is. And everyone that has this hope in Him purifies himself, even as He is pure"* (1 John 3:22,23).

2. True hope molds us into that form of obedience which is pleasing to the Lord, *"For in hope he believed...and he did not stagger at the promise of God through unbelief, but was strengthened in faith, giving glory to God, and being fully persuaded that what God has promised He is also able to do"* (Romans 4:18,20,21).

3. True hope shines the light on the filthiness of this world, and in doing so it takes off the cutting edge of our afflictions. This causes us to prefer to suffer affliction with the people of God than to have the temporary enjoyment of sin; to count the reproach which goes with believing in Christ to be greater riches than the treasures this world can give us (see Hebrews 11:24,25).

4. True hope causes us to be persistent in seeking to God for fulfillment of His promises, to be consistent in believing that His promises are being fulfilled to us every day, as well as believing that they shall all be finally fulfilled in another Day, *"It is good that a man should both hope and quietly wait for the salvation of the Lord"* (Lam. 3:26); *"in the hope of eternal life, which the God who cannot lie promised before the world began"* (Titus 1:2); *"For our citizenship is in Heaven, from which we also are looking for the Lord Jesus Christ as Savior, who will completely transform our body...for it to be made like His glorious body—according to the almighty working of His power..."* (Phil. 3:20); *"For this reason tighten up the waist of your mind. Be watchful. Hope to the end in the grace which is being brought to you in the revealing of Jesus Christ* (1 Peter 1:13).

"and iniquity stops her mouth"—The abstract is here put for the concrete. Iniquity is put for those who are full of iniquity. Before God is pictured as making them active in their own destruction; here He is making them active in silencing themselves. It is not unusual for the doing of God to leave His enemies speechless.

This stopping of their mouths is caused in two ways: (1) from shame; (2) from admiration and amazement.

(1) A man will sometimes fall silent because he is ashamed to speak. In Scripture, there are constant references to men who have been disappointed in their false hopes, and they are pictured as blushing with shame, as being pale and distraught because of shame. The Holy Spirit often puts shame and confusion of face together. And it is shame which lays its hand on their mouths, which puts their senses in a stupefied condition.

(2) The works of God are so marvelous that they will amaze and unhinge any man who is released from his sinful pride long enough to see the wonder of them. Normally, men of iniquity will do nothing but talk. They are forever boasting, censuring, slandering and destroying with their tongues, but a day comes when God's hand is lifted up. Then *"they will see and be ashamed because of their envy at God's people"* (see Isa. 26:11).

Even the works of man, those works which God works in man, will put the wicked to silence, *"that by welldoing they may put to silence the ignorance of foolish men"* (1 Pet. 2:15). The only reason ungodly men keep blaspheming God and blasting his saints is the awesome fact that God withholds their eyes from seeing His wonder, that their iniquity may become full and overflowing, to their everlasting and never-ending pain and misery.

"Behold! Happy is the man whom God corrects. Therefore do not despise the chastening of the Almighty"—Job 5:17.

Here Eliphaz begins a second branch of exhortation, and it continues to the end of the chapter. To encourage Job, he reminds him that any man who has the correcting and chastening hand of God upon him is essentially a happy man. And since this chastening hand of God is the means of happiness to an afflicted man, it ought not to be despised.

"Behold!"—Again, the Holy Spirit used this word here because something of a wondrous nature is about to be revealed. It is a call to us to pay attention, to get ready to admire the supernatural truth that is now to be announced. And what is so marvelous about the following words? They tell a truth that is contrary to all human reasoning. Natural sense cannot see, much less understand, how a man can be happy in a high degree at the very time when his affliction is the deepest and sorest. Moses was no more astonished to see a bush that burned and was unconsumed, than Satan's followers when they see a saint painfully afflicted and yet happier than ever. And, just as the Bush did not lose so much as a leaf, actually continuing to flourish in all its beauty, so the suffering saint is a godly plant on fire, yet flourishing and bearing the beautiful fruit of God's Spirit. Many is the child of God who has first really bloomed, who has first begun to bear fruit heavily when his first severe trials came upon him. Truly, such a wonder deserves our attention—Behold!

"happy is the man"—Happiness is the enjoyment of good. Perfect happiness, if it is to be such, must bring together a desire for perfect goodness and the fulfillment of that desire. Since only God is good, then only God can completely satisfy our desire for perfect goodness. Only a desire to be like God, to be completely conformed to Him, could be a perfect desire. And the crowning of that yearning to be like God cannot take place without the correcting and chastening hand of God being laid to the root of sinful men in order to burn out their corruption. Only God is perfectly happy. Only men and devils are perfectly unhappy. And of these two, only men may ever hope to be happy with that perfect happiness which characterizes God. God has chosen some to be rescued and restored. These feel His correcting hand often and with force. They are happy, both here and hereafter—not only because their sins are not imputed to them (Ps. 1), but also because the love of God brings with it healing and happiness.

The word translated *"happy"* is actually a plural word. Behold! Look at the happinesses of that man that God is good enough to correct and set right. As God is molding His own to the image of His son, Jesus Christ the Righteous, there are many happinesses setting up a glorious glow within and without. A man cannot be happy if God takes up His weapons against him. Likewise, a man cannot be unhappy if God displays His many-sided love for him. A man in his sins, still in the gall and bitterness of his rebellion against God's ways, cannot be happy without God, nor can he be happy with God. In short, such a man cannot be happy under any circumstances. O yes, he thinks himself happy if something he lacks is suddenly given to him. Or, he promises himself happiness if some great lust of his will only be fulfilled. But when did riches ever make a poor man happy? Or when did a return to health in itself make the sick man happy? Or where is the man who was made happy by being transformed from a nonentity to a famous man? These promised happinesses all turn to ashes in the mouths of the ungodly once they have sunk their teeth into them. It is a fool's game, this promising of oneself that happiness will come from this or that earthly thing. Every good and perfect gift, and that certainly would include happiness, comes down from the Father (James 1:17)—and happiness is a godly thing, it is spiritual, not earthly. And it never consists of but one main thing, it is not a single good. Happiness consists in the concurrence or meeting together of many good things. God is not a single good, nor a particular good, but He is all good, both to Himself and to His people. Now a godly man is not happy only at this particular time, or that. His happiness does not become real now and again. He is happy at all times, whether he is suffering under the hand of God, or whether he is being carressed with the love of God in some other way. Just as surely as God never leaves him nor forsakes him, that surely can it be said that his happinesses never leave him nor forsake him.

Some translate the words, *"Behold the blessednesses of that man whom God corrects,"* counting them to be in the abstract. But we translate it concretely. In either case, there is recognition that a godly man has more than one happiness. He has happiness in this life. He has happiness in the life to come. A man being corrected by God does not lose either. Both his temporal happiness and his eternal happiness increase as God educates and instructs him in the art of happiness. Of course, the words here have their application in this life. For correction and chastisement exist only in this life—there will be no rods to beat us in Heaven, nor will we any longer be children once we are there.

Lastly, the word translated *"happy"* is always dual, or plural. It is never read in the singular number in the Hebrew. And, furthermore, it is only applied to man. The word which we translate *"blessed"* is used both of God and of man, but the word here is used only in connection with man. The reason? The Lord is infinitely above either obeying or suffering.

"is the man"—There are several words for man in the Bible, and the words happy and blessed are used in connection with them in various places. In Psalm 1, *ish* is the word, signifying the excellent man, the holy and strong man. In Psalm 32:1, *adam,* the general word for man, is used, *"Blessed is the man whose iniquity is forgiven."* In Psalm 94:12, we find *geber*, the great man, the honorable man, the man of high birth or place, *"Blessed is the man whom You chasten, O Lord, and teach him out of Your Law."*

Here, however, we have the word *enosh*, a word that God uses to signify a sickly, weak, miserable man. A man that cannot help himself, one who in every worldly way is considered to be without a single reason to be happy—this miserable creature is the one that God calls happy! Starkly and nakedly God pictures the vast abyss of sinful ignorance which exists within the breast of all men who have never been made new creatures in Christ Jesus. They do not have that mind in them which was in Christ Jesus. They think a man miserable because he is weak, but not because he is wicked. They think a man unhappy because he is sick and cannot do the things he lusts to do, but not because he is proud and unwilling to do the things that God tells him to do. But God shows what a difference His grace makes between men. Before grace, there is a contradiction in thinking that a man may be happy, though miserable. After grace, the correction of faith, the benefits of conformity to God, the vantagepoint of being close to God causes a man to count himself happy in the highest degree even though he may be without any worldly thing or attribute. Men in their right minds have different values than those who have degenerated into insanity. A gracious man values God's love, His word; His values are seen only through faith, which is a grace given by God to those He loves.

"whom God corrects"—The word we translate *"correct"* signifies to reprove or to convince by arguments. We see it in Lev. 19:19, *"You shall not allow sin upon your brother; you shall surely rebuke him."* Convince him of his sin, lay his wickedness open before him so that he may be brought to repentance. So the Lord God does for His own, He does not allow sin to remain upon His children, but He rebukes and reproves until they are convinced of their need for repentance and renewal of faith. If words do not serve His purpose, He will use blows. He may dispute with a rod in His hand, bringing an argument with feeling to wake us to our sinful condition, and to the point of earnestly seeking improvement.

WHAT IS THE DIFFERENCE BETWEEN CHASTISEMENT AND PUNISHMENT?

Does not God correct and chastise every sinful man on earth? Is there a man who has not been born unto trouble as the sparks fly upward? No, and, yes! God does not correct every man on earth, but only His children. Every man is indeed troubled and afflicted, but not every man is happy either during or after his affliction—only God's people are happy. Why the difference? And, what is the difference?

FIRST, there are three ways in which there is agreement in the affliction of the righteous and the affliction of the ungodly: (1) God is the efficient cause of all affliction, both of the child of God and of the child of Satan; (2) Both the godly and the ungodly suffer the same afflictions, the same troubles come upon both groups of men; (3) There is even the degree of affliction in many cases. In fact, in some ways, affliction may lie heaviest upon the child of God.

SECONDLY, there are vast differences between chastisement and punishment: (1) There is a difference in relationship; (2) in position; (3) in the manner of affliction, and, (4) in the purpose which lies behind their affliction.

(1) Those chastised and those punished differ in their relationship of God. Those who are chastised are sons; those who are punished or judged are not sons of God, but sons of Satan (Heb. 12:5-11; John 8:44). Because God loves His children, He chastises them. Because God hates the wicked, the sons of Satan, He judges them and then punishes them.

(2) Those chastised are in Christ Jesus—identified with Him, at one with Him, buried with Him, risen with Him, inseparable from Him, protected by Him, etc. When God looks upon one for whom Christ died, He sees that one as perfected in Christ. Christ has stood judgment for him, and he is acquitted of all wrongdoing in Christ Jesus. There is need of correction and chastisement in the work of perfecting which God does upon His children in this life, but it is never punishment. On the other hand, the wicked stand before God in a state of rebellion—there is no intercessor to stand between them. To these punished ones, He is a consuming fire. They have nowhere they can hide from His wrath.

(3) The afflictions of the righteous are all acts of love. The afflictions of the ungodly are all calamities. The heart of God is turned toward His children when He corrects them. But His heart is turned away from a wicked man when He punishes him. God is portrayed as a concerned Father who feels for His children when He must chastise them (see Hosea 11:8). But the punishment of the sons of the Devil is accompanied by indignation, even laughter and mocking (see Prov. 1:26).

(4) There is a tremendous difference in purpose when God chastises or punishes. God lays the rod of affliction on His child in order to purge his sin and make him better. He punishes a man in vengeance, determining to make him miserable, in order to show forth His holiness and righteousness — *"I will laugh at your trouble, I will mock when your fear comes, when your fear comes as a wasting away, and your ruin comes like a whirlwind; when trouble and pain come upon you...for they hated knowledge and did not choose the fear of the Lord"* (Prov. 1:26).

In the case of His children, God is driving him back from further sin, while at the same time He is revealing a better, a more satisfying and happier way to live. Because *"God knows those that are His,"* because He loves with an everlasting love all those that name the name of Jesus upon themselves, He heats them in the furnace of affliction. In love, He beats them with the rod of His displeasure and molds them with His talented hands until they begin to really look and act like sons of the living God. There is a vast difference in men, though at the beginning all are born speaking lies, there are none that seek after God, and there is not one that does good. Taking this common beginning, God makes a difference between men (1 Cor. 4:7), giving to some men faith (Eph. 2:8) while others are left in their gross unbelief. Some He quickens with life, others He leaves dead in their trespasses and sins. Those that are His, those He has set His heart on, whom He has loved from the beginning (yea, from everlasting — Jer. 31:3), become known through various proofs. One of these tests is this, Are they chastised? If they are chastised, they are sons. If they are not, then they are illegitimate and not sons (Heb. 12:5-11).

The difference which God has made in men comes to light under affliction. Those that are truly God's children react to affliction by (1) freely admitting that God has a right and a duty to do what He desires with His creatures, but more than that, they sweetly melt before the warmth of His love; (2) they acknowledge that God has full and complete sovereignty, owing no explanation nor revelation to the one He is afflicting; (3) they accept affliction as proof that they are loved and wanted; they rejoice in the knowledge that God loves them enough to drive out their corruptions; (4) they seek diligently and without let-up to find out what God's will may be, desiring to find how they have failed to conform to His will, seeking strength and the desire to move away from whatever sinful position they had fallen into; and, (5) they fall upon His breast and importunely ask of Him the spiritual wisdom that they lack (James 1:5), the faith and the patience needed to gain not only relief from the pressure and heat and pain of affliction, but also to receive the lesson which always accompanies His catechising afflictions. Those that do all these things when they are afflicted may be certain that they are God's

Illegitimate offspring may be noted by a totally different reaction to God's afflicting hand. When a person is seen to defy God, to deny His right to afflict, to curse and murmur, to kick out against the instruments of affliction, then he is demonstrating that he is none of His. Those who feel hurt and mistreated, who feel that God's ways are not equal, are acting like the spoiled children of Satan. And those who assert the right to their own will, who feel God is encroaching on their sacred rights when He insists upon His way, are still in the gall and bitterness of their sins. You cannot complain and mutter about God violating your free will without revealing the fact that you are of another parentage than His, *"You are of your father the devil, and the lusts of your father you will do"* (John 8).

The total picture, then, of the man who is happy when God corrects Him is this:

1. He is always happy, whatever may be his condition, however deep an affliction may lie upon him, however long it may last, and to whatever extent it may affect his life.

2. He senses, if he does not distinctly enunciate it, that the corrections are being sent to take away his corruptions, not his comfort. He knows that he cannot expect to be comfortable in his corruption, for that would be proof that He was not God's child.

3. He tucks himself under the wings of the Almighty hiding himself in a place where he may learn how to end his affliction. He counts himself happy so long as he has His God, and the best way to receive continual assurances of the love of God is to seek His embrace. Who can be unhappy when he is holding tight to all that makes him happy? What does it matter if you lose everything, all the things you own, if your happiness does not lie in any of them? If you are happy simply because you have Christ, then you'll suffer the loss of all things besides Him, without the slightest unhappiness to blur your sense of wellbeing. Those who have their happiness in anything else but Christ will never be happy, for they will either be losing something they desire to keep, or else they will be desiring to have something they are not allowed to have — their entire life will be but a casting up of mire and dirt, a restless, wicked churning in their breasts.

4. That which keeps a man from being perfectly happy is sin — sin separates between a man and his God, making him unholy (unwilling to yield to God's will) and ungodly (unlike God in thought and in action). The child of God turns to God, turns away from sin and turns his back on it when he finds that it is causing him to be more and more separated from his Source of happiness.

"Therefore, do not despise the chastening of the Almighty"—The word translated *"despise"* has various meanings, all of which will throw light on the place we are studying:

1. It means to reject a thing; to cast it off with loathing (as when a man's stomach turns at the sight of certain kinds of food). You will find it so used in Numbers 11, *"until it comes out of your nostrils, and it is hateful (despised by) to you."* They were at first delighted to sink their teeth into the quail they had lusted after, but became queasy when their sin upset them. The least mixture of God's displeasure is enough to sour our sweetest delicacies, making our very pleasures to become loathsome to us. (Here we cannot resist drawing the comparison between the things that are of the earth, earthy, and those that are spiritual, heavenly. The best of earthly things will grow dull and finally hateful if we use them too much. Even manna from Heaven will not go down long with us. But the Manna which is not earthly, Christ Jesus the Heavenly Manna, together with all those spiritual blessings and graces which He purchased and is giving to us, grow sweeter and more delectable the more we experience of them. Does a man get sick of receiving more and more of faith? Earthly love can make a man sick, but does a godly man ever get sick of the love of God? Yearnings and hungerings after some earthly price may pall, may become hateful to us after a while, but the Christian's yearnings and hungerings for more of the Lord Jesus Christ, for the sight of Him in Heaven, grows stronger and stronger year by year).

The meaning of the word in this sense may also become clear from the picture of a physician giving good medicine in order to cure his patient. Many times that which is given is a bitter pill to take, or a distasteful liquid to drink — so much so that the patient may even turn his head and not take it at first; it may be he thinks he would rather die than to take it. But then his loved ones or the physician may persuade him, saying, "do not get angry and refuse to take the medicine, even though it is hateful to you; it is an enemy only to your disease.' So here, Eliphaz (as it were) is bringing in God as the Great Physician, like a tender mother standing by the bedside using all his knowledge and all his loving-kindness to persuade or to force the sick one to take his bitter portion. Afflictions may be found to be compared to a cup which we must drink, in Scripture, as when the Lord Jesus said, *"The cup which My Father has given Me, shall I not drink it?"* (John 18:11). That cup would have turned the stomachs of all men and of angels too, but He for our sakes (that we might be cured of our sinfulness) drank it down.

It is not to be thought that because we are children of God, and because we are willing to receive affliction at His hand, that we also are completely free of any averseness toward chastening. Even the Lord Jesus Christ prayed that if it were possible, let the cup be taken from Him — being quick and careful to say immediately, however, *"Nevertheless, not My will be done, but Yours."* Affliction is of course a bitter cup to the saint, as well as to the wicked, considering only the immediate effect of it upon the spirit of man. *"Now chastening for the present does not seem to be joyous, but grievous. Nevertheless, afterward it yields the peaceable fruit of righteousness to those who are exercised by it"* (Heb. 12:11). It is grace that persuades a man to take his spiritual medicine, and especially it is the grace of faith which makes that which is bitter become sweet to us. Just as a sick man hangs back from a distasteful medicine until his reason overcomes his sense, so a godly man may be unwilling at first to bear his affliction — until his faith overcomes his reason. There can be no quietness of his spirit until he is assured that he shall be the better servant of God because of his trials, then it is faith which is *"the substance of things hoped for, the evidence of things not seen"* (Heb. 11:1). When the apostle Paul was carried up on those eagle's wings of assurance, to see a house not made with hands, eternal in the heavens, then he groans earnestly under the burden of his earthly tabernacle and desires to depart and be with Christ. But, then, looking upon death, he saw no form nor comeliness in it that he should desire it, and therefore he seems to correct himself (at least to draw his mind plainer with the next drop of his pen,) *"not that we desire to be unclothed, but clothed upon, so that mortality might be swallowed up by life"* (2 Cor. 5:4). He speaks somewhat like a man who in a time of heat hastily strips himself to go into the water, but putting in a foot and finding the water cold, he calls for his clothes again. The apostle in a true holy heat of spirit had in his desires almost stripped himself of his body, but putting a foot out into the grave and finding it so cold, he finds he can wait until God puts a suit of glory on him before he lays down his life. The saints would rather that their mortality be swallowed up by eternal life than that their temporal life should be swallowed up by mortality. If a man has grace, he will not like the disunions of nature. As it is in the case of death (the last affliction because of sin), so it is in the case of all afflictions (which are, after all, but lesser forms of death). Though the saints embrace and kiss them (both in a holy submission to the will of God, and in an assured expectation of their own good), yet they have nothing pleasing in them, of themselves. Therefore, there may be a loathing at the beginning, so that the best of the saints may need some counsel and encouragement before they will take their spiritual medicine and be glad that they have it to take.

If, then, there is some averseness on the part of the saints to drink down the bitter cup of affliction, no wonder if there is an abhorrence in wicked men, who look upon those bitter portions as carriers of death and destruction, because mixed with God's wrath and outraged justice. When the Lord hands the unbeliever the cup, it is a mixture of judgments and plagues and punishments. He has sworn that *"all the ungodly of the earth shall wring them out and drink them."* Certainly those who have drunk so willingly and freely of the cup of sin will be nauseated when they find that for each cup of sin they shall have to drink down double that amount of the galling wrath of God—"*As much as she has glorified herself and has lived in luxury, so much torment and sorrow give her...she shall be utterly burned with fire, for strong is the Lord God who judges her*" (Revelation 18:5-9).

Secondly, the word which we translate "*despise*" denotes the rejecting of a thing as unprofitable or unuseful. If a man thinks that a thing is of no use to him, he despises it, "*the Stone which the builders refused (despised) has become the Headstone of the corner*" (see Ps. 118:22). The masterbuilders among the Jews saw no usefulness to Jesus, only trouble, therefore they despised Him. They did not want to build with such a Stone, not being living stones themselves. In this sense, the word is very applicable to our text, for it is hard for the natural mind to conceive of any usefulness for afflictions. Even the saints may at first glance refuse to admit that afflictions are useful. They may almost conclude that they can easily do without their troubles and trials. It is a rare saint indeed who has not at one time or another counted a certain ill-happening to be of no use to him and his faimily—only to find it a real cornerstone in the building up and edifying of both himself and his family at a later date. When Peter wept bitterly outside the High Priest's palace, having just fallen painfully into denying the Lord, do you think he at the moment realized just how important that heart-rending experience would be in his life thereafter? Yet, in his last days, hear him speak, "*In this you greatly rejoice, though now for a time, if need be, you are in heaviness through manifold temptations — so that the trial of your faith might be found unto praise and honor and glory at the appearing of the Jesus Christ...*" (1 Pet. 1:6). He tells them that though they may think that they are past the time when they need the rod of God upon their backs, yet it may be that there may yet be much need of heaviness of soul before they come to Heaven. Let us not despise our chastenings as of no use to us, for it may be that our corruptions must be burned or pressed out of us for many years before we enter upon our incorruptible inheritance (1 Cor. 15:50).

Thirdly the word is often applied to the rejecting of a thing or person as low, dishonorable or disgraceful. Applying this sense to our text, we would receive this message, "*Do not despise the chastenings of the Almighty,*" thinking that they dishonor you and disgrace you. Man is a proud piece of flesh, and he resents to the uttermost anything that is seemingly dishonoring to him. There are those who can easily bear the pain of the cross, but who cannot even bear the thought of shame because of the cross. Our great Example is held up to us in this point also, "*He endured the Cross, despising the shame*" (Heb. 12:2). Not only did He look upon the shame which the world attached to the Cross as a shame to be despised, but He did not count the Cross to be shameful at all. We cannot be hurt by a loss of honor, or dignity, or fame, unless we count those things worthy of our love, If a man is truly above the world, being a citizen of another World, one that far surpasses this world, then the opinions that prevail in this world will be unimportant (and shame is no more than an opinion, when it is the shame of this world). Saul was more concerned with being honored before his elders than he was for the loss of his kingdom. It is not so with those who have been translated into the kingdom of God's dear Son — to us evildoing is our shame, but it is no shame to suffer affliction at His hand.

Fourthly, to despise a thing denotes the slighting of it. In this sense, we ought not to in any way slight the chastenings of the Lord, lightly passing them by as inconsiderable or unimportant. When God lays a hand on us, we had better lay it to our hearts. Would a prisoner say to the judge, Do with me whatever you will, I do not care a whit what you do? Let him who undervalues the correcting hand of God beware, lest He find himself buried under a load of care which will drive him to distraction. To think little of God's chastening is to think little of God. And whoever dares to think God is too little to be of consequence shall find himself learning hard lessons indeed. Every affliction is a messenger from God. God will not bear it if we carelessly cast aside His message.

Lastly, it should be recognized that there is in this word, "*Do not despise,*" more than these words express. The Holy Spirit is not only saying that we should not despise His chastenings, but also that we should highly prize and esteem them. When God tells us, "*Do not despise prophecying*" (1 Thes. 5:20), do you think this means that we are to simply avoid despising prophecy, or does it not rather mean that we ought to highly prize it? Not only are you to be careful lest you despise the chastenings of the Lord, you should lay it upon your heart to highly esteem His chastening — as if they were indeed evidences of His love and affection for you.

"*the chastening*"—the original verb means to instruct, or to teach (in Job 4:3, "*you have instructed many*," it is the same word as here, only in verb form). One may give instruction by words, but also by blows. The wisdom of God calls for the mixing of His rod with His words, chastening with teaching. Therefore the word is used interchangably, here for teaching and there for chastening. God's chastening is indeed only for His children, but it still must be recognized that chastening is necessary only to correct disobedient, or unbelieving children. If you despise the words of God, taking them not to heart, then you are in need of the rod of God to drive them home. If you have a bundle of foolishness wrapped up in your breast, then it may take a bundle of chastising rods to drive them out. The Lord, too, acts upon His word, which says, "*if you spare the rod, you spoil the child.*" He wants us to know that it is a privilege to have Him for our Instructor, but we are at the same time to remember that we would not need His rod upon our backs if we were not unruly, foolish, careless or many other ways defective in holiness and reverence. (For a full exposition of this word, and a discussion in depth, see the Treasury section.)

"*of the Almighty*"—this chastening rod is in the hand of *Shaddai*, the Almighty. This is one of the glorious names of God. And He is so called first because of His power, His ability to complete what He starts, to do all that He plans. He never lacks the power to continue to the end of His purpose. Therefore, do not despise His correction, for He has the utmost power to destroy, to spoil, to lay waste, or to do any lesser thing that He decides is best. Some say that He gained this title by destroying and wasting His enemies. Others say that He got it when He overthrew and drowned the old world. The holy prophetsno doubt alluded to this when they used the expression, "*destruction from the Almighty*" *(shod* from *Shaddai* — Isa. 13:6 and Joel 1:15.)

Others derive the word from two Hebrew words, the one *(Dai)* means to suffice, or to be sufficient; the other, though it be but a letter *(Shin)* yet it supplies the part or place of the relative, which, and so the word put together expresses this much, "*Who is sufficient, or, Who is all-sufficient.*" Do not despise the chastening of Him who is All-sufficient. You are not being instructed by one who will come up short, but by One who has everything in His power and in His storehouse that you may need. He alone is sufficient of Himself, and He alone has all the sufficiency which can supply all your needs.

Some say the word comes from *Shad*, a Hebrew word meaning a breast. These would say that the text is teaching us not to despise the chastening of the Almighty, because it is He who nourishes and feeds, it is He who strengthens and blesses, it is He who makes us fruitful and multiplies us (as in Gen. 28:3 — "*God Almighty bless you and make you fruitful and multiply you.*") In the first part of this verse is pictured a man happy because *Elohim* corrects him, so here we are not to put on a despising face because it is *El Shaddai* who is supplying our need for chastisement. This All-powerful, All-sufficient, All-nourishing God is not One to be taken lightly, or rejected, or thought little of, else the despiser may well discover how powerful He is, how sufficient He is to supply Himself with weapons and painful tools of instruction, how easily He can wipe out all our supplies and withhold from us the necessities of life, until we hear the rod and kiss it.

It should be observed that even when the stroke is light, there is a great God striking. He who can deliver the heaviest of blows can also lay on the lightest of chastenings. He whose little finger can destroy a world can lay a caressing hand on His children which will remove their warts and moles and leave them without spot or wrinkle.

Again, when He takes away ever so many things from us, be they comforts or conveniences, remember that He is All-sufficient and therefore able to supply us immediately with those comforts and treasures that cannot be stolen away from us, nor made of no effect.

Lastly, He is as a tender nurse, or as a mother in all His chastenings. The mother strikes the child a little blow to correct him, but gives him the breast with the other hand. She raps him with one hand, and spoons food into his mouth with the other. God's chastening hand is but to bring you in line so that you may receive your blessings from Him. Do not ever think that He stikes in order to do you harm, even though your wound may be deep, but rather remember that He is certain to have brought healing ointment and careful dressing to bind up the wound, and that He will not leave you nor forsake, but will sit patiently at your side until your corruption has been completely drawn out and you are in full health again.

"For He makes sore, and binds up; He wounds, and His hands make whole"—Job 5:18.

This verse contains an example of the former teaching that we ought not to despise the chastening of the Lord. For some might object, saying, Where is this happiness of those God corrects? Can there be any happiness in sores and wounds, in sickness and weakness? Eliphaz seems to answer for God in this text. Who would not be glad of a wound when he knows that the Almighty Himself will be the surgeon who binds it up? The hand of the Almighty both smites and cures, and it is a privilege to be either smitten or cured by Him.

"He makes sore"—The word was translated grief in the second chapter, where it is said that Job's friends saw that his grief was very great. It is grievous to be sore. And it is a soreness of the mind and spirit when we are in grief. When both are present, as in Job's case, then the chastisement is surely worthy of the name.

"and binds up"—The word is applicable to any kind of binding, such as, (1) the binding of captives in prison with chains; (2) to the binding or ornaments on the head, etc. In this case, it is the binding of a wound that is in view, a skill which surgeons must have if they expect success from their efforts. When the Great Physician makes wounds, you would expect that He would have the skill to bind it up and cause it to heal, in due time: *"He heals the broken in heart and binds up their wounds"* (Ps. 147:3).

Of the two meanings often given these words, the first contends that the words mean that He in the very making of the sore is binding it up for the healing and restoring of the afflicted one. The healing of the wound depends a great deal on the surgeon who makes it. A great physician is thinking of the healing when he is plunging in his knife. And the wound not only is shaped for healing, but is made of the right width and length and depth to remove the corrupting agent, but not a whit more. So it is with the Almighty—He wounds with exactitude, and He heals more quickly because of His skill in making the wound. If the wounds of a friend are faithful (Prov. 27:6), how much more are those of God?

The second meaning takes the words in the plain rendering of them, so that God in two distinct acts makes sore, then again binds up. In these two acts there is a shadowing of His great attributes of justice and mercy. God is the great correcter and instructor of His own. So He is the Great Physician. The Almighty, unlike many mighty men, both breaks your head and (upon your repentance and exercise of faith) binds it up. It is not so much to make us sore, however, as it is to make us sound. It is as the surgeon must do, he must be cruel to the flesh in order to be kind to the body. If he does not cut out the corrupting agent, there may be nothing to save on another day. His cuts cure the body. So God's afflictions are the curative agents as well as the wounding agents.

"He will deliver you in six troubles; yea, in seven no evil shall touch you"—Job 5:19.

Still seeking to convince Job that he ought not to despise the chastenings of the Almighty Eliphaz continues with a general statement here in the nineteenth verse, then he enumerates some particular cases of great dangers and outward evils. Also, he desires to show the happiness of those God corrects by giving assurance of positive blessings that follow.

The word for deliver here is that deliverance which comes when a man is snatched or is pulled out of the hand of the enemy, or out of the mouth of danger. The word for trouble comes from a root which means to straiten or to make narrow and cramped — so by a metaphor, to vex and trouble (for those who are forced through ways too narrow for them are pained and troubled by it). Oftentimes in Scripture, this word is put for an enemy, because an enemy crowds and pushes you into straits too narrow for comfort. The word is also used to signify the pangs and throes of women in childbearing – pain caused by the forcing of the infant through a narrow womb.

"He will deliver you in six troubles, yea in seven"–God befriends His children by delivering them from their enemy, trouble; He enlarges your way, or He so spreads the divine anointing oil upon you, that you are able to squeeze through, intact and very much alive. The use of the figures, six and seven, is full of meaning, for there is a kind of excellency in them which becomes evident when one studies the Scriptures. These numbers have a special significance when used by the Holy Spirit, carrying the meaning of a great number or a perfect number. The number six denotes perfection, which may be seen in the work of creation – a six-day creation that was perfect. Therefore, we may see here that God is promising to give a perfect deliverance to those who have great trouble or troubles.

Seven is a famous number which implies multitude, or perfection. She who had seven children (as Hannah) were complete mothers. When the seven demons were thrown out of a woman, a multitude is denoted. But when seven spirits, the seven churches, the seven trumpets, etc. are mentioned, these are put for perfection. Some would say that Eliphaz is here mentioning the exact number of those evils which he enumerates later, (1) famine, (2) war, (3) backbiting, (4) destruction, (5) evil beasts, (6) hurtful stones. These are six, and if a seventh should come upon you, He will deliver you from that also.

However, I think these fixed numbers are put for the unfixed, certain numbers for the uncertain, and that uncertain number is a great number, greater than any one can conceive. The Scripture speaks in this way often (see Amos 1:3; Job 33:29; Proverbs in several chapters). The Almighty will deliver you in one, two, six, or any number of instances, more times than you can imagine. The power and malice of men cannot multiply your troubles faster than the power and goodness of God can multipy your deliverances. If need be, He may be pleased to perfect seven deliverances for you before they can lay the plot for the first trouble they plan for you.

1. He will deliver you, no matter what the power of your enemy. He did not send Moses to plead with Pharaoh, but to deliver to him an ultimatum. He commanded the release of His people, and Pharaoh scoffed at his peril, finally perishing for his unbelief.

2. He will deliver you no matter how many troubles beset you, or how many times you are surrounded by them. Troubles, like clouds, return, though they were complete dissipated before. Think back, how many troubles has He delivered you from already? Can you not say with Israel, *"If it had not been the Lord who was on our side when men rose up against us, they would have swallowed us up..."* God never stops delivering you because He becomes weary, but He may stop delivering you from your troubles because you become weary of Him (see Judges 10:10-13).

"no evil shall touch you"–the evil of sin, or the evil of punishment, either could be true here. The Lord will so keep up your spirit and direct your way in trouble that you shall not defile yourself with the evil of sin. Your troubles shall purge you, rather than pollute you, when the directing hand of the Lord is put to work for you. And He can so keep you that you will not be annoyed by any evil of punishment. Even if wormwood and gall are your portion for the present, He may give you honey and sweetness so that though your troubles press upon you, yet evil shall not touch you.

"shall not touch you"–this notes an exact deliverance, a complete escape. In a battle, we may count ourselves blessed if we come off with a small wound, or even the loss of a limb, but when we are not so much as touched, then had we not better thank Him for such a wonderful blessing? Yet, just as surely as the three Hebrew children came out of Nebuchadnezzar's fire without a hair of their heads singed, without even any smell of fire upon their clothes, so may you expect God to be present in your troubles so that no evil shall touch you. Just as a wicked man may be loaded down with knowledge of the goodness of God, yet not be a whit the better for it – so a godly man may be loaded with evils, yet no one of them even so much as touch him so as to do him harm. You shall have temptation,

perhaps more than any other, but God is faithful, who will not allow you to be tempted above that you are able to bear.

"In famine He shall redeem you from death; and in war from the power of the sword"— Job 5:20.

But what is it to be redeemed from famine? To redeem properly is to take a man out of the power of another, by price, or by a greater power. Redemption is a special favor, one distinguishing the redeemed one as very dear to the redeemer. When God sent flies upon Pharaoh and his people, but did not permit so much as one fly in Goshen with His people, that was an act of redemption. When others perish, but we are saved from the sword, that is a redemption. When others are starved, while we ourselves are fed, that is a redemption from famine. Famine is one of the sorest of God's judgments, yet He delivers his Jeremiahs with a share of the bread when stores are all but exhausted. He may instead, of course, put His people beyond the famine, as when Abraham went to Egypt — or, as with Elijah, He may supernaturally cause His people to be fed. Whatever the way, God does redeem His people from famine (unless it be time for them to be forever reposed in His presence). If worst comes to worst, as men count it, then you shall find yourself upheld in joy and comfort, even while others are committing the most abominable acts of sin because of the lack of food. Your insides will burn, just as theirs do — but you will not curse your God and seek to remain alive by cruel and sinful acts. Instead, you shall be kept close to Him by His word sounding in your ears, beating in your heart.

"And in war from the power of the sword"—Famine, war and pestilence have often been bosom companions in this world of woe. The word for war here is from a root which signifies a devouring and devastating agent. By a metaphor it signifies to fight, or to strike with the sword. For the sword eats up the bodies of men and drinks up their blood. And likewise war eats up and consumes the fruits of the earth. The Hebrew here reads,*"they shall be delivered out of the hand of the sword"*—sometimes Scripture has it, the face of the sword, other times, the mouth of the sword, but here, the hand of the sword. The promise is that though the powerful sword threatens to beat you, eat you, or drain you of strength, God will deliver you. How many times do you see proof of His ability to do this, as when one of His people chased a thousand, or when a Jericho was destroyed with hardly a scratch on any of God's people. Think of David killing his ten thousands — do you think that skill can preserve a man in the very midst of ten thousand enemy swords? Nothing but the power of God can keep a man alive when he is killing a thousand Philistines with the jawbone of an ass. Needless to say, nothing here would lead you to think that you could presume upon the Lord — as if you could not be killed by the sword because He is bound by His promise to protect you. No, a man of God may fall before either sword or famine, as to this life, but it shall not happen unless they are being delivered by these into God's holy embrace forever.

"You shall be hidden from the whip of the tongue; neither shall you be afraid of robbery when it comes"—Job 5:21.

There is no whip which can cut and bite into the flesh like the whip of a sharp tongue. The word for tongue here is a word which means to detract, to slander. When a man is hit with a cane, we say that he was caned. So the Hebrews, when a man was whipped or slandered by the tongue, called it by that name, they said that he was betongued.

The tongue can scourge in many ways, in many places. A man can be excoriated in public, by a judge or a tribunal. Many times the secular power has served Satan by public denunciation of one of God's best. Can you not imagine what tongue-lashing was given to Christians in Roman days, there being so much vicious persecution of another sort? But, then, was not the Lord Jesus crucified on the tongues of men long before He was crucified on the wooden cross of the Romans? *"Crucify Him!"* they cried. Yet, God delivers us from this scourge, either by causing the tongues to cease, or by causing us to cease to hear the tongues.

"from the whip," or, *"scourge"* of the tongue—Not only may we be smitten with the lash of the tongue, but we can be emotionally and mentally damaged by the rumors and alarms maliciously launched by others: *"The king of Babylon has heard the report of them, and his hands became feeble. Anguish took hold of him..."* The tongue can terrorize a person until he cannot think nor act, nor even feel. Like Nabal, one may turn to stone upon hearing of danger — even when it has passed. But God can and does deliver us from such terror (Ps. 112:7), a heart that has trembled at the voice of God does not need to be afraid of anything that evil men or devils may say. The only saints who fall before the storm of the tongue are those who have taken their eyes off of Jesus Christ (as David, when he said, *"surely I will perish by the hand of Saul")*.

The word translated whip, or, scourge, may also be translated nations — and often is. But even if nations come against us, with all the propaganda they can muster in this age of instant communication, we shall be hidden from their hurt. But however true that may be, it does not so squarely fit our context here.

Undoubtedly, the benevolent hiding which is mentioned here is from calumniation, vicious slander, lying witnessing and untrue accusations—in the mouth of the foolish is the rod of pride (Prov. 14:3). The wisest of the unbelievers is but a fool, filled up with pride and hateful toward God and His children. No whip, even a cat-of-nine-tails with steel tips could tear up a man's back as hurtfully as a backbiting tongue can rip up a man's reputation. But a Christian will survive even the destruction of his reputation; for what is reputation but the opinions of men. If God regards a man as a faithful servant, as one after His own heart, then that reputation shall not suffer from the tongues of men. Not that a man of God should allow anything in his life to be a fair target for the tongue to strike, but rather to avoid even the appearance of evil so as to prevent any evil tongue from having even the most specious excuse for evil-speaking.

No one person has been so universally calumniated, so persistently lied against, as Jesus Christ. Yet who was more innocent and pure than He? And who has triumphed over the tongues of men more than He? God takes care that goodness triumphs. No amount of temporal upset, of seeming harm, can change the testimony of history — that God is able to deliver His people out of their trials, and this includes hiding them from that world of iniquity, the tongues of men. Yes, even the gossip of the saints shall not hurt us.

"neither shall you be afraid of robbery when it comes"—The word translated robbery is a word that signifies a meeting together of all kinds of evil. When evils break in together, it is as when robbers break into a house to steal and destroy. We are not to be afraid of evil flowing together to rob us of either our property or of our ideals. To be dismayed, to be benumbed with fear, to be utterly faithless when rivers of evil seem to be pouring in to destroy you, this is sinful and excuseless before God Almighty. Read the catalog of the faithful saints in Hebrews 11, and you will see that fear did not keep them from performing their duty toward God. The whole world was destroyed, but Noah was not afraid, for he had the ark which God had told him would save him from destruction. Now, how much more ought we to trust in the Ark of God, the Lord Jesus Christ, to save us from all forms of destructions — yes, even though all is destroyed, we shall not fear.

This is not to say that a saint shall never be afraid. There may be physical fear when the highest form of spiritual courage fills the breast of one of God's heroes. The flesh will always shrink from cold steel, even when the spirit is resolved to serve God irregardless of danger. But God promises His people protection from unbelieving fear, that fear which is the daughter of despair. A saint shall never be a terror to himself, nor shall he look upon God as a terror. So long as we are at peace with ourselves, and at peace with God, no loss or destruction can travel faster toward us than the consolations and comforts of our relationship to God the Son, our Savior. What can men rob from us? That which we treasure most is beyond the reach of thieves, rust and moths. Job is being given us as an example of what loss a man may stand and yet retain his faith and integrity. Though Satan and his fellow-robbers have taken from him everything that is counted precious in this world, even his health and physical wellbeing, yet Job grows stronger in faith, becomes more famous than ever for his integrity. God's own are carried beyond the borders of fear upon the other-worldly wings of assurance, the unshakable companion of faith in God.

"At destruction and famine you shall laugh; neither shall you be afraid of the beasts of the earth"—Job 5:22.

Here God's promise is made even more merciful, for not only are we hidden from the awful destruction of the tongue, and the stripping effect of robbery, but also in the very midst of destruction and killing famine, we shall laugh! Not that there shall be an insane breaking out of laughter, or an insensible merriment, but even the heaviest of afflictions weighed against the joys that are set before us are but *"light affliction which...works for us a far more exceeding and eternal weight of glory"* Anointed with the divine eyesalve , we do not look at the things which are seen, but at the things which are not seen – for the things which are seen are temporal, but the things which are not seen are eternal (see 2 Cor. 4:15-18; Rom. 8:18). Looking at things this way, even famine and destruction may be laughed at, that is, may be despised as not worthy of our fear. Shall we like Esau sell our precious birhtright for something to fill our bellies? No, we shall laugh at famine.

The word used is indeed the word ordinarily used for laughing. As when Abraham rejoiced at the promise of the birh of a son. It is sometimes used in a good sense, sometimes it is used in an ill sense:

In a good sense, to laugh is an outward expression of inward joy and true comfort. It is proper for man to laugh when there is good reason for him to be joyful. But without a sound reason for joy, laughter is foolish, it is as the crackling of thorns under a pot.

In an ill sense, to laugh is used for scorning and deriding. As when the wild ass is said to scorn or laugh at the people of the city (Job 39:7). Or when the Lord is said to laugh at those who gather themselves together to take counsel against Him, and is said even to have them in derision (Ps. 2:4). God scorns, even derides those who join hands together to thwart His plans (but of course He does not scorn or laugh at men simply because they are helplessly entwined in the sinful cords of humanity – A Savior, the very Son of God has been provided that these may look upon Him and be saved).

Needless to say, the laughter of unbelief is an ill laughter (such as Sarah's unbelieving laughter in Gen. 18:12). We may not laugh at God's promises, as if the circumstances of our lives nullified them. It is the man who laughs at circumstances who laughs last, not he who laughingly scoffs at God's power to deliver from seemingly certain disaster.

Good laughter comes from faith – Abraham fell on his face and laughed, not considering that he was a hundred years old and his body seemingly sexually dead, not considering the deadness of Sarah's womb either, but in faith he believed the promise of God and such faith caused him to laugh joyfully. Not only did he delight in the promised fulfillment of a desire for a son with Sarah, but in the fact that the Savior would come of this seed, *"Abraham rejoiced to see My day, he saw it and was glad"* (John 8:56). A man may be said to laugh in faith when it is because he has with his faith a holy courage, a heavenly confidence. He may laugh in faith when he sees great storms of troubles approaching because he is assured that God has given him a strong ship and good spiritual tackling to ride out the storms.

In our text, certainly we may not laugh at destruction and famine out of pride, or out of self-confidence, or because we are so comfortably full of the world's provisions, or because we are dull and insensitive to what they mean. No, this laughter comes from the humble belief that God is present, from confidence that God is able to do whatever He desires in Heaven and on earth, from the consolation that all that we cherish spiritually cannot be lost to either destruction or famine, and from the lively and ever-fresh feeling that whatever evil-happening God has created for the moment can as easily be removed by Him whenever His plan has been fulfilled. He may even more positively glory in the approaching storm, feeling that God is sending it to strengthen him, to make of him a pure and holy servant – something he has not been able to attain without such trials: *"experience works out hope"* (Romans 5:4). Faith puts a silver lining on the darkest clouds of life.

"neither shall you be afraid of the beasts of the earth"—the word covers all living creatures, basically meaning life. The wild beasts being so active and full of life may properly be signified by this word. They are called here the beasts of the earth because they are of the earth, and to its dust they return.

The word for earth means the whole earth, whether habitable or uninhabitable.

Some take the words, *"the beasts of the earth"* as being men. Such usage is seen in Psalm 68:10, in a good sense. And in Ps. 68:30, we see wicked men referred to (properly translated, *"the wild beasts of the reeds"*).

But commonly the word is translated as the wild beasts of the earth, those animals which are considered dangerous to man — savage, cruel and carnivorous. God gave man dominion over these, and they once obeyed him. But when man sinned, he was immediately thrown into tension with the world and with many of its creatures. Many times men have been hurt and their property destroyed by beasts, not only those that are normally destructive but even by those who are normally domesticated. Even the weakest of creatures, such as the termite, or the locust, may be the proper source of fear. Only faith can deliver us from such fears, that the beasts or living creatures of the earth shall do us great harm.

"For you shall be in covenant with the stones of the field; and the beasts of the field shall be at peace with you"—Job 5:23.

Not only may we be delivered from the fear that the beasts shall harm us, but we also may be blessed in such a way that the stones of the field and the beasts of the field shall be so beneficial to us that we may be said to be in covenant with them. This word for covenant is one used for a covenant of reconciliation between God and man. It pictures a solemn act, and therefore it is well to ask how we could be in covenant with the beasts and stones. First, we must ask what stones these are, before we find out what kind of covenant we make with them.

Some say the stones are strong men, as in Job 6:12 an allusion of this sort is made, *"Is my strength the strength of stones?"* The Chaldee paraphrast understands the Law as the stones here, it having been written in stone by the finger of God. That is a great truth, but it is nothing but a conceit to think that this is the meaning in our text. Others say that these stones by a metonymy are put for those beasts which lie among the stones, or have their dens in hollow rocks. This may well be the meaning of this text.

Stones, whether those lying on top the ground, those buried under the soil, those made into a wall or fence, or those set up as marks and boundaries, or those fashioned with a tool and made into idols, may in many ways act as a hindrance and a troublemaking instrumentality for man.

A covenant, in the proper sense, could not be made with stones, as natural stones. So it must be an improper or allusive use of the two words together here. The context having enumerated many ways in which God will keep us from being harmed, now we have the mention of stones. A covenant would indicate that God has provided formal protection from the stones mentioned here, also that good or benefit would derive to man from it. As God made promise in Ps. 91:11 that the angels would protect the Messiah, so that He would not so much as dash His foot against a stone, so might we also be given protection. If God so will, a stony-ground farm will yield abundant harvests; walls that are erected to the hurt of God's children may be turned to their protection; marked boundaries for the purpose of self-aggrandizement may become the means of keeping intruders out of a holy man's place of worship.

Whatever we do, there is no protection, no benefits certain from it. But whatever God does, there is sure to come the greatest of benefits, including the hiding of us from hurt. That which makes the ungodly the most uncomfortable can become a great mercy and comfort to the godly. Satan admits that Jesus could turn stones into bread, and we hear it said by Him that stones could be turned into faithful witnesses — how much less is it to make the stones of the field serve us, if it pleases Him. Let not any impediment, whether physical stone, or spiritual hindrances, cause you to stumble — God has made all things so that they will work out good for you. Even the stones that killed Stephen were in covenant with him, putting the face of an angel on him before he expired, and putting him into the arms of the waiting Lord Jesus as soon as they had finished the work.

"and the beasts of the field shall be at peace with you"—that is, they shall speak peace toward you. By redemption, a man may regain this much of his original estate, he may have peace with the creatures. This is not to say that a godly man will prosper by walking into lions' dens, as if there were a promise here that he would not be hurt. But that there is no need to fear anything, not even the most fierce enemy of man among the beasts, if one has that faith that drives out fear. Just as sin makes every animal a potential enemy of man, so grace makes every animal a potential friend of man. An ungodly man's courage comes from an ungodly presumption. A godly man's courage comes from his reliance on the dependable word of God, divine reason furnishes reason enough for courage.

If under the cover of the word, *"beasts,"* here is meant those men who as so brutish and animal-like that they truly deserve to be counted among the beasts of the earth (as when the apostle Paul said that he had fought with beasts at Ephesus), then let it be known that a godly man had best believe and act upon divine reasoning in this case also. Just as Paul triumphed over those of Ephesus, so may each of us who is covered by the blood of Christ confidently expect to triumph over the most unfeeling of men. We are told in Proverbs that *"when a man's ways please the Lord, He makes even his enemies to be at peace with him"* (16:7) — so here we are told that even the beasts shall be at peace with him.

"And you shall know that your tent is in peace; and you shall visit your fold, and shall miss nothing"—Job 5:24.

In the nineteenth verse there was a promise that God will deliver out of six troubles, and no evil shall touch us in seven. Then were enumerated many ways in which God keeps us from being hurt or harmed, ways in which our fears are turned around and made into instruments of faith. Now we go back to a summation, a final assurance of profit from not despising the correcting hand of God. All the specific blessings turn into security for us. In the remainder of the chapter, there are set forth four areas of blessing: (1) a quiet and happy life; (2) many prosperous children; (3) a long, full life; (4) a sweet and comfortable death.

"You shall know"—that is, you shall see and feel that your life is quietly peaceful. Often knowledge is put for experience. We say of a rich man, that he never knew what it was like to be poor. In the same way, Christ is said never to have known sin (that is, he never experienced it, though He who had been so offended by it certainly knew all there was to know about sin, outside of experience). In this way, the godly man knows that his tent shall be in peace, he knows it by experiencing it — he feels it, he sees it. Or, it could also be said that Job would know that his tent was in peace by reasoning and debating over the things mentioned above. Again, this knowledge of peace could be that which comes in by faith. The peace brought in by faith is not a peace felt or apprehended by the senses. Lastly, knowledge is assurance. Just as Job said, *"I know that my Redeemer lives,"* thereby expressing much assurance, so Eliphaz is telling Job here that he may be assured that his life shall be in peace if he will but accept the chastening of the Almighty gladly.

"that your tent"—Tents or tabernacles were of two kinds: those for private use, and the ones used publically. Here private tents are in view, and, by a trope the entire estate and outward life of a man may be expressed under this description, his tent.

"is in peace"—Peace may be either strictly so, or largely so. As opposed to war, we may have a peace that is largely so, but it does not necessarily mean that we have peace every moment. If we yield to the chastening hand of God, then we may be delivered from being invaded by foreign forces, from the warlike actions of our neighbors, and from the spirit-depressing contentions which develop in our homes. In a larger sense, peace may signify all kinds of blessings, all those comforts which this life may experience, including those of the soul. In this sense, a man may be much troubled, yet be in peace at the same time.

Peace is a choice blessing, a special gift that comes down from the Father above: *"You will keep him whose mind is rested upon You in perfect peace, because he trusts in You"* (Isa. 26:3). And, as for the wicked, *"There is no peace, says my God, to the wicked"* (Isa. 57:21). Without the peace of God, riches are but thorns in the side, honor is an unceasing form of misery, and health is but the ability to suffer greater affliction. But with this peace which passes all natural understanding, the saints are free to pursue the grace and knowledge of the Lord Jesus Christ. While others are fighting the world, their neighbors, their friends, their families, and, not the least of all, themselves, the children of God are able to concentrate on a life that presses toward the mark for the prize of the high calling of God in Christ Jesus. While others have minds in turmoil and hearts full of hate and spite, the singleminded and singlehearted Christian can think on those things that are true, those things that are honest, those things that are right, those things that are pure, those things that are truly lovely and full of the revelation of God's goodness and grace.

It is good to have the blessed peace which comes only from the hand of God. There are three stages of deliverance in attaining to such peace: (1) the deliverance from strife, the negative part of the blessing; (2) the elevation to a tranquil and peaceful relationship with God, the positive working of God; and, (3) the promise or other form of assurance which God may give that this peace shall be a continuing and unending one. The first we receive when Christ delivers us from the prison house of sin; the second when the benefits of His intercession flow in upon us; and the third when we read in words that cannot be broken that God promises us this peace everlastingly — that there are none who can pluck us out of His hand and again bury us in the mire of sin and its terror.

"and you shall visit your fold and shall miss nothing"–The word for visit means to take care, to provide for. To visit your fold, or your house, is to carefully regulate the affairs of the home, to order and direct those who under you care for it. The word translated fold is variously translated as dwelling-place, habitation, pleasant place, etc. It means a resting-place. Here it properly means the home, the well-ordered and carefully kept.

The word for miss properly means that, to miss a mark, to err or miscarry in duty, etc. It is used of the Benjamites who could sling stones at a hair's breadth and not miss. And, because every transgressing is a missing of the mark, an erring from the straight paths of our duty, the word is also translated *"sin."*

Under the meaning, *"you shall miss nothing,"* may be meant the protecting hand of God shall keep all your possessions from robbers, destroyers or wastes. Just as David said that he and his men had watched over Nabal's flocks, and as his servants testified, nothing was missing — so God watches over us in this wilderness of sin and loss, and so long as we are gladly submitting ourselves to Him, we shall miss nothing.

Under the meaning, *"you shall not sin,"* the promise may be that you shall be of such wisdom and discretion, such divinely-guided care that you shall not sin in the affairs of your family. In this sense, it may be Eliphaz is inferring that Job has sinned in the caring of his family, and that is the reason he has lost all. In Job's case, everything is missing, he has nothing of his family left but his wife — and she is estranged from him.

"You shall also know that your seed shall be great, and your offspring as the grass of the earth"–Job 5:25.

It was of course one of the great concerns of the ancients that their children should be of the great ones in the earth. In Job's day, the promises of God for temporal blessings were still operating. It is only in New Testament days that we are taught to concentrate on spiritual blessings as the fulfillment of God's promises.

The word translated great is a word that both means many and much. The promise here is that if Job comes back to his senses and adopts the right frame of mind and spirit, then he shall have many children, and they shall also be great, honorable, important persons.

"and your offspring as the grass of the earth"–This is but an emphasis of the first phrase above, the word for offspring here being one that can be translated, bud, or fruit. To be as the grass of the earth is proverbially the same as the expressions, *"as the stars of the heav-*

ens," and, *"as the sand upon the seashore."* It is hyperbole with a middle-east flavor. And it obviously is meant to convey the thought of children of such number and such greatness as to please even the most desirous soul.

Here, it goes without saying, Eliphaz cuts deep into Job's wounds. For here is a man who has not had the time or the stable circumstances to reconcile himself to the deaths of every single one of his children, and his 'friend' brings to mind their loss by promising him a multitude of children, children who would be great and honored persons. All this, says Eliphaz, shall be yours if you will but agree with me as to the cause of your trouble, and if you will but accept my advice as to how you may recover your lost estate and family.

"You shall come to your grave in a full age, like a shock of grain comes in its season"—Job 5:26.

After peace, an ordered and pleasing home, many children who are great, what more can a man ask of God? The answer is nearly universal, he wants a long life to enjoy all these things. Therefore, in encouraging Job, in luring him to accept his solution, Eliphaz here brings in this last strong desire of man, and he gives Job the promise that he shall have a full and long life.

Along with this, there is the implication that Job shall also have a peaceful death. It was more strongly desired by the ancients, even up until recent centuries, that a man should die well. To have a blessed and happy death was considered to be an important way to witness to a man's unbreakable connection with God. So the heathen had a saying, that no man could be accounted blessed until he came to his death — and when it was seen that he died well, then they were willing to call him blessed. Needless to say, this is no infallible guide to a man's blessedness. There are indeed Stephens among us, who taste of Heaven before they go there. There are men willing to die, cheerful at the thought of going to be with Christ, as was the case with Paul. All Christians are to be of a mind where they can say with honesty and strong desire, *"Even so, come quickly, Lord Jesus."* There is no Scripture, however, which even slightly infers that we should judge a man's Christianity by the way he slips out into eternity. This is not to say that the way a man goes may not indicate strongly his spiritual condition (as with the man who is still grasping and gasping to retain all his possessions in this world until his last breath is drawn), but God sets up His own criteria for judging a man's heart — nowhere does he indicate that a man's deathbed scene is to count for any more than any other like moments of his life.

Job is perhaps also being promised here that he will come to his grave in honor. And in a full age may mean that he shall not only have fullness of age, but also fullness of wealth and honor. Job's present poverty is to turn into an abundance of everything, even unto the day he dies. The primary meaning here, however, is this, that Job would live long if he would but repent and accept his chastening. Some say that along with the fullness of days there is also the promise of lustiness, of strength and health in his old age. As Moses is said to have gotten to the age of 120 and yet have his eyes not dim nor his natural force abated, so Job is being promised here that he may come to old-age and still be comfortable and in good temper.

"like a shock of grain comes in its season"—the similtude here is to assure Job of a life that comes to a fruitful end, one which is useful and full of profit to others. A man who is cut off in the midst of his days may possibly be compared to grain cut down when it was yet green and not yet useful — though history abounds with testimony of those who died very young, full of fruitfulness in their own age, and continuing to be useful to all who have lived since. Examples of young men who died, yet still live are easy to find: men such as Abel, Enoch (comparatively young when translated), John the Baptist, Stephen, and, finally and best, the Lord Jesus Christ Himself (at age 33). Of the men who have lived and died for the Lord Jesus Christ since, space would not permit the naming of them all, but note especially Joseph Alleine (age 36) and Robert Murray McCheyne (aged 30).

Ordinarily speaking, however, it is a great blessing to be brought to the fullness of age, and to be blessed with a life of usefulness in God's cause for more than a normal span.

"Behold this; we have searched it, it is so. Hear it and know it for your good"—Job 5:27.

Eliphaz began this dispute with an elegant preface, and now he ends it with a rhetorical conclusion. It is as if he were saying, 'Job, I have spoken many things to you, now hear the sum and upshot of it all — *"Behold this; we have searched it, it is so. Hear it, etc. "*
The conclusion has two main thrusts; First, the assertion that what he has spoken is true; Secondly, the call for Job's assent.

"we have searched it"—We have not taken these things upon trust, or by an implicit faith, says Eliphaz, but we have followed our experience and have found these things to be true. We have not received them by tradition, but we have searched and tested and discovered that this is the way the matter stands in God's dispensations, both to a wicked man and to a godly man. We have learned that God does not punish the innocent; we have learned that man cannot compare in justice to God; that hypocrites shall not prosper for long; and that a man's afflictions are a direct result and in the measure of his transgressions.
The word translated *"searched"* clearly signifies a very diligent and exact scrutiny (see Deut. 13:14). It is to search as Judges search into and inquire about a crime. It is a search such as Judges make into the Law in order to determine what sentence to give. It is the serious search that might be made to determine the answer to a riddle. It was the word used when the spies were sent out to bring back information which could mean life or death to the Danites (Judges 18:2). A spy is an exact inquisitor, one who looks into all affairs in order to discover the information he must bring back. So here, Eliphaz assures Job that a thorough search has been made into the experience of those present, and into the experiences passed down from historical sources. And it is implied that there has also been a search of all the orally-transmitted Scripture. Then he announces the findings of such an exact and diligent search, *"it is so."*
Some have concluded this speech of Eliphaz to be apocryphal, a matter of mere human invention, a work of man's wit rather than of God's Spirit. For, say they, in chapter 4 he says that *"a thing was secretly brought to me,"* yet here he indicates that he knows these things by a search and study, rather than by Divine revelation. Men who are inspired by the Holy Spirit speak another language, saying such things as, *"Thus says the Lord;" "this we have received,"* etc. Scripture, say they, is given by inspiration from God, not by the disquisitions of men.
The answer: The apostle Paul has sufficiently attested the Divine authority of this discourse by alleging a proof out of it: *"He takes the wise in their own craftiness"* (1 Cor. 3:19). Secondly, that which Eliphaz states was secretly brought to him was only the one special oracle mentioned in chapter 4, verse 17, *"Shall man who dies be more just than God; Shall a man be more pure than his Maker?"* The other part of his discourse, to which these last words refer, were grounded upon the experiences which he and his friends had observed in and about the providence of God. They conclude that all God's dealings with both the godly and the wicked agree with that grand principle which Eliphaz received by immediate revelation. Therefore he is telling Job that this general position taken from the vision which was brought to him has been fully attested and corroborated by a diligent and careful search of all the records of the ages. He feels that the Lord has given His approval to these statements, and that His providential dealings with men have agreed with them. God's word is enough to assert His own justice, but His works witness with it.
"we have searched it"—He speaks in the plural number. He began his speech in the plural number, and he concludes it here in the plural number. Yet we are not to think that this was a discourse pieced together from all of them, as if they had first debated in private what to say and then elected Eliphaz to speak it. Rather, Eliphaz is indicating that he is of the opinion that what he is saying is the sense of what his two friends also believe and would subscribe to.
"Hear it"—To advise you was our part, but to hear and to act upon it is your part. But why does Eliphaz tell him now to hear it, when Job had been hearing him all this while? To hear, as Job is bid to hear here, is more than merely to hear with the ear. It is,

First, to believe and give credit to what is heard, *"I have told you already, and you did not hear. Why do you want to hear it again?"* (John 9:27). That is, you would not believe nor give credit to what you heard the first time. To hear is more than the work of the ear.

Secondly, to hear is to listen — that is, to yield and consent to what is spoken, *"Because you have listened to your wife,"* (Gen. 3:17). Barely to hear a temptation to sin is not an act of sin. Barely to hear an exhortation to do good is not an act of grace. It is because Adam not only heard with his ear but listened and consented to what Eve spoke that he was guilty of sinning against God.

Thirdly, to hear is to obey, *"Hear and your soul shall live"* (Isa. 55:3). It is not every hearing of the ear that brings life to the soul. Only obedient hearing is life-giving hearing.

So here Eliphaz is telling Job that what he has heard has been previously searched, tested and proven, therefore it behooves him to hear it, submit and consent to what has been spoken, obey and practice what he has been told.

To hear is both an act of sense and an act of reason. It is an act of nature and an act of grace. If God hears us when we pray, our prayers are granted. If we hear God's counsel and command, then we obey it. When God hears man, He grants; and when man hears God (or hears men speaking for God,) he yields and obeys.

"and know it for your good"—or, as in the original, *"know it for yourself."* Because that which a man knows for himself is for his own profit, we translate it, *"know it for your good."* That is, know this as that which will give you the greatest good. To *"know it for yourself"* does not import that thus one is to know and keep it to himself, allowing no one to partake with him. When Solomon says, *"If you are wise, you shall be wise for yourself,"* he is saying that you shall have profit by your wisdom. He does not mean that you will have a corner on wisdom, to the exclusion of others. Rather, wisdom brings in a thorough and fair review. There are many who know much and who may for a moment seem to be very wise because of what they know, but in actuality they know nothing as they ought to know it, and they are not wise at all for their own profit.

There are three sorts of knowing men;

First, some know only to know. They know, but they have no goal except the attainment of knowledge. They do not learn for the good of others, nor even for their own good. As some gain riches and honor, so some gain knowledge. The covetous man may gather riches, or honor, or fame. Many covet knowledge as a means of gaining honor or fame — they read book after book, remember point after point, delve into science after science, only that they may display knowledge to the world. And what do they do with this knowledge? They do not use it for the good of mankind or even for their own good. To know, as a mere means of knowing, is no better than not to know at all.

Secondly, Others know so that others may know; or, they know that they may guide their practice by their knowledge. These are the true ends of knowing, to communicate knowledge, and to obey knowledge. The great end of knowing should be for the profit of others, and for our own profit in holiness and obedience. So it is here, *"know it for your good;"* that is, get some advantage from your knowledge.

TRUTH DESERVES OUR MOST DILIGENT AND EXACTING SEARCH

There is a promise that we will find truth only if we search for the truth, *"You shall find wisdom;" "If you seek her...and search for her"* as you would for hidden treasures in the earth (Prov. 2:4). There are two places where you will find the veins of truth, (1) in God's word; (2) in God's work. In these two books you must search if you are to find the truth and use it for your own practice and profit, or to teach it to others.

Note this, that what we offer to others as the truth should be only those things which we have verified by a diligent, personal search. Truth that is only by hearsay, truth that we have not made our own, may be truth indeed, but it will carry no authority unless we have gained it by a diligent and exacting search of God's book and God's providence.

Those who hear well will search the Scriptures to see if those things are so (as did the Bereans, Acts 17:11). Not only are we to study carefully what we have heard, to see if it is so, but we are also to study carefully beforehand what we are going to teach for the truth. Those who receive for truth that which they never personally verify will not hold to that truth when someone begins to inquire into their grounds for believing it. Truths which are merely borrowed and taken upon trust in another man's fidelity or knowledge, will form no abiding treasure of knowledge to anyone. Yet most today can only say of all the truth they affirm that which he in 2 Kings 6:5 said to Elisha, *"Alas! master, for it was borrowed."* These snatch up one truth from this hand and another truth from that hand. They take it on credit of this reputable man, or that learned man. And it is the plague of our age that so very few of us may say, as Eliphaz has said here, *"Behold this; we have searched it."* Yet the more pains we take to find out the truth, the more pleasure we shall have from knowing the truth. It may even be questioned whether a man who merely has the truth on credit can have even a little gain or pleasure from truth gotten in such a way. The fact is, that which we sweat most for is that which is the sweetest to us. Whether we pray or study, the morsels of truth which are dipped in that sauce will both fatten and strengthen the soul the most.

How can a man be confident of the truth when he has not searched and inquired into it? It is only after you have searched it that you can say confidently and boldly, *"so it is!"* A man who has his truths second-hand will waver, he will be a double-minded man, an unstable professor of truth — let not that man think that he shall receive anything from the Lord for so despising His truth that he will not search into it.

WHAT WE KNOW FOR OURSELVES BY DILIGENT SEARCH SHOULD BE TOLD

We have searched it, says Eliphaz. Yet he is not going to put his findings under a bushel and thus hide the light of the truth. He refuses to hide his talents in a napkin and bury it. The truth should be told. For truth does not need to stand and beg for an audience. It is not necessary for truth to creep on the ground with flattering insinuations or base submissions in order to gain acceptance. Truth is imperious, it speaks in kingly fashion, saying, I will, and I demand it. It commands men, it does not beg them. Every word of the truth is a law to men, therefore it is only right that we should exhort men, *"Hear it!"*

General doctrinal truths take on form, shape and usefulness when they are given a special application to our lives. Eliphaz attempts here to apply his general set of truths to the life of Job. And although he failed much in making the application, yet he did have a set of truths which were very useful for application. At least he did not make the mistake so often made by those who proclaim the truth, the failure to apply what he had proclaimed. Eliphaz does not leave his doctrine hovering in the air, but he attempts to bring it home to the individual heart, where it will truly do good as it is laid upon the conscience. Yes, even experimental truths are to be discussed and brought home to the hearer.

THE DEVIL KNOWS MUCH, BUT WHAT HE KNOWS IS NOT FOR HIS GOOD

The devil is a world-renowned scholar. He knows much, much less than he is credited with knowing at times, but more than any other sinful creature (without the grace of God in his life). Yet what the devil has learned and knows is not for his benefit, but for his hurt. Some men think that they know most of that which is knowable. Such a one is the old serpent, no doubt. Yet he knows nothing at all which is profitable to him in the end. Not a thing is increased by the devil's knowledge, except the devil's pride. He has been puffing up with knowledge for centuries on end, yet he had not been edified one whit! With him, as with all of us, it will be found that the knowledge which puffs up will at last also puff down and cast us down with it.

For those who take pride in their knowledge of the letter of Scripture, remember this, that the devil knows his Scripture better than most — did he not quote it to the Lord? It is not enough to know the Scripture, you must hear it, then obey it. There is not one vein of truth in the Scripture which a godly man may not use for his profit. And the more he mines of this treasure, the more he may store up and later expend for the profit of all. Even truth that is about things earthly and temporal will sublimate and spiritualize a believing heart. All truths, especially those truths continued in the promises, are the portion of a godly man. Anything that is spoken for the benefit of godly men may be taken to our breasts as our portion also. Whatever a man may find in the book of God, especially the great riches and precious things in the promises, he may take for himself — nothing is too good for him, *"He who did not spare His own Son, but delivered Him up for us all, shall He not with Him also freely give us all things?"* (Rom. 8:32). On the other hand, not a word of the Scriptures will profit one who does not believe them — the very promises are threatenings to them — the very blessings of God are a curse to them. The clouds are made to pass over this and that piece of ground, then they dissolve and bring life to a third. So it is with the promises, which are full of blessings and comforts — they pass completely over a wicked man's head, not letting down so much as one drop of mercy or comfort upon him — they are like the *"barren wilderness, which does not see when good comes"* (Jer. 17:6). But when the promises pass over a man of faith, they dissolve and pour down blessings, *"to refresh and confirm the inheritance of the Lord"* (Ps. 68:9).

So, then, in this fifth chapter we have considered the latter part of the speech of Eliphaz, in which he has presented many different arguments to convince and humble Job under the hand of God. He has given him one counsel after another, presented him with one motive after another, in order to persuade him to seek to God for deliverance, by humbling himself under God's correcting hand. He has begun with a loving preface, and he has presented those things which he felt confident were true, concluding with a moving exhortation to Job. When Job begins to make his defence, he is able to scatter the charges brought against himself. But this does not mean that he has completely discredited all the things that Eliphaz has spoken for the truth in these past two chapters.

"Then Job answered and said, O that my grief were but weighed, and my ruin laid in the balances together!"—Job 6:1,2.

Eliphaz has undertaken the reproof of Job for his impatience and complaints, and he had advised him to adopt a more holy and better-tempered charge towards God, he being under His afflictions. In his reply, Job shapes and forms answers to both these things:

1. He refutes the reproofs of his impatience and complaints. And he adds his refusal to accept the counsels which had been given to him. He gives seven verses to this.

2. He renews and reinforces his complaint, expressing his grief and his desire to die. He gives six verses to this. He is not only far from satisfied with the charges spoken against him, he will not recall a word nor recant at all.

3. He then makes a charge against his friends, a censure which makes them to be rash and uncharitable; yes, even deceitful in dealing with him. For this he takes twelve verses.

4. Still he is willing to submit himself to their judgment and direction, if only they would speak reason to him at last, if they would but come home to his case. He is even willing for them to fully and candidly discover and reveal any error which he is truly guilty of committing and he states he is willing to be corrected. This he does in two verses (24 and 25), in which he is saying that he does not believe that all Eliphaz has already said is really applicable to his condition. You have mistaken my case, he is saying. Still I do not stand out against you, for it is not my will that opposes what you have spoken — it is my understanding. Therefore, if you can show me better reason why these things that have come upon me are commensurate with my guilt, then I will not lengthen out contentions, nor am I resolved to have the last word.

5. He vehemently expostulates with Eliphaz, demanding that he recognize that he is not a man who is out of his wits, a raving madman. He is aggravated that it should be thought that his words are vain and windy, words which do not deserve the attention of these men.

6. Job returns some advice to Eliphaz, and gives them an admonition, that they should carefully consider what they say before they continue their counsel and discourse with him. And in the seventh chapter he humbly acknowledges himself as unworthy that God should take notice of him, admitting to his own sinfulness and even earnestly requesting that his sin be pardoned. Yet in doing all this, he does not meet the approval of Eliphaz.

Job refutes the reproof of Eliphaz in these first four verses by showing that the reason why Eliphaz was so sharp and bitter in reproving him was due to the fact that he failed to consider Job's sorrowful condition. Surely he thought, this man is not feeling the weight of my grief, nor has he recognized the terror that has blasted my spirit. This is his argument to Eliphaz — 'You have no right to reprove or convict me for sinful impatience unless you have fully weighed my calamities, which are the cause and ground for my complaints.'

Admittedly, Job's is a difficult case to feel and understand, for who else is apt to have been so completely crushed under the destructive forces which had devastated his life—he is a wounded spirit, and as such he is hard to bear (*"a wounded spirit who can bear,"*—Proverbs 18:14). He has been shocked with the loss of his goods, then torn with grief at the death of his children. And if this were not enough, there followed onslaughts from his wife, his friends, Satan and God! He is numb with grief, he is racked with excruciating pain, and he is utterly distressed by the pat explanations and false accusations of these friends. But most of all he is terrorized by the realization that back of all this is the hand of God. He has been thrown headlong into the darkness, close to despair, by the One he loved the most, by Him that he had served with joy and gladness, and by Him to whom he had submitted himself with exact and unremitting obedience. Yet he found it hard to reasonably deny that the horrifying things that had happened and were happening to him were proof that God had thrown him over — this terrifying thought being cruelly inserted into his mind and heart by Satan, again and again and again.

It must be kept in mind, however, that Satan has not gained his point, nor does he ever. At this very point, where worship and piety seem simply impossible for Job's wounded spirit to give, his faith comes rushing in again and again to ward off every threat of collapse brought on by each new assault. Amidst grief, hurt, debilitating loneliness and terror he continues to believe in God, he will not admit that his service to God has been foolish, nor does he seek to escape from His hand. He did stagger and totter under these tremendous blows — who would not? But though it appeared certain that he would fall again and again, God secretly strengthened him each time he was at the brink of spiritual disaster. Just as Paul, left for dead at Lystra, was revived, strengthened and set on his feet again, so did God do for Job here. He was given a still greater measure of faith to fight off the greater pressures that were continually building up against him.

"Then Job answered"—He answers the charges, reproofs and arguments of Eliphaz. It is the duty of good men to answer when they are falsely charged, *"Be ready always to give an answer to every man who asks you a reason for the hope that is in you, with meekness and fear — having a good conscience — so that in the thing in which they speak against you as evildoers, they who falsely accuse your good behavior in Christ may be ashamed"* (1 Peter 3:15,16). It is to the honor of God that you meekly remove any charges of ungodly behavior against yourself. Or, if they are true, to freely admit them as sinful, giving evidence that you fully repent and rest upon the Lord for forgiveness. It would not be right to despise one's own integrity or reputation by failing to stand up for it when falsely charged. Job is resolute on this point, professing that he would hold to his integrity until the day of his death (and do not forget that God Himself had testified to Job's integrity). Again, it is our duty to answer in respect of others. We should attempt to satisfy any who may be scandalized by what we have been falsely accused of doing. Whether it is a scandal actually given, or a scandal simply presumed (as in the case of Job,) there is a duty to remove the pollution which has been cast upon a child of God, and through him upon God. When we are silent in the face of a charge, we either strengthen suspicions or cause others to completely convict us of the charge. Job, then, was duty-bound to defend his words and his actions, lest those observing may think ill of those who were under God's hand. We are to love others as we love ourselves. And since self-love is the rule of our love to others, it follows that if we neglect our own wronged honor then we are apt to neglect that of our neighbor's as well.

"O that my grief were but weighed"—Grief may be either active or passive. Passively, it is the thing that we suffer, that which is grievous to us. Affliction itself is called grief. Actively, it is the sorrow we express under the pressures of grievous afflictions. The original word is sometimes translated anger, sometimes indignation, sometimes wrath. It is the same word used by Eliphaz in Job 5:2, where he says, *"wrath kills the foolish man,"* — in which he lays a very aggravating charge of foolishness to Job. Now Job gives his answer, beginning with the first word of that charge, saying in effect, 'You told me that wrath kills the foolish man, but if my anger, my wrath, my grief were to be fully weighed, then you would quickly see that it is not the anger or wrath of a fool that you are seeing. You would find reason enough for my passion, that it is not the lack of wisdom which causes it, but it is the plentifulness and weightiness of my grief which has wrung these complaints from me.' If you should claimed to have weighed them, then surely you must have done so with false balances and a bag of deceitful weights.

The Vulgate translates, *"O that my sins,"* namely, for which I am thus afflicted were thoroughly weighed. As if the meaning of Job were to lighten his sin. But the original will not bear such a translation, nor is it scriptural to suggest that any amount of sufferings could in the least balance out the least of our sins. All the afflictions possible in this life could not be weighed against the sufferings of Christ on the cross. Nor can they be compared seriously with that *"exceeding weight of glory"* which awaits us. Therefore this rendering of the Vulgate is not at all the true one.

Our English word scale, the instrument in which we weigh, is well conceived to come from the Hebrew word used here. It signifies to weigh anything, but especially coin or money. In those days they did not count money, they weighed it. It was from this original word (*shakal*) that one special sort of Hebrew money is derived, the shekel. By a metaphor the word signifies to weigh or consider a thing exactly and fully, thus to judge it. Men of wealth weigh out gold and silver exactly, down to the last gram or grain. The Jewish scribes weighed out the law very exactly, thus are actually called *"the weigher"* (Isa. 33:18). So here Job is crying out, O that my grief were weighed, as gold and silver is carefully and exactly weighed, down to the least bit of it, then you would fully know what it is like, how heavy it lies upon me.

But the word is actually doubled here, for the original says, *"O that my grief were in weighing weighed."* And when a word is doubled, or by a Hebraism repeated, it heightens and increases the sense exceedingly. Therefore, laying all this together, it imports this, that Job asks that the entire weight of his grief be put into the scales of judgment at once. It is not right that they should take this word or that passionate outburst and spend their time judging him for those, when there is far more to be weighed and considered than the aftermath of his crushing blows. Circumstances often alter cases, and words spoken in a fit of passion should cause the judge to examine carefully the circumstances surrounding the event.

"And my ruin laid in the balances together!"—Reciprocating causes are feeding each other, in that Job's calamity causes him grief, and his grief in turn has caused him the calamity of this day, when his friends falsely accuse him and turn coldly away from any consideration of his condition. The word translated ruin is any kind of misfortune or evil-happening which is very destructive to a man's life. And the original for balances is a very elegant word, being found only in the plural (or dual) number. The same word in Hebrew signifies the ears, the organ of hearing — and the reason given is this, that as the tongue or bar between the scales is balanced, inclining toward neither side, so the ear of a fair judge will stand indifferent to both parties until he has heard their matters debated fully, with the reasons on both sides being carefully weighed before him on the scales of justice.

"laid in the balances"—actually Job desires that his side will ascend in the balances when all matters concerning his grief are laid upon the scales of justice.

"together"—there is some difference in opinion about the word. Some say he means this, that both his grief and calamity should be weighed together, not leaving half on a side to be weighed at another time. Some think that he is indicating that both his grief and his calamity should be weighed against the weight of the sand of the sea. Another says that he wants his grief put into one balance, his calamity in another, that it may be seen which of these two is the greater.

It is a fair assumption that Job wants his clamoring, passionate words, which spring out of his grief, to be weighed along with all his considerate amount of grieving emotions in one scale. In the other scale he wants his calamity to be weighed against his grief — that is, all that has happened to him, the loss of his goods, his children, the estrangement of his wife, and the loss of his wellbeing, plus the estrangement and false accusations of his friends. By such a comparison he means to prove that all his excessive grief, his passionate words, his extravagant and unwarrantable impatience, and his yearning to be put out of his misery, when weighed against his afflictions, his destroyed life, would then prove to be nothing compared to his calamities. Any fool could judge and see that he has not erupted nor boiled over nearly so much as the occasions would be expected to excite in him.

If it be thought that he means the same thing, that his grief and his calamity are one, then they together would outweigh anything that his friends may fairly put into the other side of the scale—then the meaning would appear to be that which was expressed in the first phrase, and then doubled here. It is certain that Job by all this seems to desire that his case be thoroughly canvassed and his conduct thoroughly examined, to be well-weighed and pondered in the scale of right reason and sound judgment, by men of equal and impartial characters. He at least is tacitly suggesting that his friends are not such men, therefore he yearns for one who will undertake this fair and proper judgment of his case.

"For now it would be heavier than the sand of the sea; therefore my words are swallowed up"–Job 6:3.

To prove that his calamity was heavier than his grief, he adds these words. The sand of the sea is applied three ways in Scripture:

1. It is an expression used to set forth an exceeding great number (see Gen. 22:17).

2. It is used to express the extent or capacity of a thing. The sand of the sea extends beyond the vast sea itself, so it is indicated that this sand of the sea cannot be measured (Jer. 33:22). It said that God gave Solomon *"largeness of heart as the sand of the sea,"* that is, as the sand encompasses and takes the sea into its arms, so Solomon had a heart which comprehended all the depths and oceans of knowledge (see 1 Kings 4:29).

3. The sand of the sea is applied to Scripture to note the exceeding weight and heaviness of a thing. Here Job does not merely want his calamity weighed against sand, which is heavy enough in itself, but against the sand of the sea — which is much heavier, being soaked with another heavy substance, water. But again, the word is not singular, but he suggests that his ruin is heavier than the sand of the seas — all the seas, and all the sand in and of those seas. In this hyperbole, Job reaches a high strain of eloquence, choosing out expressions which will not only add to the weight of the words, but will multipy them one by another.

To take in all three of these pregnant and fruitful meanings, we see that Job has an exceeding great number of calamities and griefs weighing him down. We see that the extent of these is immeasurable, and that his situation seems to have a capacity for unspeakable loads of grief and ruin — which seem to be still falling upon him and crushing him cruelly. And we see that his heaviness of heart is but a faint expression of the real weight that has pinned down his spirit, that his explosive remarks are but weak vents of steam which do not do justice to the pressures that have built up on and in him.

AFFLICTIONS ARE HEAVY BURDENS INDEED

The judgments of God upon wicked men are frequently called burdens (as often in the prophets). But so may afflictions upon the godly be spoken of as heavy, as burdensome, as grievous sorrows. And as affliction is because of sin, that is, no one is afflicted except sinners, or one bearing their sins, so sins in themselves are heavy, burdensome and sorrow-begetting. In a figure, even God depicts Himself (in an anthropomorphism) as being burdened by the sins of men, *"I am pressed under your sins, as a cart is pressed that is full of sheaves"* (Amos 2:13). But of all afflictions, inward afflictions are the greatest burdens. As the spirit of a man is stronger than his flesh, so afflictions which weigh down the spirit of a man are far heavier than those that are upon his flesh. The pain and ruin of his body does not trouble Job nearly so much as the wound in his spirit caused by his impression that God had inflicted him without the kind of causes suggested by his friends. Just as the pain of the nails in his body were nowhere as crushing as the thought that God had forsaken Him, in the case of the Lord Jesus in His sufferings — so here we have Job trying to keep his spiritual head above the floods of destruction and grief which are tearing at his spirit. Now his friends found Job's wounded spirit impossible to bear, that is why they weigh in so heavily upon him. But how much more difficult do you think it was for Job himself, for he must bear this wounded spirit — there was nowhere he could pass it on — and without God's help, there was nothing he himself could do to assuage it.

How proud and presumptuous is man, when he would make himself the judge of others! Here Job's friends recklessly make judgments about him without the slightest thought of taking into account his afflictions. That is to say, they were not sensible of the afflictions. They were merely observing them outwardly, and judging him as great a sinner as was his afflictions. They see that the afflictions are great, but they do not permit themselves to apply a single drop of mercy before they issue their judgments. This man's wounds are stinking, and his heart is breaking, but they feel not so much as a throb on their own heartstrings.

They see God's justice as a mechanical reaction, or as a sort of chemical reaction. When a man reacts with obvious providential pressures from God, the measure of his affliction is evidence of the extent of his sins. Given this false premise, one that they certainly did not glean from the Scripture — not even the orally transmitted Scripture, if that is all that they had — they inexorably apply this impersonal and unfeeling principle to its furtherest point of cruelty when they lay it upon Job as a truth which they claim has been searched out and corroborated. How different was He who is described as *"a Friend closer than a brother!"* He was One who was *"touched with the feeling of our infirmities, being in all points tempted as we are"* (Heb. 4:15). Let men fail in their duty to have pity and to be merciful, the Lord Jesus shall carefully weigh our griefs and our calamities against the circumstances.

For no one can ever rightly judge another until he has thoroughly weighed the condition of the other. How easy it is to be uncharitable when one does not stop to consider what may have triggered a man's fall. But even the most careful and exact weighing of a man's condition cannot result in a fair and charitable sentence unless the judge himself has felt the afflicting circumstances. He who would judge the afflicted must have been afflicted himself, else he will go astray when he does so. No more can a sandhog judge the work of an artist, than can the non-afflicted judge the culpability and sensitivity of the afflicted. Just as a man cannot know what it is to be spiritually comforted until he has been made spiritually alive, so a man cannot know what it is to be afflicted in the spirit until he has had this experience himself. Most acute is the disparity when it comes to spiritual sorrows — how impossible it is for the Christian who has never had the feeling that God has forsaken him enter into a judgment of one who has now entered this appalling experience of the terror which accompanies the hiding of God's face. It is true that God has promised that He will never leave us or forsake us, but that does not mean that He never withdraws the sense of His presence from us — as He did from the Lord Jesus on the cross. It is the utmost test of faith, and it is usually reserved for those who are His darlings — read again Psalm 51. How presumptuous then is it for another Christian to judge a man to be sinful and hypocritical when he has suffered the loss of the sense of God's presence!

On the other hand, how much comfort is afforded to such persons when they have as a counselor and helper one who has been through this fearful and awesome experience. The Lord Jesus was tempted in all points as we are. For what reason? So that He might be able to feel our infirmities, our afflictions, our calamities. So ought we to be, just like Him.

"therefore my words are swallowed up"—The Hebrew word signifies a licking up, or a swallowing down. By a metaphor it means to destroy or to consume. So here it is as if Job is complaining that as soon as he speaks he finds the words snatched away and gobbled down by the sharp teeth and devouring stomach of his grief and sorrows.

However, many constructions can be put upon the words — most of which expound the others. For instance, (1) it could mean that Job finds that language is too narrow for the vastness of his sorrows; or, (2) that his words come out bitter because he has swallowed down gall and wormwood, therefore it is no wonder if his words taste of them; or, (3) the sorrows which are in my mind and heart flow out upon my tongue; or, (4) my words fall short because there is a weight upon me which is heavier than the sand of the seas — I find it impossible to make my expressions come up to my intentions, because every time I open my mouth some of those churning, supercharged emotions gurgitate and cause my spiritual utterances to be stillborn. Like a stammerer who finds that his haste to speak eats up his words before he can get them out, so Job finds that his words are blotted out, or even corrupted by his grief as he seeks to emit them.

Passionate speech is subject to breaks and excesses. The cool, calculated, unflawed, speech is never a passionate one. Passion is the result of heat and pressure, and these two are usually able to affect a person so as to bring forth hot emissions and tearing eruptions. Therefore it was foolish to take a person in Job's position, being weighed down by incalculable destructions, being heated with the friction and pressure that attend compression into a much more restricted posture than ever experienced before, and expect from him the carefully chosen and measured words of the uninvolved.

Moreover, it may be that Job is saying that he has not yet been able to speak his mind, due to the fact that his words have been swallowed up or interrupted by his grief. Is he saying, *"even admitting that my speech thus far has been imperfect, yet do not be scandalized by it, but be patient until I can again bring up the words which have been snatched away from me and swallowed down."* Not being able to express our grief is an aggravation of it, and it may be that grief will then be multiplied by the scattered thoughts and emotionally constricted throat of the distracted one.

Lastly, the words may fairly be rendered, *"therefore my words break out with heat."* This would answer to the hot and passionate manner in which Job has spoken.

"For the arrows of the Almighty are within me, the poison of which drinks up my spirit; the terrors of God set themselves in order against me"–Job 6:4.

Though words are poor vehicles for conveying the depth and breadth of Job's grief, yet they are all that he has to work with. Therefore, he proceeds to give another dimension to the picture he is drawing of his distress, this time by comparing them with an arrow for sharpness and with an army for terribleness.

In this verse we must open up a quiver full of poisoned arrows, we must marshall an army full of divine terrors. An arrow is a deadly thing, called in Hebrew a death-dealing engine. Properly, of course, it is an instrument of death shot out of a bow. Here it is figurative, as is usual in the Scriptures, where they are taken in these many ways:

1. By arrows, the word of God is sometimes meant, *"Your arrows are sharp in the heart of the king's enemies"* (Ps. 45:5). God's words are sharp and piercing, by them He convicts and beats down sinners, either converting them or destroying them by the hammer of His word. The rider on the white horse goes out to conquer with a bow in his hand, which is conceived to be for the conveying of God's truth, that His words may triumph.

2. Arrows are put for the bitter and reproachful words of men, *"they bend their bows to shoot their arrows, even bitter words"* (Ps. 120:4).

3. They are put for any evil or mischievous purposes which a man intends to use to hurt his fellow men, *"when he bends his bow to shoot his arrows, let them be as though they were cut off"* (Ps. 58:7). Bending of the bow depicts the preparing and setting up of mischief. The arrow shot out of this bow is the mischief acted and finished.

4. Arrows are put for any kind of affliction, judgment or punishment, *"And the Lord shall be seen over them, and His arrow shall go forth as the lightning"* (Zech. 9:14). This may be a famine, *"the evil arrows of famine"* (Ezek. 5:16); for pestilence, *"You shall not be afraid for the terror by night, nor for the arrow that flees by day"* (Ps. 91:5). The next verse explains that this is pestilence. When God sends thunderbolts or hailstones from the heavens upon wicked men, these are called the arrows of His indignation (2 Sam. 22:15). Arrows from God may also signify afflictions of the mind, soul or spirit. God often shoots an arrow which pierces into the very soul, *"O Lord, do not rebuke me in Your wrath...for Your arrows stick fast in me"* (Ps. 38:1,2).

The arrows here are those afflictions, both external and internal, which God has fastened in and upon Job, galling him in body, soul and spirit. They are described in two ways: from their efficient cause, which is the Almighty; from their effect, that they drink up the spirit of Job.

They are the arrows of the Almighty (*Shaddai*). It is one of the names of God which expresses the power and omnipotence of God. It is God who bends the bow and shoots out afflictions upon and into Job. Because He is infinitely mighty and infallibly true, His arrows always hit their mark. They hit with devastating effect, making a wound exactly as deep as He had planned, and they cannot be drawn out, nor the wound from them healed until He pleases. *"He has prepared for him (the wicked) the instruments of death; He has made His arrows against the hot pursuers"* (Ps. 7:13). When God's enemies are so hit, they never get rid of God's arrows, nor can they recover from the poison of them. But when God wounds His friends with poisoned arrows, He will both draw them out and apply the antidote for the poison — besides comforting and teaching them all the while.

Arrows may be compared to afflictions in several ways, (1) both arrive speedily, (2) both come suddenly and unexpectedly. An arrow is upon a man before he knows it, and so are afflictions, (3) an arrow is felt before it is heard, it flies silently and secretly, stealing upon and wounding a man before it is seen. So it is with afflictions.

"the poison of which drinks up my spirit"—The word of the text is derived from a root which signifies to become hot or inflamed. By a metaphor it is translated anger, because angry men become hot and inflamed. And we get the meaning, poison, by a metonymy, because poisons usually heat and inflame the flesh and set the body on fire. Or it may be because an angry man seems to breathe out fire or to spit poison like an angry serpent. Whether the translation is anger or poison, the idea of inflammation is present, which will drink up the spirit of a man. Poison gets quickly to the spirit, being subtle and speedy in its progress toward a man's heart.

There are different interpretations of what the expression *"drinks up my spirit"* may mean. Some say it is the breath. As if Job says, I have been wounded by these poisoned arrows so that I am faint and cannot breathe. Others understand it more generally, taking the spirit for his strength and vigor. In which case, Job would be saying that all his powers and abilities of both body and soul were wasted and consumed by the arrows of the Almighty. The same for those who conceive that it is his reason and understanding that are meant by spirit here.

"the terrors of God set themselves in order against me"—Here we have the same thought, in different clothing. Although it could be that the arrow is put for the affliction, and terror is then put for the effect or consequent of it. The word used for terror is one that signifies a most terrible terror. Terror, of course, is the extreme of fear. These are called the terrors of God either by the common Hebraism which would distinquish them as very great terrors, or because He was the One who sent and commanded this army of terrors.

These terrors of God may be taken either actively or passively. If actively, it is that work of God in terrifying and troubling. If passively, it is for those afflictions which oppress the mind. When God leads that army against us, encamping around us with terrible instruments of affliction, then there is reason to be distracted and unhinged in our minds. A man may feel the terror of the Lord either from without, by the forces that come to bear upon the outward man; or, he may feel that terror which comes from inward forces, *"the word outside and the terror inside shall destroy both the young man and the virgin"* (Deut. 32:25).

Inwardly, the terrors of God may afflict us when our sins are set in array before the eyes of our conscience. And surely when God hides His face from us, there arises out of that darkness an army of terrors. In Job's case, there seems to have been a definite withdrawal of the comforting presence of God which was normal in his life. Along with this darkness came the astonishing events, the losses, the pains, the disappointment, the treacheries, etc. All of these could have erected themselves into fearful enemies attacking him day and night, for even relatively unafflicted people are aware of this kind of nightmare. What then must be the case with poor Job, with his whole world blasted, and his whole being one great bundle of pain and terror!

"set themselves in order against me"—He pictures the Lord as having studied to be exact and exquisite in afflicting him. An army of sorrows, griefs, pains and terrors has been especially prepared for the purpose of assaulting Job. This was not a chaotic and confused horde of bandits which happened along and set upon Job. By now we know that the first battle was set in array by Satan, who marshalled the forces which took away Job's possessions. No doubt he also set Job's wife against him, and his friends, as well as the affliction which destroyed his health. Yet when the ultimate credit is given, we see that the providence of God is seen to be the force behind it all. Job recognized this, and he sees God's hand carefully selecting out those terrors which are to be used against Job. Even if Satan is permitted to be the general in the field, it is God who drew the plans and who gave command as to what was actually to be executed against Job.

Some observations may be made from the verse before us:

1. Afflictions come sometimes by multitudes, seemingly endless and apparently infinite in their power to destroy us. There are cases where you see one man and one affliction, and there is a battle between them, perhaps for a lifetime. The apostle Paul was given but one answer when he sought the Lord's help in removing his affliction, *"My grace is sufficient for you."* Other times a man is inundated with troubles and conflicts, with a thousand temptations thrown in. Job is in such a period, when legions of evil spirits are swarming over him, leaving him no time to breath, no composure to think, no energy to act.

2. God sometimes appears as an enemy to His own servant. Job expected favor and help from God, as he had experienced times without number. The very shocking realization that God was not going to rescue and comfort him in these greater-than-ever distresses may have terrified him as much as anything else that happened to him. And consider this, that God described Job as a holy man, one who loved God and hated evil – then think of him feeling the arrows of the Almighty smashing into him, experiencing the draining of his spirit and comfort from him, and realizing that he may be the subject of God's anger. When one you love with all your heart is angry with you, how painful and grievous it is! One who for many years has been used to spiritual milk and honey cannot but find it all but impossible to survive on the polluted bread and bitter products of one's own nature.

3. If God is one's enemy, there is no holding out against His power. As soon as he realized that it was God's arrows and God's army of terrors appearing against him, how pitifully did Job cry out! This man had courage and might, and in his first battle with Satan came off clearly unscathed. But all his strength left him when his Hope left him to face the terrible forces that God arrayed against him.

But what can be said to people who have never experienced these arrows of destruction from the bow of the Lord God? You can make them understand something of plague and pestilence, of broken bones and burning fevers – they may fear and tremble over these things. But tell them of the arrows of the Almighty being shot into the spirit, of the terror of the Lord being marshalled against the inward man, of the hiding of God's face, and what do you perceive – nothing! They haven't the faintest notion what you are talking about. Only those few who have been there, who have felt these, who have sunk under such afflictions, will vicariously feel pain and sorrow when hearing of someone being hit with the arrows of the Almighty. Especially let unbelievers beware that these things do not come upon them. Yes, for the moment they may feel secure, fat and happy (by their definition of the word). But he warns in Ps. 50:21, *"I will reprove you and set your sins in array before your eyes."* When He does that, pray that it shall not be when you are standing before the judgment seat of Christ on that Day. For if He shall afflict you now, bringing you to the end of yourself, all your resources having failed you, there is hope that you will turn to Him and put your trust wholly and fully in Him.

"Does the wild ass bray when he has grass? Or does the ox low over his fodder?"–Job 6:5.

The Hebrew word for a wild ass comes from a root which means *"to bring forth,"* and the reason is because wild beasts usually are more fruitful and productive than tame animals. The word also denotes wild in general, being applied to wild and savage men, wild places, etc. The word is used when Ishmael is prophesied to become a *"wild man."*

And of course it would not be usual for a wild ass to bray when he has grass to eat. On the other hand, lacking grass, he would bray loudly. This animal is very impatient when hungry or thirsty.

"Or does the ox low over his fodder?"–The meaning is repeated here, with another animal to teach the lesson. Whether wild or tame, there is quiet and composure to those animals who have their regular provisions before them. Brute beasts do not complain, then, without a cause. But given a situation where their normal provisions are taken away, they complain loudly. Among men, of course, there are those who complain and grouse whatever their lot – though they may be provisioned far more richly than most other men. The ox knows his owner, the ass knows his master, the stork knows her appointed times,

"but My people do not know the judgment of the Lord" (Jer. 8:7). Men by nature are far worse than the beasts. The Psalmist charges it upon himself that he was as a beast (Ps. 73:22) —but when nature fails, grace will not. Grace will not bray or low, whether or not there is provision made. Still, even though Job did not fail this test when all his possessions were swept away, and even when his wife forsook him, there is a limit to a man's ability to hold back complaints — and that limit is strictly according to the grace of God operating in his life. Observe that Job failed in part, in that he complained bitterly about the uselessness in his life as it was now being lived. But his faith never failed, that is, his faith never completely failed. He staggered and tottered under the tremendous blows from God's arrows, and it may appear to the reader here that he is certain to fall if they continue. Yet God in mercy secretly strengthened him each time he was ready to give up the fight for the glory of God. His sinking spirit actually begins to get stronger as he survives each new onslaught.

"Can that which has no taste be eaten without salt? Or is there any taste in the white of an egg?"—Job 6:6.

Continuing with his defense, Job follows his argument that he can reasonably be expected to complain when his provisions have been removed with this one, that he cannot be expected to be senseless and stony when he is being fed tasteless and unseasoned food. How much more then could he be expected to complain when he is having bitter and disgusting things thrust down his throat.

"Can that which has no taste"—the word is the same one used in Job 1:22, where it is said that Job did not charge God foolishly. He was not tasteless or unsavory in his comments upon God, or in his thoughts about Him. The word has three applications mainly, (1) it is applied to unpleasant food, (2) to untempered mortar, (3) to indiscreet speeches, which lack the seasoning of wit, wisdom and truth. The lying visions of false prophets are described with this word (Lam 2:14).

Seasoning makes tasteless things into desirable food. And as salt gives a relish to food, so gracious wisdom gives a relish to our words. In Latin, in fact, gracious speech and salt are expressed by the same word.

"or is there any taste in the white of an egg?"—none at all. These words are much obscured by most translators. One may find almost as many expositions as expositors. The Vulgate, for instance, translates it thus, *"Is there any taste in that which being taken brings death."* However, to clear up the meaning as they give it, they made the Hebrew word that we translate *"egg"* to be a compound which signifies to die. Others translate it, *"Is there any taste in the spittle of a healthy man,"* making the word which we translate white to signify spittle or froth (as in 1 Sam. 21:13). But this to me is a very diseased interpretation.

The word signifies strictly the white or the spittle of the yolk. The root word means to become fat or strong, and therefore is taken for the yolk of the egg because that is the fatter, most condensed part of the egg. However, the white of an egg is the emblem of things without taste, and the sum of this proverbial speech (as I see it) is to note that the tasteless and insipid things being presented to Job have no relish at all for him. He heightens the antipathy in the next words.

"My soul refuses to touch them; they are as sorrowful food to me"—Job 6:7.

In this verse we get the application and explication of both the former similitudes. The things which Job's soul refused are those things which he could not abide. To desire with the soul implies the sweetest delight (Isa. 26:9), so to refuse with the soul imports the strongest and bitterest averseness. This word translated refuse in this context would be used to picture nausea. Job's stomach has been turned by the things that he must swallow in his affliction.

"they are as sorrowful food to me"—That which a man finds too filthy to touch with his finger, he surely will not put into his mouth and chew it, let alone swallow it down willingly. So Job's meaning seems to be this, that what he desired to be the greatest stranger from was now being offered to him daily as his familiar acquaintance. He was now being

forced to eat that which he would not before touch, therefore it is called sorrowful food.

The right application of these words is as difficult as the translation of them. At least two of them appear to be most likely; (1) that all these unsavory, tasteless, sorrowful foods which Job mentions are but the shadows of his afflictions and troubles received from the hand of God; (2) or, that they are shadows of the counsels and reproofs which he had just received from the mouth of Eliphaz.

1. Some refer and apply all to the troubles which were upon Job. Then these words are a fuller justification of himself, he is telling why he has cause to complain, because his grass and his fodder (that is, his comforts) were taken from him. Now, he calls attention to the fact that he is being forced upon a diet of sorrow; a distasteful, grievous, galling and bitter life of affliction. From this sense we may note that the things that we hate today may be made our steady diet at another time. There is a saying, that one man's meat is another man's poison — but the day may come when the same man's meat may be his own poison. Those in Lamentations are a good example (they were brought up in scarlet, but they embraced dunghills). Secondly, we learn here that the things which makes afflictions most grievous to us is the unsuitableness of our spirits to those afflictions. Delight and contentment come only when our affections and desires meet with objects that suit them. God offers spiritual food to the natural man, but his soul refuses even to touch it. He hates heavenly food, he quickly becomes weary of the manna of the word of God. The precious gospel, the very bread of true life, is an affliction to an unbeliever, because his heart is not fitted to receive it. How miserable will these be at the last, when they find that they will have as their sorrowful food forever that which their souls abominate most — the never-ending witness of the word of God to their rebellious and sinful natures. Those who hate Jesus Christ and His ways will find nothing in the end to please their corrupt palates — that which is most contrary to their appetite shall be their daily portion.

2. But these words may all be applied to Eliphaz as well. Job's ready submission to the afflicting hand of God in the first and second chapters argues that afflictions were not the things which his soul refused to touch — however grievous they may be. Therefore, it may fairly be doubted whether the falling from a position of authority and riches, of delicate living and blooming health, is at the bottom of these words of Job. Perhaps the Septuagint translation better shows his meaning, for there we read, *"Is there any taste in vain words?"* In which case, the words of Eliphaz are being compared to the white of an egg, to meat without salt, and to other nauseating fare. It appears to be bold and unwarrantable for these Greek translators to so depart from the original text, putting down what they judged was the meaning, instead of actually translating the words. Yet it is evident that they strongly felt that this is the meaning of Job's words here. And most of the Greek writers held to this view, that the counsels and speeches of Eliphaz lacked the seasoning of wisdom and prudence — that they were unsound and untrue as applied to the spirit of a man as sick as was Job.

One has paraphrased Job's words along these lines, as follows: 'I would not have complained of the things which you have spoken if they had been meat suitable for my consumption. But I assure you that your counsels are not nourishing to me. I can find no food, much less any sweetness or fatness in them. Your counsels lack the due seasoning of wisdom, the right temperament of holy zeal, the warmth of lovingkindness. They are tasteless and unsavory. Not only are they not refreshing, but they are a burden to me. And the remedy you prescribe is worse than the disease. How can I submit and subscribe to your advise when it does not fit my state or my spirit any more than saltless meat suits my taste. Therefore my soul refuses and rejects what you have spoken. Instead of mitigating my sorrows, you have added to them.'

An objection has been entered against this, one ancient commentator being angry with those who make this application to the counsels of Eliphaz — for, says he, 'Let no man think that this holy man despised the counsel of his friend, who himself was humble,' To which this answer may be given: The counsels of Eliphaz were good and savory doctrine which may have been wholesome food for someone else. But in Job's case, he was quite mistaken in applying these truths to the man. Therefore, without doubt, he managed to trouble the man instead of easing his pain. A physician could possibly give a sick patient medicine which was very good indeed, but this good medicine given to the wrong patient could result in death for the patient, instead of a cure. The only truly useful and successful physician is the one who is wise enough to give the right medicine to the right patient. If, then, a man sets up a practice of curing souls, as a spiritual physician, then he must bend all his efforts and skills to learn enough about his patients that will enable him to give the right prescription. If he does not do so, that which he intends to give spiritual quickening may actually prove to be spiritually deadening. Even Christ, talking to his spiritually blessed disciples, said this, *"I have many things to say to you, but you cannot bear them now"* (John 16:10). There are times when a man may bear that which before he was too weak to receive. The apostle Paul was made all things to all men (1 Cor. 9:2) so that he might become wise in prescribing spiritual medicine for the wise and the foolish, for the weak and the strong, speaking the right truths to every degree and sort of men at the right time. To rightly divide the word of God may include not only making the right interpretation of the words themselves, but also the right application of them to the right person at the right time.

Plainly, in the case of Job, Eliphaz has not prescribed the right spiritual medicine. However well earned his reputation as a wise man may have been, to Job he was a physician of no value! A healer who brings the wrong portion, mistakes the kind and extent of the disease, then forces this nauseous brew down the throat of the protesting patient, is not only of no value, he is a menace to the wellbeing of the patient. Words that are true in themselves may by the wrong application of them become a dangerous, even deadly false accusation. The apostle warns us, *"Let your speech be always with grace, seasoned with salt"* (Col. 4:6). Our advice must not only be seasoned with the salt of truth, but with the salt of wisdom and discretion as well. God Himself tells us in Job 42:7 that Eliphaz lacked this salt in his speeches to Job, *"You have not spoken of Me what is right,"* — as Job did.

"O that I might have my desire, and that God would grant me the thing that I long for!" —Job 6:8.

Job has been defending his right to complain, or at least excusing himself for having been guilty of speaking unadvisedly with his lips. Now he begins to renew and reinforce his desire to depart from the land of the living. He not only maintains and justifies what he has already said, but he again begins to beg for death as heartily and importunately as he did in the third chapter. He begins in this verse and continues in the next to express his strong desire to be taken away from this world. In verses 10 through 12 he gives his reasons.

"O that I might have my desire"—It appears that Job in this passage is assuring his companions that his faith is firm and his comforts flowing from it were sweet — that it was not impatience caused by his troubles in his life which caused him to yearn for death, but rather that it was the comforts of the next life which pulled him on to that longing. He has such a strong assurance of the comforts of this next life that he triumphs and glories even in the midst of his most painful approaches to death. And these hopes made him able to despise all the hopes of this life. These hopes held out to him by Eliphaz, of being restored to health and wealth in this life, seem pale to him now, for he has gotten hold of a better world, one where temporal happiness cannot be even compared to that eternal happiness which is so real to him. The thing that he longs for is not the grave, but that which lies beyond the grave. It is not so much that he longs to escape the misery of this life, it is that he lustily desires the presence of God. What physical health can be compared to that spiritual health which comes from being in the bosom of God? What worldly wealth can be compared to the riches and treasures that are in God Himself? That Job did not consider these things to be a fancy or a dream can be easily seen by His words, for he shows that he believes he has good proof and real evidence of the life and communion he is shortly to have with God.

The original Hebrew is literally, *"O that my petition might come."* He has sent up a request, an earnest prayer for death, and he yearned to receive the answer from God. As is so often the case, every hour seems to be a year when one is waiting for something he desires with all his heart. The word here denotes a very strong desire, a strong cry, a mighty longing, such as are accredited to Christ, *"in the days of His flesh, when He had offered up prayers and supplications with strong cryings and tears to Him who was able to save Him from death, and was heard in that He feared"* (Heb. 5:7). Only Job's cries are that he may be delivered up unto death. And there is no doubt but what he was heard, in that he also feared God with a holy faith — but God did not specifically grant him his request.

"and that God would grant me the thing that I long for"—He repeats his desire in other words, a multiplication and intensifying of the thought according to Hebrew usage. He is not only importunate in prayer, it is obvious that he expects an answer. A man who puts up a prayer should be like a man who sows a seed in the earth, he should expect something to come of it, and that it should be exceedingly beyond all that he sowed (prayed). Like Habakkuk, Job is set upon an answer, *"I will stand upon my watch and set myself upon the tower, and I will watch to see what He will say to me"* (Hab. 2:1). Furthermore, Job shows himself a better exegete than most, for he sees the answer to prayer as a grant, an undeserved favor from God. Nothing stands between Job and the thing he desired but the will of God! Let Him say, I will! Then let some man presume to defeat His purpose! But then God often finds it not according to His will that the exact request of His children be granted. Like earthly fathers, the heavenly Father finds altogether too often that His children ask amiss, or ask that they may spend upon their lusts, or ask ignorantly because they have not taken the time to study His word and His person. Still He hears, and there is a sense in which He always gives an answer to every prayer put up in faith, in accordance with His word and will. Such an answer He gave to Paul, not what he requested, not what he longed for, but this, *"My grace is sufficient for you."* Sometimes there will come a strengthening of faith, or some other fruit of the Spirit will become more abundant in the heart and life of the petitioner, which may properly be called an answer to any prayer which carried at the end of it that most important ingredient, *"Your will be done, not mine."*

"Even that it would please God to destroy me; that He would loose His hand and cut me off"—Job 6:9.

Some would read it, *"that He who has begun would now make an end in destroying me."* For the word can mean both to be willing to do a thing and to begin to do it. Job, of course, considered himself on the brink of the grave. So it would be in context to read it in this way, that he wanted God to finish the job which He had started, the carrying of Job off the stage of life.

But rather take it in the other sense, as we translate it, that Job is praying for God to destroy him, to cut him-off. In this sense, he would be praying that it might be God's will. In the other sense, he would be presuming to know God's will.

The word translated destroy is one that is used for beating a thing to powder, to pieces. As the Psalmist said of his enemy, that he had beaten him into the dirt (the same word as here), so Job here longs for the Lord to beat him back into the dust he was formed out of. It is a word (*daka*) variously translated, to bruise, to be broken, etc. An especially interesting translation is that in Isaiah 57:15, *"I dwell in the high and holy place, even with him who is of a contrite and humble spirit."* That which is translated contrite is the word here. God dwells with those who have their spirits beaten to powder, for a broken and contrite heart best equip them for dwelling in His presence. And Job's contrition is apparent to all who will but study his words, from the beginning until the end. This was no sudden fit of longing to be out from under his burden. His call for death is not a hasty one, one that he would withdraw if his circumstances were to improve. Rather we find it is a settled desire on his part, he woos destruction. His is a sad condition indeed, lying there under all these varied and innumerable weights, but instead of crying to have them removed, as would be expected, he cries again and again, 'More weight! Please put on more weight that I may be crushed to pieces, that I may be returned to dust. Some of the martyrs experienced a similar situation, having a strong desire to depart and be with the Lord Jesus, they cried out, More fire! More fire! counting the cruel flame their friend for sending them to Heaven. As dear Latimer suffered in the fire, he complained, 'O, I cannot burn!' So here Job is crying and complaining, 'O, I cannot die!'

"that He would loose His hand and cut me off!"—Again the petition is doubled in order to make it most emphatic. The picture is of one loosing the bonds so that another might use his hands and feet — we see it in Psalm 146:7, *"The Lord lets the prisoners loose."* Job depicts the Lord as if He had His hand bound, but the truth is that God can (so to speak)— overmatch anyone with but a word from His mouth. But Job prays that God will unloose His hand and cut him off from the living. Or, it could possibly be that he is asking that Satan may be let loose to cut him off, remembering those words of God, *"spare his life."* The word translated *"cut off"* is one meaning to cut off with an insatiable appetite for revenge. As if he should say, Do not spare my blood, let Satan that bloodsucker come and do his worst against me.

From this we see that God acts as He pleases. He may loose His hand, or not, as He will. He controls our estates, our bodies, our very lives. When He *"opens the hand of mercy, He satisfies the desire of every living thing"* (Ps. 145:2); and when He looses the hand of His judgments, He takes away anything and everything that He desires to cut off from us.

"Then I should yet have comfort; yea, I would rejoice in pain, though He did not spare me; for I have not hidden the words of the Holy One"—Job 6:10.

First, he spelled out his request. Now he tells us his reasons, what would be the effect if his request is granted. He is certain that if God will grant him his desire it will be a great comfort to him. Nothing is so comforting, so cheering, so encouraging to a man as the knowledge that he has had his most importunate prayer answered. Job obviously believes that there is no comfort left for him this side of the great divide, and he does not even want to travel the path back which Eliphaz has consistently held out to him as his hope — he wants to go on quickly, to rest in peace, to enjoy himself in the bosom of God.

"yea, I would rejoice in pain, though He did not spare me"—There are many ways that this can be translated, and therefore there is great diversity of comment also. There are three major ways these two phrases are translated:

1. *"Yea, I would harden myself in sorrow — let Him not spare,"*—KJV
2. *"though I should scorch (or parch) with pain, and though God should not spare me"* —Broughton, many other older commentators, translators.
3. *"Yea, I would rejoice in pain, though He did not spare me"*—KJVT, Septuagint, RSV, many others.

Taking it as the first of these three, *"I would harden myself in sorrow,"*—then Job is saying that if he only had the comfort of knowing that his death would soon come, he could harden himself in his sorrow and endure gladly to the end. It is easier to bear pain and all forms of misery if we know that the end is coming soon. In such cases, it is possible to put on a hardened layer cushioned by hope, and to continue to the end without complaint. The sharpest pangs, the most piercing arrows for the afflicted are those thoughts that this time of horror upon horror shall never end—it will be one of the severest judgments upon those who have despised and trampled under foot the Lord Jesus that they shall be in torment, both from the flames of Hell and from the hopelessness of Hell.

Taking the second of these, *"though I should scorch with pain, and though God should not spare me"*—The original word in question, that which is being variously translated as *"harden," "scorch," "rejoice,"* or *"exult"* is a rare word, being in Scripture only this one time. The Jewish writers give us also a third possible meaning, *"to pray."* Though the pains should become even more scorching, and though God should not spare him any of a great number of other torments, Job thinks that he could pray and be comforted by the knowledge that God was going to loose His hand and cut him off. Or, taking the idea of heat, it may be that Job regards this good news that might come, that his days would soon end, as a warm blanket which would comfort him and keep him from fainting. It is more likely that if this meaning is adopted, there is the thought that even if God heats Job's furnace of afflictions seven times hotter, not sparing him one whit, yet he would have comfort in the thought that it would all soon end.

The third meaning, that which is in *King James Version, II*, and in other places, would carry this signification: Job is saying that the comforting thought of his early demise would be sufficient for him to leap for joy, to exult and rejoice exceedingly. Even if God did not spare His whip, His legions of afflictions could not keep Job from exulting and rejoicing, for his encouragement would overweigh all these things. The Septuagint and the Targum note that the word means to leap. The word in the Arabic language is used of a prancing and pawing horse, one who strikes with his foot and makes the ground shake, mocking at fear and exulting in his power to overcome the spear and shield. Job should not be thought to be proud and overly confident of his powers as a mere man — he shows this in the next and other verses. His comfort comes from God's power, and the knowledge that he was to be delivered from his present woes would cause him to exult and to rejoice only if he was confident that this was God's will for him, that he should now be given his reward, his good things in the life beyond.

"though He did not spare"—That it is possible to be comforted, even to exult and leap for joy in the face of God's impending blows can be seen in the case of the Lord Jesus Christ, who for the joy that was set before Him endured the pain and the shame of the Cross. God did not spare His only Son (Rom 8:32), yet Jesus was comforted in the jaws of His providentially prepared end, because He was aware of God's will and His part in fulfilling that will.

"for I have not hidden the words of the Holy One"—Job had the testimony of a good conscience, notwithstanding all the troubles which were upon him, even in the face of the harsh and false accusations splattered upon him by Eliphaz. No man, no force on earth can take that away from you. Satan himself, with the help of the Sabeans, Job's wife, a child-destroying whirlwind, and three pitiless friends could not destroy within the breast of Job the assurance that he had in sincerity, in pure conscience obeyed the will of God. Experience of grace may at some fleeting moment take on an unreal quality, but it will never prevail in one who has walked with God, obeyed His word and displayed His word to all who would listen to them. God testified to Job's fidelity, that he had been faithful in God's cause, to His truth, that he had been holy and forthright in declaring that truth.

There are four ways by which the word of God is sinfully hidden, and Job was innocent of them all, (1) We can conceal God's word by being silent, by not revealing them when God gives us the opportunity to give our witness by them — we should all be able to say with the apostle Paul, *"I have not shunned to declare to you the whole counsel of God.... I have kept nothing back that was profitable to you"* (Acts 20:20,27); (2) We can conceal God's word by silencing others — there are those who for their own selfish reasons keep back the words of God, and they will not endure others who would highlight this perfidy by speaking the word themselves, so they silence them by whatever means they may — as the chief priests and rulers ordered Peter and John not to speak or teach in Jesus' name; (3) God's word is most often hidden under false interpretations, given a shine and a gloss which the original word never favored — it is amazing how many who call themselves Christians will repeat old wives tales, will use heathen expressions (such as 'luck') and put forth for truth the commandments or proverbs of men (such as, God helps those who help themselves) — This is a most dangerous way of treating the words of the Holy One and let those who are following this foolhardy practice read in the Scriptures what happened to the Pharisees; (4) Our lives can hide the words of the Holy One — though we speak the word truly, even with the elegance and winsomeness of an angel's voice, we do most reprehensibly conceal the truth by acting as if we did not believe a word we speak in God's name — it is not enough to hold the truth, it is not enough to speak the truth, we must also be doers of the truth if we are truly to reveal the power of God's word to a corrupted and dying world. Job made his life such that he made God's word visible.

On the whole verse, contrast Job's strong grasp on the hopes of life after death, and his willingness to quickly pass over into that life, with good king Hezekiah. When told to prepare himself for death, Hezekiah turned his head to the wall and wept with a great weeping (2 Kings 20:3). He had this in common with Job, having just prayed these words to God (and no one ever contradicted them,) *"Remember now how I have walked before You in truth and with a sincere heart, and I have done good in Your sight."* Job also could pray this prayer. But Job goes a long step further than Hezekiah, praying earnestly that God would loose His hands and cut him off from this life. Yet of the two, Hezekiah had by far the advantage, having had the written Scriptures, the witness of God's dealings with His chosen people, whereas Job had only the oral transmission of Scripture.

"the Holy One"—It is a paraphrasis for God. The title is too big for any but God. Only God is truly holy. All holiness is in God. God is called the Holy One in three aspects, (1) In His nature, His essence is purity; He is essential purity; (2) He is holy in His word; (3) He is holy in His works; not the least imaginable stain or defilement has ever been on anything that He has done.

Putting the three together, God is holy in His person, His word and His works, therefore He is glorious in holiness, the Holy One who is our example, *"Be holy, even as I am holy."* That is also our motivation toward holiness, that He is holy. In His works, He is absolutely perfect in holiness — it cannot be otherwise, for God is holy in essence, therefore all His works being but extensions of Himself are so. Only God is thus holy. Angels are holy by an addition to their nature — for when they lost their first estate and became devils, they continued to be angels. Therefore an angel can be unholy. Angels, then, are not holy in essence. They are naturally angels, but they are not naturally holy. Likewise in men the holiness they have is a grace, a gift of God. When Adam lost his holiness, he did not lose his manhood. After all, holiness in man is but his conformity to God. We are denominated holy when we have become partakers of the divine nature, when we have become conformed to His image, when we have been brought into a voluntary obedience to His will. Only God can do all things to please Himself and still be holy. For man to be holy, he must do all things to please God, and he must not do things for the purpose of pleasing himself. No act of man is a holy act unless it is done for the glory of God, and that means that it must be done in order to please God. The measure of the holiness is in exact proportion to the willingness to completely abdicate one's own selfish desires in favor of the desires of God. Holy David was so because he was *"a man according to God's own heart"* (Acts 13:22).

If conformity to the nature of God, and conformity to the will of God makes a man to be holy, then the opposite is true of the unholy and the impure sons of men. If a man's garment has become dirty, it is said to be unclean. So inwardly, when a man in his mind and heart cleaves to anything which is not God, then that man becomes ungodly in direct proportion to the love and attention he gives to ungodly things. It does not matter if the object of his affection is clean in itself, the fact that this thing is held in esteem for any other reason than that it gives glory to God is enough to make it an unholy affection. A man so occupied with other things than God will find the distance between God and himself increasing at a rate of speed commensurate with his inattention to God's will. But if we with open face look upon the glory of the Lord, and seek His presence and His pleasure, then we shall *"be changed into the same image,"* (2 Cor. 3:18) and shall find ourselves becoming holy as He is holy. When Christ appears, we shall be like Him for we shall see Him as He is. But we need not wait so long, for if we will use all the means of grace available to us now to see Him as He is, to know Him as He can be known, then we shall be like Him more and more until that Day when He shall appear.

Here is a test of holiness. By this you can know whether you love the Holy One of Israel: If you will set your mind on Heaven, and for a concentrated time dwell upon the fact that all who go to that place shall be entirely, constantly and intensively taken with the presence of God. None will be permitted to do anything in Heaven except to continually please God. Are you happy at that thought? Are you willing to be like a candle against the sun, forever?

Or does it bother you that you will not have any personal recognition by others who are present. Do you feel just a little twinge of regret when you think of that day when you will never again be able to do anything simply to please yourself? Then remember this, that you thereby fail the test of holiness so far as you feel that way. A truly holy man not only should be able to say, *"Even so, come, Lord Jesus,"* he should also be far enough along in holiness to say and to feel that the greatest pleasure possible to a man is the pleasure of always and forever being dedicated to pleasing God, and Him only.

So Job finishes his first reason why he feels he can rightly call upon God to end his life.

"What is my strength, that I should hope? And what is my end, that I should be patient?" —Job 6:11.

Here Job appends two more reasons why he thinks he should be allowed to die, and why he feels he is ready to die, (1) he had no hope that he could live long, nor was there any strength left in him to enforce such a hope; (2) he did have a hope that he would live in another world, and he was convinced that death would be a gain, not a damage to him. Why should he desire to prolong a life which was being attended by a progressive weakening of the flesh, when he had a better end in view and a better hope as well?

"What is my strength, that I should hope?"—Eliphaz had advised Job to seek unto God, to commit his cause to Him, to seek help at His hands. Perhaps Job is saying here, Why do you think that I have not done that all this while? Do you believe that I have borne all these assaults in my own strength? Surely, even you should be able to see that I have been held up by the power of God, that God has put His everlasting arms under me. For what is my strength that I should be able to hope, or to bear these burdens this long? (These last words can be translated, *"that I should bear."*)

The basic meaning of the word being hope, however, and it implies a patient waiting combined with a hopeful trusting. To wait with hope is not easy at any time, for anyone. The depressing seeds of sin are within us, and when we hope it is necessary that we hope against hope with that faith which enthroned Abraham as the father of the faithful (see Romans 4:18). Abraham staggered not at the promise of God through unbelief. Neither do we see Job here stagger at the promise of God through unbelief, but rather he is fully persuaded that what God had promised He was also able to perform. Therefore it has for many millenniums been imputed to him for righteousness – yea, for all millenniums! The Job who is speaking is not the calm, cool, collected and intelligible Job who had been the chosen champion of God set forth in the first chapter of this Book. He has been hellishly assaulted with weapons both earthly and unearthly, he has been shattered by principalities and powers who are experts at taking sinners apart and causing them to curse God. To expect a man to stand against Satan, his hordes of fiendish angels, his multifaced army of unfeeling human beings (both avowed enemies and avowed friends), is to expect more than a man can do? Yet in all his distraction, amidst all his pains, even in spite of all his doubts, Job does stand against them all! For what is impossible to a man is not the question being asked in the book of Job. The question is this, what is possible for a man who hopes in God? What Job cannot do, God can do. For nothing is impossible with God.

"that I should hope"—The word is *yachal*, and it is this very same word that Job uses in his second most-quoted sentence, *"Though He slay me, yet will I trust in Him"* (13:15). For it is this same word that fits our meaning here, *"Even though He slay"* Job, *"yet even then he would still hope in Him."* But what is there to hope for when one is watching his last moments of life slipping away? Can one lie smitten and miserable at the portals of death, yet express David's hope, *"But I will always hope and will yet praise Thee more and more"*? Hope does not survive the grave, for if one goes into torment, there is no hope there – and if one goes into the presence of the Lord Jesus, there is no longer any need for hope, *"for what a man sees, why does he still hope for it?"* (see Ps. 71:14; Rom. 8:24). But it cannot be denied that as long as Job draws breath he also always hopes. As for praising God, that will leap the grave – yes, we shall priase him more and more forever and ever.

"and what is my end that I should be patient?"—Or, as in the original, *"that I should lengthen out my soul"*—The word which we translate life may be taken also for desire. For desire is a vehement act of the soul. The soul expresses itself so much in desires that the same word may express both. And so we may render Job's sense in this way also, 'What is my end that I should extend or prolong my desires any more after the things of this world'—or, 'that I should defer and put off my desires after the things of the world to come. Is there anything in this life worth my struggle to hold on to it, or anything so worthless in the next world that I should not wish to immediately begin enjoying it?' The word is often used in this sense, as in Gen. 23:8, and in Prov. 23:2 (*"if you are a man given to appetite"*—that is, if you are one whose desires are your lord and master).

"end"—This may be considered in two ways: (1) for the end of this life; (2) for the end of his troubles; or, (2) for the termination of his life, the last term of life.

(1) His end may be taken for that latter part of his life which Eliphaz had promised would be comfortable and very long, *"You shall come to your grave in a full age, like a shock of grain comes in its season."* But Job may be saying in response, your promise of good days and long life does not compare well with the usual state of a man in his last years. For then (as Barzillai said to David, 2 Sam. 19:35), the taste of meat and drink, the sound of music, etc. do not have the same pleasure-giving power that they had when one is in the Spring of life. In the Winter of life, there is cold and cloudiness and darkness. Is there a reason, says Job, that I should stretch out my life for that?

(2) But, rather, the meaning is this, the very last term of life. Not that latter part or condition of a man's life, troublesome old age, nor even a renewed estate here, but the termination of life is the end Job has in sight. What is my death that I should desire to live, he may well be saying. There is no evil in death that I should be afraid to have my life ended here and now. Nothing about dying can make me wish to spin out this troublesome life any longer. Surely the trouble and pain of death is not so much as the present trouble and pain of my life. What is this end, that I should desire to prolong my life?

MAN'S HOPE

In a man's greenest years, at the very peak of his strength in body, mind and soul, there is no reason for him to hope. What is youth, or strength, or beauty? They are all but temporary fruits to adorn man, having no lasting foundation for a man's hope, *"man in his best estate is altogether vanity"* (Ps. 39:5). He that hopes to live upon any of these things, anything in this life, is hoping in a vain thing, is trusting in shadows. Even our hope to live this natural life must be in the living God. How much more must our spiritual and eternal hopes be in Him? Death sits upon our shoulders when we are at the height of our strength and beauty. As our days grow longer, our days grow shorter. As we grow up, we are on our way out of this life. Even when we are flowering, we are withering. A truly wise man is he who regards this life as a short passage to death, and one who prepares for that death. Who is more miserable than the man who has hope only in this life? Who is happier than the man whose hope is in the life to come? Only He who is *"the Life"* can give a life that is never-ending, a life that is worth living for, a life that is worth dying for!

Death has no fears for a godly man. All the bitterness of death is removed, it is sweetened by Christ. Death may truly be the king of terror to a man in his sins, but it is a welcome doorway to everlasting felicity to a man whose sins have not been imputed to him. The Prince of life has abolished death for these, He has brought life and immortality to light by the Gospel. For the good news is this, that all the fears of death and the grace were buried with Christ in His grave, *"O death, where is your sting? O grave, where is your victory?"* (1 Cor. 15:55). When one who hopes in Christ attends his funeral, it is the funeral of his sorrows. And it is the resurrection of his joys. The man whose hopes are in this world says this, What is my end, that I should desire to die? He has reason to be afraid to die. Even Lot, though tormented with the filthy behavior of the wicked, showed that he had a mind to stay in Sodom. Yet he was persuaded by the heavenly messengers to leave.

But the natural men who live in the Sodom of this world cannot be persuaded that their best interests lie in another world. If they can, they put themselves out of hearing, so that they cannot hear the bells toll for them. They run behind the door, or hang onto some imaginary anchor, and they are many times still cursing and screeching when God finally thrusts them out of this world. It seems incredible that a man would not want to exchange this suit of clay for a suit of glory, to be clothed upon with immortality, with garments of everlasting praise! Yet all those who make themselves the objects of their affection have in doing so despised such a marvelously beneficent exchange.

"Is my strength the strength of stones? Or is my flesh of brass?"—Job 6:12.

These words may refer to the former part of the last verse, *"What is my strength that I should hope?"* What is this strength? Let us seriously examine and consider it. Is my strength the strength of stones? Or is it of brass. Am I strong enough to endure anything? Stones and brass are hard and heavy bodies that can bear blows and knocks without breaking. They do not yield easily to the hammer. It is hard to make an impression on them, even with violent strokes. To say a man is strong as a stone or as strong as brass is to give a man too much. Beasts are stronger than man, and they can endure more blows than he. Trees are stronger than beasts, and they can endure more. But stones are still stronger, a great many more blows must be struck to harm a stone. Therefore, when Job asks if his strength is supposed to be that of stones or brass, he is putting it to the utmost. He is saying. Even if a man had the strength of beasts, trees, stones and brass, he could not stand out against these crushing blows which have fallen upon me. But I am a man without the strength of these, and I am likewise one who feels the blows that rain upon him. A stone cannot feel the hammer. Brass cannot be pained. Am I a stone? Am I as brass, that I can be expected to feel all these things that are happening to me and yet not desire my end? I am made of flesh, he says, and I cannot fight everlastingly with these afflictions.

Man by nature is sensible of affliction and can be subdued by it. This body of clay is not an impregnable castle. Even a man's spirit, which is far stronger than his flesh, cannot hold out forever. Even the condemned ones shall be strengthened so that they may bear the wrath of God forever — flesh and blood would fail, their spirits would fail and faint at the first encounter with the everlasting burnings. They shall be made immalleable, their sense of pain shall be admirably quickened and yet they shall continue to be conscious of it. For without the strengthening hand of God, however, no man could stand even the afflictions of this world, the fires of affliction would consume him and he would perish.

"Is not my help in me? And is wisdom fully driven away from me?"—Job 6:13.

This and the next verse are of a very difficult construction, therefore hard to be understood. This is so much so that one learned interpreter said, If there is any hard text in the whole book of Job, it is this one. After all his thoughts had been marshalled and applied to this text, he had this further to say, I do not yet understand what it means.

As we first read it, the text seems to carry a harsh connection with the foregoing words. There Job asks, *"Is my strength the strength of stones?"* Yet immediately he says, *"Is not my help in me?"* It sounds incongruous. For if he had help in himself, he had strength. Job has said with one breath that he had no strength in which he could hope, and in the next he seems to say that he had strength, in that he said, *"Is not my help in me?"* But, in fact, no man has his help in himself, not even enough to enable him to do any natural work, much less any spiritual work. Most of all, he has none for upholding his heart under affliction, much less to deliver himself from it. We must say with one voice, Our help is in the name of the Lord. Or with David, we cry out, *"The Lord is my helper."* Man has strength enough to ruin himself, but he has not enough to help himself. That which man so confidently, yet foolishly, quotes for Scripture, that God helps those that help themselves, is a lie. The fact is, the very opposite is true, that God helps those who cannot help themselves (2 Cor. 3:5).

If it cannot mean that Job was claiming strength to help himself, then what does it mean? To clear it, consider the different readings. Some read it, *"Was not my help in me?"* And so they make the meaning to be this, Did I not help myself as much as I could? Was I faint-hearted and cowardly? Did I not put myself forth to the uttermost in order to stand under these troubles and afflictions? Of course there are many who do not help themselves even as much as they might. Their spirits sink and their hearts fail even before their strength fails. This certainly was not so in Job's case. And he could well say such a thing.

The Septuagint refers these words to God making Job speak in this way, *"Did I not trust in Him"* As if he had said, I never put my trust in myself, nor did I promise myself anything great. For, alas! what is my strength? I know well enough my own frailty. I have trusted to God and to His help, now it seems that He has forsaken me and withdrawn His assistance from me. This, to me, seems to have but little in it. It does not fit the context.

The Vulgate translates the whole verse negatively, whereas we read it interrogatively, *"Behold, my help is not in me, and my friends who should help me have departed from me."* That which we translate wisdom is by them translated, *"my friends, who should be my helpers."* And so the meaning of all this would be as if Job had said, *"I cannot help myself, and they who should help me have deserted me."* Thus it would connect with that which went before, *"What is my strength that I should hope?"* This does make out a good sense.

Another rendering is this, *"What though I do not have any help in me? Is wisdom then completely driven from me?"* Though I do not have any strength, and do not have any help in myself, yet I have not lost all my wisdom because of that. It is as if he had said, Will you conclude that I am a wicked man, a hypocrite and a fool because I am not able to help myself and deliver myself out of these troubles? This also makes a clear sense.

Considering the words as we translate them (with which most of the Rabbins and Jewish writers concur, although they usually express the sentence affirmatively instead of inter-rogatively,) the statement is an affirmation. Job is saying, *"My help is in me,"* and, *"Wisdom has not departed from me."* And if this is his statement, then it may be taken in this way, *"Do I not have in me that which will be a help to me, notwithstanding all the objec-tions and assaults which you have made against me? Do I not have in me that which may furnish me with wisdom to answer all the exceptions which you have taken to my com-plaints?"* Mr. Broughton's translation favors this sense, *"Do I not have my defence? And is judgment driven away from me?"* That is to say, Do I not have a defence for my desire to die? Is there nothing to say for my request? Do I not have arguments to help myself defend my words? Do you think I have been deserted by God and bereft of the wisdom He has given me simply because you and the world have deserted me? In which case, Job would be referring to his innocency and integrity of heart. There was no help in himself, his flesh being of tottering, crumbling clay — but the help that he had outside of himself had indeed implanted within him something which would be of help to him in all his af-flictions. He had been given grace, hope, the testimony of a good conscience, the witness of the Spirit with his spirit that he was a child of God. And all these things make a man wise, giving him not only comfort but the ability to deal with the greatest assaults that man or devil could launch. The Sabeans, the Chaldeans, and the Devil had robbed him of much, but they had not taken these things from him. His help was in him, though it was not within his power to help himself. Job did not hope in his strength, nor did he have any desire to wait for his end, not having the strength of stones or brass, but he still had help from those fruits of the Spirit which had been so abundantly nurtured within him. These gave him wisdom enough to answer the false charges of his friends.

The word translated *"wisdom"* is one which may be, and often is, translated in other ways. One renders it, *"The Law is not departed from me?"* as if his meaning were, I never forsook the Law of God. Another reads, *"Was my duty driven from me?"* as if his mean-ing were, I always kept close to the rule of my place and calling. A third says, *"Is my sub-sistence driven from me?"* And a fourth, *"Is my ability to subsist gone from me?"* As if he was saying, Can I not live because I do not have the world to live upon? To which sense the words of Christ would apply, *"A man's life does not consist in the abundance of the things that he owns"* (Luke 12:15). All of these interpretations can meet to make up a complete apology for Job's piety, constancy, patience, and undying resolutions and faith even in the face of his dying, withering condition. He had lost all his earthly substance, and the assistance of all earthly persons and powers, but he had not lost his love for the Law of God, he had not lost his devotion to duty, and he still had that substantial deposit which the Holy Spirit of God had dripped into him, line upon line, precept upon precept. For when a godly man has lost all his outward helps, there is that which still remains. Even if he himself seems to be strayed and decayed, there shall still be in him truth, *"as an oak whose stock remains, when they cast their leaves — so the holy seed shall be its trunk"* (Isa. 6:13). A man's substance may disappear, and it may even appear that he has lost all spiritual substance for a time, but he still has invisible supports. He has riches laid up beyond the reach of men, beyond the reach of Satan. Even when the outward man is swept with withering winds, the inward man is renewed with sweet refreshings and strong consolations day by day. The spirit of a man will bear his infirmities when his body cannot — and the godly man can bear still more because of his grace and truth. For grace does not wear out nor wane, nor can it be spent or exhausted. Afflictions are but the higher services and employments of grace. Faith and a good conscience are our best helps in trouble, and Job has these to assure him that there is still help and wisdom which he can call upon.

Still, Christians must take warily the truth that we always have a holy deposit within us for our help. Grace and holiness, faith and a good conscience are evidences of God's work within us, but they are not God — they cannot be trusted upon any more than riches or outward means of any sort. There are those who try to make an idol of their faith, a vain thing of a good conscience. Rather, faith and a good conscience are our best helps and friends, because faith carries us to Christ, who is our Help indeed. A good conscience will feast us in the favor of God. Faith alone is no help, but faith is our help because it is not alone. Faith feeds upon Christ, else it is not true faith. It is that which knits us together with Christ, conforms us to His image and keeps us under His wings. We are helped by the graces within us, but the graces within us are not our help.

A godly man in the darkest affliction or night of sorrow finds a light of holy wisdom to answer all the objections of his enemies, as well as the suspicions of his friends. In the midst of a thousand evils. Job can plead his own integrity in the throng of many jealousies, and contradictions. The truth is that sometimes God leaves His servants in so much darkness in order to try and exercise their graces. It is not until they can no longer swim against the current of troubles that they begin to exercise their graces, to cry out for God (as did David, Asaph and the other Psalmists). As our sins can sometimes hide themselves from our view, so also there are times when we cannot see our graces either. But if a man becomes encompassed with a multitude of afflictions, his redeemed spirit will be able to make judgment of his own interests in Christ, though black clouds hang forebodingly all about him. No distraction or confusion can in the end prevent a godly man's graces from shining through, and they eventually come through on top of all circumstances — for whatever has been born of God overcomes the world (and the flesh, and the Devil). Once the eye of faith becomes accustomed to the darkness of affliction and sorrow, it takes on a quickness, a liveliness and a confidence which cannot be understood by those who are on the sidelines watching it flourish. Does it not strike you that it is in this very rich soil of affliction that faith grows best, becoming an astounding and shining star which sheds forth the light of the gospel more and more each day it persists. Look at Job's faith, how it grew and grew, until it was stronger than any of those who sought either to destroy him or to defame him.

"To him who is afflicted, pity is due from his friends, but he forsakes the fear of the Almighty"—Job 6:14.

Here Job begins the third section of his reply to the words of Eliphaz. And he finds it necessary to draw up a strong charge against his friends, then to present a *prima facie* case of uncharitable behavior on their part: (1) He refutes and answers their objections against him, in verses one through eight; (2) He renews his complaint, which had originally been the ground of their objections, verses eight through thirteen; (3) Now he lodges his charge of unkindness, indiscretion, even cruelty, against them. By way of preface, he affirms, *"To him who is afflicted, pity is due from his friends, but he forsakes the fear of the Almighty."* It is as if he had said, You should have dealt with me differently than you did. God has given me the light of His Spirit, He has given me wisdom enough to discern my condition, but you were no help to me in this matter. I found no help in you, my friends. You have been pitiless toward me, you have opposed me, you have forsaken that duty which the fear of the Almighty teaches you. From this he proceeds to teach by similitude.

"To him who is afflicted"—Or, *"To him who is melted"*—Affliction dissolves the spirit of a man, as it were it melts his heart, therefore it is called the *"fire of affliction."* To be dissolved or melted, and to be afflicted, are the same, *"My heart is like wax, it is melted in the midst of my bowels"* (says David in the Messianic Psalm 22, verse 15). The friction of affliction causes great heat, and the anguish of one's spirit will add great compression.

"pity is due from his friends"—The word in the Hebrew denotes a sacred, sweet affection of mercy, good-heartedness and piety. And by contraries (in which sense words are often used in that language), it denotes such things as reproach (Prov. 14:34); impiety and cruelty, harshness and severity; and even the most abominable wickedness, *"a wicked thing"* is incest, says Moses — it is this same word that he there uses to express it. The word expresses a strong feeling, one more than a bare act of pity or commiseration. Pity in the weak sense given it by hard hearts is no more than a compassionate feeling for one who is in misery, a sorrowful feeling and an accompanying wordy expression of pity. But pity here and in all cases between brothers in the faith should be these plus much more, the actual, unrelenting attempt to relieve the pitied one and to restore him to full spiritual or physical health. There are times when words are a comfort (and Job would no doubt welcome some comforting words at this time,) but words alone are seldom enough to express a true feeling of lovingkindness — which is the way this word is translated most in the A.V. The apostle John issues the same kind of strong rebuke to those of the faithful who are inclined to be slack in fulfilling their duty to fellow-believers, *"But whoever has this world's goods and sees his brother has a need and shuts up his bowels from him, how does the love of God dwell in him? My children, let us not love in word or in tongue, but in deed and in truth. And by this we know that we are of the truth and shall assure our hearts before Him"* (1 John 3:17-19). And if he who withholds this world's goods shows a lack of love, then how much more may he who withholds spiritual comforts from the afflicted be considered hard-hearted and hateful (hate is the opposite of love, is it not?)

The failings of Job's friend, Eliphaz, flood over us when considered in the light of these truths. Job was not even given so much as the sound of pity, not even the expressions of commiseration which would be ordinary in a worldling! Eliphaz shut up his bowels of mercy against Job, he did not show that the love of God dwelt in him — he not only did not show love in deed and in truth, but he did not even show love in word and in tongue. How then could he know that he was of the truth? How then could he assure himself before God? A godly man will have a disposition to discharge his duty toward those who are in a pitiful state, especially to those who are of the household of faith (Gal. 6:10). This word for pity here in the concrete is a word translated, *"a godly man."* For who is a godly man but he who has received pity, lovingkindness and grace from the Lord? For this reason alone, pity is then due to all. In fact, the holy proverb assures us *"that a good man is merciful to his beast."* How much more, then, should he be so to a brother in the faith!

In Jewish thought, there were three sorts of men — to which the apostle Paul alludes in Romans 5:6,7. First, there were ungodly men, the profane. Secondly, there were righteous men, ethical men. Thirdly, there were good men, those who were loving, kind, merciful and pitying in their approach to others. The apostle makes this comparison, *"For when we were still without strength, in due time Christ died for the ungodly"*—there is the first sort of men; *"for one will hardly die for a righteous man"*—there is the second sort; *"yet perhaps someone would even dare to die for a good man"*—there is the third and best sort of man. If a man has shown lovingkindness toward others, then there will be many who would desire that he continue living. However, in God's case, He commended *"His love toward us in that while we were yet sinners* (ungodly, profane, the worst sort of men) *Christ died for us"* (Rom. 5:8). No one ever had a love like that, that they would be willing to give up their own lives for those who were the worst sort of men, except Christ Jesus. But even natural men, those who know not the grace of God, having none of the love of God shed abroad in their hearts by God the Holy Spirit, can show pity to those who are afflicted.

What is it that Job asks of his friends? He wants them to get close enough to his problems that they will become involved with his feelings. He yearns for them to love him and to extend the utmost mercy to him. It is not that he expects them to relieve his bodily ills or even his losses of worldly goods, but he expects them to fulfill the promise of their reputation as godly and wise men, to excite his spirit toward God, to nurse his wounded spirit back toward health — thus enabling him to better draw strength from the Almighty. But Job's friends have not proven to be friends to him, or friends of God. They are not acting like they are His. What good is it for Eliphaz to say, *"I would seek unto God,"* when he himself is not applying the first principles of godliness toward his friend? It is no proof of friendship to quote the Scriptures to a man in trouble, unless we quote the right Scriptures for the occasion and make the right application to the man in trouble. It is of little comfort to Job that they profess to seek his good, or even to set about bringing him back into the outward favor of God — while they at the same time are using God's word to rasp him raw. The sword of the Lord can be a terrible weapon in the hands of those who through bias or opinion prove to be unskillful in its use. Is this love, for Eliphaz to misapply God's word so as to depress and prey upon the mind and spirit of Job, one who is already so far afflicted and distracted as to be almost beside himself with grief and pain?

"but he forsakes the fear of the Almighty"—The charge is this, that Eliphaz had forsaken all godliness, goodness and true religion, for the fear of God takes in all that is good. Pity is a gift which God the Holy Spirit gives to the children of God, it is one of His fruits (see Gal. 5:22, where goodness, gentleness and longsuffering express the meaning of the pity which Job is asking of his friends). Every good and perfect gift comes down from the Father of lights (James 1:17). To fear God, to reverence Him, to hang upon his breast as His trusting child, is the beginning of all good things which may come to you. To forsake this fear of God is to cease to keep our minds and eyes on Him continually — and this is apt to bring a fall which will tumble us into evil, hard, even unthinkable acts of cruelty to our fellow men. Such a thing has apparently happened to Eliphaz and his friends here.

There are many interpretations of this verse, with nearly as many translations:

1. *"He that has taken away pity from his friend has forsaken the Almighty"*—which is a truth, and a good sense, but it is not so clear to the letter of the text.

2. *"By him whose mercy is melted toward his friend, and who leaves the fear of the Almighty"*—joining the melting to mercy, and not the man, with this meaning: 'Do I not have a defence? Is judgment driven away from me by you whose mercy has melted away and who has forsaken the fear of the Almighty?'

3. Some render it in the contrary sense, *"should reproaches be cast upon a man that is afflicted by his friends; should he be told that he has forsaken the fear of the Almighty?"* Job, according to this sense, found his friends dealing with him reproachfully, giving him vinegar to drink when he is thirsty, or gall for food when he is hungry. They are giving him reproaches instead of comforts, slanders instead of refreshing encouragements.

4. *"Shall he that is perishing by the reproaches of his friends also forsake the fear of the Almighty?"*—The meaning then would be this, Do you think that all men whose riches and comforts are lost have also lost their reason and judgment? Do you think that because a man is reproached by other men he has also lost the fear of God? It is the world's judgment that there are none wise but those that are rich; and, akin to this, that they fear God most who rejoice most (outwardly). But Job's practice and example here, in his opinion,

will let the world know that a man who is consumed and spent by the reproaches of men, or even by the strokes of God, may yet fear God, not only keeping all his holiness and wisdom through it all, but actually gaining in those graces that God gives.

5. Some refer the words to this, that the false pity being displayed by Job's friend is in fact melting him away, causing him to perish. Then he would be saying, *"Shall he who is being consumed by the love of his friends be also charged to have forsaken the fear of the Almighty?"* As the mercies of the wicked are always cruel, so sometimes the mercies of the godly are also cruel — especially when they give preposterous and indiscreet counsel to a friend in dire straits. This interpretation would suit well with Job's conclusion in chapter 16, *"You are all miserable comforters."* Your efforts to comfort me do not show that wisdom which God gives, therefore your learned tongue and your good intentions have only added to my miseries.

6. There is a reading which gives the sense very fair and easy, *"To him who is afflicted, pity is due from his friends, otherwise he forsakes the fear of the Almighty"* —where the word *"otherwise"* is substituted for *"but"* in the translation. If a man does not show pity to his friend who is melted in affliction, then that man proves by his lack of pity that he has forsaken the fear of the Almighty.

Interpreters and translators are much divided on this verse, but there is truth in every sense given, and their variety may teach us to adore the fullness of the holy language, as it can lead our thoughts in so many different ways (in order to deal with our diversity of character and need). Let us all be humbled by our blindness of mind and narrowness of heart, that we see and comprehend so little of the mind of God because of our failings.

The last meaning is the clearest meaning of Job, and the others more or less reduce to this meaning. There are three observations which can be made to expound the text:

1. It is the common duty of a friend, and the special duty of a godly friend, to pity and to help those who are afflicted. Pity without help is not the answer to our duty, for if we do not actually assist those who are afflicted to escape the oppression of his burdens, we have not fulfilled our obligation to the law of love. Faith without works does not justify, does not qualify as true faith, living faith. So pity which does not also work cannot be justified nor qualified as true pity.

2. The fear of God is always joined with love toward our brothers. The apostle John so warns that if you say you love God and yet withhold love and kindness from your brothers, then you are a liar. What if Christ had merely affirmed His love for us, but had not taken our distresses to heart? What if He had expressed great pity for our condition, but had not made Himself of no reputation, had not taken upon Himself the form of a servant, had not agreed to be found in fashion as a man? Even then, what good would it have done us if He had not also loved so much that He humbled Himself and became obedient to the shameful death on the Cross? That is true pity, that is true fear and reverence for God!

WHO, THEN, IS A BROTHER?

There are brothers many: (1) brothers in the flesh; (2) brothers from the same blood line; (3) brothers in spirit, those who are knit to us in affection, in likeness, in disposition, etc.; (4) brothers in a common cause or pursuit, such as men of the same nation.

In brotherhood, there is a nearness, a likeness, a oneness. These things are only shadowed out in the brotherhood which is common to this world. Blood-brothers may be near, may be alike, and may even have some common purposes and common feelings — but they can be trusted only as far as their own selfish interests go. Brothers in Christ, on the other hand, have the utmost reason to trust one another, in that they both trust Him and are identified with Him who is the same today, yesterday and forever. We may change, but He never changes. We may suffer from inconstancy, but we are constant in Him by whom we consist. And there is all the nearness, likeness and oneness of true brotherhood built into our relationship with Christ Jesus. If you are like Christ, and if your brother is like Him, then who is more like you than your brother? Are you not both being conformed to the image of Christ Jesus? Has not God worked in both of you to will and to do of His good pleasure? Then you are also sharers in a oneness of purpose, that all-pervading purpose of the saints, the determination to do all to the glory of God. Having this common and glorious purpose, it is not too much to ask of us that we help each other, *"A friend loves at all time, and a brother is born for the time of trouble"* (Prov. 17:17).

A true friend can hardly be discovered in a time of prosperity, and a false friend can hardly be hidden in a time of adversity. Are not Christians all of one body? When the toe hurts, does not the rest of the body ache with it? Shall a brother be in affliction, in pain, in misery, and yet not cause anyone in the church to hurt? Yes, everyone in the church should feel twinges and heavinesses, if not severe pain and burdensome troubles, when a fellow-saint is being heated and molded by afflictions from the hand of God. If you are like Christ, then you will befriend such a one as Job, for Christ is *"a Friend who sticks closer than a brother."*

"My brothers have dealt deceitfully as a brook, as the streams of brooks they pass away; brooks which are black because of the ice, and in which the snow is hidden. When they become warm, they go away; when it is hot, they vanish out of their place. The paths of their way are turned aside; they go to nothing and are lost. The troops of Tema looked, the companies of Sheba hoped for them. They were ashamed because they had hoped; they came there and were ashamed. For now you are like them – you see my casting down and are afraid."–Job 6:15-21.

Job in the former verse had begun to charge his friends with the lack of charity toward him, and now he proceeds in this context to illustrate his charge by a similitude. This is to make visible to them the position they were in, a position which would expose them to the displeasure of God. And since the comparison runs to seven verses, it is well to look at them all at once before taking them verse by verse.

The sum of the similitude is this, that Job had looked upon his friends as alleviating instruments of God, thinking that they would surely attempt to refresh him. For he was parched and scorched in those hot regions and fiery climates of affliction. Yet they did not so much as give him a drop of water to cool his tongue or to ease his complaints. This is why he compares them to a brook, one of those mountain brooks or desert streams, which promise much when there is no lack of water, but which vanish away when great need arises. There are four parts to these verses:

1. Job's charge that these men had dealt deceitfully with him (verse 15);

2. His explanation of what he means by a deceitful brook (verses 16-18);

3. His confirming application, that certain ones had found the brook deceitful (verses 19 and 20);

4. His specific application to his friends (verse 21).

"My brothers"–The first signification of the word is that of natural, blood-brothers. In this place, of course, the term brother is applied because there is a supposed nearness, oneness and likeness between Job and his friends. He is still willing to call them brothers, even while he is rebuking them for not acting like brothers. There are those who will read anyone, even everyone, out of the kingdom of God when they are displeased with those persons. God has a man in Job, a mature believer, who will both charge his brothers with their lack of godly behavior and still love them as brothers at the same time. As Paul rebuked Peter in the presence of others for dissembling, so Job rebukes his friends here for their lack of pity.

"have dealt deceitfully with me"–the word imports a perfidious or treacherous dealing of any kind (as in Isa. 21:3, *"the treacherous dealer deals treacherously"*). It is applied to those relationships which are the highest in earthly life. It is a deceiving of one who trusts you. It is a deceiving of one who has hope that you will bless them and do you good (so it is used in the husband-wife relationship, *"Surely, as a wife treacherously departs from her husband, so you have dealt treacherously with Me"*–Jeremiah 3:20). The original and basic meaning of the word, in the verb, is that of a garment which men wear. A learned Hebrician explains. Garments were never worn by men when they were pure and holy, but men

began to wear clothing at the time when they first dealt deceitfully and treacherously with God. When man sinned, he became one with a heart that was deceitful. The donning of clothing, of covering, was an effort to hide his shame, to deceive himself into thinking that his case was not much worse than before. However much men and women now may pose and strut in their luxurious clothing, it is in truth a reminder of their perfidy, their deceitful and treacherous treatment of God, their shameful rebellion and falling away from Him. This is the word that Job applies to his friends. And although only Eliphaz has spoken thus far, he uses the plural, applying the term equally to all his friends. That he was not unfairly judging the other two can easily be seen when you look forward and see what they say to him later.

From these words we learn that, (1) However near a relationship may be, however binding an obligation may be, an evil heart will deceitfully and wickedly break his bond. It is not only true of unbelievers, that they will deceive those who trust them implicitly, but it is also true of believers when the carnal nature erupts. Not only did Absalom deceitfully betray his father David, but it was a chastisement to David because he had dealt so treacherously with Uriah — first by taking his wife, then by causing his death. (2) It is evil to deal deceitfully with anyone, but it is worse to deceive those who trust us. When a brother deceives, the sin of the deceit is doubled. In fact, deceit from a brother in the faith is more than double unfaithfulness, as is witnessed by David's complaint against Ahithophel, *"It was not an enemy who reviled me, then I could have borne it. Neither was it he who hated me who magnified himself against me, then I would have hidden myself from him. But it was you, a man my equal, my guide and my friend."* (Ps. 55:12,13). Again, it was God's way of chastising David for his deceitful dealings in the matter of Bathsheba, for Ahithophel was the grandfather of Bathsheba, and had secretly turned away from David because of this ungodly course of action with his granddaughter. How much more wicked is it when we deal deceitfully with God, when we dig out cisterns for ourselves and deceive ourselves into thinking that the Fountain of living waters has done but very little for us. God voices such a complaint again and again, as in Isaiah 1:2, *"I have nursed and brought up children, and they have rebelled against Me."*

"like a brook"—Job explains by this similitude, that his friends' deceit is comparable to a brook that disappears in time of need. The word signifies both a brook and a valley, because streams usually run in valleys. The same word also means to inherit, and some have joined the three words together in this way: Valleys inherit the brooks which descend to them from the mountains—*"He sends the springs into the valleys, which run among the hills"* (Ps. 104:10). This brook which Job mentions is not a spring-fed brook, however. This is the kind of brook or stream which is fed by torrential rain or melting snow. For a spring-fed brook does not deceive, but one depending on seasonal sources often will.

"as the streams of brooks they pass away"—Brooks have a narrow channel, and they also have a wider channel which is used at times when it is swollen above its banks. When they are at flood-level, then they are streams of brooks. These streams get their name in Hebrew from their impetuous, violent strength, for they run violently and quickly spend their strength. That which is violent cannot be permanent, much less perpetual. Job compares his brothers to such a stream, they being quick to run him down, impetuous and violent in their treatment of him. But, he says, they pass away. As strong as their torrents were, so they pass away with the same strong motion. They run fast and quickly run themselves into nothingness. Many times the Scriptures treat one who passes away as if he were not (see Ps. 37:36). Anyone who has seen the dry bed of a stream high in the mountains in the summertime, or deep in the desert in the dry season, will have this impression: How can they call it a stream when there is no water in it?

"brooks which are black because of the ice, and in which the snow is hidden."—Job 6:16. After a rainy fall season, the water congeals and traps both the water and the debris that is in the brook — they are surprised by cold and cannot get away. Then the snow falls and covers them up, and there they stay until the time of year when warmer weather thaws

them. At this time they seem to have a permanency, they seem to offer treasures of life-giving water.

"When they become warm, they go away; when it is hot, they vanish out of their place" —Job 6:17.

When it becomes warm, they go away. Here only is this word used, to become warm. It has the meaning of scattering or dissipating. These brooks are scattered and then dissipate as soon as it becomes warm. They go away, they go to nothing and are lost. The further they go, the further they get from their source, which at best is only a surface supply. At first they are a torrential stream, but soon they are but rivulets. And rivulets are quickly swallowed up by that hungry pair of enemies, the ground and the air. Soon they vanish from the face of the earth, and there is little, if any evidence that they ever were. Men are like that by nature, they promise much, they appear to be full of usefulness to us, but when the thaw comes they are soon gone.

"The paths of their way are turned aside; they go to nothing and are lost"—Job 6:18.

He repeats, they vanish and are gone, they go to nothing and are lost. This is for emphasis to his friends, that the heat of his afflictions have caused them to thaw and run out on him, to vanish out of their rightful place as friends. The word for turned is a word which pictures the gathering together of all of one's strength. It is the word used of Samson when he *"turned himself with all his might"* in order to pull down the pillars of the Philistine stadium. Here the brooks gather their strength into one channel and try to protect themselves from that great river-drier, the sun. They go to nothing and are lost. It is the word used in Gen. 1:2. There was a nothingness upon that confused heap before God stamped a form upon it. The Jews called an idol by this word, a useless *"nothing in the world"* (1 Cor. 8).

Without that *"well of water springing up into everlasting life"* within us, we are useless, we are nothing, we are lost. There must be this inward source to keep us supplied with grace and life. Even a worldling must have some kind of inward principle to keep him in a constant course. How much more so is this of spiritual endeavors! It is asked of the hypocrite, *"Will he always call upon God?"* (Job 27:10). No, he will not, because he does not have streams of living water in his belly to feed his desires after God. That is why the new birth is necessary, that is why there must be a new creation within us. For all the outward sources of strength of purpose will fail man. Whatever temporary good may be extracted from him by motivation, by hopes or fears, by threatenings or promises, by rewards or punishments, there will be no lasting good come of it. There must be a new heart or else all will vanish and come to nothing.

"The troops of Tema looked, the companies of Sheba hoped for them"—Job 6:19.

Job having explained his similitude, showing what he means by a deceitful brook, now gives us a confirmation by an actual experiment. Here we have the troops of Tema trying to find these waters. These *"troops"* were travellers who came in great companies from Tema (which means, sunburnt), a city of Arabia. These passed through those deserts which surround them, and there they found frozen streams in wintertime. To themselves, they said, Here I shall find water when I return this way. But when they came and looked again, this brook had dealt deceitfully with them by vanishing out of its place. The companies of Sheba are also from that area, and they also are pictured as hoping in vain because their hopes were in a brook that was deceitful.

"They were ashamed because they had hoped; they came there and were ashamed"— Job 6:20.

They were ashamed and confounded, they blushed and became pale because they had put their trust in a deceitful brook. Disappointments of our hope will perplex us, and many times makes us ashamed. There is also in this word a further meaning, this is that kind of shame which makes us want to dig a hole and hide in it — or to run into a cave and wish that the rocks would fall and cover the mouth of it.

Deceived hopes will trouble us more than the lack of the things we need. This is why the burden of sorrow is so heavy, it is why the portion of those in Hell will be so intolerable — for the hope that there shall be overflowing streams of happiness from the things of the world makes the grief to be far greater when all these hopes turn to the ashes of regret. To lack something that is needed is a present smart, but deceived hopes are a perpetual wound, a running sore of disappointment, and ever-growing mountain of reproach. Deceived hopes fill us with shame, they make us want to hide our heads. Shame arises either from doing a thing against common principles, or from losing a thing against common expectation. The Lord warns the Israelites, *"you shall be ashamed of the oaks which you have desired and you shall be confounded because of the gardens which you have chosen."* They had forsaken the trustworthy and dependable God for these fool-reared idols.

"For now you are like them; you see my casting down and are afraid"—Job 6:21.

Job now makes his application of the similitude. He points the finger at them and says, You are the men! You have been deceitful like these brooks. You have dealt treacherously with me, as these brooks disappointed others. If we render the Hebrew word for word, it is this, *"you were not."* Just as he had said that the brooks pass away and are not, so he applies this to his friends, they passed away, vanished when he was in need (though, alas! still present to trouble him), they were nothing to him. You are not what I took you to be. You have deceived me, for I hoped for floods of comfort from you, for streams of consolation, but so far I have not had a drop of good from you. A man who does not fulfill the purpose for which he exists is nothing to the ones he is supposed to serve. A friend is not a friend unless he fulfills the duties of a friend. He is useless, therefore he is nothing. The friends of Job are nothing to him, because they are useless. Yet he calls them brothers. But they may as well not be brothers, or friends, as to be brothers and friends who are worth nothing as brothers and friends. Looking down into the dry bed of that brook that runs only in the springtime, you might in a sense say that there was a brook there, though dry. But since the purpose of a brook is to supply water, you may well say also that there is not a brook there—it is nothing because it does not fulfill its purpose. There are many who believe that they are something when they are nothing, they only deceive themselves (Gal. 6:3). These are apt to think that they are not worthless as long as they are useful to themselves. But, alas! it is not so! To be worth something, you must be useful to others, and ultimately you must be related to God. The words of Paul describe the goal we all should seek, *"not seeking my own profit, but the profit of many, so that they may be saved"* (1 Cor. 10:31,33). Just as a tool is counted as nothing when it is broken and cannot fulfill its purpose, so men are nothing when their usefulness is nullified by sin. Just as a piece of fruit is worthless when it is rotten, so a friend and a brother may be neither of these until he has been purged from the corruption self-love and its lusts.

"you see my casting down"—Job's friends had seen his misery, his dejection, his discouragement, his consternation and confusion, his heart-fallen state. And what did they do? Forsaking the fear of the Almighty, they refused to exercise their graces and be loving, kind and merciful to him. They acknowledged what he had been, then they brought all the Scriptures they could marshall in order to bear down on him and make him admit to spiritual guilt which he did not feel. Never did they admit that there was a possibility that he was as innocent as they were (for he did not claim complete innocence, he only claimed that he was no more of a sinner than they). He had hoped in them, but they deceived him by being useless, even worse than useless, a burden to him. Twice thus far they have deceived him, and they have become a pain to him equal to any other pain that he had until now. They had traveled a long, hard journey in order to be helpful to him. Now they have proven to be useless and harmful. Why?

"and are afraid"—The three friends came up and observed Job in his troubles for seven days and nights, and they were afraid. Why? Did they fear that they would be infected by Job's disease? Or did they see what God could do to a man who led an upright and useful life? Did this in turn cause fear to well up in them, the fear that even worse might be done

to them? Could this deceitful and treacherous defection of Job's friends be laid to the fear that they must either convict Job of heinous, secret sins or else admit that their own hopes for a pleasant and comfortable life were ill-grounded? Was not their proposition, that a man suffers in exact proportion to the magnitude of his sins, a protective belief which they had deceitfully devised for comfort's sake?

One thing is plain at once, holy Job is able to bear more than these three friends can even stand to look upon. He is only alternately afraid, as his troubles overwhelm him from time to time, but they are afraid just by looking at this unsightly saint. Some men are more afraid when they look at a man bleeding from wounds he received in a battle than the man who has suffered the fears and wounds of war. A fearful man, a cowardly man dies a thousand deaths — each one worse then the death of a saint who dies in the battle against iniquity.

A selfish friend, one who is primarily interested in his own welfare, one who desires to keep his skirts clear from the disaster that is engulfing his friend, soon becomes a burden to himself, as well as to his friend. The less he does his duty toward his neighbors and his friends, the more he becomes spiritually deranged. Next, he finds no more springs of refreshment to his spirit within himself, only poisoned and venomus pus. He then turns to others, to draw from them. And it is not long before he tries to take from them even what they need. Such is the case here, at least, they are trying to take from Job what he needs. Just as the five virgins without oil in their lamps were quite willing to make up for their sloth and faithlessness by taking the oil from the lamps of the faithful virgins, so these men are doing to Job. They have been slothful in the formation of their beliefs and opinions, learning only the letter of the portion of the Scriptures which they had. This is proven by their false accusations against Job, their failure to make the right application of God's word. It is also proven by this willingness to convict him of sins which they could not in any sense justifiably lay to him. The Pharisee and the Levite were despised by God because they would not be merciful and compassionate, as was the Good Samaritan. How much more cruel and inhuman it would have been for the priest and the Levite to walk up to the wounded man and start to belabor him with accusations of sin! Suppose the man in his dazed condition had uttered something hastily, something not in accord with their view of the Scriptures. Is that reason enough to enter into a long, bitter and accusatory argument with the man as he lay there bleeding and beaten inside and out? But is this not what Job's friends are doing to him?

Job could not have been more hurt if they had taken sticks and knives to him. They are working hard to pull out from under Job the only hope that he has left — the hope that he is God's. God has not left him anything but his faith. Job clings to this faith, it is the only thing which keeps him from drowning in the floods of sorrows which are billowing over his soul. Then his godly friends appear. How much hope and joy must have filled his breast! They come up and put on the robes of commiseration, sitting with him and contemplating the depth of his desperate condition. Then, taking convenient offence at Job's opening speech, they began to beat him with their tongues — they tug and tear and wrest at the faith that is keeping him from perishing in Satan's snare. Unknowingly, they do their utmost to force Job to submit to Satan and to curse the God who had given him his faith and hope.

It should be noted here that there is a great difference between the love of God and that of most men. God is the best friend we have at all times. But God is best of all to us in the worst times. He is a best friend to us when we have no other friends — and if Job has any friends at this time, they are nowhere to be seen. Yet there is no excuse for any to be less a friend than God is. There have been times when the Scriptures have been fulfilled in the lives of men. For instance, the heathen marveled in primitive Christian times at the great love that Christians had toward one another. They did not hesitate to put their lives into jeopardy for the sake of others of their brothers. Today, alas! The heathen are more apt to say, See how the Christians hate each other. When they should be helping, they fall to accusing one another! O that we might stop being deceitful brooks to our fellow-saints!

"Did I say, Give to me? or, Offer a bribe for me from your wealth?"—Job 6:22.

Job has charged his friends directly with a lack of lovingkindness toward him, with a deceitfulness which ought not to be. They had promised him something when they called him their friend. They had failed to keep that promise. Now in verse 22, Job further shows the unfaithfulness of his friends by his own modesty in seeking to them for supplies.

"Did I say, Give to me?"—Eliphaz has hinted broadly (by dwelling long upon the earthly benefits that would accrue to Job if he would but commit his cause unto God) that Job is both impatient and sinfully distracted because of his loss of estate and position. Here he asks them to prove that he is guilty of this, by asking them this, *"Did I say, give to me?"* If a man's heart is set on his possessions, then when his possessions are lost he will exert all his energies to regain them. The man who considers fame and position the most important thing in his life will never be satisfied to be without honor and influence. If these are taken from him, he will study day and night the ways and means that will restore him to his former position. And such men are not the least bit reluctant to use their friends and acquaintances to the very hilt in order to regain their losses.

Job affirms by this question that he had not asked his friends for anything. He was so modest, so trusting in God, so thoughtful of his friends, that he asked nothing of them but their compassion, their comforting reminders of God's promises to the faithful. They instead put on a false front and paraded as servants of God, pretending to be interested only in preserving His reputation and glory — and at the same time they were being pitiless and even cruel to their friend. Their counsel therefore was of no value to Job, not being dipped in the holy healing ointment of the Holy Spirit.

These men no doubt had some substance. And it would not have been wrong for Job to ask of them a little seed-grain, a pair of this kind of animal, etc. It is no sin to ask a friend for help, even if it may take half the goods of a friend to satisfy a legitimate need. But not one request for their substance did Job utter. None of his losses were to be made theirs.

"Offer a bribe for me from your wealth"—The word translated reward by many is actually a bribing reward, such as would be given to a judge by one party in a suit. The bribe is for the purpose of making the judge take the side of the giver. It is the meaning of the original word that this reward is to make the receiver 'one' with the giver. But it is many times put for any gift or help, any subsidy or supply of another's want. The word translated *"wealth"* is one which implies the natural strength of a thing, that which supplies the needs and supports of the body (see Lev. 26:20). Riches, estates, etc. are the source of civil strength to their holders, therefore this word is translated wealth, estate, or substance. Job reinforces his first question with a second, *"Did I say to you, offer a bribe for me from your substance?"* No, he had not asked anything of them, nothing but spiritual encouragement.

"Or, Deliver me from the enemy's hand? or, Redeem me from the hand of the mighty?"—Job 6:23.

The Hebrew word here translated *"enemy"* is a word that pictures a narrow way, a strait which endangers one. Being in the hand of the enemy is comparable to being in such a tight circumstance or position. Paul uses a Greek word to express the Hebrew meaning here, *"We are not troubled, we are not distressed"*—that is, we are not straightened. Job's ills and evil circumstances were bearing in on him, he was in the hand of enemies to his comfort and sense of wellbeing. But in spite of that, he never asked his friends to deliver him. He spares them even one plea for this kind of help.

"Or, Redeem me out of the hand of the mighty (the terrible)"—Job's goods had been carried off by marauding bands. Perhaps they could have been redeemed. But Job does not ask them to do anything to retrieve these goods. The meaning of the word *"redeem"* here is this: to cause a think or a person to be brought back by an agreement or contract, usually including the payment of a price. To redeem may also mean to bring back a person or thing by force. So Christ Jesus redeemed His people, not only by an agreement

and covenant with God the Father, but also by force out of the hands of Satan. He spoiled the principalities and powers, making a show of them openly (see Col. 2:15). But Job had neither asked his friends to redeem his goods by agreement or by force from the terrible ones who had carried them off.

Some say that Job may mean here that he did not ask his friends to deliver him from his affliction, seeing Job's affliction as the terrible one that held him captive. If so, it would answer to that in Proverbs, *"So shall poverty come, as one that travels, and your want as an armed man"* (Prov. 6:11). There a man's poverty is called *"an armed man,"* here Job's affliction may fairly be called, *"the terrible"* enemy that holds him in distressed circumstances, afflictions of the mind and spirit.

These are the observations on this verse:

1. It is an aggravation of unkindness when we see a man in need, yet not asking us for anything at all, then to fail to make any effort to fill that need. If we have the kind of love that never fails, the true love of a brother and friend, there should be no need for one to ask us for help. And especially we should be moved to help him who asks us nothing, for this is usually a sign of true godliness.

2. Job is not guilty of inordinate love for the things of this world. Not only did he not sin against God when his possessions were taken away, but he even now continues to consider them as dung. His main concern is to maintain his hope in God, to salvage his faith in the love of God. In accusing him of being cast down because of his losses, his friends are cruelly oppressing this good man, who sinned not with his lips when his were lost. In failing to help Job by buoying up his hope in God, in believing God's hand is against Job and is crushing him for his sins, his friends are heartlessly gouging his afflicted spirit. If he had been seeking their funds and the sacrifice of their wellbeing in order to recover his possessions, then they could perhaps have some grounds to suspect that he loved God only for the gain that he got from his relationship to God. This is what Satan had said. This is what his friends evidently have concluded. And if they have not, then why are they not upholding the man in his struggle, instead of pushing him down from every perch which he manages to get hold of?

3. It is well to notice the working of a gracious heart when great loss is suffered. Such a heart will not look to man as his ultimate helper, but will expect God to be his Helper, his Repairer, his Restorer, his Redeemer. Did not David, that man after God's own heart, say so innumerable times in the Psalms? (see Psalm 3). It is not unlawful for those who are in need to make their needs known to friends and brothers. It may well even be a duty, so that they may not lack the opportunity to prove themselves to be true friends and saints. But it is usual for a child to run to his father when he is in trouble, and a child of God is certain to run to his Father in such times. If God has decreed that a brother shall be his helper, then God will move the brother onto the scene to offer his help and to vigorously support the one in need.

4. If you are one that happens to be full, blessed with strength and means, it is your duty to give to your less-favored brothers, those that are weak or poor. Did not Barnabas do so? He sold all his goods and gave them to the poor in the church. And there were many others who *"sold their possessions and goods and divided them to all, as anyone had need"* (Acts 2:44). And never has anyone on earth been any happier than these people of God who are willing to give sacrificially of themselves and their goods.

"Teach me, and I will be silent; and cause me to understand where I have gone astray."
—Job 6:24.

This is the fourth branch of Job's answer to the speech of Eliphaz. First, he has told him that only one who had suffered what he is suffering could speak accusing and rebuking words with any force. Secondly, he told him that there was no desire on his part to remain here in this world, that he had a hope beyond the grave which made him want God to deliver him from the pain and misery of this earth. Thirdly, he told him and his friends that he was due pity, mercy, tender-hearted concern and help from them, but that instead they had been deceitful, void of all good to him, worthless as friends, and worse, a burden to him.

"Teach me"—the original word here in its strict sense denotes the casting or throwing of a thing, such as a dart or stone. This may be done downward, upward or outward. So by a metaphor, it signifies rain, and it is sometimes translated rain. This is because rain is cast forth from the clouds sometimes with such force as to seem to dart out of the clouds. Also by a metaphor once more removed, it signifies teaching. As seen in Ezekiel 20:46, teachers of the word of God may be said to be raining truth, *"Son of man...drop your word toward the south..."*

Doctrines, truths, wholesome instructions from God are instilled in and distilled within the teacher, who then drops them down upon God's people, dripping truths into their spiritual bloodstreams, giving life and godliness with each drop.

So Job is saying here, O my friends, rain down God's truths upon me, teach me in the way everlasting, and I will be silent. God shows us this picture, *"My teaching shall drop as the rain; My speech shall drop down as the dew, as the small rain upon the tender plant, and as the showers upon the grass..."* (Deut. 32:2). God's doctrine, every drop of His precious teachings are like rain in four different ways:

1. Rain is from God. It is one of those good gifts that come down from the Father. Men may act upon the clouds in such a way as to evoke the fall of moisture from them, but only God can put the rain in the clouds. Likewise, the teachings of God represent the whole truth, and none other than God Himself can give us any truth. Men may cause the truth to fall here, or there, under God, but they cannot ever be the originators of one shred of truth. He said truly, *"I am the truth, etc."*

2. Rain refreshes the earth. Though it may be barren, parched, etc., the rain will renew and refresh it. So it is with God's truth. Though the people may be languishing and fainting in ignorance and error, God's truth will drop down upon them and into them, causing them to become lively, laughing and singing, receiving the word with joy.

3. Rain makes the earth bring forth fruit. It is amazing what can be grown in a desert after it has been irrigated. Where there was nothing of value to man before, suddenly there is life-giving food as far as the eye can see. So it is with God's truth, where it is withheld and is despised and ignored, there is barrenness, waste, fruitlessness. But let's God's truth come in among the people and the fruit of the Holy Spirit begins to spring up, beyond all conception, some bringing forth fruit thirtyfold, some sixtyfold and some a hundredfold!

4. The word of God taught is like rain in a fourth way – it can be softly rained down. It can be sharply slung as a stone to slay a Goliath. It can be cast out with thunder and lightning, threatening to inundate the person who refuses to seek refuge in God. There are some who will drink in the rain of God's truth gladly, having a hungry, parched heart that is all prepared and opened to receive His droplets of truth. There are others who are giants in their own conceit, who harden their hearts against the truth, who must be pierced by the word of God, who must be shattered by the hammer of that word. There are still others who fear men but not God, who think that God is altogether such a one as they themselves are. These are content with a god who in their minds is full of mercy and love, but a god who has a total lack of concern about their spiritual fruitlessness. These need to know that God is a God of majestic power and fearful threatenings, who demands that His truth be received and believed. There must be thunder and lightning mixed with their rain. Those teachers who are always thundering instead of raining mistake their work. But those teachers who think that they can minister God's word without ever thundering from the pulpit are also mistaken. There must be teaching if a ministry is to succeed. And there must be more than teaching in his ministry, there must be ways and means of delivering his message to various kinds of people. Fire sometimes must mingle with the rain of truth, and some need terror with their instruction to bore their ears ahead of the truth. It is the duty of each teacher to know when to use this method, when to use that – he must know how to give each one his portion from the word of God. Some must be saved by compassion, others must be saved with fear, pulling them forcefully out of the fire (Jude 22,23).

"and I will be silent"—The original word properly taken signifies to dig or to plow. It is sometimes used to express the act of meditation. And it implies much thoughtfulness because a musing, meditating, thoughtful man is always digging into matters. He does not rest upon surface data, but he puts in his plow deep to turn up the very bottom of a matter. From this, by one step further into the metaphor, it is translated to signify silence, or to be quiet. This is because those who meditate much and think deeply usually have few words. Musing men are not great talkers. When the mind is much at work, the tongue usually does little.

Job's promise to be silent may have a threefold reference, (1) He promises to be a learner and to silently listen if they will teach him; (2) He promises to give over complaining if they will but teach him better than they have managed to do until now; (3) He promises to be silent, to listen carefully, and also promises not to gainsay what they say if they will but teach him aright. From these the following observations can be made:

1. A gracious spirit is a teachable spirit. It is grace that moves a man to say, *"Teach me, and I will hold my tongue."* A gracious heart wants to be strengthened, and the words of the Lord strengthen a man when he is taught them. A soul that is honestly ignorant will pray, Lord instruct me, that I may understand You. Give me the wisdom of the prudent so that I may understand my way, and I shall walk in Your ways. A godly man does not love to be at his own disposal, much less does he desire to be his own tutor. For a man who learns nothing from others is certain to have a fool for a teacher. If all eternity will not suffice to teach us all the glorious truths that we may know about God, then how can any but a man wise in his own conceit be content to waste a moment that could be used to learn some of this thrilling knowledge while still in this life?

2. A teachable spirit is an excellent spirit. A man that is willing to be taught is in a far better condition than most. And he is even in a better condition than many of those who are called teachers. It argues a holier temper of the heart to be willing to be taught than is true of him who is merely able to teach. And it is far worse to be unwilling to learn than not to be learned. In short, unteachableness is more dangerous than ignorance. It is sad to consider how unteachable many are. They refuse to be taught, or worse, they think they have already learned all they need to know. Some deceived souls act as if they had a spirit of infallibility. What? Teach them? They are above being taught. But it is truly a sweet frame of spirit when a man sees that he may be out of frame. He who acknowledges that he may be in error is in a fair way to learn what is right. He who presumes that he cannot be wrong is certainly out of the way of truth. Whatever a man's learning accomplishments may be, the Apostle Paul resolves it, *"If any man thinks that he knows anything, he knows nothing yet as he ought to know"* (1 Cor. 8:2). The apostle does not mean that all knowledge is inconclusive, that we should halt between two opinions and hang like the stars in space. Nor does he commend to us that proud modesty which will not let us acknowledge that we know what we know. But this is his mind, that one must not think that he knows anything so well that he need not know it better. He who thinks himself so good that he cannot be better was never as good as he should have been. It is best to be fixed in judgment, but it is very ill to be fixed in opinion. It is to be feared that man who is so married to his own formulations that he resolves that nothing but death shall part him and his opinion is a man who is divorced from right reason. Opinionated men often espouse their own fancies, rather than the truth — and being so certain of their opinions, they never leave any room for the truth to enter. These friends of Job are men who never seemed to have learned a single thing from Job's learned answers to their charges. It is well to be fixed on the truth as it is revealed in God's word. But to be so fixed that a man may be frozen in error is as dangerous as the man who is so unfixed that he cannot be stabilized upon any truth. To be so unstable, movable, and wavering in goodness is within one degree of falling into great evil. But it is equally foolish to be firmly fixed and resolved when things are still doubtful, being still under differing dispute. The apostle warns the Ephesians that they should not be *"carried about with every wind of doctrine."* Yet an equal rebuke

can be given to those who refuse to be moved by any wind of doctrine – that is, let never so powerful and forcible a wind of truth breathe and blow upon them, they will not be convinced or moved in judgment by it.

3. Silence becomes those who are learning. Yet it is not right to be silent completely. There is a speaking which can be helpful to learning. Doubts must be removed if one is to resolve them, and questions are the readiest means for instruction. But he who talks all the time has no time left to listen, and he shall have but little profit. The seasonable stopping of our mouths is a ready means to open our understandings. To be *"swift to hear and slow to speak"* is the speediest way to attain wisdom.

4. He who has been shown his error should speak no more, he should sit down convinced. Job says, *"Teach me, and I will be silent."* He will not reply any more if they will but show him his fault. He will not excuse error or apologize for mistakes, but these must be shown to him. Some are witty enough to make a fair cover for and put a respectable gloss upon the most deformed, the grossest of errors. There was never any ill-based opinion in the world but some have been found to second it and undertake its protection. Once the conscience has been şilenced, wit will be very talkative. When reason has been rejected, some can wrangle everlastingly. A subtle sophisticate will dispute anything, and he can bring probable arguments (if man's reason is the sole judge) against the most undoubted truths. But the proverb tells us, *"If you have done foolishly in lifting yourself up, or if you have thought evil* (or maintained evil), *lay your hand on your mouth"* (Prov. 30:32). Never be an advocate in a bad cause, even though it may be your own. An honest man, and certainly a humble man, will shut his mouth when his faults are demonstrated to him.

"and cause me to understand where I have gone astray"–Some would have it that Job is here showing some doubt as to his cause, or some hesitancy in his spirit. This speech does not imply that he either doubted himself or that he admitted to any error. Job is using the orator's methodology, for the wise disputant will, when he is sure of a point, yet grant a little doubtfulness – he will raise doubts so that he can confidently carry the point by allaying them one by one. It is an ordinary thing for us to suppose, even when we have no question as to the truth of a matter. Job is not acknowledging error when he challenges his friends to cause him to see where he had erred. But not being a man who believed in his own infallibility, Job shows a willingness to submit in case he had erred – he is willing to concede that he might err.

The words, *"cause me to understand"* come from but one original word, and it signifies to convince by reason or argument. That is, do not feel that you can force my opinion, nor can you do violence to my judgment, neither can you club me down with great words and clamorous threats – you must silence me by solid arguments, you must demonstrate by reason that I have erred. Do it by good counsel, not by bitter reproach and invective. You must deal with my understanding, not barely with my affections and passions.

"my error"–it means those errors which are human, usually bodily errors or wanderings. It sometimes is used for the wandering of the mind, sometimes of the judgment and affections, as when Solomon advised the husband, *"rejoice with the wife of your youth, like the loving hind and pleasant roe, let her breasts satisfy you at all times, and be ravished always with her love"*–our word is here in that last phrase, saying, *"and always err with her."* That is to say, Let all your wandering, erring thoughts and affections be reduced and brought home to the wife God has given to you. And the next words so interpret it, *"why will you, my son, be ravished with a strange woman"*–it is our word again, saying, Do not wander after a strange woman, but let all your wanderings, all your delights, all your ravishments be toward the wife of your youth.

Further, it signifies erring or wandering out of mere ignorance. This word is often used in Leviticus for the sin of ignorance (see 4:2; 5:18; 22:14). The sins a man commits out of ignorance and inadvertency cannot always be understood (see Ps. 19:12), therefore it is well to imitate Job's sweet spirit here and admit to possible errors, to pray David's prayer, *"O make me pure from secret faults"* (Ps. 19:12). He does not mean sins he has committed privately, sins he knows, but sins he had committed in ignorance, not realizing he sinned.

It is not enough to beg an erring brother or friend to leave his error, we must also make him understand what his error is. Error should not be left before it is known to be error. A man may sin in leaving an error, for all who lay down an error while they still think it may be right are guilty of despising the truth. For if they do not know what is true, or even which is true, then they are not leaving the error for the truth. A man should believe and obey the truth simply because it is the truth. Likewise, a man should leave off the believing and practicing of error simply because it is an error. It may be that he will sin in believing the truth, if he believes it without being convinced it is the truth. Contrariwise, it may be that he will sin in ceasing to err, if he ceases without being convinced that there is anything wrong with it. There is but one Lawgiver, and He it is that claims to be *"the Truth"*—He alone can one day examine you before the Judgment seat as to whether or not you believed His words and acted upon them. The word of none other can be accepted, as the truth, unless it is seen to be a true reflection from God's word. Unless we know personally what is right and what is true, we may find that our good deeds are not credited to us as good — because we did not do them out of conviction that they were in accordance with God's written Law, the Bible.

"Right words are powerful, but what does your arguing argue?"—Job 6:25.

The words may also be read, *"How forcible are right words! But what does your disputation dispute?"* Or, *"How potent are the words of an upright man!"*

The word translated *"powerful,"* or, *"forcible"* is used to denote a mighty force which cannot be contained. This is a force that is applied with sharpness, which grinds in and makes its mark, causing great damage or change. Shimei cursed David with a powerful, smarting curse. So evil words may be powerful in this sense, too, but right words are so much more powerful that the comparison would be like that of the sunlight to the moonlight.

Why are right words powerful? Why do right words burrow in and lodge forever in the heart of a man? It is because right words are true, and the truth hurts those who lie against the truth and live as if there were no truth. For the believer, on the other hand, the truth is like a holy preferment, it comforts and nourishes, it cheers and encourages. So, (1) Right words are powerful because they are true; (2) Words are true and right because they are in accordance with God's word; (3) Only God is true, therefore only His words are true, *"Yea, let God be true and every man a liar;"* (4) A man can no more get rid of the true words of God than he can obliterate God Himself; (5) God's word written is the standard of truth, a measure to measure by, so that we may be brought back from our speculations and imaginations, *"For the word of God is living and powerful and sharper than any two-edged sword, piercing even to the dividing apart of soul and spirit, and of the joints and marrow, and is a discerner of the thoughts and intents of the heart"* (Heb. 4:12).

The words of God are powerful in at least four different ways:
1. They search the heart.
2. They convince and powerfully affect the conscience.
3. They comfort and encourage godly hearts.
4. They convert the hearer, making a powerful change in those who hear it.

1. Right words search the heart, *"I the Lord search the heart"* (Jer. 17:10); He does it by His word, as was noted in Hebrews 12. God's word is powerful in that it tells us things about ourselves which we hoped no one knew but us, or perhaps had even submerged below our consciousness. This was the experience of the woman of Samaria (John 4). It also tells us things about ourselves which we never knew or realized. Only God can search the murky depths of the human heart, and only God can reveal it to us. Satan cannot wade in those waters, nor could he if he desired reveal the filthiness of our flesh to us. Man cannot fathom his own depths. Only God's word can plumb the depths of wickedness, perversity and deceit in our hearts. It is the truth, right words, which draws a detailed portrait of us. transmitting to us the horror of our nature, giving us the pungent smell of the rottenness which is in us (see Jer. 17:9).

2. Not only does the powerful word of God search and reveal our hearts to us, but it also convinces and convicts us of our corruption, that *"we are as an unclean thing, and all our righteousnesses are as filthy rags"* (Isaiah 64:6). The Scriptures say that Paul was blameless in his performance of outward duties, yet he was convinced that they were worse than worthless, *"I count them but dung in order that I might gain Christ and be found in Him, not having my own righteousness, but that which is through the faith of Christ..."* (Phil. 3:8). The conscience is especially fitted to be acted upon by right words. If there is any tenderness left in a man's conscience, then he will be affected powerfully by those words which reflect God's ways and judgments.

A. To the objection offered, that many remain apparently unmoved and unconvinced by God's word, the Scriptures acknowledge it — up to a point! *"For the gospel was preached to us, as well as to them. But the word preached did not profit them, not being mixed with faith in those who heard it. For we who believed do enter into rest...the works were finished from the foundation of the world"* (Heb. 4:2,3). Some are not moved by powerful and right words because they lack faith, and they lack faith because it was, (1) rejected by them as a way of life, and (2) it was not given to them, for faith is the gift of God — not of works, not by works of righteousness which they had done, or not done — not given because not chosen, for *"God knows those that are His"* (2 Tim. 2:19). Some are vessels of wrath fitted for destruction (Rom. 9:21-23; Jude 4), ordained to condemnation.

Some will perhaps say that the word of God is truly not all that powerful if it cannot convert all that it brings pressure upon. Does that prove it is not powerful?—*"For the word of God is living and powerful and sharper than any two-edged sword, piercing even to the dividing apart of soul and spirit, and of the joints and marrow, and is a discerner of the thoughts and intents of the heart"* (Heb. 4:12). Has fire no heat because it did not burn the three Hebrew children in Nebuchadnezzar's fire? Is the sun to be despised because it hardens clay, softens butter and melts sugar? God's word does not return to Him void simply because He alone decides beforehand whether it shall be a *"savor of death unto death,"* or, *"the savor of life unto life,"* (2 Cor. 2:16). Some He deliberately hardens, it may be even by His word hammering against the one hardened, *"Even for this same purpose I have raised you up, that I might show My power in you and that My name might be declared throughout all the earth. Therefore He has mercy on whom He will have mercy, and whom He will He hardens"* (Rom. 9:17,18). Right words are powerful, and it is God's prerogative as to what they will powerfully effect in the lives of men.

3. Right words comfort and encourage, *"He sent His word and healed them"* (Ps. 107:20). *"Your comforts delight my soul"* (Ps. 94:20). *"I will not leave you comfortless...I will ask the Father and He shall give you another Comforter..,..the Spirit of truth..He shall teach you all things and bring all things to your memory, whatever I have said to you"* (John 14:15-26). Discomfort and discouragement are the seeds of sin, and those who intricately weave presumption, ill-assumption and 'human logic' into a covering for their sins will meet with these two giants at every turn — yes, even a greater one will stalk their steps, the giant, Despair. But even such men as these, if they will but repent of their evil ways and words, turning to the Lord Jesus as their deliverer and healer, have hope for endless days of comfort and encouragment and cheerful obedience to Him.

4. Right words convert the hearer, making a powerful change in those who hear it, *"whose heart the Lord opened, so that she listened to the things which were spoken by Paul"* (Acts 16:14) — *"He who has ears to hear, let him hear"* (Matt. 13:43). There are those who hear God's word, and there are those who cannot, *"Why do you not understand My words? Because you cannot hear My word! You are of your father the devil, and the lusts of your father you lust to do"* (John 8:43). But so powerful are the words of God when He directs them to convert the hearer, that even the dead hear the voice of the Son of God, *"and they who hear will live"* (John 5:25). He who made the seeing eye also made the hearing ear, and He is able to make that ear hear whenever and wherever He chooses — yes, even the wicked must hear and fulfill His will, if He pleases (Rev. 17'17).

MAN'S DEFENCE AGAINST RIGHT WORDS

The secret will of God is not known to those of us who are charged with speaking His word toward ears that seemingly hear nothing we say. It may be helpful to understand at least a few ways that men turn aside the words of truth, of which we will mention five:

1. The proverbs (commandments) of men are used to nullify and disarm right words.

2. The traditions, rituals and tribal customs of the human race are designed to slow and eventually stop the penetration of the words of God, by friction, sublimation, etc.

3. God's outward dealings with men are used as arguments to make God's word void.

4. Spiritual privileges and practices are perverted into acts which hypocrites may perform.

5. Scripture is used to deny those scriptures which demand perfection and absolute purity, those words which condemn and strip man down to one who drinks iniquity like water.

1. For every proverb in the God-breathed Bible, there is a proverb of man which denies, perverts, or lightens what God has said. To these have been added the impediments of all the unbelieving hearts of the army of philosophers since the dawn of time, neatly packaged into lying proverbs. And if this were not enough, to these have been added the accretions and secretions of filthy men, those whose *"every imagination* (notion, fancy, concept, scheme, idea) *of the thoughts of his heart was only evil continually"* (Gen. 6:5). From Confucius to Mao, from Nimrod to Russell and Huxley, men have been coining counterfeit proverbs as a means of nullifying and disarming the words of God. On the face of it, with little objection possible, one would have to say that men as a whole group, or as each particular representative of the race, are culpably ignorant of what God has said to men. Yet, seemingly paradoxically, there is not a man on the face of the earth who cannot tell you what God has said to men – if you do not believe this, just ask him. As long as you will still sit and listen to him, he will unwind to you his cobwebian beliefs, a mixture of untruths, lies and perversions which will defy all efforts to sort them out and trace their origin. They will tell you that God helps those who help themselves, that all who live by the golden rule will go to Heaven, that if you do the best you can you will be accepted before God as well as the next man, etc., *ad infinitum.* The cast of the civilization will determine how far from Biblical teaching these proverbs will be. The Pharisees kept their perversions steeped in the generalizations which men make from God's word. The savages have but the barest vestiges of God's commandments written upon their hearts today, so their best proverbs do not reflect much of the original truths revealed by God to man.

The key to teaching sinners, be they converted or yet in the gall and bitterness of their sinful souls, is to remember that *"all men are liars,"* and to determine to *"let God be true and every man be a liar,"* (Ps. 116:11; Rom. 3:4). Those who *"are according to the flesh mind the things of the flesh, but they who are according to the Spirit mind the things of the Spirit"* (Rom. 8:5). If you speak right words, keeping them in the context of the Scriptures, then you may be sure that they will have their effect upon your hearers.

2. Besides the counterfeit proverbs coined by men to make God's word of no effect, a profuse use of ritual, custom and tradition proved to be a great way to make an unholy marriage between man's religious nature and his desire to be a god to himself. The first sign of departure from the true word of God is usually this permission of ritual in the church. Nothing in God's word leads one to do anything by rote. Every rewardable act by a believer must be a voluntary, conscious act of faith toward God, individually conceived and personally desired. In those groups where tradition is allowed to spread its pervasive grey cover of assumptions, sin never again appears to be pitch black, and purity is never again required to be perfectly white. Once man's religion becomes customized to the ungodly desires of the heart of man, the truth is systematically squeezed out of all his activities and thoughts – and whatever is then put in the place of God, whether it be ancestor worship or the hoary traditions of the catholic church, will be patched and tailored by generations of men – but always using the same pattern, the wicked and deceitful heart of man (Jeremiah 17:9). If a man wants to be sensitive to the word of God, it

would be well for him to remember that anything which appeals to his sensual appetite is going to make it more difficult for him to discern the truth and to make judgments about things that differ.

3. God's outward dealings with men, His love, mercy, goodness and forbearance, are used as an excuse to avoid the right and powerful words of God. *"Because sentence against an evil work is not executed speedily, then the heart of the sons of men is fully set in them to do evil"* (Eccles. 8:11). The tender mercies of the Lord are over all His works (Ps. 145:9), and there is a sense in which He is merciful to all — *"Our God is a consuming fire"* — *"It is of the Lord's mercy that we are not consumed"* (Heb. 12:20; Lam. 3:22). Some presume upon this general blanket of mercy which the Lord has spread over the race of men, thinking that because His rain of goodness falls upon the wicked as well as upon the godly then in the day of judgment there is hope that He will not be severe with those who were not precise in obeying Him. These are *"willingly ignorant"* of God's limiting words, *"I will have mercy on whom I desire to have mercy,"* and on the others may come a hardening influence made up out of the very same mercy which blesses God's chosen vessels. Of course those scoffers who walk in their own lusts are going to pretend that there is no difference between the mercy which God shows toward them and the love and grace He showers upon those who believe. Because all share His mercy, they promise themselves that all also share God's favor. But God does not love everybody, therefore He does not give His grace to everybody. God is rich in mercy, but it is because of *"His great love with which He loved us* (even when we were dead in sins) *that He has made us alive together with Christ...and has raised us up together and made us sit together in heavenly places in Christ Jesus, so that in the ages to come He might show the exceeding riches of His grace"* to those that are His. It is toward the *"beloved"* that He is *"longsuffering."* He truly is not slack concerning His promise — but, then, His promise is not to all men, but to us whom He has ordained to believe (Acts 13:48). And since He keeps His promises, He is longsuffering toward us — He is NOT longsuffering toward THEM! Therefore, He will not allow any of us to perish, for He is not willing that any one of those He *"from the beginning"* chose *"to salvation through sanctification of the Spirit and belief of the truth,"* to be lost from His embrace or presence. From *"the foundation of the world"* He wrote the names of all His chosen ones in the *"Book of Life of the Lamb"* and it is certain that though a mother may forget her sucking child the Lord God will not forget a single one of those He has loved from everlasting (Jeremiah 31:3). Therefore, He shall grant to each and every one of those chosen vessels the gift of repentance (Acts 11:18), and they shall all be saved — not one of them shall be lost, there is not a single son of perdition among them!

4. There are those who are abundantly privileged, being under the hearing of the word of God, being reared in the company of those who are faithful, being befriended by the true children of God constantly. Why do they not hear and obey the word? It would appear that they would not be able to withstand the power of those words which they so readily admit to be the very words of God. But there are those who are *"hearers only,"* deceiving themselves into thinking that because they acknowledge the words to be from God they need not be doers of the word. The Lord Jesus described several groups who heard, but did not profit because of it, (1) Those who heard but did not understand it, because their heart was gross and their ears dull of hearing — the wicked one comes and catches away all the seed of the word that has been sown in such hearts, as easily as one takes candy from a baby; (2) Those who heard with joy, but not having the root of the matter in themselves, they stumbled and lost it when they had to suffer tribulation or persecution because of the word; (3) Those who heard and apparently received the word into their lives, but soon found their care for the world, for its riches, etc. choked the word right out of them again.

There is still among us a multitude of groups who deceive themselves, saying, *"We are the seed of Abraham,"* meaning they are baptized into the 'church' as infants and hold some inviolable right to the name of Christian. Many times Jesus answered these, saying, *"If you were Abraham's seed, you would do the works of Abraham"* — beginning, of course, with Abraham's faith. *"Why do you not understand My words? Because you cannot hear My word...He who is of God hears God's words. Therefore you do not hear them because you are not of God."* (John 8:39-17). These depend as much on their baptism as the Jews depended on their circumcision. Just as the Jew counted himself to be a true Jew because he was circumcised, so these count themselves to be true Christians because they are baptized. But as the apostle Paul told those Jews, *"he is not a Jew who is one outwardly, nor is that circumcision which is outward in the flesh; but he is a Jew who is one inwardly, and circumcision is that of the heart, in the spirit and not in the letter"*— so must we tell these baptized ones, however faithful their parents, that, 'he is not a Christian who is one outwardly, nor is that baptism which is but sprinkled upon the flesh; but he is a Christian who is one inwardly, and baptism is illicit unless one is buried with Christ in baptism, and unless one rises from that baptism with Christ through a faith which is worked in him by the almighty working of God' (Rom. 2:25; Col. 2:12). Neither baptism, nor any other outward act will avail anything. Only a new creation is able to give validity to the claim of any man to that love name, Christian (Galatians 6:15).

There are those who believe in salvation by works. Since words mean nothing to them, and their works are all that count with them, they throw off even the most powerful words with reckless abandon. These carefully form themselves into a godly mold, or what they consider to be a godly mold — but since their entire concept of salvation is one which they can fashion themselves, they are condemned by the word of God as *"lovers of their own selves,"* and, *"lovers of pleasure rather than lovers of God."* Of course, they react violently to these accusations, presenting an impressive array of proof that they sacrifice themselves selflessly, that they carefully avoid worldly entertainment, worldly self-indulgence, etc. Yet it must be asked, For whom do they do this? For what do they do this? If they deny themselves ever so much, if they force themselves into however much of a contorted religious position, and do it because it pleases them to do it, they are guilty of being *"lovers of their own selves,"* and, *"lovers of pleasure more than of God."* One can wear a different dress, cultivate different habits, fly in the face of the world's values, speak in a tongue unknown to any other and give all his goods to the poor, yet remain nothing more than a worldling, gain nothing more than self-adulation, or the plaudits of some fellow practioners of this low-grade spiritual art. It is not only that we must not be conformed to this world, it is also that we must be renewed and transformed until we have in us that mind which was in Christ Jesus — who, contrary to the popular view, lived a life of faith based on every word that proceeded from the mouth of God from everlasting to everlasting. That which these proud self-saviors call love of God shall one day be seen for what it is, an adulterated extension of their own self-love.

There are those who believe that what all men agree upon must surely have some authenticity in the eyes of God. Yet God's word is explicit to these, *"Do not follow a multitude to do evil,"* *"whatever is highly esteemed among men is abominable to God,"* *"whoever desires to be a friend of the world is the enemy of God,"* etc. (Exod. 23:2; Luke 16:15; James 4:5).

5. Some are such astute learners from their father, the Devil, that they use his method of avoiding the force of powerful scriptures — they quote the Bible against the Bible. There are a host of men who spend their time digging up what they denominate 'errors' or at least, 'discrepancies,' in the word of God. These do not seem to realize that in doing so, in determining for themselves that God's word is imperfect, they are setting themselves up as the infallible ones — that is, they are the ones who determine what is perfect, what is not. If a thing is imperfect, using their set of rules, their logic, and, more importantly, their limited views, then these 'gods' make this the law of their lives. One cannot but be astounded as he watches them substitute their words for the pure words of God, then summarily

demand that all bow to their exalted excrescences.

Another form of this ungodliness, exampled by Satan in the Temptation of Christ, is the quotation of a scripture out of context in order to induce a sinful action. Not only will they search for full verses to use in establishing their errors, but they become very adept at using half-verses to teach a lie. A perusal of any sectarian commentary, and especially of their 'translations,' will turn up myriads of such perversions – and some, like Origen, will quote a verse one way this week and another way next week, for expediency. For example, unbelievers bask themselves in the warmth of Romans 8:28, *"all things work together for good"* – many of them stop quoting it there. Others add, *"to those who love God"* amd congratulate themselves upon the fact that they love God (and who does not, if their own claims are all the authentication that is needed?). But only a handful of faithful men will add the qualifying clause which excludes the vast majority of the sons of men, *"to those who are the called according to His purpose."*) Acts 2:38,39 has been the womb from which some have claimed to extract the Bible-denying doctrines of salvation via baptism, the denial of salvation to all who are not water-baptized, and the false view that there are specific promises to all children of believers – yet the entire verses themselves belie these doctrines (take the latter case, *"the promise is to you and to your children"*–yes, but to what children, *"as many as the Lord God shall call"*).

It should be remembered that the Pharisees used the Scriptures to prove that Christ was not the Messiah, nor even a prophet! Be careful that you do not wrest the Scriptures in order to prove your own beliefs to be the right set of beliefs, and your construction of the truth to be the only construction of the truth. Leave the windows of your mind open toward God, that the light of truth as it is in Jesus may shine in upon you. All too often the truth loses by the patronage and defence that some give it – we must not only know it, we must study to make ourselves able to present it in its Biblical context. But especially the truth loses by the tongues of those men who have no grace in their hearts, as witness again, the Pharisees. Truth in the mouth of a wicked man is weakened by the falseness of his heart and the filthiness of his life. God may allow hypocrites to sit in Moses' chair, but their words will not have power, only the word of God will have power when they speak them to believing hearts.

"What does your arguing argue?"–Job is saying that the words of Eliphaz are discredited because they are not right words – at least they are not the right words for his case. The rebuke could have been timely and on target, as was later proven by Elihu and by God Himself. The arguments of Eliphaz are not arguments at all if they do not apply to Job. Would one spend his time proving the basic principles of mathematics to a mathematician? All the good Eliphaz has said is of no use to Job, being but what he already knew and in fact could express better. Will a man admit to murder when he has murdered no one? No more can Job admit to the kind of sins which his friends imply that he 'must have committed. in order to bring upon himself such severe affliction. Let them argue until they are blue in their faces, they will never prove a thing to a man who is not guilty of their charges.

"Do you intend to criticize words, and the speeches of one who is hopeless, that are wind?"–Job 6:25.

Job having made an humble submission of himself to the better counsel and instruction of his friends, asking only that they show him in what way he had erred, he now begins to expostulate with his friends about their attitude toward him, and he admonishes them to be more moderate and considerate in what they yet intend to say to him.

First, he taxes them for making light of what he had said. They are reproving him for his words, for his speeches, yet they have not given any weight to the fact that he is a hopeless and desperately disturbed man. Secondly, he rebukes them for laying such a heavy load upon one who already was overloaded with cares and considerations far deeper and hurtful than they seemed to realize.

"Do you intend to criticize words"–Are you here to turn a critical eye on my every

word? Do you imagine that God sent you here to reprove my words? Is it your scheme to turn the spotlight on my words and carefully to pick up every little waver from the path of absolute righteousness? Did you come all this distance to search for a twig in my eye, and do you think that you have God's command to remove it? The original word pictures a very curious, exquisite and elaborate invention of anything. Could it be that these men had come there for the purpose of proving themselves logicians and orators, rather than as loving friends? If not, then why did they insisting upon wording it out with Job? Why did they spin out carefully devised and ill-disguised charges of great sin upon Job, phrasing them in polished and close-knit arguments? And why did they so despise Job's words as to completely ignore them in making these charges? You do not see them saying, 'you said,' and in answer to this, 'I say,' or, 'God says.' Instead they treated Job's words as so many empty syllables, or, worse, as a frothing of the mouth from a madman. Was there not a single word of truth and reason in all of that speech?

"the speeches of one who is hopeless," or, *"desperate"*—The word signifies a person that is quite without hope, who thinks his estate is past remedy, his wound incurable, his loss irreparable, and his breaks so wide that they can never be healed (see Jer. 2:25). Before they were charged with thinking Job's words unworthy of their attention, now he comes with a further reproachful charge, that they believe he is a hopeless case, a desperate one. Because he had lost all, his possessions, his children, his friends, and his health, they were acting as if he also had lost his wits and his faith. It is easy to throw off all a man's words by simply declaring him mad. However cogent and forceful his arguments may be, there are usually many who will join you in saying that he is out of his mind — such was the case with Festus when he declared to Paul, *"much learning has made you mad."* If a poor man cannot get his wisdom before the people, how much less can a man accused of madness be in hope of a fair hearing? (Eccl. 9:16).

"that they are wind"—It is common in the Scriptures to put light, vain and unprofitable words under this expression, that they are as wind. The Jews were accused by Jeremiah of having such a view of the prophets, *"And the prophets shall become wind, and the word is not in them"* — that is, the words of the prophets are no words, they are but wind. To which the Lord replied, *"I will make My words...fire, and I will make this people wood, and it shall devour them"* (Jer. 5:13,14). *"Ephraim feeds on wind"*—and what was this wind? They were vain words and promises which he had built into hopes, *"he daily increases lies"* (Hosea 12:1). Truly, if we do not have the spirit of reason, that which comes from our mouths is nothing more than *"great swelling words of vanity"* (2 Peter 2:18). Wise men speak great things, but fools only speak great words. But Job was no such fool.

Windy, empty words will of course not convince or convert anyone. They are like the bubbles that float through the air, finally bursting upon any solid object they contact. But it is uncharitable to assume that the words of a man sorely afflicted are bound to be nothing more than windy speeches. It is easy to think that such a man complains more than is necessary, and that he talks more than he ought. In fact, it may be very sinful indeed not to listen to one who is heavily afflicted by God. If his every word is drenched and steeped in sorrows, if his every sentence comes, as it were, bleeding from a wounded spirit, then compassion and love should flow as freely from our hearts toward him.

It should not pass notice that Job describes his case as hopeless, though denying that he is hopeless in the sense that he can make no sense with his words. He never quite fell to making Jacob's error, of saying, *"all these things are against me;"* or David's error, *"I shall one day perish by the hand of Saul,"* yet he sees himself as a man who had no strength to hold on to life, and in fact as one who had no desire to do so. His hopes were not here any more.

Job's words in chapter three should be studied. They are not the words of a madman. It may be that they were excessive, that they call for spiritual correction, that even his ill-condition cannot cover all the unrelieved complaints that he made, but they are not at all words of no value, windy speeches, or irrational emissions.

"Yea, you cause anger to fall on the fatherless, and you dig a pit for your friend"—Job 6:27.
After his charge of uncharitableness, he now adds this further degree to it, that they had overwhelmed him with the hardness of their blows, with the sharpness of their expression. And he does it by charging them with two odious acts of cruelty: (1) the undoing of an orphan; (2) the digging of a pit for a friend.

"you overwhelm the fatherless"—The original is full of emphasis. It may be translated, *"you throw yourselves on the fatherless,"* an allusion to hunters who hunt down their prey and after wounding them severely fall upon them heavily. A dog jumps upon a rabbit once he has caught it. Here, of course, Job accuses them of hunting him down as one who is already crippled, wounded and weak, then falling upon him. For the word means this, to run upon one with violence (so giants are called *nephilim* in the Hebrew, because they are big enough to be heavy oppressors and to overwhelm the weaker with force and with violence). It is possible also to translate the words, *"you lay a snare for the orphan"*—in which case the oppression would be one of subtle and secret planning. It can also in such a case perhaps be compared with the word in the New Testament which means, to scandalize. There are those who set out to entangle a man and cause him to lose his reputation.

"the fatherless"—The word strictly taken is put for an orphan, but here by fatherless it is evidently put for one who is destitute of help. He that is friendless and comfortless is in a very real sense an orphan. When Christ promised the disciples the Comforter, He in the original said, *"I will not leave you orphans,"* or, *"fatherless."* For orphans are usually full of sorrows, without the comfort of parents, without the light of counsel and direction given by those more wise than themselves. So these are accused of overwhelming and heavily bearing down upon one who is poor, destitute and helpless.

"and you dig a pit for your friend"—or, literally word for word, *"you dig for your friend."* This fits well with the translation, *"you lay a snare for the fatherless."* For it is normal to dig a pit when laying a snare. False and fallacious arguments are traps in which the innocent may easily become entangled. Job may have supposed that his friends are trying to cast him down into the pit of despair by charging him with hypocrisy and rottenness of heart in his profession. It is evil to dig pits and lay snares for anyone, but it is an aggravated sin to oppress those who are so weakened and heavy-laden as to be unable to defend themselves. As Solomon warned the rich, *"Do not rob the poor because he is poor,"* (Prov. 22:22) so may the strong be warned in like manner. Do not fall upon the weak because he is weak. When we help those who cannot help themselves, doing it as we ought in God's name, by the enablement of God, then God gets much glory from our act. But if we hurt those who cannot defend themselves, will not God's name be dishonored? And will not God Himself be likely to take his part and give us our deserved reward?—*"their Redeemer is mighty, He shall plead their case with you."*

If it is twice evil to dig a pit and attempt to ensnare one who is unable to protect himself, then it is thrice evil to do so to a friend. How much more is it an aggravation of unkindness when we try to hurt those who we are bound by many commands to love and comfort!

"And now please look upon me; for if I lie, it is before your face"—Job 6:28,
Job begins to humble himself and moderate his charges against his friends as he now asks them to moderate their views of him. He wants them to look more favorably upon him, to uncloud their brows, soften their faces and become the friends they always had been.
Or, it could be that Job is saying, Look me in the face and see if you can find there any evidence that I am lying to you when I say I am not guilty of the things you charge. Again, it may be that he is saying, I am not afraid to look you in the face, so look upon me and then you will have to say that I lied looking you in the eye.

"For if I lie, it is before your face"—Some think that there is a secret imprecation in this speech, as if he had said, 'Do not let the Lord be merciful to me if I am being false-hearted and lying to you.' It is not unusual to see such an oath in the Hebrew.

To lie may be taken two ways, either strictly, to speak that which is false in order to deceive; or, to lie in the sense that one falls short of being what is expected from them. The word is so used in Hab. 3:17, *"though the labor of the olive should fail"*—it is this word, *"should lie"*—meaning, that if one would come for the fruit of the olive it, would fail to produce what was expected of it. In either of these cases we may understand it as being an evident thing to those who would but look in Job's face, whether he was lying in order to deceive, or whether he was failing to meet with their expectations. He gives them a like challenge in 24:25, *"who will make me a liar and make my speech worth nothing."*

Just as the eyelids of the Lord *"try the children of men,"* so do we look carefully and long into the faces of those we suspect of lying. Just as the judge must eye his defendent, so must we at least have the courtesy to search the faces of those we intend to accuse. There are those who are able to bear the heavy weight of guilt without betraying themselves with an eye or an expression of the face, but it is usual for those who are guilty to be ill at ease and lacking in confidence.

Uprightness has much boldness. He that has a good cause and a good conscience is not afraid to be searched to the very bottom. He invites inspection. David would say to God *"search me and try me, and see if there is any wickedness in me"* (Ps. 139:23).

A lie cannot usually be hidden for long. If the first lie does not betray itself, the second lie to cover it will reveal it.

"Turn back, I beg of you, let there be no sin; yea, return again, my righteousness is in this matter"—Job 6:29.

The word does mean to return from a place, but it is also used metaphorically as a returning from anger, *"His anger is not turned away, the Lord did not turn back from His fierce wrath."* Some understand it so here, this is, *"I beseech you not to be so angry."*

Also there can be a meaning of desisting from our purpose, changing our minds. And in this sense it would be the same as repenting, and the Scriptures abound with the use of the word in this sense. In which case, Job would be saying, *"I beg of you, repent of your former way of dealing with me, for my righteousness is in this matter."*

Again, there is a possibility that he is saying, Turn back and have another look, lest there be sin. Give over your hard censures and wounded language before it is too late to turn back.

"let there be no sin"—Some see it as meaning, Do not speak unrighteously against me. Others say it means, Do not deal so unequally, so unjustly, and hardly with me. The Hebrew particle does not always forbid, but it often denotes a simple denial— so some translate it here, *"there shall not be iniquity,"* that is, in my words, or in that which I shall speak.

"yea, return again"—This repetition of the plea to turn back doubles the vehemency of the beggar. It expresses an opinion that a weighty and necessary point is being made. Pay doubly close attention, for this is important! So the word return is often doubled, as is the word rejoice.

"My righteousness is in it"—Job was not known to boast of his righteousness, for he was an humble man, so described by God. Therefore, when this humble man declares flatly and confidently that he is righteously making this claim of innocence, this plea for fair appraisal, it is binding upon his best friends to show themselves friendly and heed his call. If they brush aside his claim to righteousness, then if they are wrong the wrong they do him will be many times multiplied. If you turn back, he is saying, you will find that I am in the right, that I am not to blame in this business as you think that I am — I have not broken the rules of justice nor departed from a good conscience.

To persist in evil is worse than the bare commission of evil. Once warned that evil is being done, it is best that we turn back and reconsider our steps carefully to make certain that we have not gone astray from the will of God. It is common to man to sin. It is peculiar to the Devil and his followers to persist in sin even after being plainly warned of the wrong being done. Many have in passion gone beyond the bounds laid down by God, but it is a usual thing for the conscience to warn us to turn back. Thus anger will abate, and appetite will be slaked, but devilishness will persist in wickedness. Oftentimes the Lord lays this as the heaviest charge of all upon His people, that they will not turn back from their course of sin, *"but you have said, There is no hope; no, for I have loved strangers and after them I will go"* (Jer. 2:25). *"I have smitten you, yet you have not returned to Me."* Impenitency seals the stone of destruction upon both persons and nations.

Every sin is a sin, as the least drop of water is water. But in a strict sense, not every sin is an iniquity. The nature is the same, but the degree varies. A sin repeated, unrepented of, is going to be iniquity.

It is remarkable that Job is able to move far enough away from his own troubles, his own complaints, to offer some excellent advice to his friends. And more, he is showing concern for them in trying to keep them back from sin. He does not rail at them, and certainly he does not revile them in the way they have been reviling him. But he begs them to reconsider their course and to look carefully at him, so that they may avoid further sinfulness.

It is not only charitable and wise, it is also prudent to consider carefully a man's condition before we pass judgment on him and condemn him as a gross sinner — yes, it would be the better part of wisdom to consider twice before doing so. If we must give account for every idle word (Matt. 12:36), then how much more shall we be called into judgment for every unjust censure, for each mistaken condemnation — even of an enemy, much less a friend!

"Is there perversity in my tongue? Cannot my taste tell things that are wrong?"—Job 6:30.

Job insists upon some answer which has reference to his words. If there is any perversity, any wresting of the Scriptures, any iniquitous utterance which would call into question the rule of God, then he asks that they reveal it to him. He is not aware that he has said anything mischievous, nor desired anything unlawful.

"Cannot my taste tell"—or, *"understand"*—It is not unusual in God's word to read of an understanding tongue, or hand, as well as mind. There is a great affinity between reason and speech, and therefore the tongue, the instrument of speech, is honored with the work of the understanding. Speech is, or ought to be, the immediate issue of reason. Words are, so to speak, conceived in the mind and born at the tongue. These words are the image of the mind. The mind and the heart become known, what shape they are in, by what issues from the tongue. There is a second reason why acts of the understanding are ascribed to the tongue, or to the other senses. It is because a well-spoken word reveals a well-ordered understanding, one well-furnished and informed.

Further, it is frequent in Scripture to metaphorically translate things which are only acted or apprehended by the inward sense to the outward senses. Taste is properly of meat and drink, yet here Job speaks of doctrines, or of actions. If a thing is perversely spoken, cannot I discern it and tell that it is wrong? In another place Job varies the metaphor, saying, *"Does not the ear try words?"* (12:11).

"things that are wrong"—or, as others translate, *"Cannot my taste tell when desirable things are in it?"* The original word can mean desire, as well. Either way, whether tasting desirable things, or things that are distasteful, there is an understanding that it is so.

The tongue oftentimes reveals the iniquity and perversity of the heart. If the heart is evil, the tongue will blister with its poison. For the tongue is a fire, a world of iniquity (James 3:6), but it could not be so of itself. It has to be set on fire by the carnal nature of man. It is out of the abundance of evil that is in the heart that the mouth speaks (Matt. 12:34). As the girl accused Peter, *"your speech betrays you"* (Matt. 26:73), so it is with most.

Job claims, and rightly so, that a man who has perversity in his tongue will know it. Although it is not always so that a believer has a clear sight of his own integrity and uprightness (many a soul is a false witness to himself,) yet for the most part sincerity has the ability to witness of itself, and holiness carries a light by which it is seen to him who has it. Furthermore, it is a duty of the righteous to maintain his own integrity. It is not right to accept false accusations against one's person, else the ungodly may conclude, as the Devil charged against Job, that the only reason a person holds to the obedience of a holy God is because there is some kind of gain involved in his service.

A CHRISTIAN HAS A GOD-GIVEN TASTE TO DISCERN ERROR FROM TRUTH.

Kings have servants to taste food before they will eat it, lest there may be poison in the pot. Likewise, it is our duty when we are at a full table of knowledge, where there is a variety of doctrines and opinions being served up to us, to pray for a spiritual taste to enable us to distinguish those things which are truly according to the word of God. If we do not guard against poisonous teachings, then we may be spiritually retarded, crippled or corrupted before we have gotten our spiritual wits about us. Even one wild gourd among good herbs in the pot may put death into the pot. Therefore we must taste, comparing all opinions and teachings to the word of God. For there is a woe attached to failure in this duty, *"Woe to those who call evil good and good evil, who put darkness for light and light for darkness — woe unto those who are wise in their own eyes and bright in their own sight! ...as the fire devours the stubble and the flame burns up the chaff, so their root shall be like rottenness and their blossom shall go up like dust — because they have cast away the law of the Lord of hosts and have despised the word of the Holy One of Israel"* (Isa. 5:20).

There is also woe to those who will not give others the right to discern for themselves what is good or evil. Those, and they are many, who do not think that there is anything true unless they have digested it with their own bellies shall one day discover that God is the one and only Lawgiver, and He will tell each of His children what is right, *"If anyone desires to do His will, He shall know of the doctrine, whether it is of God"* (John 7:17). It is no better to let another taste for us than it is for us to allow another to live for us.

Then he who will not take the pains to develop a taste for spiritual things, so as to be able to discern between good and evil things, will have not much less woe than he who encourages this kind of attitude toward God's word. These indifferent fools are as apt to pronounce evil doctrine to be wholesome and tasty as they are to call good teaching bitter and unsavory. Bring them a false doctrine, a lie, a dream, a fancy, any mere human invention, and they apply a taster that is ruined by lust and made rusty by disuse —they will call them all alike good. Then there is the one who has a truly reprobate mind, one who knows those things that are right and true, yet one who determines he shall do all that is in his evil heart. He shall have the heaviest curse, being guilty of the perversity of devils, sinning willfully against knowledge.

It is a sadness which ought never to have been, but which comes sometimes into the life of the Christian — he loses his spiritual senses. These are usually those who have wantonly wasted their opportunities to know God's word in a measure not offered to many. These usually are walking deliberately below the truths that they know, being content to do less than they know is plainly commanded. The closer these have walked with God, the further they may be allowed to stray from Him. Consider David, a man after God's own heart, a man who became the sweet Psalmist of Israel long before he ever saw Bathsheba. Never has a man fallen so far so fast as this one, who went upon his rooftop to idle away his time, and came down from there with his spiritual senses corrupted by the sight of a beautiful woman bathing. The adultery, the robbing of Uriah, first of his wife, then of his life, the lies and deceit that went between—who would have thought that David would ever have been affected by the sight of a woman so much that he would lose all his ability to tell right from wrong? When our tastes are not exercised, we lose them — *"For everyone who uses milk is unskillful in the word of righteousness...but solid food belongs to those who are of full age, even those who because of use have their senses exercised to discern both good and evil"* (Heb. 5:13, 14). It is he who uses his spiritual senses that is able to keep his ability to discern the things that are of God, and those that are not.

Even true doctrine falsely applied is a perverse thing, and Job claims that he has the taste to tell when such a thing is being done to him. False teaching will pervert reason, and it will corrupt understanding. Even in the church of Ephesus, where Paul taught for so long, men arose *"speaking perverse things, to draw away disciples after them"* (Acts 20:30). Holy teachings will draw God's men, but false doctrine will draw men who are not close to God. As itching ears heap teachers to themselves, so do false tongues.

"Is there not a warfare to man upon earth? Are not his days also like the days of a hire--ling?"—Job 7:1.

Because the connection between this and the former chapter does not lie on the surface, there is a great deal of conjecture about it:

1. It may be conceived that Job in this discourse refutes that tenet of Eliphaz, that he who suffers much is being punished and scourged for his wickedness. By showing that it is the common condition of man to be afflicted in one way or another, Job proves that affliction is not directly the result of wickedness or sinfulness as to its degree or measure.

2. Some say that Job is confuting the promise which Eliphaz made in the twentieth verse of chapter five, by proving that it is inconsistent with the present estate of mortals to look for uninterrupted happiness, or even troublefree days.

3. The connection may be made with those words which he had spoken in verse twenty-four of the last chapter in which he claimed that he was teachable. In line with this, he then admits here that *"man is born unto trouble as the sparks fly upward."* And later in the chapter he also seeks unto God, in verses seventeen and twenty.

4. But lastly, and most probably, Job has in the former chapter refuted those arguments by which Eliphaz had sought to convict him of a heavy load of guilt, and now he proceeds to confirm his first request to die and lays some groundwork to justify the request.

First, he notes that all of life on earth is a continuous warfare. Why should he desire it?

Secondly, even a servant may look for this much reward for his work, the cessation of his service, therefore is there not good reason for Job to desire to end his work on earth?

Thirdly, his own special condition, which seems to him to be the very last fleeting scene which he will see in this life, convinces him that it would be far better to depart and be with the Lord.

Fourthly, he begins again to renew his former complaints.

Lastly, in this chapter, he abases himself before God as unworthy that God should take any notice of him, not so much as to bestow a thought or even a chastisement upon him. He concludes the chapter with a confession of sin, an earnest desire for pardon.

"Is there not a warfare to man upon earth?"—or, *"Is there not an appointed time to man on earth?"*—Affirmatively, as the question-form would suggest, it is this, *"There is a warfare to man on earth."*

Just as surely as man is born unto trouble, he is born to fight in a war which has continued from the day Adam sinned until now. This would be a sad circumstance even if he were born to fight on the side of good, on the side of power, with the hope of eventually winning this war and achieving some peace and tranquility for himself. But, alas! There has been only one fleeting period of time when this earth has known peace and tranquility — that short time when Adam was content and satisfied with God and by God alone. Never again on THIS earth shall there by any peace and tranquility for the whole race at any time, nor for anyone for any long period of time.

MAN FINDS HIMSELF FIGHTING A WAR ON FOUR FRONTS AT ONCE

This war is not imposed upon him, but it is a war of his own choosing. And, sadly, any one of the enemies he has chosen to fight is too hard for him — he cannot even defeat the weakest of them. How then could he expect to win a contest with God Almighty?

1. Men are at war against God.
2. Men are at war against Satan and his angels, principalities and powers.
3. Men are at war with all other men.
4. Men are at war with themselves.

In spite of this impossible entanglement in wars he cannot win, man is so full of evil imagination, so blinded by pride, so deceived by false reasoning, that he has delusions and hallucinations in which he sees himself the victor over all his foes. Is this not like a dying soldier, feverish and out of his head, boasting loudly how he has conquered his foes, how he will punish them with fiendish delight as soon as he recovers from his wounds.

1. MEN ARE AT WAR AGAINST GOD.

We are all born with a carnal mind, which *"is enmity against God, for it is not subject to the law of God, neither indeed can it be"* (Rom. 8:7). *"For if when we were enemies we were reconciled to God by the death of His Son"* (Rom 5:10)—in which we see the flat statement that we were enemies; *"you who were once alienated and enemies in your mind by wicked works"* (Col. 1:21); *"My Spirit shall not always strive with man"* (Gen. 6:3). Men in the flesh are continually lusting against God the Holy Spirit, as well as God the Father and the Son (Gal. 5:17).

It was lust which started the war between man and God, for Adam desired (lusted) to be wise, to be as God, and thereby became a sinner at war with God. Thus man, through his appointed representative, Adam, chose war with his Maker rather than to give over his lust to be a god to himself.

It is lust which keeps man at war with God. For God, in His infinite goodness and rich mercy provided for man that which He never gave His angels, a Savior to deliver them from their state of rebellion, with complete pardon for their guilt and restoration of their former excellencies (Eph. 4:24). Yes, more, He now added the unspeakable privilege of being partakers of the divine nature, of being fully and finally conformed to the image of Jesus Christ, his God and his Lord. Again, more, they were now given the opportunity to become members of His own beloved family, to rest in His bosom forevermore. But man, corrupted and rotten in his nature, would not accept his peace from the One he considered his enemy. He, like the gladiator of old, must slay and completely destroy his foe. He feels that a surrender to God even on His generous peace terms would be to lose all. He is certain that existence without those things he is warring to obtain would be far more miserable than his troublesome life of warfare at present. It is self-love that rules supreme within him, and self-love tells him that there is no god and no degree of godliness that is worth the giving up of himself, the yielding to a complete new creation which will leave him a new and different man.

2. MEN ARE AT WAR AGAINST SATAN.

"be vigilant, for your adversary the devil walks about like a roaring lion, seeking whom he may devour" (1 Pet. 5:8). The entire book of Job is proof that Satan wars against men. Satan lives to make men miserable, to stand and accuse them, to take them captive and enslave them for his own foul purposes. Because they are captive to his will through their lusts, they are not able to fulfill all their lusts as they wish. This makes them hate their adversary, the devil. You would perhaps wonder why man does not make peace with the devil, and vice versa, they being the common enemy of God. It is lust that keeps man at the throat of Satan, and it is lust that keeps Satan undermining man through his rotten nature − the lust for pre-eminence, the lust for predominance, the lust for power to lay all in the dust who would raise a hand against him.

But carnal warfare, the kind that exists between Satan and mankind, is waged with the weapons of sophisticated intelligence and strength. The angels being of a higher order than man are both wiser in the ways of this world and stronger than the man of this world. The devils know the weakness of their enemy, man, and this is the greatest advantage in warfare. If a man has a weakness, such as a lust for strong drink, then to make it possible for him to obtain it is to win the battle over him. He can then easily be made to do the will of Satan. Men are diverse, but they all have lusts for myriads of varying things, for things that comfort and sensually please the body, for things that please the eye and the eyes of other men, for things that make him proud and glorious (John 2:15). Satan, by his rulership of this wicked world, is able to provide man with his drops of 'pleasure.' the easing of his painful lusts for a time, trading each one for a victory, for some service a-against God. Having drunk these fitful pleasures, man becomes putty in the hands of the Devil. He controls them through their lusts, whether it be gambling, illicit sex, lying, etc.

3. MEN ARE AT WAR WITH OTHER MEN.

"Where do wars and fightings among you come from? Do they not come from this, from your lusts which war in your members? You desire, and do not have. You kill, and are envious and cannot obtain. You fight and war, yet you have not because you ask not. You ask and do not receive because you ask amiss, so that you may consume it upon your lusts. Adulterers and adulteresses! Do you not know that the friendship of the world is enmity with God? Therefore, whoever desires to be a friend of the world is the enemy of God"– James 4:1-4.

"Now the works of the flesh are clearly seen, which are...hatred, fightings, jealousies, feelings of anger, strifes, sedition, heresies, envyings, murders...and things like these" –Gal. 5:19.

"For out of the heart come evil thoughts, murders, adulteries, fornications, thefts, false witness, blasphemies"–Matthew 15:19.

Not only does the flesh lust against the Spirit (Gal. 5:17), but the flesh lusts against the fleshly. Hatred, strife and fighting come out of the heart just as venom comes from a serpent's fangs, naturally, as the expected fruit of an unbelieving and ungodly nature. They are the offspring of man's lust to do as he pleases, when he pleases – he perversely claims it as his right, thereby putting himself in direct contradiction to the words of God.

Men may make peace for a time, but even when their words are smooth there is war in their hearts (Ps. 55:21). When every man is a god to himself, when everyone regards himself as the center of the universe, about which all persons and things must revolve, then there cannot be any peace. Conflicting desires bring conflict. Since all unbelievers by their very nature seek to enthrall the whole world and cause each one to sacrifice to their drag, evil sparks will forever fly when iron will strikes against another's iron will. There may be short periods of cease-fire while each seeks to bring up those weapons which will overcome the opposition, but as long as there are two sinners on the face of the earth, there will be *"a warfare to man upon earth."*

4. MEN ARE AT WAR WITH THEMSELVES.

"I beg you, as strangers and pilgrims, abstain from fleshly lusts which war against the soul"–1 Peter 2:11.

"but I see another law in my members warring against the law of my mind and leading me captive to the law of sin which is in my members. O wretched man that I am!"–Rom. 7:23,24a.

Lusts are strong desires – the Lord Jesus *"lusted to eat the Passover"* with His disciples. But the lusts of the flesh are many and varied, all of them strong and lusty, all of them warring against the good of a man's soul. Of the many ways that a man is at war with himself, we can only mention three: (1) he is at war with his conscience – every fleshly lust is at war with the conscience. God's witness is placed within man so that he might not sin without a testimony to the wickedness of that sin. Even a seared conscience will have traces of God's standards embedded in it, causing conflict and guilt (however sublimated) to rise in the heart of the ungodly. Herod was troubled for his rash oath in ordering the murder of John the Baptist. Yet it is not to be thought that the conscience is any kind of unerring guide (it being defiled–Titus 1:15), only that it will set up opposition within a man to many of the things that he lusts to do. Sometimes the conscience will connive with a man to cover or excuse certain sins, but it is always true that in some measure the unbeliever is at war with his conscience; (2) he is at war with his reason – it is not reasonable to think that a man can sin against an almighty and completely unlimited God and still be doing what is best for himself. Though his mind is corrupt and defiled also, there will always be thoughts within a man that warn him that he is acting foolishly, unreasonably following his lusts instead of his best interests. This sets up a conflict within him, for he cannot do what he wants to do without fearing the consequences. Such conflicts in every life will take their toll, bringing some to the state of insanity as they try to escape the inevitable results of their unreasoning sinful acts; (3) he is at war within himself, with one lust warring against another lust – he wants to greedily fill himself with two sinful pleasures at one time (e.g. one cannot both gamble and commit adultery at one time),so the two dominant lusts will come out on top and fight one another for the time or opportunity to fulfill itself. A man can be torn between pleasure and fear, both lusts in an ungodly one – he wants to soothe his burning lusts, but he is afraid he will have to pay too high a price for the respite achieved, and so he wavers back and forth with a double mind and a troubled mind until the decision is made. Then oftentime the battle is rejoined when one lust has been fulfilled and the other's fear comes to fruition – the man then fights himself as to whether or not he should have done what he did do. There is no end to this war in a man's own mind and heart – as long as he lives without God and Christ he eats his own flesh and boils his own blood, with pain and stultification constant companions.

The question may then be asked, Are godly men not free from this warfare which is ordained for men upon earth? No, they are not. The apostle Paul makes it clear in many of his epistles, Romans 7 being the best known case. In all four points they still fall into lusts which cause them distress and pain: (1) David lusted against God in the matter of Bathsheba, *"Against You and You only have I sinned;"* Peter was called Satan when he advised the Lord Jesus to oppose God's will – was this not because he lusted against God? (2) No one would deny that the saint is at war with Satan all his redeemed days upon earth; (3) The Lord Jesus warned that the kind of men who hated Him would also hate us, therefore it is evident that we are at war with other men also; (4) And certainly no truehearted man would deny that he is constantly at war within himself, as Paul declares so clearly in Romans 7:23; 1 Timothy 1:18; 2 Tim. 2:3; 1 Tim. 7:12; 2 Tim. 4:7; 1 Cor. 9:25 also show Paul's testimony as to a Christian's warfare. There are two places where he more fully arms us for this war, Ephesians 6:10-18 and 2 Corinthians 10:4, where he says, *"For the weapons of our warfare are not carnal, but mighty through God to the pulling down of strongholds, casting down imaginations and every high thing that exalts itself against the knowledge of God, and bringing into captivity every thought to the obedience of Christ; and having a readiness to revenge all disobedience, when your obedience is fulfilled."*

CHRISTIAN WARFARE

The classic passage on the warfare of the Christian, after Romans 7, is that one so wonderfully inscribed for our encouragement in Ephesians 6:10-18 [see Treasury section for a summation of some of William Gurnall's unmatchable points on the various phases of our Christian warfare]. There is another place in Job worthy of our notice here, *"O that You would hide me in the grave, that You would keep me secret until Your wrath is past, that You would set me a fixed time and remember me! If a man die, shall he live again? All the days of my warfare I will wait, until my change come"*–Job 14:13,14.

The classic example, as always, is seen in the life of Him who lived a life of faith for us and having fought the good fight of faith to the uttermost, He gave us the final example by sacrificing Himself for us – as we will see after we consider the alternative reading:

"There is," or, *"Is there not an appointed time to man upon earth?"*–Job 7:1a, an equally well-grounded translation of the original. For there is no real conflict between being born to a warfare on earth, and having our times appointed on earth – both are by God's ordination. There is an appointed time to war, a special season when it is most suitable. Also, men go to war at a certain appointed age, a time when he is most fit to bear arms.

THERE IS AN APPOINTED TIME ON EARTH FOR EACH MAN

1. God is the Owner of the earth, and He farms it out to men.

A. We all work for wages. It is really a question of what wage we work for. The Lord Jesus endured *"for the joy that was set before Him."*

2. God is the holder of life, and He measures it out to men.

A. He tells that there is a time for us to be born, to bear our burdens, and a time to die. The thread of our lives has a definite length.

1. He who tries to seize the reins will be paid quickly, *"the wages of sin are death."*

2. He who patiently endures — in faith and trust shall be rewarded, in God's time, *"the gift of God is eternal life."*

3. No one has the power to shorten your life on earth.

A. Our hairs are numbered and our days are no less numbered. We need not fear man whose breath is in his nostrils.

4. When God calls, then we should die willingly, it is certain that we shall die. For all the while you are dying unwillingly He is able to make you wish you were dead.

While we live, He has appointed the bounds of our limitations — where we shall live, what we shall do or not do, with whom we shall live and enjoy life, or endure in our misery: *"He Himself giving to all life, breath and all things. For He had ordained the times and boundaries of their living place, which He before determined"*—Acts 17:26. Just as surely as the sea has never gone beyond the bounds set by God (*"You shall come this far, but no further; and here the pride of your waves shall stop"*—Job 38:11), that certain is it that no man has ever gone beyond the bounds which God has set for him. Even he who wickedly shortens his life is living out all the time God gave to him. We live in these houses of clay only so long as He has determined to permit our tenancy. He is the Lord of time, and our times are in His hand (Ps. 31:15).

Most men fall into the foolishness of thinking that they have something to do with the term of their lease on life. They speak as if their tongues and their time were their own, *"Tomorrow shall be as today, and it shall be much more abundant."* But even if they say, as they ought, *"God willing, tomorrow, etc.,"* tomorrow may never come at all for them—for when we pass over into eternity, there are no tomorrows.

Some use decrees and final determinations of God as an excuse to become careless with their lives. In our temporal lives, it is as in our spiritual lives. Though only the elect are saved, yet none are saved by their election. The decree of God appoints us to salvation but the decree does not save us. Every one of the second causes and means must be run through. In temporal life, God has appointed our days. but He has also appointed the means for us to live out our days. We are under His orders as to how we live our lives, as well as under an inflexible order as to how long we shall live them. There is not the slightest warrant for any man to cast himself upon needless dangers, or to forbear necessary helps for the sustaining of his life simply because he reads that God has appointed his days on earth. There is comfort for Job in knowing that he has an appointed time, and he is hoping that those days are ended for him. Men cannot prolong our sorrows, but God has reserved that right to Himself.

Since our hairs and our days are numbered, ought we not to honor God and have only good thoughts of Him? For whether our days on earth be fair or foul, calm or stormy, they are appointed by Him who does all things well.

CHRIST, OUR GREAT EXAMPLE, WAS APPOINTED TO A WARFARE ON EARTH

Yes, the King of kings and Lord of lords freely chose to join the ranks of the soldiers of God, enduring all the hardships of war alongside of and for the benefit of His chosen ones for the exact time appointed to Him for that purpose. His hour came when He was *"delived...by the before-determined counsel and foreknowledge of God,"* and Herod, Pontius Pilate, the Gentiles, and the people of Israel, then gathered *"together in order to do whatever God's hand and counsel determined before to be done"* (Acts 2:23; 4:27,28).

There are several things common to war, (1) In war, all combatants are subject to their commander-in-chief; (2) A soldier has no permanent resting place, whether he is marching or waiting, he has nowhere he can call his own; (3) All who war must be ever wary —they must watch carefully that the enemy does not surprise them and cause them to be guilty of losing the war for all the others who fight alongside of them; (4) Each warrior has his appointed place, and he must keep his rank and file — he must stand his ground

— though it be no more than a bean patch to be defended, we must fight as Shammah fought the troop of Philistines (2 Sam. 23:11); (5) War is full of hazards, troubles and labors — hardship is the lot of all who war with all their might; (6) Every war has its end, either in victory or defeat — either we overcome, or we are conquered and made captive to the will of Satan.

In all these ways the Lord Jesus Christ fought through a life of wartime, an appointed time, foredetermined days:

1. He said, *"Lo, I come to do Your will, O God"* (Heb. 10:7). It was written in God's book that He should do so, yet He came willingly to make Himself of no reputation and to put Himself at the service of the great Commander-in-chief of us all.

2. He said, *"the son of man has nowhere to lay his head"* (Matt. 8:20). He who had been the constant companion of God from the beginning, He who owned all the world together, put Himself into the warfare on earth knowing that He would be without a place to call His own.

3. He warily watched Satan lay his snares in the wilderness temptations, and this was but an example of how His days went. For the moment never passed that He a was not tempted in the same way as we are, yet without sin. He could allow not even a stray thought, for to do so would be to lose the entire war for every one of God's children. What a strain it must be, to have so many precious persons depending upon every single thought and violation for every day of every year for an entire lifetime! Yet He never slipped or slept when the enemy came to surprise Him into betraying us all.

4. When He went to the feast, He sat at the lowest place at the table. Never did He aspire to thrones and possessions, fame or fortune, nor even leadership among the mighty. No, He was a rank and file soldier in His appointed place, standing firm in the face of the assaults of Satan and his armies of devils, in the teeth of men who cursed Him.

5. As to hazards, troubles and hardships, *"His visage was marred more than any man, and His form more than the sons of men"* (Isa. 52:14). Men were astonished at His wasted appearance, He endured so much hardship in laboring for us by day, and in praying for us by night, that there was no beauty left in Him for men to see (that is, physical beauty). Try to think of a life that had fewer physical comforts than the life of Jesus.

6. But it is written, *"stripping the rulers and the authorities, He made a show of them publicly, triumphing over them in it, "* and, *"When He went up on high He led captivity captive and gave gifts to men"* (Col 2:15; Eph. 4:8). His triumph was complete. There could be no victory which was as great or as far-reaching as this victory, for Christ Jesus destroyed the devil and his works, and His enemies were placed as a footstool for His feet.

It was this One, this faithful and hardy soldier of God, by whom all things were made, and by whom all things consist, whose days were appointed beforehand — just as ours. *"And when they had fulfilled all that was written of Him, they took Him down from the tree and laid Him in a tomb. But God raised Him from the dead..."* (Acts 13:29,30a). He could say again, *"I have finished the work You gave Me to do"* (John 17:4). Now He sits again as King over all. And if we claim that we have His royal blood in our veins, if we say we are partakers of the divine nature, then we must prove our pedigree by the same courageous and heroic spirit which He had, to dare to be holy in spite of men and devils.

"Are not his days also like the days of a hireling?"—Job 7:1.

A hireling is one who works for a set time, for a set reward. So this clause of the verse is a doubling of the first. His days are appointed days, he toils for a certain wage. There are also mercenary or hired soldiers, so that the picture of warfare is included in this part of the verse also. Job here includes all men in his observations. All have a warfare. All have certain appointed days to do a particular work. There is work for all, none are exempted. We must fight to survive, even if we do not have to work to eat. But it is the general desire of God that men should labor, as He evidenced in putting even holy Adam to work in the Garden of Eden. He does not intend for us to forget it, as He reminded us in 2 Thess.

3:10, *"If any man does not work, then let him not eat."*

Now that we acting in our father Adam have made our work harder, a work of toil and sweat unknown in the Garden, there is no reason to murmur at our labors or the wearisomeness of it. Just as the Lord cannot bear that we should murmur at our spiritual work, saying, 'What a weariness it is to have to do God's will,' so our ordinary work in life is also His appointment and we have no right to murmur or complain of it. It is our own corruption which makes our work so hard. The servility and drudgery of it is due to our sinfulness. All forms of temptation and trial are common to man (1 Cor. 10:13). Again, the Lord Jesus Christ was not exempted. He said, *"It is necessary for Me to work the works of Him who sent Me while it is day,"* and, *"The works which I do in the name of the Father, these witness about Me"* (John 9:4; 10:25). For the joy that was set before Him, He despised the shame of an ignominious death on the Cross and finished the work which He was appointed to do. In His case, He freely willed to hire out to God for this strange work of living in humiliating circumstances and dying under scandalous conditions. He gladly and fervently enlisted under the banner of God, and He found it a pleasure to fight His warfare upon earth — not because it was easy, but because it was for the glory of God. Let every man be as free in his desire to do God service, and let each one of us be as fervent in our work, that we also might give Him the utmost glory.

There are wages, or a reward to all of us. Each one shall receive according to his works. Those that have done evil shall be rewarded evil for evil, multiplied and increased, with eternal torments which they have not the will or the body to bear in this life. Those that have done God's will shall receive the crown of life, their reward being the presence of God and the knowledge of His riches of glory. The wicked earn wages and put them in a bag full of holes while they are in this life, but each lost opportunity will return and will haunt them for an eternity of separation from the goodness of God. They loved the wage which unrighteousness gave them, they promised themselves liberty all the while they were actually the slaves of corruption (2 Peter 2:13-19), but they earned for themselves the second death, a horrible existence without God and without hope.

While a hireling works for his wages, he also works for his master. If he does good work, both shall prosper by it. Those who are careless in their work are a drain on their masters. If we neglect to do what we are ordered to do by the Lord, then we are not only not adding to His glory, we are detracting from it.

The reason for Job bringing in this comparision seems to be this, that he feels his work is done, his appointed days are over. Therefore, he sees no reason why he should be so harshly criticized and suspected simply because he desires to depart from this toilsome existence and take up another which has been promised to him for a reward. He regards life on earth as painful, troubling, dangerous and toilsome, at best. Now that these adjectives will hardly describe his life, without the greatest amplification that man can imagine, he does not feel guilty for thinking that his appointed time has come, that his wages are due. He feels he has many evidences and symptoms of death, that he has heard the message and received the summons to proceed to the grave. Why, says he, should you insist that I should lengthen these miserable days? Why do you hold out hope of more days to me? Does not man have a warfare on earth? And is there not a day when it is ended? Does not the hireling work in hope of the day of rest and reward? And have I not good reason to believe that these have arrived for me?

"As a servant earnestly desires the shadow, and as a hireling looks for his wages"–Job 7:2.

To desire earnestly is but one word in the original, a word that is so full of sense that we cannot empty it in our language with only one word. Literally, it is this, *"As a servant breathes after the shadow,"* because a man that earnestly longs for a thing is often pictured as panting after it — he gasps after it, breathes after it. The word signifies to gape and draw in the air pantingly, and thus to desire earnestly.

"the shadow"–some understand it of the night, when the servant comes to rest after his

long day of labor — night being but a great shadow. Others take it for the shadow of the day, as when a servant is hot from toiling in the open field and goes looking for a bush or a tree to throw a shadow over him for a short time of rest. Again, the shadow may be taken for the house, for to come into a mans house is called a coming under his shadow (see Gen 19:8). Then, too, the shadow is used in Scripture to note protection and God-given mercy (see Isa. 4:6). The Lord promises us that He will be *"as the shadow of a great rock in a weary land to His people."* And David flees to this shadow for safety, *"Under the shadow of Your wings shall be my refuge, until these calamities are past"* (Ps. 57:1).

So that in these words Job means that he earnestly desires to get out of the heat of this life and to hide himself under the restful shadow of God.

"and as a hireling looks for his wages"—A hireling desires rest, and he desires reward. When he is hot, the shadow refreshes him. When he is hungry, his pay refreshes him. All the while he works, his heart is upon the wages he will receive when he has finished. He looks, that is he expects his reward. So God has decreed that the hired servant is to be given his hire, that the sun should not go down upon it. He has his heart set on it.

"for his wages"—the Hebrew is, *"for his work."* Why? He had work enough before, all the day long he has had work. In the Scriptures, the word work signifies three things, (1) the very act of labor; (2) the effect of labor, the thing worked for, the product of it; (3) the wages which a man receives for his labor. Many times the word is translated reward, but the original is work (see Lev. 19:13; Ps. 109:20). It is usual to put prayer for the thing prayed for, as Hannah said, *"The Lord has given me my prayer,"* whereas she meant that the Lord had given her the child she prayed for. Cain complained, *"My sin is greater than I can bear,"* but he meant that his punishment for sin was too great to bear. In this way is work translated into reward, wages being the normal end of work.

"so I am made to possess months of vanity, and weary nights are appointed to me"— Job 7:3.

It looks like a very unlikely similitude — *"As a servant desires the shadow...so am I made to possess months of vanity."* To clear this, we must remember that this is a similitude with a dissimilitude. The similitude is concealed, while the dissimilitude is expressed. We may make it out in this way, 'As a servant desires the shadow and a hireling looks for his wages, so I who am laboring in the heat of these afflictions am earnestly desiring a shadow and, likewise, I who am at work am looking for a reward. That is, I long to see the end and issue of these troubles. But (here is the dissimilitude), instead, I am made to possess months of vanity, and weary nights are appointed to me.

It is as if Job said, 'When the servant has worked all day and is weary, he can lie down at night to quietly rest himself. But, alas! The night is as troublesome and laborious to me as the day. When the hireling has labored and taken pains to do his work well, he receives a reward at evening, but my wages have been months of vanity, my rewards so far have been nights of weariness.

"I am made"—I am an heir to months of vanity. This is our inheritance from Adam, our father, who represented us before God, who sinned away our righteousness, our holiness, and our ability to know and enjoy God. An inheritance of labor, weariness, sorrow, etc.

"Made to possess"—There is no choice when God chooses to afflict. God holds the man in one hand and the afflictive agent in the other, bringing them together as long as is needful to His purpose — with as much or as little abrasion, or melting, or pressure as is deemed good in His sight.

"months of vanity"—It is true that men are altogether vanity (Ps. 39:5). That is to say the same as these words of the Lord Jesus, *"Apart from Me you can do nothing,"*—nothing good that is. But there is vanity and there is vanity. There are graduations of vanity. Then, too, there are those days that seem to be in vain, but which in fact are filled with gain. Here

months of vanity may well mean months empty of good. There may be months which have no comfort in them, months which are without form and void of any discernible alignment with God's purpose. Men live their lives in search of refreshment, joy, enlightenment, contentment, accomplishment — of which it can be said that they are rewards from God. But there is the vanity of men, that they should expect these things apart from God. It is vain for men to wish to escape the wages of sin, and in their place to reap the rewards of sinless, unselfish and fervent-hearted labor for God.

Even those who are God's own, those for whom Jesus died, those for whom Jesus prays that their faith fail not — even those have their times of affliction, sorrow, grief, mixed with their times of refreshment, joy, enlightenment, contentment, and accomplishment. In fact, if true sight is given us, it will be seen that we need to be measured out for larger doses of the former in order to bring us into God's will long enough to receive and enjoy the latter. For of all the men who have inhabited the earth, only one, the Lord Jesus, has run his race without vanity.

The lives of many afflicted saints are painted for us in the words of Scripture. Job has much company in the type of affliction which he is now suffering. And of these, Job is not the only one to have sought death at the hand of God as an escape, and in cases not so oppressive or so distracting as Job's. Elijah prayed that God would take away his life when he ran for fear of Jezebel. Jeremiah prayed in circumstances similar to Job's (see Lam. 3:4-15), and the similarity of his word's are very remarkable: *"Cursed is the day in which I was born. Let not the day in which my mother bore me be blessed. Cursed is the man who brought news to my father, saying, A man child is born to you, making him very glad. And let that man be as the cities which the Lord overthrew, and repented not. And let him hear the cry in the morning and the shouting at noontide, because he did not kill me from the womb, or that my mother might have been my grave and her womb to be always great with me. Why did I come forth from the womb to see labor and sorrow, that my days should be ended in shame?"* (Jer. 20:14; see also 1 Kings 19:4; Ps. 6:6; 55:4 and 77:2 for comparison with Job's case). Yet none of these had the calamities in his life or the pains in his body that Job had. Nor did they have the crushing weight of the thought that God's hand was against him, and that without any cause known to him. It is relatively easy to have all the hands of men against you, but, then, when God's hand appears to be with them — this is the greatest obstacle to faith of all. And, lastly, it must not be forgotten that Job lived in a time when there was no written revelation. He could go only to his memory, he did not have the 750,000 God-breathed words of comfort which we enjoy today.

"months of vanity"—that is, *"lying months,"* or, *"deceitful months"*—months that have not produced the reward that I had hoped for. The hireling has his time appointed and his reward promised. But, says, Job, I have labored my day, as the hireling, and when the time came for me to receive my reward. I did not get anything for my pains. Like the Israelites who spent the day slogging wearily through the sand of the wilderness, up the mountain, through the thickets, perhaps as many as three million of them, yet at the end of each day they were oftentimes no nearer the promised land. In fact, whether they were near to Canaan or far from it did not matter, for God was determined that they should not enter into rest — because of their adamant, flinty, corrupted hearts. All such men wander around; yea, they are led by the nose hither and thither through the wilderness of this life without coming to the knowledge of the truth. They never receive those refreshing rewards which their father in unbelief, Satan, promises them.

But as the children of Israel were led and misled until such time as God was pleased to bless those of them in whom He was well pleased, so it is in this life. There are those He has marked out beforehand for condemnation (Jude 4). And there are those He has marked out for adoption as His children (Eph. 1:5). Both are made to spend months of vanity in this world. but there is method in every age, for God has planned it so that some lives are fruitful, rewarding and eternally blissful. It is part of His plan to reveal His grace and His glory to both angels and men by the giving of just punishment to those who despise God and do not seek after His will.

"and wearisome nights are appointed to me"—Job 7:3b.

The hireling, all laborers in fact, may hope for some rest and respite when night falls. If days are weary, there is hope that night will at least give a parenthesis to the sorrowful trek through life: *"man goes forth to his labor and to his work until the evening"*—Psalm 104:23.

But Job, and others who are sorely sick, discovered his nights (if not more) as much labor than his days. Activity ceasing all around him, silence surrounding him, the sick one falls to closely examining his sorrowful condition. This induces sleeplessness, often fearsomeness (often due to an awakened conscience,) and other kindred disturbances, such as worry, excitement, feverishness, etc.

"are appointed to me"—are subtracted out and assigned to me. God numbers not only our hairs, but our days and nights, which he subtracts from the whole and assigns to us. He measures out so many of this kind and so many of that kind. He has taken the days and nights together and He has carefully taken from the pile a number of wearisome nights, which now are appearing in Job's life.

It is said of Christ that He was *"numbered"* among the transgressors. It is the same as here — He was appointed to be among the transgressors. God subtracted Him from among the innocent (all of·whom·were in Heaven—and set Him over among the transgressors. He was set apart for this purpose. He suffered the reward of transgressions, that those given to Him might be rewarded with everlasting, never-ending joy and glory which God has appointed to all who would believe in Jesus and live godly.

"wearisome nights"—were appointed to Job so that the purpose of God might be known and so that it might stand. God, the all-wise Disposer and Master-planner, had weighed out so much sorrow and trouble and grief and vanity to Job. Now he is carefully measuring out from this pile all that is needed by Job in order to make him spiritually fit and healthy for the many remaining years of his life. Nights like these make lasting impression upon the sufferer.

God is to be praised for giving to us a taste of what we deserve — and along with it the repentance and faith in the shed blood of our Lord Jesus Christ which will cause our appreciation to increase and multiply. Job's suffering is hard to understand simply because such suffering is extraordinary in the annals of a history of suffering, as he states time and again, as in Job 30:17, *"My bones are pierced in me in the night, and the gnawing pain takes no rest."*

"When I lie down, I say, When shall I arise? But the night is long, and I am full of tossing to and fro until the dawning of the day"—Job 7:4.

That night must be wearisome which has a man wishing to get up as soon as he has lain down.

"When shall I arise? But the night is long,"—or, *"When shall the night be gone?"*—The Hebrew holds forth a picture of a thing being measured, as cloth or a piece of ground is measured by a rod. It also signifies the measurement of time, the observation of hours. It is as if Job had said, 'I lie awake all night and count the hours as the clock chimes.' O the tediousness of those hours when a man is too sick to sleep soundly, when he is pained to the point of anguished sleeplessness! He turns and he tosses to and fro. He is full of tossings as a man is full of food, uncomfortably so.

"and I am full of tossing to and fro"—These are great inward agitations in the heart and mind, as Asaph wrote for us, *"In the day of my trouble.I sought the Lord. My sore ran in*

the night and never ceased. My soul refused to be comforted. I remembered God and was troubled. I complained and my spirit fainted. You kept my eyes awake! I am so troubled I cannot speak"—Psalm 77:2. Along with these inward tossings to and fro went those outward movements of the body seeking to ease the pain for just a second or two.

"until the dawning of the day"—The word can signify both the evening and the morning with our translators choosing the latter. It may more properly here be kept to that time when darkness begins to depart and give way to the prevailing light.

Nights usually bring a cessation of conflict, when we can make a truce with troubles to wait for another day. Each day has enough evil in it, so none is needed for the night. The sleep of night is designed as medicine for our bodies, it is a time when everything slows to a more comfortable pace and the body is refreshed by the rest that comes. To Job, however, the night brings no such refreshing. To a man in as much pain of body and soul as this man, there is a tendency to look upon every time as a better time than the present time of pain. So he asks as soon as he lies down, When shall I arise; And when he arises, he asks, When shall I lie down? What was prophesied in Deuteronomy was true of Job's case on this day, for in the morning he says, *"I wish that God would make it evening,"* and in the evening, *"I wish that God would make it morning."*

A change of place is no guarantee of ease from pain. Pained bodies try a change of position. Pained spirits try a change of place. A man that is sick in his soul will change from this duty to that duty, trying what he may do to ease his guilt. But unless he comes bowing down to the Physician of souls, it is all in vain. It is the same in bodily pain, only God can ease it. Drugs and ointments may seem to mollify the pain, but they do not cure unless they get God's command to do so.

Therefore, let it be known that all your months will be comfortable and profitable if God wills it. And if you find your bed giving you rest, bless God for it. It is not possible for the softest bed, that which is called the most comfortable, to ease you and give you rest if God has appointed to you wearisome nights. It is not the bed that gives rest, it is God!

"My flesh is clothed with worms and clods of dust. My skin is broken and has run afresh" —Job 7:5.

His restless nights were not without reason, his unquiet body was clothed with worms and his skin was broken and running pus. He puts *"flesh"* for *"body"* but it is very interesting to note the original word for flesh here. It is a word which signifies to bring good news (therefore the gospel is expressed by it). Some critics give this reason why a word which means to publish good tidings should be translated flesh — They say it is because there should be a taking of flesh, namely the incarnation of our Lord Jesus Christ, which should be the best news, the most joyful news that the world ever heard of.

"is clothed with worms"—That seems a very fit and suitable suit of clothes for the grave. For is this not what happens after the body is in the grave? He speaks as if he were in Heman's words, *"free among the dead,"* a member of that corporation, a brother of that society already. He has a gown of worms set or embroidered with clods of dust.

It is frequently seen in Scripture, when the Holy Spirit would heighten the sense of what we are, or what we enjoy, or what abundance there is in a thing, or how a man is dressed, or with what one may be defiled, He expresses it under the notion of clothing. Even God is described as clothed with majesty — because He is majestic all over, there is nothing but glory upon Him. Elsewhere He is also described as clothed with judgment and justice. Why? Because these are His honor and His ornament, He is justice and judgment all over. Job described himself in a different clothing later on, *"I put on righteousness, and it clothed me, my judgment was like a robe and a diadem."* In past days, he says he was full of righteousness. To be clothed with humility, to be clothed with the Spirit, to be clothed with

Christ — all these are phrases of the same import. On the other hand, to be clothed with pride, with shame, with dishonor (Ps. 109:29) is to be full of these, to be covered with these so that nothing else can be seen. That which strips a man naked is in this sense called his clothing, a man is clothed with desolation when he is stripped of consolation. So here we understand Job to be saying that these worms spread themselves all over him, a filthy and loathsome garment covering his whole body, thus covering or hiding his natural flesh. And besides this figure, Job spoke properly that while he was so full of sores and botches and boils, he was clothed with worms. For it is not unusual for such sores to breed worms (remembering that he lived in a day when virtually nothing was known about controlling diseases), and worms are a disease in the flesh, as well as in the bowels. Such diseases are, as you know, the filthiest and foulest of diseases to the sight and smell. Is it any wonder that Job abhorred himself? With putrefaction breeding worms in his skin, is it any wonder that he felt ready to die and have such a thing behind him?

The reference in Isaiah and Mark to the worm that will not die is the spiritual equivalent of these putrefaction-bearing red worms of the flesh. Why does the Holy Spirit say of these men who were never washed nor healed of their sin-sores, their soul-sickness and pollutions —that when they depart from this life they shall have a worm that will not die? It is an allusion to this, that as there is a rottenness in the bodily flesh that breeds worms that feed on it, so there is a corrupt conscience and a filthy soul which will refuse to be washed in the blood of Christ and will breed undying worms that will gnaw and torment the soul ever.

"and clods of dust"—A strange material to be clothed with! Some conceive that Job sat in the dust and therefore the dust gathered around him, covering him like a garment. Others say that these clods of dust refer to the scrapings from his sores (for he says elsewhere that he scraped them with sherds of pottery). Carry on the allusion, his skin was his garment, which had been broken and had become loathsome — its most noticeable adornment being worms and clods of dust. A few days before Job's picture was quite different from this, for he was clothed with silk and scarlet, adorned with precious jewels. His skin had been smooth and beautiful, his face cheerful and manly, but now it is broken and running with rottenness.

However marvelously God works day by day to preserve them, it can be easily seen here why they are called corrupt. Being filled with the seeds of destruction, sins within have eaten away all but the outward appearance of healthiness, our bodies are vile and ready to break out in running sores of spiritual putrefaction. All can say, as Job did, *"I have said to rottenness, You are my father, and to the worm, You are my mother"* (Job 17:14). Only the Holy One, Jesus, was not corrupt in body and soul, only He escaped corruption (Acts 2:31).

Is it not strange then that so many take pride in their bodies and in their beauty, to say nothing of their mere clothing? Only a day ot two can provide the proof that under that outward beauty, and because of that very pride, lies a sin-sickness which has completely corrupted every one of us — *"there is none good, no, not one!"* (Rom. 3:10-17). Take no thought of your days, whatever beauty you behold in them, but put your hope in your tomorrow, when Jesus shall have appeared and you shall become like Him! All that you now are, all that you wear now, all that you can adorn yourself with (except that which is spiritual), is but dust and will return to dust in a time that is even now leaping upon you. Array yourself with the precious Lord Jesus Christ and His graces, that you indeed shall have a glorious appearance, both now and forever.

"My days are swifter than a weaver's shuttle and are ended without hope"—Job 7:6.

In the *Septuagint*, it is, *"My days are more nimble than a word."* Nothing moves faster or passes away more quickly than a word. You but speak it, and it is gone. So the Psalmists say in effect, *"we spend our days as a tale that is told"* (Ps. 90:9)—it is true of life that it comes and goes as suddenly and as quickly as a few words. A discourse spoken is quick to depart from the mind and a discourse in the minds even quicker to escape from us.

But the word properly signifies a weaver's shuttle, an instrument which is noted for being very swift in its motion. That word which we render *"swifter"* is one which means any light thing (because things which are light usually go swiftest). Thus horses that are swift are called in the Hebrew light of foot.

In the third and sixth chapters, Job had complained that his life was so prolonged and slow-paced that it was very tedious for him. Now he makes it as swift as a weaver's shuttle? To answer, his days here are to be understood as his good days. Those days of comfort and prosperity, of peace and of plenty, had slipped away as swiftly as a weaver's shuttle from the hand of the weaver. When he had complained of his life being slow-footed, on the other hand, he means these days of sorrow and trouble, of pain and misery. Those first pleasant days now live only in his memory, but these present days of grief and lamentation seem to live on and on in reality.

"and they ended without hope"—The word which is translated *"ended"* can mean both consumption and consummation — it can be the end, being spent and completely consumed; or, it can be the perfecting of a thing. God so speaks when He says, *"And the heavens and the earth were finished."*—it is the same word, they were ended. There God ended His work by way of perfection, He made His work complete. But here, and often in Scripture, it denotes an ending by way of consumption (*"I will consume them by the sword"*—Jer. 14:12).

To show how deep a consumption was upon him, Job tells us that it had devoured and eaten up all his hope — and it is worse to have our hope ended than to have our days ended. Some translate it, *"my days are spent and I do not have any hope."* This hopelessness may refer two ways: (1) I have no hope of length of days, for I am afflicted with this obviously killing disease; (2) I have no hope of being in a better condition, of having my estates and my health restored, so why speak to me of these things as a certain reward that is for me if I take your advice? In both senses, as he saw the thread of his days being cut off, so he saw the thread of his hope in this life being cut off. He felt he was near death, therefore, the earthly hopes which he had entertained were also dead.

Here, then, he begins what amounts to a discourse on the shortness of time. Time is fleeting, however long it may seem at the moment. No man is master of even one day, and he is a servant only for a few short days. The Holy Spirit gives us many reminders of this — it is an argument God uses constantly. It is a wonder that such a plain and common truth should be handled so often, that the Holy Spirit should labor to bring up so many similitudes to convince us of the transitoriousness of nature, when there is not even the dullest of men who can deny it. It is because of this, that the temporary quality of earthly life is easy to be known, but it is very hard to be believed. Everyone subscribes to it, but how few actually live as if they believed it! And surely the Holy Spirit would not spend so many words on it if it were not most important to our faith. Is it not the most common of principles that we usually slight? Preach a sermon on this subject of the shortness of our lives, the speed of time, and the insecurity which we all enjoy, and you will find that the people will regard it as the longest sermon they have ever heard. Why, it is likely they will say, It is a theme for children. But the truth is that men would live holier lives, perhaps even longer lives, if they but believed what they say about the shortness of time. In this connection, it should be remembered that when we neglect a common truth, that which everyone knows to be true, then we cause a neglect of all truth, of every truth, to develop within us. If we had more serious thoughts of Heaven and Hell, and of how each thought and act of ours drives us toward the one or the other, then surely we would more profitably improve the few hours that we have left on earth. If we have only time and talents to trade with, then should we not use them to be about our Father's business?

It should be noted here that hope is the last refuge of the soul. When a man has lost his hope, he is like a dead man. It is hope that makes life lively. Just as hope is the anchor of the soul, sure and steadfast (Heb. 6:19), so hope is the anchor of the unbeliever's life also. When comfort is gone, hope can be our comforter. But when hope is gone, there is no comfort.

Here we see that in some sense a godly man's hope may lie prostrate. It is not to be thought that every godly man has the same strength of faith that Abraham enjoyed when it was said to him *"that against hope he believed in hope"* (Rom. 4:18). Nor did Abraham have such an experience each time he was faced with trial and temptation. There are weaknesses in the strongest of us. That man who has the strongest hope may find a day or days when his hope seems weakest. There are ebbings and flowings, declinings as well as the greatest of heights reached by graces within our soul.

Having made his complaint plain and clear to his friends, Job now turns to address God. For the next words are generally understood to be an interjectional speech, an apostrophe to God.

"O remember that my life is a breath; my eye shall no more see good"—Job 7:7.

Why should Job ask God to remember? How can God remember when He knows all things; yea, even the end from the beginning? It may be said that God remembers in three ways:

1. God remembers in judgment, *"Remember, O Lord, the children of Edom"* (Ps. 137:7). They have mocked Israel, and God remembers them. He calls up His judgment which He had decreed against them for doing so.

2. God remembers in affection. When we love someone, we remember them and never forget them. It is not that they cannot drop out of our memory — we being sinners with a defective memory — but these are the ones that we particularly remember with our memory working. God, however, never forgets. *"Can a woman forget her suckling child......? Yea, they may forget, yet I will not forget you"* (Isa. 49:15). But more, He remembers us continually. We are always in His thoughts. And,

3. God remembers by having His mind upon the present decree that is to be fulfilled; *"so that it might be fulfilled which was spoken by Isaiah the prophet saying, Behold My Servant whom I have chosen, etc."* It is marvelous, beyond all praise, that God never forgets to fulfill His word. His promises are yea and amen. What if God had not remembered when the time had come for Christ to be born of a woman? What if He did not remember that which is next to be fulfilled in your life? What if He did not work in us to will and to do of His good pleasure, as He has promised?

Obviously you will not pray that God remember you in judgment, and thus get what you deserve instead of what Christ deserves. But you will pray that His affection might be known to you. And to experience the sight and joy of God's remembrance of us, we must remember that it is sinful to magnify and to be always remembering ourselves first. If we humble ourselves, if we are contrite in our hearts, then He will come and dwell with us and speak to us comfortably. Job here is humbly praying, asking God to remember how frail he is, as Ethan did, *"Remember how short my time is. Why have you made all men for vanity? What man lives and never sees death? Shall he (who is strong) deliver his soul from the hand of the grave?"* (Ps. 89:47).

God remembers us always, but we will know that He remembers us in warm affection when we remember who we are, whence we come, and what we are by nature.

"O remember that my life is a breath," or, *"wind"*—Because the wind or breath is of an invisible nature, swift in the case of the wind, and life-giving in the case of the breath, it is applied to the Holy Spirit. The operation of the Holy Spirit is also shadowed out by the figure of wind or breath, *"Christ breathed upon His disciples, saying, Receive the Holy Spirit"* (John 20:22). And when the Holy Spirit came at Pentecost, He came as *"a mighty rushing wind"* (Acts 2:2). When Job says, *"remember that my life is a wind,"* he means

it as a similitude, not an assertion. The life of man is like the wind in two things: (1) the wind passes away speedily; (2) the wind once past does not return again, *"He remembered that they were but flesh, a wind that passes away and does not come again"* (Psalm 78:39). It is in this sense that Job calls his life a wind, it passes away and will not return again.

But it is to be observed that Job does not say that his soul was a wind. Some have philosophized the soul into a wind, a mere blast or a breath. These tell us that the soul goes like the soul of a beast, that life and soul are the very same thing — that when the life is gone, then the soul is gone and does not exist any more. Then, they say, it is restored again with the body at the resurrection. How dishonorable this is to the noble constitution of man, and how dissonant to Scripture, is proved in the very mentioning of it. We do acknowledge that life which is the union of soul and body is as a wind that passes away. In all the learned languages (Hebrew, Greek and Latin) the word which signifies spirit or life has its original from respiring. So when one says that his breath was gone, or almost beaten out of his body, the meaning is that his life was gone or almost gone. In the Creation, God *"breathed into man the breath of life,"* or, *"lives,"* implying the many operations and faculties of life. And inasmuch as the body of man was first formed, then his life was breathed into him afterward in order to act and move it, this is an abundant proof that the soul of man is not any temperament of the body (for the body was completed before it had any life). Whereas beasts (to whom these beastly philosophers compare man in his creation) had living bodies as soon as they had bodies, their total form being but an extract from the matter.

To those who bring in Eccles. 3:19-21, it should be remembered that it is the Atheist who draws this conclusion from those confused oppressions which he had observed in the world. He had seen men carry themselves so much like beasts, preying upon one another, that he (who had nothing but carnal reason to judge by) presently resolves, *"that which happens to the sons of men also happens to beasts; even one thing happens to them. As the one dies, so dies the other; yea, they all have one breath; so that a man has no advantage over a beast — for all is vanity. All go to one place. All are of the dust, and all return to dust again."* And though the Atheist had heard some speak of the ascent of man's spirit after this life, he puts it off as but talk and guessing, *"Who knows the spirit of man that goes upward and the spirit of the beast that goes downward?"* That is, who can tell that there is such a difference between the spirit of a man and a beast? Who ever saw the one ascending or the other descending. Or from what textbook was this to be learned? So the Atheist derides the doctrine of the soul, and he laughs and is merry so long as his body lasts. But this is not so strange as that there are many who are sober, Bible-believing Christians who would be so foolish as to plant their opinions in this soil of atheism — foolishly making that a proof of their faith which Solomon brings in only as a proof of some men's infidelity! The preacher in this book personated those he hated, and he sometimes speaks the practices of other men, not his own opinion. There is no more reason to ground this unsound tenet of the soul's mortality upon Eccles. 3:19-21 than there is to ground intemperance in the words of Eccles. 11:9, *"Rejoice, O young man, in your youth and let your heart cheer you in the days of your youth, and walk in the ways of your heart and in the sight of your eyes,"* or in that of the apostle, *"Let us eat and drink for tomorrow we die"* (1 Cor. 15:32). If anyone wants to learn Solomon's own sense on this point, let him read it — it is as plain as words can make it, *"Then the dust shall return to the earth as it was, and the spirit shall return to God who gave it"* (Eccles. 12:7).

So then in the text before us, the soul is not a wind, but it is the life that is as wind. And all those scriptures where life is compared to wind, and where dying is compared to the passing of life like the wind that does not return, are denying the return of the soul to a natural life — they do not deny the eternal life of the soul. They imply the short stay of the soul in the body, the certain departure from it, but do not give any credence to the theory that the soul ceases to exist when the body dies. The soul and the body must part, and when they do part the body will cease to live – and the two shall never again return to the same estate again – this is the teaching of the Scripture.

"My eye shall no more see good"–Or, *"I shall not return to see good,"* which answers perfectly to the metaphor of the breath or wind above.

To see, in this place as in many others, is to enjoy (*"I shall not enjoy good"*–Ps. 4:6). *"Who will show us any good"*–that is, who will cause us to see any good. It was not the bare sight of good which they desired, but the enjoyment of it. To see good is a mercy, but to see it and not enjoy it may well be a curse. Therefore, those who thought themselves to be so high in the favor of God, but were in truth under His wrath, are told that they shall see *"Abraham, Isaac and Jacob in the kingdom of God,"* but, alas! they shall not be there enjoying themselves with these saints. When it is said that Christ shall not see corruption (Ps. 16:10), it means of course that He would not partake of corruption – for who would dare to say that He who is perfectly pure could not see the corruption that abounds in all other men.

The good which Job will not see any more is that little good which may be seen while we are in this life. The greatest good, that which he will see again and again, is that good which we see when we die and are carried into the bosom of Christ Jesus, our God. It is not Job's meaning that he shall see no good when he has departed this life, for he says in another place, *"I know that my Redeemer lives...whom I shall see for myself, and my eyes shall behold, and not another's"* (Job 19:26,27). His meaning is this, that his eye shall see no more earthly good, none of these things which we call good in this world. He expects to be above the smart of earthly sorrows, and above the sense of earthly joys. Good may be either natural, civil or spiritual. When God created the world, He looked upon all that He had made and pronounced it very good. It is good when there is order, peace and prosperity in the world – a good that stops when death comes to the body. But that which is eternally good, spiritually good, cannot be stopped by bodily death – the eye of the redeemed soul cannot be dimmed by carnal expiration.

So the atheists have no argument here for their imagination that the soul ceases to be, or ceases to be awake, until the resurrection. Job is speaking only of the sphere and course of nature, when man dies naturally, and thus cannot enjoy those things which are naturally good.

From the fact that Job turns to present his complaint to God, we learn that it is better to cry to God than to men. Although God is usually the last we turn to, yet He is always the best refuge. When we have laid out our tale of woe to all the men who will listen, it will yet be the sweetest story when we have told it to God and He has answered us. The men we know are but creatures, and creatures cannot rise above creaturehood. When they have done their best for us, it may be that they can do no good for us. That man is most to be bemoaned who can only make his moan to men. A man who does not know to take his complaint to God is the saddest of all men. But as long as we have a God to turn to and spread our case before, though men turn from us and refuse to listen or help, yet it is enough for us to cry, O Lord remember.

Secondly, Job is using the argument which will most effectually draw out the affections of God. either in regard to our spiritual or temporal estate, the argument that we are weak and frail, that we cannot help ourselves, *"But He, full of pity, forgave their stubborn sins...For He remembered that they were but flesh"* (Ps. 78:38,39). Consider which will move God first, the pleading of our holiness, our zeal, our prayers – or the pleading of our frailty and weakness. To tell God that we are sinful will gain us more than for us to tell Him that we are righteous. It is true that Hezekiah and Nehemiah both prayed their perfections as a plea for action from God. But this does not prove that these were the best and most effectual pleadings to God. Both these men in the very same context are seen to humble themselves and to confess their sins, begging for mercy instead of asking for their earnings.

"The eye of him who has seen me shall see me no more; Your eyes are upon me and I am gone"—Job 7:8.

Job has just said that his eye shall no more see the good of the world. That is, he says that he shall no longer enjoy it. Much of the comfort of this world is by way of sight. Now he says that other men shall no longer see him either. Altogether too much of the enjoyment we have in this world is from seeing and being seen. We are desolate if we believe that no one sees us. Thirdly, he brings in the eye of God, that He will see him no more — again meaning that he will not be seen on earth any more. He is saying that he will not be seen by himself, by men, or by God. It does not actually say that God shall not see Job any more, but that God's eyes are upon Job when suddenly he will not be here on earth any more — he will vanish like a cloud, he will go down into the land of Sheol, the grave, never to come again on the earth — his house and his place shall never again know him. It is as if he had said, 'Lord, You will not have a Job to help if You do not help Your Job. Your eyes are upon me, searching me, trying me, but, alas! I am not able to stand before Your justice and Your pure eyes. Yet I appeal to You, help me or else I shall not be here to help.

"I am gone"—That is, *"I am not"*—Not to be does not import a not being, but a not appearing. Rachel wept for her children because they were not. Joseph's brethren said to their father, Joseph is not. And Job says, *"You shall seek me in the morning and I shall not be"* (7:21).

"As the cloud falls and vanishes away, so he who goes down to the grave shall come up no more"—Job 7:9.

Job having moved the Lord to take notice of him and his transitory condition now gives us another comparison, to the same sense and purpose.

"As the cloud falls and vanishes away," or, *"as the cloud walks across the sky and vanishes"*—Clouds are made of vapor which is very condensed and congealed until it hangs between heaven and earth like a dark curtain. Yet it is made by the sun, and it can be made to dissipate by the sun. It is blown into position by the wind, and it can be scattered by the wind. Both of these, the sun and the wind, however, are but doing the work of God. For it is He who appoints the place and the time and the strength of the cloud. It goes where He wants it, it stays for as long as He desires, and it continues or dissipates as He pleases.

Scripture often compares those things which are temporary and vanishing to clouds. A notable place is Isa. 44:22, where the sins of the saints are compared to clouds, *"I have blotted out as a thick cloud your transgressions, and as a cloud your sins,"* Just as a cloud blots out the sight of the sun, so the clouds of sin blot out a man's sight of the Son. The sun is there even if you cannot see it. The Son is there even if you will not look to Him or hope in Him, that He might blot out the clouds of sin that defile your soul and blind your spiritual eyes. Sins in themselves are as dark clouds which hang ominously over the sinner and threaten his life and wellbeing, but the sins of the saints should be but vanishing clouds, for they need but call upon their Lord to have them scattered and dissipated.

There are those who refuse to look to Christ for help, (1) those who do not see any clouds of sin at all, (2) those who see their black sins but much prefer the sins and the trouble that goes with them to the surrender of heart and soul to Christ [*"the Light has come into the world, and men loved the darkness rather than the Light, for their works were evil"*—John 3:19]. To these the clouds of sin will become solid mountains of misery, the full weight of which will be an ever-increasing burden to them as they make the horrible discovery that there are depths of pain and despair that never before entered into their minds or hearts.

So Job compares his life to a cloud, a vapor, as does James, *"For what is your life? It is a vapor which appears for a little while and then vanishes away"* (James 4:14).

"so he who goes down to the grave shall come up no more"—The grave is a descent. The word used here is *Sheol,* about which innumerable disputes have arisen among the learned. The root of the word signifies to desire, to crave earnestly or hungrily. And the reason given is this, that the grave is always inordinately craving and demanding to be filled. The grave has devoured its hundreds of millions of men, but it is as hungry as if it were asking for the first body. It is never satisfied (Prov. 30:16). Sheol is taken five ways in the Bible:

1. It is the place of those that are condemned, *"Hell and destruction are before the Lord —how much more then all the hearts of the children of men"* (Prov. 15:11). Sheol here is the place of destruction appointed by God.

2. In a metaphor, it is put for great and extreme danger; those miseries which seem to be without end or recovery. These are called *"hell"* because it is well understood that hell is a place which allows no recovery. All changes are on earth. Neither Heaven nor Hell will see any change. David praises the Lord, *"You have delivered my soul from the lowest hell"*—that is, his life on earth was at such a low ebb and seemed so remediless that he considered it be as Sheol.

3. It signifies the lower parts of the earth, without relation to punishment, *"If I go down to hell, You are there,"* He is saying, *"If I go down to the lowest part of the earth, God is there."*

4. It is taken for the state of the dead, whether they are formally interred in a grave or not, and whether or not they are saints or sinners. It is actually more readily understood as the *"unseen"* world. This is seen in the illustration of David in Psalm 16:10, which is repeated by Paul, *"You will not leave my soul in Sheol, neither will You allow Your Holy One to see corruption"* (Acts. 2:31). This being a Messianic Psalm, it appears that Christ went to Sheol, that is, to the unseen world, the state of the dead. Anyone studying the original meaning will not be deceived into thinking Christ went down into Hell — for He did not, not for any reason. But there is this much that is different about Christ going to Sheol — His is the only body that went there and did not corrupt and disintegrate; it did not go back to dust as a result of rotting away.

5. Sheol may properly be designated as *"the grave,"* but it is the grave in general, that place that receives him after he leaves this life — it is not that place chiseled out of the earth to receive him in his coffin, *"before I go where I shall not return, even to the land of darkness and the shadow of death; a land of thick darkness, as darkness itself...without any order, and where the light is as darkness"* (Job 10:21,22).

"shall come up no more"—If his hopes are in this world, they are buried with him. His fears are not buried with him, his retribution for sins will not perish with his body, but any hope of a better and more enduring life will vanish with his last breath, unless he has transferred his hope to the Blessed Hope who gave Himself that He might redeem the remnant of grace from all iniquity and to purify them as a peculiar people.

"He shall return no more to his house, neither shall his place know him any more"—Job 7:10.

This verse extends and explains the latter part of the last verse. Job has not denied that a dying man's hope is vain, but he has stated that he shall not return to the life that has just departed from him. He shall have no more to do with this world, with worldly business and contentments.

"neither shall his place know him any more"—His place may be taken in three ways: (1) for the calling and condition of a man in this life, that is the place of a man; or, (2) locally, for his house or his estate where he lived; or, (3) Place may be taken for dignity, for

the eminency of a man's calling — we say of a great man, he is a man of place and rank. In all these senses, his place shall know him no more.

Places, of course, are without life and sense, and much more without knowledge. There is a double figure in this place: some understand it by a hypallage or transmutation of the words, meaning, that Job shall not know his place any more — as in Psalm 37:10, where it is said, *"you shall carefully look at his place and it shall not be,"* that is, he shall not be in his place, for the place shall be there as long as the earth remains. Secondly, it can be understood by a prosopopeia, a meaning-filled personification, which is frequent in the Scripture — the inanimate things of life are made to imitate animate things with life —— when a place takes upon itself the qualities and abilities of a man, as if it has a man's reason and senses. In the Psalms, for instance, the little hills are said to rejoice at the showers. So here in Job, his place will not see him or know him any more.

It is notable that when God desires to humble man He so often brings in the inanimate creatures. These preach what man is, and they testify as to the greatness of God, *"When I look at Your heavens, the work of Your fingers, the moon and the stars which You have ordained — what is man that You are mindful of Him? and the son of man that You visit him?"* (Ps. 8:3,4). *"The heavens declare the glory of God and the firmament shows His handiwork," "because that which is known about God is clearly known within them, for God clearly showed it to them. For the unseen things of Him from the creation of the world are clearly seen, being understood by the things that are made, both His eternal power and Godhead, so that they might be without excuse"* (Rom. 1:19,20; Ps. 19:1). But as the heavens declare the handiwork and marvelous creative powers of God, they also declare the weakness and worthlessness of man.

"Therefore I will not hold my mouth; I will speak in the trouble of my spirit; I will complain in the bitterness of my soul"—Job 7:11.

In the next six verses, Job resolves to complain, makes his complaint, amplifies his sorrows and then renews his pleadings to be taken from this life.

"Therefore"—What he says now is based on what has been said before. Job says, *"I will not hold my mouth"* because, (1) my grief is heavier than the sand; (2) the arrows of the Almighty are eating me up within with the poison and terrors of my existence; (3) my friends are without pity and full of deceit, refusing to give me that which is due from true friends; (4) my appointed days to war on this earth are finished, my days of hire are over and I have reason to desire earnestly the shadow of death; (5) my days now are vain and worthless, there is no more good that I can do on this earth; (6) my fleeting life is spent, and I am in pain and distress, both of my body and of my soul — *"therefore I will not hold my mouth."*

Because he sees himself at the end of his journey on earth, his body is past cure, his estate is irrecoverable, and his spirit is distressed, he presses God to remember that only a breath separates him from this miserable existence and that glorious existence which shall be his when he crosses the black divide of death. He is saying, 'Hasten Me, O Lord, through the paths of sorrows, speed me through the pass of death, that I may have that comfort which You have promised me all my life.'

"I will not hold"—This word *"hold"* comes from a word meaning to prohibit, or to inhibit. Job will not prohibit his mouth from speaking or crying out that which fills his mind and heart. He gives the picture of a vessel that has been heated until it is filled with steam; it has reached the point where it must vent itself by spewing out and spilling over its contents. Job's afflictions have heated his passions, and his passions are threatening to run wildly through his being, therefore he feels that he must find some ease for himself by spouting words from his mouth to God. He claims the right to do so.

"I will speak in the trouble of my spirit"—Job is in a strait, all these things which he has

been describing have compressed him. He sees them as walls closing in upon him, causing him to break out in anguish of spirit. He feels that unless he opens his mouth

been describing have compressed him. He 'sees them as walls closing in upon him, causing him to break out in anguish of spirit. He feels that unless he opens his mouth to vent some of this pent-up compression, his heart will surely break. The two distressing desires of Paul straitened him (Phil. 1:23), and how much more could possibly be bothering Job here? Paul had the confidence that if he were to be required to remain here in the flesh it would be for the purpose of serving God's children. Job has no such confidence. Because he is being tried to the uttermost by Satan, no helps or comforts are allowed to him.

"I will complain in the bitterness of my soul"—The word translated "complain" signifies to meditate. God very plainly is telling us by the use of this word that Job is not merely spouting words from the top of his head. Rather, Job is speaking these words deliberately and after much forethought. He has framed and worked them out by meditation. Rash speech is for fools. The wisest of men are foolish when they speak rashly—that is, with no meditation beforehand. This word is also sometimes translated "prayer," because prayer should always be the result of meditation. A man's prayer should be the considered emission of heartfelt requests which have been the product of reading God's words and thinking God's thoughts after Him. Even men think little of words that issue from a man without forethought. Who cares for any statement which a man does not speak from his heart? What good are words which come tumbling out of a man without being preformed by meditation?

Hannah uses this same word, *"I have spoken out of the abundance of my meditation and grief"*—that is, *"my complaint and grief."* She was troubled by her lack of children, and she had meditated upon what she should ask of God. Though-grief-stricken, yet she had carefully considered what she should say to God. Her words were not just the expression of mere passions, but of the deepest feelings of her heart.

"I will complain in the bitterness of my soul"—The depth and the strength of Job's distress as such that he calls it bitterness of soul. It is more than a bitterness which is caused in many by mere bodily misery. It is a bitterness which also affects his soul. And, as Mr. Spurgeon said, when you have soul trouble, you have the very soul of trouble. To relieve this bitterness, Job considers it expedient and wise to vent it through his mouth.

AN AFFLICTED SOUL DOES FIND SOME EASE IN COMPLAINING

A complaint that is meditated upon, then directed to God in purity and fullness of faith, may well be without censure from God. That such complaints are rare among men is due to the innate sinfulness of man, their natural unbelief. The usual complaint that issues from a man is one of impatience, distrust and censure of God. Such complaints are sinful, hurtful. As such they bring God's correcting hand down hard upon the complainant. It is well to remember that though we are permitted to sue in God's court, we are not allowed to sue the Judge. God Himself is the judge of what is right and wrong, we may not accuse Him who can do no wrong.

But there are an abundance of examples where complaints were not only allowed, but where there is good reason to believe that they were justified complaints which had God's approval. Of course those most easily assumed to be so are the complaints of the Messiah in the messianic Psalms, *"My God, My God, why have You forsaken Me, and are far from My help at the words of My cry? O My God, I cry in the daytime, but You do not hear; and in the nighttime and am not silent. But You are holy..."* (Ps. 22:1-3). There were the usual times when the Lord Jesus suffered His humiliations and deprivations, *"as a sheep before the shearer, dumb, opening not His mouth"* — but there were times when He too cried in faith to His God for a just and premeditated complaint. Job was suffering mainly because he was being tried, because Satan must be taught that a man of faith will never curse his God, not even where there is no apparent gain in continuing to adhere to God. As this champion, a fact unknown to Job, he is made to suffer many things, some which do not have direct reference to his relative faithfulness. Others have far less faith, but the fact is that they also have far less pain. It does not make sense to Job's friends, therefore they are certain that he has done many dark deeds not known to anyone but Job himself. It does not make sense to Job, for he knows that he has not done any of the heinous things which are attributed to him simply because he is suffering so severely. In this context, not in the full context of a sinner and his God, but in the context of a sufferer who sees not why he suffers so much more than another less gracious. Job has a complaint. It gives him this much right, the right to come before the Judge and apply for relief from his oppressing circumstances. If he is willing for God to be the sole arbiter of the matter, and if he is willing for God to continue the ill circumstances for as long as He judged them to be good and needful, then he is permitted to come and make his complaint.

Alas! Job proved here to be a man subject to like passions as we are. Not that he did not show more faith than most any man that you could find today, even those who have been blessed with much knowledge of the complete and perfect body of truth, the Bible, but that as he fell to seeking his cure through complaints, he missed his godly course now and then. Like the sheep that may be caught in the thicket, he harms himself by charging this way and that to free himself, thus digging his horns deeper into his own flesh. In the main, Job kept close to God. Certainly he never gave Satan his wish by cursing God. But he can be seen entangling himself further by his all-too-human complaints. That is, he sometimes in the bitterness of his soul makes bitter complaints. In his impatience, Job makes impatient complaints. Likewise, he makes distrustful complaints and censorious complaints.

1. There are complaints which are bitter. Though we may have some cause for complaining, we never have any right to be bitter. Man may be permitted to complain to God, but He has no permission to be bitter in his complaints. A bitter complaint is one which has the underlying claim of undeservedness. We are bitter when we get more affliction than we think we deserve. Yet why should a living man complain? (Lam. 3:39). Is it possible for a sinful man to get more affliction, or even devastating punishment, than he deserves? For just one sin he deserves all the pain and misery of hell forevermore.

2. There is every reason to believe we can come before God with our troubles, but He never gives us a right to be impatient as we come before Him. Any relief He gives us will be according to His timetable, not ours. You may rightly ask for relief, but it is not your right to specify when you shall receive it. Job is in effect trying to determine his own lifespan. He thinks he knows that it is at an end. Yet he is so far wrong that he is actually going to live almost as long again, long enough to beget another family of ten children. Do not all of us make this mistake all the time – and without Job's distressing circumstances, too? Did you ever complain because God does not deliver you when you think He ought? Do you murmur when you see that you are having to pay for one mistake all your lifetime? If there is one thing that is common to all men, it is this, impatience. And the one thing which God says is the cure is trial, *"the proving of your faith works patience."* So He tells us to jump for joy and to exult when we fall into different kinds of temptations (see James 1:2-5).

3. There are also distrustful complaints. When we are not being bitter with our circumstances, or impatient because of them, we often are expressing a stupid distrust of God's handling of our lives (*"a man's heart plans his way, but the Lord directs his steps"*-Prov. 16:9). Every time you complain about the weather you are putting up a distrustful complaint against God. If you don't like your looks, or if you murmur about your in-laws, you are being distrustful of the God who gave them to you. Truly faith is a gift of God, for by nature a man never leaves off thinking that he is wiser than his Maker.

4. Sadly, it must also be admitted that man emits censorious complaints. It is bad when we complain we do not deserve our afflictions, when we insist that they should not last any longer than we desire, when we infer that God has unwisely ordered such trouble to come upon us – but it is another thing, a far more wicked thing, when we censor God.

for doing such a thing. And if you censor God for allowing a thing, it is the same. Hard thoughts of God are common to man, but they are the least defensible. It was the judgment of the Pharisees that Christ should die, and that He should die in shame and disgrace, in pain and in misery. They put their censorious complaint into action. They devised a way to get Him crucified. Your censorious behavior begins in the same way. You are not pleased with the providential dealings of God in your life, then you think hard of Him. Next, you censure Him. Next, you sit in judgment on Him and you judge Him to be at fault. You then condemn Him as wrong, and whether you believe it or not, the next thing you would do if you could is this, you would sentence Him to die. An honest and truly believing heart will admit that he has such censorious complaints at times, and will repent of them.

Sorrow hanging about us for a long time will all too often become boisterous and presumptuous. Job has three *"wills"* in this verse—(1) I will not refrain; (2) I will speak (3) I will complain in bitterness. His reason had been turned into will and his will into passion. He had become resolved upon his own will, not giving proper precedence and weight to the will of God. Still, his will was more strong than pertinacious. It was not his considered intention to oppose the will of God, though it was his considered intention to complain.

"Am I like the sea, or a whale, that You set a watch over me?"—Job 7:12.

Of all the inanimate creatures, what is more boisterous, what is more violent and hard to control than the sea? And of all the animate creatures, what is more formidable and hard to control than the whale? These two appear here as good examples of the power of God, for God is pictured here as an all-powerful One who sets a watch over the sea and over the whale, saying, *"This far you may come, and you may go no further."*

The wicked are said to be like the troubled sea in that they are greatly troubled and turbulent. The sea is so stormy and unruly that it threatens to overwhelm all things, the land and all that lives on it. The sea no doubt played a major part in the great Flood, as is witnesses by any number of destroyed and marred points of the earth. In our own day we see the destructive power of the sea from time to time, when the great deep roars its tidal waves into inhabited communities, wiping out lives by the thousands. These floods and destructions are a reminder to us that God has locked up the sea with positive control, as He says in Job 38:8-10. He shuts the sea up with doors, He sets His limit on it.

Likewise God controls men, even turbulent, unruly, stormy and God-despising. He permits them to be violent, to display their temper and tyranny in child-like fits, but He says to them like words, *"This far you may come, or go, and no further;"* *"The king's heart is in the hand of the Lord as the rivers of water; He turns it wherever He will"* (Prov. 21:1). If God was able to tell Satan in Job 1:12 and 2:6 how far he could go and what he could do, then how can it be doubted that He can completely control weak, puny, ineffective, foolish, and ungodly men?

Not only is the sea turbulent, but it is capacious. The mind of man cannot comprehend the vastness of the sea. There are places which may be 250,000 feet deep. There are sea-forms of such magnitude, sea-life of such abundance, that it would boggle the mind of the wisest man. It may be, then, that Job is saying that he is not so capacious as a sea. He is not able to drink in all these afflictions and sorrows. His capacity for affliction was far greater than others, far greater than mine or yours, yet he sees that he cannot absorb all that is pushing upon him.

The sea has great strength. We may say, 'weak as water,' but water for all of its unstable qualities is one of the greatest forces on earth. It will wear away the hardest rock. And in the end, when it has destroyed all other forces with its dynamic power, it will suffer no loss thereby. It is not only still the sea, it even has the same content as before, the same basic degree of coverage of the earth (71%) after all these years of power.

Job, then may be saying to God, 'Am I like the sea that I should not wear away, that I should not lose my senses and my bearings under all this affliction?'

"Am I like a whale"—Remember the giant fish which swallowed Jonah? When did he do that? Was it not when Jonah was thrown over the side of the storm-tossed ship? That ship had followed an absolutely erratic course during the preceding storm. How did that giant fish happen to be there? Would not the ungodly call it luck, for lack of a God to credit? It was God who prepared the fish, and it was God who so controled the fish that it arrived at exactly the same time that Jonah hit the water. Then, to make us realize how completely the fish was under the will of God, Jonah was spit out at exactly the right time and place in order to set him on his way to Ninevah. Could a man put a bridle on a whale and turn him wherever he wanted him to go? No, but God can.

Job, then, is teaching us that God sets a watch over the whale. God sets a watch over the sea lest it hurt His people, He sets a watch over man lest he hurt himself and other men. He sets a watch over our mouths, keeping the door of our lips (Ps. 141:3). James described the tongue as an unruly evil which could not be controlled by man. Yet God can and does control it.

"that You should hedge me in with troubles"—Job may be saying that he considers himself imprisoned, shut up with his troubles so that he cannot escape from them, thus giving them leave to bear in on him and overwhelm his spirit. The sea is such a prisoner. The whale is a prisoner in the sea. The whale cannot simply decide that it is tired of being a sea-creature, that it will change God's will for it and become a land-animal. Many times men feel that they are God's prisoners, that they are locked up by His providence, that they are unable to escape from their circumstances, from the consequences of their sins. Men are prisoners, Jesus Christ came that He might deliver the captives from prison. He is the great Deliverer from the circumstances of life and the consequences of sin. But the cords of hell and the cords of sorrows may not be taken from around a man's neck without a direct command from God. Men will continue to be strangled by their sins until the time comes for them to be delivered by God through Jesus Christ.

Thank God that He does set a watch over men. Words will not describe the viciousness of man by nature. What would wicked men not do to one another if they were not restrained by the Holy Spirit of God? God rules men by circumstance, by reason, by force and by suggestion. If you will not use the reasoning power He gave you, then He rigorously whips you into place and the attitude that you need to be in, *"Because you rage against Me and your tumult has come up into My ears, therefore I will put My hook in your nose and My bridle in your lips. And I will turn you back by the way by which you came"*—it was the powerful, conquering king of Assyria who thus felt the lash of God's power. This earthly great one had conquered the habitable earth, but, *"thus says the Lord...He shall not come into this city, not shoot an arrow there, nor come before it with shield.. For I will defend this city to save it for My own sake..."* That very night the Lord sent His angels to kill 185,000 of Sennacherib's fierce warriors. And the next morning He ordered the great king to go back to Nineveh to meet his death at the hands of his own sons.

Men are like the sea in many ways.

1. The sea is vast, almost boundless. Man is naturally vast and boundless in his lusts.

2. The sea is unstable, always fleeting and moving. The heart of man is such a movable thing, ebbing and flowing, forward and backward, tumbling up and down, restless as the sea.

3. The sea is often provoked with storms and tempests. So there are many winds striving upon the sea of a man's heart continually, so that he is boisterous and stormy. Men serve many different lusts and pleasures, all of them together whipping them into a foaming rage of unreasonable action. And, like the sea, man is most turbulent and tempestuous when he is restrained. He rages and smashes when he is stopped. Even holy Job here is be-

coming unquiet because he has been hemmed in by his many calamities and afflictions.

4. The sea casts up mire and dirt from its bottom. So does man, his native corruption is seemingly endless, and his capacity for casting his filth is prodigious.

This further observation from this verse, that man is apt to have good thoughts of himself — Job thought he ought not to be put into the same position as the sea or the whale. Also man is apt to judge that God lays more on him than there is need — Job cannot understand why God should bound him with his afflictions and put such a rod on his back. He does not think that he needs all this. But the most wise God never lays more on a man than he needs. When God straitens us with afflictions, it is to strengthen and instruct us with those afflictions. If there are many afflictions, there is much need. Or, as in the case of Job, if there is to be a very great man; if faith is to be blown to its furthest heights; if the example is to be for a very long time, then the afflictions must be great and deep and wide and prolonged. God was making a Job, a man whose fame for patience would live through thousands of years, for the benefit of billions upon billions of men. This required more than an ordinary measure of trial. And though Job does not know this, God still works His great work upon Him.

"When I say, my bed shall comfort me, my couch shall ease my complaint"—Job 7:13. Now he begins to amplify his sorrows on this general ground, that they were such as he could not ease or abate — not at any time, not by any means. He considered his grief and pain to be so remediless that nothing, either artificial or natural, would be of help to him. He instances in those things which usually give some abatement or intermission to sick and distempered bodies. In this verse it is his bed, which usually will ease the sick.

"When I say my bed shall comfort me"—The word signifies to mourn or repent, as well as to comfort. This is because comfort usually follows holy mourning and repenting. Godly sorrow is the mother of spiritual joy. Here again He personifies his bed, accusing it of not comforting him. Or it may be he is putting one thing for another, picturing the bed as comforting because ordinarily we find comfort from the bed.

"My couch shall ease my complaint"—the words both can be translated *"bed,"* but if we take them distinctly, then the bed is the place where we rest at night, and the couch is the place where we rest in the daytime. The word is an expression of easing by lifting up a stone, Give that man rest — then we shall rest upon a stone. Did not Jacob do so? The most probable means cannot help us of themselves — and yet a word from God will make the most improbable means help us — even the destructive can be ordered to save us.

From this we must realize that rest and sleep are blessings from the Lord, as are all good and perfect gifts: *"for so He gives His beloved sleep;"* (Psalm 127:2).

"then You scare me with dreams and terrify me with visions"—Job 7:14.

The word translated *"scare"* has the fullest meaning of the word, it denotes such a fright as will leave a man weak, prostrate and fearful in the most horrible manner. It is the kind of fear that comes upon a man when he feels doom bearing inexorable down on him (as in the case of Belshazzar).

The word *"dreams"* comes from a word which is descriptive of the way dreams come to us, the drugging of the mind and the body by vapors of sleep.

"terrify me with visions"—again a tautology, telling of the terror, of the pictures and the visions of the imagination, the kind that make the hair stand up on one's head.

DREAMS

1. A dream is a product of the imagination (or, in an older form, the fancy).

2. Dreams are naturally fleshly, therefore they are self-glorifying as opposed to God-glorifying motions.

3. As in all our faculties, God may take charge of our imagination, appropriating it for

the purpose of conveying His word and/or purpose to us. That He has done this in times past is evidenced by multitudes of Scriptures. His use of this form of communication in these days, since the word of God is now complete and perfect, is certainly limited — and it may be that He does not any more communicate His will and word by dreams. But if He does use the dream as a vehicle for communication, one thing must be surely noted to differentiate such a dream from the ordinary — it must be God-glorifying, and it must be in absolute accordance with the God-breathed words of the Bible. No additional or further revelation is given to man beyond the Bible, nor could there be, for else God could not then judge us strictly according to His word — something He promises He will do.

Dreams are the product of the imagination. The imagination is the photographic library of a man, but more than this, it is a creative faculty which can take the bits and pieces of memory and the conceptions of the mind to weld together a proposed vision of the future. Man was given imagination to help his understanding, that he might more fully be convicted and convinced by the pictures which went with his understanding of a thing. In perfect Adam, the imagination was under the strict control of his right reason. It was not allowed to run wild, presenting ungodly, fleshly scenes to the pure mind of Adam. In fallen Adam, and in all of us who are born in Adam's image, the imagination has become the evil servant of the lusts of a wicked and deceitful heart (Jer. 17:9), *"And God saw that the wickedness of man was great in the earth — that every imagination of the thoughts of his heart was only evil continually"* (Gen. 6:5). And the Lord hates this, for among the six things that He says He hates is this, *"a heart that devises wicked imaginations"* (Prov. 6:18).

That dreams are of the imagination can be seen by the fact that without pictures and representations of form and shape there is no dream. Only the imagination can draw these figures for the mind. Dreams are usually considered a product of the imagination at night, but the Scriptures also mention those that dream in the daytime, even while a man is a-wake.

Dreams come from various causes: (1) they may come from the natural temper of the body — some are more disposed to dream than others; (2) distresses of the body or the mind have a tendency to produce dreams; (3) outside agents, such as certain foods, drugs, etc. may cause dreams; (4) tense concentration upon the things in one's life may bring dreams about those things — those we care most about most often people our dreams, as well as those we fear most; (5) dreams can be sent by God, but in the New Testament we have only two instances, that of Joseph in Matthew 1 and 2, and that of Pilate's wife in Acts 2:17, and the sobering epithet of Jude 8, *"these filthy dreamers defile the flesh."* Paul tells us of seeing things too wonderful, too other-worldly for him to relate, saying he did not know if he was out of the body or in the body — but this does not necessarily mean that he was dreaming these things. They would appear to be actual happenings, not conceptions of the imagination; real events observed by him in a state not natural to man. (6) dreams could possibly be used as a vehicle by Satan, for here we have Job telling of terrifying dreams at a time when he is being tried and afflicted by Satan. It is not God in His person who is scaring Job with dreams, though He may be permitting the immediate agent to send these frightening, horrifying dreams.

Dreams are fleshly, therefore self-glorifying. If the imaginations of men are only evil continually, and they are, then the product of their evil imaginations must also be evil — who can bring a clean thing out of an unclean?—*"that which is born of the flesh is flesh,"* so all that comes from the evil imagination is going to be fleshly, carnal and selfish. The fact that good objects and good purposes appear in our dreams do not make them good dreams. A man may dream of going to Heaven, of meeting God, of associating with the apostles and prophets, all for the purpose of convincing himself that he is eminent and fits well there. A thing is ungodly when God is not the principal object and purpose of the thing. That the wicked dreams are not godly is evident, but we should also examine those dreams which we consider to be good and see if God is at the center of them, and to make certain that the entire scene is not being staged that we may be glorified. *"For in the multitude of dreams and many words there are also many different vanities. But you should fear God"* (Eccles. 5:7).

God often took charge of the dreams of men of old: (1) they usually were dreams in a deep sleep, however, not the natural dreams of man; (2) they were plain and clear, not disjointed and full of absurdities. Much that was hard to understand, some that was very mysterious may have been part of the dream, but there was a complete and undistorted message conveyed; (3) those dreams always came to pass — so much so that a false prophet could be known by the fact that he prophesied dreams which did not ever come true.

"so that my soul chooses strangling and death rather than my life"—Job 7:15.

Job is so disenchanted with this life and so anxious to enter the life to come that he is willing to suffer any kind of violent death, even strangling, in order to depart. Remember that Job is now talking to God, not to his three frail and foolish friends. And he is saying to the One who can bring it to pass, *"my soul chooses strangling and death rather than my life"* Some take the view that Job's horrifying dreams had perhaps distracted him to the point of madness, and some even suggest that he entertained desperate thoughts of destroying himself. This does not have any ground in this context. He puts his soul for his whole man, and he states clearly that he would prefer death. But in no way does he hint that he intended to pre-empt God's right to choose the time of his death.

"and death rather than my life"—or, *"death rather than my bones"*—some make it his bones choosing death, that is, that all of him, his soul and his bones choose death. It is common for David to use the like expression, *"All my bones shall say, Who is like the Lord?"* (Ps. 35:10). It may be he brings in his bones because they are sore and painful bones, Satan having said, *"touch his flesh and his bone and he will curse You to Your face."* And lastly, some say that Job had nothing left but bones, thus he brings in his bones as desiring death.

"I despise it. I would not live always. Let me alone, for my days are vanity"—Job 7:16.

Job hates his life. And if it were your life, you would hate it too! This word is the very strongest word that God ever uses to express aversion to a thing. It is the same word He uses to express loathing for the hypocrisy of the Jews in their offerings (Amos 5:21).

To loath a food is to have no appetite for it, but, further, that thing turns the stomach so that it will not go down. Whether it is in fact a delectable morsel does not matter. The stomach that loathes it is the sole judge of its desirability. There are spiritual appetites, too, and these determine whether or not we receive good or bad into our spiritual stomachs.

Job is saying, I do not have any appetite for this life any more. It may be great for you, but I despise it. I do not want to live always. The idea of a perpetual and never-ending life on this earth is hateful to him, and he will not entertain the idea at all — it turns his spiritual stomach to think of it. He has found that this life does not any longer satisfy him. It is vain, empty, worthless. It is painful, tormenting, miserable, and sorrowful. He hates to think of another day, for it will mean a continuance of the river of dissatisfaction that is flooding his soul. Why does Job now choose strangling rather than life? When did he make that choice? It was not because his children were taken away. It was not when his possessions melted away. It was not when he saw his wife forsaking him. It was not when his friends so heartlessly deserted him. He spoke good, God-pleasing words all along when these things happened. Why then had he now lost his appetite for life? It was this, that he now could no longer feel that God is with him. God has now withdrawn far enough that he cannot seem to draw on His strength. It is written, *"If God is for you, who can be against you."* But then this too could be said, If God is against you, who can make your life worth living? It is God that *"satisfies the longing of every creature."* Jesus Himself in that unspeakable moment of darkness at the Cross cried out, *"My God, My God, why have You forsaken Me?"* Then what? Then *"Jesus cried with a loud voice and gave up the spirit"* (Mark 15:34,37).

If you love this life, then thank God that He gives you the satisfaction to so love it. If you find your life full of dissatisfaction, then realize that it is so because you have so little of God in your life. You can fill your life with people, with things, with fame and fortune and pleasures, but there is no satisfaction in any of these. If God will test you in the matter, you too will find yourself choosing strangling rather than life.

"Let me alone, for my days are vanity"—or, *"cease from me"*—which is taken two ways: (1) cease to prolong my days, do not stand by and assist me to keep my life whole within me; (2) Let me alone, that is, stop holding me in this woe-filled condition.

"for my days are vanity"—There is trouble enough in my life, even when the greatest of ease is given to me it is but vanity. He is calling his days nothing but a bubble, a puff of smoke. The root word imports a vanishing or disappearing. He sees his days as fleeting, vanishing away, and he desires to be left alone to expire. The life of man is a vain life, for there are two things in vanity: (1) it is empty; (2) It is full. It is empty of comfort and it is full of vexation and torment, *"all is vanity and troubling of spirit"* (Eccles. 1:14).

The vanity of man's days may be demonstrated in four ways:

1. They are vain comparatively, *"my age is nothing before You"* (Ps. 39:5). We cannot form an apprehension of our life to take in how little it is; we cannot reach so low in our thoughts as to reach the bottom of man's vanity. Just as we are not able to raise our heart so high as to feel the excellency of that estate which we have by Christ, no man's mind has thoughts big enough to comprehend it. We are less than nothing. How little that is, to be less than nothing.

2. Our days are vanity, because they are so inconstant and changeable, so subject to motion and alteration. Anything that is ever changing is certain to be vain. The opposite of ever-changing man is the never changing God, *"with Him there is no variableness nor shadow of turning"* (James 1:17).

3. The vanity of our days appear in this, they are unsatisfying days. That thing which fails to satisfy, which fails to fulfill its purpose in life, is a vain thing. Since our fall in our father Adam, there has been no fulfilling of the purpose for which we were created — except as the Lord Jesus has recovered and restored us in righteousness, holiness and true knowledge.

4. The vanity of our days appears in that they are deceitful days. That which promises us something but delivers us nothing is deceitful, and therefore is useless and empty of all good. The things in this life promise us much, but they give us nothing. Just as apart from Christ we can do nothing, so apart from Him we can enjoy nothing. All is vanity and vexation of spirit. It would be better not to expect anything, than to be promised satisfaction by that which is not able to deliver it.

"Surely every man walks about like a shadow! Surely they are in an uproar for nothing" "every man at his best estate is altogether vanity" (Psalm 39:5,6). Truly life is a stage on which deceitful creatures pose as this and as that, but none are really worth anything. If the days of man of themselves are so vain, then let us set our eyes and hearts upon that which is something, upon that which is all, upon that which is lasting, upon that which is everlasting, upon that which is true, upon that which will not deceive and cannot do so. Spiritual life not only promises much, it delivers more, *"abundantly more than we ask or think."* Although it cannot be said of God's word, that *"the half of those good things"* were not told, yet it can be said that we do not yet know the half, nor even the smallest fraction of that fruition which we shall have when we are with Him and like Him.

"What is man that You should magnify Him, and that You should set Your heart upon him?"—Job 7:17.

The next three verses contain further argument, in which Job seeks to strengthen his complaint. The sum of the argument is taken from the comparision of the power, majesty and greatness of God, with the meanness and misery, with the lowness and poverty of man. Why should the great, the wise, the all-powerful and glorious God contend and strive with weak, miserable, vain man? How unequal is such a match!

There are three magnifications of man which are set before you:

1. God magnified man when He created him. That God should think enough of us to create us is a magnificent and remarkable thing in itself. And He in this creation set man at the head of it, that all things in the earth and in the heavens should have been made to serve man — this is further magnification of man. God did not need to do so.

2. After man had tried to seize the crown off of God's head, to declare himself worthy of his own service and love, man became a vexatious vanity, a monstrous mist that permeated the earth with death (so much so that the whole creation groans and travails in pain until the day when God will burn up this sinful old earth and bring forth His *"new heavens and new earth"* (Rom. 8:21-23). Yet man was magnified again, in that God sent Christ Jesus, His very own, only-begotten Son from out of His bosom to become our God and Savior. This provision of redemption is a far greater magnification than the mere making of Adam and those of us who have followed from his loins. Here was love of an unspeakable variety, that God should be willing to empty Himself and take upon Himself the form of a servant and to be made in the likeness of men. O more! That He should be willing to humble Himself and allow men to berate Him and mistreat Him, to spit upon Him (the Lord of glory!) and finally to nail Him painfully to a tree — how can we ignore the inexpressible magnitude of this free gift of God? How can we be so monstrously unfeeling when we see how much God has magnified man by providing for them a Redeemer to redeem them from their self-destroying sin? He did not do it for angels. Why men?

3. This still was not enough. Though man had been twice magnified, men yet despised God, both the Father and the Son, as well as the Holy Spirit. God Himself testifies to it, *"In the beginning was the Word, and the Word was with God, and the Word was God!"* He was in the beginning with God. All things came into being through Him. And without Him not even one thing was made that came into being. In Him was life...And the Word became flesh and lived among us. He was in the world, and the world was made through Him, and the world did not know Him! He came to that which was His own, but His own did not receive Him! O the wickedness of man, the vileness and filthiness of man! That he refused to receive the greatest of all gifts, the Lord Jesus Christ, God with us! He came down out of eternal bliss to redeem His people, but His people refused to have Him. It was only after God magnified man a third time that man would recognize and begin to love the God who gave and the God who offered Himself. For it was when God gave man a new life and a new heart that he was magnified the third time.

When the life-giving Son gave life, all things became new. Christ revealed the Father to these new-born children (Matt. 11:26) and they began to nourish themselves at His breast with joy. What did man do to deserve such magnification. Nothing at all. Apart from Christ they can do nothing. It was God who did it all. He first loved them with an everlasting love (Jer. 31:3), then He determined to magnify them. Even after they had fallen, the whole man becoming corrupt and worthless, God determined to magnify His chosen ones. Though they were dead in trespasses and sins, poisoned by their own sinful lusts, God yet passed by and said to them, Live! And when God says, Live! even the dust rushes together and forms itself into a living and breathing creature.

But more than this, God could have created man, redeemed him, recreated him in the image of God, still leaving him alone to feed upon the husks of this world, without God and without any future hope. But this was not His plan, for He intended to magnify man so far as to make him a *"partaker of the divine nature."* Could there by any further magnification than that? Could a traitor be raised any higher than that? But further, God has promised this mere man, this recreated but still lowly man, that he shall reign with Him, *"for if we died together with Him, we also shall live with Him. If we endure, we shall also reign with Him"* (2 Tim. 2:11,12). Still more, for *"when He shall appear, we shall be like Him"* (1 John 3:2).

That would surely seem to be enough magnification even for the inordinate desires of men — man created, redeemed, recreated, adopted, made like God, reigning with God? No, though that is more than our sin-crippled minds can comprehend, that was not yet the unutterable extent of the love of God. There is yet another magnification, one that Job has glimpsed, one that fascinates him here more than any other:

4. God has magnified man in that He has set His heart upon Him, and that in such a way as to purify him by the fires of affliction and the trial of his graces every moment. Suppose this, that God has recreated you, has given you holy affection for Him, has cleansed you from guilt, has delivered you from filthy lusts — would that be enough to please you? What would you be like if God left you to your own devices now, did not remind you through the Holy Spirit and your renewed conscience that you were not yet what you ought to be? Where do you get the urge to become more pure, more loving, more righteous, more diligent? Is it not from God's word? No, it would not be enough to be left in your recreated state without further instruction, constraint and superintendence.

It is one of the most certain signs of God's everlasting love that He will not leave you in your present state. You are recreated, but you still stand there virtually without spiritual form, void of the graces which serve to make men like God. The angels are watching, that they may see God's manifold wisdom unfolding in your life (Eph. 3:10). *"to whom it was revealed that they were not ministering those things to themselves, but to us...which things now have been made known to you...into which things the angels desire to look"* (1 Pet. 1:11,12). They are no doubt astonished at the minute attention and the marvelous magnification you are getting from God.

The further magnification of man seen by Job is this, that God continues to love and to instruct, to correct and to sculpture us until we are conformed to the image of Christ Jesus, the perfect Man. And of those who were most magnified was this man Job. There are only 33 men whose names appear on a book of the Bible. One of those is this man who so little recognized his magnification that he chose strangling rather than to go on in this life which was afterward to become so famous!

"What is man"—the word used is *enosh,* the Hebrew word for man in his most miserable and weakest condition. This man is a sorrowful figure. He is vanity. And will God magnify such a man as this? God describes man in many ways, but among them are these, *"man is grass,"* and *"man is a lie"* (Isa. 40:6; Ps. 62:9). Yet God magnifies him.

All the worth and dignity of man lies outside of himself. Of himself, he is worse than nothing. Outside of himself, God setting His love upon him, he is great, he is magnified far beyond anything that he could even conceive.

If God magnifies man, then how can one man dare to vilify and debase another man? Is the estimate of a mere man to be set above the estimate of God? It is very dangerous to abase those whom God magnifies, to despise those whom God has made great. So very strongly does God feel on this point that He demands that we love our neighbor as ourselves, and that Christians love their brothers in order to prove that they actually love Him.

"that You should set Your heart upon him"—It is as if he had said, *"What is man that you should magnify him by setting Your heart upon him?"* When God sets His heart upon a man, that certainly is a great and marvelous magnification in itself. The very act of setting His heart upon one is enough to make that one great. It is an exaltation that cannot be nullified. There is no greater honor than this, that God should set His heart upon you. This is because setting the heart upon a thing is the highest exaltation that we can give it. And the Lord calls upon us to set our hearts upon Him, because that is the highest honor we can offer to Him. How much more, though, does His setting His heart on us wonderfully magnify us! If *"He humbles Himself to behold the things that are in Heaven and in earth"* (Ps. 113:6), then how much more does it speak of His love if He looks upon us in the filthiness of our flesh and speaks us into life and comformity to Him.

To set the heart upon a man imports four things in the Scriptures:

1. It tells us of God's great care and loving attention toward us.

2. It tells us that there is affection and desire – of God toward us, and of us toward Him.

3. It denotes a high esteem and account – it is more than a bare love and affection.

In all these ways God sets His heart upon man. He cares, He attends to us, He loves and desires us, He esteems us and accounts us worth the giving of His Son for us.

If this is so, then should we not the more set our heart upon God? Should we not care, attend closely to His words, love and desire Him, esteem and account Him worthy of all our heart and mind and soul and strength?

"that You should remember him every morning and try him every moment?"–Job 7:18.

There are here two more acts of God which Job questions: (1) God's visitation to man; (2) God's trial of man.

To visit is first to afflict, to chasten, even to punish. The highest judgments in Scripture come under the notion of visitations, *"visiting the iniquity of the fathers upon the children"* (Exod. 34:7). And in the prophets, *"Shall I not visit for this? Shall not My soul be avenged...?"* (Jer. 48:44). So afflictions are visitations, being called so because it is then that God comes to search our hearts and lives. By afflictions God examines us, and then He instructs in the same way. For when God starts lighting up every corner of a man, it is time for him to start assisting in the search for his iniquity, his infirmity, his carelessness, etc. Woe to those who will not search and try their ways when God visits them.

It is also wise for us to visit God when He visits us in afflictions, *"Lord, in trouble they have visited You. They poured out a prayer when Your chastening was upon them"* (Isa. 26:16). If we will pay a visit to God through prayer, then His instruction begins sooner. The sooner He begins to reveal His will to us, the sooner we learn – and that means that our affliction will end that much sooner. For God does not afflict any longer than is absolutely necessary.

2. To visit in a good sense signifies to show mercy, to refresh, to deliver and to bless:

"Naomi heard how the Lord had visited His people and had given them bread" (Ruth 1:6). –*"The Lord visted Sarah and she conceived"* (Exod. 3:16). When God comes in kindness and love to do us good, He visits us. And these mercies are called visitations because, (1) God comes near to us when He does us good. Mercy is a drawing near to a soul. When God visits with punishment, it is a withdrawal, a going away. But when He visits to do us good, it is a coming near to us; (2) These mercies are visitations because they are freely and liberally given. A visit is one of the free things in the world. There is no obligation except love to make a visit. I visit a man because he is my friend and I love him. So that act of grace which God put forth in redeeming the world is properly called a visitation – it was an act freely and voluntarily done, out of love and mercy toward God's chosen. In no way was God under any obligation, nor was Jesus Christ under any obligation to us.

3. To visit imports an act of care and inspection, of tutorage and direction, *"Pure religion and undefiled is this, to visit the fatherless and widows in their afflictions"* (James 1:27). Christ pronounces a blessing on those who visited Him when He was in prison, and this was not a case where the visitors merely came to see Christ in prison, but rather it was an expression of care and helpfulness for Him. In this sense our present verse would fit well, *"What is man...that You should visit him every morning?"* It is wonderful that God should take care to come and inspect us, look us over narrowly and then provide for us.

"every morning"–The Hebrew is, *"in the mornings"*–and the word used here for morning is a very full word. There is a twofold morning, the Jews distinguished each exactly by the watch. One morning was that which they counted from an hour before sunrise, from the very first breaking of the day until the sun appeared above the horizon – which is about the space of an hour. And the word which they use for it is one which means to be dark or black; it is because that first morning is somewhat dark. The other morning was for the hour after sunrise, and the root of that word signifies to seek or to inquire diligently. The reason for this being that they saw the sun as the lamp by which we may seek and search about our business. The height of the day they called the body, or the

strength of the day (that which we call the heat of the day).

In this text either morning may be meant, though it may be more proper to understand the latter. As soon as the sun is up, Job says, God visits man. As soon as there is light to sees us, He comes to visit us: It is an extraordinary thing to visit one so early in the mornin, but God's visits are always extraordinary, however often they may be — and, according to this text, He visits us every morning. There is not a morning that He forgets us.

To do a thing every morning denotes the doing of it always; or, it could be, the certain doing of it. As surely and as certain as the sunrise that certain is it that God will visit us. Or, it can express the speed, the haste that God makes to visit us. He comes the first thing in the morning, without delay, *"God shall hear her in the morning"* (Ps. 46:5)—-that is, speedily.

In this sense, Job is saying that God visits man every morning, like a shepherd going to see about his flock as soon as there is light to see them by. God's mercies are renewed every morning as He visits us. And it must be so, for yesterday's mercies will not be enough for today's trials — each day has its own evil, and that evil must be overcome by faith, a faith that believes that when the first light arrives God will arrive with it, to solve our sore problems and to provide us with the wisdom and strength to give Him the glory He is due.

"and try him every moment"—It is of the same sense with the former. The word expresses an exact and thorough trial. Some take it to be an allusion to the practice of those who set the watch in armies, who left their sentinels, then later revisited them to make certain they were being faithful and watchful. Or, it may be the kind of trial by which a scholar is tried, an examination. God comes to examine and to probe to see what proficiency we have acquired since yesterday. How have you improved the time? Did you learn more of yourself, of God and of Jesus Christ since I was here yesterday morning? Or, it may also be a trial of affliction. In the case of the unbeliever, God tries him before He sentences him to such and such punishment for failing to believe and obey for the past day of his life. But for believers, there is a trial for chastisement, and one for correction — actually both of these achieve the other. Then there is trial in the sense of temptation, a testing as to whether or not we will adhere to God's word, follow our teaching, obey that which we claim to believe.

By trial the Lord proves that there is grace in the heart, and at the same time He uncovers the corruption that is there. Job's trial is to prove that he has such grace that nothing Satan can do will elicit from him a cursing of God. In the proving of His point, God also is discovering to Job and to us that in the holiest and most faithful of men there is a defilement which builds up from our corrupt nature. There are some degrees of grace which cannot be known without such a trial. We ourselves would not believe what strength of faith we may have until God proves it to us by sorely trying our hearts and souls. On the other hand, it is virtually impossible to convince us of our pride, or our hard-heartedness, without severe trial by affliction. God knows what is in our heart. We do not know until He reveals it to us, and then we will not believe Him until He proves it to us beyond all doubt of a sincere heart. At the same time He proves His own sufficiency to supply our needs, even those graces which flourish and overcome in the midst of trial.

God also tries us by our prosperity or comfort. A man may be faithful to the utmost in the midst of affliction, but give him just a little ease and he corrupts like manna on the Sabbath. If you get riches or honor or credit, then watch how you use them — for God is by these things proving whether or not you are the believing servant that you think you are.

From this we learn that awesome truth, that the temper and state of our hearts are so various that we must be tried every moment in order to keep us in the way of grace. It is sad but true that the frame of our heart an hour ago will not necessarily foretell what it is like this moment. From belief to unbelief, from humility to pride, from lovingkindness to utter selfishness, etc., is the matter of only a moment except God keeps His correcting hand upon us continually. As quickly as one thought jumps in front of another, we can go from grace to fleshliness. As the physician tries the pulse of a sick man many times an

230

hour, so God must try our pulse every moment, that we do not relapse into those sinful ways which filled our yesterdays. Only when we have been carried up to meet with the Lord Jesus Christ, when we have been made like Him, when we have been put into the frame of glory, will He no longer need to try us every moment. Then will come stability.

"Will you never look away from me, nor let me alone until I swallow down my spittle"— Job 7:19.

Job now makes application of the two former verses. It is as if he had said, Since man is a creature so weak and unworthy in himself, and since I am such a man why do You visit me and try me every moment? How long shall it be before You depart from me? Or, How long will it be until You look away from me?

The original word signifies to look upon a man with respect and complacency, *"The Lord had respect to Abel and his offering"* (Gen. 4:5). There He looked toward Abel, but here He is to look away, as in Isa. 22:4, *"Look away from me; I will weep bitterly."* And because they who withdraw their eyes from us are ready also to withdraw their presence the word also means to depart. —

But is this the voice of Job? Is he burdened with the presence of God? It is the wicked who say to God, *"Depart from us"* (21:14). This is no mercy, it is that which the Lord often threatens to do to those who will not give Him glory. Instead He promises the faithful, *"I will never leave you or forsake you."* Will a man in darkness tell the sun to go away? Will Job in the midst of his fiery trials ask God to depart from him? To understand it, it must be understood that the Lord's presence may be considered in two ways, (1) His comforting presense; (2) His angry, afflicting presence. Job intends to ask God to take away His afflicting hand, as did David, *"Remove Your stroke away from me. I am destroyed by the blow of Your hand"* (Ps. 39:10). So some translate here, *"How long before You will spare me?"* Or it may be as Job speaks of a third person, *"look away from him so that he may rest, until he shall finish his day, like a hireling"* (14:6), which fits very well into this context. And it is the sense of the next clause of the verse.

"nor let me alone until I swallow down my spittle?"—This is not a refusal of God's support. He does not ask that God should stop upholding him. If He ¹by whom all things consist were to let us alone in that way, we could not even swallow down our spittle. Not only do we depend upon God moment by moment for spiritual energy, but also for each breath and each bit of energy for our natural acts. The word translated *"let me alone"* is one which means to loosen or untie that which is bound. From this comes also the meanings, to deal gently or tenderly. The word is used sometimes in a good sense to express the way that God has bound us to Himself, how He has tied the knot of His own love and free-grace about us. It is also used of an onslaught of unbelief, *"If you faint in the day of trial, your strength is small"* (Prov. 24:10)—that is, if you are loosened or untied from God, then your strength is going to be small.

Job, then, is asking to be let loose from the bonds of his affliction. He wants God to take him off the rack of his tortures and troubles. As we are girded with strength, so we also may be girded with weakness, as Job speaks of God, *"He weakens the strength of the mighty"* (12:21)—the Hebrew is, *"He loosens the girdle of the strong."* The same God who loosens the girdle of our strength is He who loosens the bands of our infirmity.

Note that God can and sometimes does make His own presence to be grievous to His servants. It is true that, *"In His presence there is fullness of joy,"* but there can also be the fullness of sorrow and pain in His presence. He can be a Sun to warm His people, but He can also be like a fire to burn them — a shield to defend them, or a sword to wound. It is well to value His presence, even if it means much grief and misery for the time.

Troublesome times are very tedious times to the saints. It has always been so, as can be seen in the Psalms, *"Has the Lord forgotten to be gracious" "Will the Lord cast off forever?"* etc.

Afflictions are like bonds, they bind us tight to experiences which we would refuse if we were not chained to them until they have worked out an abundance of grace in us. It is well to remember that while they are so binding us, they are also holding us back from sinful acts which we might well be committing against God if we were not afflicted. And we soon learn that we ourselves cannot loosen these bands of affliction. If God binds the affliction to us, no one but God can set us free from it, *"He opens and no one shuts; He shuts and no one opens"* (Rev. 3:7). So those of you who are striving and struggling with God, watch lest your bands be made strong (Isa. 28:22).

It must be said that Job does not attempt to break the cords, nor to cut them in two. It is not his intention to untie these knots, but he wants God to do it.

"until I swallow down my spittle?"—Laying aside the speculations as to any literal meaning which Job intends, there are two proverbial ways these words can be taken:

1. It can denote the shortest time, no more time than it takes a man to swallow. In this case Job is saying, O let me have a little intermission, a little respite. Let me have at least enough time of ease as it will take me to swallow my spittle. Let me know once more what it is to be without pain, even if it is but a moment.

2. It can denote a very strict watch set over another, to watch a man in all his motions, so that he cannot stir a finger, or move his tongue in his mouth unobserved. So Job would be saying, I cannot stir my tongue or swallow my spittle (which is one of the most unperceivable acts of man) without Your notice. O please do not hold so strict a hand and so curious an eye upon me. Let me have a little liberty. Do not examine my every failing or question me on the least infirmity.

From the former it is true that afflictions are continued upon some without any intermission. Job did not have very much whole skin for anyone to set a pin upon, nor so much as a moment of time he could call his own so that he could even spit. Every second brought its wound with it. The renewal of each moment also renewed his afflictions.

Again, a short refreshing may be a great mercy. Dives did not desire a large drink but a mere drop of water. But he also knew it would have eased him but for a heartbeat or two. Yet he sought even such little respite, no longer than it takes for a man to swallow. The eternity of pain in hell will not find even that much abatement, either in time or degree. But those afflictions which have no intermission may sometimes seem to be like hell to us on earth, when there are no comforts or any sort of ease to interrupt them. In the very same way, our comforts in Christ also may seem like Heaven when they continue unbroken for a long period of time.

From the latter, God counts our steps and watches all our motions, even those that are secret. He has searched us and has known us (Ps. 139:1,2). He goes into our inner rooms, into those secret recesses of the heart, into the most fleeting of thoughts, and watches as they form and come toward us.

"I have sinned. What shall I do to You, O watcher of men? Why have You set me as a mark against You, so that I am a burden to myself?"—Job 7:20.

In the first part of Job's answer to Eliphaz, he strongly contests the implication that his excruciating pain and the agony of his soul is due to the fact that he has committed sins commensurate with his suffering. Here in chapter 7 he has been expostulating with God for leaving him in this condition. Now he assumes a different posture, humbling himself before God and making confession of his sin.

"I have sinned"—The words may be taken in two ways: (1) as a prayerful confession; or, (2) as a concession.

1. As a prayerful confession, Job is in effect saying, 'Lord if You are holding me on the rack of affliction in order to obtain a confession, I am ready to confess that I have sinned.' The word for sin here is one that means to miss the mark we aimed to hit; or, to miss the way we intended to follow.

But is such a general confession of sin acceptable to God? Did not Pharoah, hard-hearted and defiant as he was, also confess that he had sinned. Did not false-hearted Saul do so? Did not Judas the traitor also confess it? (Ex. 9:25; 1 Sam. 15:24; Matt. 27:4).

A. A general confession may be a sound confession. It depends upon the matter, the manner and the reason for the confession. If these be right, then a general confession does not need any particular details of sin in order to make it an acceptable one. Those who hide their sins in their excuses, in their idleness, in their ignorance, in their forgetfulness, cannot absolve themselves by merely exclaiming, 'I have sinned.' Where Pharaoh, Saul and Judas failed, Job and the Publican succeeded in making a holy confession to God, smiting the breast and saying, *"God, be merciful to me a sinner."* They differed from that unholy threesome only in the matter, the manner and the reason for their confession.

1. The matter of a confession is important to its success, for it must include four things: (1) true confessors not only acknowledge the fact of sin, but the blot, the filthiness and defilement, the blackness in every sin; (2) True confessors confess the fault, that they realize that they are liable to the fullest penalty of God's law for what they have done. Faithfully confessing such guilt, they put themselves into the hands of God's justice and trust in the Lord Jesus Christ and His work to take them out of the hands of God's justice — and to put them into the hands of God's mercy; (4) True saints accept all the punishments threatened in God's word as properly due to their sin, openly declaring, *"O Lord, righteousness belongs to You, but unto us confusion of face...,"* (Dan. 9:7). None, like Cain, dare cry out, *"My punishment is greater than I can bear,"* seeking to ameliorate the suffering, but instead they flee to their Refuge, Christ Jesus. They believe that He has borne their punishment once for all and that the Father will not again require it at their hand.

2. The manner of a confession is equally important, for at least five ways of confession may be noted in a saint's prayer for forgiveness: (1) True confession must be made freely. Pain, trouble and threatening may extort a confession from a Pharoah or a Saul, but even on their best days the saints are ready to speak the worst of themselves. In those seasons when the unbeliever is reaping the best fruits of this world, he despises *"the riches of God's goodness and forbearance and longsuffering."* But the faithful are never so humbled as in those times when the *"goodness of God leads them to repentance"* (Rom. 2:4). (2) True confession is done feelingly. When they say they have sinned, they taste the bitterness of sin, they groan under its burden. Confessions run through a natural man like water through a pipe, leaving no impression whatever. The natural man feels nothing while confessing, unless the hot breath of God is on his neck and he fears immediate retribution if he does not confess with a show of feeling. (3) True confession must be offered sincerely, *"Blessed is the man in whose spirit there is no deceit"* (Ps. 32:2). The unholy ones will dump their sins by confession the way seamen dump their goods overboard in a storm — they unhappily part with them, sadly wishing that there could be a way to recover them when the storm has passed. They may cast out an evil spirit, but they keep his place decorated and swept in the hope that he may come again. But the true saint feels filthy with sin, and he washes it off with repentance, issuing forth in confession in order to be rid of it forever. He then bars the door, seeking for all helps from God's word to prevent that sin from ever returning again. (4) True confession is offered in faith. One eye may be on the sorrow that emanates from sin, but the other is on Christ. Judas, when he was convicted of his heinous sin, confessed that he had betrayed innocent blood. But Judas did not believe that his sin could be washed away in that same innocent blood — so he defiled himself further with his own blood, murdering himself. Any man who trusts in the shed blood of Jesus Christ to wash, renew and to regenerate him will also believingly continue to trust in that blood to cleanse him from those defilements which come to all who walk through this life. (5) True confessors do so knowingly. A godly man may maintain his innocency and justify himself when accused by men, but before God he willingly acknowledges his weakness and judges himself to be a sinner before God. Job had spent much time in washing off the aspersions cast on him by his friends. But here he charges himself with his failings in the sight of God. It may be that God will speak well of his servants, as He did of Job (1:21), but they dare not do so themselves. Only a hypocrite has unrelieved good thoughts of himself, boasting of his own spiritual beauty, flattering *"himself in his*

own eyes until his iniquity is uncovered" (Ps. 36:2). Godliness goes with lowliness, as the life of the Lord Jesus Christ proves beyond doubt.

3. The reason behind a confession is very important. Not only is confession our reasonable service, a duty owed to God, but it is reasonable to confess because of the benefits that accrue to us from this duty: (1) Confession is commanded because confession pumps sin out of our system. The line of sinning is as long as the line of life. The best of the saints take on sin like a leaking ship takes on water, and while the ship leaks, shall the pump stand idle? As long as we are taking in the poison of sin, there is need for vomiting it out with our confession; (2) Confession is a soul-humbling duty which the best have need of. The Lord sends us the buffetings of temptation by Satan, allows us to see the results of our deeds and thoughts, so that we may be humbled by them — so that we may be brought to purge ourselves by confession; (3) Confession affects the heart with sin, engaging the heart against it. Each confession brings with it an obligation not to do it any more. A tender heart avoids the pain of sin, and it is confession that keeps the heart tender. (4) Confession shows us our need of mercy, endears that mercy to us. How sweet and how good is the mercy of God when we have tasted evil and have the bitterness of it permeating our lives! How welcome and how beautiful is His pardon which He gives according to His promise when we confess. (5) Confession of sin advances Christ in our hearts. How wonderfully is Christ revealed to us when we unashamedly cleave to Him and beg of Him to remove the crushing debt which we have contracted by our sins, O how we appreciate His healing virtue when we are bent over and warped by our sins, confessing to Him that we have suffered mortal wounds and incurable sicknesses which only He can cure.

"what shall I do unto You"—The word which we translate *"do"* expresses working or doing under a twofold qualification.

1. Working with great willingness and readiness of mind, and so it may be applied to the workings of sin in natural men, who work with the greatest freedom. Man sins naturally and therefore freely. He is carried on with a full swing, with tide and wind. Nothing within him contradicts or gives a contrary vote to him when he proposes to sin. He is a true worker of iniquity (Ps. 5:5).

2. Working with energy and success, and the doing of a thing not only effectually, but willingly. When God works, He works thoroughly. He does not do business by halves. So when Job asks, *"What shall I do,"* it is a questioning as to what shall be done willingly and readily, as well as effectually and thoroughly. He is in earnest. What is to be done?

The question as to what to do when one has sinned is a point of the highest consideration to every one of us. If we ever need counsel, it is in this matter of what to do when we have sinned. Such is the nature of sin and the consequences of it, that it calls us to the highest level of effective action in order to do something about it. Sin sends its ripples all the way into eternity. If anything is worthy of your serious thoughts, it is in this matter of what to do about your sins.

Note that the sincere confession of sin will make the soul very active and inquisitive as to the remedies of sin. Many make confession of sin, but do not seem to be much troubled about the cure of sin. If you say, *"Lord, I have sinned,"* then the very next question must be, *"what shall I do."* When the Jews heard what they had done in crucifying Christ, they were stabbed in the heart, and they said to Peter and the other apostles, *"what shall we do?"* (Acts 2:37). When the Philippian jailor realized how marvelously he had been saved from certain death, his life being forfeited if a single prisoner had escaped, then his sins crowded in upon him and he rushed up to Paul and Silas and said, *"Sirs, what must I do..."* (Acts 16:29,30).

A soul that is sensible of sin, that realizes what sin really means, will be ready to submit to any terms which God shall put upon it. Let Him merely say what is to be done, there will be no negotiations, no picking and choosing amongst alternatives — there will be no debate but a yielding and immediate haste to do those things which will take sin off and bring peace in. And although we may know that we have sinned, we do not always know to what extent we have sinned. It is needful for us to ask God to tell us both what we have done, and what it is that we must do. It is God that is offended by sin. David cried, *"Against You and You only have I sinned"* (Ps. 51:4). Therefore, it is only God who can relieve us of that sin, who can direct us what we must do to remove the effects of that sin. He alone knows what will please Him. And He alone knows His word well enough to direct us to this or that passage of Scripture for our direction. If we attempt to amend for our sin without His direction, we may in fact go in the wrong direction — then we may further offend and sin against Him, missing the mark again and again because of our presumptuous foolishness.

Taking the question negatively, there may be two senses in it:

1. Some render it, *"what have I done against You?"*—then the meaning is this, I have done nothing against You; or, I have not hurt You by sinning. In what way have I injured You, that You lay Your hand so severely upon me in these grievous afflictions, both upon my soul and upon my body? I am hurt, but in what have I hurt You? There is a truth in that, but it is not the truth of this place. A man may say when he has sinned, What have I done to hurt God? Yet all the hurt and wrong which God receives is by sin. Our sins are no hurt to God in that they lessen His happiness or fullness or essential honor. All the poisonous darts of sin fall short of reaching God. We must not think that anything can in truth annoy God. We have that expressly stated in this book, *"If you sin, what do you do against Him? Or if your transgressions are multiplied, what do you do to Him?"* (35:6). But, on the other side, if a man is ever so holy and good, if he does never so many acts of righteousness, still God will not gain a whit by them. We can neither subtract from God nor add to God, *"Is it any pleasure to the Almighty that you are righteous? Or any gain to Him that you make your ways perfect?"* (22:3). When the Scriptures say that He is delighted in the services of the saints and take pleasure in His people, we must understand them in the same sense as those scriptures which describe Him as displeased with the sins of men, angry and grieved, etc. All the expressions of God's delight or grief are only expressions towards the creature, not any impressions upon Himself.

2. Taking the question in this way, *"what can I do to You?"*—as in the Septuagint, the answer would be, Nothing! If Job is saying, 'Lord I have sinned, and if You seek for satisfaction at my hands, I am not able to make any.' He has nothing to give.

3. He may be saying that he can do nothing to escape God's power. He cannot get away.

4. He may be indicating that he can do nothing to satisfy God's justice.

5. He may be saying that he can do nothing to pacify God's anger.

There is a threefold deficiency in all that a man can do to satisfy the justice of God: (1) All is imperfect and defiled. Our services smell of the vessel through which they have passed. The taste is of the barrel from which they pour. There is a stamp of our sinfulness on all that we do, even upon our holiest efforts. And can that which is sinful satisfy for sin? (2) Whatever we do is a debt before we do it. All our duties are owed before we perform them. Then can we pay the debt of sin by those duties which we already owed? For they were due before the sin was ever committed. (3) The greatest deficiency is this, that our works lack the stamp of God's appointment for that purpose. God has nowhere set up man's righteousness as satisfaction for man's unrighteousness — that is a human concept. If it would be possible for us to perform perfect acts of righteousness which fully conform to the whole will of God, yet these would not satisfy the offended justice of God unless God has said that He would accept them as a way of satisfaction. It is God who appoints those things which will be acceptable to Himself. Surely, all that Jesus Christ did or suffered for us in the flesh would not have satisfied the justice of God if God had not first appointed that Christ should come to do and suffer those things for the express purpose of satisfying His justice! It was the agreement between Christ and His Father that made Him a Savior, *"Sacrifice and offering You did not desire"* (Heb. 10:4). God refused sacrifices because they could not purge sin. Instead, God prepared a body for Him, and with magnificent wisdom He devised the only way that there could be any sacrifice for sin which would actually expunge guilt and make it possible for sinners to come into the presence of God, *"we are sanctified by that will through the offering of the body of Jesus once for all"*—inferring that the offering of the body of Jesus Christ could not save us but by the will and ordination of God.

Pardon and forgiveness of sin come in at the door of free-grace. It is simply because of the freely given grace of God that any are saved and pardoned. We must come without money and without price, depending and resting only in the merciful provisions of God. Those who trust in good works to purchase pardon and forgiveness of their sins are of all men most miserable, for a good work trusted in is as mortal as an unrepented sin.

There is something to be done when we have sinned, but there is nothing to be paid. It is gospel-language to say, 'What shall I do?' — the Jews were told to repent, to believe. These are the ways in which salvation is tendered to us, not for works that we have done. It is a dangerous error to lift up the grace of God so as to deny the industry of man through grace. Because he can do nothing in the way of satisfaction does not mean that man can do nothing at all. Never did the apostles answer this question, *"what shall I do"* with a *"There is nothing you can do."* They always told them to do something. They did not allow them to think that all they must do is to talk or pose. They told them to confess, to repent, to believe, to obey, to mourn, to humble themselves, to renew their vows, to present themselves a living sacrifice, to be conformed to Christ Jesus. Beware of those who pretend to lift up the grace of Christ while they are merely seeking cover for doing nothing. There are those who readily deny that they have any righteousness, freely confessing that only God is righteous, but who are not much interested in seeking to live righteously. Our righteousness is dung and dross in justification before God, but they are gold and precious things in sanctification. Without them we cannot walk worthy of our holy calling.

"O watcher of men"—or, *"O preserver of men"*—The word means both to preserve and to observe, and it is often applied to God, *"He kept him as the apple of His eye"* (Deut. 32:10). As the Watcher of men, God looks right through us, He misses nothing about us or in us. He that ponders the heart, considers it and keeps it, does He not know? As the preserver of men, He keeps him safe, or keeps him so that he cannot escape. As the watcher of men, Job may be addressing God, saying, *"What shall I do to cause You to look upon me with favor,"* or, *"to allow me to escape Your accusing gaze."* In the speaking of words to that import, Job would be speaking as Jeremiah did, *"He has built against me. He has compassed me about, He has made my chain heavy on me."*

As the preserver of men, Job credits God as the savior and protector to whom he has to present his questions. He cannot understand why affliction after affliction is falling upon him when he knows that he is under God's promises and protection, *"The Lord preserves the faithful"* (Ps. 31:23). And it is good that he does, for man needs most of all someone who will keep him safe, and keep him holy, pleasing to God. If a pure Adam could not preserve himself, how much less can we who are so ungodly by nature? We walk in the midst of enemies, and there are a multitude of enemies in our own breasts — in both cases we desperately need to be protected by our great Preserver and Protector.

1. He preserves by His own hand and outstretched arm, *"I will be to Jerusalem a wall of fire all around"* (Zech. 2:5).

2. He preserves by the hands of others, preserving man by man, and even sometimes by the beasts of the field and the fowls of the air. To complete the creation, He also has used angels to preserve and protect His own.

To preserve men requires the strength of God, the wisdom of God and the patience of God. Thankfulness is due to Him that He should so use His attributes and His creatures for our preservation, and that from unbelievers as well as believers. Of all persons, only God preserves and is merciful to His enemies. But God is the preserver of His own in a special way, *"the savior of all men,"* that is, *"the preserver of all men, especially of those who believe"* because (1) They are more precious to Him than all the world, they are His jewels (Mal. 3:16); (2) He is a near relative of theirs, their Father, and the Church is the spouse of Christ. And this preservation is perpetual, never ending and never intermitted.

"Why have You set me as a mark against You?"—The word signifies to meet one, to come the opposite way. From this we translate, *"why have You set me contrary to Yourself?"* Others, *"Why have You put me as an object against You?"* The word may be taken simply for an enemy or adversary, one who stands in opposition to us in his actions and designs. This translation of ours suits the sense of the word fully, because a mark at which a man aims is set in direct opposition to him. We level our arrows or bullets at the mark right before us. Job thought himself to be placed as a target or mark at which God was shooting His arrows. He believes that God has set him out as if he were an enemy. He is expostulating or complaining before God that he was the man chosen out among all the men of the world to be the mark and butt against which God shot His afflictions. How revealing this is of the foolishness of men, of man's inability to discern the intentions of God in His providential dealings! Job was indeed a man chosen to be a mark, and He who chose him was God. But he was the mark of Satan, chosen By God to be the mark because he was not an easy mark. Job does not know this, but in pleading with God to remove His hand, in begging God not to make him His mark any more, he is actually praying against his own best interests, both here and hereafter.

Men are quite inquisitive into the reasons for God's dealings. His ways are past finding out, but this does not stop men from seeking and searching into them. This may be because it is some satisfaction and ease to the mind smitten by the hand of God to know that there is a reason why He wounds and smites. Yet, in this case, for God to tell Job the answer to his question would defeat the entire purpose of God in setting Job up as a mark in the first place. To have Job quit now would be to hand the victory to Satan, or at least to turn the contest into no contest. Many times it would be an ease to our pain if we but knew the reason behind it. But there are more important things in God's providence than our ease, and many times those things take precedence over our present comfort. In actuality, this little interlude of time when we live on this earth is nothing more than a testing ground — it was not the lot of Christ Jesus to have comfort and ease here for His lifetime on earth, and we have no right to demand it for ourselves either. Those who regard themselves as pilgrims and strangers, who think of their home and their life as being above, are not so apt to expect God to make a heaven for them on this earth. It is this group which is so quick and free in saying, *"it was good for us that we were afflicted."*

God sometimes does seem to be an enemy of His faithful servants. The Lord oftentimes takes upon Himself the posture of the enemy because it is the best way to conform them to His image. And when He is acting as One who is shooting at us. He is very accurate and true with His shots — they hit the mark, and do make the changes that He intends.

Man in sinning runs contrary to God, and in effect he is setting himself up as a mark for God to shoot at. God in affliction runs contrary to man, in man's mind, but in actuality God is truly befriending and perfecting the saints when He afflicts them. When we sin we assume the position of the wicked man who is described in Job 15:25,26, *"because he stretches out his hand against God, and sets himself against the Almighty. He runs upon Him with a stiff neck, with the thick layers of his shields."* If we are not to suffer the same fierce blows from God that the wicked receive, then we need to repent of our sins and remove ourselves from his posture.

"so that I am a burden to myself?"—The former words are the cause, these the effect. You have set me as a mark, and O I am a burden to myself! The *Septuagint* reads, *"I am a burden to You,"* in which case the meaning would be, *"Lord, You have set me as a mark against You and now I am a burden to You."* The Jewish writings take this for the ancient reading of the text, saying that the scribes made the alteration to our reading, *"a burden to myself."* They conceived that it was unbecoming of the majesty of God that Job should say that he was a burden to himself. But our translation carries the sense more fairly. God had thrown Job upon himself so heavily that he had become a burden to himself. Outward afflictions, poverty, sickness, etc. are burdens and may well make a man a

burden to himself. The very removing of our comforts can act like a heavy weight upon our spirits. The removing of health from the body is a weight upon the soul. Fear is a burden, care is a burden, pain is a burden, etc. So God tells us to cast all these burdens on Him (Ps. 55:22).

The fact is, man left to himself is not able to bear himself. Natural corruption is enough to sink any man. We all have a *"weight, the sin that so easily besets us"*(Heb. 12:1). And when he advises us to cast our burdens on the Lord *"and He shall sustain you,"* he is saying that we cannot sustain ourselves.

The thing that burdens Job most of all is of course his apprehension that God is against him. The poison that was in God's arrows was the fact that they were God's arrows – as such they drank up his spirit. When it was merely the Sabeans and the Chaldeans that set themselves against him, Job bore it well indeed. From an enemy one can bear blows, but from a familiar friend they become burdens that one cannot bear – as David and his A-hithophel, and Christ and His Judas. In the next verse, in the last breath of this answer, Job points out what it is that is pinching him.

"And why do You not pardon my transgression and take away my iniquity?For now I shall sleep in the dust and You shall seek me in the morning, but I shall not be"–Job 7:21.

Now Job sues for the pardon of those sins and the removal of sorrows which will follow. He hopes thereby to unbend God's bow and to stop any more arrows from being shot into his breast. He asks for speed and expedition, lest help being retarded may come too late. For he professes that he cannot hold out much longer, and if God tarried, then He shall find that His servant is gone.

"Why do You not pardon my transgression"–The words may be taken in two ways:
1. In the form of them, they are a vehement expostulation. Job's spirit has been heating up with the fire of his suffering, and here he speaks in the heat of his spirit — he breathes out fiery desires after mercy. He keeps up his heart to the same height and tenor still. He had said, *"Why have You set me as a mark,"* now he asks, *"Why do you not pardon."* He wants to change himself from being a mark for God's arrows to the point where he will be a mark for God's mercies. Job's expostulation is in effect Job's plaintive prayer. He says, *"Why do You not pardon,"* but he is praying, *"O that You would pardon my transgression."* A man who is deeply wounded will not be cold and nice in asking for a surgeon — he will be hot and he will call loudly for the one who has the wisdom to save his life — and if the word does not reach the surgeon, the patient may be gone before he arrives. Sins are deep wounds, and God is the only surgeon who can remove the missile that caused them, the only physician that can cure the wounds and make the man whole again.

"Why do You not pardon" –The *Septuagint* reads, *"Why do You not forget my transgression"*–bury it in the grave of oblivion. The word can mean to forget, as well as to take away. But generally, it carries the meaning of lifting up, or taking away that which lies heavily upon us, either in a moral or in a natural way. Because pardon is the taking away or lifting off of sin, it is often put for the act of pardoning. Christ, the substance of all the sacrifices, is said to be lifted up, and He Himself said it, *"so must the Son of man be lifted up."* When the Lord is said to forgive, it is a lifting up of iniquity or transgressions (Ex. 34:7; Ps. 32:1). But not only is there the picture of a lifting off of a burden, but the taking on and bearing of that burden by another, – this is the full meaning of pardon. For pardon is not the taking away of sin from a man, laying it down who knows where. But pardon is the taking away of sin off of a man and laying it down upon the shoulders of the Lord Jesus Christ – *"the Lord has laid on Him the iniquity of us all"* (Isa. 53:6). *"Surely He has borne our griefs and carried our sorrows."* *"Who Himself bore our sins in His own body on the tree, so that we...might live unto righteousness"* (1 Pet. 2:24).

Pardon is not only a taking away, a lifting off, and a bearing of sin by another – it is also pictured by the putting away of sin, or the passing away of sin, or the casting of sin behind the back. So the word is translated now and again. Then again, the word is applied to the committing of sin, as well as to the pardoning of sin. For when it it joined with words, the commandments of God, the statutes of God, the word of God, etc., it signifies the violation of those, the breaking out of bounds, trangressing. For in sinning a man passes by the word and commandments of God.

Of course when pardon is complete, when sin is taken away, put away, or is caused to pass away, all the punishments due to sin go out with it. A pardoned sinner will never feel the weight of God's little finger in judgment — He will pass over such a one when He comes to take vengeance.

"transgression and take away my iniquity"—Transgressions and iniquity are words of great signification, for in them all kinds of sin, especially the most weighty sins, are comprehended. A transgression is a violation of the command of God. It is a going beyond, a deliberate, high-handed rebellious act which expresses the mind, the spirit and the heart of the transgressor. There is a spice of pride in every sin, for in sinning we are proudly refusing the will of God while we are at the same time setting up our own will as worthy.

Iniquity imports the crookedness and inequality of a thing, when it turns this way or that way and does not extend in a straight or right line. So it is applied to the perversity and vitiosity of man. Our nature is a crooked piece and it makes everything in our lives to be crooked. So this word also implies more than a bare act of sin, arising from infirmity, weakness or inadvertency. It rather notes out those sins which are committed from a perverse nature and a crooked purpose, from an ill bent of the heart. It is a case where the mind sees God's standard, that which is right and good, just and straight, but perversely determines not to follow it. Instead it turns to crooked paths in order to do that which is different from God's word.

Job addresses himself to God because it is only God who can pardon transgression and iniquity. These gross sins must be met by a longsuffering, a merciful and gracious God who is both able and willing to pardon, *"Who is a God like You, pardoning iniquity"* (see Micah 7:18). The greatest sins fall within the compass of God's pardoning mercy. Job is not speaking in a diminutive language, he is willing to lay the full load of his sins upon himself. Those whose hearts are right will not stand mincing about the size of their sin —there are no truly small sins because there is no small God to sin against—but they will admit to all those sins which are considered to be the greatest among men. A godly man may be guilty of committing most any of the sins which a wicked man commits, except the sin against the Holy Spirit. These Job was willing to confess, as will any perceptive and tenderhearted saint. The grace of the gospel is as large as any evil of sin. The grace of the gospel is as large as the curse of the Law. Whatever the Law can call a sin, the gospel can show a pardon for it. Whatever the Law can bind us with, the gospel can unloose. The Mercy-seat covered the whole Ark — it covered completely the Ark where the Law was put. It is not the malignity of the sin but the malignity of the sinner that makes it incurable. The sin against the Holy Spirit is not unpardonable because there is not sufficient mercy to pardon it, but because such mercy is refused, the medicine to heal is despised.

But does Job ask pardon? Was he never pardoned until now? Job was according to the testimony of God a just and upright man, one that feared God and hated evil — such a man surely had been pardoned before such things could be said of him. Yet those whose sins are pardoned must still pray for the pardon of their sins. Nathan told David, *"God has put away your sin,"* and no doubt that godly man believed that gracious message. Yet in his pentitential Psalm he prays earnestly for pardon, again and again. He was assured he had been pardoned, but still he prayed for pardon? Why? Think of this, that Christ was fully assured of the love of His Father, yet He cried, *"My God, My God, why have You forsaken Me?"* Again, Christ knew that those given to Him, His sheep would continue forever, that none could take them out of His hand. Yet in the high-priestly prayer (John 17) He prays for them abundantly and in various aspects. Then too, He was assured that He would be delivered and upheld in death, *"Yet in the days of His flesh He offered up pray-*

ers and supplications with strong cries and tears to Him that was able to save Him from death" (Heb. 5:7). He was certain of the issue and knew he could carry the work through against all the armies of hell, yet He prays with strong cries. So then, it is no argument because a believer knows his sin is pardoned that therefore he should not pray for pardon.

Further we may answer that matters of faith are of two sorts:

1. Such as are fully accomplished, acted and completed in all the parts and circumstance of them — for these things we are not to pray. No one is to pray for the redemption of the world, for redemption is an accomplished thing — yet it is a matter of faith. But, 2, the pardon of sin, though it is complete in itself and a matter of faith to us, yet it is being completed and perfected every day more and more. Pardon is given to us, yet we do not feel all which pardon gives. It is a settled act on God's part, yet it is in motion on our part; that is, it is in a perfective motion. Therefore, though we are assured that our sins are pardoned and shall stand pardoned forever, yet we may pray for the pardon of them.

3. Suppose a man knows his sins are pardoned, yet he may pray to know it more. He may desire that the evidence that his sins are pardoned may be made clear to him. For though sin cannot be more pardoned in respect of God at one time than at another, yet in regard to man it may. That is, he apprehends the pardon of his sin more now than before; and he may hereafter apprehend it more than he does now. And it is worthwhile to bestow pains in prayer for pardon, to have the pardon a little more enlightened. The degrees of any grace or favor, as well as the matter and substance of them, are worthy of all our seekings and most serious inquiries at the throne of grace.

4. He that has assurance of the pardon of sin is to pray for the pardon of sin because he continues to sin. And though it is true that still uncommitted sins are pardoned in the decree and purpose of God, yet we must not walk by the decrees of God but by His commandments and rules. His decree pardons sin from all eternity, but His rule is that we should pray for pardon every day. We must not say that God has pardoned all sin at once and therefore we need not ask it again. So long as we sin it becomes us to pray for the pardon of sin. He that has ceased to sin may cease to ask for forgiveness of sin.

In having breathed his spirit in arguings, complaints and prayers, Job moves the Lord to give him a speedy end and gracious answer. Otherwise, he sees no way but to breathe back his spirit into the hands of the Lord who gave it and lay his body in the dust.

"For now I shall sleep in the dust"—Chapter 3:13 tells what he means by this sleep, and at that place it has been shown why death is called a sleep and in what manner it is. The word here properly means to lie down. But the sense is the same, for men lie down when they compose themselves and get ready to sleep. And the dead are called 'those who lie down' as well as sleepers in the Hebrew. David's is a similar statement, *"You have brought me to the dust of death"* (Ps. 22:15).

It is well to realize where we are all traveling before long. Those whose heads are highest, even the ones who lie in beds of ivory, must lie down in a bed of earth and rest their heads on a pillow of dust. Most lay asleep in the dust while they live, but all must sleep in the dust when they die. Earthly men have earthly minds and they cannot rest except it be buried in the earth. Only he who has laid up his heart in Heaven can comfortably think of laying down his head in the dust.

"You shall seek me in the morning, but I shall not be"—In the Hebrew it is, *"You shall seek me in the morning"* all contained in one word. To English it would be, *"If You morning me"*—that is, if you come to seek me in the morning, You will not find Job alive in the earth to bestow Your mercies upon.

"I shall not be"—The Hebrew is, *"And not I"*—that is, I shall not be alive. He refers to a non-existence, not a nonessence. He would have a being, but He would not appear to be. It is as if he had said, 'Lord, I shall not be a subject capable of outward deliverance and bodily comforts unless they come speedily. Lord, If You will give me any help, give it, for death hastens upon me, as if it hoped to be too nimble for me, and too nimble for You if it outruns Your succours.

CHAPTER VIII

"Then Bildad the Shuhite answered and said"—Job 8:1.

The first discourse of Eliphaz has been answered by Job. But now a second and a third combatant, or accuser, are ready to enter the battle against him. And when these three have tried their skill and strength on him, they all three charge him afresh in a second round of charges. Then two of them renew those charges a third time. All three agree in calling Job a hypocrite. And the name of a hypocrite (like that of a heretic) is such that no man ought to be patient under it.

This is the first of three speeches by Bildad. Not once does Bildad entertain the slightest doubt as to Job's guilt. He judges him to be a hypocrite deserving all that has come upon him. Bildad presents himself as an advocate for God (which, if it were true, would be very commendable), and he conceived that there was need for someone to answer Job on the justice of God — for he thought Job had wronged God in the matter of His justice.

There are four parts in this opening speech of Bildad:

1. Bildad censures all that Job has said (verse 2).

2. He gives an assertive question, to demonstrate that God is just (verse 3).

3. He proves God's justice by three examples: Job's children, the voice of the past; and from nature (the rush, the spider-web and the tree—verses 4-19).

4. He sets forth God's favor to the faithful and sincere, proclaiming God's goodness to repenting sinners.

"How long will you speak these things, since the words of your mouth are like a strong wind?"—Job 8:2.

It may be that Bildad speaks in wonder, saying, How long can a man twist out such a thread of sinful discourse! Or, it may be that he is indignant, saying, How long can you expect us to bear these things which we find so contrary to our judgment, so grating upon our spiritual nerves? Or, he may intend to accuse Job, saying, How long are you going to speak these empty, foolish words which so indiscreetly and falsely impute injustice to God?

It is proper to speak in this manner. David asked questions like these in Psalm 4:2. Wisdom also asks, How long will you simple ones love simplicity? (Proverbs 1:22).

"these things"—He considers them to be fruitless, frothy, crude and undigested matter which is injurious to God's reputation, besides being dissatisfying and useless to men.

Though Bildad's charge against Job is false, we may learn from his words, (1) that to speak evil just once is once too often; (2) that perseverance in evil-speaking is a multiplying of sin; (3) that it is our duty to be watchful over our words, for if we refuse to apply God's word to tame our tongues, then another may be sent by God to stop our mouths with Scripture. Paul wrote to Titus, *"there are many unruly and vain talkers among you,"* then, *"whose mouths must be stopped, who subvert whole houses,...!"* (Titus 1:10,11). It is our duty to put the muzzle of Scripture over the mouths of those whose evil words *"corrupt good behavior."* If we do not, then they may subvert whole houses.

We must be careful that we do not make Bildad's mistake, to base our rebukes on our own misconceptions and false assumptions. Once he made the fatal error of judging Job by his outward condition, after only a fleeting glance, it was but a small step to the conclusion that there was nothing Job could say to extricate himself from the charge of gross sin and obvious hypocrisy. It is all too apparent that Bildad did not follow Job's words, did not see their scope or catch their drift. More than likely he simply stopped his ears while Job spoke. Then, without taking up any particular of what the man had spoken at length, Bildad clothed Job's speech in a dress of his own making and proceeded to reprove and censure Job accordingly. One of the amazing proofs of the depravity of man is this willingness of all men to disfigure the opinions and teachings of others with conceits that are strictly their own. They not only put words into the mouths of others, but they put thoughts into their heads. Then they attach their own caricature instead of the true opinions of their opponents. Bildad truly showed no pity for Job, but rather dealt deceitfully with him (Job 6:14,15).

"since the words of your mouth are like a strong wind?"—Job had said that *"right words are powerful,"* which was demonstrated first in the beginning, *"By the word of the Lord were the heavens made, and all the host of them by the breath of His mouth"* (Ps. 33:6). Words are air or breath formed and articulated by the instruments of speech. All Scripture is God-breathed (2 Tim. 3:16). And so they are powerful simply because they are God's words. He slays the wicked by His words (Isa. 11:4; Hosea 6:5). Even mere men have learned to turn energy into matter, and matter back into energy. Is it then too hard to imagine God breathing out powerful words to create a universe? Likewise, there is substance and power in His word yesterday, today, and forever — power enough to turn the world upside down.

But how can Bildad compare Job's words to a strong wind? Even ungodly words may be compared to a strong wind in several ways, (1) Bold, firm, vigorous, robust and resolute words have a strength to move and to sway people; (2) Many words spoken fiercely on many sides of an argument are often strong enough to blow others off course; (3) Words fitted to the heart of the hearer pass swiftly into thoughts, desires and action, thus becoming a mighty rushing wind to sweep all before them; (4) Light words have no weight or substance, they are like the light breezes that blow.

As to (1), Job's words indeed were bold, vigorous and resolute. Bildad was not moved by them, however. He obviously does not think they were strong in this way. As to (2), the word translated *"great"* or, *"strong,"* signifies both multitude and magnitude. Many words may be strong because they are stormy and tempestuous. For the tempest of the tongue is one of the greatest tempests in the world. Stormy words from passionate men are forever making the world unquiet. Winds may have no substance in them, yet they may bear down the trees of a vast forest. Ill winds of doctrine may subvert whole houses; yea, whole nations — they may bear down and root up all but the very elect (who are rooted and grounded in the love of Christ and through faith are able to grasp firmly the breadth and length and depth and height of that love—Eph. 3:17,18). Thank God that we who are in Christ Jesus may not be tossed to and fro by every wind of doctrine. It cannot be said that Job's words bore down or rooted up Bildad's beliefs. As to (3), Peter's words on the day of Pentecost ran swiftly into the newly prepared hearts of his hearers, conducting truth into thousands at once. But the winds of words may blow both good and evil. We are exhorted to be swift to hear those words that are good, slow to hear those that are evil. But, alas! We are perverse and so apt to hear swiftly that which is evil, whereas that which is good is heard but dully. The swiftness of Job's words did not succeed in penetrating Bildad's apparently closed mind. As to (4), it is Bildad's contention that Job's words are light, empty of substance, for even strong winds are light and empty of any substance.

"Does God pervert judgment? Or does the Almighty pervert justice?"—Job 8:3.

There are five words to be distinguished here, *"God" (El)*, *"Almighty" (Shaddai)*, *"judgment" (mishpat)*, *"justice" (tsedeq)*, and *"pervert" (avath)*.

When the Hebrew word *El* is used, it signifies the strong God, One who is mighty and powerful to carry out His will against all opposition.

Shaddai, on the other hand, denotes God as all-sufficient. He is sufficient within Himself to please Himself, to be happy apart from any or all. He has a sufficiency to do what He pleases, to effect what He designs, to direct all His actions and the actions of His creatures according to His own judgment. He has an abundance, a fullness in Himself sufficient not only for Himself but for all He may desire to fill — though there may be myriads of universes full of creatures. He can fill them all and be not the least diminished by doing so. *Shaddai* also denotes God as the maker of all things, He who gives everything number, weight and measure. Being such an all-sufficient God, He cannot of course pervert justice. *"Shall not the judge of all the earth do right?"* It is impossible for God who judges all men to do an act of injustice to any man.

Judgment and justice are often put in Scripture for the same, and when they are put together the latter is as an ephitet to the former, *"I have done judgment and justice"* (Ps. 119:121)—that is, I have done judgment justly, exactly, to a close tolerance. Sometimes they are distinctly different:

1. Judgment signifies that right which every man ought to do at all times (Ps. 106:3).

2. The Law or rule itself according to which every man is to do right is a judgment. God calls all His laws judgments, because they are all most just and equal. Judgment has a threefold opposition, by which we may understand the nature of it, (1) Judgment is opposed to anger, rigor and severity, *"Correct me, O Lord, but with judgment, not in Your anger"* (Jer. 10:24). That is, Correct me mercifully, moderately and in measure. Do not allow Your whole displeasure to arise. In this sense the judgments of God upon wicked men in hell shall be without judgment. So to do a thing without judgment is all one as to do it without mercy. (2) Judgment is opposed to foolishness, Judgment is wisdom. When we say, Such a person is a man of judgment, we mean that he is a wise man. So judgment is an ability to judge. (3) Judgment is opposed to injustice and wrong, which is the common meaning.

We may take it in any of these senses here. As judgment is opposed to anger, so it is moderation in justice, *"Will the Lord pervert judgment?"*—that is, will He not be as moderate in executing judgment as equity can admit? *"I will not execute the fierceness of My anger"* (Hos. 11:9).

Again, judgment is wisdom. God walks exactly by the rule of wisdom, of the highest and purest wisdom. There are no mists or clouds of ignorance before the eye of His understanding. And as He has no darkness, so no false lights.

Lastly, judgment is opposed to injustice. The Lord will not wrong anyone. He will not be partial, or a respecter of persons.

To make the distinction between judgment and justice, (1) Judgment signifies due order in trying and finding out the state of a cause. And justice is the giving of sentence upon the completion of that trial. (2) Judgment is a clear knowledge of what ought to be done, and justice is the doing of that which we know. Justice is an evenness and uprightness of conscience, in passing everything according to received light. (3) Some distinguish them in this way: that judgment is in condemning those that are guilty, whereas justice is in absolving and acquitting those that are innocent, or rewarding those who have done well. (4) So judgment respects capital causes which are for life, and justice respects civil causes which are for the estate or liberty.

Take them in any of these senses, or under whatever other distinction, they are of considerable importance. The Lord God is no perverter of either judgment or justice. He never disturbs or clogs the order of trial. He is no hinderer of the sentence from due execution. He exactly understands every cause, and He awards what is due to every person. He will wrong no one in life or limb, in estate or liberty.

Now as to what it is to pervert judgment and justice, the same word is used in both.

"Does God pervert"—some translate it, *"Does God supplant justice."* In which case it would import secret, cunning ways of injustice. For to supplant is properly to come behind a man and to catch him unawares and cast him down, or to lay something in his way to make him trip or stumble and fall. God does not supplant justice. He lays no plots, He sets no snares to entangle or overthrow a man in his cause.

More largely, the word *"perverse"* means to make crooked. So it well answers the point in hand. Judgment and justice are both carried by a straight line. They are the rectitude of our actions. To pervert judgment is to make crooked lines. So we have the lines, *"that which is crooked cannot be made straight"* (Eccles. 1:16)—he means it of civil, not of natural things. Some may cure natural crookedness, but no one can cure all civil ends. It is especially true that none *"can make straight that which God has made crooked."* So then to pervert judgment is to make judgment crooked, or to make judgment to bow or bend. To pervert justice is to cripple justice, to make it lame and halt.

Judgment may be perverted in two ways: (1) by subtilty; (2) by power.

1. Some pervert judgment by subtilty. They are wise to do evil. The Lord has infinite wisdom and so is able to go beyond and overreach all creatures. He is wise enough to outwit the whole world. But he is not wise to do evil. His wisdom is not a trap or a snare to others, but an unerring guide and light to Himself.

2. Some pervert judgment by violence and force. If they cannot untie the knot by craftiness, they will cut it in two by power. And if they do not have a law for it, they will replace the law with will, to which they add a strong arm and do what they desire. The Lord has power to do that which He wills, but He has no will to do that which is evil and unlawful. He can put forth as much strength as he desires, but He has no desire to pervert justice, or to act His power to overawe and master it.

Further, to pervert judgment and justice has these two things in it, (1) To darken and obscure the rule of judgment; (2) To torture or misinterpret the rule of judgment.

1. Judgment is perverted by darkening and obscuring the law or rule of justice. God will not do so. He never casts a mist before His word, or a veil over it, so that He may act against it.

2. Neither does He misinterpret His law. A good law may be ill-expounded and made the warrant of an evil judgment. A gloss corrupting the text of the law corrupts justice. Where tongue and conscience are put up for sale, the wit must find out some way to help the market.

From these words we learn that God is most exact in judgment — He is a just God. It is a high truth, one we should adore, that whatever God does is done justly. When reason cannot reach a thing, or make it out, then faith must. We must honor God in what we cannot understand. The Lord is righteous in all His ways, though His ways are past finding out.

God hears every cause before He judges it. He does not judge one side before He knows the other, *"I will go down and see whether they have done altogether according to the cry of it, which has come to Me. And if not, I will know"* (Gen. 18:21). God does not need any intelligence to be brought to Him, nor does He that fills all places actually go to any place to inform Himself. But He speaks in this way to inform us, that He is exact in point of justice. He puts these things in man's context, so that we may know that man is not more just than God in judging matters.

God examines and receives the confessions of men before He judges. With our first parents, did He not go down into the Garden and question them, asking for and receiving their excuses before He judged them?

God proceeds by the evidence of law, as well as by the evidence of the fact. These two things make judgment perfect. You must not only have the evidence of the fact, that such a thing is done, but you must have the evidence of the law condemning such a deed! God Himself is an everlasting law, only He can be and is a law unto Himself. Yet He has given out a law which gives the knowledge of sin, *"But I did not know sin except through the Law. For I would not have recognized lust unless the Law had said, 'You shall not lust.'"* (Rom. 7:7,8).

God is impartial in giving judgment. He does not strike one and spare another who is under the same condemnation. Nothing can sway or bias Him. Nothing can preponderate the balance of justice in His hand. You cannot put in any consideration to sway His beam besides the right.

There are three things which usually cause men to pervert justice. The Lord is free from them all.

1. Fear of greatness. Some would do justice if they dared. But to do so seems to them like taking a bear by the tooth or a lion by the paw. But the Lord fears nothing and no one. He is the Almighty, and the all-powerful One who cares not for any man's greatness.

2. Hope of reward. Many pervert judgment in hope of some reward. A bribe taken or promised clogs and obstructs the course of justice. The Lord is above all gifts. He has all

sufficiency within Himself.

3. Affection and nearness of relation pervert judgment. Many have clean hands, not taking bribes or fearing any one, but they are overcome with affection when they are called upon to judge their relatives. The Lord loves as no man can love, and He acknowledges His relationship to His children more than any lover among men. Yet He will not pervert judgment for any of them — no, not even for His beloved Son, the only-begotten one from His bosom.

God is exact, both in judgment and in justice. He carefully searches out each cause in order to give exactly the right judgment. He is as ready to acquit the innocent as to condemn the guilty; as zealous in rewarding those who deserve well as in punishing those who do evil (for not to reward is as great an injustice as not to punish). He neither discourages goodness by neglecting it, nor encourages sin by winking at it.

Further, Bildad, speaking upon supposition that Job has wronged God, teaches us that it is a duty to vindicate the justice of God whenever we hear it wronged. If any man wound God as to His faithfulness, truth or justice, we should immediately stand up to plead for Him the plain truths that appear in the Scriptures.

The judgments of God may be secrets to us, but they are never injurious to us. Justice is in all the dealings of God, but His justice is not always visible. His judgments are founded on reason, being expressions of His will, and His will is the highest reason in itself. God cannot be unjust, and He always punishes those who are. He does not approve when men subvert justice, but He sees it and punishes it.

"If your children have sinned against Him, and if He has cast them away for their transgression,"—Job 8:4.

The next four verses contain the first confirmation which Bildad alleges in favor of his general position that God is just, that He does not pervert judgment and justice, therefore that which has happened to Job is just, and contrariwise these have happened to Job because he is a gross sinner. Bildad considers the death of Job's children to be a judgment upon them and upon Job. He argues that God will be seen to be One who does not pervert judgment, that He will relieve the innocent, provided Job will repent and wait for God to do him good.

"If your children have sinned against Him"—This may mean, *"although your children have sinned against Him, and although He has given them into the hand of their transgressions, still if you would but seek earnestly to God and pray to the Almighty in purity and uprightness, surely He would now awake for you and prosper you."*

Or, more likely, it means this, *"As your children have sinned against Him."* That is to say, Consider this, that your children have sinned against God in a most wicked way, and take note that God has for their obstinate sins sent them away in the clutches of their horrible transgressions, even so you are about to be cast away if you do not seek earnestly to God.

Job's children are said to have sinned against God, or, before God. The Hebrew actually reads, *"have sinned to Him."*

If they are said to have sinned against God, then of course we see the picutre of all sinners busily marring the face of God. Sin is contrary to God. Sin is a transgressing of the law of God. Sin is the doing of one's own will without any deference to the prior will of God. In this way we are all in the same boat that Bildad casts Job's children into. All have sinned and come short of the glory of God. Death comes upon all men as the wages of sin. None live another day simply because they are 'lesser' sinners, nor do any die a day sooner because they are the 'greatest' sinners on earth. Paul described himself as the *"chief of sinners,"* yet he still walked the earth far longer than holy Stephen (who had such a seraphic face that the Pharisees gnawed at their own hearts when they looked upon him). If this is Bildad's meaning, then he certainly errs here.

Job's children were sinners. It may well be that they were gross sinners. It is certain that they had not the care toward God that Job had. Yet we are not told expressly that they were wicked above all the other men on the face of the earth. Neither had Bildad observed them in such courses of sin, for if he had done so would he not have brought particular charges against them here? Is not Bildad making the mistake that we all make so freely? He is imputing sin, presuming sin, because of outward circumstances. Jesus rebuked the Jews on this point when He asked them if the men who died under the tower in Siloam were sinners above all men who lived. No, He answered, but unless you repent, you will all likewise perish. So we see that Bildad's message is a good one in this way, that his example of those that had died was proper so long as it was brought in only to bring Job to repentance. But he went too far in making the application to Job, in that he charged Job's children with sin beyond the sins of other men — extraordinary sin, which he in turn was intended to lay on Job's back.

"If your children have sinned before God"—In this sense, that Job's children sinned before God, or in God's presence. David sees himself in such a position when he cries aloud, *"Against You and You only have I sinned."* All men saw David's sin in some degree, but God alone was able to observe what unspeakable sins David committed in this matter of Bathsheba and Uriah. It is God's eye that should trouble us most, for the very thought that we are committing these filthy sins in God's presence will tear out the heart of a true believer. No sin is secret before God, though many may be unknown to other men. God sits on the circle of the earth and watches all that we do. He is everywhere, even in the secret recesses of our being, in those places where our ungodly thoughts go to hide. We are never out of the glare of God's holiness. All our fornications are in the plain sight of His majesty the King, even the Almighty God.

"and if He has cast them away for their transgression,"—There is in this the accusation that Job's children were sinners of the worst stripe, the kind that voluntarily studies to sin. They are being accused of deliberately provoking their sinful nature to do its utmost to desecrate God. They were cast away for their transgressions, in the sense that all men are. No one ever perished except he was a sinner, save the Lord Jesus Christ. And even in His case He perished because of sins which He took upon Himself to bear for His own.

The Hebrew reads, *"He has sent them away in the hand of their transgression,"*—There are two things here, things which may be true of men in general, even though they may not have been true of Job's children in particular:

1. God may and oftentimes does send men away from Himself, permitting them to accompany their sins off into the darkness. This He does either as a punishment to them, or as a chastisement to them — depending upon whether they may be of His elect or not. Sinful men lust after evil. The lusts of sinful men lead them captive, rush them headlong into all kinds of hurtful situations. Now God sometimes sends them away. Or, as it appears to the sinner in his evil imaginations, permits the sinner to steal away with his paramour of the moment. Sometimes God casts them away violently, or drops them suddenly into the fullest experience of their sins. The word here could bear all these interpretations and nuances.

As God may be said to send us away, He is pictured as sending us away in the clutches of our transgression. There is justice in sight here, giving us just what we deserve for our transgression — even the giving of us into the power of that transgression. Just as a child left to his childishness will do himself harm, just as a fool left to his foolishness will entangle himself, so a sinner left to his sinfulness will be grievously enslaved and demeaned by his sin. Paul preached to the heathen that God in times past allowed all nations to walk in their own ways (Acts 14:16). In Romans, chapter one, we see that the wrath of God was revealed when He *"gave them up to uncleanness through the lusts of their own hearts, to dishonor their own bodies between themselves — for they changed the truth of God into a lie, and they worshipped and served the creature more than the Creator...for this reason God gave them up to vile affections"* (Rom. 1:18,24,26).

An adulterer left to his adultery comes to the point where he cannot cease from his sin.

A liar left to his lying becomes such a chronic liar that he cannot tell the truth, though he tries hard to do so. Sin is its own punishment in this life. It is not all the punishment a man may receive, but in itself it is a horrible punishment. It is a punishment which would make men stop sinning if they were not so desperately wicked. The Psalmist describes the scene before us, *"My people would not listen to My voice...so I gave them up to their own hearts' lust; and they walked in their own purposes"* (Ps. 81:11,12). The Hebrew there says, *"I sent them into the pentinacy of their hearts"*—they who seek counsel of themselves have a fool for an instructor, and God will turn them over to their own direction as a judgment upon them.

2. The sense which our translation holds out is this, *"you have sent them into the hand of their transgression"*—that is, you have left them in those evils which their transgression deserved. Hands and power are ascribed to sin because God gives men over to those punishments which their sin challenges at His hands. Some sins have a louder voice than other sins, but every sin unpardoned cries to God for vengeance, and God often puts the sinner into the hand of sin that he may at once receive a reward for and from his own foolishness. One of the fearful things about falling into the hands of God is this, that He may give you into the hands of your sins. What a dreadful thing it is to be under the power and tyranny of our own wicked hearts! When God took up a resolution against His people Israel, He said, *"Those who are for death, go to death, and those for the sword, to the sword; and those who are for the famine, to the famine; and those who are for captivity, to the captivity"* (Jer. 15:2)—that is a dreadful sentence, but that He should turn each man over into the hands of his sins is far more dreadful than those natural calamities.

"If you would seek earnestly to God and make your prayer to the Almighty"—Job 8:5.

Bildad is saying, God has been just in punishing your children, and now He will be merciful in pardoning you if you will seek to God and pray to Him. He is repeating the counsel of Eliphaz, agreeing that the reason for Job's sufferings is plainly and clearly the fact that Job is a gross sinner who will not repent and humble himself at God's feet.

There are two parts to Bildad's counsel, (1) He tells Job to humble himself in prayer; (2) He tells him to purge himself by repentance.

Or we may look upon this counsel as a pattern of repentance and turning to God:

1. To seek to God.
2. To acknowledge our own unworthiness to receive any mercy from God.
3. To be sincere and upright-hearted with God in both.

"If you would seek earnestly to God"—We have met with the word more than once before. Literally it is, *"If you would morning God,"* or, *"seek Him early."* It may be taken for an earnest, diligent seeking to God in any part of the day. To seek God softly and gently in the night is according to this Hebraism a seeking to Him in the morning.

It was an ancient custom to seek God early in the morning, *"my voice you shall hear in the morning, O Lord,"* (Ps. 5:3). Even the heathen took this course by the light of nature, especially the sun-worshippers. Pliny reported to Trajan that Christians were known for rising before daybreak to pray and call upon God.

Praying is a seeking to God. Our work is to get near to God, to find God. For every soul that prays does so because it feels itself at a loss for something which God can provide. In God all that we lack may be found, and that is why He invites us to seek Him. In this life the saints are a generation of seekers. In the next life they will be a generation of enjoyers. Once God is fully found, there will be nothing more to be sought. Having Him, we shall have all.

God must be sought without delay. We must *"seek Him while He may be found"* (Isa. 5:5). Any delay may take us further from Him, may make it longer before we gain what we seek from Him.

God must be sought diligently. It is not a slight inquiry which will find God. He is found by some who do not seek Him, but it is not written anywhere that He is found by those who seek Him negligently.

"and make your supplication to the Almighty"—The word which we translate *"make your supplication"* is very significant in telling us how we should seek to God — that is, that we should bottom ourselves upon free-grace alone, rolling ourselves over onto God. A thought of our own worth at the time we supplicate God would be inconsistent with our doing so. It is pity, help, relief, freely given that we seek. And to achieve this wonderful result we must acknowledge that there is nothing in us worthy of the least of His mercies. That adverb used in the first chapter and repeated in the second, where the Devil objects, *"Does Job serve God for nothing"*—it is an adverb which comes from this verb. As we ought to serve God (in this sense) for nothing, and not be like mercenaries who serve for hire, so God helps us for nothing in us — He does not hire out to us either. Solomon says, *"the poor speaks humble requests"*—it is our word here, *"makes supplications,"*—because the poor has nothing to offer, he must supplicate. Likewise, we who are poor of spirit, we who have nothing to offer to God which is of any encouragement to Him to respond, we must diligently make our supplication to Him as the Almighty. He will be gracious to whomever He desires. And Bildad's counsel is correct, though misplaced in Job's case, it is not possible for us to stand on our own terms and plead our own integrity and good works to God. We must humbly bow and make supplication if we are to receive anything at His hand. Abraham *"believed in Him that justifies the ungodly"* (Rom. 4:5). Even Abraham, after he was justified in the sight of God through faith, looked upon himself as ungodly in reference to his own works.

Looking at the fourth and fifth verses together, we should learn that the falls of others into sin, or under judgment, should be warnings to us. Parents may learn to fear God by observing God's judgment on their children. Children may learn to fear God by attending to God's dealings with their parents. The apostle uses the judgments of God upon the Israelites in the wilderness as an exhortation to us, saying, *"these things happened as examples to them and were written for our warning"* (1 Cor. 10:11). God let them fall so that we might learn to keep our feet. The Greek word is very expressive of this sense. The things that happened to them were types for us. A type is such a form or representation of a thing as is made by hard impressions or strokes upon it. It is the leaving of a mark with a blow, or with pressure. This implies that the Lord in those strokes upon His people in the wilderness left marks upon them (or printed letters, for the Greek word for a printer is a typewriter). And these marks made upon them are legible to us, their posterity even to this day.

"If you were pure and upright, surely now He would awake for you and make the dwelling place of your righteousness blessed"—Job 8:6.

Bildad has counseled Job to seek to God, yet he puts in this caution, that Job should not approach God as if he were pure and upright. Rather he should make his prayers pure and upright, that God may be awakened by them. He formerly gave advice as to what Job should do, now he tells him how to do it. He must seek God, but he must do it with a pure heart.

"pure and upright"—The word means to shine or to glisten, noting that the purity of our lives in holiness shines like the light, *"let your light so shine before men"* (Matt. 5). The works of the saints should be clear as crystal. There is a twofold purity, (1) The purity of our natures, which is received at conversion; (2) the purity of our lives, which is renewed by repentence. Both of these, or either of them, may be understood in this place.

1. Holy persons are fit for holy duties, and only they are prepared for them. Sin in our separation from God, and holy duties are acts of communion with Him. How then shall sin and duty stand together?

Job is told to make supplication to God, but to be pure and upright in doing it. What have unholy persons to do about holy things? God cannot like the services of those who are unlike Him. Prayer purifies, yet purifying must be a preparative to prayer. *"If I regard iniquity in my heart, God will not hear me"* (Ps. 66:18). The blind man expressed this truth, *"God does not hear sinners"* (John 9:31). We are commanded to pray, *"lifting up pure hands"* (1 Tim. 2:8). A heathen man being at sea in a great storm looked upon the wicked wretches who were with him in this extremity, and he said to them, 'O please do not pray; hold your tongues, for I do not want the gods to take notice that you are here — for if they do, then they will surely drown us all.' If the heathen by the light of corrupt nature could say that much, how much more should be our realization that we ought not to spread forth filthy hands in supplication to God.

But the prayers of a pure and upright man will prevail, *"the effectual, fervent prayer of a righteous man avails much"* (James 5:16). Fervency alone will gain nothing, but coupled with righteousness it avails much. God is not melted into compassion by the heat of our words, but by the holiness of our hearts — a holiness which makes us like Him, giving Him an interest in answering to it.

It is not contrary to the doctrine of free-grace to say that we must be holy if we desire to have our prayers heard. Bildad's doctrine here is an excellent piece of divinity, left by itself, without the application to Job's suffering. We are not heard because we are pure and upright, but none can come with any warrantable confidence that he will be heard in his impurity and hypocrisy. It is imprudence, not confidence, to make supplication to God with a secret resolve to go on in sin. The greatest sinners in the world may come to God, even those who are most impure and filthy may find favor — yet they, and every man who comes to God, must come with this desire to have his impurities removed and his backslidings healed. It does not cross the doctrine of grace when with the same breath we say, God will do us good freely for His own name's sake, and yet we must be pure and upright when we come to God — *"with the pure You will show Yourself pure, and with the upright You will show Yourself upright, but with the perverse You will show Yourself perverse"* (Ps. 18:25,26). It is not that the Lord takes color from everyone He meets, or that He changes as His company changes. God is pure and upright with the unclean and the hypocritical, as well as with the pure and upright, and His actions prove Him to be so. But when a man deals perversely with God, God sends him away in the hands of his perversity — He will not accept anything from them, but He rejects them so long as they remain perverse. It is pure and upright of God to do so. But when He shows Himself pure with the pure and deals with them as He has promised, when He hears them and accepts them, He also is being pure and upright. Still there is nothing in purity and sincerity which deserves mercy, therefore God does still deal with us in mercy when He is pure with us in our purity. Yet we cannot expect mercy without seeking to be pure and upright when we seek it.

There is a threefold gradation of mercy laid out by Bildad here, (1) If Job were pure and upright, then God would awake for him; (2) then God would prosper him and give him peace; (3) God would abundantly increase and multiply him in his latter end.

1. God will awake for the pure and upright. It is a certainty, it is without a doubt. It will come speedily, He will do it "now!" It would be a great benefit, it will be a blessing when God awakes. God does watch over some for evil (Jer. 44:27), but it is not so with the pure and upright ones. The word *"awake,"* means both to awake and to arise. Some take the words transitively, *"He will awake for you."* These say that it is not Job awakening God by prayer, but God awakening prosperity and stirring up blessings for Job. Then it would be as if Bildad said, 'Job, your blessings are now asleep, but if you pray God will awaken them for you.' As a man's spirits, gifts, and even his graces are sometimes dormant, asleep, needing awakening, so also are our outward comforts at times.

But rather understand it of God awakening. He will awake for you. The Psalmist tells us, *"He that keeps Israel shall neither slumber nor sleep."* Then how can it be said that He will awake? God is said to sleep when He does not answer our prayers. When He hears our prayers, then He said to awake. Again, God does not sleep in regard to the act, but in regard to the consequences of sleep. Natural sleep is the binding or locking up of the senses (but the eye and ear of God are never so bound). To man, however, it seems that the affairs of the world go on without the observation of God — they not seeing Him intervene. When His providential dealings call for such apparent retirement from the happenings in the world, then it is that God is said metaphorically to sleep, *"Awake! Why do You sleep, O Lord? Arise! Do not cast us off forever! Why do You hide Your face and forget our affliction and our oppression"* (Ps. 44:23). On the other hand, when God in the workings of His providence searches out the wicked and brings them to their deserved destruction, breaking their designs and turning their counsels backwards, then He is said to awake, *"He gave His people over to the sword and was angry with His inheritance. The fire burned up their young men and their maidens were not given in marriage. Their priests fell by the sword and their widows were not able to weep. Then the Lord awakened like one out of sleep, and like a mighty man who cries aloud from wind. And He struck His enemies"* (Ps. 78:62-66). God's sleeping or waking, then, note out only the changes in His providence.

2. Holy prayer will awaken God and then He will prosper and bless. When the disciples awakened Christ, saying, *"Master! Save us! We are perishing!"*—He awoke and rebuked the stormy waves that threatened them, and peace was immediately restored, so much so that they marveled. Some of the Jewish writers claim that it is the soul that shall prosper here, because the soul is the proper seat of righteousness and holiness. Others of the Jews take this dwelling-place of the righteous to be the body, because the body is the dwelling place of the soul.

But rather take the word *"dwelling-place"* in the two ordinary Biblical senses, either strictly for the place where Job lived, or more largely for all that belonged to him. The dwelling-place of a man is all his estate, and all that pertains to it. The Chaldee Paraphrase reads, *"He will make your beautiful place to be prosperous,"* the word signifying beauty as well as a habitation.

"of your righteousness"—that is, the dwelling-place where righteousness flourishes, that place in which you live righteously. But what is righteousness? Righteousness is distinct from holiness and piety. Righteousness relates to men, holiness to God (Luke 1:75; Titus 2:12). God's grace teaches us to live soberly, in opposition to the intemperance of our bodies; righteously, in opposition to wrong in our actions; godly, in opposition to all impiety and profaneness of mind.

But righteousness here takes in our whole duty, whether toward God or man. Righteous duty toward man is twofold, (1) distributive justice, giving every one his due; (2) commutative justice, giving every one his due in commerce, as a neighbor.

"blessed"—That is, He shall make your dwelling-place peaceful and quiet, settled and established. The word means peace, plenty and prosperity. He shall pacify all for you. See these three things in the word, (1) Quiet —there shall be quiet and peace and unity in the family of the pure and upright man who seeks earnestly to God; (2) Abundance — there is fruitfulness and great increase in the family of such a man; (3) Enjoyment — the good things of this life shall be given to such a man.

Bildad by statement and implication is saying this to Job, 'Your dwelling-place has heretofore been the habitation of unrighteousness; your house has been filled with impiety and sin. But now, Job, if you will make yourself pure and upright, you shall see a different life, righteousness shall now come and dwell with you. You shall be blessed.'

"Though your beginning was small, yet your end should greatly increase"—Job 8:7.

This is the third gradation. God will not only awake for you and make you prosperous, but he will greatly increase you. You shall not only be set back in as good a condition as you were, but in a better one.

"Though your beginning was small" — The word *"small"* denotes a smallness in either quantity or quality. It is opposed to greatness in quantity or in quality. It is questionable as to how we are to make this comparison between Job's beginning and end. Are we to refer it to his estate which he owned before he was afflicted and compare it to what he is to have after his affliction as compared to what it will be when he comes to his final end. Either way it is a good comparison.

As to the former, how could Job's estate in the beginning be said to be small, when we have seen what a large inventory of his possessions were given us? He was the greatest of all the men in the East in the beginning, how then can that be said to be small? However much he may have had, it was not the whole world. Comparatively, it could still be small. The moon is a great light, but compared to the sun that light is mere darkness. In the end, as God describes it, Job had twice as much as he had before (Job 42:10), and it is said, *"The Lord blessed the latter end of Job more than the beginning."* So comparatively, the increase of Job was according to Bildad's promise here, but not because Bildad was right in his promise.

The Lord is able to repair all our losses with abundant additions, no matter what great amounts we have lost. And it is His way to give great repairs to those who have lost much for His sake. He will not allow us to put Him in our debt, but will in spiritual things give us exceeding abundantly over all we ask or think.

In our latter end, when we are in glory, we shall be greatly increased — there will simply be no comparison between what we are now, what we have now in the way of graces. Whoever you are, whatever you are, whatever you have, all these things are but small in comparison to what soon will be. Therefore, do not be like Elijah's servant, who thought the cloud as big as a man's hand meant nothing. Instead be an Elijah who sees that this small favor which we enjoy now shall become an abundant flood of blessings before we can begin to make ready to receive it.

"For, I beg of you, do not ask of the former age and prepare yourself to the search of their fathers"—Job 8:8.

Bildad's first argument that God is just is ended, and now he gives his second general argument to prove his former assertion. This one is grounded upon the testimony and the authority of the ancients. He is then saying, 'I will not press you with my own bare judgment, saying this with my own reason and authority, but I ask you to search the records of former times, to consult the wisest and holiest men that ever lived, and then let them judge in this case.' Bildad, you will note, is managing his counsel in the same way that Eliphaz had used before him. For Eliphaz said to Job, *"Call now — is there anyone who will answer you? And to which of the saints will you turn"* (Job 5:1).

Bildad then makes the strength of this argument to be this, (1) That when the holiest and wisest men in all antiquity agree with one mouth and consent, then that thing is true; (2) But the holiest and wisest of men of old agree in this, that God is just; (3) therefore this is a truth, that God deals justly and does not pervert judgment. But then he infers that God was dealing in justice with Job in consuming his estate, in destroying his children, in afflicting his person. And in inferring this, he also is assuming that God is not dealing so with these wise and eminent friends of Job in the same way because they are pure and upright in comparison to Job. *"Ask of the former age"*—This again is a very earnest and diligent search, one made with industry and energy; yea, with persistence. In an age when histories and testimonies were mostly confined to oral transmission, it would indeed require all of these to determine what the ancients had agreed upon. By the former age we are not to understand those that immediately preceded Job's generation—our immediate predecessors are not usually considered to be eminent authorities to us. Rather, this probe was to begin at the first of the generations and to proceed down through the ages in as much detail as possible.

"age—This word age is taken in three ways, (1) For the whole space of a man's life, and

when the word is doubled, it means a very long life (Ps. 61:7); (2) For some special part of a man's life. One's life is divided into four parts, perhaps alluding to the four parts of the year — infancy or childhood, youth, manhood, and old-age; (3) For an age of men, or the state of the time present. So Christ calls the scribes and Pharisees, *"a generation of vipers, and an adulterous generation."* The prophet writes, *"Who shall declare his generation?"*—it is the word of the text. Who can speak for his entire generation. You can easily write up the days that Christ lived here on earth, they were but few. But who can speak for His generation? What pen would have the lively colors and special skills to describe the wickedness and tyrannies of that age, the wonders and the marvels which were set afoot in the world when He was here?

The age which Bildad asks Job to inquire into is not a part of a man's life, or the whole life of a man, or one age of men, but it is the whole space of time from the very beginnings of all things and persons. And the reason why he begs him to so inquire is this, that he is certain that traditional teachings will prove what he says to be true. These oral transmissions were the sole authority in the day of Job, but after the written Word came into being it is noteworthy that no one is ever told to search into the traditions or experiences of those former ages — rather, we are told, *"to the law and to the testimony, if they do not speak according to this Word it is because there is no light in them"* (Isa. 8:20).

"and prepare yourself to the search of their fathers" —He is telling Job to lay a good and firm foundation for this search by preparing himself. The word also means to fix, *"fix your heart upon this work,"* he is saying.

It is good for all to carefully search the past records that we might observe the dealings of God with other generations. If history were of no use to us presently, then God would not have filled His book so full of history. The administrations of God in one age are for the instruction of all ages. God spoke with Jacob only in person at Bethel, yet later we read, *"He found him in Bethel, and there He spoke with us"*—Jacob's posterity was able to say that God had spoken to them when He spoke to Jacob. So with our fathers in the faith, when God spoke to them, when He pressed His truths upon them, when He blessed them, He was doing all these things for us too, *"Ask now of the days that are past, which were before you, since the day that God created man upon the earth, and ask from the one side of heaven to the other, where has there been any such thing as this great thing is, or has there been heard anything like it?"* (Deut. 4:32).

By God's overruling providence, it is remarkable true that there is always a testimony to the truth in ancient records. Every old way is not a good way, but in every good old way we may walk safely and see the footsteps of truth. The proverb which says that that which is oldest is best is true, but only when you consider that the teaching which is the oldest is that which began in eternity past. Truth is as old as God Himself, for truth is no more than a revelation of the mind of God. And this truth was with God from everlasting. Needless to say, there is a great abuse of the principle that the past must teach the present. To believe everything that was believed in antiquity would be to fly in the face of all that God has taught us since. Even if all of it were true, it would still lack the perspective of the revelations which followed (as, for instance, compare the Old Testament truths as the Jews saw them with those same truths as we New Testament saints see them).

Consider then to what antiquity and to what fathers you appeal. If Josiah had merely consulted his immediate predecessors in Israel, it could never have been said of him that *"there was not held such a Passover from the days of the judges who judged Israel, nor in all the days of the kings of Judah"* (2 Kings 23:22). Think how many times Jesus contradicted and reduced to error the sayings of the Jews, *"you have heard that it has been said to the men of old, etc.,"* *"but I say to you, etc."* The opinions of many men will be found to be laced with error, not with the truth of the ages. If you are not going to distinquish between things that differ, you will find there is not any difference between those who itch after novelties and those who dote upon antiquities. Old fables and young fancies can be alarmingly alike in leading us away from the truth. The old is better than the new only if it reflects everlasting truths better than the new.

As to preparing oneself to search, it must not be thought that God strews His truths on the surface, so that we need merely take a little time out from being wise in our own conceits in order to gather truth. Truth, like all precious things, must be diligently sought, *"If you cry after knowledge and lift up your voice for understanding; if you dig for it as silver and search for it as for hidden treasures"* (**Prov. 2:3**).

Four things are required, then, if we are to find the truth and make it our own:

1. It takes humility. God does not teach the proud, He resists them (James 4:6). It is to the humble that He gives more grace. A man that is meek and lowly shall know the mind of Christ, and he shall have it.

2. It takes holiness. Only by submitting to God and practicing the truth that we know will prepare us for receiving more of the truth. He that does the will of Christ shall know of His teachings (John 7:17).

3. It takes prayer, *"Does any of you lack wisdom, then let him ask it from God, who freely gives, etc."* (James 1:5). Truth is the offspring of God, and He will not bestow her upon us unless we ask for her hand.

4. It takes love of the truth. Nothing is more beautiful than truth, she deserves our love. To love the truth is to love the Author of the truth. And if we say that we love Him, we will keep His commandments — one of which is this, that we should buy the truth and sell it not — and another, we should study to show ourselves approved. To set out on a search for truth when we do not love it is a dishonor to truth and to God. The reason so many apostatize and fall away from the truth is that they despise it, they do not love it. They taste it, even recognize that it is good, but, alas! They trample upon it and upon the Son of God who teaches it.

"For we are but of yesterday and know nothing, because our days upon earth are a shadow"—Job 8:9.

It is as if he were saying, The reason we refer you to the former ages is this, that we who are here are but of yesterday and know nothing.

"yesterday"—Commonly this means the day that immediately preceded this one. It is sometimes put for that time which was lately. It is sometimes put for all time, however long that may be (Heb. 13:8). In this place we are not to understand it as all times past, nor the time immediately past, but of final time past, that is, we have lived but a little while in the world, the knowledge that is acquired in our days is not sufficient to challenge that of past ages. Bildad styles himself and his friends as being short-lived, though they were aged men. Some have counted Bildad to be a hundred and forty years old, Eliphaz even older. They were old enough to be the father of Job himself (15:10). The meaning here is this, that the longest of lives are comparatively short, especially when compared to the early inhabitants of the earth. Furthermore, truth distilled from many ages should be a greater body of truth than any one man, or few men, could gather in a lifetime.

"we know nothing"—Again it is a comparative. There is a vast ocean of truths to be known, especially in these days of the gospel, but we are small-necked vessels who can take only a drop of the truth at a time, and when we are at our fullest, we hold but little of the body of truth. Our only hope is that by diligent search and earnest prayer we may be expanded by God to receive multiplied myriads of truths which we are not now able to receive, and that He will sit upon us constantly to work in us to improve our time so that the day of plenty shall not be delayed.

Bildad speaks modestly of himself and his friends. These were known for wise men, yet they claim to know nothing. It is good to admit that what we know is comparatively not anything to boast of, *"he who thinks he knows anything knows nothing yet as he ought to know it"* (1 Cor. 8:2). You may be sure that he who thinks that he knows nearly everything is not very knowledgable at all. After one knows, one must know how to use what he knows. In this Bildad and his friends certainly were not accomplished, for their applications of the truth in the case of Job were very unwise. To this Elihu testifies vehemently, *"I said, Days should speak, and the multitude of years should teach wisdom. But there is a spirit in man; and the inspiration of the Almighty gives them understanding Great men are not always wise; neither do the aged understand judgment....I waited for your words; I listened to your reasons, while you searched out what to say...and, behold! there was not one of you who proved Job to be wrong, or who answered his words"* (**Job 32:8;12**).

"our days upon earth are a shadow" But were not the days of all the fathers a shadow also? Yes, the longest life is but a long shadow. Again, he means their lives were comparatively shorter than the early men on earth.

1. The life of man is as a shadow because it has little in it that is substantial, a shadow is opposed to a substance. Our life rather seems to be, then is, it is so quickly gone.

2. A shadow (though it sometimes is put for protection and safety) implies unsettledness and uncertainty. If a man stands or rests under a shadow, the shadow will leave him — it will be gone from him before long, leaving him under the scorching sun. For a shadow does not stay long in one place. There is such an uncertainty in the life of man. It will not remain the same, it does not stay in the same state long, there is a deceitfulness in it, it is ever changing.

In general, our lives being like a shadow teaches us that it is very short, movable and inconstant. Therefore we must improve this shadow to gain assurance of eternal light. Life here is but a fleeting shadow, but that to come is an abiding substance. Shall we for the pleasures and comforts of a life which is no more enduring than a shadow risk the pleasures and comforts of that life to come, which endures forever? A man does not have even the shadow of reason, true wisdom and understanding, who will spend out this shadowy life in those things which endure but for the wisp of time that is left for him here.

"Shall they not teach you and tell you, and speak words out of their heart"—Job 8:10.

You shall lose your labor in laboriously combing the records of ancient times, for they will teach you. How? They were dead and gone, they could no longer speak. But, as it was said of Abel, that he being dead yet speaks — so it is said of the good counsel of the past, it yet speaks to us.

"speak words out of their hearts"—The meaning is, either the general truth that the real conceptions of those minds of old will speak sincerely to you when you hear what they said; or, that they will speak wisely and judiciously to you about these things — you need not suspect them of being biased against you, nor misled as to your particular circumstances. A wise man's mouth is in his heart, when he speaks it is from the heart. That is, he rich man, *"if they do not hear Moses and the prophets, then they will not be persuaded though one rose from the dead."* But Moses and the prophets were dead and gone. Still there *his heart he will bring forth good things."* And, thanks be unto God, he is a singlehearted man, one who will give you the pure truth, without confusion. The hypocrite, on the other hand, speaks from a double heart, from a heart and a heart. You'll get no true help from him. And as for the fool, he has no heart at all.

These words may be taken as a secret reproof of Job, 'If you will look to these fathers and search them, they will not speak as you have, rashly, unadvisedly and indiscreetly. They will speak from their hearts, they will utter things of weight and serious consideration.' This would certainly be in context.

That dead men may speak to us today may be seen easily in the Bible. Christ told the rich man, *"If they do not hear Moses and the prophets, then they will not be persuaded though one rose from the dead."* But Moses and the prophets were dead and gone. Still there were writings and recorded works, and in this case they were preserved for us by God Himself that we might read and learn and believe and obey.

But if Moses and the prophets may be heard when dead and gone, then how much more should we listen to Christ, who died but has risen and sits now on the right hand of God! If Abraham could settle the matter of the rich man's request with a *"let them hear Moses and the prophets,"* then how much more should all of our matters be settled with a hearing of Christ and the apostles. Do you say that if Christ and His apostles were to come to your church, or to your home, and there tell you what to do, that you would do it. Then do it, for in the Scriptures these do come into your church, and they do come into your home. If He were to come in person and found you despising the words which He speaks in the Bible, you would get no such instruction as you think.

"Can the rush grow up without mire? Can the reed-grass grow without water?"—Job 8:11.

From the eleventh to the twentieth verse, Bildad seeks to illustrate the former argument against Job. He does this from a threefold similitude, (1) of a rush, (2) of a spider-web, (3) of a luxurious, flourishing tree. In sum, he is saying, 'It is as equal and ordinary in the course of divine justice to destroy wicked men as it is in the course of nature for a rush to wither when water is taken from it. Or, as it is natural for a spider-web to break when it is leaned upon, or for a tree to be cut down when it either outgrows the owner's house, or when its boughs darken the windows of it, so it is normal for God to do with men.'

The rush cannot grow without mire. The original word for a rush speaks its nature, the root signifying to suck and drink in, to always be guzzling down. The rush lives in a place of much moisture, and it is always drinking. The word translated 'grow' pictures something growing with strength, luster and beauty — a growing with a kind of pride.

To ask if the rush can grow without mire is no more than to ask if a man can live without food. Mire is meat and drink to the rush. You will see why he asks this when he applies this in the latter part of the chapter.

"Can the reed-grass grow without water?"—The word signifies any fertile place for grass, such as a meadow. The answer is the same as before, it cannot — and for the same reason.

"While it is yet in its greenness, and not cut down, it dries out before any other herb"—Job 8:12.

Even while it is shooting up in its stem, even though you do not cut it down, it will begin to wither if its moisture is cut off from it. Other plants may endure for a while, some for quite a while because they store moisture within themselves, but the rush withers as soon as moisture departs from its roots.

"So are the paths of all who forget God; and the hope of the ungodly shall perish"—Job 8:13.

Bildad now applies his similitude, making it out in three ways, (1) That hypocrites are kept in life and luster by outward, earthly supplies only. As the rush is kept in health by water, and as it fails when its supply of water is cut off, so the hypocrite withers when his worldly supplies are cut off; (2) As the rush has roots only in the mire, not established in the earth, so is the hypocrite, having his roots only in this world; (3) As a rush may be flourishing today and withering tomorrow, so may the seeming graces of the hypocrite vanish in a moment.

Here we may see again that God uses nature to teach us spiritual lessons, *"When I consider the heavens, the work of Your fingers, etc."* Likewise, when we behold the grass and the flowers of the field, we may find many spiritual truths — as did Christ when He was teaching His disciples. No figure from nature is used more often than this one, however, that man is as grass that flourishes today and withers tomorrow. With the addition of grace, he may become a tree, *"planted by the rivers of water, that brings forth its fruit in its season."*

THE HYPOCRITE

Since Bildad is unwisely charging Job with being a hypocrite, using these similitudes to draw the net around him, to immobilize him and demoralize him from defending himself, it would be well for us to understand what a hypocrite is, how he acts and how he may be discerned.

First, as to the comparision at hand, a hypocrite is like the rush. The rush is a very hollow, spongy, insubstantial plant. A hypocrite is likewise a hollow-hearted man, spongy of character, and lacking in substance or solidity. In a high wind the rush or the reed will bend with the wind. The storm will not harm it because it yields to the storm and lets the wind blow where it desires. Likewise, the hypocrite will shift, yield and bend to any powerful force. That which destroys many good men because they take a strong stand against forces of evil has no such effect on the hypocrite. He will still have his honor and his preferment whatever changes may come about. He sways but never breaks. His principles are the same as any other kind of wicked man, therefore he finds it easy to give over any adopted principles which he may have. The bulrush in a time of storm will seem to hang down its head, *"Is this the fast that I have chosen, a day for a man to afflict his soul? Is it to bow down the head like a bulrush?"* (Isa. 58:5). So it is with the hypocrite in times of public humiliation, they will hang their heads and seem to lay their mouths in the dust, with a mock-mourning which will nearly make the truehearted ones envious. But when the danger is over, the hypocrite builds again the things which he had taken down in order to avoid being hurt by the storm.

Once more, the rush being heavy drinkers of moisture have a kind of sensuality in them. They must have their appetites pleased every moment, else they die. So it is with the hypocrite, he must be filling his own belly, he must be drinking in and sopping up all the honor that can be had, he will not go if he will not gain. Lastly, rushes bear no fruit. The rush makes a fair show, appearing to be something of value, but it bears no fruit at all. So it is with the hypocrite, however green they may appear, however much they seem to shine, they shall yield no fruit of holiness to anyone, not to themselves, nor to any other.

A HYPOCRITE IS AN ACTOR WHO INPERSONATES ANOTHER PERSON

(verse 2); They delight to know God's ways (2); They ask God for rules to follow and take delight in drawing near to Him (3); They fast, afflict their souls (3); They do many other things that a child of God will do.

And what does God say to these diligent, zealous servants? How does He answer their prayers? He says that they fast for strife and debate, in order to strike with the fist of wickedness. He says that they afflict themselves, bowing down the head like a bulrush, that they spread sackcloth and ashes under themselves. But He goes on to say that they do these things as a mere pretence which does not undo the bands of wickedness, or remove heavy burdens, or free those who are oppressed, or break the yoke of Satan.

A HYPOCRITE BOTH SIMULATES AND DISSIMULATES

1. He wants to appear what he is not.
2. He does not want to appear as he is.

Therefore, (1) he carefully trims his ways and conforms himself to the image of a Christian. That is, he acts like a Christian is supposed to act, depending on the opinions prevailing in his circles. By no means does he dare to act the hypocrite. He will still have his honor and his preferment whatever changes may come about. He sways but never can he live wholly and solely for the glory of God and of Christ, attributing all his good and all his works to God. For these are the things that are his own glory, they are his very life.

And, (2) he carefully dissimulates so that none can see through his deception, his mists and his myths of holiness, with which he surrounds himself.

Thus you see that he simulates a Christian, putting on an act to do so. And then he dissimuates so that his act may not be detected.

A HYPOCRITE'S HOPE SHALL PERISH

So our text says, *"the hope of the ungodly shall perish,"* or, *"the hope of the hypocrite shall perish"*—and so it certainly will be. The word which is translated *"ungodly"* or *"hypocrite"* comes from a root which signifies close and covered, and by a methaphor, polluted. A hypocrite fits this picture because he is outwardly covered, beautifully painted over, yet he is defiled and contaminated, his covering being vile in the eyes of God.

1. A hypocrite does have hope — that is, his expectations abound and they are high. Most of them have their hopes in this world only, for they do not believe in a world to come. Some, however, believe in an imaginary heaven, a place which squares with their fleshly lusts, where they shall go for their reward. Here they believe they will sit like the king of Tyre, as a prince of golden attire and unspeakable glory, ruling over the poor fools who failed to give him his proper glory during this life.

2. A hypocrite also has confidence — such strong confidence that he is willing to rest his entire life and future on the ground of his hope — and the ground of his hope is in himself. He has confidence in himself. But, as in our next verse, *"his hope shall be cut off, and his trust shall be as a spider's web. He shall lean upon his house and it shall not stand. He shall hold it fast, but it shall not endure"* The word here translated *"hope"* is one which means confidence. Or, it can also mean folly or foolish. In the hypocrite's case, it is certainly a foolish confidence. The word translated *"cut off"* is one which means to fail or to languish. The meaning then is this:

The hypocrite has a hope, and his hope is in another than God, or else in another god. This delightful expectation of his shall perish, it shall not last, like a deceitful brook it shall vanish away. The hypocrite has confidence in himself, in his ability to spin out a web of pretences and duties which will gain him his expectations. This confidence shall weaken, it shall fail and shall be cut off — for though the spider spins a beautiful structure, adequate for both living quarters and for the trapping of the food he needs, it is but a light fabrication out of her own bowels — any confidence she has in such a structure is bound to be cut off. Just as no one can lean on a spider's web, so no one can lean on a hypocrites hope. He may hold fast to these hopes, but no matter how clever or how strong he may be, they shall endure only for a moment.

The hypocrite is the greatest fool of all, for he takes pains and makes great sacrifices in order to live up to a profession of faith in Christ Jesus. He oftentimes lays himself open to persecution, and he hazards his reputation, his estate, his liberty and sometimes even his life. Not believing that Christ is all the He says that He is, the hypocrite is of all men most miserable (1 Cor. 15:19), for he believes that it is in this life only that we have hope in Christ. Yet he curiously spins out his web of false hopes and carefully constructs his world out of his imagination, sometimes earning the admiration of men for his efforts. But his foolish confidence shall be cut off, and he shall discover that he has been deceiving himself (James 1:22). And when his confidence fails, he will be as displeased with himself as was Judas, who was unable to resist the temptation to throw himself off of a cliff. Is it any wonder that one who has lived in the presence of God, but who has put his hope and confidence in himself, should throw himself down when he discovers that he has been leaning upon a mere hypocrite's web for his hope, instead of Jesus Christ, our living and lively Hope.

When dreams satisfy hunger and thirst, the hypocrite's hope shall be satisfied. He will have that dream, believing he shall be filled and happy with everything his wicked heart desires. But all dreams come to an end, and when he awakes he shall find that his hopes will vanish with his dreams. The christ on which they leaned was but a shadow, a fanciful imagination, a mere idol of their own making.

Hope and confidence are properly built upon promises. The hypocrite builds up hope on his own promises to himself. Or, if he sees himself well enough to know that he is insufficient for such confidence, he will make up a god who can be made to promise him the things that he hopes to obtain. To these he will add those promises from the Bible which strike his fancy. He will appropriate especially all those precious promises that promise everlasting life, peace and tranquility, and other things which can be perverted into flesh-pleasing dreams. The hypocrites' Bible is of course not the same as that of the obedient Christian. The unbeliever looks upon the Bible as a great and wonderful table spread for his benefit, one from which he may choose freely all that he desires. From this he will select out peace, comfort, enjoyment, security, glory etc. But he also believes that there are many things in the Bible which he may freely reject, that they are there only for such as may desire them. When God promises humility, for instance, the hypocrite rejects that promise. When God promises freedom from the pleasures of sin, things such as victory over covetousness, triumph over self-love, the hypocrite is willing to leave such things to those who are fools enough to desire them. When God promises to work in us to will and to do of His good pleasure, the unbeliever quickly gasps out a quick and emphatic, No, thank you. And when there is mention that we may have spiritual power to be excellent slaves to Christ Jesus, he looks straight past such promises, lest he see them and have to wrestle with them before he is able to cast them off again.

THE HYPOCRITE PROMISES HIMSELF PEACE AND SECURITY

God promises to those whose mind is stayed on Him continually that they shall have perfect peace. Such a person will lean upon God, for God is his staff of life. This trust in God brings the believer into perfect safety, as well as into perfect peace. A mind wholly taken up with the beauty and loveliness of Christ will find also joy, love, hope, etc.

The hypocrite, however, promises himself peace and security, these in his case being based on his own productions. Like the spider spinning webs from her own bowels, he spins out hopes and promises for himself from within himself. In doing so, he looks at the children of God carefully. He studies them, he imitates them, all the while promising himself all that they expect. That is, he expects all the rewards of the righteous, and he also expects all the rewards of this world. To obtain the best of both these worlds, he will adopt the methods of both worlds. Do God's children pray, so does he. Do they hear, so does he (but only what he wants to hear). Do they fast, or make vows, or give themselves to be burned? So does he. Do they have faith? He has more! Do they fear God? He fears with a flourish. And as for zeal, he has more than anyone. He burns hotter, and he will be by far the most dedicated destroyer of the profane. Talk of grace and glory? None can match him in these. He may even tell you that he is glorious.

But how can the hypocrite promise himself such things as heavenly peace and security?

1. They believe in their own worth. They make much of the fact that they were made in the image of God. And many, like the Mormons, promise themselves that by their good works they shall in time actually become a God - in all the beauty and glory that entails.

2. They believe in their works, that they earn rewards equal to their desires.

3. They believe in their gifts. To them the gifts they have by nature, plus the gifts they have attained for themselves, are proofs of God's love — they have the heathen notion that they are children of destiny, and as such that all things work together for their good. The more astounding the gift of the hypocrite, the greater will be their punishment. But he looks past such things, lest he see them and have to acknowledge and wrestle with them.

This is the hypocrite's house. And until the day comes when he shall lean upon it, he is very well satisfied with it. Actually he has two houses, a worldly house, and a spiritual house: (1) His worldly house is made of earthly materials, such as riches, favors, relationships, fame, reputation, political ties, etc.; (2) His spiritual house is made of gifts (knowledge, understanding, prayer, healing, discernment, special revelation, etc.); of holy duties such as prayer, hearing, almsgiving, teaching, witnessing, 'soul-winning,'; and of pretending grace, such as faith, hope, love, patience, humility (of which he makes much, trumpeting it for all the attention it can get), temperance, mock-sorrow for sin, etc.

These are the things he leans on. And these are the things that shall perish. Sometimes they perish with him, that is, they perish when he dies. More often, however, these things perish with his reputation — for it is seldom that a hypocrite makes it all the way to the grave before he is discovered. The Devil tries to help him, for none are more helpful to Satan than the well-hidden hypocrite, but the corruption and pollution of a hypocrite will erupt, it must come out, and when it does the Devil loses a good slave.

"His confidence shall be cut off, and his trust shall be in a spider's web"—Job 8:14.

Hope and trust are often taken promiscuously. There is a gradual difference between them, not an essential one. Trust being the strength of hope, or the acting of a strong faith. The original word here expresses a very quiet, secure, settled trust as when a man trusts upon a thing so completely as never to have even one jealous thought about it. When the hypocrite trusts, he never suspects himself. His heart tells him that all is well, and he believes it implicitly. He has the same attitude as that famed mother of harlots who said in her heart, *"I sit as a queen and am not a widow; and, I will in no way see sorrow"* (Revelation 18:6). Yet in one day death and sorrow and hungering shall come upon her. So it is with the hypocrite.

This verse having been largely handled in the last verse, we refer you to verse 13.

Bildad goes on to bring down his similitude to this particular. The spider rests upon his house, and the hypocrite rests upon his house, both are satisfied with their building efforts. But neither the web nor the fool's edifice shall stand.

The leaning here is that leaning which one may do upon a staff, as Saul leaning upon his spear to keep from falling (1 Sam. 1:6). The same word is used in 2 Sam. 22:19, *"the Lord is my stay."*

"it shall not stand"—It is a word that means to stand firmly and strongly. He thought that the materials which he had brought together and the hopes which he had raised them on would be a strong and reliable foundation. But it shall not stand. It may stand until that day when Christ will say to him, *"Depart from Me, I never knew you."* The Jews put their trust in the Temple until it was pulled down around their ears.

"He shall hold fast to it, but it shall not endure"—It is of the same importance as the last clause, but the sense is somewhat heightened. Not only does the hypocrite lean upon his house, but he takes strong hold on it. As Job held fast to his integrity (2:9), so the hypocrite holds fast to his false hopes.

"it shall not endure"—it shall not be established to him. The hypocrite establishes his own rules, legislated laws according to his own desires, but they shall not endure.

"He is green before the sun, and his branches shoot forth in his garden"—Job 8:16.

The context of these next four verses hold forth to us the third similitude by which Bildad illustrates the condition of a hypocrite. Now he compares the hypocrite to a luxurious tree. In this similitude, the hypocrite is granted the best of his condition, he is put into a posture that is as fair as possible. Yet for all of this he proves to be nothing; his root is rotten; his blossom falls into the dust. It is as if Bildad had said, 'If you think that I have spoken too little and too low, or have debased the hypocrite more than was right, then take him in his highest motion and let him be compared to a green, flourishing tree that fastens his roots and spreads out his branches — yet you shall see that at last his end shall be destruction. This is the only 'joy' that his way can give.'

Three things are held forth in this similitude concerning the hypocrite, (1) He has an outward happiness and a flourishing estate in this world; (2) He has a hurtful effect on his neighbors and brethren; (3) He shall be cut down and destroyed in the end.

"He is green before the sun"—The word green here means to be moist, juicy, full of sap,

as is proper to trees. The word is used again in Job 24:8, *"they are wet with the showers of the mountain"*—wet, moist. A tree that is green, full of sap, etc. is in the height of its strength and beauty. Juice and sap to a tree are as blood to the veins and marrow to the bones of a man. The hypocrite may be such a flourishing tree, temporally strong.

"before the sun"—Or, *"before the face of the sun"*—The word signifies a minister or servant, because the sun is the great servant of the world, ministering those benefits of heat, light, etc. which God intended for it to give.

Some take this *"before the sun"* to be this, openly, conspicuously and in the sight of all. For to do a thing before the sun is to do it without secrecy. So the hypocrite may be flourishing in the sight of all. But *"before the sun"* may also be a description of spring. In which case he would be saying, 'As a tree when the sun comes toward it in the spring and shines hot upon it in the summer makes a beautiful picture, so the hypocrite may be full of carnal joy and contentment while he has the sun of prosperity shining upon him. While those warm rays of outward comforts nourish him, he may flourish. Others say that before the sun means this, that he is green before the sun starts to scorch and to wither him. For a hypocrite cannot stand the extreme heat of persecution, etc. Before can refer both to time and to presence.

"and his branches shoot forth in his garden"—The word for branches comes from a root which signifies a little sucking infant. The reason is of course because branches come from a tree, sucking out moisture and sap from the trunk much like an infant does from his mother's breast. That is why suckers, branches which sprout from a fruit-bearing tree must be cut off, because they draw too much from the tree and hinder the fruit. These branches could be a hypocrites children, his honors, his relations, or his reputation.

"in his garden"—That is, in that place which he has fenced for himself. A garden is a plot separated and enclosed from those places which are open and in common. He then may appear to be beautiful and glorious, green, flourishing and stately in dignity and honor. The hypocrites' garden is where he keeps and preserves his worldly comforts.

A hypocrite may appear to be more godly than a truly godly man, if nothing but outward show and appearance is seen. Like those typical hypocrites, the Pharisees, they pray often, they pray publicly, they give alms with a flourish, and none can fail to know that they make a strong profession of faith. Like Jehu, they say, *"Come and see my zeal for the Lord."* And like Jehu, they may be very zealous in killing the prophets of Baal, very fierce against other false religionists.

"His roots are wrapped around the heap, and he sees the place of stones"—Job 8:17.

The root of this hypocritical tree is that by which he fastens himself. That is, any accommodation or strength which he has in the world, such as credit, riches, friends, etc. will be the things he fastens himself on and in. Getting thus set firmly, he puts out his roots as far as they will go.

"wrapped around the heap"—The word means to roll, or to bring things together, to put them into a heap. So the verb is used for the act of the soul in believing, by which a Christian gathers himself together with all that he has and rolls it upon the Lord (see Ps. 22:8 in the Hebrew). So it is sometimes translated as a tempest, when the winds roll and are enfolded together; other places as a wave of the sea, which is a rolling water. Here as a heap, because in a heap there are a great many stones or other things gathered and rolled together.

Lastly, as is applied to this text by some interpreters, the word signifies a spring or a fountain, because springs and fountains are as the gathering together of waters. So these translate, *"His roots are wrapped about the fountain"*—further setting forth the seemingly sure and steadfast estate of the hypocrite, who seemingly is as established beside the waters as is the godly man (who is described as a tree planted by the river).

But most go with our translation, His roots are wrapped around the heap, which may have three meanings:

1. It may denote his thriving against all opposition, here shadowed by heaps of stones. Heaps of stones are hindrances to growing trees. But to show that he may even overcome and conquer these difficulties which arise to hinder him, it is said that his roots wrap around the heaps. According to this sense, Bildad is saying that the hypocrite can grow amidst difficulty and great disadvantage.

2. Or it may denote that he thrives even though, and even because, he is a hindrance to others. For by the heap some understand the foundation of a house, where stones are artificially heaped or laid together — it not being a natural or accidental heap. Trees that grow near a house will shoot its roots under the foundation of the house and become dangerous to the whole house. So the hypocrite will grow mighty at the expense of others, by wrapping and entwining himself about the foundation of another man's house — he will build his reputation at the expense of anyone who will serve him for that purpose. Hypocrites do not care if they injure someone, just so they themselves may thrive.

3. Or it may denote the firmness and the seeming strength of his standing. He is rooted, not in some loose and sandy earth, or in clay, but his roots are wrapped about a heap of stones. So hypocrites pretend to be founded upon Christ, they say they have wrapped themselves around the Rock.

"and he sees the places of stones"—Or, *"he dwells in the place of stones"*—Or, *"he plants himself among the stones"*—thus carrying the sense of the last clause. There are many renderings, but all these will come to a fair agreement, and the result is this, that he lives, converses or lodges where there seems to be the least probability, in the place (or house) of stones. Yet for all of that, though he be made firm among the stones, his house is a tottering one, it will not be able to stand.

"If he is destroyed from his place, then it shall deny him. I have not seen you"—Job 8:18. Who is the *"he?"* There is no antecedent expressed in the Hebrew. Some understand it in this way, *"if He,"* that is, the Lord, *"came to take vengeance, etc."* then he who seems to be a tree, so high and so deeply rooted, etc. Others say, it is the Gardener — if the Master or owner of that ground or place, seeing a tree so luxuriant, growing so near the foundation of his house, if he come to destroy him, it shall deny him. Again, some say it is the sun that will destroy him.

The word which we translate *"destroy"* is one which means properly to swallow down. It is that swallowing which comes about when a man is very hungry and thus eats greedily. Food thus eaten is of course consumed and destroyed in the stomach.

The meaning in context would seem to have it as the Husbandman who comes, who quickly destroys it from its place, even though it is grown, rooted, etc. The destruction of hypocrites and wicked men often comes very quickly upon them, in the very height of their prosperity. Even while they are green and flourishing, they suddenly are gone. As a forest fire hits the green trees and by its fierce heat and force devours them, so the fires of affliction and persecution can quickly destroy a whole army of hypocrites. We have a good description in Job 20:22, *"In the fullness of his plenty he shall be in trouble."*

"it shall deny him. I have not seen you"—Here is a further aggravation of his misery, when he is destroyed, *"it shall deny him."* What shall deny him? Some say, *"his place shall deny him."* The Hebrew is, *"the place shall lie"*—that is, the place shall pretend, saying, we have not seen him.

"I have not seen you"—We have nearly the same words in Psalm 37:35, where the flourishing estate of a wicked man is shadowed under the notion of a tree, *"I have seen the wicked flourish like a green bay-tree. Yet he passed away, and lo, he is not; and I looked for him, but he could not be found."* "No place is capacious enough for the saints, and it is certain that the place will not forget those who have been there. But any place where the hypocrite has been will easily forget him.

Bildad having thus enlarged his similitude, in all the parts of it, has at last laid the hypocrite as low as forgetfulness, so low that no man will remember seeing him. Now he gives his conclusion against him.

"Behold, this is the joy of his way, and out of the earth shall others grow" —Job 18:19.
The word translated *"joy"* is one that describes the highest joy, a leaping for joy. It is an allusion to dogs who come and leap upon their masters when they come home. It is an exulting joy. But the only joy a hypocrite has is in the exultation he feels in earthly advance and worldly accomplishment — it is the kind of joy that Haman felt the day he believed the queen honored him when he was invited to the banquet with the king, Ahasuerus.

"of his way"—that is, his course, his purpose, that way which he holds in the world. This is it. The particle is demonstrative. This is it which I have told you. From which we may learn three things:

1. A hypocrite may have much joy in his own way. He my rejoice much in his condition and think that all is well. False faith and false hopes produce false joys. In fact, the imagined faith brings forth false joy more abundantly than true faith brings forth true joy — or, rather, it may be more evident and effusive to observers. Satan encourages this hypocritical joy, and for a time God may not hinder it. The stony ground received the word with joy, which endured for a little while. The senses and reason of a hypocrite may find the promises of God a matter of joy when strained through his own interpretation. His heaven being on earth, he may at times feel he is in his heaven and therefore will feel that there is great cause for joy.

What is joy? It is his worldly comforts, his flourishing outward condition.

2. The hypocrites have joy chiefly in their outward things. They do not rejoice in the Lord, though they may rejoice because they think they are favorites of the Lord. He has much joy from his green boughs, from his strong roots, from his beautiful (in appearance) fruit.

3. The joy of the hypocrite is but for a moment. This is his joy; and it is best that you look quickly to see it, for in a moment his greenness will be turned into withering, his root will dry up and his fruit will fall off. Soon he will be like those in Judah, *"twice dead, plucked up by the roots."* He was naturally dead in sin, then he became judicially dead under wrath. He was born spiritually dead, and his whole life has been a passage to his eternal death. *"the portion of hypocrites is weeping and gnashing of teeth"* (Matt. 24:51)—their joy is but for a morning of a day, then their weeping comes.

"and out of the earth shall others grow"—There shall then come others to take their place and possess their dwellings. He follows the similitude of a tree, where one may be pulled up, but another is planted there and grows up in its room.

Further, the words may carry this sense, that when wicked men are taken away, the righteous shall grow in their place. Pull up the briars and the thorns and the vines and figtrees, the lillies and the roses will flourish. When wicked men are removed, good men will prosper.

Again, it may mean that out of the meanest and lowest condition others shall grow. In this case there would be an opposition between the hypocrite being rooted up and the godly man who was planted.

"Behold, God will not cast away an innocent man, neither will He help the evildoers"—Job 8:20.

These next three verses close up Bildad's argument against Job. He has argued that God is just, and that He does not pervert judgment. Then in a clear reference to Job, beginning with his children, he paints the sad plight of the hypocrite who would not seek earnestly to God and make his prayer to the Almighty. Now he brings up his heavy artillery to batter Job back into line with what he considers to be the truth, warning him that he must repent and take himself out of the position of an evildoer.

Here Bildad is saying, 'God will not cast out a perfect man. Job, you may see by what I have spoken that God is not an enemy to the righteous, nor a friend to wickedness. You see what the portion of wicked man is from God. Yet know this, that mercy shall act as gloriously in the hand of God as His justice does, for God is not unjust so as to favor hypocrites, so neither will He be unjust to forget the righteous and perfect man. The hypocrite shall perish, but He will fill the mouth of a godly man with laughter and his lips with rejoicing.'

Or, if we consider his speech more distinctly, we may see the negative acts of justice, one toward the perfect, the other toward the hypocrite, with the effects of both.

His justice acts towards the perfect man in that *"He will not cast him away."* The effect of this is that *"the filling of his mouth with laughter and his lips with rejoicing"* shall follow.

His justice acts towards the hypocrite in this way, *"He will not help the evildoers."* The effect of this is, *"evildoers shall be clothed in shame and their tents shall be no more."*

As to the general application, Bildad is saying this, He is a God that does not cast away a perfect man, He is just and righteous in His dealings and administrations with him. But God does not cast away a perfect man. Therefore He is just and righteous in His dealings.

As to the particular case of Job, he is saying, God is a God who does not cast away a perfect man, therefore if you are perfect He will not cast you away. Then, Job, return and make your way perfect before God and He will not cast you away. Or, inferentially, he is saying, God does not cast away a perfect man, therefore, Job, you have a great deal of imperfection or insincerity in you because God has cast you off and laid you aside.

"Behold, God will not cast away an innocent man"—Behold! It is a strong affirmation, worthy of our special notice. The strong God, He who has infinite power, will not lay out that power to cast away an innocent man. The word translated *"cast away"* is also translated *"despise"* and *"cut off."* God will not despise, reprobate or cast away an innocent. Of course, more is intended than is expressed in such a statement, for God not only does not cast them away, He also highly esteems and prizes them. And this casting away may be either here in time, or eternally. But God will not cast away such a man either here or hereafter.

"an innocent man"—or, *"a perfect man"*—the same word that God used to describe Job in the first chapter. By this use of the very same word Bildad shows how little he knows about Job, and he is proven to be directly wrong in his estimate of Job. God regards Job as a perfect man. Bildad does not regard him as a perfect man.

"He will not help them"—Some read it, *"He will not put forth His hand to evildoers"* —So the letter of the Hebrew imports. And there may be a threefold sense given of that reading, (1) Our taking men into society, fellowship and familiarity with us. When we desire to show a man how much we love him we will take him by the hand. God will not take an evildoer by the hand in this way, to welcome or entertain him; (2) He will not put forth His hand to receive a gift or an offering from wicked men. When a gift or a present is brought, the receiver (if he would show his liking and acceptance of it) puts forth his hand to take it. Now, says Bildad, God will put forth his hand to receive any offering or gift from wicked men — the sacrifice of the wicked is an abomination to the Lord. (3) It rather refers to God's refusal to assist wicked men. To put forth or stretch out the hand, according to the Hebrew phrase, implies strong holding, or the taking of strong hold upon a thing. A man that would give assistance to another puts forth his hand to assist him. When we want to help, we put forth our hand. When we desire help, we ask, Lend me your hand. But when the Lord refuses to put forth His hand, then it is plain that He bears no favor to them, he gives them no encouragement and he will not deliver or rescue them.

"evildoers"—These are not to be thought of as every man who does something evil — for then whom would God ever help? We may then say with reverence, God helps us indeed. But the evildoer is a man who is notoriously, professedly, studiously wicked. He is one that acts and devises evil against God and His ways. A man who does evil in any one act cannot thus make himself an evildoer.

There are common helps which God will give to an evildoer, as to all men on earth:

1. He gives a negative help, by calling in the power to do good, or by not giving them the power to avoid evil. When He departed from Saul, Saul went on getting worse and worse. Before Saul had managed to avoid doing so much evil, though he slipped and fell into a great deal of it. When God does not assist such a man against the evil of his heart and the pollutions or temptations of the world, then this lays them open to much more sin then they otherwise would have committed. Yet the sin that he then commits cannot be laid to God, nor charged to Him than the darkness of the night can be charged for allowing the sun to go down. Sin follows divine desertion, not as an effect does the cause; but as a consequent does its antecedent.

2. He delivers or gives them up; first, to Satan, secondly; to their own counsels, to a reprobate mind and vile affections (Ps. 81:12; Rom 1:24,26). This is more than a mere desertion. It is a spiritual judgment when God makes a man's own wickedness active against him. It would be better to be put into the hands of all the tyrants in the world than into the hands of our own lusts and passions. God does not implant a reprobate mind or vile affections, but He does give some up to them.

3. Evildoers do not spring any surprises on God, nor do they escape His directing hand. He directs and orders the steps of every man. Wicked men run beyond the line of obedience, but they cannot run beyond the line of providence. God limits and circumscribes the acts of wicked men, for every wicked man would be an uncontrollable monster if he were left alone to develop his evil propensities. The sinfulness of men would be not only immeasurably intensive in sin, but it would be immeasurably extensive in sin if God did not keep it in bounds. There is a sea of wickedness in the heart of every man, and if God did not have control of that man's actions, iniquity would truly overwhelm and overflow all of us. If God could not turn the wicked man's actions into good for the saints, then it would not be true that *"all things work for good to those who love God."* It would be of no avail to pray for God to keep you safe from the depradations of evildoers if He could not say to them, *"This far and no further may you go."*

4. God gives the strength for every man's motions, therefore it may be said that the motions of sin are committed by God's assisting strength in that sense. But the motions to sin do not come from God, nor the sinfulness of any motion. All strength is from the Lord, but God does not strengthen the hand of an evildoer. To eat was a natural act in our first parents, and this was from God. But to eat against the command was a moral act, and that was not from God.

God does not help evildoers by instilling the least motion of evil into them. Instead He casts in and infuses holy thoughts and motions into the hearts of His own people, to prepare them for holy acts.

The Lord does not excite or stir up that natural, inherent corruption that is in a wicked man. He does not provoke him to blow up his lusts. He does excite the graces of His own people and work in them to do any good that they do.

God always resists wicked men in their evil deeds. This does not mean that He lays out all His natural powers to stop them from doing evil. But He consistently and continually impedes them as they are committing evil. He declares them wrong, and He gives them His disapproval that they may be judged for doing so.

"until He fills your mouth with laughter, and your lips with rejoicing"—Job 8:21.

The *"until"* here notes a continued act. It is as much as to say, He will never cast them off. The word both in the Hebrew and the Greek often expresses everlastingness. God made a promise to Jacob in this form, *"I will never leave you until I have done that which I have spoken."* Would He then leave him. When it is said to Christ, *"Sit on My right hand until I make Your enemies Your footstool"* (Ps. 110:1), it does not infer that when Christ's enemies have been made His footstool then He will have to move from the right hand of God. No, but He will always and forever be at God's right hand.

"your mouth"—Observe here the change of the person. Before he spoke in the third person, now he brings it home and applies it to Job. This allows us to see that he meant all foregoing remarks for Job. The laughter that he promises is that which comes in with much joy, the kind of joy that the heart cannot hold without some outward expression. True joy is from the heart and it cannot be pretended. This would be a comforting and encouraging promise indeed if Bildad were not false accusing Job and basing his remedy upon a sickness that did not exist. It would be good for Job to have such a comfort in his heart that he could not hold back the laughter. No doubt that day will soon come, though he does not yet know it, when laughter will once more fill the mouth of Job.

"and your lips with rejoicing"—The word properly expresses, *"a joyful sound,"* as it is translated in Ps. 89:15, *"Blessed is the people that know the joyful sound that is made by the lips."* The main use of the word is in describing the shouting of soldiers after a victory, an exultation — it was the shout at Jericho. Thus Bildad is promising Job that if he will follow his good advice then the comfort that shall come to him shall be very great, heart-felt laughter shall fill his mouth and exultation his lips.

Joy, of course, is one of the delightful graces which belong to the people of God. It is a fruit of the Holy Spirit of God, and it is promised to them innumerable times. True joy is for the godly only. Only they have anything to exult about. Laughter may be thought to be more common, less distinctive — we read of the *"laughter of fools,"* etc. But the laughter in this text is also to be appropriated by the godly and completely God-centered man only. A wicked man's laugh is but madness, for who but a mad man would laugh in the face of certain doom? The joy promised here arises in two ways:

1. Joy rises from the greatness of the blessing. The least mercy is such a great blessing that joy should follow in its wake. Our joys will normally take their measure from our estimate of the blessing we have received. For this reason, those who see Christ in all of His greatness, and His sacrifice in the true magnitude, as well as their own filthiness of the flesh in all its depth, will have the greatest joy. The closer one is to God, the larger and more magnificent He becomes to them. And the greater your God, the greater your blessing will become to you. As your blessings and your God grow, your joy grows with them. It is a pity to find a Christian that has been crippled by false doctrine or self-indulgence until they have tipped over their cup of joy and lost most of it for the moment.

2. Joy also arises when we realize the greatness of the judgments which are poured out on the enemies of God and of the saints. The overthrow of Pharaoh at the Red Sea was followed by a filing up with joy in the hearts of God's true children. And, though some wince at the thought and take sides with the man-centered philosophers when they hear it, there shall be great rejoicing among the saints when the greatness and purity of the Lord Jesus Christ is revealed as He casts His enemies in the Lake of Fire at judgment (see 1 Thess. 1:7-10).

"Those who hate you shall be clothed with shame; and the tent of the wicked shall be no more"—Job 8:22

God resists and will not put forth His hand to evildoers, and in the end they shall be put to shame. Shame is the opposite of laughter. He who rejoices can hold up his head and have no care as to who sees him. But he who is ashamed holds down his head and cannot endure to be seen.

"Those who hate you"—It can have two meanings, (1) The putting forth of bitter hatred by a malicious man; (2) The withholding of due love. He who lacks the heat and height that should be an integral part of love may be said in some sense to hate. In this way Leah was hated, that is, Jacob did not think as much of her as of Rachel. To be loved less, to be in effect despised and thought little of, may appear to be hate to the person who is so slighted. In our text, those who do not love and esteem the righteous and perfect man are guilty of hating them, and they shall be clothed with shame.

To be ashamed at all is a great punishment. What then would it be to be clothed with shame; Shame is the fruit of sin. When there was no sin in the world, there was no shame. Innocency can know no shame, and there will be none in glory. The presence of shame reveals the presence of sin. It is God's way of reminding us that we have sinned, and it is intended as a corrective pressure on us. The perturbing effects of shame, the troubling of the mind, the confusion of the heart, many times break out into the outward signs of holding down the head and blushing in the face and neck. It arises in three ways:

1. From doing something against the light of common knowledge. Every act of evil has shame in it, but men being naturally coarsened by sin are not usually ashamed unless the thing they do is against the light of nature. Not to be ashamed of such sins is to put out the light of nature. Those who are not ashamed when they sin against light are called impudent in the Scriptures. Much more ashamed should they be who sin against the light of Scripture.

2. Shame arises from long delay, as when an expectation is long overdue in being fulfilled. When Moses stayed in the mountain so long, the people were ashamed. When one has promised that such and such a thing will happen at a certain time, and it does not come to pass, shame rises and grows the longer it is delayed.

3. Shame arises from utter disappointments. If hope is deferred, it causes shame. When a man puts his trust in something or someone, and when that trust proved to be misplaced, then he becomes ashamed. To publicly hope and to be publicly proven wrong in that hope brings still greater shame, being multiplied by the greatness of the hope and the magnitude of the persons involved, as well as by the number of persons who know of it.

Evildoers shall be ashamed upon all three of these grounds. They regularly sin against light. They cannot deny that the major part of their desires go unfulfilled. And they shall yet be revealed as fools who put their trust and hope in persons and things that were as wicked and worthless as themselves.

"clothed with shame," – To be clothed with shame applies both to their ornamentation and to their dishonor. The Scriptures reveal three degrees of expression about shame: (1) Barely to be ashamed, that is the lowest degree; (2) To have the face covered with shame, "for Your sake I have borne reproach, shame has covered my face" (Ps. 69:7). How much more will those who have worshipped themselves be covered with shame! (3) To be clothed with shame implies the whole man is shrouded in a covering of disgrace. If Job was right in saying that his own clothes abhorred him (9:31), then how much more will the wicked say it when they realize the extent of their corruption.

There is an abundance in being clothed with shame. Just as to be clothed with honor is to have much honor, so it is with shame. There is a public exposure when one is clothed with shame. A man may hide the better part of his filthiness of the flesh, but he cannot hide his clothing of shame. Servants are clothed by their masters. They wear clothing that pleases their masters. The unbeliever serves Satan, and he is the one that suits them up in this clothing of shame.

That which evil men glory in will be matter for their abasement, as the apostle says, "they glory in their shame" (Phil. 3:19). No man can glory in anything under the notion of shame, but many glory in that which is in itself shameful and will prove to be to their shame. The Hebrew expresses an idol by a word that means shame, or a shameful thing (and it is the root of the word in our text), because idols always eventually make their worshippers ashamed. The idols that men have are not all stocks and stones. The ungodly idolize myriads of things above God, and they glory in them as if they were gods.

It can be proven from our text that wicked men hate the righteous. Being haters of God, they must of course be haters of all those who bear the image of God. Natural men are such haters of holiness that they hate even the hypocrite, though he but acts out a false holiness.

"and the tent of the wicked shall be no more" – The meaning is that his whole estate is to be brought to nought. Everything he has, everything he loves, shall cease to be.

CHAPTER IX

"Then Job answered and said,"—Job 9:1.

It is remarkable that Job is not by now frothing at the mouth, for *"surely oppression makes a wise man mad"* (Eccl. 7:7). Bildad has made clear his assumption that Job is a gross hypocrite, therefore his threefold advice, however generally true, does not fit Job's case. Not being suited to the occasion, and there being an assumption of unproven guilt, this advice is tailored more to provoke this poor sufferer than to restore him to health.

1. Bildad has advised Job to get his thinking right about the justice and judgment of God.

2. He has advised him to humble himself and to seek to God.

3. He has advised him to stop complaining of his own troubled life and to cease desiring his death.

Now Job shapes his answer to these three heads of Bildad's advice in the following two chapters:

1. He reveals his thoughts about God's justice, and he highly magnifies it.

2. He renounces all his own righteousness, with obviously true humility, and then he proves that a man cannot be judged by God's present dealings with him.

3. He renews and justifices his complaint against his life, and his wishes for death, by many arguments in the tenth chapter.

In most of these points he answers exactly, in strict accordance to the laws and rules of disputation.

First, he repeats his opponent's argument. Then he yields what is true and denies what is false. Then he distinguishes what is doubtful. This he does with so much accuteness and vigor, with so much strength and clearness in reason and judgment, that one of the fathers exultingly exclaimed, 'O how much philosophy (I may say, how much logic) has Job shown in this reply to the argument of Bildad!' (Chrysostom).

Bildad's argument runs in this vein, God who has punished you is just, therefore you are unjust. Job answers by granting the antecedent, but he denies the consequent. He is full in granting that God is just, (1) from His wisdom; (2) from His power. At the twenty-second verse Job begins to prove that he is not being punished for being unjust, saying in effect, 'This is not argument, that I am a wicked man because God has destroyed my estate and my children. In this sense, God destroys both the righteous and the wicked. It cannot be proven that I am wicked because God has afflicted me, or even that God has afflicted me because of my wickedness. There is another way to acquit the justice of God and to declare Him righteous, though I do not join with you in condemning and judging myself unrighteous.'

"Truly I know it is so, but how should man be just with God?"—Job 9:2.

The word has a double force in it. Sometimes it is a bare but strong declaration, and it is sometimes an oath. Truly I know it is so! This is so much of a truth that I will swear it is a truth, I will dare to take an oath on it. As a declaration, it is a vehement Amen. It is here a sealing to the former truth delivered by both Bildad and Eliphaz (4:17; 8:3). Does the Almighty pervert judgment. No! A thousand times, No!

'Bildad,' Job is saying, 'do not think that I have ill thoughts of the justice of God. I never did think that the justice of God was perverted simply because He was afflicting me. I acknowledge what you have truly said, that God does not pervert judgment. And I accept that you are faithful in counseling me to seek to God and to make my supplication to Him. But, alas! Who am I that I should contend with God? What am I that I should dispute with Him concerning my troubles, or concerning His dealings with me. If I should be so rash and foolhardy as to attempt such a thing, I could not answer Him even one thing.

1. All disputes and controversies should be conducted so as to have the disputants admit and yield to that which is right. It is good to agree as far as we can, if we cannot agree in all. Let us walk with the adversary the first mile, even if we cannot go with him for two. Job gives us a good example: as soon as he hears a truth, he falls down before it. Never does he speak a word against the truth of God, even though it comes from proud men in an erroneous setting. He will always be a friend of the truth, even if it is brought by his enemies. Many disputes would fall to the ground if only this much imitation of Job would take effect in the lives of the debaters. As some out of love to men are apt to follow them in their errors, so some out of hatred to men (or simple displeasure toward them) will reject their truths. Errors cannot be adorned, no matter how skillfully one may try. Truths cannot truly be daubed and besmirched so as to make them appear as errors. A willingness to embrace and receive a truth from those whose errors we most zealously oppose is the due temper of a true champion of the truth.

2. A godly man is a knowing man. He is established in truths, especially in the great and necessary truths. He will not neglect the vitals and fundamentals of religion. Job had for a long time been well acquainted with this principle, that God is just, and that every man must abase himself before Him. After life come light in the new creature. Proof that one is a new creature may be seen by observing him, whether or not he begins to learn to discern between things that differ (Phil. 1:10). Bring a truth to a godly man and he will find something in himself to answer to that truth.

3. Even in the midst of pain, and racked by the misery of his suffering, Job does not hesitate even a second in giving honor to God. A gracious heart will give testimony to the righteousness of God even though it is severely chastened under the hand of God at the time. When God deals most hardly with the soul, or with the body, or both, a holy heart still will not have hard thoughts of God. Let those who curse God stop calling themselves godly. Not only will a good man acknowledge that God was just when He punished others, but also when He afflicted him.

The common argument of Job's friends in proving God just is this: God is righteous, for He deals with men according to what they deserve. But Job argues this way: God is righteous, whatever way He deals with men. If the men are righteous, or if they are wicked, whatever God does to them, and for whatever reason, God is righteous. When we see God breaking the wicked, we see He is just. But the saints proceed on principles more pure and sublime than this: they hold that God is just even when He afflicts a just and holy man. To them, the righteousness of God shine through the darkest sufferings of righteous men. The righteousness of God is not grounded upon the object He is dealing with, whether it is righteous or unrighteous. The righteousness of God is grounded upon the act of His own will; yea, upon the pleasure of His own will. His righteousness proceeds from Himself. His acts are righteous because they are His, not because of the object He acts upon. There is no need to say that God is just because He punishes the guilty. God is just even if He afflicts the innocent. It is not inconsistent for Job to maintain his own innocency and the justice of God even while he lays bleeding and sore under his severe scourges.

"but how should man be just with God?"—He is saying, You talk of justice under such a notion as will render it impossible for any man to be just before God. In some sense a man may be righteous before God, but in your sense it would be impossible for anyone to be just. Would you have us believe that no man can call himself just unless he is completely without sin? If you take just to be the same as being without an indwelling sin, then no man can appear just before God. But man may be just and righteous before God, though he has sin dwelling in him, and that is my notion of justice in this dispute.

Justice is either inherent or imputed. By inherent justice, no man is just before God.

According to imputed justice, a man may be just and is just before God. So these two propositions are reconciled, 'No one is just before God,' yet, 'Every believer is just before God.' Our translation, using the discretive, But, seems to carry this meaning, that no one can be just before God by inherent justice. And the next verse implies the same.

The words taken in this sense are the same with the question of Eliphaz, *"Shall man who dies be more just than God?"* (4:17). There Eliphaz speaks comparatively, in the way of excess, *"more just than God,"* or, *"just rather than God."* Here Job speaks comparatively in a way of equality, How can a man be just with God? He cannot compare with God at all. Yet the sense is the same, and the denial of man's perfect, inherent righteousness is the subject of both. A just man will deprive himself of all his justice if he compares himself with God. He will become a nothing if he tries to be what God is.

The way for us to humble ourselves for our own sinfulness is to look up and consider the purity and holiness of God. If we take up a position close to Him, O how vile and rotten we begin to appear! His fullness convinces us of our emptiness. His purity shows us our spots. His all-sufficiency reveals our nothingness. Men comparing themselves with other men may conclude that they are very much like God Himself. But if they look up to God, O how the thoughts of their hearts fall! The Pharisee did not hesitate to give in a good judgment of himself in comparision with other men *"God be thankful that I am not as other men are"* (Luke 18). But was he God? A quick look upwards will bring pride down. Men comparing themselves to other men are condemned by the apostle in these appropriate words, *"they, measuring themselves by themselves, and comparing themselves among themselves, are not wise"*–they were not bringing together the right things. One does not measure the straightness of a stick by a crooked stick. It is the great Standard that declares the rightness of things, *"For not he who commends himself is approved, but he whom the Lord commends"* (2 Cor. 10:12-18). Though man in regeneration is made a *"partaker of the divine nature,"* (2 Pet. 1:4) yet his nature cannot bear the perfections of the divine nature.

"If he will argue with Him, he cannot answer Him one of a thousand"–Job 9:3.

This is to confirm what he had just said. Job is acknowledging that no man can be just by inherent righteousness before God, and to bring that statement into focus he gives us this one, *"if he desires to contend with Him, he cannot answer Him one of a thousand."* For this is a case where it is being posed whether a man has a mind or a delight to argue with God. If it pleases him to have a go at God, then he will find that he has his hands full, and his belly full, too. From this word, the church is called Hephzibah (My delight is in her). So here, if anyone takes some delight in seeking a contest with God, then he shall get more than he is bargaining for.

Man by nature loves contending – he will argue at the drop of a hat. *"If anyone seems to be contentious"*–what man isn't? (1 Cor. 11:16). Contentious spirits love victory more than they love truth, they love to overcome more than they love teaching or learning. And man, proud as he is, will often challenge those who are far beyond them. As in the days of Amaziah, the thistles are still challenging the cedars. It is foolishness for a man to contend with any man as a matter of pride, and it is even more foolish for him to proudly challenge those who are above him. But how mad, how full of foolishness and pride must a man be who will attempt to argue with God?

"he cannot answer Him one of a thousand"–a thousand is a great number, here used because it is a full number and thus is put for all great numbers. It is a leading number, there being in the Hebrew word the idea of leading. This number, then, is a chief number, a king among the numbers. Job is saying that God cannot be answered once no matter how many arguments we may give Him. This expression, *"one of a thousand"* is used to

mark out a man among men, an excellent one, a choice man from amongst all (Job 33:23). If the meaning here is taken from that, we would have the contentious man making a choice from among all the hard questions in the world that could be asked of God. Then, says Job, he would find that he had a foolish argument. And if God were to choose one of a thousand questions to ask of the man, he could not answer Him even that once.

Some refer it to the person, that no man can answer God. Other refer it to the matter, that he cannot answer that which is brought against him by God. Some refer it to God Himself. If God delights to contend with him, he would not be able to answer Him one of a thousand. Some men draw up their skirts and refuse to answer questions merely because of their position, their royal highness. But God does not and need not avoid any question, He can answer all of them, to the confusion of him who dares to set himself up as an opponent to God. But God does have the privilege of ignoring questions put to Him. His majesty is so great that there is no claim that a man can bring which will require God to submit Himself to examination.

But rather, let it refer to man. This contentious man cannot answer one of a thousand. He will have to shut his mouth, put up his books and go hide his face if he tries it. Job in the fourteenth verse rephrases it in this way, *"How much less shall I answer Him and choose my arguments with Him!"* There are men who will reply against God (Romans 9:20), but these fools hardly need an answer. They could answer themselves if they only would exchange the pride and strife in their hearts for a new heart.

The things that a man usually delights to question God about are those daily rules which God has given him to live by. Men always have their doubts as to God's wisdom – this rule is unreasonable, that one is hard, and a third one is unprofitable. One does not have to wait long to find that *"the carnal mind is enmity against God, it is not subject to the law of God, neither indeed can it be"* (Rom. 8:6,7). Men are dead set against God's will, by their very nature they are in opposition to Him in a way so vicious that only a complete change of nature can cure them of it. As a man, he does not desire to know God's will, and if he knows what God requires he secretly wishes that he were ignorant of it. A hypocrite will contend with God as to his good works, *"Why have we fasted and You did not see it"* (Isa. 58:3). Carnal men will even dare to criticize God, *"You say that the way of the Lord is not equal"* (Ezekiel 18:25).

Men are not able to maintain any of their causes against God, they cannot argue with Him about His works or about their own works. And *"woe to him who strives with his Maker,"* for he will be crushed if God is pleased to answer him. Sometimes He may not be pleased to answer, as Elihu told Job, *"Why do you fight against Him? For He does not give an account of any of His matters"* (33:13). Later, however, God was pleased to personally answer Job, and when He did there was a quick end to the matter.

"He is wise in heart and mighty in strength. Who has hardened himself against Him and been blessed" – Job 9:4.

These words are intended as a further illustration both of the justice of God and of man's duty to humble himself before God. There is a double proof in the words:

1. There is proof of God's justice. Why? *"He is wise in heart,"* therefore He knows how to do right. *"He is mighty in strength,"* therefore He does not need to pervert judgment or do wrong for fear of man. Fear of a higher power usually biases and powerfully influences those who are in power. These two attributes of divine judgment are in proper poise, therefore there is no turning of Him out of the path of justice.

2. It is a proof of the need for man to humble himself before God. It would be dangerous to contend or contest with God. Why? Because He is wise in heart and mighty in power. Shall an ignorant, foolish man challenge the all-wise God? Shall a weak, ineffectual man set himself against the almighty God? Can a man be a match for God?

There are two ways that a controversy can be carried on: (1) by wit and policy; (2) by strength and power. If a man would try to use the weapon of wisdom and cleverness against God, trying either to outwit Him or dispute with Him, God will make him look like the fool that he is. And if he should arm himself to the teeth, set his shoulders, and attack God with power, he will be shown to be a poor, infirm creature indeed.

These two attributes render God at once the most dreadful adversary and the most desirable friend. It is a hard choice whether to have wit or power in an enemy, for we do not want him to have either. But who does not want his friend to have both wisdom and power? Under either of the two views of God here, any intelligent man would find Him to be dreadful − for what can strike fear into a man more than an enemy who will surely be able to outwit and overpower him? Before such an adversary, it is wise to humble oneself.

"He is wise in heart"−It is spoken after the manner of men. The heart is the principal organ in a man by nature. The heart in man is the seat of all that is important to man. To say that God is wise in heart, then, is to say that He is most wise, and that at the very center of His being. A man may be said to be holy in heart, humble in heart, upright, etc. In this way God is said to be wise in heart. We are to understand that He has deep, solid, rooted wisdom. What is not expressed here, but is made plain elsewhere, is that God is infinitely wise − He is all wisdom, and there is no end to His wisdom− His ways are past finding out, for His wisdom is illimitable, immeasureable and unendable. There is a twofold act of wisdom, both of them most eminent in God. There is the knowledge of the nature of things. Then there is the knowledge of how to order and dispose of things so as to cause them to do our will. They may properly be called science and prudence. When a man has much knowledge about the nature of things, but lacks prudence to apply that knowledge, he becomes like a ship with a very large sail but no rudder to bring him to the place he wants to go. Such a thing cannot happen to the Lord, for He not only knows all things as they are, but He knows exactly how to cause them to do whatever He will in both Heaven and earth (Dan. 4:36).

"He is mighty in strength"−It would be a great compliment indeed to say such a thing of any man, but no words have the power to describe the almightiness, the all-powerfulness and all-sufficiency of God. The word for strength here is one that imports great natural power and lively vigor, which in man is the strength which nurses and feeds him with continual supplies of energy for his activities. The Lord has an everlasting spring of strength in Him, but in His case there is never any loss of strength, not even for a moment. He may expend as much strength as it takes to make a world in six days, or as much as to raise His Son from the dead, or as much as it takes to make a pure, new creature from an impure and wicked man − but when He is through, He will have as much strength as He had immediately before He acted, *"Have you not known? Have you not heard, that the everlasting God, the Lord, the Creator of the ends of the earth, does not grow weak nor weary. There is no searching of His understanding"* (Isa. 40:28).

"Who has hardened himself against Him and been blessed"−Having described the Lord in His wisdom and power, he now challenges all the world to show him a man who has ever set himself against God and still had been blessed and prospered. Job not only had no thoughts of challenging God, of throwing his weak body or wisdom against the strength and wisdom of God, but he states that he never knew or heard of a man who had done so with impunity.

Hardening under a natural consideration comes by withdrawing moisture from a substance. Then this substance becomes usually condensed, stiff and unyielding to the touch. Therefore that is called hard which will not easily submit to impressions from without. In a moral sense, to harden is to settle the spirit, or to immovably resolve upon the doing or not doing of a thing. When a man purposely resolves upon a thing and resolvedly purposes to carry it to an end, then it may be said that he hardens himself to do it. The word is used in both a good and ill sense. In a good sense, when a man is resolute to do the will of God, when he grows so resolved that he will not be moved by hopes or fears, by promises or by threats to do anything but the will of God, then such a man is hard and firmly established. He cannot be swayed, he is fixed and firm like a rock, he has a spirit hardened to do good. Ezekiel was such a man, for when the Lord told him that Israel had stopped their ears against His messengers and hardened their hearts against Him, he gave Ezekiel a promise: *"Behold, I have made your face strong against their faces and your forehead strong against their foreheads. I have made your forehead as an adamant harder than flint; do not fear them..."*-(Ezek. 3:8,9). As being hardened in sin is worse than sinning, so to be hardened in doing good is better than doing good. Sin and grace display their glory most when they are acting against virile opposition.

But usually hardening is taken in an ill sense. To harden the spirit is, (1) to resolve in sin whatever God may say or do. To sin against the word and works of God is proof of a hardening of the heart, and this is far more dangerous than the very much feared hardening of the arteries. When a man is determined to go his own way, even when the threat of divine judgment hangs over his head, and even when the words of God are resounding in his ears, then such a man is hardened in sin. (2) A man also hardens himself against God when he speaks strongly against Him. The hardness of the heart can appear in the tongue. *"Your words have been hard against Me, says the Lord"* (Mal. 3:13). (3) We harden ourselves against God when we are displeased with what God does, boldly adventuring to demand our own pleasure instead of His, *"lovers of pleasure, more than of God."* (4) There is a degree of hardening in us equal to the amount of dissatisfaction that we have with God's providential acts. Discontentment and unquietness of spirit will harden us to oppose God. (5) To pay no attention to giving glory to God is a hardening influence in our lives. He that will not give God glory in what He commands is hardened each time he fails to do so, *"blessed is the man who continually fears, but he who hardens himself shall fall into mischief"* (Prov. 28:14). A man who fears God quickly takes impressions from the Word of God. To this man, the will and works of God are as caresses to a lover, they send pleasant sensations through his whole being.

That which is chiefly meant here is the grosser act of hardness, when men either speak or go on in their way acting against God. The Word seemingly makes no impression on such a man (though one day he may suddenly shatter and disintegrate). This hardening may be natural, acquired, or supernatural:

1. It may be that natural hardening of heart which is common to all men. God takes away the heart of stone when He gives a tender, loving heart to His new creatures.

2. It may be acquired hardness. Men start with a hard heart against God, but they are able to add to their former hardness by practicing evil wit and acts against God; these *"stretch out his hand against God and strengthens himself against the Almighty"* (Job 15:25). There is a growth in sin as well as a growth in grace. Many hard acts make hardness more habitual.

3. There is a judicial hardening of the heart, when God as a righteous judge hardens the heart of a man who knowingly opposes Him. When a man is determined to harden his heart against God, he will find God in agreement that his heart should be hardened. This we see plainly in Paul's discourse, *"For the Scripture says to Pharaoh, Even for this purpose I have raised you up that I might show My power in you and that My name might be declared throughout all the earth. Therefore He has mercy on whom He will have mercy, and whom He will He hardens"* (Rom. 9:17,18). And how did God judicially harden the heart of Pharaoh? Was it not by the ministry of His word by Moses and Aaron? So then we can cultivate hardness of heart, to add to that hardness of heart which we have as a legacy from our father Adam. Then, too, the Lord may in wrath, in order to have His word glorified and His will done, harden a man's heart — and that is the hardest of all hearts, when He has finished.

There is an active hardening of heart, when man hastens the process by his own obdurate acts. This was true of Pharaoh when he took attitudes and spoke words which were bound to harden his heart, saying, *"Who is the Lord that I should let Israel go."'* and, *"Who is the Lord? I do not know the Lord."* Every act of sin hardens the heart of man, but the heat of blasphemy at once shows and puts it into the extremity of hardness. In four major ways, a man may harden his heart:

1. Presuming upon mercy is very efficient in the hardening of one's heart. Many do evil because they hear that God is good and merciful, thus turning God's goodness into wantonness. They do not fear the Lord, being assured that God will be merciful to them whatever they may do. Needless to say, these fools are deliberately deceiving themselves

2. God's longsuffering is another excuse used by man to give him false hope while he is hardening his heart against God. If God delays His judgment, if He is slow to strike, then they are swift to sin, *"Because sentence against an evil work is not executed speedily, therefore the heart of the sons of men is fully set in them to do evil"* (Eccl. 8:11). Such men do not have any questioning and debating in their minds as to whether they should do a God-defying act, they are so full of themselves, so full of lust to do what pleases themselves, that they have no room in their hearts for better thoughts or counsels. If we preach the gospel to them, then they become *"scoffers walking in their own lusts and saying, Where is the promise of His coming? For since the fathers fell asleep all things continue as they were from the beginning of creation. For they are willingly ignorant of this, that by the word of God the heavens were of old...but the present heavens and the earth are kept in store by the same word, being kept for fire until the day of judgment and perdition of ungodly men...But, beloved...The Lord is not slack concerning His promise...but He is long suffering to US, not willing that any should perish, but that all (of us) should come to repentance"* (2 Pet. 3:3-9). There are those who read this without care, who fail to note that God is talking to His beloved, from the beginning of the book of 2 Peter to the end, and that He is careful to tell us that it is toward us that He is longsuffering — that He is not willing that any one of His beloved and elect ones should perish. He does not say, nor in any way imply that He is longsuffering toward those scoffers. He is very careful to keep *"us"* separated from *"them."* He does not say that He is not willing for any of them to perish, but that He is not willing for any of US to perish. If there were no context, then some may have some figment of imagination to fix their view of universal salvation upon, but the context is very plain in 2 Peter. He writes to the beloved and elect children of God, and he gives promises to them, encouragement to them, and to them alone. There are no promises to those who are not of God, to the unbeliever there is no hope to be found by a careful reading of Peter's God-breathed words. Any notion that God is not willing for the ungodly to perish would surely disappear when they read, *"The Lord knows how to deliver the godly out of temptations and to reserve the unjust to the day of judgment to be punished...they shall utterly perish in their own corruption and shall receive the reward of unrighteousness"* (2 Pet. 2:9,12).

In Romans 9:22 only is there any hint that God is longsuffering toward those who are ungodly, and then it is plainly stated that it is for the benefit of the godly that He forbears, *"What if God, willing to show His wrath and to make His power known, endured with much longsuffering the vessels of wrath fitted for destruction — and that He might make known the riches of His glory on the vessels of mercy which He had before prepared to glory, even us whom He has called..."* Note carefully that it was to show His wrath and to make His power known that He endured with much longsuffering the vessels of wrath fitted to destruction. Their presumption that He is waiting and waiting, hoping and wishing that they will soften their hearts and become more pliant in His hands, is a fiction from their own continually evil imaginations (Gen. 6:5). No Scripture in the Old or New Testament will give even a hint of hope to the ungodly that He will give them a whit less than they deserve for hardening their hearts.

3. Gross ignorance is a hardening influence. Men are wilfully ignorant of themselves, and of God. Not knowing what the full effect of their acts will do to their lives, they boldly

act on their ignorant foundation and do those things which will send them toward hell in an ever-accelerating vehicle of foolishness. Not knowing what God will do as the result of their acts, they do not care nor even look to see what it is that God has threatened.

4. Hardness of heart in sinning may be contracted from following a multitude of the ones who openly commit such a sin or sins. If all do it, then shall any suffer? But the word of God is explicit, *"You shall not follow a multitude to do evil"* (Exod. 23:2). The heart is always ready to flatter itself into the opinion that God will not be angry with someone who is doing nothing more than what has become common practice. It never seems to cross the minds of most men that a man is valuable to God only if he is pleasing to God — and this holds even if all men in the world commit the same sins, for was not the Flood a case where God slew all the men in the world, save eight persons, to put to rest the notion that God cannot abide the thought of a world without men. There are three major excuses offered by those who profess to sin because of the example of others:

Excuse 1. If the famous and the honorable go this way, then who am I to say that it is wrong and that I should not do it? The heathen, hearing that their gods and goddesses committed adulteries, said as an excuse for their own adulteries, If the gods do it, then why should I not do it?

Excuse 2. If the wise and learned men go that way, then who am I, ignorant and unlearned as I am, that I should conclude they do not know what is right?

Excuse 3. If godly men have done such things, then who may not? The failings of the saints appear to give wicked men some excuse for their follies. They scorn the ones who make it their heart's work to exactly follow God's commandments, and they will not imitate them in that way of doing things. But let them see or hear of a godly one who has fallen into such and such a sin, then see how many of them will begin to claim them as their example. They will imitate the falls and sins of those whose repentance they would never think of imitating. Many have hardened their hearts by doing what David did, without having any thought of repenting as he did — their hearts did not break, their concern for God's glory did not multiply, as was the case with David. But when all stand at the Judgment Seat, if not before, it will be known that the excuse of those who have followed the saints into sin will not hold. It will but be another gross sin to be rewarded along with the other, with unspeakable pain.

There are no hard hearts that developed into a scandalous hardness in a day. There are usually several steps which will lead one to a heart of adamant.

Step 1. The first step is seemingly but a little one, the leaving of the mind to idle thoughts, or the heart to covetous or other lustful desires. Vain and selfish thoughts will start the hardening of the heart.

Step 2. Stolen 'joys' which come from seeking pleasure against the will of God are certain to harden the heart. The so-called pleasures of sin can bring a natural kind of exultation, but the aftermath is a lessening of sensuality — that which pleased the senses will soon please it less, then another form of pleasure must be sought, until one day it is found that there is no pleasure to be found in anything. As it is with pleasures of the senses, so with the lusts of the eye and the pride of life. There is no real pleasure in greed, so the greedy will find that the thing that he gets abundantly is the displeasure of God. Whatever the fleshly sin, it will war against the soul and harden the heart.

Step 3. When a sin becomes a custom, when it is performed out of habit, then it is proven that the heart has hardened dangerously. When a man comes off seemingly safe after committing a sin, he will often venture again, until at last he thinks there is no real danger in sinning at all. Every life should be examined to see if any such habitual course of sin is in it.

Step 4. When a man comes to the point where he is willing to attempt to defend his sin, then that man has a heart mightily hardened. He has so long spoken against God's word in his heart that now he can speak against it with his tongue before everyone. Before he was a practicer of sin, now he becomes its patron and advocate.

Step 5. The harder hearts grow angry and passionate with anyone who will advise them to give up their sins. He is resolved, and a man that is resolved in his way is always angry when someone tries to move them out of that way. He who loves his sin will hate his reprover.

Step 6. Those hearts that sit constantly under the hammer of the word may become the hardest hearts to be found. A man in armor does not feel the stroke of a sword. A man who has hardened his heart against God's word hundreds of times becomes as it were armored against it. He becomes sermon-proof. He gets to where he is past feeling anything in moral matters. *"Some being often reproved harden their hearts"* (Prov. 29:1) until their hearts are too hard for all reproofs.

Step 7. If you have hardened your heart until the sword of affliction does not pierce it, then you have become judgment-proof — that is, you have gotten to the point that judgments will not do you good. But you will not have escaped the great Judgment.

Step 8. The hardest of hearts are scorning hearts. These deride the Word, mock at God's judgments and scoff at the Savior. They may be found also opposing good men. If evil is done, they laugh. These are at the end of that strange catalog of wickedness listed by Paul, *"who, knowing the judgment of God, that they who commit such things are worthy of death, not only do the same, but have pleasure in those who do them"* (Rom. 1:32). And they cannot but hate those who are conformed to the image of the Lord, for they who have hated Him will surely hate all who are like Him.

These men who have made their hearts hard in these several ways shall not prosper, they shall not be blessed.

It must be realized that the steps toward the hardening of the heart are not taken only by the Pharaohs, Sennacheribs, Pharisees and apostates. The saints may fall into these things, and they are thus warned by the apostle, *"Take heed lest any of your hearts be hardened through the deceitfulness of sin"* (Heb. 3:13). If the wicked do not prosper when they harden their hearts, then shall the saints be blessed by doing so? It is mercy that God will not give peace to His children when they sin. He will not allow them to thrive on it. If the saints fall into a time of hardening their hearts against God, then God (in a sense) will harden His heart against them — that is, He will not appear to be tender-hearted and compassionate towards them in reference to present comforts and graces. If they harden themselves to sin and provoke, then He will harden Himself to afflict and chasten. It must not be denied, those who are close to God do sometimes harden themselves against Him — they entertain thoughts not worthy of a follower of Christ — they partially obey a command, in the footsteps of Saul — they pretend to accept an easy interpretation of a hard piece of Scripture — in many ways they foolishly depart from the living God and go a little ways apart. Then God begins to make their hearts ache. He breaks their spiritual bones (Ps. 51:8) and He intensely pursues them in their consciences until they feel the rod on their backs and the burn in their spirits and return to Him, repenting, believing and obeying.

"He who removes the mountains, and they do not know it, when He overturns them in His anger"—Job 9:5.

Having in general asserted the power and wisdom of God, Job now descends to make a particular proof of it. The argument may be formed in this way, He is infinite in power and wisdom, and this is proven by His ability to move the mountains, to shake the earth, to command the sun, to spread out the heavens, to dispose of the stars, etc. But it is the Lord God who does all these things, therefore it is He who is mighty in power and infinite in wisdom.'

He starts with the minor proofs, those things which are physical, requiring wisdom and might far beyond that of any man, but less than other things God does.

"He moves mountains"—The *Septuagint* has it, *"Who makes the mountains become old-*, *"*—The word does signify to become old and strong, because things as they grow old become strong. Also that which *"becomes old is ready to vanish away"* (Heb. 8:13), that is, it is ready to be moved and taken away (as the ceremonial law was). And because growing old implies a kind of motion, therefore the word is used to describe motion, even local motion, a moving from or out of a place (Gen. 12:4). This local motion may be either natural or violent. This in our text is violent motion.

There are natural mountains, and there are metaphorical or figurative mountains. It is an act of the mighty power of God to remove either, and He does move both. He has thrown down mountains in the form of men, such as kings and conquerors; nations like Babylon (Jer. 1:25), and the mountains of the soul, *"Every mountain and hill shall be made low"* (Isa. 40:4)—it is foretold as something Jesus would do. But He did not throw down the outward power of men, He allowed Herod and Pilate to remain on their thrones and to prevail for the moment. But He threw down mountains and hills of sin and unbelief in the soul. These things that blocked up His passage into the soul must be removed. These mountains of high proud thoughts must become His servants, *"casting down imaginations, and every high thing, and bringing into captivity every thought to the obedience of Christ"* (2 Cor. 10:14). These are metaphorical mountains that God has and does remove. But in our text we have natural mountains, as is consistent with all the following strictly natural illustrations of God's power.

The moving of mountains spoken of here is a violent motion which tears mountains out by the roots and casts them somewhere else. He has His witnesses that He has done so in the existing mountains — it does not take much observation to see that a violent upheaval has taken place to move this mountain or that one. Sometimes He does it by earthquakes. Sometimes He does it by floods (and surely by the great Flood He did so). Sometimes He may have done it without any common force, but by the direct forthputting of His power. If it pleased God, He could move a mountain by merely speaking to it to move — He who created a world with a few words surely can be granted the ability to move a mere mountain in the same way.

This much is meant, however, that God is so mighty that He can alter the entire world, even to the moving of the mountains out of their places — He can do whatever He desires. You will see later in this book of Job that God Himself chose natural phenomena to confound Job and bring him to repentance for spiritual errors. It needs a great deal of study, but God assures us that the invisible things of God may be seen in the visible things, even up to and including His eternal power and Godhood. (Rom. 1:20).

"and they do not know it"—They? Who? Are these the mountains that do not know it? Some say, yes, it is the mountains (being a figure attributed the ability to know—a not uncommon thing in Scripture). Others say the antecedent is man, then He is said to move mountains in a way that men do not know. Men may not know because they are ignorant. Or they may not know because God does the thing in secrecy. It would be easy to illustrate how God removes metaphorical mountains without the knowledge of men, but since these are natural mountains in our text, it should be restricted to this: The mountains did not know that God intended to move them; or, they did not know they had been moved; or, men did not know how they were moved; or, men did not know that they were to be moved beforehand.

"when He overturns them in His anger"—This is that form of overturning which will change the way a thing appears, or the way it is made up. It can be an overturning that brings a thing to nothing. God may not only turn mountains into molehills, but He may even turn them into plains, or into pits (leaving a monstrous hole to testify to the former presence of the mountain). It takes might to move a mountain, but is it not more evidence of power to cause it to disappear completely?

"in His anger"—Anger in man is a mixed affection, made up chiefly of sorrow and revenge. The word in the text means the nostrils, and the Scripture often employs it to express anger. Anger is seen and made visible in the nostrils, for instance quick breathing is a sign of anger. God is of course without parts and passions. He is not in any way angry in the way that a man may be. But He is said to be angry when He does those things which men do when they are angry. The Lord is not moved or stirred by anger, but He is angry when He makes motions and stirrings in the creature. We see the effects of His anger, but He does not have the passion, much less the perturbation of anger.

Therefore, consider that when some part of God's creation is hurled this way or that way, or violently removed and put into another place, this is an argument that God is angry, *"Was Your anger against the rivers? Was Your wrath against the sea?"* (Hab. 3:8) He may act in anger to protect or establish one of his saints (Ps. 18:7).

"He who shakes the earth out of its place, and the pillars of it tremble"—Job 9:6.

This is a higher expression of the power of God. Mountains are great, bulky bodies, and they are not easy to move. But no mountain is as great as the whole earth, which He is here to shake. The word for shake is one which imports a violent motion of the mind, causing either by fear (Deut. 2:25) or grief (2 Sam. 18:33). It is also applied to civil shakings and commotions by the troublesome spirits of men (Prov. 30:21). Some expound this of a natural motion. But the text says that He shakes the earth out of its place, but an earthquake shakes the earth in her place. Did the Lord ever shake the earth out of its place? It may be that He did in the days of Hezekiah, when He made the shadow of the sun go back up the steps of the sundial. At this time it is recorded that sunworshippers were forced to rebuild temples so that the sun could be seen out of the gates of it, the earth apparently having been tilted that much. But whether or not the Lord has done so, He can do so. The earth may be here today and gone tomorrow, if God would so desire it. One day it shall melt with a fervent heat, and there shall come down a new heaven and a new earth — is that not another evidence of His power?

"and the pillars of it tremble"—The word means to stand upright, to be erect. Pillars may be ornament or for strength. They may support something, or they may be supported by something. The mountains, for instance, could be understood as pillars. If God shook the earth, these pillars would surely tremble. And if He shook the earth that which supports the crust of the earth would surely tremble. Whatever pillars there may be, either under the earth, or upon the earth, these tremble when God shakes. Since the other parts of the text and context are dealing with natural things, it does not seem that the pillars here should be expounded as those other pillars of the earth, the great men of it.

"He who commands the sun and it does not rise; and He who seals up the stars"—Job 9:7.

Now Job rises another notch and describes a still greater exercise of power on the part of God. Here in the heavens stand a far greater ball than the relatively smaller earth. Here Job tells of an act greater than the shaking of the earth, God commanding the sun not to rise. He is pictured as a mighty master who speaks to His servant, for that is what the sun is, God's servant. He speaks to the sun, and the sun does what He says!

"and it does not rise"—The phrase implies an ordinary event. But when was there such an event as this? Again, it could be that He is being described as He might be. He could order the sun not to rise. Again, there have been times of great darkness on earth, when there was no evidence of the sun (as Exod. 10:21). It could be the days when all the earth, or the vast majority of it, is shrouded in clouds, and the sun does not appear to rise. But here it appears to be that God has ordered the sun to be still, relatively. As an axis for the other heavenly bodies, it must remain stable. If, for instance, the sun were to stray too far from its relative position to the earth, all of us would die — the distance from the sun, and the position of the sun in relation to the earth, is of the utmost importance to life on this planet. For an example, huge, 'prehistoric' animals have been found

in Siberia with undigested food in their stomachs, frozen completely, and perhaps instantly. Why? There must have been a sudden change in the influence of the sun upon that region of the earth. One scholar believes that it happened when Hezekiah's shadow ran back up the sundial.

"and seals up the stars"—Some think that the former clause and this one tell us that it is God who commands the day and the night, with the sun for light in the daytime and the stars at night. Other would have it that God seals up the sun so that the stars may shine. But it would be best to keep the seal upon the stars. This may be in two ways:

1. He keeps the stars safe, that is He preserves the stars in their orbits. Sealed is often used for assurance and safekeeping (Daniel's lions were sealed so that they should not hurt him). In a spiritual sense, the sealing of the Holy Spirit is to make the soul safe in the love and favor of God. He makes the stars firm and fast in their spheres.

2. Sealing is more often used for secrecy, for the hiding of a thing (Deut. 32:34; Job 14:17). So the Lord seals up the stars when He clouds or obscures them and will not let them be seen. Some make it an allusion to a book. The heavens are a great volume in which many truths of God are written. His name is there. And the stars are as so many characters or letters of His name. He often seals up this great volume and so blots these letters that no one can read or distinguish them.

Another interpretation would have it that He keeps in and closes up the influences of the stars. In which case the teaching would be that the influences of the heavens are in the hand of God, to let them out or keep them in, as He pleases. As He can seal up the spiritual treasures so that we receive no light, comfort or refreshing from them until He please, so He also can seal up the natural influences of the heavens so that the earth may not receive the fruits and benefits of them.

"Who alone stretches out the heavens and walks upon the waves of the sea"—Job 9:8.

Here is a further argument of the mighty power of God. Job's discourses have moved from earth to the heavens, and back again. He searches for the wonders of God's power and wisdom in every place where they are so bountifully displayed.

The heavens in reference to the earth are the upper part of the world. The heavens are a great, brilliant canopy over our heads. The word is dual, having these meanings:

1. Some derive it from a word which signifies a name, a name of honor and dignity, Shem — men of renown (Gen. 6:4). The heavens are the most glorious, beautiful and renowned part of the creation. Their name is above every name of inanimate creatures.

Others, because there are waters above in these heavens, derive the word from *sham,* which is an adverb of place meaning waters. Then it would be as much as to say, there are waters, or there is the place where God has set fountains and stores of water. All His waters are not upon the earth, He has waters and springs in the heavens.

A third opinion takes it for a simple word, not a compound word. In this case, it would note only superiority in place, high or above.

A fourth opinion derives it from a word which means to be amazed. And the reason given is this, that the heavens are such a vast body that a man will be amazed if he is blessed with the full impact of them.

But what are these heavens that He has stretched out for us? The heavens which we see were extracted out of the first earth — the sun, the moon, the stars, even the very light itself were made out of that earth, that general heap of matter which the Lord created at first. In the Scriptures, we find the heavens put for the starry heavens or the firmament. (Gen. 1:17; Ps. 8:7; 19:1). Again, there are heavens which include that which is below the moon, for the air and the clouds. So the birds are said to fly in the heavens. Also it is written that the rain from the heavens was restrained (Gen. 8:2), but there is no rain in those heavens which are above the moon.

All of these heavens are stretched out by the Almighty God. Now stretching may be done in several ways, (1) By beating out and spreading thin; (2) by melting, then stretching, or melting and running out. *("Have you spread out the sky with Him, which is as strong as a molded mirror?"*–Job 37:18); or (3) By unfolding the parts, like a tent or curtains, *"O Lord, You are clothed with honor and majesty, You stretch out the heavens like a curtain"*(Ps. 104:1,2).

So the stretching out is either an exposition of the nature of the heavens (*"The Lord said, Let there be an expansion,"* or a stretching forth – see Gen. 1:8). Or it may refer to the words going before, in which case it is shown that God stretched out the heavens, and that is why He is able to command all that is in them. And of course if it is He who stretched them out, then it must needs have been He alone who did it. It is an axiom in divinity, that no creature can be an instrument in Creation.

"and walks upon the waves of the sea"–The sea is a fluid body, therefore it is a marvel when anyone walks upon its waves. This is said that we may see that God also has complete command over the sea, either to quiet it, or to firm it up for His tread. ⸱ To walk upon a thing is to have that thing under our power or in subjection to us. When all things are put under God's feet, it is to say that all things are made subject to Him. All things today are under the feet of God, the Son, but they do not appear to be so. All men would not agree today that this is so. But there will come that day when He will make it so evident that none will be able to raise an objection to this universal subjection of all creatures under Him.

"Who made the Bear, Orion and Pleiades, and the chambers of the south"–Job 9:9.

Having given God the glory for mightily stretching out the heavens, we now have a particular instance given, of a giant star and of two well-known groups of stars. The Bear, or Arcturus, is a fixed star of the first magnitude in the constellation Bootes. Orion is one of the fifteen southern constellations which may be seen at some season of the year in every land, and it is particularly conspicuous in the winter sky. Pleiades is the name for the seven stars in the neck of the constellation Taurus. This great and wise Artist has created all this giant canvas of wonders, and particularly He has ornamented it with these beautiful and famed stars, the Bear, Orion and Pleiades. Mythology has it that these particularly named stars had a great and special power over the sea. As usual, mythology is drawing on the Bible without knowing that they have confused the divine history. Long before the story was invented that Jupiter set these stars in the sky, Job had given that glory to the proper Creator, even God Almighty.

"and the chambers of the south"–to take in very great numbers of other stars, to expand the magnitude of the Creator's work, and perhaps to take in the other season – for some believe these are put for the four seasons. So that the Lord by His powerful strength and wisdom orders and appoints the motions of the heavens, in all the quadrants of the heavens, and by them also orders the seasons and the weather. Needless to say, these are also put synecdochically, that is the part that is put for the whole, that God made all that is in the heavens.

By all this may be seen the unspeakable and inconceivable power and wisdom of God. They shine out of every star in the heavens. There is so much of God in the heavens that the heathen; yea, and the Jews, the covenant people of the Old Testament; worshiped the hosts of the heavens, *"Beware lest you lift up your eyes to the heavens and see the sun and the moon and the stars, even all the hosts of the heavens, that you should be driven to worship them and serve them"* (Deut. 4:19). If we are not careful to look above the stars and see Him who made them, we are apt to place our attention and give the glory to those lesser bodies. It is indeed impressive to study the stars, to realize their immensity – so many of them being many times the size of the entire earth. Add to this the distance from the stars to the earth, and one cannot but become overcome with the wonder that God should have made His expanse so expansive. The size of the universe is some help to us in realizing the magnitude and the power of God. He did not lack for ability to create, leaving off the making of more stars only when He deemed it wise — until then He both spoke into being the matter they were made of, and wisely placed each one at the proper place in the universe, giving each its orbit and its usefulness. Add another dimension by considering the time, that these gigantic bodies have been treading the same path through the heavens so long that all national histories agree upon the major stars and their positions. God only stretched out the heavens, and only God could have kept them in their exact order and duties for these ages and ages, *"the stars in their courses fought against Sisera"* (Judges 5:20). It is unusual to find persons who have considered that the very stars are the servants of God. Diviners of old, and altogether too many astronomers of our day, would have us serve the stars. But we serve God, and the stars serve God, or under God, the stars serve us. It is purely heathen to think that we should serve the host of the heavens. It is good to be a star-beholder, to see there the marvelous handiwork of God. But it is wicked to be a star-gazer, to look there in order to divine what you should or should not do on a given day.

It should be noted that a truly learned man was Job, who knew virtually all that was revealed in his day. A godly man who attends to the teachings of God will always be philosophically and astronomically aware, while at the same time being kept back from fruitless and corrupting speculations.

"Who does great things past finding out; yea, marvelous things without number"—Job 9:10.

Job repeats these words from Eliphaz (5:9), and he is seeking to gather together his former illustrations of God's wisdom and power as he does so. For the particular words of this verse, see Job 5:9 and our exposition there. But observe this:

A godly man labors to exalt God, both in his thoughts and in his word, with heart and with tongue, whether God is depressing him or blessing him in this world. Which one of you would be so careful to give God His due glory if you were in Job's pitiful condition? These friends of Job would not be reacting so violently to his pinnings if there were alongside him in his afflictions also. To most the removal of all the family, goods and health that one had would be evidence that God was not able to do what He pleases — that God failed to have the power to protect those He had chosen. No such fall happened to Job. Here he is, wounded and sore, sorrowful and grief-stricked, bereaved and naked of all that he once called dear, being falsely accused by those he thought to be his best friends, and what does he do? He spends the better part of his time giving God as his portion and his hope both on earth and in heaven. In all of his distempered moments, his heart still stood right with God. Whatever evil befell him, he never spoke evil of God — though he was fully aware that all these things were in God's providence and bore God's personal stamp of approval.

From this we learn that though God uses His power to afflict us, yet we have reason to glory in that power. If He will emply His wisdom to completely undo and impoverish us, yet a gracious man will have enlarged thoughts (not lesser thoughts) of His marvelous wisdom. For God is as wise in troubling us as He is in delivering us. But natural hearts will curse God if He does not use His power, His wisdom, and all His glorious attributes to do for us those things which we cannot do for ourselves. It is our nature to wish to be above God, to be in a position to deny Him or defy Him when we are not pleased with Him. Being a partaker of the divine nature makes us wholly new creatures, for then we desire for God to be so far above us and so much free of all human influence that He can do whatever He pleases — for instance, only then is it possible for God to make all things work together for our good, for the good of those who are His called-out ones. By grace we can lift up God the highest when He is casting us down the lowest — it is a proof of true grace, and it is an instructor to our graces.

"Lo, He goes by me and I do not see Him; He passes on also, but I do not perceive Him"—Job 9:11.

Having in the foregoing context exalted the power and wisdom of God in many instances, Job closed with the inspiring fact that the things God does are both past finding out and innumerable. To demonstrate, he now acknowledges that the invisible God passes by him times without number and he does not know it. He works, but it is hard to search out all His great and wonderful works, since we cannot always see Him when He works.

"He goes by me and I do not see Him"—The Lord is said to go by us, but it is not in any local movement, for He fills all places and needs move to none, *"Does not He fill heaven and earth?"* (Jer. 23:24). God said that to convince the Israelites that no one can hide himself in a place so secret that the Lord cannot see him. The motion of God is not local, but providential. God does not move to act, but His acting is His moving. He goes by us, doing marvelous things for us, but we do not see Him when He is doing it nor even see what He is doing.

The other word here is of the same sense, yet more peculiar and proper to the motion of spirits. We had it in Job 4:15, *"a spirit passed me."* It means to change and to vary, either one's place or condition. The transitory changableness of the creature is expressed by this word (Ps. 102:27). The creatures pass on, as from place to place, and from condition to condition, *"for the fashion of this world passes away"* (1 Cor. 7:31). They not only have a perfective change, but a corruptive change. So the original word expresses any change or motion. The Lord passes on and makes changes, working sometimes to perfect, sometimes to destroy. But it is not possible for us to see which He is doing at the time.

Here, then, we have two words, one referring to sense, the other to understanding — *"He goes by me and I do not see Him"* — that is, my sense cannot find Him — *"He passes on also, but I do not perceive Him"* — that is, He roots up, destroys, builds, plants, but I am not able to understand what He is doing. I cannot unravel the meaning of His wonderful works, *"He does great things past finding out, yea, marvelous things without number."*

Some interpret Job's discourse here as still being about the natural works of God, the earth, the heavens etc. God is about us, ever working in nature, but we do not see Him doing it.

Others say that His going and passing are acts of His favor or disfavor. He goes by me in bestowing His favors, and He passes on in taking them away. To pass by sometimes is put for sparing, pardoning or showing mercy.

Then there are those who take the words as an argument to prove the power and wisdom of God. He would then be setting the Lord infinitely above all that is in the creature, and he does it here by an argument drawn from God's nature. What is His nature? He is a spirit, without any mixture, without any composition, without any materiality. He is invisible. So bodily eyes cannot behold Him. Man being a material substance is not able to see the Lord, so then how could he contend with Him, much less to conquer Him. This interpretation would make God invisible therefore invincible.

Still another interpretation would have the words teaching the general truth that there is an infinite distance between God and man. The Lord is omnipresent, He is going by, He is passing on, He is in all places, and He acts His power and wisdom where He pleases. Poor man is confined to one place, so that when he is here, he cannot be there. But God is everywhere. And though God be everywhere, yet He cannot be seen anywhere. God sees all, but no one can see Him. He fills all places, but His presence is unperceived. Nothing is hidden from Him, yet He is hidden to everything except the faith of His own people. So the whole is a confirmation and proof that the Lord is infinite in power and wisdom, whereas man is an ignorant, narrow-hearted and blind creature compared to God. He is weak and ignorant in comparision to God who cannot see or comprehend where God is or what God does. But man is not able to comprehend or see where God is or what God does. Therefore man is weak and ignorant in comparision to God. How then could he match wits and power with God?

Yet this must not be taken so strictly as to leave man without any perception or understanding of what God does. Job in the former context gave us a large account of the works of God, what wonders He had done. The saints find out some of God's doings in the world, though the blind world does not see anything He does. Job speaks comparatively when he says that the Lord passes on and we do not perceive it. It is very little of the workings of God that we ever see, even the best of us. Many do not see Him at all. He who does see Him sees but very little of all that God does. Some do not see because they do not want to see, *"Lord, when Your hand is lifted up, they will not see it"* (Isa. 26:10).

It is evident that Job teaches here that God is invisible in His essence and incomprehensible in many of His actions. Man's eye cannot see Him, either with the natural eye or with the eye of the mind. But why does Job speak in this way if it is the common condition of mankind? When Moses desired to see God's face, he was told, *"No one can see My face and live"* (Exod. 33:20). It would be death to see the living God in His essence or nature. But yet His hind parts may be seen, as in that same place in Exodus. We are permitted to see much of His glory shining forth, as much as we can bear while we are in the flesh, as much as will satisfy us. We see Him in His manifestations and glorious workings, as Isaiah did (Isa. 6:5). Yet by the eye of faith, that same Moses who was told that He could not see God is said in Heb. 11:24 to have seen God, *"that he saw Him who was invisible."* To faith the essence of God is as plain as any of His works are to our senses. God comes near to their spirits and lifts them above means and shows them His love and their interest in Him by an immediate witness of the Spirit of God (1 John 5:8).

What sight we have of God is in Christ. Christ is the express image of His person and the brightness of His glory. He is the medium by which we see God now, and some have the thought that we shall see God only in Christ forever. It is certain that we shall not see God here in this life except we see Him in Christ. God is too far above us, only Christ can bring Him near enough for us to see Him, Without Him, God goes by us and we do not see Him; He may pass on forever and we would never perceive Him.

The foolishness of those who would sit in judgment on God's dealings in the world can be seen when you consider that you are judging One that you cannot even see, One who works beyond your understanding. Would you judge another man that you had never seen, nor even had a witness to what he had done?

"Behold, He takes away – who can turn Him back? Who will say to Him, what are You doing?"–Job 9:12.

This and the next verse prove man's weakness as the former does man's ignorance and blindness. Men are so weak they cannot hinder God from taking away what He will. Yea, man is so little able to stop God in what He is doing, he does not even have the right to ask God what He is doing. Man is not strong enough to stop Him nor righteous enough to question Him. This is the total denial of any possibility in man to deal with God.

"Behold, He takes away"–The word means to take away by violence or force. It is as if he said, The Lord comes and takes a thing from you by open violence, but you cannot turn Him back. Augustine, following the Chaldee, translates, *"If He take one out of the world, who can hinder Him?"* The word is used of such a situation. Job may be admitting that though God had taken away everything but his life, there was that yet that He could do – and none could turn Him back.

Observe from this text, then, the following extracts for our learning:

1. Power cannot hinder nor stop the Lord from taking away. When the Babylonians encamped around Jerusalem, God warned them that they would not deliver themselves, because He had sent them to take away their city and state, *"And though they were all wounded men, yet they shall rise up and take your city"* (Isa. 43:13). And did He not later in an even greater display of His wonderful strength take away Babylon from the Babylonian king, even announcing it by the mouth of Daniel a few hours before it happened?

Policy nor wit can hinder God – no counsel shall ever stop Him. There were those who took counsel and resolved to go up against Judah and destroy it. But God answered them, *"It shall not stand, neither shall it come to pass"* (Isa. 7:6,7). There is no counsel against the Lord, for any who desire to outwit Him will find that it is an ill wit that tries it. *"Who will say to Him, What are You doing?"*—Job poses a question all ought to carefully consider. Not only are you not able to stop the Lord from doing what He pleases, but the question is, Do you have a right to even ask Him what He is doing? The answer is plainly stated here and elsewhere in the Scriptures. You do not have any right to ask Him what He is doing, nor what He has done, nor even why He has done anything. Only one who is superior may demand an accounting. Therefore only God can ask, What are you doing? As inferiors men have neither the right not the encouragement to ask God what He is doing. According to the apostle Paul, you are replying and acting against God when you simply ask Him such a question, *"Shall the thing formed say to Him who formed it, Why have You made me this way"* (Romans 9:20). No, you may not ask Him this, nor any other thing beyond a simply prayer, If it be Your will, Lord, reveal to me what I am to do under these circumstances. An humble and contrite heart will weigh in heavily with Him, and He will tell you what to do if asked in that vein — though it may be that He will tell you to do nothing at the time. But a presumptuous questioning of Him who need give an account to no one will bring only your own blood and misery upon your hands. When David said, *"I did not open my mouth because You did it,"* this would not only include the fact that he did not complain nor murmur, but also that he did not ask the Lord, What are You doing?

The Lord never silences those who speak in His name according to His words. But He will not hold him guiltless who speaks against His works. Take Nebuchadnezzar's advice and give God His due glory by not asking Him, What are You doing (4:35). For by this time that great king had found that it was not by his own strength that he had built that magnificent city, Babylon. When his heart was lifted up the highest, the Lord God brought him down to his lowest point, and he was taught with thorns that God is an absolute sovereign. He will brook no interference. He has the power of life and death over us breath by breath. One may petition such an awesome Ruler, but one does not say to Him, What are You doing?

,*"God will not withdraw His anger; the helpers of pride stoop under Him"*—Job 9:13.

An undeniable fact and a plain and clear warning are in this verse, for not only can God not be stopped from doing what He desires, and not only are we not able to rightfully demand to know what He is doing, but if He has set Himself to punish or chastise in His anger, there are none who may withdraw Him from His purpose. If some who consider themselves powerful and wise would undertake to protect the object of God's anger, then they finally will bend to His will and will be forced to stoop under His power.

The letter of the Hebrew is, *"If the Lord will not turn away His nostrils (His face)."* This is taken for anger, as in other places in the Scriptures, because there is such an appearance of anger in the face and nostrils. Therefore to turn away the face or nostrils is to turn away from anger (Ps. 78:38). When the Lord is angry, the turning of His face toward a man shows that He is reconciled. But when He is angry and does not turn away His face, then it witnesses that He is resolved to preceed in anger — that man who is under such anger is in a sad case, and those who endeavor to help him will have to stoop and fall away. *"He is of one mind, and who can turn Him? And what His soul desires, even that He does"* (Job 23:13).

"the helpers of pride stoop under Him"—It is a Hebraism to express those who think themselves most powerful and able to help. The same word is translated *"strength"* in some places, and *"pride"* in other places. If a man has a little strength in the world—strength in friends or riches or body or mind or understanding or memory, then he has a very strong temptation to be proud. Pride is one of the greatest weaknesses a man may have, yet it is always grounded upon some supposed strength.

But who are these proud helpers? Some understand it of the good angels, for they stoop under the power of God as well as men. Others expound these strong helpers to be devils, those who are evil angels, to whom evil men seek sometimes for help. If the Lord will not turn away His anger, even though men seek to the devil for help (as Saul did), then that helper shall surely stoop under Him. Others understand these strong helpers to be godly men. If the Lord will not turn away His anger, then the righteous will stoop under Him — that is, they shall not be able to rescue a person from the anger of God, by prayer, or by the utmost improvements of their relationship to God. There have been places that have fallen because there were no godly men to support them. Others have fallen even though they had godly men to support them. The Vulgate Latin translations renders it, *"They that bear up the pillars of the world shall fall."* Godly men bear up the pillars of the world. Though the Hebrew will not bear their translation, yet the sense is good. Men of god are continually helping the world, swallowing up those floods of God's displeasure which would drown them otherwise. It was because there were so few such men that the world was drowned in Noah's day. Because there could not be found even ten good men in it, Sodom was burned by the fire that came down from Heaven. God looks for saints many times to stand in the gap and save a kingdom (Ezek. 22:30; Jer. 5:1). Yet it is so that in some ages a kingdom is not saved even though there are many godly men to stand in the gap. For unless God turn away His anger from them, they would surely stoop under Him and fail to preserve the world from falling.

Further, more generally these proud helpers are supposed to be kings and nations, joined in strongest confederacies. Then the sense is, If God comes against a nation, that nation shall not escape loss and punishment, even though many kings join with them and try to save them.

There is yet another interpretation which restrains and limits the word to Egypt, *'Unless the Lord turn away His anger, helpers out of Egypt shall stoop under Him.''* Frequently in the Scriptures of the Old Testament, Egypt is meant by this same word which we translate *"pride."* For both Egypt and Babylon are matched together and made to stand for pride and for oppression (Isa. 51:9). These then would make that text in Job 26:12 and this text here to be an argument that this book of Job was written after the people of Israel were delivered out of Egypt. Then, they say, this and the other passage refers to God's mighty work in destroying the Egyptians at the Red Sea. (Job 26:12 says, *"He divided the sea by His power"*—thus the Red Sea can be glossed into the text easily.) A group who take these texts to say Egypt still do not believe that it is inferred thereby that Job wrote after the Exodus. Rather, they say, he said this prophetically. For even at this date Egypt was known as a place to which many sought for help. A good sense may be made from this translation, but it is doubtful that this is the true one.

The word for *"stoop"* also imports a casting down or humiliation. Because we in the worship of God ought to be lowered and humbled before Him, we may well stoop before Him. The meaning of all of this is plainly, 'that except the Lord Himself suspend His own act and restrain His anger, then no power in the earth or the heavens (however strong, proud and confident they may be) shall be able to force Him to alter His course of action. Those who count themselves strong enough to help shall find that they are not even able to help themselves, much less those to whose help they come. They shall stoop instead of succeed when they go against the mind and purpose of God.' Then observe:

1. Those passions which are ascribed to God are fully under the command of God.

The passion of anger is ascribed by God, yet the anger which we say is in God has no power over God. Anger in a man will usually master him and cause him to do things that are not to his own best interests. But God is master of His anger; that is, he can turn and withdraw His anger when He pleases. God cannot be perturbed. When He is offended, He is not moved. His motions are all upon the creatures, He has no motions in His own bosom. The passions of the Lord are His most serious counsels and determinations. So it is said that He is angry because His counsels caused Him to take actions which to us appear to be the effects of anger.

2. It is not in the power of man to turn away the anger of God. Even prayer will not stop it. Prayer may be said in a sense to appease the wrath of God, as when Moses stood

between an angry God and the wicked Israelites — but it was the will of God which caused His anger not to be visited upon the objects of His anger, it was not the force of Moses's prayers nor the graces in his person. It was God's plan to, (1) create an evil situation; (2) permit the people to sin grievously, partly by withdrawing Moses from their presence; (3) work in Moses to will and to do of His good purpose, in this case to plead for the people by reminding God that His glory was involved; (4) to appear to be angry; (5) yet to have Moses pray and prevail; and, (6) then to forgive most of the people, though a token destruction of three thousand people was ordered by Him so that they might realize His displeasure with their sin. When God stirs up the heart of His child to pray for a certain thing to be done, then it is that His decree may become known to us — for only then, when we have prayed and when we have seen our prayers answered, can we see that God had purposes from the beginning to do that thing for us in our day.

"How much less shall I answer Him and choose my arguments with Him?"—Job 9:14.

Having in the former verses lifted up the glory and majesty of God, His power and His justice, Job now draws his speech nearer home, calling his thoughts away from those far reaches of the universe, from the depths of the sea, etc. He now gets down to his own case in order to answer the false charges which have been laid against him, and the evil inferences which are so evident to him. He sets out to prove that He did not intend to set himself against God, nor did he pretend that he could turn God from any purpose which He had been following. His argument to extract himself from their foolish charges proceeds from the greater to the lesser, saying:

'He who is so strong, so wise and so just that all the powers in Heaven and earth are not able to oppose or stop Him, surely He cannot be opposed by one who is so weak as I am, both in power and in wisdom I find myself unable to challenge Him. But as is clear from those former instances I have given, God is so strong, so wise and so just that all the powers of Heaven, the sea, the earth and the universe, not to mention those relatively weaker powers that prevail among men, are not able to resist Him. Therefore, I being such a poor and weak creature shall not in this sad condition presume to reason with Him about what He is doing to me (not that I have any desire to do it in any case).

Only the conclusion of this logical and undebatable argument are presented here, the premises of the syllogism being in the foregoing verses. But Job brings himself in considerably below that strength and wisdom which is mentioned in the premises — presenting himself as so low and weak and unwise as not being able to even hold discourse with God. He says in effect, Not only do I not have any power to oppose God, I have not even any words to oppose Him.

"How much less"—It is an expression of Eliphaz in the fourth chapter, *"How much less in those who dwell in houses of clay."* Both texts bear the same sense. If angels are not able to oppose God, then how much less the children of men can contend with Him.

"shall I answer" There is a twofold answering, both applicable to this text:

1. There is an answering by way of fact, a real answer, or answering to a condition. So one man answers another that is of equal power and strength, of the same measure in abilities and gifts with him. So bodies and buildings answer to one another, when they have the same dimensions. So money answers all things, because it bears value with all.

2. There is answering by word, which may be either contradictory or satisfactory. Servants may not contradict their masters by words (Titus 2:9), else they will displease them and Him who is their ultimate Master. It is this kind of answer which the apostle Peter charges upon all Christians, *"Be always ready to give an answer to everyone who asks you for a reason of the hope that is in you, with meekness and fear"* (1 Pet. 3:15). This is the duty of everyone, both toward God and toward man. On the other hand, to answer by contradicting the command of God would be rebellion. To answer by satisfying the demands of God is a duty. To answer by a proportion to the power and wisdom of God is

infinitely beyond man's ability. He sees himself as no match for God, and he is not inclined to try to reason with God, not being able to so much as choose out the words to reason with Him.

From this it may be seen that a godly man is apt to have low views of himself. Job had gone through several series of the creatures, finding them unable to contend with God. And now he concludes himself more unable than they. No doubt he could answer God in the manner of men as well as any of us. If any godly man could have contended with God, Job would have been an able champion for them. Did not God choose Job as His champion to demonstrate to Satan that a man of faith will not curse the God he believes in. From this we may note that they of whom God has the highest thoughts have the lowest thoughts of themselves. For the more we know God, the more humble we become. It was because Job knew God so well that he felt so insufficient to choose out words to reason with Him. There is a reason that men become full of pride, it is because they do not know God. If they could know what He was thinking of them as they boasted, then they would tremble and fall to repenting. Even Job, once God had revealed Himself to him in the latter chapters of this book, became far more humble, saying, *"I am vile. What shall I answer You? I will lay my hand upon my mouth."* (Job 40:4). Then after another short burst of truth from the Lord, he went further and said, *"I have heard of You by the hearing of the ear, but now my eye sees You. Therefore I despise myself and repent in dust and ashes"* (Job 42:6). He abhorred himself. Abhorrence is a perturbation of the mind arising from vehement dislike, or extreme disesteem. Abhorrence, strictly taken, is hatred wound up to the highest height. As exulting is the highest joy and delighting the highest act of love, so abhorring is the deepest act of hatred. Job not only disliked himself, despised himself, but he hated himself when he compared himself to the Lord.

When the sun shines into a room, the least bit of dust will appear. When the glory of God irradiates the soul of a man, then he can see all the specks and atoms of sin. Then the least spot and unevenness of our hearts or lives will show up plainly. The more we know of God, the more we honor Him — and the less we think of ourselves. If He increases in our esteem, then we must decrease. Who was it that called himself *"the least of the apostles," "less than the least of all saints,"* and, *"the chief of sinners"* (1 Cor. 15:9; Eph. 3:8; 1 Thess. 1:15)? It was Paul who had been the only man ever taken up into the third heaven and yet allowed to return, he who personally taught *"as one born out of time"* by the Lord Jesus Christ.

"and choose my arguments with Him"—The word signifies a choice after exact trial. It is used in that sense when Moses told Joshua to choose out men to go and fight Amalek. He did not take everyone as they came to hand, nor press them into service, but he carefully considered all of them and then picked out the man he thought best for that service. In the same way, David chose carefully the five stones which he would need for the defeat of Goliath. Here Job denies that he could choose arguments against God. He does not think that he can set words in any kind of frame and thus to prevail against God. In the spiritual world, it is not rhetoric and eloquence which prevails. The apostle Paul refused to use them, *"my speech and my preaching was not with enticing words of men's wisdom, but in demonstration of the Spirit,"* and he again says it in verse thirteen, *"not in words which man's wisdom teaches, but which the Holy Spirit teaches"* (1 Cor. 2:4,13). To be successful in carrying men by the ears, the words of eloquence and oratorical craft may be what one needs. But to use style and craft in choosing out words for God would be to greatly offend Him — it would argue that one did not know the One he opposes. If words are to be chosen for the most effective arguments, shall not the all-wise and all-knowing God be able to better choose the words which will be most effective?

But if Job here will not choose out words to argue with God, then why does he later say, *"Surely I would speak to the Almighty, and I desire to argue my case before God"*

(13:3)? The answer is this, that there is a twofold reasoning with God, (1) there is the reasoning of declaration, and there is (2) a reasoning of contestation. When Job declines here to choose out words to reason with God, it is because he does not wish to enter a contest with Him. When he later says he desires to reason with God, his meaning there is this, that he desires to declare and set forth his case and condition before him. God will allow us to reason with Him by way of narrative, to plaintively tell our story and wait upon Him for relief. There in the thirteenth chapter Job is speaking comparatively, showing how he would rather declare his case to God than to his unfeeling and pitiless friends.

Then there is that question which would arise from Isa. 1:18, *"Come, let us reason together,"* says the Lord. If the Lord, then, calls us to reason with Him, may we not then reason with Him? Is it not sinful modesty to refuse what God offers? The answer lies in this, that there are two ways in which we may not reason with God, (1) We must not reason with Him in our own strength; and (2) We must not reason with Him upon our own worth. Here Job refuses to reason with God in his own strength, and He will not advance his own worth in a contest with God. However, in prayer there is a reasoning with God. In fact, the reasonings and pleadings that are in prayer are the life and strength of our prayers. For prayer is not only a bare manifestation of our mind to God, but it is (or ought to be) a holy arguing with God about the matter which we declare to Him. It is right for us to bring out and to urge all the reasons and motives by which we think to move Him to grant what we ask. The prayers of the saints recorded in the Scriptures are full of arguments. However, God is a spirit. And as such, only spiritual arguments will prevail with Him – in fact, only those arguments which are of the Holy Spirit will prevail. Test this with the case of Jacob, who was so afraid of Esau and his army of men. He fled to God's presence at Peniel, where he wrestled with Him in prayer until daybreak. At the beginning he had used no less then seven arguments to stir God up to deliver him, (1) the argument that God's covenant with Abraham still was in effect and covered Jacob; (2) the argument that God had himself ordered this journey; (3) that God had promised him to deal well with him; (4) the argument that he was unworthy, and thus the kind that God helps; (5) the acknowledgment of the streams of mercies which God had already given him; (6) that he was in great peril, such as could be conquered only by the Almighty God; (7) the promise again, that God would do him good. Jacob did reason with God, and it was said of him (after the Holy Spirit had proven Jacob unable to conquer – that he had prevailed with God).

Now that the Scriptures are complete, and replete with examples for us, we may see the fullness of God's promises and instructions to us. There are many stones in that stream of truth which we may deliberately choose out and send up to God, asking that we be blessed in the same way that others have been in the same kind of circumstances. We can now much more confidently reason with God, He having not spared His only beloved Son, promising that with Him He would give us all things. Let us then reason from the proper topics, with the very words of the Holy Spirit wherever possible, heading our arguments with, (1) the freeness of grace of God; (2) the firmness of His promises, (3) the greatness of our need; (4) the concernments of His own glory, that it will be served; (5) the involvement of the cause of Christ.

It must be remembered, however, that no man can answer what God may bring as an objection against him. The Lord has myriads of arguments which we are not able to in any way answer.

"Whom, though I were righteous, yet I would not answer, but for my judgment I pray to Him"–Job 9:15.

This brings the matter to the very height. Why? Would I reason and try to make a case with God? No! For even if I were righteous, I still would not try to answer Him. It is as if Job said, 'I am so far from entering a contest with God that I profess strongly that I would not do it. For even if I had the greatest advantage and fitness to do it of anyone in the world; yea, though I were perfectly righteous, I would not do it. I do not say that the reason why I would not plead with God is because I am wicked, sinful and more unrighteous than my neighbors, but however righteous I might be, I still would not do it.'

Job speaks as one who knows the strength of God, and he will not enter a contest with this all-powerful and all-wise One in any way, for any reason. Righteousness, of course, would be the best armor for a man to wear if he were to approach God. As the apostle Paul assumed this and that high act of man to be insufficient (1 Cor. 13) to be called by the name of love, so here Job assumes that even if he were righteous, it would be impossible for him to contend with God.

"though I were righteous"—He does not say that he was righteous. He shows that he considers himself to be unrighteous and unclean, but he will not admit that even a righteous man can answer God. Job does say later that he had put on righteousness (29:14). But he does not claim thereby to be righteous. There are two ways that man may be considered righteous, comparatively, (1) in comparision to the wicked of the earth — the profane ones, the hypocrites, and the oppressors — Job was not profane, he was perfect and upright and therefore no hypocrite, and he was not an oppressor; (2) in comparision with the imperfect, that which has any failing or lack in it — in this sense Job was not righteous and that is why he says in effect here that he is not righteous.

Righteousness is twofold, (1) There is a righteousness of the person; and, (2)—There is a righteousness of the cause. Job does not forsake the righteousness of his cause, but he does disclaim the righteousness of his person. No created righteousness can answer God — He even charges His angels with foolishness, that is, He saw defects in them when compared to Himself. Even if man had remained innocent, he could not have answered God. For created righteousness will never answer to the inherent righteousness of the eternal God. There is a righteousness in which we many answer God, and Job's supposition does not exclude that. It is the righteousness of faith which we have by Christ. Man may answer God by the righteousness of Christ which is imputed to Him. For faith does not bring man to answer God, but it brings God to answer God. Christ can answer God fully to all the demands of justice, without any abatement. Christ has not compounded with our creditor for our debts, but He has paid them to uttermost depths and heights — there is nothing that is due to God's justice, He has paid it all. When a believer asks God's pardon for his sins every day, he offers the righteousness of Jesus Christ. The believer can ask God to try him to the uttermost, to see if there is any imprefection or flaw in the righteousness which he has to offer — and there will not be — then he may venture his soul upon it, that God will find the righteousness of Christ to be the full and complete answer.

"yet I would not answer"—As righteous is a judicial word, so is answer. It implies that Job would not only answer God when He was objecting or reasoning, but also that he would not answer Him when he was accusing or charging him, when He was judging or sentencing him. He acknowledges that he is what God judges him to be, and he admits that he is worthy to suffer what God judges is right for him to suffer.

From this observe that Job is bringing to mind that all the infirmities and weaknesses of man are the issues and effects of the sin of man. Man is an unrighteous creature, therefore a weak creature. Job argues from the effect to the cause, from the fruit to the root. Man is infirm and weak, therefore he must be a sinner. Where there is no sin, there is strength. Where there is no sin, there is knowledge. Perfect holiness scatters all the clouds of darkness and ignorance.

Also we see that unrighteous men cannot answer God. It is no wonder that David said, *"The wicked shall not stand in judgment"* (Ps. 1:5), for in a sense the righteous cannot stand in judgment either — that is, they cannot plead from their own righteousness before God. The ungodly have nothing to help them, and no one to help them, neither help within or help outside themselves. It goes well with the apostle Peter's argument, *"If the righteous are scarcely saved, where shall the ungodly and sinner appear?"* If Abel is not able to answer God, then how can Cain.

It is well to note the vast difference between the spirit and temper of a godly man and that of an ungodly one. Look at Job's humility here, as he will not justify either his own righteousness, nor himself in his righteousness. A Saul will try to justify his disobedience, but a Job will not do so. An ungodly man will still cling to the claim that he is righteous more than unrighteous, even if God tells him to his face a thousand times that he is vile and filthy. Yet perfect and upright Job, who sinned not against God when all was stripped away from him, will not dare to claim anything for himself.

A righteous man, that is, one who is godly by faith, looks upon his own righteousness as no righteousness. Job's supposition, *"though I were righteous,"* has a negation in it. He did not deny the work of the Spirit, or the grace of God in him, but he would not own them in his pleadings with God in regard to his chastisements. With men he could stand upon his character and behavior and come off quite well, but before God he had nothing to mention but Christ. In reference to the higher degree of grace for sanctification, we must forget all that is behind and press on to that which is before us. And in reference to the whole grace of justification, we must forget all our sanctification — however far it may have progressed. The less we remember our own righteousness, the more righteous we are in Christ. Only a hypocrite tries to increase himself instead of Christ in himself. The Lord draws a picture of a hypocrite in His parable of the Pharisee and the publican — and keep in mind that the reason Christ told the parable was that none might trust in his own righteousness. The Pharisee presumed to tell. The saints love to do well, and they love to hear well of others, but they know from experience that it is not good to hear others speak too well of their saintly deeds. They love to do good, even more than to receive good, and much more than to speak good of themselves. When Christ is represented as sitting in judgment, He tells the faithful of all their good deeds, their acts of love. But how did these good men answer Him? *"When did we see You hungry and feed You? When were You thirsty and we gave You something to drink?"* etc. (Matt. 25:37). The Lord keeps a faithful record of what his people do, but they themselves do not attempt to do so. It is our duty to remember to do good, but it is God's part to remember the good that we have done, and, *',The Lord is not unrighteous to forget our labor of love"* (Heb. 6:10). But if we think it is so important to remember the good we do, it may be that God will think it unimportant to remember it. The servants of God know full well what they do good, for to do good in ignorance would be a degree of evil. But when the good has been done, then they put but little importance upon remembering it.

Hezekiah did remind the Lord of his good deeds (Isa. 38:3), because he wanted to remind God of His grace which had been operated in the person and life of His servant. It is one thing to remember what we have done historically, as Hezekiah, and another to remember it legally. It is good to say to the Lord that we remember the work of His own grace in us, but it is not good to bring to His attention our works in order to obtain His grace.

"but for my judgment I pray to Him"—Job is saying in effect, 'I am not without hope because I have no hope in myself. I am not lost because I am lost to myself. I still have a sure and certain way left to me, *"I will make supplication to my Judge."'* It is as if he had said, 'Though justice cast me off, yet mercy will relieve me. Mercy will help me to honor God more.'

The word pictures the humblest submission, as when a man begs for his life. Job is not unwilling to obey Bildad's advice, when he said, *"if you would seek earnestly to God and make your prayer to the Almighty"* (8:5) — in fact he is in this verse praying earnestly to God. Not all prayer is supplication, but all petitionary prayer is supplication. When we are very much abased and brought low, then the prayer we lift up to God is called properly supplication. Solomon made such a difference when he prayed at the dedication of the Temple.

No weapon will prevail with God, but prayerful supplication will often be blessed with spiritual triumph. Even Christ did not conquer by the powerful use of the weapons of His command, but He conquered by dying. So we cannot prevail except by submitting ourselves to the will of God. Yet it is not our supplication, as our act, but supplication as an ordinance of God that causes it to prevail. True prayer is God's ordained means, and He honors it because He has planned to do so from the beginning.

Job is in a great contest with men, but he makes it clear that men are not his judges, but God is. And it is a comfort to him to know that God is his Judge, for surely these men were not sufficiently wise to give him the justice he was due. For God is not only just, He is also compassionate and forgiving.

"If I had called and He had answered me, yet I would not believe that He had listened to my voice"—Job 9:16.

Job had abased himself by disclaiming all ability and righteousness, and he had shown that he had no intention of contending with God in any way. Now he confirms his lowly and humble spirit by these words. Not only will he not try to choose words to argue with God, but he can hardly believe that God would even take the time and trouble to answer him.

There are many interpretations, and almost as many translations of these words. The *Septuagint* reads it negatively, *"If I had called and He had not answered me, I would not believe"* etc. The majority of the Jewish writers fall very hard upon Job and accuse him harshly. They take the attitude that Job is a plain unbeliever because he is denying the providence of God in these verses (they say). They take it that he is denying that God is willing to take notice of men and their acts. Others take it that Job is in deep despair, and that these words show that he has lost all hope of receiving any further favors from God. But these aspersions are unworthily cast upon Job, a man full of humility and submission to the will of God. So frequently does he apply himself to God in prayer that all these foolish objections are confuted easily. The Jewish commentators are all along very rigid towards this holy man, cruelly putting the worst constructions upon all passages where they are able to do so — even putting ill meanings upon those passages which are plainly good.

There is a difficulty about the grammatical meaning of one word in the text, which may carry the sense two ways: *"If I had called and He had answered me"*—The Hebrew word which we translate call sometimes means to pray, sometimes to plead or to challenge. An act of invocation may be meant, or an act of provocation. It is translated both ways here. Most have it as we do, *"If I had called;"* but others have it the other way, *"If I had sent in my plea, or challenge."* Now if it is taken as the latter, for a challenge, it could still have a good sense: 'If I had challenged God and He had answered me, then I would not believe that He had condescended to give me an account of His ways. I would not believe that He had listened to my voice, that He had yielded to me or acknowledged that He had done me any wrong. Shall such a one as I am, dust and ashes, prevail in a suit against God?'

In the other sense, it may be that there could be two or three fair interpretations:

1. Some who favor Job conceive here that he is speaking through the infirmity of the flesh. They believe that it was sin in him that is speaking these words, since it would be sinful to disbelieve that God would answer prayer.

2. It may refer to the manner of his prayer or invocation, as not coming up to the desired height and measure of the duty, thus not fulfilling that law of prayer which the Lord requires. Therefore, his prayers being weak and imperfect, he would not believe that God would take notice of him and hear his voice. Then it would be as if he had said, 'You advise me to make my supplication, but if I do, yet I will not believe that God takes notice of my prayers — they being but cold, weak, distracted prayers from a distempered heart.'

3. But, rather, take the sense in this way, that Job in these words breathes out the humility of His spirit. He is saying, 'I am far from standing upon my own terms with God, as if I had hopes to prevail with Him by contending with Him, that though I come in the humblest manner to call upon His name, and though I find Him so gracious and merciful to me in answering my requests, yet I will not believe that He has listened to my voice be-

cause of any worthiness in me, in my works, or in my prayers – I will not believe that the answer I received from above is obtained by any value which my person may have with God.'

Job bends over backwards to give all the glory to God. Yet in doing so he is not denying that God hears men, or that God hears men who pray, or that God hears him when he prays. He denies that God hears men simply because they pray (God hates the prayers of the wicked), or for any reason that lies in themselves. Rather he believes that God listens to the voice of the Mediator, not to the voice of men. It is the voice of His own free grace that pleases God. The motions and intercessions of God the Holy Spirit is that which is heard by God the Father, as well as the motions and intercessions of God the Son. With two such voices as these speaking, why would God listen to the voice of a sinful man?

"believe"–The word means both to believe and to establish. This is because faith settles the heart. An unbeliever has no bottom, he is built without a foundation, his spirit is not anchored in anyone or anything, it wanders about. Faith believes what God has spoken, both historically and logically – that such a thing was said by God, and that such a thing is true because God said it. Job here is saying that he would not assent to God listening to his voice simply for his sake, but he is not saying that God would not listen at all to his voice.

"that He had listened to my voice"–To listen is more than to hear. It carries with it the inclination of the mind, rather than the attention of the ear. When one stops his ear he is shutting his heart against obedience, and not merely shutting the ear against hearing. To tell a tale to a deaf man is to speak to one who can hear but who will not hear what one is saying.

When one prays, he is calling on God. Therefore he ought to listen. How can we expect God to hear when we will not call upon ourselves to listen. God may answer our prayers in many ways. Sometimes He answers by His providential acts, by His works. There is not to be an answer by voice, but by dispensations. But faith is a necessary ingredient of prayer. When one prays without believing that he shall receive the answer to that prayer, he should fall to praying for faith to believe – *"Lord, I believe! Help my unbelief!"* Faith is the strength of prayer, therefore we must not allow the clouds and darkness of unbelief to weaken it. Instead, *"whatever you ask in prayer, believing, you shall receive it."* Prayer without faith is no better than a gun without a bullet – it will make a noise but it will not get any results. We must put forth more than our voice in prayer, we must put forth our heart also. The Word of God coming to us will do us no good unless it is mixed with faith and moves the heart. *"The word preached did not profit them, not being mixed with faith in those that heard it"* (Heb. 4:2). So the word that goes out from us, the word of prayer, will not prevail at all with God, it will obtain nothing from Him, unless it is mixed with faith. All the promises are made to believers, *"All things are possible to those that believe."* *"Ask in faith, wavering in nothing, for he that wavers is like a wave of the sea, driven with the wind and tossed"* (Mark 9:23; James 1:6). Believers often doubt, but all sound believers are without wavering. The Greek word means to question or dispute a thing, which is a degree beyond doubting. It is as when a man is sometimes of one mind and sometimes of another, being between two opinions, not knowing which way to take. We find the word in the opposite setting in Romans 4:20, *"Abraham did not stagger at the promise of God through unbelief."* Abraham was not tossed back and forth between waves of unbelief, today believing, tomorrow disbelieving what God had said. He was no double-minded man. No promises are made to such unbelievers, he shall not receive anything of the Lord, because he does not ask it in faith.

But though a godly man prays in faith, yet he may still have no faith that his prayer deserves an answer. Christ loves prayer, it is music in His ears. Faith is what makes our prayers melodious. But it is not our faith, that is something from ourselves. And it is not right to expect God to give us the particular answer we seek because we have prayed the right way, in faith. As it may be said after all is done that we are *"unprofitable servants,"* so it may be said after we have prayed well that we are always short of what we should have done. So God does not reward us because we have a surplus of good works — we are always short of what we should have done. So God does not reward us because we have put up a perfected prayer — we are always short of what we should have prayed and what we should have believed. Therefore, when He answers us, it is not because of our perfection in prayer, but because of Christ Jesus who ever lives to make intercession for us.

It is true that a godly man often doubts that his prayer has been heard, even when it was heard. The Jews expressed it as a dream when they returned from Babylon, *"When You turned our captivity, we were as those that dream"* (Ps. 126:2). They found it incredible. The church in Mary's house prayed without ceasing for Peter's deliverance from prison — yet when Peter pounded on the door to be let in, they called Rhoda crazy for believing that God would do anything for him, however marvelous and great. But a believer knows what is in himself, and he can hardly believe the unspeakable things which God has done for him. Their faith is often below His workings, they find themselves unable to take in the mercies as fast as they come. Faith widens the soul very much, yet God can pour in more than any faithful soul can receive.

Again, alas! faith has its decays. There are days when faith is not at the same height as it was before. One day we may believe that God has answered us, when He has not. Another day we may believe that God has not answered when He has. Sometimes it is *"Before they call I will answer."* Other times it is, *"Before the Lord gives, I know that He will give it."* Faith gives substance to the promises of God, they become real even before they are actually fulfilled. Yet the same heart that believed the day before may fall into unbelief in other matters today. David believed God when He anointed him to be king over Israel. Yet one day he muttered, *"I shall one day perish by the hand of Saul."*

There is a further possible understanding of the words, as you will see when we take in the next words:

"He who breaks me with a tempest and multiplies my wounds without cause"—Job 9:17.

Job's sorrows bring out the richest expressions, those which carry force and meaning from his vocabulary. He reaches for another height of expression and brings in a tempest.

The word we translate break is one which means a total ruining of a thing or person, the dashing to pieces of the thing or one broken. This is the work used of Christ when it is said that He will *"bruise,"* that is, *"break"* the head of the devil (Gen. 3:16). Christ with His infinite power not only bruised and broke the head of the devil, but he utterly destroyed the serpent's power — He spoiled and ruined him forever (Col. 2:15). He took away the souls he had taken captive and then led the devils away as prisoners of war. The devil also tried to break Christ into pieces and ruin Him, but he was limited to the heel of Christ.

"With a tempest"—The word not only means storms and tempests but also a little hair or twined thread. So the Chaldee Paraphrase translates it here, *"He contends with me to a hair,"* making the sense to be that God will not allow the smallest instance to go by without debating with Job, therefore he cannot believe that God is answering him. As Abraham said to the king of Sodom, *"I will not take anything that is yours, from a thread to a latchet"* (Gen. 14:23). He would not take the smallest gain from him. So to dispute to a hair is to contend about the very smallest differences one can find.

But generally the word is translated a tempest or a storm. God is often described as contending with man in this way, *"His way is in the whirlwinds and in the storm and the clouds..."* So Job here is saying that he was being broken by a tempest sent by God in using a common figure in Scripture.

To break with a tempest implies at least two things, (1) A sudden and unexpected affliction. Tempests are never welcome, and it is seldom that one knows they are coming.

When the sea is so calm and smooth that you can throw a die upon it, a storm may arise in a moment and put the ship in great danger; (2) It depicts the fierceness and violence of an affliction. Tempests are the most violent motions. They come with power. A tempest is irresistible. Who can stand before it? Who can contest with storms and great winds? When the Lord made total conquests of His enemies, He contended (this word here) by storms and tempests, as in 1 Sam. 7:10, *"When the Philistines drew near to battles against Israel, the Lord thundered with a great thunder that day upon the Philistines and troubled them."* The word is used figuratively in war, when besiegers come upon a town or fort, they are said to storm the place, or, to take it by storm. The prophet alludes to this, *"When the blast of the fearful ones is like a storm against the wall"* (Isa. 25:4). In that case God was picturing Himself as a refuge from the storm which men set against His own. Here we see that same God who saves man from the storms of men breaking Job with a storm.

Job was stormed, yet he supposes that his prayer was answered. Prayers may be heard and answered when the greatest afflictions are upon us. Yea, the greatest prayers are usually issued when the greatest trials beset us. It is not to be thought that prayers are lost simply because our comforts are lost. It does not follow that God does not hear you because He does not immediately relieve you of your burdens. His forbearance does not mean that He is denying you what you ask. His answer must be to your profit, but not to your comfort. He answers to our spiritual interests, making all things work out to our spiritual good, but there is no promise for your bodily and worldly interests. The sick man calls to the physician to take away the bitter medicine; the wounded man calls to the surgeon to forbear those torturing operations; but the physician gives him medicine and the surgeon uses the knife to make him better. These are not to torment the patient, but to bring the patient to the point where he will no longer be ill. Health and soundess of the body are more important than ease. So it is in spiritual things, the Lord heals us by wounding us. He removes our corruption by plunging the knife of afflictions into our spiritual sores. He is answering our prayer to remove the afflictions at the same time He is repairing our spiritual health by afflicting us. He goes down deep to the source of our troubles and removes that source.

We must learn to keep to our duty even while God may be dealing with us in a stormy way. It is no release to us when He does so, we still owe Him all that is due. Whether we are in calm or in storm, then, we must pray. And however more He may break us, that much more it behooves us to pray. He may not remove the storm, but He will remove our doubts as to His lovingkindness toward us.

It is only a seeming paradox, that the Lord lays the sorest afflictions and the heaviest storms upon those that He loves most. The same scourges that He lays upon His enemies are laid upon his best friends, and oftentimes they are applied with more strength and greater weight upon those He loves. To his enemies, he is fearful, breaking them and scattering them only that they might avoid putting themselves in the position of His enemies. He lays terrible strokes and blows to those who lie in His arms and live in His embraces, because it is His desire to remove far from them all that hinders them from enjoying His embrace. Therefore, it is impossible to distinguish the godly from the ungodly, the enemies of God from the loved ones of God, by the way they are afflicted; nor can they be distinguished by the measure of their afflictions. That which is a judgment to one is but a chastening to another. He wounds a friend and destroys an enemy with the same weapon.

Why would Job not believe that God had listened to his voice? It is easy to fall into this snare of the devil, that we may think that afflictions mean that God is greatly displeased with us — that is, more displeased with us than with the one who is not under heavy affliction. It is the hardest trial for faith, to be forced to believe that every outward sign points to the opposite conclusion. It is for that reason the highest proof of faith that a man will believe at the same time he is being broken with a tempest. It is very difficult indeed for one to be calm in untroubled faith when one is all blown up in a storm of affliction — but this untroubled exercise of faith is God's witness that the root of the matter is in us, and when we see that we can believe even when it appears that we are perishing, then we may know that God has given us a precious gift that none can take away. Therefore, let not His clouds of trouble obscure your view of His glory — by faith you can see right through them to the sight of God calmly applying to you, with love, the most disturbing affliction that is known to man. Then the serpent's whispers, then the pain of your wounds, then the passions of your earthly self, fade into the background and you find yourself detached from your troubles and attached to God.

It is not unusual for one to conclude that his prayers are not answered when afflictions continue, sometimes even multiplying after his prayers. But it is the eye of the fleshly mind, the uninstructed reasoning power of the sinful creature, which brings such a conclusion. No one versed in the Bible can prove such a conclusion to be warranted. It is only in the unreasoning passions of the flesh that such conclusions can be based. God has not so dealt with any of His servants, that He has left their prayers unanswered, as it were hanging in air, while He laid on more afflictions. Instead, it should be concluded that He is answering prayers by laying on more afflictions — for the thing that we pray for, if we do not pray amiss, is spiritual strength and wisdom — *"if anyone lack wisdom"* — that is, spiritual wisdom, *"let him ask of God, who gives to all liberally"* (James 1:5). In that place it is clear that God wants us to exult in our afflictions because they bring us such glorious spiritual results.

"He multiplies my wounds without cause" —Is this not a claim of injustice, that now achieved his purpose, to cause Job to curse God? No! The Hebrew word which is translated *"without cause::"* has been dealt with in 1:9 and 2:3. This complaint of Job's here is not a charge of injustice upon God. His heart was far from the least thought of that, as the former words will easily prove. Instead, it is an acknowledgement of the sovereignty of God. He is saying, in effect, *"Though He has wounded me already, yet He still has the right to wound me more; whether I have given him a specific cause at this time, or whether He gives me a reason, or does not give me a reason, He can and He is (rightly and properly) multiplying my wounds."* God need not yield simply because we contend with Him. He does not need to give us a running account as to why He is doing these things while He is doing them. The entire context deals with Job's contention that he cannot call God into account, that He has a position which is unreachable by anything that Job can do or think to do. If we will but follow Job's argument, we will find that Job is his own expositor. He is picturing for us some of the mysteries that lie in God's providential dealings with men. Job is answering the charge that he is a man so full of guilt that the greatest tempest of afflictions were due to him, and are being applied to him. He shows that God deals so with men because it is His right to do so, it is the proper application of His wisdom and power. This is not a case where God is dealing with Job as a malefactor, as a punishment for guilt. God is probing and testing Job, that all may see what is in his heart, that all may see that a godly man may stand in faith even those things that ruin and destroy the ungodly. Therefore, Job says this, *"He multiplies my wounds without cause"* —that is, without the cause that you say underlies His actions.

To multiply wounds denotes the afflicting hand giving numerous and manifold blows. These are various kinds of wounds, inflicted for various kinds or reasons, in order to achieve various results in the heart and soul of Job. Job's wounds were deep, deadly wounds. He was afflicted both within and without. Yet. they were not inflicted because of any specific course of sin he had indulged in. Nor yet were they inflicted unjustly. It was seen in the third verse of chapter two that God did not afflict Job because he was more sinful than another. There may be three more points raised here:

1. Whenever the Lord takes a thing from anyone, He is taking that which is His own. If He wounds, He has a right to wound, whoever the wounded person may be. If He could smite the sinless and perfect Christ, His only-begotten Son, then what injustice could

there be in the smiting of a sinful and imperfect creature? He is lord over all. All that we have is His. There is a foolish notion amoung man, one that is widely propagated and believed, that God has transmitted to men certain rights, certain areas of action, as well as complete ownership of this or that possesion. This is but the evil imagination of man (Gen. 6:5). All the earth is the Lord's and the fullness of it is still completely in His possession. If He needs anything, He does not need to tell us, nor will He humiliate Himself by asking us if He may take something which He has loaned to us (for whether it is for today or for a lifetime, all that we call our own is no more than something He has loaned to us for that short period of time which we call a lifetime). He has never given over a single iota of His rights or His possessions to men. Therefore it is not wrong for Him to dispose of what He owns as He pleases. Even if man were without sin, yet it would not be an injustice. For take the case of a man and his dog. What belongs to the dog belongs to the man. What the man gives to his dog can be taken from him, even though the dog has done nothing to precipitate that action. There is nothing morally wrong in removing that which belongs to oneself, however much the inferior creature may howl at the loss.

Suppose that a man could say that what he had was his own, that he had a right to his health, his strength, his possessions. God could still take them away and do that man no injustice. States and kingdoms regularly practice this principle, for do they not in a time of war, of danger to the entire citizenry, commandeer the entire populace in that war effort? Do they not take those things that are necessary for the general protection of all? And do they not do so without any excuse or apology? The citizen has done nothing to suffer this loss, yet he is not wronged when the loss is ordered by the state. In fact, it may justly be called a privilege to have something which may be taken for the common good. The Philippians were told, *"to you it is given to suffer for His sake,"* a gift that most would not wish for themselves. It was a special privilege to have something to give, even though it were suffering that they had to give. In time of war, thousands and thousands may give their lives for the public good — men do not count it unjust to ask it. If, then, according to the line of men this is not injustice, much less is it injustice in God (who is without line or rule) to act for the common good of all by repossessing those things which He has given us for our use for a time.

3. The Lord may multiply wounds and yet do it without wrong to the wounded. If he intends to heal the man by wounding him, then it is not wrong to do so. If He takes away something of lesser value in order to give that which is of far greater value, all will agree that He has not done any harm to the loser. In the case before us, there can be no doubt that God is wounding in order to heal, that God is taking away in order to give more to Job. It is true that a man may not without cause suddenly crack another man's head in order to heal him, or wrest from him something he owns with the intention of giving him something of more value, but God can do these things for no reasons more than His own will. Man has no right to wound another man or take away from another man — he did not give that man life and breath, and he does not with each breath maintain that life. But God the Creator and Sustainer of life has all rights, has every right, to do as He pleases with that which He created, *"who are you that answers against God?...does not the Potter have authority over the clay?"* (Rom. 9:20,21). God makes no idle promise when He says He will heal, for He has both power and wisdom to do so—yet it is not on this premise that He wounds whom He will — it is because they are His to do with as He pleases. He who can give anything and all things to a man does not need to apologize when He takes something from him in order to give him something of more value — yet God does not proceed on this premise when He takes away anything that He pleases to take away. He who owns all things need not give a reason when He takes it into His own hands again. If God has made it His eternal promise and purpose to make all things work together in such

a way as to benefit us at every turn (in spiritual matters only), then this is a special privilege and favor to us, one for which we should give thanks forevermore. It is not our duty. It is not His duty. It is free grace that He should do this further thing for those he loves.

AFFLICTIONS ARE NO ARGUMENT THAT GOD DOES NOT LOVE US

As the Lord has a multitude of mercies in His heart, so He may have a multitude of afflictions in His hand. Not only may a multitude of afflictions consist with a multitude of mercies, but the one may be necessary to the other. Those visible armies of sorrows and opposers may be surrounded by an invisible army of comforts and protections. If God by faith opens your eyes and allows you to see those myriads of angels, those innumerable applications of His power to turn the hearts of men wherever He desires, then rejoice and be glad that He has granted you this comfort. But if He gives you no insight into what He is doing, it does not mean that He is doing nothing to relieve you of your trials. By spiritual hindsight all can see that God has done such things for their good. Would any offer to give back all those benefits which he has received in the midst of complete ignorance of God's purpose? Would any agree to return all the comforts he has received in the midst of doubt? What? Is God always acting according to our inconstant and ill-advised minds? Would there be a quicker or a better way to prove to us that He did not love us?

"Who will not allow me to take my breath, but fills me with bitterness"—Job 9:18.
This implies the total lack of any intermission in Job's afflictions — they are continual, perpetual, unending and without intermission. No respite is given, not so much as a returning breath is allowed except it bring with it another reminder of the afflictions of God upon him.

Some interpret this of a bodily distemper or disease, that God had brought such a sickness upon him that even his breath was affected. But we may take it figuratively, that his sorrows left him breathless. Not only is there no period when his trouble will stop, there is no period or pause between his troubles. He speaks in that high strain of rhetoric which is called hyperbole. For in the strictness of the letter, it would be a complete destruction of a man not to allow him to take his breath — he would die. This is an expression of the continual nature of his sorrows, not the expiration of his days.

Again, not to allow a man to take his breath before he had done such a thing is a proverb for doing a thing speedily. God will not allow Job to take his breath because every second counts in this great work which he is doing with Job. Job finds the suffering long, and by comparison to the sufferings of most men, it is long. But God by intensifying Job's sufferings, by getting His work in Job done in the shortest possible time, is actually making the time of Job's suffering.shorter. And if he but knew what God was about Job would not ask for any respite between sufferings.

"He fills me with bitterness"—It is a word opened before in chapter 3, verse 10. In the Scriptures sweetness implies all comfort, so bitterness implies all trouble and sorrow. God complains about the services of His people, *"Your sacrifices are not sweet to Me"* (Jer. 6:20)—the original is, Your sacrifices are not acceptable to Me, not pleasing to Me. As sweet things are pleasant, so bitter things are unpleasant, *"no affliction for the present is joyous, but grievous"*(Heb. 12:11). Bitterness is put for the most extreme affliction. In the original here, it is, *"bitternesses,"* implying all kinds of afflictions. To be filled with bitternesses is to be afflicted with superfluity, an abundance which overflows the soul. Job's had his belly full of trouble, the gall and the wormwood of afflictions are eating and gnawing at his spirit.

The Lord sometimes mixes a bitter cup, but bitterness for the saints is a medicine which has no substitute. There are things which God does best with bitter experience in the life of one He loves. Not only does He mix a cup of bitters which will punish the wicked and make him to know how unwisely he has despised God, but He mixes a cup much like it for the godly, that they may not despise the One who loves them. In both cases, He may find it necessary to force the bitter cup through their lips and force the medicine down their throats. But the one is done out of love, the other out of wrath, therefore the results are different. When everlasting love is mingled into a bitter cup, the bitterness in the mouth becomes a sweetness in the stomach of the saint. Saints never drink pure wrath, just as the wicked can never drink pure love.

Job had now climbed down four steps, coming to the climax that we have here:

1. He has acknowledged that he was unable to answer the Lord;

2. He has professed that even if he could, he would not answer — but, rather, he would humble himself before Him.

3. If in mercy God should answer his petition, yet he would not be confident at all (in regard to himself) that God had heard him.

4. He acknowledged that God might go on to afflict him still more (for some read this text in the future tense — *"He will multiply my sounds and continue to afflict me without cause; He will fill me with bitterness"*). A godly man counts up his afflictions as well as his comforts to the praise and honor of God. The more God afflicts him, the more a saint humbles himself saying, Let Him do what seems good in His sight. But it does not follow that he will admit that he is worse than other men because God afflicts him so severely.

"If I speak of strength, lo, He is mighty! And if of judgment, who shall set me a time?"
—Job 9:19.

Job has not yet laid himself as low as he will. He now gives an additional proof that man cannot contend with God either in regard to strength, or in regard to justice.

"If I speak of strength, lo, He is mighty"—There are two ways by which a man proves strong against another man, (1) by the strength of his arm and his skill in using it; and, (2) by the equity of his cause, the goodness of his conscience. Job professes his inability to deal with God in either. There is great emphasis expressed in these words, that God is mighty!

There are five words in the Hebrew which express strength. The first speaks of strength in general. The second is that strength which is needed to endure labor. The third is a strength to be effective. The fourth is the strength to be vigorous. And the fifth is that which is in our text, the strength or might to be superior, the force needed to prevail. The Lord is more than merely strong. He is the strongest of all. All these strengths are in Him in such abundance that He overwhelms all the strong. Christ in the Gospel speaks of the devil as a strong man who keeps his house from being broken into, but, says He, when He who is stronger comes, then He spoils him and takes away his armor and his goods. When the Holy Spirit talks of God being mighty, however, there is the plain meaning that there are none who can force his way into God's province, nor take away anything at all from Him or His children. The word here is the same one used in 2 Sam. 22:18, *"He delivered me from my strong enemy and from those that hated me, for they were too strong for me."* They were prevailingly strong against me, yet my Help was so prevailing strong against them that He delivered me.

God is infinite and insuperable in strength. Anyone among men may have more malice and wickedness and presumption than God, but none may oppose Him — will a fly challenge the sun? Only the fool, only a man so wicked as to have his wits unhinged, would try to overcome, subdue, or even to hold at bay He who is almighty. And if He is able to overcome and overwhelm all who breathe, then who is so foolish as to resist His will? Only one who believes that God is either weak or that He has foolishly hamstrung Himself would dare to resist God's command. Not only does He have the strength, but He has the right and the authority to smite every man without cause or reason being given. A man may have strength to do those things for which they have no authority (as to oppress and to rob), but God has both strength and authority. He is sovereign, He has authority to do as much as He can and He has strength to do as much as He desires. His insuperable strength appears in three things, (1) He has strength to do whatever He desires, nothing is too hard for the Lord; (2) He has strength to refrain from doing a thing — for the Lord is able to do far more than He ever will do. He could scrap all the world and all that are in it, creating for Himself another world, an inconceivable (to us) universe full of obedient and wise creatures. But He does not take immediate vengeance upon us, visiting our sins upon us in fury; (3) He is so strong that He can do all His will, and only His will. To do a thing which we do not desire to do is a sign of weakness. God never is forced to do anything. He does only as much as He planned to do, only as much as will fulfill all His desire as it was from the beginning.

"And if of judgment, who shall set me a time?"—If I cannot by force and power do what I will, then perhaps I may do it by subtlety and wit? No! We cannot deal with God in the fields with the sword, nor can we deal with him at the bar, at the judgment seat. There are two words in the Hebrew which are used for judging, (1) Dan, the name of one of the sons of Jacob, he who was to judge his people (Gen. 49:16). That word in strictness signifies to doom or sentence in a cause; (2) the other word is that in the text, which means more especially the doing of what is right, or the righting of a man in any controversy. The Greek word takes in both meanings. Which judgment does Job mean? Judgment may be taken in three ways:

1. For the rule of judging, or the law by which we judge. It is said that Samuel, after he had anointed Saul, told the people how the kingdom should be. He even wrote it in a book so that judgments could be made (1 Sam. 10:25).

2. Judgment is put for an ability or a fitness to judge, to discern and weigh things, to scan a cause and to develop the uttermost truth from every circumstance. So judgment has to do with the ability of the one who is to judge.

3. Judgment is taken for the sentence which is given after the evidence has been developed, heard and judged. Judgment in this sense is the result of the former two judgments. For when the rules and laws have been applied, and then the ability of the judge has been applied, the judgment given shall be according to both these judgments.

"If of judgment"—that is, if I bring my cause to be tried by God's laws, and if I bring my cause to be tried by the only just and wise Judge, then I shall not be relieved nor shall I overcome. He will still be too much for me, even in judgment.

Some at this place take judgment to be only afflictions upon a person, not a judicial or forensic term. These are called the judgments of God, *"How unsearchable are His judgments"* (Rom. 11:33). His providential dealings with men are past finding out. In this sense Job would be saying that he could not face God with His providential acts and ask Him for an answer. Who is able to plead his cause before Him who does all these things?

"who shall set me a time?"—It is one word, but the sense is very large and various. It means to appoint, to constitute, to prescribe a time, a place, or a person, or all of these things. Some take it here as a setting of a time; others of the setting of a place. The people of God are to meet at certain places and times, therefore the word here is used to designate a congregation. It is used to depict any meeting or assembly (Ps. 48:4; Amos 3:3). In 2 Sam. 24:15, it is put for a set time. Again, the word is put for any covenant, pact, or mutual agreement. So the tabernacle is indifferently called, *"the tabernacle of the testimony,"* *"the tabernacle of the congregation."* It was there that God confirmed and settled His covenant and agreement with His people. It was there His people met to-

gether to have the articles of that covenant made good to them by His own appointment. There is an appointed time for man on earth. Likewise, there is a place where he ought to be at all times. He has set the times of us all, and He has bounded our habitations as well. This will be so always, even after we have gone to our eternal destiny.

For a clearer understanding of this, it may have an allusion to that course which is seen in courts of justice, where one may have a counsel appointed to plead for him if he so petitions the court. And when our judges appoint counsel, they set the time and place as to when and where the pleading shall be done. Thus Job may be saying, If I come to judgment, the time and the place of judgment, then who will plead for me. Will anyone stand up to plead for me against the Lord?

There is another understanding of the word, as having reference to the testimony or witness which is brought in. In this sense, no one would be so bold as to offer evidence for Job against God.

Taking in all these senses, if there are none who will give evidence for me, if there are none to plead for me, if there is none to assign counsel for me, if no one will appoint a time and a place for a hearing, then how can I contend with God? I may as well contend with Him in strength as in judgment.

"If I justify myself, my own mouth shall condemn me; though I am perfect, He shall prove me perverse"—Job 9:20.

If there is no witness, no counsel, no judge to help me, and if I then justify myself, then my own mouth shall condemn me. My tongue will cut out my own throat if I try to make myself more just than God. Well might a warning be given to men that whatever they may say could be used against them, for all men will be judged by God for every vile word, all the words they said which were not for the glory of God. Any plea which Job might make before God would merely display his sin. If I should put my cause into the hands of the best of men, or even in the hands of angels, they could not justify me. How much less could I justify myself?

There are three things which prove that a man would be condemned by his own mouth if he should try to plead against God:

1. Man is not sufficient for these things. Even the saintliest of men, the apostle Paul as an example, can say, *"not that we are sufficient of ourselves to think anything as of ourselves, but our sufficiency is of God"* (2. Cor. 3:5). Man at his best is weak, ignorant and unrighteous, then how could he plead his cause with God, who is infinite in wisdom, righteousness, strength and holiness? Even while a man frames a *"not guilty"* with his lips, the words will come out strongly, *"guilty!"*

2. He who justifies himself must appear in his own commendation. He will have to plead his own good works, boasting of his excellencies. What man can do so without condemning himself? Even the heathen could say by the corrupt light of nature that 'a man's praises are sullied by passing through his own lips. To sound our own praise is to sound our own shame.' To plead a man's excellencies before God is to bring them into the presence of God for comparison — there is no man who can stand such a comparison, for even the angels are not clean and pure in the presence of God. There are none spotless in that light!

3. A man's own testimony is not legal to prove his own cause. A man must not be both a witness and a party to a cause. He that justifies himself condemns himself because his very self-justification is an accusation of himself. It we are to take a man's witness of himself, then who will ever be condemned? When the Pharisees said to Christ, *"You bear record of Yourself, Your record is not true."* they spoke upon a legal ground or maxim. Christ answered them, *"Though I bear record of Myself, My record is true...My judgment is true, for I am not alone, but I and the Father who sent Me"* (John 8:14,16). His own witness would have been insufficient, but together with the witness of the Father, it was enough to prove that it was true.

"my own mouth shall condemn me"—Of what? Surely, it would convict him of foolishness. One may justify himself before men, as did Paul (2 Cor. 12:11), but even then it must be said, *"I have become a fool in glorying."* Though he was forced by them to take up his own defense, and though it was his duty to throw off their allegations, yet he felt himself to be a fool for speaking his own glory. Two questions arise here, (1) Why may not Job justify himself; (2) Why does Job say here that he would not justify himself?

1. The Lord had justified Job to Satan, saying that he was a perfect and upright man. Yet in the next expression, Job says that he would be perverse if he would say that he was perfect. Solomon resolves this question for us, *"Let another man praise you, and not your mouth; a stranger, and not your lips"* (Prov. 27:2). Man must not speak the evil he knows of others, unless called upon to do so by the proper authority. Neither must he speak the good that he knows of himself. To speak good of ourselves with our own mouths is much like doing good by other men's hands. We must not act things praiseworthy by proxy, for to claim glory for such deeds would be gross hypocrisy. Likewise, we cannot claim praise by our own mouths without condemning ourselves. It is *"not he who commends himself that is approved, but he whom the Lord commends"* (2 Cor. 10:18).

2. In other places Job justifies himself, as in chapter 29 and 30, but here he will not attempt to justify himself. There he describes himself as a just man, a holy man, a righteous man, a merciful man, etc. Why, them, is he so modest here? It is the difference between men and God. Job will not plead any personal perfection in the sight of God. But in comparison to men, he will state what he has done in order to deny their false charges against him. To them he can say, 'You accuse me of hypocrisy, you censure me deeply, but I can justify myself and plead innocence before you. It is true that I dare not say a word to justify myself before God, for in His light I cannot be but ashamed. But as for you, my friends, I will justify myself in your sight, I am not the man that you say that I am.'

To understand Job, a close attention to the argument is absolutely essential. He stands upon his integrity with his friends, for he need not take a back seat when it came to them. But he cannot stand upon his integrity with God, he must humble himself and see himself as vile and worthless to God, he must see and bewail his sinfulness. The apostle Paul is another instance of a godly man who found himself saying soulfully, *"O wretched man that I am! Who shall deliver me from this body of sin and of death?...I thank God, through the Lord Jesus Christ"* (Rom. 7:24). He admits that he knows *"nothing by myself,"* yet he justified himself against his false accusers among the Jews. A man may be conscious of his own natural corruption, yet he may be confident of his own practical integrity. In the case of Job, God Himself had testified to his integrity (2:3).

"though I am perfect, He shall prove me perverse"—These words in strictness of sense refer to the inward purpose of his heart, the bend of his mind (as the former did to the outward way of his life). There could be no meditated obliquity in his heart, no intention of going astray, no secret hypocrisy or falseness there, yet God would easily prove that he was perverse. And the very saying, that I am perfect, could prove me perverse.

The word which is translated *"perverse"* is one which means to wander, especially the wandering of the mind when it is supposed to be fixed upon a single object, or the wandering of the feet when it has a very narrow path to follow in order to maintain life. What would ever prove Job to be such a person? Only God could prove it, but He could easily prove that Job was perverse, that any one of us is perverse. It is that famous Gospel teaching which first appeared in the Old Testament. *"No one can be justified before God by the works of the law."* It is as noble a proof of free justification in the Old Testament as any there is in the New. The saints have been acquainted with this truth from the beginning, that man is nothing in himself, and that free grace does it all. The doctrine of free grace is not a new doctrine, but the doctrine of free will is, *"Who can say, I have made my heart clean, I am pure from my sin?"* (Prov. 20:9). For he who justifies himself before God must be prepared to say such a thing. Everyone who thinks he can justify himself is forced to express himself in legal terms. Yet all have sinned and come short of fulfilling the law of God. Therefore, it is too hard for men, this making of their own hearts clean and pure. Yea, even the angels in Heaven cannot make one heart clean. Only Jesus Christ is able to remove all the filthiness of man, the pollution of our spirits, and that only because He is both God and man, both Creator and servant to the law of God. Anyone who knows himself and knows the word of God will never say, I am clean, let alone, I have made my heart clean.

Secondly, it is important that God had testified to Job's excellent spirit. He, of the few who have ever lived, could produce testimonial letters subscribed by the hand of Heaven, that he was a just and perfect man, one that feared God and hated evil. Yet this man will not speak well of himself to God. It is usual in good men that those who have the most real worth and holiness in them are the least in their own eyes. Think of that Man who was the man among men, the Lord Jesus, for it is said of Him that He was *"meek and lowly."* Compare for a moment in your minds what He could have said, with what He did say while on earth.

"Though I were perfect, yet I would not know my soul. I would despise my life"—Job 9:21.

There is a difference of opinion among interpreters as to which part of the chapter this verse addresses — whether to that which went just before or to that which immediately follows. Considering it as belonging to those verses which went before, observe the gradation: He has said before, If I plead with God and justify myself, I shall be condemned and proved perverse. But if my case were pleaded at its very best, that even if the Lord were to accept my self-justification, yet I could take no joy in this. If the Lord should condescend to know me under that notion, yet I would not adventure to know my own soul under the notion of perfection.

Why not? Why would he not know his own soul? There are two senses given, (1) If I were to plead and debate with God and come off perfect in my own judgment, certainly then I would have to say that I did not know my own soul. This sense would fall in well with the last verse, acknowledging that ignorance of ourselves is the cause of proud and high thoughts of ourselves. Any man that truly knows himself must surely know that he is imperfect. It is the greatest perfection in this life to know our own imperfections. It is proverbial that he who knows not himself knows not God, for the knowledge of God will bring us a comparative knowledge of ourselves. If a man walks in the light of God's word, he will see evils in himself that he never dreamed existed, that he would not have believed if he had not seen them for himself by the eye of faith. If a man sees no evil spots in himself, it is evidence enough that he is walking in darkness, having not the light of God in his life.

Again, *"though I were perfect,"* though someone told me that I was perfect. I would not know my own soul — that is, I would not take notice of myself as perfect, I would be a stranger to myself under such a title as that. Anyone who entertains notions of perfection is an enemy to his own soul, therefore I would take great pains to shake such a notion out of my mind as part of the sin and corruption of my evil imagination.

So then, *"I would not know my soul"* imports elected knowledge, not affected ignorance. Job was no stranger to his own soul, he had studied himself and was well versed in his own imperfections. There is a double knowledge which we may have of ourselves (1) the knowledge of our sinful self, our sins and our failings (2) the knowledge of our renewed self, our virtues and our graces.

It is sinful and corrupt ignorance when we do not know how frail we are, how full of sinful lusts we are, how perverse we are in all matters which concern God. Likewise, the saint must know his virtues and graces, what the work of the Spirit has done within him, what the new nature means to him. It is the state of a beast not to reflect upon our own estate. The new creature is light, and he carries within the light to discover itself. And it is not intuition, nor logical reasoning, but scriptural revelation that makes us know what we are, what we can be, and what we shall be. Those who profess to be Christians and yet are found preening themselves on what they judge to be perfections only place a question mark beside their profession. One may not entertain pride even in one's own mind, even though not a word or an expression is allowed to convey it to others.

A gracious heart rejoices in nothing but in the righteousness of Christ alone. He will refuse to know his own soul in his own perfections. A godly man would have God know him at his very worst, but he will not know himself at the very best. He would not have a single sin hidden from God, but he will pray for him to search him and try him in order to find the least imperfection in his life. Like the apostle, he will *"count all things but loss for the excellency of the knowledge of Christ Jesus,"* and he will say with Job here, *"not having my own righteousness, which is of the law"* (Phil. 3:8,9). Paul the apostle refused to know Paul the Pharisee. Legal righteousness was no gain to him, but loss, a total loss when he found Christ. That which he had counted to be perfection before now became as dung to him when he came to see with the eyes of faith that righteousness which was in Christ Jesus. As a leader among the Pharisees, he had his ledger full of 'good deeds' and he had coined a mint of legal righteousnesses. But when he met Christ, he said that they were all counterfeit riches, he threw them into the spiritual garbage where they belonged.

"Though I were perfect, yet I would not know my soul. I would despise my life"—taking it as belonging to the following verses, it then would be a supposition in order to set up the following words. This, then has met with different interpretations:

1. My heart is upright and I have always prized and valued my own integrity so much that in comparision to these things I have not prized my own life or soul at all (some would have Job to be saying). It is a comparison between his natural life and his spiritual life. He would not value the first if it must be compared to the second. In the same sense that Levi is said not to have known his father and mother, so here. That is, Levi in comparison to his duties to God, would not allow his father and mother to take precedence over them. These then conceive Job to be saying that he would allow nothing to stand between him and obedience to God. It would be akin to what the apostle Paul said, *"none of these things move me, neither do I count my life dear to myself, so that I might finish my course with joy and the ministry which I received from the Lord Jesus Christ, to testify fully the gospel of the grace of God"* (Acts 20:24).

2. Then there are those who say Job is so pressed and overwhelmed with his afflictions that he cannot feel, he scarcely knows whether he is alive or dead. It is as if he were saying, 'I do not know where I am, my soul does not acts its offices, it is benumbed; there is no vigor or liveliness in my spirit — I despise such a life as this is, for who would want to live a life which is no more than a continued earth?'

There is truth in this. For as extreme and excessive joys carry a man so far beyond himself that he hardly knows whether he is alive or not, so some in the excesses of sorrow and anguish have come to where they hardly know if they are alive or not.

3. Then one expounds the words as an admiration, 'Do you think that I am not acquainted with myself? Am I a stranger at home? Have I so despised my life that I take no notice of it, that I do not care how things go with me? It is a countercharge to the friends, for they had charged Job again and again with things that he had denied.Therefore, they are putting themselves into the position of knowing Job better than he knew himself.

4. Others understand it in this way, and this appears the fairest and most suitable of the interpretations, that Job is saying, 'I am not conscious of any evil in my soul. I know of no secret guilt or corruption hidden there.' In this case, science is being put for conscience. I know not is actually, I am not aware of any evil that my soul delights in, either

against God or man, yet such evils are upon me that I despise my life. Solomon says that *"the spirit of a man will bear his infirmity,"* then what a load of infirmity presses that man whose life is a burden to him! Troubles of conscience do often make the most peaceable estate of this life to be troublesome. Troubles in the outward estate alone may make those who have peace in their consciences weary of this life for a time.

These words are a transition to the second part of his answer to Bildad's charges. Having before given glory to God by acknowledging His justice, wisdom, power and sovereignty in all His actings, he passes to an apology for himself, or a defense of his own integrity against the insults, suspicions and accusations of his friends. He has tried to save the person of God from the least touch of an uncomely thought, let alone any rude and proud contentions with Him. But he cannot in good conscience allow them to plaster their hypocrite label upon him either, though he is perfectly willing to humbly lower himself to the lowest rung of God's children. He is proceeding to the argument, which is in this form.

The proof of the minor proposition or assumption is contained in the three following verses. The discussion and opening of these will give both light and strength to his argument.

"It is all the same, therefore I say, He destroys the perfect and the wicked"—Job 9:11.

One learned interpreter was exceedingly troubled when he read these words, conceiving them to be impious and blasphemous because he thought Job had mingled the state of the wicked and of the righteous into one. But it can easily be shown that Job did no such thing, not in any way denying God's distinctive and wise handling of the wicked and the righteous.

"It is all the same, therefore I say"—You have spoken to me many things about the power, the greatness, the justice and the wisdom of God, and I agree with you – there is no difference on these points, for I too have always thought highly of God and I try to think humbly of myself, But there is one thing on which I must disagree. It is here that Job's thinking diverges widely from the thoughts of his friends. On this point, there cannot be any glossing over of their differences. Therefore, he must say it – it is a vehement statement, a free and bold speech in which he uncovers his mind on a point that he has well considered and long held – it is the truth, it must be said, and it cannot be given over simply because of wild charges and glowering faces.

The truth is ever the same. It does not vary from person to person, nor from age to age. Because the truth is ever the same, therefore our statement of the truth should ever be the same – allowing for only one change, the statement of additional truth that we have learned since last stating it.. This truth that Job is stating next is the hinge of this dispute. Therefore he has good reason to be resolute in clearly stating it. It is no bargain to buy a little truth at the expense of much peace. There are no terms which are honorable enough to cause us to give up even a shred of the truth. We ought to contend earnestly for the faith that was once delivered to the saints.

Job has a principle here, and he is going to base his counterattack on this one principle. From this we can learn that one truth rightly held will refute and repel all objections that can be brought against it. A whole army of errors will be scattered by one truth well-held and well-managed. This is Job's one-truth defense, or, as it may be, his one-truth offense:

"He destroys the perfect and the wicked"—It is a hard teaching, but a good one. God is to be honored even if He is destroying, and He must have His honor though it is the perfect that He is destroying. The word we translated *"destroy"* is one that means an utter blasting, a total consumption, of a thing. It is intended to show that the outward dispensations of God may be severe and terrible to the perfect, as well as to the wicked. He does not say that the Lord afflicts the perfect and destroys the wicked, or that He chastens the perfect and consumes the wicked – no, but he says that the Lord destroys, consumes both the wicked and the perfect.

"the perfect"—In chapter one, there has been a full description of what is meant by this

word. The perfect man is the man in the highest form of holiness, a man full of spiritual knowledge, faith and good works, one who belongs among the first three in God's grace. But though he be the first of the first three, yet he shall have no security against God's destroying dispensations.

"and the wicked"—That is, the unsettled, unquiet, tumultuous man. He has no anchor, no resting place, because he has refused to know Christ. Wicked men are ever unquiet, they are as the restless sea, casting up mire and dirt. They trouble and torment others, but the ones they trouble and torment the most are themselves.

So Job categorically denies Bildad's assertion that *"God will not cast away a righteous man."* Though that statement may have a true sense, yet Bildad gave it in the false sense as regards to Job, for it is plainly his contention that God will not cast a godly man away in this life, that He will not totally destroy him in the things of this life. Job contradicts this sense, stating that not only may a godly man be cast away in this life, but he may even be destroyed in the same way the wicked man is destroyed. It would appear that Bildad saw further than Eliphaz, who had the belief that a man may not be afflicted except for his wickedness, seeing that God could afflict a man to exercise his graces. But he was very confident that God never allowed a righteous man to be overwhelmed with affliction. It was his belief that after some short, though perhaps sharp, assaults God would restore the godly man to health and happiness. Bildad would never have admitted, however, that a godly man might be destroyed. Job continually holds the contrary principle, that a godly man may be so afflicted as to be destroyed, that he may be utterly and irreversibly stripped of all his worldly comforts so long as he might live.

A godly man has a spiritual estate that is so strong, so ordered and so connected to the life of God that he cannot lose it. Grace is above the hazards that are spiritually destructive. But the tempral estate of a righteous man may be lost, both totally and finally. It does not matter who is the master of riches, honor, comforts, health, etc., they are vain things and they may vanish overnight. The righteous man will be a better steward of these things, and if he is wise will know that he has them only for a short time, however long that may be in his life-span. Let any man observe any part of man's history, he will find God destroying both the wicked and the godly. The prophets are very full in describing God's dealings, when He not only threatened pestilence, destruction, humiliation, etc. to the heathen, to His chosen people in Israel, but also to His Jeremiah's, so far as temporal life was concerned, *"I will cut off from you the righteous and the wicked."* Both the good figs and bad figs went into captivity to Babylon (Jeremiah 24:1-3).

However, though they fall under the same destruction, yet their case under that destruction is as different as the persons are. Faith and holy reason distinguish where sense cannot. Judgments upon wicked men for the satisfaction of God's justice. They who are heirs of eternal death receive part of their inheritance in this life. All their punishments are but down-payments. The foretastes and beginnings of further sorrows often touch the wicked man. But the judgments upon the saints are for the purpose of correcting them, for purging them and making them more fruitful. These hopes are not destroyed alongside their bodies or estates. Their afflictions may be healed, they may even heal when they kill. Though God destroys both the one and the other, we must not wrap up God's dispensations to the godly and to the wicked in the same understanding. His act is the same toward both, but His meaning is not the same. See the seventeenth verse of chapter five for further discussion of the difference between the afflictions of the righteous and the wicked.

"If the whip kills suddenly, He will mock at the calamity of the innocent"—Job 9:23.

Job goes on to confirm his statement by a further argument. For if any should deny that God destroys both the righteous and the wicked, he proves that such a denial is foolish, for God laughs or mocks at the innocent in their trials as He does at the wicked. These words not only confirm, but aggravate what he said before.

If the former words gave offense to some minds, who conceived them to be inconsistent with grace and holiness, more will be offended by these words. In the letter the language is indeed strange, *"The Lord mocks at the calamity of the innocent!"* One learned writer has concluded these words, along with those in chapter 7, *"so that my soul chooses strangling,"* to be the most difficult words that Job speaks. He believes that Job has these two in mind when he says, *"Once I have spoken, but I will not answer; yea, twice, but I will go no further"* (42:5) It is a witty theory, but too heavy for the circumstances. Job needs no apology for these words.

"If the whip kills suddenly"—The verb signifies to encompass or to encircle a thing, to twine around it. So it alludes to the way a scourge looks when it goes around a man's body. The whip or scourge in Scripture is put for any affliction, plague, famine, etc. (see Isa. 10:26). What kind of whip does Job have in mind? The next words expound it, for it is not a whip of cords or wires, but of swords and spears. The Jews had a descriptive scourge, *"an overflowing scourge,"* that is, a common, spreading sweeping judgment which like an overflowing river encompasses and circles about one, taking in all that it encircles (Isa. 28:15).

Not every whip kills, and many that do kill do not do it suddenly. There is usually the sound before we feel the bite of the whip, and some scourges are heard a long way off, before they ever smite. This whip is one that kills suddenly. Some take the suddenness of this whip for a mitigation of the judgment, others for the heightening of it. If it is a mitigation, it is because the whip does its work quickly and thus the suffering is not for long. In Lamentations 4:6, we see them complaining that their afflictions were not as quick to do their work as was the smiting of Sodom and Gomorrah. So a sudden scourge may in a sense be a kind of mercy. It is better to die quickly than to die always.

But here the scourge slaying suddenly is a judgment which comes unexpectedly. Those who sleep secure in their sins seldom dream of scourges. But God can and often does send death and affliction in a moment. When they say, *"Peace and safety! Then sudden destruction comes upon them"*(1 Thess. 5:3).

"He will mock at the calamity of the innocent"—The Hebrew word may spring either from a root which signifies to tempt and try, or from another root which means to melt and dissolve. Therefore, one translates, *"He scorns at the melting away of the innocent."* Afflictions are hot and they melt us and all that we have — they dissolve our comforts, the stability of our lives often melts and runs out when afflictions come in.

Taking it as a mocking at the trial of the innocent, how can God laugh at such a trial? The word carries with it the idea of derision and scorn, *"He who sits in the heavens shall laugh, the Lord shall laugh at them"* (Ps. 2:4). But how can we fit this into the business at hand? Will the Lord scorn and deride the innocent when he is being probed and tried? The Vulgate seems to have been so pressed to make out the sense that the translator of it rendered it negatively, *"If the whip kills suddenly, he will not laugh at the trial of the innocent."* Others render it as an interrogation, *"If the whip kill suddenly, will He laugh at the trial of the innocent?"* No, they conclude, He will not do such a thing as deride the innocent when they are being tried. But most of the learned Hebraists find it impossible to depart from the affirmative, *"He will laugh at the trial of the innocent."*

Some then would dispute as to who it is who will laugh. These think that this scorning and deriding of the innocent is too low and dishonorable to be ascribed to God, so they carry it down low enough to ascribe it to the devil. That is a truth, but it is not necessarily the truth intended here. Others make the antecedent to "he" to be a wicked man. It is again true that the ungodly scoff and scorn and deride the godly when they seemingly get nothing for their pains but the whip. But it need not be the truth of this text.

We need not ease the text by such wrestling, there is no difficulty which needs that kind of relief. Let the relative be God Himself and see how we can make out the sense in a way that gives Him honor and glory:

1. God does not laugh or deride properly at the afflictions of His people. Instead, He is tender, gracious and merciful to His people at all times, and most tender to them when they are in the hottest afflictions. Therefore, as laughing or mocking implies hardheartedness or unnatural harshness of spirit, it cannot be said that the Lord laughs at His afflicted saints in that way. What, then, does He laugh at? First, it must be noted that Job's point is this, that the Lord carries Himself in an evenhanded way toward both the good and the evil, dealing out equal destruction to both. Now there can be no doubt that the Lord derides the wicked, *"I will laugh at their destruction and mock when their fear comes"* (Prov. 1:28). There is of course no laughter in the real sense of the word in God. He expresses Himself as a man to convey a truth to us. In His providential dealings, He may dispense to men a storm of affliction which affects all in a city or a nation. When either the wicked or the relatively innocent ones cry to Him to lift the afflictions, He does not answer them, and it may well seem to those afflicted that He laughs and mocks them by instead adding more and more scourges and storms of troubles. See how He dealt with His chosen spokeman, the one by whom He said He would tear down Judah, Jeremiah. When the famine came, when all suffered severely, where was Jeremiah? Was he hidden, away by the brook Cherith being fed by the ravens? No! He was down at the bottom of a dank and dangerously unhealthy well, being fed the same bread rations as those above,but considerably more uncomfortable than the most of them. He may well have cried with the Psalmist, *"In the day of my trouble I sought the Lord; my sore ran in the night and never stopped; my soul refused to be comforted"*—it must have seemed to Jeremiah that God was mocking at his trials. He not only lay there in discomfort, but in much danger of being killed by the king's nobles – of all people in the city, those most wicked and most deserving of these destructive afflictions, Jeremiah was in most danger of being suddenly killed! When the Lord did not deliver him, it may well be said that in a sense He despised him and laughed at his calamity. The more God laid on him, the more He slighted him.

Again, the Lord may be said to laugh at the trial of the innocent in regard to the effects and outcome of that trial. If it is the godly who is on trial, then those words of James are certainly appropriate, *"exult when you fall into different kinds of trials, knowing that the trying of your faith works patience...so that you may be perfect and entire, lacking nothing"* (James 1:2-4). If we are to laugh, to exult, then well may God laugh when He knows full well all the spiritual benefits that will accrue to us as the result of our trials. Then He would be said to mock, or to scorn, or to deride, in the sense that these are insignificant and unimportant things, things which offer no real obstacle to the success He is achieving. As the warhorse mocks at spears, so the Lord God mocks at obstacles which threaten to turn the trial of the saints into a disaster. And well should He laugh, knowing what result He is achieving, *"that the trial of our faith, being much more precious than of gold that perishes, shall be found unto praise and honor and glory at the appearing of Jesus Christ"* (1 Pet. 1:6,7).

Then, see this, that while we may think the Lord is mocking at us in our trials, He is in fact laughing at our trials, It is not the innocent He mocks, but He mocks at the calamity! For those who have weak spiritual stomachs, consider that *"It pleased the Lord to bruise"* the Lord Jesus Christ. The Father was delighted to bruise His Son because that was the very thing they had agreed upon, that He would travail in pain, being wounded for the transgressions of His chosen ones, being bruised for their iniquities, so that He might receive the fruit of the travail of His souls and be fully satisfied when He saw His seed healed and transformed into the image of God. God was no more the cruel tyrant for having been pleased in crushing the innocent Savior than He is in this text, laughing at the trial of the innocent.

There are two more interpretations given for these words, (1) He laughs at the fears and sad forecasts of His people, who not being able to look through second causes to see the end of the things they are suffering are apt to conclude that all is lost, etc. But God, who knows the end from the beginning, looks through all these black clouds and stormy winds and see exactly what He planned to see at each period of time that the trial proceeds. (2) God laughs at laughter and derides the joy of wicked men as they watch his innocent ones being tried. They say in their hearts that they are happy not to have such a whipping come upon them; or, it may be, that now their day of triumph has come. But God laughs when He hears such foolish talk, thinking how these wretches have deceived themselves.

So Job concludes that there is a destruction of both the wicked and the perfect, and a mocking which appears at the trial of the innocent — something which was directly contrary to the conclusions of his friends. Now he shows them something else which they will not like to believe.

"The earth is given into the hand of the wicked. He covers the faces of its judges. If it is not He, then who is it?"—Job 9:24.

The earth may be taken strictly for the element of earth, as it is opposed to fire, water and air. But here it is put for all earthly things (as in Ps. 115:6). Or, it could be that earth here takes in all the inhabitants of the earth, for the rulers of the earth are of the earthly sort. God has given the earth over into the hands of the earthly sons of men *"the whole world lies in wickedness."* There can be a gift by providence, or a gift by promise. Here it is that common providential gift by which God disposes of all things to men. Everything a man has is a gift from God. Wicked Jeroboam received his kingdom as a gift from God, as did Jehu and Hazael. The gift of promises is a special gift for believers only, *"He that spared not His own Son, but gave Him to die for us, will He not with Him also freely give us all things?"* (Rom. 8:32). Even worldly things are included in that promise, as He sees fit to deal them out to us, *"all is yours, for you are Christ's."* Believers enjoy earthly things by a heavenly title. In this sense the earth is not given to the wicked.

In every way that the wicked come into control of earthly things, it is a gift of God — whether it is by inheritance, by violence, by deceit, or by whatever means, it is a gift of God.

"of the wicked"'—there is some question as to who these wicked ones may be. Some expound the text as if it were to the wicked one, the prince of the power of the air, he who rules this world so thoroughly that he even presumed to give it to Christ. But the text is plainly to all wicked men those who are taken captive at the will of Satan. The argument of Job will be served only if it is kept in mind, that he has set out to prove that in affliction there is no difference between the wicked and the perfect. He is proving to his friends that there can be no judgment made as to a man's innocence or guilt from observing the destructive and ruinous afflictions which are visited upon him. Who can doubt that the providential dealings of God, giving the opulence of the earth to the worst sort, giving poverty and all the scourging afflictions of the earth to the best sort, cannot be read without reference to the teachings of God. One would have to conclude that there was no moral force at work, no certain punishment for those who are wicked, if one were to take all his impressions from observing the dispensations of this world. Those who have most of earth in their hands have nothing of Heaven in their hearts. Yet, by their standards, they have the best of it, by far. They govern, even enslave, the innocent. They, as Job points out later, often have little in their lives to wrinkle their brows — but at the worst, in their worst afflictions, they excuse themselves by observing that those who cry most to God seem to suffer the same kind and sometimes a greater degree of discomfort.

The most high and most wise God has all things in His hands to dispose, and He does it with infinite wisdom. He gives the good things of this earth into the hands of the wicked. He gives the good things of the new earth and the everlasting life into the hands of the godly. Let them have their dissatisfying earth, we shall have a most satisfying life hereafter. Will you trade your pardon for sin with a wicked man for his gold? If you but knew the price that the wicked will pay for their portion of the earth, then you would not want to trade with him. What they own is as much theirs as a thing can be on this earth. They have it as a gift of God. But how they use what they own shall be the cause of much pain and gnashing of teeth.

"He covers the faces of its judges"—Again some would have the antecedent to he to be a wicked man, but again it appears that God is the one who covers the faces of its judges. There is of course a common practice among the wicked of covering the faces of the judges who sit in judgment upon their causes. They do this by bribes, by threatenings and fear, by shaming or disgracing them, and sometimes by putting them to death.

God, of course, often opens the eyes of judges and uncovers their faces so that they may discern between an evil cause and a good cause. But He also at His will covers the faces of judges so that they cannot discern between an evil cause and a good cause. He also has various ways of covering the faces of judges, (1) by hardening the heart and blinding the eye of the judge, removing His light far enough away that they cannot see clearly (Ps. 82:5); (2) by giving the judge into the hands of those who bribe, or threaten; (3) by removing the judge from the case, etc.

"covers the faces"—It may be their faces are covered with ignorance or blindness; by inhumanity and cruelty; or, by making them partial to one party of the suit. If the judge's face is covered, they will not even look upon the case of a poor man. Many judges, being bribed, weigh in on the side of one party so heavily that the scales of justice tip crazily. Some are queasy in applying such gross disabling to those who must judge between the guilty and the innocent. It is an old and a wide argument. It always resolves itself in the same shape, that *"The Lord of glory"* shall do right. He is pure from all sin, but He may visit impurity upon the impure. He is just in giving men over to unjust men.

"If it is not He, then who is it?"—For those who overlay God's righteousness with their own, not admitting that He can do anything but what they allow to be right, here is the question: If it is not the Lord who does this, then who is it? There is a threefold understanding of these words:

1. Some again make the antecedent to be the wicked. They think to acquit God, thinking that it would be blasphemy to attribute to Him the covering of the judges' faces. As is usual in such cases, what they say is true up to the point of their own understanding — It would be blasphemous to ascribe to God a sinful action, but we need not use our carefulness in this area for a subterfuge. We may lay more of an aspersion upon His justice and His holiness, not to mention His wisdom and His righteousness, by insisting that He cannot do this or that without committing sin. God can and does leave men to their own evil imaginations without any thought or touch of evil in Himself. For those who stick at this verse, there is a verse which will put the matter quite out of their reach, one which they cannot wrest without a flat denial of the purity of the Scriptures: *"For God has put into their hearts to fulfill His will, and to agree, and to give their kingdoms to the beast until the words of God shall be fulfilled"* (Rev. 17:17).

2. Others interpret this question as a challenge, *"It is so, if it is not, then where and who is he?"* Who and where is the man that will argue or implead that I have falsely stated the case? Who will convict me of error in this teaching which I have delivered? If anyone thinks that these things are not so, then let him appear and charge me with error. Then let him tell me who it is that causes these things to be done.

3. But, rather, it should be taken in the sense before given. If it is not the Lord who does this, then show me who it is. There is a grace and conciseness in the Hebrew, which says only this much, *"If not, where He?"* The sense is as given above. The words are an exclusion of any other power, ordering and disposing the things of the world. Isaac used these words when he was disappointed in his intention to give the blessing to Esau, trembling, he said, *"Who, Where is he?"* (Gen. 27:33). He was confused by the deceit of Jacob and his mother. Job here is saying much the same, he is confused if there is any other who disposes things than God. What could cause greater confusion than this, to take away Him who orders and disposes all things, and to put in His place a question mark? Instead,

understand that it is God who orders even the greatest confusions in the world. There is an instance in this verse, for what could cause greater confusion than to give the world into the hands of the wicked? By this we see that even those things which seem to have no order are ordered by Him who orders all things, *"A man's heart plans his way, but the Lord directs his steps"* -even the wicked man's heart cannot carry out his plans except the Lord's plan calls for him to do those things—*"The ordering of the heart in man and the answer of the tongue is from the Lord;" "The lot is cast into the lap, but the whole ordering of it is from the Lord;" "There are many purposes in a man's heart, but the counsel of the Lord shall stand"* (Proverbs 16:9; 1:33; 19:21).

The confusions in the world argue the power of God. For if it is not He who keeps the world from being destroyed by the wicked, who is it? And if it is not He who keeps His saints from being consumed, who is it? Will not the wicked go as far as he can go? Will he not do all he can do to make everything in the world subservient to him? Yet he cannot do the things that he would. Not even saintly Paul could do that, when it was good that he wanted to do (Romans 7). So it must be concluded that the mysteries of God's providence are not all known to us, His ways are past finding out until He reveals them to us in another world. A man cannot do good except God enable him to do it. A man likewise cannot do evil except God supply the power and the permission for him to do it. Our book of Job is the purest proof of God's overruling hand in evil-happenings. For did not God order and put into operation the malicious mind of Satan? If He did not do it, then who did? Did not Satan go as far as God permitted him? Did he go any further? But did he not complain that he was not allowed to go far enough to make Job curse? Then did he not get permission to go as far as God permitted again? *"Behold, he is in your hand, but save his life!"* Was not God ordering the steps of Satan? And in the case of Job, was it Satan or God that ordered these normally unbearable afflictions? Was it not God who brought the name of Job into view, setting him up as His champion for the Devil to shoot at? If weak, sickly, depressed, crushed, sore-ridden Job was able to tell who it was that ordered these afflictions upon him, then how can there be any doubt in the minds of those who can read the entire story from beginning to end? Can you find one place where Job blames Satan for his troubles? Do you not find innumerable places where Job acknowledges that it is God who is afflicting him?

It is an unspeakable comfort to know that He whom we love is the One who holds all things in His hand, dealing out wisely and justly both good and evil so that all things will work together for good to those that are called the called-out ones.

"Now my days are swifter than a runner, They flee away, they see no good"—Job 9:25.

Job seeks here to confirm what he has said, that the wicked are exalted oftentimes, that the innocent are afflicted sorely oftentimes. He uses his own experience as proof of this.

Job uses this similitude to show how uncertain his prosperity was, how quickly it blew away. In this and the next verse, he inquires into three of the four elements, the earth, the air, the water — a runner on earth, a ship on the water, an eagle in the air, all to witness what he says is true.

"Now my days"—that is, my prosperous days, *"are swifter than a runner"*—that is, lighter than a runner, for light things are quick and swift (what is faster than the speed of light in itself?). Time flies, days fly swifter than the fastest runner on earth. Many live as if they could not get rid of their time, as if time were on their hands and they know not how to spend it. Yet when it is too late to redeem that time, it will be seen that those long days flew swiftly away, or, as in our text, ran away like a fugitive from hard labor. You may have labored hard to get rid of the days, but the days also labored hard to get away from you and your wasting of them. There are many ways in which swiftly passing days are like a runner or messenger, (1) The messenger runs as fast as he can run; (2) he paces himself so as to get the utmost out of his strength; (3) he rests only long enough to refuel himself with food and to recharge his energy with sleep; (4) he keeps his mind on his

business as if his life depended on it; (5) he allows no one to hold him back from proceeding to do what he came to do. Job complains that his days were like that, (1) they ran away as fast as they could go; (2) they would allow no one to hold them back from departing.

The best things in the world are movable, they are passing away, *"And the world passes away"* (1 John 2:17). All created things perish with the using. If we are to enjoy them, if we are to improve them and cause them to give glory to God, then we must hasten to do so — for they will flee away from us so swiftly that we will wonder how they could go so fast.

"they see no good"—Not to see good is not to have the least experience of good. For the eye takes in its objects and judges them sooner than any other sense. The eye is not long about its business. Job is saying that the good things of this life are so transient that he can barely see them before they are gone, let alone feel them and taste them. The runner cannot stop and study anything, he gets only a glimpse of things as he goes by on his business. Besides, to see good is to enjoy good. Job is saying that he saw no good in his days. Little good can be seen in vanishing days, vain days, days that will not wait for one to enjoy them. There is so much inconceivable happiness in Heaven because all the good in Heaven will be fixed — we shall have all eternity to study and to enjoy them, for though time flies away, eternity stands still for us. Eternity is an ever-fixed Now.

"They have passed away like the swift ships, like the eagle who swoops on the prey"—Job 9:26.

This passing away is like a thing that swiftly glides by one. When a ship is far away, it appears to move slowly, but when it glides by a point close to us, it is gone before we know it. A ship is like our days in that it is never quiet. These days may be called faster, in that a ship never stops, never has to refuel (the ships were sailing in the wind in Job's day) and never has to replenish its energy. Not only does Job compare his days to a ship, but to a swift ship — a word that indicates a ship that moves in a swift river, having both the wind and the swift current of the river to carry it away quickly. Others derive it from another word which means desire — *"my days have passed away like ships of desire"* — those ships which are laden with riches and which carry all our fortunes in them, which are driven as fast as they will go toward the port where we expect to enjoy them. The Chaldee Paraphrase derives it from a word which signifies a stalk, one bringing forth the first ripe fruit of any kind. So then it would be, *"my days have passed away like the ship which carries early fruit"*—which ships of course must be driven swiftly to their destinations, lest the fruit should perish.

"like the eagle who swoops on the prey"—A runner runs fast, a ship moves swiftly, but the eagle goes at a speed that makes these others seem slow. The Scriptures make much of the eagle, extolling them for strength, for keen sight and for speed of wing. One of the most conforting promises uses the eagle as the comparative object, *"They shall renew their strength, they shall mount up with wings as eagles"* (Isa. 40:31). The similitude in this place compares not only to an eagle, but to an eagle swooping toward its prey — that swooping at such speed that the bird looks almost like a huge dart. She will fly so high that the eye of man does not discern her, then when she spots a carcase which arouses her greed, she will plunge at tremendous speed all the way to the ground. So Job describes his properous days, they passed away as swiftly as an eagle's plunge toward its prey.

Some would criticize Job, saying, There is no excuse for Job to speak so lightly of those days of prosperity, for he was exceedingly blessed with such rich possessions that he was an eyesore even to the Devil. Now will he make nothing of it? Is he not being very forgetful and exceedingly thankless in regards to God's gifts to him? Should he not have said that he remembered with satisfaction those days when God had prospered him? As usual, a jaundiced eye cannot see that which is good, only that which is evil. Job has not spit in the eye of God, much less has he become forgetful and thankless for God's blessings. He is engaged in throwing off the scurrilous and abusive charges of his friends. His argument is this, that the estate of a godly man in this life is as transitory and as brittle as the estate of the wicked man, and that therefore there can be no distinction made between men by their outward dispensations from God. He is enforcing this argument with experiential similitudes which can be recognized as patently true by most anyone. It is not his purpose here to keep himself from other abuse by us, his posterity. If these friends had asked him a question as to the blessedness of his former estate, he would have been quick and full in giving God glory for it.

"Truly, every man at his best state is altogether vanity," writes David in days that were a great deal less evil than these days of Job. David's crown and kingdom were fading, vanishing flowers; Abraham and all the patriarchs had *"no continuing city here."* The godly man need not think that the things of this world will be petrified in his hands and become continual sources of comfort or enjoyment to him. All things happen alike, to both the wicked and the godly, the fashion of this world is passing away swiftly.

"If I say, I will forget my complaint, I will depart from my heaviness and be of good cheer"—Job 9:27.

Now Job is proving the latter part of his assumption. He has said that both an innocent and a wicked man may alike lose their outward comforts, which he has just illustrated in three similtidues. Now he is proving that he may become entangled with afflictions beyond any hope of escape and yet be as free from guilt as any man. To do this, it is now necessary for him to show just how deeply he is wounded, and just how hopeless his case appears to him. Job may be paraphrased in these surrounding verses as follows:

'I, stricken with poverty, grief, and deep affliction, yet study to forget the troubles which are upon me. I labor to refresh and revive myself with hopes of some deliverance, laying aside all anger, passion and discontentment which you charge is upon me. But while I am endeavoring to do this, my sorrows assault me afresh, my grief and my pain overwhelm my infant hopes, my budding comforts and night terrors take hold of me. Now I even despair of recovery out of the hand of any of my afflictions. I am persuaded that I shall not be delivered and proven to be pure and innocent as to your charges, but I fear that my continued and deepening afflictions may prove to be a further argument to you that I am wicked. Then I shall have the fierce troubles of the present banded to me for whatever future I may have. Why then should I deceive myself with hopes that I shall be delivered? Should I expect that God will awake for me now and make the habitation of my righteousness prosperous? When I believe that as pure and guiltless as I am of your charges, yet it seems impossible for me to wash and cleanse myself well enough that God will not immediately throw me into the ditch again. It is clear that God intends to try me further, even to the uttermost, casting me again into the ditch before I have wiped off my former filth. If He will but take His rod away from me and cease to make me afraid, then I would speak and not fear Him'

Job, like the apostles is at this point *"Appointed to death,"* *"a spectacle to the world, and to angels and men"* (1 Cor. 4:9).

"If I say, I will forget my complaint"—Job is answering Bildad's charge in 8:2, where he tells Job to stop spouting words like an east-wind. Job answers, If I should say that I would not complain any more, what then? Would it be as you say? No, but instead I am afraid of all my sorrows and almost assured that they will return upon me in greater measure than ever before.

"I will forget"—There may be a threefold forgetfulness, (1) That forgetfulness which comes from the neglect of our natural abilities, when we are careless and take no care to remember; (2) That forgetfulness arising from the weakness of our natural abilities, when we cannot remember however careful and diligent we may be; (3) That forgetfulness which Job means here, when we study and court forgetfulness, when we do not desire to remember a thing. If Job decides that he will try to forget his complaint, yet he cannot

blank out all his sorrows, etc. There are times when we cannot forget, however hard we may try. Think of those in hell, how much they must strive to forget even one idle word that they spoke, yet they cannot. They cannot forget past guilt nor present pain.

"my complaint"—There is a mournful meditation pictured here, a breathing forth in mournful expressions. The same word was used in 7:13, *"When I say, My bed will comfort me and my couch shall ease my complaint."* Forgetfulness is a cure for some diseases, but it is not permitted to Job even for a moment.

"I will depart from my heaviness and be of good cheer"—The Hebrew word for word is, *"I will lay aside my face"*—for that which strictly and literally signified the face of a man also depicts anger and wrath, sorrow and heaviness. And the reason, of course, is that the face of man reflects his anger, wrath, sorrow and heaviness. Some learn to disguise these passions, going deep into hypocrisy in order to become artful at deceit. But most men cannot hide them, and their efforts to depart from heaviness, for example are obviously unsuccessful. Job would have gladly washed his face and his heaviness with it, but he would not — his sorrows were renewed to him moment by moment, there was no departure from them so far as he could see. Sorrow, as anyone who has been exceedingly sorrowful will know, is not easily laid aside. It is the most skillful act the hypocrite performs, this dissembling of sorrow. A man can forget his sins far more easily than he can forget his sorrows. He can pretend holiness and succeed before many, but his pretence of cheer in the midst of sorrow simply will not come off. Grief will win out, heaviness will weigh down the spirits of a man until it falls out at his face. A man may laugh on the outside while he is crying on the inside, but one may see his crying heart in his face while he laughs.

"and be of good cheer"—Comfort is the very life of our lives, the light of our days, the sun in our sky, the complement of mercy. Therefore Christ gave us that great gift, the sum of mercy, the Holy Comforter. Comfort is not a commodity to be found in the hand or power of man, therefore some criticize Job for suggesting that he should cheer himself. The great God is of course the source of all comfort, for He alone is the *"God of all comfort."* Spiritual comfort, worldly comfort, sensual comfort, all of them are directly from that God of whom it is written, *"Every good and perfect gift comes down from the Father of lights above"* (James 1:17). A man may be comforted by another, who conveys to him the promises of God. A man may be able to cheer himself in the same way, by reading or remembering God's words of comfort. Though a man may not comfort himself ultimately, yet God has appointed some means and expects men to use them.

There are those who add to their afflictions, aggravating and increasing them. They make their night darker and obscure the light of any good counsel that is brought to them. The black melancholy vapors of their own hearts stifle the consolations that are administered to them by family and friends. Like Rachel, they refuse to be comforted. Some seek ease from sorrow, which the Devil hates with great passion. Then there are worldly sorrows of an unlawful kind, sinful sorrows, which the Devil loves dearly. Some men are such good servants of Satan that they joy in the same things, yet in this passion of sorrow they do not have a kinship with Satan, for he laughs when they cry.

In Job's case, he may have deepened his sorrows, added to his heaviness, by forgetting the good that could not be taken from him by these things. He was not ignorant of what God meant to him, but in the midst of these memory-destroying passions he easily could forget those things which would act to cheer him. He is now near his deepest depression over his condition.

"I am afraid in all my sorrows, I know that You will not hold me innocent"—Job 9:28.

It is a word which expresses trembling and shaking with fear. The sorrows here are of double depth, the sorrows of grief, the sorrows of tormenting thoughts which at the same time closed off hopes and reminded him of his sinfulness. No sooner does Job speak to comfort himself than his sorrows throng him again. They jump up before his face and make such a ghastly apparition that he is frightened by them.

Afflictions naturally cause us to fear. The arrival of evil heightens our fear that evil will come, and this fear will grow more boisterous and inordinate as afflictions take hold. Godly men are not protected against these fears. Christ Himself, when He was in our nature and clothed with our flesh, was afraid of all His sorrows, *"My soul is exceedingly sorrowful, even to death"* (Matt. 26:38). It is said in another place that He was heard in that He feared. His sorrow was a sorrow which none of us shall ever know, for that Man of sorrows took upon Himself all the suns and griefs and pains and sorrows of the myriads of saints for all of time. In order that He might have a perfect and acceptable life to give us, it was necessary that He should be tempted in all points as we are, yet without sin. So the Savior suffered fear, not a sinful fear, yet a real and certain fear. Now if Christ Himself in our flesh was afraid of His sorrows, which He knew He would overcome, how much more may the fear of sorrows come upon our sin-weakened flesh?

"I know that You will not hold me innocent"—How did he know it? Who told him that God would not hold him innocent? A wicked man cannot know that He is not of God's elect, he cannot know that he will certainly go to hell. So it is here with Job, he has no more than a suspicion, at the very best he but conjectures. It is the language of fear, for suspicion and fear go hand in glove. The best of men sometimes speak from their worst part, there may be a total lack of grace appearing in a man's speech even though he has much grace within him. When the flesh is in great pain, it is particularly hard to get the spirit to act its part. If Job had not been under such a crushing load of afflictions, in the jaws of that tyrant fear, then he could have avoided this offensive statement.

The word translated *"innocent"* comes from a root which means pure and clean. Innocence is the purity or cleanness of a person. And it is common in Scripture to *"hold"* persons either innocent or guilty (1 Kings 1:9), etc. There are two interpretations of this phrase, turning on the word, *"you."* Some say the antecedent is God, some say it is Bildad who will not hold Job innocent.

Referring it to God, it may be he is saying, 'You will not cleanse my body from this filthiness, from these diseases that are wasting me away.' Or taking it tropically, as we translate it, it is a judicial cleansing or purification — *"You will not hold me innocent."* Such sorrows and troubles are upon Job that he fears God will not pronounce him innocent of the charges his friends lay against him, or of sin in response to their false charges, or of sin which arises from the multitude of afflictions which are assaulting him. One cannot be innocent in fact unless he has been declared innocent by that great Judge of us all. So we see that even a most godly man may in the midst of heavy affliction have misgivings about God's mercy and grace. There is a sinful seed in man which makes him doubt especially that he will ever be released from punishment. David experienced it when he unbelievingly said, *"I shall one day perish by the hand of Saul"* Until this fear of guilt is removed, there can be no removing of trouble. Job was not seeing very clearly at the moment, else he would have kept the pardon of his sins in the eye of his mind. And if he could not plainly see his pardon written by the hand of God forever, then he could not of course see the end of his punishment. Of course it must be remembered that the wealth of the Scriptures which we now have was not known by Job, The Mediatorship itself still being wreathed in mysterious types and shadows. It is only under the gospel that we find saints in God's word exulting and rejoicing in suffering and afflictions, and that is because we have a clear picture of the pardon of our sins in the New Testament.

It cannot but be said, God often deals with His best servants in their outward troubles as if they were guilty — that is, as severely as He would if they were guilty. As the Ruler of all the earth dealt with His Son, so He deals with all His servants. God the Father dealt with Jesus Christ as if He were a guilty person. He was numbered among the transgressors. He made His grave with the wicked. He suffered agonies so beyond our possible experience that we cannot truly sympathize with them. So long as He was taking sin upon Him,

He was treated like a sinner. Job is not called a type of Christ, yet he was like Him. There is a parallel in those two lives which will yield many observations. In this place we see Job being numbered with the transgressors by his friends, and we see him being treated as if he were guilty by God. And no one can argue that God did not love Job simply by the fact that God was destroying Job's life and reputation at the moment. If they did so, the example of the Lord Jesus Christ would rise up and haunt them until they repented. God handles His Son roughly in order to redeem sinners. He so handles His servants at times that He may purge them from sin, sometimes to try and build up their graces, and always to make them finer vessels for displaying His glory. We cannot by the weightiest of afflictions earn anything toward glory, yet in God's hands *"these light afflictions...work for us a far more exceeding and eternal weight of glory."*

If the antecedent is Bildad, then it is true (as we later may see) that Bildad is not going to hold Job innocent in any sense of that word. He is violating the command of Christ to us, *"Judge not according to appearance, but judge righteous judgment"* (John 7:24). We cannot hardly judge what is right if we judge by what appears. Men are not what they appear to be.

"I shall become condemned, why then should I labor in vain?"–Job 9:29.

Job is not admitting to his friends that he is coming to the same ill opinion of himself as they had. Yet he positively affirms here that he will be accounted wicked. But he means only to say that he expects to be handled like a wicked man, to suffer the same severity that comes to the wicked. Or, it may be, he sees that whatever he says there will be no change in his friends, though they will surely condemn him.

"why then should I labor in vain?" – This word expresses the hardest labor, travail. Why should he with pain and much toil labor to extricate himself from his sufferings, or to clear himself from the prejudice of his friends? Why should he labor to find apologies or arguments to defend himself when God is going to continue to treat him severely? Bildad had told Job to seek to God, here Job seems to answer him, Why should I labor since it will be lost labor.

For the better understanding of this, we may consider the words as an argument by way of dilemma, *"If I am to be accounted wicked, then why should I labor in vain? If I wash myself with snow water and make my hands ever so clean, yet You will plunge me into the ditch."* It is as if he had said, 'Either I am wicked, or I am clean and pure. If I am wicked, as you say I am, then I deserve more punishment, then my labor to be eased of my afflictions will be in vain. If I am pure and clean, God will yet cast me into the ditch of affliction. So, then, I am between two walls, hemmed in on both sides: For wickedness would certainly ruin me, yet my righteousness will not deliver me. Why, then, should I labor to whip up vain hopes of deliverance, if my righteousness will not relieve me of the same degree of afflictions that the wicked suffer?' So he concludes Bildad's promise that God would awake for him if he would but be pure and upright to be a false and unwarranted representation of God's way of doing things.

There are those who see Job contesting with God here. These think that Job is casting into God's teeth the claim that he has carefully walked in holy ways, yet he cannot see that God has placed him among the godly – and, therefore, he has concluded that he may as well cease laboring for that goal. This I must lay aside.

Others see this as Job's answer to Bildad, saying, 'If I am wicked, as you say, then it is a vain thing for me to seek the Lord, as you advise me. Why will you set me on a course that will be fruitless?' The thought expressed in John 9:31 was no doubt well known in Job's time, *"Now we know that God does not hear sinners."* Such a sinner as Job's pitiless friends claimed he was could never be heard by God, therefore their advice that he should petition God and that he should seek to God was not consistent with their evil charges against him. If he is wicked, then he may not seek to God. To obey your counsel would be to labor in vain.

There is a sense in which it is vain for a wicked man to seek to God. Then there is a sense in which it is not in vain for him to seek to God. These should be distinguished: If a man is wicked, it is vain for him to seek to God while he still loves wickedness, *"If I regard iniquity in my heart, the Lord will not hear my prayer;" "the sacrifice of the wicked is a hateful thing to the Lord"* (Ps. 66:2; Prov. 15:8). It is vain to labor to pray or to sacrifice to the Lord if you will not depart from iniquity. In Psalm 50, God says to the wicked, *"What is it to you...that you should take My covenant in your mouth?"* But for whom is the covenant made, if it is not made for those who are wicked? If men were not wicked, then would there be any need for a covenant of grace? The covenant is for the wicked, and it is to bring grace enough to pardon those who are greatest in wickedness. Why then does God say to the wicked that they are displeasing Him in taking His covenant into their mouths? He expounds it immediately afterward, *"since you hate to be taught, and you toss My words behind you"* (Ps. 50:16,17). A wicked man will labor in vain, he will never lay hold on the covenant of God so long as he is determined to hold on to his sin.

However, if a wicked man will *"forsake his way and the unrighteous man his thoughts; and will return to the Lord, then He will have mercy upon him"* (Isa. 55:7). Christ died for the ungodly while they were yet ungodly. God justifies the ungodly (Rom. 5:6; 4:5). They shall not be heard for their much speaking, nor shall they attain because of their hard labor, but their wickedness will not keep them from pardon if they will repent and believe, forsaking their own ways and embracing God's ways.

"I shall become condemned"—The meaning may be this, that Job considers these men to have blasted his reputation, and if he will then be reputed by men to be wicked, then why should he labor in vain to seek to again erect his reputation. Reputation, after all, is merely the opinion of men. When all is said for it, it is not worth any more than the men whose opinions make the reputation. Those who will make Job a wicked man for these sentiments and words will again have to look at Asaph, who said much the same thing in circumstances not so dire as Job's, *"Truly I have made my heart pure in vain, and I have washed my hands in innocence. For all the day long I have been plagued"* (Ps. 73:13). From all of these it may be observed that when hope fails, then all labor will cease too. If Job has no hope of getting out from under the wicked charges of his friends, then he will not try. If Job has no hope of getting out from under his afflictions, then he will not try. When the heart sinks, the hands hang down and the knees become feeble.

Lastly, taking the words (as in the original) absolutely, without any supposition, with Job acknowledging that he is wicked, not in the opinion of men only, but indeed and in fact − then, note these things: (1) If the fullest and most rigorous application of the justice of God is to be made to Job, then it would be vain for Job to seek any comfort, for no flesh can be justified in His sight; (2) Then the supposition of Bildad, *"If you were pure, etc."* would be a mockery, for neither Job nor Bildad nor anyone else could ever be pure with God − for when the Lord comes to examine for purity, He shall find the most pure to be most impure. This sense falls in with the following verse, where Job observes that however clean he might make himself, he still would be plunged into the ditch by God's purity.

"If I wash myself with snow water, and make my hands ever so clean"—Job 9:30.

Washing is an act proper to the cleansing of the body, or of bodily things. In the Bible we find civil washings and ceremonial washings − the first to take away dirt, the second in a figure to take away sin. So the apostle described the Jewish worship and the different parts of it, saying that it consisted of *"meats and drinks and different kinds of washings."* The Lord alludes to this when He says, *"I will sprinkle you with clean water;"* and the apostle Peter speaks of *"the sprinkling of the blood of Christ"* —Paul of *"the washing of regeneration"* (See Heb. 9:10; Ezek. 36:25; 1 Peter 1:2; Titus 3:5). The saints who came out of great tribulation are said to have washed their robes and to have made them white in the blood of the Lamb (Rev. 7:14). Sanctification, which is cleansing from the filth of sin, and justification (which is cleansing from the guilt of sin) are pictured as washings in the Scripture (1 Corinthians 6:11).

But why does Job mention washing with snow water? Some say it is the purest of water, the kind that comes from springs, from crystal streams, and not merely snow water here. Others think that it is an allusion to a peculiar rite of those times, when they took snow water for washing because it was conceived to be from the heavens, not from the earth below, therefore more excellent in its nature. Still others think snow water is specified because in those countries the river water was not pure, so they had to preserve snow as a means of retaining clean water for washing. Lastly, he may be saying, *"If I wash myself with snow water"* because he wanted to express the cleanest washing possible. White as snow is proverbial for the most resplendent whiteness (Isaiah 1:18).

"and make my hands ever so clean"—The Hebrew text is very emphatic, clearly meaning, *"though I wash my hands in purity,"* Our translation is not to the letter of the Hebrew, but it does reveal the sense. The former expression had referred to internal holiness, and this now refers to external. The hands in Scripture note our outward works, for they execute the motions of the heart. The apostle James calls for holiness of the outward man, saying, *"Clean your hands, sinners, and purify your hearts, you double-minded ones" (4:8).*

"Yet You will plunge me into the ditch, and my own clothes shall despise me"—Job 9:31.

The word which we translate plunge signifies a dipping or immersion, rather than to dye or to stain and then to cleanse (see Ezekiel 23:15). There are two interpretations here:

1. These words may be understood as meaning that God would judge him to be sinful in spite of all his purifyings. Then it would answer the expression of the latter clause of these 30, and would be as if he had said, Though I make myself as clean as I can, yet You may justly count me to be unclean. Yea, Job may be saying, The more I labor to justify myself, the more unclean you may judge me to be, and You will plunge me into the ditch. The plunging into a ditch here denotes the greatest defilement, it imports a man being defiled all over.

2. The word which we translate ditch sometimes has the meaning of corruption only, as in Psalm 16:10, *"You will not allow Your holy One to see corruption."* It can also signify a pit dug and prepared for corrupting carcases (Ps. 94:13). So to be cast into a ditch may picture any great humbling or affliction, any reproach or contemptuous treatment.

We may take it here in either sense, that God will plunge Job into filth and corruption if he tries to cleanse himself; or, that God will plunge him into the greatest afflictions even if he purifies himself with snow water — it is His right, and He may be just in doing so.

From this we may learn that those who seek to make themselves most holy by their own doings will appear most unholy before God. The very thought of our own purity will prove us impure. We are never so black before God as when we are the whitest in our own eyes. The Pharisee made himself out to be ever so clean, while the poor Publican plunged himself into the ditch, judging himself fit only to be thrown into the mire. But which one went down to his house justified? God tells the Jews, *"though you wash yourself with soda and take much soap for yourself, yet your sin is marked before Me"* (Jer. 2:22). It means the same as our words here. The Holy Spirit intends to condemn hypocritical washing which is performed in order to excuse or deny our sins. We cannot by substituting an imaginative forgery of holiness expect to paint over and obliterate the sins God has marked down.

"and my own clothes shall despise me"—It is the same word that appeared in 8:14, which in that place were translated *"cut off"*—taken properly these words import, (1) His degradation from all his former dignities; in the estimation of men he had been degraded, and he expresses this by the change in his clothing (which ornately decorated him in the height of his fame, which now smells of sickness and death); (2) these words may be taken as a circumlocution of death.

You will plunge me into the ditch — that is, I shall die and my own clothes will despise me (in which case he would be stripped).

Taken figuratively, (1) the words may be a picturization of his friends and the way they despise him now — then it would be a case where God plunges him into the ditch and thereby causes his friends to flee from him, even those who were as close to him as the clothes on his back; or, (2) It may express his works, that his own works shall no longer claim any acquaintance with him; or, (3) It may have respect to lepers, whose clothes despise them (lepers have nearly always worn some mark of difference upon their garments to indicate that they are to be shunned).

But, rather, take it in a general way to mean extreme pollution. He is saying that if he justifies himself before God, then he will be unclean, filthy, polluted, so that even his clothes would hate to touch him. We can be said to be clothed with shame, and here it is said that our clothes may be ashamed of us, which is an even greater dishonor.

This being plunged into the ditch and the subsequent figure of his clothes despising him are no doubt meant to convey to us his conviction that if he should make himself ever so pure, yet the Lord would still plunge him again and again into that ditch of affliction which had been his habitat for days and nights without end. It needs the eye of faith to see it, but God is plunging us again and again into the fire to refine us — for He is determined that we shall not go on with pollutted and rotten lives, with weak faith and inconstant fervor, but rather that we shall become purer and purer, going from one state of glory to a higher state of glory until we come to that glory which is glory indeed.

To those who pretend not to understand how God can so severely chastise His beloved children, the question might be asked, Which tree bears the most fruit, the one that has been pruned and purged, or the one that is allowed to grow wild and uncultivated? If you answer, the pruned tree produces most fruit (as you must), then the question might be asked, And is there a rule that a tree may only be pruned once? The comparison is not a close one, for the Christian both needs more purging and can stand far more purging — not to mention the fact that he can bring forth precious fruit that no tree has ever produced — and the Christian grows in the grace and knowledge of the Lord Jesus Christ almost in direct ratio with his trials.

"For He is not a man, as I am, that I should answer Him, that we should come together in judgment"—Job 9:32.

To close out this chapter, Job does two things, (1) He again renounces all intent to make any answer to God, either by his worthiness or goodness. His aggravating friends appear to think that he has thrown himself athwart the path of God and will remain in opposition to Him until he is destroyed, but Job again and again plainly shows that this is not true. He wants to clear himself, but he does not respond by countercharges against his friends. He humbles himself, and then he speaks that which is true. (2) In the last two verses he prays to the Lord that He should condescend to lighten his pain, and that He might in this way give him hope in throwing off the evil charges of his friends.

"For He is not a man, as I am"—He does not say that God is not such a man as he is. He says that God is not a man. He seeks to bring out, (1) that there is a difference between God and himself in qualifications; (2) there is a difference in nature. So, then, Job desires to humble himself to the uttermost, acknowledging freely that he is not as God is, wise, holy, just, pure, etc.

Job cannot wash himself clean, even with snow water (that is, with the purest of water). But God can wash him clean (though his sins be as scarlet, they shall be as white as wool).

If God were a man, He might not inflict Job more and more without wronging him. But God is not a man as Job is, therefore He can fill him full of wounds and stripes, full of troubles and burning afflictions — for He is of purer eyes than to look upon sin — and He loves with an everlasting love which will not allow even the slightest speck of blame or fault to be upon the champion that He has chosen to defeat Satan.

God works like God. Men work iniquity, like men. God works purely and perfectly, righteously and holily, like the pure, perfect, righteous and holy being that He is. Any being acts like the nature or essence that is possessed by him. God having a higher nature and higher thoughts from that nature will always work above man, (1) In that He is above any wrongdoing, He cannot be charged, much less convicted, so as to lower Him; (2) He may strike down and keep down a man because He loves him, because He desires to see him go from grace to grace, until he is filled with grace on top of grace. He is not a man that He must judge by wrongdoing, evidence, proof, and other criminal proceedings. He may judge a man and have no proceedings at all, no prosecution, no jury, no guilt or innocence proven.

"that I should answer Him"—It is a judicial word, as in answering to a charge. If the Lord God should bring a charge against him, Job would remember that he is a man and not on the level of God, therefore he would not answer Him. We may also look at it as if he had said, *"that I should give Him any satisfaction."* We are expected to be ready always to give a reason for the hope that is within us (1 Pet. 3:15), but who among us can give a reason for the suffering that is upon him? Yet in not knowing all that is in God's infinite mind when He chastises, we do not feel that He has no reasons for doing so — His actions are never arbitrary.

ALL MAN'S TROUBLES WITH GOD COME FROM IMAGINING HE IS EQUAL

God personally asks Job the question later, *"Have you an arm like God? Or can you thunder with a voice like Him?"* There we see that even though Job has these many times clearly expressed his conviction that he is not the equal of God in any sense, upon any ground, and that he dare not place himself in opposition to the great and mighty God under any circumstances, yet God finds it necessary to ask Job to compare himself and see if he was equal. There was some residual pride in . Job, else the question need never have been asked of him. It is the oldest sin of man presuming himself to be as God. This is what ruined us in the beginning, and that is what corrupts us still. God put it to the Jews just as plainly as this: *"To whom will you compare Me and make Me equal, that we may be alike?...Remember the former things of old, for I am God and there is no other; I am God, and there is none like Me, declaring the end from the beginning...saying, My purpose shall stand and I will do all My pleasure"* (Isa. 46:5,9,10). Presumptuous thoughts in the minds of men make them think that they are in some way like God, equal to Him in their right to please themselves, in their right to plan their own lives, etc.

1. Man develops an unholy boldness by imagining that God is holy in the same way that a man is holy. He makes himself the standard of what is holy, so that the Spirit of God is holy in exactly the way that a man thinks of holiness. This proud and despiteful attitude toward God causes a man to do many things contrary to the Spirit of God. The psalmist tells us what a man is like when he thinks that God is a man-like being, *"you hate to be taught, you toss My words behind you. When you saw a thief, you were pleased to be with him, and you have taken part with adulterers. You give your mouth to evil and your tongue frames deceit"*—and you have done these things because 'I was silent and did not rebuke you, says God, then *"you thought that I was one like yourself"* (see Ps. 50:17-21). A man will not sin unless he thinks that transgressing God's law is nothing to be concerned about. This in turn proves that he thinks that God's goodness is not worth being concerned with — he thinks little of God, therefore he thinks little of sinning against God. If a man has a little God, then he thinks that there is no harm in despising Him, and no penalty of any significance can then be visited upon him. Because He does not execute His judgment against sin immediately, wicked men promise themselves that there is nothing for them to worry about.

2. Murmuring against God implies that we believe that He is like us, or that we are little gods that have nothing to fear from criticizing Him in His person, in His family, in His providential works, etc. Nothing that God is or does will be pleasing to us until we come to the firm and irrevocable conviction that God is God and therefore He does not have to please us in anything, or ever! Contrariwise, nothing that we are or can do will be pleasing

to God until we have come to the firm conviction that all that we are and all that we do is strictly and only for the glory of God — however humiliating and presently dissatisfying that may appear to be.

3. Relying upon our own strength or wit, or upon that of other men in times of danger is a vanity which comes from our belief that God's arm is as short as ours and that His wisdom is as foolish as ours. God asked that question of the Jews also, *"Has My arm been shortened that I cannot save?"* Can God be God and yet run the world so badly that He gets us into a dangerous position from which He cannot deliver us? What a commentary on a man's unbelief it is when he falls into thinking of God as if He were a poor man who is unable to deliver His friends from trouble (however much he would like to do so)! It is the same in the matter of gross sin, can a man sin until there is no mercy and grace to cover those sins? Because there are things which can be done against fellow men to put them beyond the point where they will ever forgive, there are those who think that God is such a man, that He has a point of no return in the matter of forgiveness. God never says so, but He does say this, *"Let the wicked forsake his way and the unrighteous man his thoughts, and let him return to the Lord, and He will have mercy upon him; and to our God, for He will abundantly pardon. For My thoughts are not as your thoughts, neither are your ways My ways, says the Lord. For as the heavens are higher than the earth, so are My ways higher than your ways and My thoughts than your thoughts"* (Isa. 55:7-9). Man's thoughts are below God's mercy as far as man's ways are below God's holiness.

When man lost the image of God in which he was created, he thought to attain equality with God by imagining that God was made in the image of man. Untold myriads have gone on to meet God and to discover with certainty that God is not a man when He sits in judgment of those men who thought that God was altogether such a one as they were. It is better to discover here and now that men do not have enough line to measure God by. The Lord God excels man in all, not only being above man's weakness, but being far above all of the perfections to which man may attain. Only a superior being can truly take the measure of another being. Just as among men, the ignorant cannot judge the knowledge of the learned, nor the foolish the wisdom of the wise, so men are not equipped to understand God's ways. He is not only far above them, as we are, but is a simple and unadulterated spirit. There is nothing in man like the Spirit of God. Therefore vain man, do not think that you can measure God by your little mind, by your attributes or qualities. Particularly, beware of measuring Him in these ways:

1. Do not think that you have a right to meddle in God's right to choose whom He will have as His companions forevermore. Man by his natural reason sets up a man's idea of what is just and what is not, then when his presumption overcomes the better part of his judgment, he hauls God before his bar and condemns Him for what He has said in His word about the mysterious matter of election.

For a classic example of how God handles such presumptuous men, see Romans 9:16-23 where God answers without answering, with a question, *"No, but, O Man, who are you who replies against God?"* You are only a man, so who are you that you think you can answer God? Job humbly says here that he would not presume to answer God. But the proud spirit of man would have it that he has a right to question God about the things that He does out of His own freedom of choice. But God shatters such illusions by saying plainly that a man has no more right to question what God does than a pot has to ask the potter what he is doing! Not only will He not brook any interference with what He does, He will not even permit any man to question Him as to what He is doing. Since a man compared to God is wholly unable to understand what God is doing, it would be useless for God to answer him anyhow. But God prefers to stand upon His prerogative. He is the Creator who has formed every man, and the thing formed has not the slightest right to question Him as to how He made him, or where He placed him.

2. Therefore, make certain that you do not question God as to His providential dealings with you. Job does not, neither should you. In fact, it can be put in a much more concrete way: You had better not presume to tell God what to do, or even so much as ask Him what He is doing! It may be that you are involved, but in spite of that, God makes it plain that it is not your place to even judge the good or bad of anything He has done in your life.

3. That is the third thing, make sure you do not judge God in anything. Do not make the age-old mistake of erecting in your mind a conception of what God should be like, then insisting upon God being like that if He is to have your obedience. His word tells us what He wants us to know about Himself. That is the kind of person He is. Whether you like it or not, He is all those things that are written of Him. You may not pick this part of the Scriptures to believe, but disbelieve that other part. God today is the same as He was yesterday, all the yesterdays: He is the God who loved some out of the whole lump of men from everlasting, the God who elected them and decreed both the Way and the means of saving them, the God who delivered His people and the God who destroyed His people (outwardly), the God who told the Israelites to kill every man, woman and baby of the Canaanites, the God who wiped out the great populated cities time and time again, etc. Yes, He is the God of all grace. Yes, He is merciful and kind. But what would those attributes be worth if He were not almighty, all-wise, holy, just and good? And what would all these be worth to us if He then put all of these superior attributes under the hand of man? Can you pray to a God who cannot do all that He desires? Suppose that He desires to do what you ask Him to do in your prayer? If He cannot do all that He desires, it does not matter that He wants to do what you ask. Whoever it is that thwarts His power is the one you should be praying to, for such a one would be stronger than He. It is utter nonsense to talk of God being thwarted by or subject to any of the whims of men (which is called popularly their free-will).

God does not seek your approval of Him. He will not even approve your approval of Him, except that kind of approval which comes from an humble and contrite mind, bowed down before Him, looking at Him through the eyes of faith. Neither does He permit you to make your own approval of His servants. You are to approve them because they are His servants, and not because you are pleased with them for your own sake. Take heed that you do not make Cain's mistake and conclude that God will surely like anything that you believe sincerely to be honoring to Him. Nothing is honoring to Him which He has not commanded you to do in honor of Him. The great and most magnificent honor that you can give Him is to obey His word and to approve of those things which He says are excellent — whether they appear to be excellent to your mind or not.

"that we should come together in judgment" —Judgment may be taken three ways, (1) For pleading, which is the preparatory part of judgment, when a pleading of guilty or innocent is made, etc; (2) For the decision and determination of the case according to the ruling law, the award; (3) For the execution of the sentence which was given when judgment was made.

Here Job intends the first, that God is not a man, therefore he, Job, could not plead before Him as if He were a man. Should he come before the Almighty and argue or debate with Him? Would not God ask him, Who are you that replies against God? The literal words will allow a translation which fits the former clause better, *that we should come a-like to judgment."* We are not both men. We are not alike in our natures or in our positions. Therefore we would be most unnaturally and unequally matched in judgment.

Job, then, cannot accept the advice of his friends, that he should make himself pure and then present himself before God to receive his rewards. Instead, he sees that there is no way that he is able to secure an acquittal by means of a public judgment. For he cannot stand in judgment with God, God is of another class and station, the supreme Judge who will not permit a mere man to meet Him in judgment matters. He will be the sole judge for all of us in all our matters.

"Neither is there any mediator between us, who might lay his hand on us both"—Job 9:33.

Since no public judgment can be sought, there is only the hope of finding someone to mediate between God and himself. But says he, there is no such person to be found, The *Septuagint* renders this as a prayer, *"O, that there were a daysman between us, that could lay his hand upon us both!"* But the original is better translated negatively.

The word which we translate *"mediator"* comes from a root which means to argue or to reprove. Some, then, conclude that Job is saying that there is not any one who can argue for him. God often appears for us in this role, as when it is said,*"He allowed no one to do them wrong, yea, He reproved kings for their sakes"* (Ps. 105:14) — He was the one who stood between and reproved for their sakes. A mediator in order to do his work properly should have the power, authority and wisdom to reprove either party in a dispute. If both do not agree to abide by his decision, then the entire business is certain to fail. Here are the five important things in regard to one who is chosen to stand between two unreconciled parties:

1. He must be agreed upon and accepted by both parties.
2. He must be fully acquainted with both sides of the question.
3. He must be able to interrogate the parties.
4. He must have the power to determine what the differences are between them.
5. His decision must be binding upon both parties.

"who might lay his hand on us both"—Some would have it that Job means here a person to mediate between him and his friends, but the text refers clearly to God. To lay on hands in the Scripture sense is to put forth power, either in an ill sense or a good one:

1. In an ill sense, that is, to strike with the hand of power, as when Reuben pleaded for the life of Joseph, *"Shed no blood. Throw him into this pit that is in the wilderness and lay no hand upon him (so that he might rescue him out of their hands)"* (Gen. 37:22). The laying on of hands may denote any violent act, whether it be from zeal or for justice. Out of envy, *"the chief priests and the scribes sought to lay hands on Him"* (Luke 20:19). Haman thought to lay hands on Mordecai, but instead, when the king thought Haman was trying to lay hands on queen Esther, the life of Haman was forfeited.

2. In a good sense, the laying on of hands may be good in three ways, (1) In the giving of benedictions, as when Christ laid His hands upon little children and blessed them; as under the Law (Lev. 1:4; 4:15). Peter and John laid hands upon the people of Samaria and they received the Holy Spirit (Acts 8:17). It may be a sign of healing, *"lay Your hand upon her and she shall live"* (Matt. 9:18). (2) Laying on of hands was used in the ceremony setting men apart for some office, *"children of Israel laid their hands on the Levites"* (Num. 8:10). In such a case, it was either a testimony that these had given up their own carnal and wordly interests in order to present themselves wholly for God's service, or it was an approval of the office they were to take and the administration they were to give it. In the appointment of officers in the gospel age we see the same, *"Do not neglect the gift that is in you, which was given to you by prophecy, with the laying on of the hands of the elders,"* (ITim. 4:14). Then again in that same book, *"Lay hands on no man suddenly"* (5:22). Even the apostle Paul, with Barnabas, was sent away with *"the laying on of hands"* (Acts 13:3). Lastly, (3) the civil power may be said to lay on hands in a good sense, for the laying on of hands may imply the authority which God has given to one man over another, for his civil good (Ps. 89:25).

This last sense is the one for our text, for Job marks up this point, that there is no one to act as a mediator between him and God, one with sufficient authority to put his hand on both parties and resolve the matter completely. To impose the hand, in the case of a go-between, is to dispose of the matter by composing the difference, (1) He puts forth his hand toward the parties to draw them together, to bring them into consent on the point that they do so desire to find common ground. This you may not do with those who are ungodly, *"You shall not put your hand with the wicked"* (Ex. 23:1). (2) The skilled daysman will lay his hand first on the one and then on the other, noting carefully their temper or distemper, using his best verbal skills, his sense, and his expression of face to beg of them to be reconciled to one another. (3) When this mediator draws to the end of his work, if he has found one part faulty, then he will lay his hand upon his head and so indicate. There was a possibility that both parties were at fault, in which case he would lay his hand upon first the one and make known the fault, then on the others for the telling of his fault.

In our text, nothing more is meant than a mediator in the civil sense, one who composes differences between two or more parties. It is not to be thought for a moment that Job is speaking in unbelief and denying that there is a Mediator between God and men, even the Lord Jesus Christ. He is not speaking in such a way at all. He is speaking as if it were an impossible thing for any person to stand between him and God in the ordinary sense of mediation, saying something to this sense, *"I would gladly refer this matter to arbitration, but the Lord is above the arbitration of men, or angels, or any other creatures. I dare not call upon any creature to meddle with any of His matters further than they are called, and there are none called to act in this kind of matter for me."*

It must be realized that even the Lord Jesus Christ does not act as a mediator in these matters, that is, He does not intercede between God and His loved ones with authority, as if He could hold God back from His purposes. Our Mediator will not lighten our affliction in the sense that He will cause God to abandon His fierce trials or to change His wise counsels. They are at one on these matters, both loving the saints with an everlasting love, a love which calls for the severest trials and the strongest application of wise (though presently grievous) afflictions in order to perfect them. Although He suffered for us, it was not that we might altogether escape the suffering that is in this life. We shall escape the suffering that the ungodly ones shall receive for their sins, a never-ending punishment. If the Mediator were meant to give us rest and quiet, complete deliverance from the pain that goes with sinfulness, then He would have removed our sins completely — we would have been fully sanctified at the same time we were fully justified — this is the error of some, but it is not the teaching of the Scriptures.

That Christ could not mediate between God and Job in the sense of the text may be seen when you realize, (1) that the mediator Job speaks of must be wiser than both parties; (2) this mediator must have power to compel both parties. Jesus Christ is God, but He is not above God, not wiser, nor more powerful — it would be foolishness to say it is so. God has appointed Him to act for us in all matters having to do with our salvation, not to overlook God's providential dealings with us and to soften them for our pleasure.

It should be noted how highly Job speaks of God, yet how humble he regards himself. The greater his afflictions become, the purer is the language of Job. He bows to God's will.

"Let Him take His rod away from me, and let not His fear make me afraid"—Job 9:34.

We have seen Job strongly protesting that he is in no way contending with God, nor does he dare to even ask Him what He is doing. Now we see him fervently desiring that God should not contend with him, so that he might speak at least about his condition and to ask what it is that he should do under these circumstances.

"Let Him take His rod away from me" —The rod has different kinds of meaning in the Hebrew. It may strictly be taken for a branch, a bough or even a sprig, because a rod or a staff is made from the branch of a tree. It may also mean a scepter, any kind of scepter, that which a king has and uses as a an emblem of his power. Many of the early scepters

were made in the form or shape of a rod. By a metonymy the scepter imports dominion, rule and government, *"I will cut off the one who holds the scepter"* (Amos 1:8). Again, the word is often used in Scripture to signify a tribe, or a family of persons, because a tribe is as a branch which has come from one stock. Lastly, the word expresses punishment or correction. For rods have many times been the instruments used to execute punishment, or to give correcting instruction,*"the rod and reproof give wisdom"* (Prov. 29:15).

The rod which Job desires to be removed is that sore affliction which the sovereign power of God had laid to his back. This man is human, and being a man he desires very much to see his hurt removed — though he seeks it in the way of death, rather than a lessening of the rod upon him. He recognized that God has the right to deal with him in this severe manner, but he cannot but sue for peace. In later verses he puts it like this, *"Only do not do two things to me, then I will not hide myself from You: Withdraw Your hand far from me, and do not let Your fear make me afraid"* (13:20.21). As for the ungodly, he speaks of them far differently, *"Their houses are safe from fear, neither is the rod of God upon them"* (21.9).

Affliction is called a rod in three ways:

1. A rod cuts and causes us to smart. Afflictions are painful in the same way.

2. Affliction is called a rod in regard to the hand that uses it. A sword is in the hand of a judge, but the rod is in the hand of a father. God corrects His people as a father, He afflicts them in order to drive the corruption and foolishness out of them — *"and a rod for the back of fools."* All our sins are foolish, and God is wise to know how to drive out our foolishness. He shall never spare the rod and spoil His children!

3. Affliction is called a rod in regard to the end for which it is sent. A rod is prepared to correct, but it is not an instrument of cruelty, much less is it meant to kill. It is possible to destroy with a rod, and God speaks of destroying such a rod (Isa. 9:4), but in God's hand the rod does not oppress or destroy His people.

It is lawful to pray that our afflictions be removed. Even though we are to be patient under God's afflicting hand; yea, we are to exult when we fall into many different kinds of afflictions (James 1:2-4), yet we may pray for God to remove them without fear that He will rebuke us. When Paul prayed that his thorn in the flesh might be removed, God did not reprove him for wrongful praying,though he prayed this prayer three times. But God did tell him to cease and desist, saying, *"My grace is sufficient for you"* (2 Cor. 10:9) and He even gave Paul an explanation, saying, *"for My strength is made perfect in weakness."* This in turn caused Paul to rejoice in his weakness, for he wanted very much to be perfected by the power of Christ — but he could rejoice in these, in reproaches, in persecutions, etc. only for Christ's sake. As to the lawfulness of it, besides the proof in the case of Paul, remember that we may pray that afflictions do not come upon us. And if it is lawful to pray that they do not come, then it is lawful to pray that they go from us. It is lawful to pray for the removal of affliction because it often happens that the Lord has sent his afflictions for that very reason, to cause us to be enlivened and to pray with fervency and feeling. A sluggish soul will be awakened by the voice of the rod, and the smarting sinner will then begin to cry mightily to the Lord to give him an opportunity to mend his ways. Just as it is an ill sign when a child will take his punishment as it grows more severe by the minute, yet he will not cry out for mercy, asking forgiveness — so it is with the child of God, it is an ill sign when he will not cry out for mercy, asking forgiveness for his sins, and seeking the end of his chastisement. There is a greater contempt toward God in lying under affliction and refusing to ask Him for relief than there is in a continual crying for relief.

Of course, there is need to be cautious here, for we must not pray absolutely for deliverance, or the removal of afflictions at once and completely — we must allow for the will of God to continue, yes, even to deepen our afflictions. There must be a readiness to submit to his will. A believer may say to the Lord, *"I will not let You go unless You bless me"* (as did Jacob), but he must not say, I will not let You go unless You deliver me now. Let the afflicted one remember that there is more than one way for God to relieve him, (1) He can lessen the affliction – it is a relief when the extremity of our troubles is removed and a less severe degree of affliction is substituted; (2) He can sanctify the rod to cause it to do us good – the saints die, yet death is abolished by the death of Christ(2 Tim. 1:10) because Christ has plucked the sting out of death and made it a gain to them – so that at the very time that Christ causes us to suffer loss of goods or of health, He is adding to our spiritual estate; (3) He can make the affliction of no strength by giving to us the strength to bear it – nothing grieves us in either active or passive obedience but what is either against our wills or above our power, a burden to a midget is not a burden to a giant, so it is with the saints when they are given extraordinary power to bear up under their afflictions. God in His wisdom both glorifies Himself and convinces us of His power to empower us when He gives us first a burden that we cannot bear by our own strength, then gives us the strength to bear that which we before could not lift. It is far more satisfying and much better for the building of the morale if we have an enemy and conquer him, than if we have no enemy to conquer.

"and do not let Your fear terrify me"–This rod upon Job was no ordinary rod, it was a fierce beating that that man had taken, and was still taking. The word which we translate *"fear"* comes from a root which expresses that which is very formidable and terrible. *"Fear and dread shall fall upon them"* (Ex. 15:16), that is, they shall be extremely afraid, all but dead with fear, as the next words import, *"they shall be still as a stone, etc."* There is a letter added to the word used by Moses, to express the excess of fear. Giants are called by this name *Emims*, because they are of a dreadful aspect (Deut. 2:11). The whole army of Israel trembled at the sight of Goliath.

Job's fear was not a needless one, he was not terrified with a figment of his imagination. His imagination could not but have been aroused and very active under these severe and mighty afflictions, but the fear he expresses here is not that kind of fear (for there is a real and terrifying fear which comes from our imagination, when we scare ourselves by what we imagine is going to happen to us). This fear of Job is that terrible fear which comes upon us when we are overwhelmed at a sight of one who is gigantic, one who is obviously able to inflict great wounds upon us. Job at the sight of God falls into a fear that he will be brought under an affliction equal to his sins against God – he is frightened to the very border of madness.

Some expound this fear with reference to the two former verses, especially the last: that if a daysman were found to stand between him and God, then his sentence would not be one that would be a terror to him. But the first is no doubt the meaning here.

At the sight of God, when He would appear in one form or another in the Old Testament, it was common for the party seeing Him to be terrified (as Samson's mother, in Judges 13:6; as Abraham, in Gen. 15:2; as Daniel, in Daniel 10:8). The same God who is a joy to His people is also a terror to them. As He lets out the rays and beams of His majesty they fill us with wonder and fear, love and terror. The nearer He comes to one of His loved ones, the more terrible He seems. Those who claim that they have never been afraid of God reveal themselves – that they have never been very close to that great and terrible Being who is our Maker and Ruler and Judge.

"Then would I speak and not fear Him, for it is not so with me"–Job 9:35.

There is an apparent inconsistency in Job's statement that he is terrified by God–then this, that if God would but lift His rod then he would not fear Him at all. Job is characterized by God in the first chapter as a God-fearing man. Now will he say that he will cease to fear Him? The fear of God is the beginning of wisdom, then has Job lost his senses? To answer, Fear may be taken in two ways: Either for the grace of fear, or for the perturbation of fear. When Job says here that he would speak and not fear God, he does not mean to say that he will lay down that fear of God which acts as a bridle for his soul, to keep it from sin. Nor does he mean that he will cease from his reverential affection for God, that which fits us to act in every holy duty we perform to God. The thing that Job desires to be freed from is the perturbating fright, the distracting terror which was keeping him from seeing God as the loving Friend that he knew Him to be. Sanctifying and humbling fear he would have welcomed gladly. His mind is plainly running along these lines: 'If the Lord will be entreated to reduce the extremity of my afflictions and remove the terrors which are disabling me, then I would be able to speak to Him both boldly and cheerfully. I would then set out the truth of my case and declare my innocency from these false charges of my friends. But violent passions are hindering my reason, and I cannot easily speak until I am eased of my throbbing pains. I cannot tell how it is with me as long as this distracting fear continues to perturb me.'

Who will say that he can speak well, or at all, when he is frightened half to death? It is unreasonable to expect reasonable speech from one who is unspeakably afraid. It is well to tremble when we speak to God, for such tremblers are best equipped to speak to Him, but one can tremble too much to speak at all. It is only when the Lord quiets and composes our hearts that we can utter our hearts and declare our minds to Him.

"for it is not so with me" —There are many opinions as to the meaning and translation of these words. One translates it, *"I am not so with myself as God's scourge seems to make me"* — the *Septuagint "I am not so conscious to myself."* The Hebrew word for word reads, *"for not so I with myself."* Some read *"but,"* most read *"for. '* The original is rather causal than exceptive.

But the word which causes the greatest difference is that which we translate *"so"* —The Hebrew word has two principal significations, (1) right, or just; (2) adverbially, in which case it would be, *"it is not with me"* —that is, it not so as you imagine it is with me.

The word can be applied to things, as in Jer. 8:6, where it is said that no one spoke aright. There are things which are not used in the right way, and the word is used with those things. Or it can be applied to persons, noting that a man is upright, faithful and honest in his conscience and behavior.

Upon both these meanings and uses of the word, different interpretations are grounded:

1. Taking the word to denote an upright man, Job is conceived to be speaking interrogatively, as if he put the question, *"For am I not right in myself?"* Uprightness feeds boldness into a man, and Job may be claiming here that he still has that upright quality which has always characterized him.

2. Some read it negatively, *"For am I not right in myself."* Then the sense may be made out in this way, 'I have not tried to justify myself until now, I have not stood on my own righteousness pleading with God. If my righteousness were in myself, then I might fear to speak with God (even if He were to take away His rod and even if His fear should terrify me) — but I have a better bottom than my own, I am not right in myself but right in the free grace of God, in the righteousness of my Redeemer.'

3. For those who say, *"I am not right in myself,"* there are some who say Job is admitting that he is unsettled and lacking in composure of spirit, therefore he desires God to remove his fear and mitigate his afflictions so that he might speak. The Vulgate gives an interpretation instead of a translation, *"For I cannot answer while I am afraid"*

Our translation, however, translates it adverbially, *"For it is not so with me."* This may give us a threefold interpretation: (1) With the former words, *"Let Him take His rod away from me,...then I will speak...for it is not so with me,"*—that is, I am not so low in spirit and of such little acquaintance with God that I do not know how to speak to Him, or that I am afraid to speak to Him. It is that the Lord is dazzling me with the blinding and distracting brightness of His majesty and at the same time beating me with His rod of pain. If He would but let up on these, then I would speak and not be fearful to do so. (2)

We may rather refer it to the false and unkind opinion of his friends, who judged him to be a wicked man, a hypocrite. He here denies it saying, *"It is not so with me."* Job will not admit that which they suspect of him, and his words explain why it is that he cannot go to God and get from Him corroboration of his claims to be no more guilty of gross sin than anyone else. Put a defendent before the judge and the jury, then terrorize him and beat him at the same time! Would you expect such a man to be able to give a good defence to the false charges placed against him? Could you expect him to say anything at all? So it is with Job, he has more to fight then false accusations of his friends, he has all that disturbing load of afflictions, fears on the inside, sores on the outside, and with them the terrifying sight of God standing over him with a rod to inflict some more wounds! Note that a godly man may be certain of his own integrity, and it is lawful for him to defend it, even when there is slander and gossip from both friend and foe all around him. (3) There may be another meaning, that he has sought the Lord to ask that He abate his afflictions, that He remove his rod, but, alas! *"It is not so with me"* —that is, the Lord has not done it.

"My soul is weary of my life. I will leave my complaint upon myself. I will speak in the bitterness of my soul" —Job 10:1.

In the last chapter Job had justified God in afflicting him, yet he had maintained his own integrity in spite of those afflictions. Now he returns to the work of seeking rest from his affliction, he again begins to breathe out his afflicted spirit in sad complainings. He not only renews his former lamentations (as in the third, sixth and seventh chapters), but he pleads more fully with God here to deal less severely with him. His complaint is beautiful rhetoric, as he reaches high strains of appeal to God's goodness. In the end of the chapter, he allows his passion to get away with him and he expostulates with God in language reminiscent of his third-chapter excesses. Still he knits together his complaints with some solid arguments. His questions put the point resolutely, yet humbly, as He asks God to show the reason why He is dealing so violently with him, compared to his former times.

"My soul is weary of my life" —The argument may be formed in the following way:

Any man who has afflictions so heavy and so bitter that he has reason to be weary of his life also has reason to complain of his afflictions — But Job had afflictions that made him weary of his life — therefore he believes that he has reason to complain.

The assumption is in these first words, *"My soul is weary of my life."* The conclusion is next, *"I will leave my complaint upon myself. I will speak in the bitterness of my soul."* Life and soul are often put promiscuously for one another in the Scriptures. Both are at places opposed to the body. Sometimes for the whole man consisting of both body and soul (in which case he is saying no more than this, that he is weary of his life, and that he would like to have his soul and body separated so that he could go on to the grave. Again, life may be taken for the manner of life (then the sense would be that he is weary of the state of life that he is in at present). The circumstances of life are called life, as in that statement, 'what a life he leads!'

"My soul is weary"—The word varies the understanding of this sentence. It properly expresses a weakening or melting which dissipates the strength of a thing. But it is most commonly applied to that weariness which arises from unpleasant and irksome considerations in a man's mind. All burdens on the body are light compared with those that lie heavily upon the soul. There are three things which weary the soul and load it down:

1. The filth and guilt of our sins weary our souls, *"I will sprinkle you with clean water, etc."* says the Lord. But to what effect? *"then you will remember your own evil ways and be weary of yourselves because of your abominations"* (Ezek. 36:31). Before a man is converted he is not wearied by his sins nearly so much as he is after he has been cleansed and given the eye of faith to see what ugly spots sins make upon our souls.

2. The perverseness of other men corrupts their manners and their dispositions so that they weary the soul (as was Lot in Sodom — see 2 Pet. 2:8). God expresses Himself as being wearied by the way the Israelites acted in the Wilderness. The perverseness of our own nature also is a weariness to our souls.

3. The pains and troubles which afflict the body also cause much grief of mind, so as to bring about an extreme weariness to the soul. That is the meaning of this text. Job's life is filled with such troubles that his soul has become weary.

Many of the Jewish doctors tell us that the most strict and proper meaning of this word is to contend or to strive, to chide or to wrangle. Then the meaning would be this, that Job's soul contended and disputed that it should not have to be wearied by remaining bound to his pain-wracked, weakened and useless body any longer, but rather it should be allowed to escape and go beyond the reach of these afflictions.

Job had erred three times before on this point, yet now we hear him complaining as if

326

he had never before complained. This was his infirmity. Much has been said, and more may still be said to refute the aspersions which Job's friends have cast upon him for his complaining, yet it cannot be denied that there was sin in some of his complaints. In the multitude of words from the lips of any man, there will be sin. Job's spirit has been slashed and stabbed in so many ways, from so many directions, that he is distraught, his words come gushing out at his wounds—bitter words, words which contain gall and brimstone. It is part of the teaching of the Book, that God can and does heal up these wounds. He can and does shut off the complaints of His children — yea, more, He turns their complaints into happy songs of deliverance, beautiful songs of repentance and faith.

By Job's continual complaints may be seen that a godly man can fall into the same sin again and again — there is a sin that easily besets us, spoiling the pattern. Where grace has taken hold of our hearts, it breaks the habits of sin, it spoils the pattern of sin which was in our lives. Yet a godly man may be seen to sin the same sin again and again. Never does he follow his old pattern of contriving to sin, of devising ways, of plotting deceitfully to commit any sin (for those acts clearly prove one to be still in the gall and bitterness of his sins, a true worker of iniquity). When a man commits a sin, if He is God's child, he will run to his Father and repent, begging His pardon for being unbelieving and disobedient. He will even condemn his sin and himself for committing it, joining with God in carrying out any sentence He may decree against him. Because of the serious approach the godly man makes to sin, it is not to be thought that he will lightly fall into heavy, gross and scandalous sins again and again. God teaches us with the thorns of sin, but He does not allow us to receive grievous wounds in depth again and again. Noah was not often drunk, nor did David commit murder but once. The grace of God taught Job to deny ungodliness and worldly lusts, just as He does in New Testament times. You have seen and will yet see that Job does not lie at ease in his sins when he sins by complaining — there are many repentings, many views of God's glory, many evidences that he can rise out of the depths by faith, until at last we see his faith conquer all as he says. *"I will lay my hand upon my mouth. Once I have spoken, but I will not answer; yea, twice, but I will go no further"* (40:4,5).

For those who would be too severe with Job for those particles of sin which cling to his complainings, compare this good man with David, who was called by God, *"a man after His own heart."* David professes sincerely, *"I have chosen the way of truth"* (Ps. 119:30). Yet not once, nor twice, but several times it is reported plainly in the Scriptures that David lied — he slipped when he took his eyes off of God, and instead of the truth he loved, he told that which he hated, an untruth. When he told Ahimelech that the king had commanded him to leave hastily to go on a bit of business for him, he did not tell even a half-truth. He did not tell the whole truth, if any of it , when he told king Achish that he had ridden against *"the south of Judah"* He who had slain Goliath was overcome by fear of a mere Achish — it is an evidence of a course of sin, however intermitted it may be. There are those who foolishly take heart from David's sin, to do the same with supposedly the same excuses, but a good man is not privileged to commit any sin under any circumstances. God does not keep us back from all sin, for it is not His way of perfecting us, but He does not give any excuse to even the most godly man to commit a single sin. Our sins are to remind us of what happens to us when we act in unbelief,for *"what is not of faith is sin."* When there is no dependence on Christ, there is a dependence on self, or on another impotent and sinful man — that is pure unbelief, and it will surely lead to spiritual bloodshed. The reservoirs of grace within us must be renewed moment by moment, day by day, else we run dry of grace and start running on our own sinful motivations again. Yes, compared to David, Job does not come off second best, though he sins again and again with his lips under the most tyrannical of manifold afflictions. Compared to you and me, is there one of us who will be so proud as to step into the limelight of the Scriptures and be compared with Job?

THE SOUL

However, it may be sometimes true that the soul is put for the whole man, as was touched on in the opening of the words. The Holy Spirit does not denominate all of man by that name. It is a fleshly, brutish opinion which some have, that the soul is nothing – that is, nothing else but the life that we have on earth, that the soul of man is no more than the life of a beast, which dies when the beast dies. These opinionists will attempt to cover their trail and hide their weakness by claiming that the body shall rise again by the power of God, but this would not satisfy for the loss of the immortality of the soul. Nor does the immortality of the soul contradict the death of the whole man. For death does not consist in annihilation, but in the separation of those parts of man, the soul and the body, so that earthly life is untied and vanishes with the separation. Death, in the spiritual sense is separation from God, not annihilation (which is a filthy imagination of man, devised in order to catch those fools who desire to live in the rottenness of the flesh to the fullest, without penalty at any time). Death, in the physical sense, is the separation of the body and soul.

For those who mock because there are times when the saints are not mounting up toward Heaven with wings of faith and hymns of praise, there are legitimate and spiritual reasons why a man may be weary of his life:

1. The violence of the temptations of this world, and of Satan, can make the soul to be weary and to yearn to be rid of the body. Hear the cry of godly Paul, *"O wretched man that I am. Who shall deliver me from the body of this death?"* (Rom. 7:24). There is a devil everywhere but in Paradise. Only those who are the willing slaves to the Tempter will be so content as to not complain in the midst of temptation. It is only God who will prevent us from being tempted beyond what we are able to bear, and only He can deliver us from sin in the midst of a trial. When we are wrestling with those who are more than flesh and blood, then we need more strength than flesh and blood can furnish us. If, as in the case of Job, God leaves us in a painful position, all bent over, temporarily bent out of shape, it is that we may come to know that nothing is impossible with God. He can deliver us from the mightiest of enemies, from the direst of circumstances. He can restore us when there is but a frayed thread of life left in us when there seems to be no more than the running, putrid sores of sin left in us, He proves His wisdom and His power by making us spiritual sound and inutterably more wealthy in the riches of His mercy.

2. The saints are wearied with the weight of their sinful hearts. Inward corruptions burdens us more than all of our outward temptations. In fact, if there were no inward corruption, there would be no outward temptation – for did not Satan fail to tempt the Lord Jesus Christ because he could find *"nothing at all in Him"* to tempt? It is the traitorous old man within us which opens the gates for the Devil, and it is our own smoldering embers of sinfulness which he enflames. The lusts and vanities of the flesh, the perverse workings of our minds, these are the things that respond to the outward temptations. Is it any wonder that a man who loves God and hates sin, as Job does, should want to die rather than to continue to sin against Him he loves? Though it is not recorded that David asked for death, see how broken up and drained of the love of life is this good man in Psalm 51. He prays to be purged of guilt, to be washed, to be renewed and restored, to be given a willing spirit again, so that he might teach transgressors not to go the way he had just traveled.

3. Some saints become weary of life because they are tormented by the wickedness of the people around them, as Lot, for that good man *"was tormented with the filthy behavior of the wicked"* Sodomites (2 Pet. 2:7). Rebekah was weary of her life because of the daughters of Heth that Esau married (Gen. 27:46). Jeremiah was wearied of his life

because of the traitors and adulterers in Judah, and he did pray that his life be removed from him.

4. There are those who get such an assurance and evidence through faith of a better life to come that they become quite weary of this one. When one tastes something that is far better, he does not then desire again that which is comparatively tasteless (Luke 5:39). A true sight of Heaven makes the earth turn pale and uninviting, it is no longer a good place to live. Paul got such a sight and he stated plainly that he thought it should be far better to depart and be with God, yet he was willing to remain for the sake of that same God. We may groan earnestly, *"desiring to be clothed with our house which is from Heaven,"* but however much we groan under the burdens of his life, it is not ours to determine when this life should end and the next one to continue in Heaven. Christ has already gone there to adorn a place for us, but we must not seek to go there until He comes and leads us into our heavenly home.

5. The saints can easily become weary of their lives when they are heavily afflicted, when there is none of the juice of joyous sap of even the physical life. This is the case with our text, Job has sickness and pain, poverty and emptiness, reproaches and cruel kindnesses, abandonment by his loved ones and mockery from those who once professed to be friends and admirers. Is it any wonder that he found his life a weary and burdensome one?

"I will leave my complaint upon myself"—He is not going to carry his complaint any further, for it will trouble no one but himself. The original also expresses a strengthening or fortifying (Neh. 3:8), so the sense of Job may be this, 'My pains do not lessen, why then should I lessen my complaint. I will strengthen and fortify my complaint as long as my sorrows continue to grow stronger.'

The word translated *"complaint"* has been explained before. It is an inward as well as an outward complaint. Some translated it, *"I will groan in silence with myself."* But the text requires rather that we interpret it of an external complaint which we form up into words. Most interpret it to be a vocal declaration of his mind, as the Seventy, and Augustine.

The greatest difficulty lies in those words,*"upon myself,"* so that one renders it, *"I will leave it aside from myself."* His following words prove that he did not intend to lay aside his complaints. Some think that Job is speaking in the face of danger, that he is venturing to complain, whatever may happen to him. The Hebrew preposition may be translated, *"upon," "with", "against," "concerning."*

Any of these may be applied, and all of them may be taken in, as if Job were saying, 'I do not intend to speak a word against God, I will not charge the Almighty with injustice, or with undue rigor, for to do so would be the highest wickedness. But I do intend to complain, but my complaint will be only upon myself, with myself, against myself, concerning myself. I will not utter a word against the wisdom of God, nor will I accuse His providence. It is not my intention to murmur against Heaven.'

There are two ways that we may leave our complaints upon ourselves:

1. When we let them lie wholly upon ourselves, not going to God for strength or patience or wisdom to bear them. Who can sufficiently mourn over his afflictions, if they leave their complaints upon themselves? It is sinful and foolish to do so. It is a duty rather to roll them upon God, to pour them into the bosom of God, that He should either ease us or give us the strength to bear them, being willing to gladly obey whatever He may say. The burden of merely ordinary cares will break our backs if we leave them upon ourselves. How much more will we find it impossible to bear such extraordinary afflictions as these that are encircling and bearing down on poor Job!

2. We leave our complaint upon ourselves when we make no excuses or evasion, but plainly charge the fault upon ourselves. This is the way we ought to treat all our complaints. It is sinful and foolish to charge any of them upon the Devil, much less upon

God. An honest heart will take them home and say, God is righteous, but I am a wicked transgressor of His law. He does all things justly, but I have not been right in my deeds. This is what Job is doing in this text.

"I will speak in the bitterness of my soul"—If the soul is bitter, it is to be expected that bitter words will pour forth. Out of the abundance of the heart, the mouth will speak. The lines and images of a man's mind and head are drawn upon his words. Whether he is joyful, sorrowful, angry, profane, holy, etc., these may be seen by examining his words. Not only should the saints be especially careful that no filthy speaking, not even any jesting, should come from their lips, but they should heed the call of the apostle Paul, *"Let your speech be always with grace, seasoned with salt, that you may know how you ought to answer"* (Eph. 5:3-6; Col. 4:6). Bitter speech and gracious speech ought not to come forth from the same lips, *"Out of the same mouth comes blessing and cursing. My brothers, these things ought not to be so"* (James 3:10).

For an explanation of Job's bitterness, see both 3:7 and 7:11. Either he means that he will proceed to let out the sorrows of his heart by his tongue, or that he is making some apology for the words he spoke. It may be that he is saying that it is the bitterness in him that is speaking, as when Paul said it, *"Now then it is no more I that do it, but sin that dwells in me"* (Rom. 7:17). Speaking in the bitterness of one's soul may indicate the excess or magnitude of a complaint, or it may indicate the cause and spring of it. It cannnot be said that Job was the kind of man who ordinarily complained, being absolved by that scene in chapter one when he did not open his mouth to complain when all his goods and more, all his children were taken suddenly away from him.

One thing which should be noticed is this, that when Job begins to complain he turns to God. He does not murmur and spread his aches out for the sake of men, but he puts himself humbly in the presence of God — he does it in chapter seven, again here.

"I will say to God, Do not condemn me. Make me to know why You contend with me"—Job 10:2.

Job begins the complaint that he has resolved upon in verse one. He has a double request (1) that God would not condemn him; (2) that God would instruct and convince him. He is not seeking alienation but reconciliation. He lacks understanding, but he seeks to know how he can knit up his spirit and become whole in his faith again.

"Do not condemn me"—The Seventy have a very different rendering of this clause, *"Do not teach me to be wicked"*—To this must be objected the thought that surely it would be the blackest and most hellish kind of wickedness to suggest that the Lord could teach it. Of course, it was the mind of those Greek translators that the wicked were learning wickedness by being ensnared in sin of their own emission, rather than that the Lord was teaching it. They would have Job's request here to be akin to that in the Lord's prayer, *"Lead us not into temptation, but deliver us from evil."* Good King Agar prayed that the Lord not make him poor, lest he steal; nor rich lest he take the name of his God in vain (Prov. 30:9). Many sin when suddenly dumped into sinful situations, circumstances which tempt a man sorely are easily turned by sinful men into sinful situations.

2. These words may be understood as a preface to Job's bill of complaint, as if he had said, 'Lord, it may be that through the tediousness of my pain and the burdens of my sorrows I will let slip from me words for which I cannot give a good account. Yet, Lord, do not condemn me if I speak to excuse myself, for I do not intend to accuse You. If I speak in my own defense, do not let it be an offense to You.' Abraham spoke in this way, *"Let not the Lord be angry, and I will speak, and I will speak yet this once"* (Gen. 18). Strong passions, which tumble over one another in their eagerness to escape, will make an unruly orator. It is the work of pity and mercy in us to bear with a speaker who is bearing much affliction in his body and in his breast.

3. The words may be taken as a plain deprecation, as they read, *"Do not condemn me"* —The Hebrew is literally, *"Do not wicked me,"* which means, Do not count me as one that

is wicked, or, Do not cast me among the wicked. But did the Lord account Job as one of the wicked? Did Job think that the Lord counted him among the wicked? No, but rather did Job think that these afflictions were not on account of his wickedness. Instead he had hopes, perhaps even assurances, that the Lord had justified and acquitted him. Why then does he say, Do not condemn me? First, it may be expounded in this way, that he prays that the Lord will keep the world from having any occasion to condemn him. Do not lay Your hand upon me so heavily that the world will understand me to be one of the wicked.Though Job was assured that he had a witness above, a record on high, yet he saw that men were taking occasion by his afflictions to say that he was one of the wicked. So he feels compelled to pray that God will not allow this to be so.

The words may also have this meaning, that Job is praying that God do whatever He desires to him, but that He not condemn him. He is willing to submit to any indignity, any sorrow, any pain, but not to condemnation from God Himself;

Condemnation has three things in it to make it very grievous to us, (1)The penalty of the sentence itself; (2) The disfavor of the Judge; (3) The stain upon the integrity of the condemned one. As regards the providential dealings of God, Job had shown that he could bear the penalty, because of his realization that he deserved it and more for his sins. But he could not bring himself to bear the disfavor of his Judge, and here in our text he is showing that he did not escape being troubled that his integrity was being stained in the eyes of the world. Spiritual speaking Job was of course secured against the penalty for sin, and at the same time he was fixed in the favor of God forever, by his union with the Lord Jesus Christ. But even the saints may sometimes be asked to bear stains upon their integrity in the eyes of the world for a period of time commensurate with the judgments of God.

THE WORLD IS QUICK TO CONDEMN GOOD MEN AS WICKED, IF AFFLICTED

When Paul had escaped death in the storm and shipwreak, and then a viper subsequently fixed its fangs in his hand, the worldlings were quick to condemn him as one so wicked that God would not allow him to live. Those who died when the Tower of Siloam fell were accounted sinners above and beyond all others, but Christ rebukes those who concluded that it must be so. It is such a common thing for the world to judge all things by what they term success. They have an opinion that the godly should gain and thrive in the things of the world, in the ease and comforts of the world. In spite of the fact that both Job and Jeremiah speaking by the Holy Spirit have warned us that the wicked are prosperous and without doubt or worry (more times than the godly), man continues to think that a prosperous man is one favored by God, that a man who is troubled is in disfavor with God. Yet the opinions of men cannot contradict the God-breathed words of the Holy Spirit. Just because men think so will not make it in fact to be so. Look at what they thought of Christ Jesus, who was God over all, Creator and Sustainer of life, pure, holy, just and good: He was *"esteemed stricken, smitten of God and afflicted"* (Isa. 53). Read the story of His life if you do not think that Christ was considered to be not only a sinner, but an imposter, a hypocrite who claimed godhood while His weak and marred face and body gave his claims the lie. God smote Him, yet He was in the highest favor with God. He had nowhere to lay His head, yet God loved Him more than any other. He was too weak to carry His cross, yet He even then was too good for this world and was on His way to deliverance from it as He delivered us from it. The centurion, one of the thieves and a handful of followers. recognized Him for a good man, but the rest of the world was certain that He was a wicked blasphemer and imposer upon God. Does it matter to us any more than it mattered to Him, that we should be condemned as He was? Of course, there is more reason to condemn us, but we need not be exercised in mind and heart except toward God.

Let the saints remember this, *"there is therefore no condemnation to those who are in Christ Jesus"(Romans 8:1).*

"Make me to know why You contend with me"—As his second request, Job asks that God give him some intelligence as to why He is crushing him under all these blows.

"Make me to know"—It is a word that signifies to have something made plain to the understanding. Job asks for some light for his reason, even if there must be heaviness in all the rest of his being.

"Why You contend with me" —The word expresses contention or striving between two or more parties, not the final sentence from the judge. The parties to a suit contend with one another, but they do not have authority vested in them to condemn the other parties. The judge, on the other hand, has the authority to condemn, but he does not enter the dispute and contend with either side. Job speaks in the style of both, desiring the Lord not to act as a judge and condemn him; yet asking why the Lord appeared to be an opponent contending with him. In some sense, at least, the Lord does contend, for He says, *"I will not contend forever"* (Isa. 57:16), and He is said to have had a controversy with the inhabitants of Israel (Hosea 4:1);

Job was seeking to know the cause for his afflictions. His friends were not troubled to know, for they were dead certain that they knew the cause of his afflictions — gross and extraordinary sin. Job does not have the answer, but he knows full well that their answer is false. He is puzzled as to God's intention, but he is not the least puzzled by his friends. In asking God why, Job wants to know at least three things, (1) If it is his sin for which God visits him with affliction; (2) And if so, what sin or sins is it that causes such sore afflictions; (3) But if it is not some specific sin or sins, then what else could it be? Some have asked, Is it lawful for Job to query the Lord. Should he not be praying for wisdom to be patient under his burdens, rather than for the intelligence as to the cause of them?

It should be credited to Job that he was not asking merely to satisfy his curiosity — it was his conscience which he wanted to satisfy. He was not prying into God's secrets, trying to unlock the cabinet of His counsel to see what he might discover to be there. He was asking that the secrets of his own heart be opened, that he might discover whatever might be lurking there. Like David, he sought to know if there was any wicked way in him. Again, he did not want the answer for his own satisfaction, that he might smirk and say, I have done no wrong. He wanted the answer in order to show the world that hypocrites, fools and rash critics did not have reason to condemn a man merely because he was afflicted more than any other man they had ever seen. He hurts in his body, he hurts in his soul, he hurts in his spirit, but most of all the hurts that he feels most are those that come from observing the world dishonor God by making Him the executioner of their opinions.

An afflicted saint will be very solicitous about the reason for his affliction. A child of light does not like to be left in the dark. All men hate riddles, but godly men dislike being left in uncertainty most when it is a question of sin in the matter. Evil men will deceive themselves and hide under the most transparent excuses in order to escape knowing that they have sinned. But godly men will search through all the heavens and the earth in order to get enough light to see their sins. Job seeks knowledge in order to apply the right remedy, repentance

Yet God will often leave a godly man in the dark as to His purposes and providential dealings. A man may labor and give some account of his own heart and ways to God, but it is not often that he is able to understand and give and account of God's ways toward him. The ways of God are past finding out. We can no more see what way He has come than we can see the way the eagle has flown, in most cases. Only God can give a commentary on our lives, making clear and plain what He was doing for us and to us. Sometimes this becomes plain in time, surely all will become plain as we sit at His feet for a blessed eternity. There is no sin in asking God for light on our paths, though He may not be prepared to give it, and though we must be bound by His will in either case. Job's awesome wounds cried aloud for him to cry to God about them. How unfeeling he would have been if he never sought to God to know what lay behind them? He was not a careless worldling, but a careful son of the living God, one who wanted to walk circumspectly in His sight.

"Is it good to You that You should press down, that You should despise the work of Your hands and shine upon the wisdom of the wicked?"—Job 10:3.

He is certain that it is not good, that God does not despise His work nor shine upon the wisdom of the wicked. But Job is going to enumerate some of the ways that men pervert justice, and he is one by one going to remove them from the pure and just God that he loved. This may be done by affirmation, or by well-constructed questions which obviously call for negative answers. These interrogations of Job are vehement negations, they flatly and peremptorily deny what they seem to doubtingly ask. The sense is this, that no one would dare say that it is good for God to oppress, to despise His own work, to shine on the counsel of the wicked. He hates these things, and He cannot despise His own work.

"Is it good to You that You should press down"—The Hebrew expresses three things, (1) That which is profitable (2) That which is pleasant; (3) That which is just, right, honorable, and reputable.

Is it profitable to God to oppress or press down? Could there be any advantage for God in crushing Job? No, no advantage or profit to God, but this does not mean that there is no profit or advantage for Job. Then is it pleasing or delightful to God to do so? No, He does not do these things for pleasure, but this is not to say that He does them against His will. He does it for our good, not for His delight. Yet He does purposely plan to do them and exactly adds the burdens until just the right weight is put upon us — for change is usually made by pressure, by heat, etc. Lastly, does it add to God's reputation and honor for Him to press down upon us? No, but it is much more glory to Him when He passes by a transgression. Again, He acts for the eventual good of Job, and as we shall see even to the restoration of Job's reputation and honor among men.

"that You should press down"—It is a word with a double signification, (1) Oppression by words; (2) oppression by actions. The tongue is a great oppressor, and the apostle James complains that men have never tamed it. The hand oppresses both by blows and by withholding that which is due and needed. The word is often used and is very broad in its use. Job is certain that God would not oppress him with either words or actions, in any evil sense of that word. Any acts of God which seem unsuitable to His nature are only seemingly so. Men, being either blind or all but blind, cannot see well enough to tell whether or not God is acting according to His nature or not — but they have every reason to believe that He does, for He never changes, nor does He ever do wrong, etc. Among men, "The best of them is like a briar; the most upright is sharper than a hedge of thorn," but God is not so, and none have a right to think so.

"that You should despise the work of Your hands"—It has a connection with and some similar meaning to the former clause. The word *"despise"* is that one which we have had several times before, it means a loathing, an abhorring of a thing. There is also the idea of rejection expressed in the word. Again, Job does not believe that God would so despise and reject that which He has laboriously put together for His own pleasure and glory. It is in the interest of man's understanding that it is called work, for in actuality the workings of God are not in any sense laborious to Him. For the same reason, we see hands ascribed to God, that we may grasp something of what He is conveying to us. Man is called the work of God's hands in three ways, (1) Because he came immediately from God, without any intermediary means being used; (2) because there is an exactitude evident in the making of man, he is an intricate work of art which only God could make; (3) Because it is a complete work, one to which no one can add any perfection that is not there.

There are three cautions necessary to man in his sinful condition in regards to this truth, that man is the work of God's hands:

1. Do not be proud that you are thus and thus excellent, for all that is excellent in you is the work of God. Are you beautiful? Are you wise? Are you extraordinary in any way? It is God's doings, not ours. Whether your excellencies are natural or supernatural, they are to the glory of God, not to any glory of your own. Even the Lord Jesus Christ could say, *"the Father who dwells in Me, He does the works"* (John 14:10). How much more can we who are so much less than He say that all we are is to God's glory, and all that we do?

2. Do not despise yourself, for it is a sin to despise that which is the work of God's hands. Many are ashamed of the way they look, or ashamed of those who are their parents. The very ones who have reason to be ashamed of what they have become through sin, of the ugliness and deformities of their inner man, concentrate most on what appears only on the outside. They put artificial beauty on at the shops in order to supply the defects of their bodies, but they never give a thought as to how they may gain spiritual beauty to supply the defects of their supernatural being. The crookednesses, the distortions, the blackness and ugliness of the soul are most deplorable, yet they are not at all deplored. If the same care that goes into mending the body by art would go into mending the soul by grace, there would be a day when you would be beautiful indeed! God made men upright. They sought out many inventions in order to escape obeying Him who made them. Now only God can remake them, only this time He will mold them by loving hands until they are far and away more beautiful than Adam or Eve — for they are promised that when the Lord Jesus shall appear, they shall be like Him — if they will only believe, repent and be saved.

Job uses a wise argument when he calls to God's mind the fact that he is the work of God's hands. David does it afterwards, *"Do not forsake the work of Your own hands"* (Ps. 138:8). It is common to be attentive to one's own works. In this God is not different He teaches us through His word to remind Him of His creatorship, *"we are all the work of Your hand, do not be so very angry, O Lord"* (Isa. 64:8). There is only one argument which is certain to bring more mercy to us than this one, and that is the reminder to Him that we are redeemed by the precious blood of our Savior, His Son. Woe to him who strives with his Maker, but grace to him who recognizes God as his Maker and gives to Him proper submission and obedience.

"and shine upon the wisdom of the wicked" —God is light. If anyone has any light it is because God has given it to him — whether it be the light of nature or the light of grace. To shine upon the counsel of the wicked would mean three things, (1) To favor or delight in them; (2) To assist them and help them; (3) to make them prosperous and successful in fulfilling their plans. Therefore David prays against his enemies, *"Let their way be dark and slippery"* (Ps. 35:6). To darken counsel is to hinder and trouble one, so to shine upon counsel is just the opposite. Will God then shine upon the wisdom of the wicked. Job is flatly denying that it is even the remotest possibility. But does not God prosper and give success to the doers of evil? The answer is this, that God makes His sun shine upon both the fruitful field and the thorn-patch, likewise upon both evil and good men. But God does not ever shine upon the evil, giving them favor, assisting them in evil, etc.

There is a twofold light, (1) The light of God's providence; (2) The light of God's countenance. The light of God's face does not ever shine upon the counsel of the wicked. They have the light of providence only, and that only because there are myriads of acts and thoughts which must come into being and run their courses before God can judge the evildoer and bless the faithful only. A man may have great prosperity in those things which he calls good, but with all of them not a single ray of good will come from God. Even the cloudy and dark mysteries that cover the counsel of the wicked. For God only shines on the righteous. He may vary His dispensations often, but He never varies His affection — He has loved His chosen people from everlasting, and He never hates them or dislikes them even when all those things which they call evil are happening to them. Contrariwise, He hates the wicked every day, and there is never a time that He loves those who are not ordained to believe (Acts 13:48) and to be covered by the blood of Christ Jesus.

But who are the wicked mentioned in this text? Some say he speaks of his friends, that he refuses to believe that God will shine upon their ill counsels and sinful censures. It is true that Job found no comfort in his friends during this trial, but it cannot be said that they gave him evil counsel, or that they took counsel together to do so. The Lord removed them, saying, *"You have not spoken of Me what is right, as My servant Job has,"* but He does not charge them with giving Job wicked counsel. Job charged them with speaking wickedly for God (13.7) but even if that were so, it could be an error in judgment at the moment and not truly a thing counseled and determined by the application of their best wisdom. Then there are those who think that Job is speaking of the Devil and his angels. He denies that God will take the part of those wicked beings. Again, others will have the wicked here to be the Sabeans and Chaldeans who stole his possessions. However, it is to be taken in a general way, for all those who are properly denominated wicked, who so freely claim that God shines upon their counsel when they succeed in the ways of this world. For God does apparently do them good when they prosper, as men think of good. While men are walking in pleasing ways , they are oftentimes walking in evil ways as God sees them. He will allow them their carnal delights when He has no delight in them at all. In fact, the Lord hates the counsels of evil men. While they are contriving to please themselves with some trifle from this world, despising Him and all His treasures, He is *"very greatly displeased"* with them (Zech. 1:15). Each time they grasp some part of this world into their greedy hands they are gathering fuel for the flames of later affliction, whether while still in this world, or whether in the world to come, or both.

"Have You eyes of flesh? Or do You see as a man sees?"—Job 10:4:

Job goes on with the same argument. In the third verse he removed three things which would be inconsistent with and dishonorable to God. So now he goes on to remove two more in this and the next verse. Again the question speaks negations. God is not one who has eyes of flesh; He does not see as a man does. These men who sit in judgment upon him merely see with the eyes of a man, they cannot see beneath his skin and outward expression. But God sees into every atom of man, He scans the inward parts where truth is supposed to be dwelling (Ps. 51:6). They suspect him because they have eyes of flesh. He knows because He does not see as a man sees.

God, of course, is a Spirit. He has no special organ or member by which He sees. But for all of that, He sees — it is something He ascribes to Himself times without number. The knowledge of God is the eye of God; or, The eye of God is the knowledge of God. He does not have to peer down at us, for He knows what we are, what we have been in His mind's eye from all eternity, what we have been from conception until this day, all that we have been, all that we have not been.

There are seven differences which may be mentioned here between the eye of man and the eye of God: (1) Man's eye is but a means, an instrument of knowledge; whereas the eye of God is His knowledge. The act and the faculty are not distinct in God, for all in God is act — whatever is ascribed to God is God. That is to say, the eye of God is God seeing, the knowledge of God is God knowing, the love of God is God loving, etc.; (2) Many must have both inward light and an outward light in order to see — without either he cannot see. God sees by His own inward light alone. He does not need any outward light — the darkness and the light are alike to Him, there is no darkness to Him (34:22). (3) Man sees one thing after another, for he is not able to concentrate his view upon more than one at a time. But God sees all things at once, His eye takes in all persons and all objects together — and they are always in His sight, being carefully observed and attended, *"The Lord looks from Heaven and sees all the sons of men"* (Psalm 33:13). (4) An eye of flesh sees at a distance, and it cannot see anything which is brought up too near it.

At the same time, man's eye cannot see when an object is too far off. Yet again, the eye may see a thing and still not know what it is that it sees. All these things are not so with the Lord, for he sees all that is near or far, and He knows all that He sees. (5) Man sees only the outside of a thing, but the Lord sees both outside and inside, and into every particle as well. (6) An eye of flesh may be deceived, for even that which he sees clearly may be distorted by a man's mind or imagination. But there are no possible deceptions which can stop God from either seeing or knowing what He sees. (7) Let the eye of a man gather in all that it can see, yet he has been only since yesterday, he shall know but an infinite small part of what he has seen, and even less of what there is to be known. It is not so with God, who needs no experience to know. He knew the end from the beginning. He does not look in order to discover something He did not before know, but instead is pictured to us as looking and watching so that we may realize that He knows all things at all times.

"Are Your days like the days of a man? Are Your years like man's days?" —Job 10:5.

Job proceeds to give another negative by his questions, that God is not a man that He should have days and years of existence. The word for man used here is that word which should have days and years of existence. The word for man used here is that word which depicts man in his worst estate, poor, miserably weak and sinfully sick man. Could God's existence be like such a man's? Certainly not. Even the longest living among men are but a puff of vapor on the sands of time, how much less then in comparison to God who has always been, is, and always shall be. God is not only called *"the Ancient of days"* because He has existed all the days that have ever been, but because He existed before there were any such things as days — He is older than all the days, so His days cannot be compared to the days of a mere man.

It may be that Job is in the center of these days, that he is referring to God's dealings with himself. Then it would be as if he had said,'Lord, why do You examine me? Why do you incessantly follow me with afflictions? Lord, You do not need to fear that time will be lost, that You will not have opportunity to know all about me. Man's day is short and he needs all of them to gain but a little knowledge, but You need no time to know. You are the Lord of time, You can lengthen it or shorten it, or even suspend it. Why then do You deal so severely with me, as if there were no more days to examine me than this month or this year?'

Again, he may mean to convey that a man's day is always changing — there are cloudy periods and there are some bright and sunny times. Somedays are wholly unpleasant, etc. But with God the days mean nothing to Him, they are all the same to Him.

"Are Your years like man's days?" —Job varies the comparison in this clause, comparing God's years to man's day, instead of man's years. The time of man is so short that it is not worthy of having years mentioned in the same breath with it. Moses makes the same sort of variation, both saying that we have seventy years only, but saying, *"the days of our years are seventy,"* (Ps. 90:10).

Another difference appears here in that a different word for man is used, this one being the word for a strong man, a mighty man, a man's man, one who has vigor and ability. So, then, Job says, God's days are not like those of a sick and weak man, neither are they like those of the strong and vigorous man — they are far above and beyond either.

God's day is the day of eternity. Not only does He inhabit eternity, being without beginning and without end, but He never inhabits time. Not only are a thousand days as one day to Him, but all the days are but one day to Him. He lives in the ever-present now, all things are done today so far as God is concerned — *"You are My Son, today I have begotten You"* (Ps. 2:7). Was it the day that the baby Jesus was born on earth? No, it was the eternal generation of the Son which was being detailed in that Psalm. Man's day was, is, and shall be. God's day always is, not being a period of time which He created.

Because God's day is different, is the ever-present now, there are no periods of time for

Him to be happy or unhappy but He is always happy because everything to Him is now. A man's days bring comforts or discomforts, happinesses and troubles, his day is filled with a succession of ill and pleasant happenings. God has all at once, all happiness without succession or progression. He enjoys as much in one of our days as He does in another, for they are all one with Him. He enjoys all at once because He sees all at once. There is not one thing after another to God, but all is at once and together. Eternity is filled with blessedness, for God inhabits eternity — where He is, there is blessedness.

Because all is not to God, He does not need to be precipitate in any of His actions. He does not pace Himself, nor does He plan periods of time when He will do this or that. A man has not a single day he can call his own, which he can rule and bend to his wishes. God makes all days to blend into His one day, everything is ruled by Him without end. Men are creatures of time, so God has divided their lives up into times, of which a day is but a short part, yet a not inconsiderable part if it is divided into the short span of life. God looks upon time as nothing, *"My age is nothing to You"* said David.

"that You seek out my iniquity and search for my sin?"—Job 10:6.

Now we shall see why Job asks so many negative questions. It is as if he had said, 'Lord, surely You do not need to search and examine me in this way, since none of these things are true of You — You do not love to press me down, You do not despise the work of Your hands. You do not shine upon the counsels of the wicked. You do not see with the eyes of a man.'

"that You seek out"—The original expresses an inquiry in two ways, (1) by word; (2) by actions. A man may examine or seek with words, or with actions. There is additionally the picture of one speaking and acting with intensive care and with a passionate desire to find what is being sought. Inquisition by torture is one use of the word, and it would fit well with Job's question to the Lord, 'Is it necessary, Lord, for You to bring such sore and terrible judgments upon me in order to find me out?'

"and search for my sin" —The word here for *"search"* is a word of similar import with the former. but there are some who distinguish them in this way: (1)The former inquiry by recalling to memory, or by examining ourselves — the question then is, *"You are recalling to Your mind all my iniquity."* (2) The second word then would express a search which was diligently carried out by digging, by uncovering sin, by close observation and minute detection. Then Job is saying, 'Why do You search for my sin, when You know all things, You know that I have no secret sins which I am hiding in my bosom.'

God does not seek us out and search us in order that He may discover something about us that He did not know. Rather, God searches us that we might know, that we might discover something about Him or about us which we did not previously know. When a brilliant light is shined upon even a well-lit room, we will see many, many things which we never realized were there before. How much more do we discover in the dark recesses of our minds and hearts when God shines His light in and starts to search out our sins there!

There is no instrument so much used to search us as is affliction. God searches Job for sin by afflicting him. Job learned about sin in himself which he never dreamed was there. There is filthiness in all of us, corrupting and poisoning our lives from their hidden corners, and God uses the rod to beat it out of us. Either He beats us, so that our filthiness begins to stink in our spiritual nostrils, or He beats us, so that our filthiness scalds us and causes us to cast it out. It is a sad thing that God must come and seek out our sins, throwing the searchlight of His word upon them. Why do we not examine ourselves, to see if we are in the faith? Is it nothing to us that we are filled with vicious bits of ungodliness? Are we to be allowed contentment when we are so little concerned to be conformed to the image of Christ Jesus, and to have that mind which was in Him? If we do not search out our sins, if God does not search out our sins, then our sins will find us out. Sin will not lie dormant and neither tip our spiritual scales backward or forward. Sin is rebellion against God, and it is ever working in us to cause us to oppose the Spirit of God. Will we allow such an enemy to use us for a lurking place from which it can attack God?

338

Let it not be said!

"You know that I am not wicked, and there is none who can deliver out of Your hand"
—Job 10:7.

Mark this verse. It contains one of the main questions of the grand controversy which the book of Job handles for our benefit. His friends say that Job is wicked, that he must be, else God would not visit him with these severe, lengthy and unintermitted afflictions. Satan originated that charge against Job, that he was a hypocrite who only served God for what he could get out of it. God tells us that He set up the challenge to Satan, whether or not he thought Job was a holy and upright man, one who feared God and turned away from evil. Job, knowing none of this, now appeals to the Lord God, whose knowledge he knows to be perfect and without defect, saying, *"You know that I am not wicked."* The Hebrew is word for word this, *"It is upon Your knowledge that I am not wicked."*

It is important to note that Job does not say that he is not a sinner, nor does he say that God knows he has not sinned. Some who presume to comment thus about this good man seem never to have read this Book. It is not his opinion that he is the best of the saints, as if he were too good to deserve that which God has been doing to him. Even the worst of the saints are not wicked, though the best of them still are but sinners. No one who is a partaker of the divine nature may be called wicked. They get their name from their better part, saints — not from their worst part, sinners.

Many translate, it, *"You know that I have not done wickedly,"* since the original is in the verb form. But the sense is the same, for a man is in action what he is in being. He who is not wicked in his state will not be doing wickedly. It is in this way that we understand that difficult verse of the apostle John,*"he who commits sin is of the Devil"* (1 John 3:8).

God knows all of us, the exact state of every man and every thing, exactly and accurately, *"God knows those that are His,"* (2 Tim. 2:19) and in Job's case He knows that he is not one of the wicked, but one of His. To know in that verse is to know in a loving way. The opposite, then, is true, that God does not know those that are not His in a loving way, *"I never knew you,"* the Lord Jesus will say to many. But in Job's sense, God knows all men, what is in them, what is not in them. All things are naked and open before Him. He knows our persons, our acts, how we acted, with what motive and intention, the means we use, and what will be the consequence of it all.

It is a matter of much consolation to Job, apparently, that God knows that he is not wicked. How wonderful it is that we do not have to live in a world where no one knows us, where there are none who can state positively and with complete knowledge that we are not wicked. As long as God knows, it is enough. Our comfort and our cheer are in Him, and it is His opinion which we truly value. Let men forget what we have done, God will never forget. Let men despise us for what we are, we shall never be despised by God, for we are His children. Let men deliberately misinterpret our motives or our acts, God knows that we intended well and that we have done well. Let our own misty conscience condemn us, God yet may acquit us — for only God knows what is right and wrong, and only God knows whether we have done right or wrong.

HOW CAN THE WICKED BE DIFFERENTIATED FROM THE GODLY?

1. Sin reigns in the wicked man; yea, it lords it over him, *"Do not let sin be king in your mortal body, to obey it in its evil desires..for sin shall not lord it over you, for you are not any longer under law, but under grace"* (Rom. 6:12,14). The Holy Spirit there tells us the difference plainly, that we are slaves to sin or slaves to righteousness, saying of the godly, *"But thanks be to God that you were the slaves of sin, but you obeyed from the heart the form of teaching to which you were delivered up. And being set free from sin, you became slaves to righteousness"* (Rom. 6:16,17). Sin reigned, then grace reigned. But the wicked man continues to submit himself to sin, he is a slave to all forms of sin, being

especially in love with certain types of sin. He may cease all outward forms of sin for a time, but he is still the slave of sin and will upon occasion return to his vomit. A saint, on the other hand,, may fall into sin while he is a slave to righteousness, but he will not fall down and serve sin again, nor will he remain in it. Christ is a jealous God, He will not permit one of His own to be both His servant and the servant of sin.

2. A wicked man sins by custom, he drives all the time in a course of sin, sin is a habit with him. A godly man does not habitually sin, but even if he falls into a sin the second time he will break its hold on him by repenting and resting in God's power to gain the victory over it. Wicked men plead for opportunity to continue their sin. Godly men plead for God to break off their sin and to cast it away from them. Wicked men make provision for the lists of the flesh, but godly men watch carefully for lusts to rear their ugly heads within them, so that they can enlist God to mortify them.

3. A wicked man carefully preserves within himself a purpose to sin. He may pray, he may protest against his sin, but he secretly intends to indulge himself in it again. That blessed saint, Augustine, confessed that before his conversion he would pray and secretly hope that God would not grant his prayer to kill off his passions. A godly man will sin, but it is never his purpose to sin. Just as an honest traveler intends to keep straight on his way in order to arrive at his destination, so the godly man tries to keep himself in the way of holiness. If he misses his way, it is not intentional. If he wanders from the way, even then he may hear the voice of the Holy Spirit whispering in his ear, *"turn to the left; turn to the right"* so that you do not go astray from the Way of Holiness (Isa. 35:8); A case exactly to the point is the sin of Peter in denying the Lord. Peter did not purpose to deny Him. In fact, Peter purposed not to deny Him, he even promised he would not deny Him. Yea, he said in his heart that he would rather die than to deny Christ. Judas purposed to make a deal with the Pharisees, but Peter did not make any bargain with anyone. Peter fell into a violent temptation, fear for his life, after he had boldly followed the Lord right into the halls of the enemy. He did fail to put his full trust in Christ, perhaps somewhat bewildered and beset by doubts because his mighty Master was being manhandled and spit upon as if He were no more than a weak man. Yet he did not deliberately sin, a godly man never does. He left himself open for an attack, and invasion by sin, and he fell before it. But he also fell to repenting afterwards, weeping bitterly over his carnal surrender. And his life became one of the finest testimonies to the power and glory of God of any that has lived and served Jesus Christ, our Lord and our God.

4. A wicked man clearly and fully consents to sin. He may have things which he conceives he will not do, but he never determines in his heart that he will not sin against God in any way. There may be some kind of late consent when a godly man sins, but there is no premeditation to do what pleases himself come what may. Just as a wicked man will upon occasion hear the word, pray, and consent to good acts, yet he never is willing to make his life conform to God's commands — so the godly man may indulge in some acts common to wicked men, but he is never willing to make his life conform to sin's commands. A godly man will resist the devils when they tempt toward sin, but a wicked man is taken captive freely, with the consent to the will, by the Devil and his evil cohorts

Job appeals to God to make known what He knows, that no such wickedness had been in his heart at any time, so as to cause these crushing blows to rain upon him. It is important to observe that Job is certain, that he is confident of his comparative innocence, and of God's approving knowledge. This is not a halting step which he takes to see if he can resolve his doubts. He is not in doubt, he knows that God knows he is not wicked. Doubts are not impossible in the mind of the saint, but they are not to be thought of as normal. A doubting Christian is a weak Christian, and it may be that he is not the man he thinks he is. Certainly those associations who call themselves Christian yet teach that doubting is the most honoring attitude toward salvation are of very doubtful origin themselves. The Scriptures show us again and again men who are as certain of their salvation as they are of their Savior.

A godly man may know that he is so by the workings of his heart, *"By this we know that we know Him, if we keep His commandments;" "We know that we have passed from death to life because we love the brothers"* (1 John 2:3; 3:14). We are justified by faith alone, so far as our justification before God is concerned. But before men we are justified by our works, *"show me your faith apart from your works, and I will show you my faith from my works... faith apart from works is dead. Was not our father Abraham declared just by works when he had offered his son Isaac on the altar? You see that faith was working with his works. And his faith was made complete by works"* (James 2:18-22). Faith works by love. If you see a man who claims to have God's grace, then by his fruits you shall know him — does he have the works of grace in his life? If he has not, then put a question mark behind his confession until he has. Grace is the image of Christ stamped upon the soul. If you do not see the lowliness, the meekness, the self-sacrifice and self-humiliation that was in Christ Jesus, then put a question mark behind your name until you can ask God to make your calling and election sure to you.

A godly man may know that he is so by the testimony of the Holy Spirit with his heart. *"Now He who made us fit for this same thing is God, who also has given to us the first fruit of the Spirit." "The Spirit Himself bears witness with our spirit that we are the children of God"* (2 Cor. 5:5; Rom. 8:16). The Spirit plants and conveys grace in the soul. He also acts and helps us to exercise the graces He plants there. He shines upon and enlightens those graces, sometimes by arguments and inferences, most times by his presence and influence,, *"we have received the Spirit which is of Christ, that we may know the things that are freely given to us by God"* (1 Cor. 2:12).

Even while Job was racked with pain, crushed by affliction, pushed by his unbelieving friends, he dared to look up to God and say to Him, *"You know that I am not wicked."* What a joy it would be to know that all of us could do as much as that good man.

"and there is none that can deliver out of Your hand," —That is, there are no creatures who can do so, for Christ is said in many places to have delivered us. The hand of God is the power of God, so that for anyone to deliver out of His hand they must overcome His power. There is no difficulty in the words, but there is some difference about the intent of them. There are those who substitute nothing for none, thus joining these words to the former as an argument of the insufficiency of man's righteousness, *"You know that I am not wicked and that there is nothing that can deliver out of Your hand"*—that is, nothing in my righteousness that can deliver. Most believe that Job is seeking to move the Lord to compassion, to stir up His bowels of pity toward him. Job is breathing out a very heroic and magnamimous spirit in these words. He is resolved to honor God and hold on to his integrity as long as he he lives. If I never am delivered, says Job, I still shall never curse my God.

"Your hands have made me and shaped me, together all around. Yet You destroy me"—Job 10:8.

He now illustrates the middle clause of the third verse, saying, 'Lord, since you will not despise the work of Your hands, why should You despise me? Am I not made by Your hands? Have they not fashioned me all around? Yet now You destroy me?" From this he goes into detail, having here the forming or making of him; in the ninth verse the matter out of which he is made; in the tenth verse his conception; the putting together of his parts in the eleventh verse; the giving of life to his parts in the twelfth verse; the preservation of that life in the same verse.

There are three opinions concerning the connection or bond of these words with those that went before:

1. Some believe that Job persists in the same matter handled in the words immediately foregoing, exalting the knowledge of God because God made man. So, then, God knows that he is not wicked because it was God Himself who made him, etc. It is a strong argument, that the God who formed man is One who knows man and also One who may

dispose of man as He sees fit.

2. Job may be explaining some of those things he had put into question from earlier, as here when he answers his own question from verse 3. If it is God's work, then He may do with it as He pleases, even destroy it. For the copulative in the original which we translate *"yet"* may be and often is translated *"and"* in the Scriptures. Then this verse would read, *"Your hands have made me...and You destroy me."*

3. The words may carry the sense of a strong motive to prevail with God, to cause Him to handle Job more gently, or at least to deal more tenderly with him as He keeps him on the rack. The argument is, that if God took such pains to make him and fashion him just so, then God will surely pity and spare him. Every intelligent agent that makes something is naturally inclined to preserve it. God's creation was followed by God's preserving providence. David and Isaiah both prayed to God the mercies and kindnesses which He had done for them in order to preface the request for more. Job here is acknowledging tha care of the Lord in fashioning his body, in preface to his asking for more care of it. In this sense, some render the last clause as an interrogation, *"Your hands have made me...and do You destroy me?"*

"Your hands".—The hands that laid the foundation of the earth, that flung the stars into space, and spanned the heavens, also formed and fashioned man in a work of creative art which dwarfs those larger operations. A multitude of opinions have arisen from the statement that the hands of God formed and fashioned man. Some think that as God said, *"Let us make man,"* in the plural, that the hands of all three of the Persons in the Trinity were involved in this work of making man. Others expound it literally and formally, not as if God had hands but that when God at first formed man, the Son took upon Himself an outward shape of a man, and so (they say) Christ in the form of man formed man.

The hands of God are all second causes, is another opinion, and God uses these second causes to produce His effects. Man's making since Adam has not been immediate, but mediate, yet it is still the work of God who is working by these second causes. But we believe that the best sense is this, that the hands of God are generally taken for the power and wisdom of God. The hand of power acts what the hand of wisdom contrives. Whatever is put into one's hand is presumed to be in one's power, as when God said to Satan in the second chapter, *"Behold, he is in your hand – but save his life."*

"have made me and shaped me"—Here are two words which some distinquish by referring the one to the body the other to the soul. We do not need to be so accurate as that. But this much is plainly noted in them, that the Lord was exceedingly accurate in this work of making man. Both these words have their special significations:

1. The word we translate *"made"* means more than to merely make – it is a making with exactitude and skill, with care and with wisdom. God uses such a word that we may know that He did not make man with half a mind, with but little concern.

2. The word translated *"shaped"* is a word that expresses the outward forming of a thing. Man not only got his nature from God, but his figure as well. It is a word used to express to trim or to polish, to make attractive with beautiful lines, etc.

"all around"—Think not that this is a mere superfluity of speech, it is added to express further the exactness of God in making man, that He would not trust the least part of the work to the hand of any other – His hands made us and formed us all around.

It is an allusion, perhaps, of the work of the potter, who as he fashions a pot will turn it round and round so as to prefect and beautify it. Some understand this *"all around"* to express all those things which man has around him. But it is more likely that God has altogether made man, inside and out, through and through, with exact skill and foredetermined planning.

Then let those who despise the body remember that we are *"fearfully and wonderfully made,"* for God has with much care and skill formed it and shaped it within and without.

It is true that the body is called vile, but it is only in comparison to that glorious body which shall be. We know not what it shall be like, only that when He appears, we shall be like Him. For now, however, we know that what we have is a body especially prepared for us by our Maker.

Again, let those be careful who are inclined to laugh and mock at some whose bodies do not meet with their approval. It is God that made that body which you find so laughable! Do you laugh at His purpose in making it so? Who are you that you should know what is a right appearance? Did He make you the inspector of bodily forms, that you should reject some that He had made? Beware, lest He give you good measure for your derision, double-barreled pain for each of your mocking remarks about His handiwork! And as for yourself, you may not complain about your looks or your form either, for *"let not the thing formed say to Him that formed it, Why have You made me this way"* (Rom 9:20). All the things which you find to criticize, even if they seem to you to be perfectly legitimate complaints, are subject to the will and purpose of God. In other words, He may have had a very good purpose in making you the way you are. Do you have a weak constitution, a sluggish mind, a crippled part, etc.? Then instead of being discontented and displeasing to God, seek to find out what good can come to you because of these things, for there are usually compensations to be found without much of a search in your life. But if you search and cannot find out the reason, believe this, that He who is the only truly reasonable One, He who made you reason, certainly did have a reason for making you as you are.

If God made us, then let us all be Davids who will pray to Him, *"Your hands have made me and formed me. Give me understanding so that I may learn Your commandments"* (Ps. 119:73). All that we are and all that we have should be dedicated to Him who made us for His glory. We are not our own, we are His, our bodies and our spirits are His, and they should be ever at work to serve Him.

"Yet You destroy me"—It is a word which means to swallow up with greediness. The Holy Spirit expresses our final victory over death by a word which reaches this sense, *"Death is swallowed up in victory"* (1 Cor. 15:54). Job has seen his estate swallowed up, his children consumed, his health eaten away, etc. Even his very breath seems in danger of being swallowed by his increasing afflictions. He is being swallowed down as it were piece by piece, and an utter end, a total consumption of him is in prospect. Read as a question, the sense is quickened and the tone is more pathetic, *"and do You destroy me?"* Do You who have made me so carefully now destroy me?

It should not be missed that the best of men may suffer the greatest destruction from the hand of Him who made him the best of men — that is, the destruction of his outward man. God never destroys the spiritual creature which He has created by the hand of His grace. God seldom acts according to our minds, that is to say, we seldom can get our minds into God's thinking far enough to understand what He will do and why. It is only as we get close to Him, so that we can view things from His viewpoint, that we are able to follow His thinking at all. Even when we believe a thing because it is written in the Scriptures, we often do not understand it unless we become so familiar with the Scriptures that we begin to depart from our own natural thinking processes and begin instead to think in the grooves which God's word has made in us.

"Remember, I beg You, that You have formed me as the clay; and will You bring me into the dust again?" —Job 10:9.

The original word is applied to a senstive act, as well as to a rational act, *"The Lord remember"* (Ps. 20:3). Memory is the savor or scent of things that are preserved in the mind. As such, memory, or the act of remembering, is improperly applied to God. Nothing is past to God, but all things are present. Memory is a storehouse into which we put those experiences which have made the greatest impressions upon us, generally speaking. God has no experiences which have made impressions upon Him. He sees everything that happens, whether in the year one or in the final year, as happening all at once — without the frustration of having some piece of some life missing for the moment. But in order to meet with the understanding of man, God speaks of Himself as remembering or forgetting. When He says that He remembers, it implies two things, (1) a serious attention to the person, a consideration of the thing which He formerly seemed to slight or to pass by without interest; (2) a speedy supply of those things which are lacking to us, or a quick deliverance from peril. God remembers us when He favors us, when He rescues us.

It is our duty to remember God, and it is our privilege to ask Him to remember us. It is a privilege because there is no natural right for us to ask it of Him. God is willing that we should speak to Him according to the manner of men, but we must not think of Him as if He were only a man like we are. Because we forget, we must not think that He actually could forget. There are four things which the saints usually ask the Lord to remember, (1) His own mercies, *"Remember, O Lord, Your tender mercies"* (Ps. 25:6); (2) His covenant, *"He will always be mindful of His covenant"* (Ps. lll:5), yet He loves for us to remember it and then to remind Him to do so. (3) His enemies and theirs, for it is a prayer often seen in God's word, that He remember the enemies of His people (Ps. 74:l8; 137:7). (4) It is common for the saints to remind God of their own frailty, both that which is natural and that which is spiritual. Here Job is reminding God of his natural frailty, that He has made him of clay, a substance that has no great stability.

"that You have formed me as the clay"—The word refers to cement or mortar which is a mixture of earth and water. Originally the making of man was described in this way, *"The Lord God formed man of the dust of the ground"* (Gen. 2:7). Job says here that He formed him as the clay, or of the clay, for the sense is the same either way. Job is of course speaking of himself with respect to creation, for, according to the ordinary course of nature, man is not made of clay. The first man was made of clay or dust, and all other men are from him. We derive our pedigree from the dirt, but now we are made as the clay — that is, we are frail, brittle and weak. We are composed of materials which will quickly crack and shatter. When the Holy Spirit desired to describe how easily Christ can shatter all the opposites of His kingdom, He said, *"He shall dash them in pieces like a potter's vessel"* (Ps. 2:9). That we are made of clay intimates three things, (1) that man's frame has an excellence, for he is not thrust together like a rude lump or mass of earth. He is *"curiously wrought."* To make a vessel of clay requires both pains and skill. (2) That God has made us of a material which will not allow us to contend with Him. For can clay withstand His strokes? (3) Our origin of clay argues that we can be easily overcome by temptation, that we are exceedingly susceptible to sin. Sin, in its kind, is as spiritual as grace is, yet our sinful corruption is figuratively called *"the flesh."* One reason may be this, that flesh when taken properly is an occasion of sin. The flesh being sensitive is a snare to the rational man, much more to the spiritual man.

Taking up this sense, Job may be saying to the Lord, 'Suppose that I have sinned, You know that I am not wicked. But suppose that I have sinned and have failed You, yet, Lord, remember that You have made me as the clay. I am not a pure spirit, as the angels are. I have this body of earth which clogs and hinders me in every duty, which makes me such as easy prey for every sin.' God Himself takes up this as an argument to spare sinful men, *" yea, many times He turned His anger away and did not stir up all His wrath For He remembered that they were but flesh, a wind that passes away and does not come again"* (Ps. 78:38,39). Again in Psalm l03:14, He allows this argument, *"so the Lord pities those that fear Him. For He knows their frame, He remembers that they are dust."* As if the matter from which man was first made, though itself without sin, were some disadvantage to him in the resisting of sin. It was a disadvantage before man had any sin in him, how much more is it now when most men have nothing at all in them but sin — even the best men have very much sin. Some imagine that God was so irreconcilably angry with the angels that fell because there was not this excuse for them, that they were made as the clay or formed out of the dust — for they were pure spirits, without any fleshly hindrances in the performance of their duties. They had no clogs of flesh and blood, no fogs, no mists vaporizing from a sensitive part to their intellectual part. They had the more power to continue pure because they were free from any earthly and elementary mixtures. Their sin was a compound of more evils because their nature was so simple. Angels had nothing within them to tempt them, but they turned themselves away from God merely upon the choice of their wills. As every good action is so much the better when it has a free concurrence of the will, so every evil action is that much worse when it has the pure and free concurrence of the will. The sin we commit is the greater by how much we have the less provocation to commit it. The sin of our first parents was aggravated in that God had given them such plenty and variety, but it was lessened in comparison to the sin of the angels because they had more provocation to sin. Our first parents were of the earth, therefore they were delighted with earthly objects. There was a temptation to the eye in the forbidden fruit, a temptation to the taste, etc. Of course a sinner in dust and clay cannot be excused because he is such, but he is more to be pitied than is the case with a spirit that sins against God.

"Will You bring me into the dust again?" —To be brought to the dust is a roundabout way of describing death; To be brought to the dust is also a description of any low and poor condition (Ps. 22:29). Job saw himself brought to the dust of a low condition of poverty and of disgrace, and he feared that he would be brought to the dust of death. He had not been brought out of the dust of affliction, so he could not ask if he would be brought out of the dust again. The words are read three ways by various interpreters, (1) as an assertion, (2) as an interrogation, (3) as an admiration.

As an assertion, it reads, *"You will bring me into the dust again."* As an interrogation, it reads, *"Will You bring me into the dust again?"* As an admiration, it reads, *"You have made me as the clay, and (what?) will You bring me into the dust again!"*

As to the first, as an assertion it may have reference to the decree of God concerning man, as if he said, By creation and natural constitution — I am frail and weak, being made of clay, and by Your purpose and decree I am appointed to death. You will certainly bring me into the dust again, therefore spare me for the short time I yet have to live.

As to the second, as an interrogation, it may be that Job intended the question to mitigate the severity of the Lord's afflictions upon him, as if he had said, 'You have made me of clay but a little while ago, and now will You bring me into the dust again already? O spare me a little before I go back to dust.'

"Have You not poured me out like milk and curdled me like cheese?" —Job 10:10. Under the modest shadow of this verse, that great natural mystery of man's generation and conception is contained. The former word signifies not only the pouring forth of liquids, but the melting and dissolving of the hardest of metals so that they can be poured forth. And as this one expresses the softening and melting of that which is hard, the next word signifies the hardening or thickening of that which is soft and fluid. Moses uses it in describing the miraculous dividing of the Red Sea, *"the depths were curdled in the heart of the sea"* (Exod. 15:8). These two expressive words may be applied fairly to that special contribution which God has charged upon each parent, towards that great work, the continuation of their kind, the raising up of posterity to serve God and their own generations.

Man has a reason to be humbled by the earthiness of his origin. Can a man be proud when he has been poured out like milk and curdled like cheese? As a picture of natural conception, we see that God is given the credit for natural conception, with no mention being made of the father or mother which the Lord had worked in as the immediate power to beget children. More is ascribed to God in the next verse.

"You have clothed me with skin and flesh and have fenced me with bones and sinews" —Job 10:11.

Job carries on his step by step description of the production of man. After man is poured out in liquid form, then curdled like cheese, he begins to be formed and shaped into the parts and lineaments of his organic body.

"with skin and flesh"—The original word comes from a root meaning naked. We commonly say he is naked who has nothing on but his skin. Skin is man's natural clothing, all that he needed until he sinned. Flesh here is probably a description of the clothing God provides for the parts of man, his heart, liver, brain, and bowels. And the bones and sinews are to fence these in so that they suffer no hurt. So, then, the skin and the flesh are two layers of clothing which God has provided for the more important parts of the body.

"and have fenced me with bones and sinews"—These are armor God has provided to keep the vital parts from being harmed. Bones are for strength, and sinews are for motion. These are the principle parts for this purpose, being put for the muscles, the ligaments, etc.

Some have thought to quarrel with God for turning man loose in the world without clothing and without arms, but God did not do such a thing, for we are both clothed and armed by nature with skin and flesh, with bones and sinews. Besides this man is given a brain capable of inventing all else that he needs, even when he has practically incapacitated himself by sin.

Among the many marvels of the body, which could be made into a multi-volume encyclopedia of wonders, is this, that God has made all these various parts of the body — whether hard, mucuous, membraneous, fatty, soft, etc. all from the same material — from clay or dust;

"You have granted me life and favor and Your providence has preserved my spirit"—Job 10:12.

Like Ezekiel's dry bones, these are but dead bodies even when they have all their parts — God still must give life and preserve it. The letter of the Hebrew here is, *"You have fitted me out for life and favor."* The soul is the ornament of the body, life is the luster of the clay. The frame of the body is an exquisite frame, but the frame, faculties, powers, actings and motions of the soul are far more to be admired. The inhabitant is more noble than the house, the jewel is more to be desired than the cabinet it is in.

"You have granted me life"—Life is here put for the soul, of which it is an effect. We translate the singular number, but the Hebrew is plural, *"You have granted me lives."* But does a man have more lives than one? Some understand Job to be speaking of both the corporal and the spiritual life — as our natural life is the salt of the body to keep it from corrupting, so spiritual life is the salt of the soul to keep it from corrupting.

Others refer the plural *"lives"* to temporal life and eternal life. But lives may be taken also for the great powers of life. Man has but one life, but it consists of three distinct lives, (1) there is a life of vegetation and growth, as in plants; (2) there is a life of sense and motion, as in the beasts, fowls and fishes; (3) there is a life of reason, as in the angels, by which they understand. These three lives are divided among other creatures of God, but they are all brought together and compacted into the life of man.

Observe that life is granted to us, it is a gift of God. From Him we receive life and breath (Acts 17:25), in Him we live and move and have our beings (Acts 17:28), and He is the one who sustains life in us, holding us together, supplying every breath (Col. 1:17). God the Son, the Word, made every being, and not any being that has come into the world has originated by-any other — *"In Him was life, and the life was the light of men,"* the *"Son quickens and makes alive whomever He will."*

"and favor"—The word expresses the purest, sincerest and most tender kindness. It has in it an exuberancy of kindness, such a kindness as breaks all bounds and exceeds even the ordinary laws of love. This favor is thought by some to be that favor which we receive in the womb, the favor to be born, and that of course is a very great favor indeed. But it may refer to the fact that life itself is a favor, for it is fair to interpret it as an adjunct or adverb, showing how the Lord granted life to him. It is a great favor to be given life. A very large catalog of creatures without life could be made. But not only has God given life to man, He has given him the highest degree of life. So valuable is that life that Satan thought he had the advantage when he said, *"all that a man has he will give for his life."* All that has life is more valuable than that which does not. A worm is a more noble creature than the sun. A leaf is more excellent than a diamond. A living dog is better than a dead lion. Life is the best of all natural gifts.

By favor may be meant or included also all those things which are made for the comfort and accommodation of life — such things as health, strength, liberty, plenty, education, etc. Then there are spiritual and eternal favors which may be meant by Job also.

"And Your providence has preserved my spirit" —The Hebrew word depicts a visitation from a superior, one who comes to order the lives of inferiors. There may be three things included in this, (1) A visitation for condemnation, for the taking of vengeance on those who have despised warnings and authority; (2) A visitation for correction, for the purpose of laying the rod to those who have transgressed and need instruction and improvement; (3) A visitation of consolation, for the purpose of delivering those who have fallen into some ill bondage, either temporal or spiritual.

There is a providential protection also included in this picture — it was a providential hedge that had kept Satan from getting at Job all those years he enjoyed prosperity. *"has preserved"*—The word means to preserve by strength and by watchfulness.

What God grants, God preserves. It is a part of His grant that He will preserve. If it were otherwise, the greatest mercies granted to us would leak out the bottom of our sinful selves, for the erosions of sin have left even the best of us full of holes big enough for us to lose all our graces in a fleeting instant of time. God's creation was followed by His providence — Providence is continued creation. And though we long ago lost all right to His protection, He still encourages us to trust in Him to preserve us, *"The Lord is your keeper...The Lord shall keep you from all evil. He shall keep your soul. The Lord shall keep your going out and your coming in, from this time forth, and even forevermore"* (Ps. 121:5,7,8).

Not only our being depends upon God, who preserves life in us moment by moment, but our well-being also hangs suspended upon Him entirely. None can be consoled, cheered, encouraged, lively, hopeful, living, kind, gentle, joyful, etc. except He work it in them.

"Do not be anxious in anything, but in everything by prayer and supplication let your requests be known to God" —Job 10:13.

Some read the first clause as an interrogation, *"And have You hidden these things in Your heart?"* The heart of God is the will, purpose or decree of God.

What things? (1) Some say that the antecedent is Job's afflictions — God has hidden in His heart the afflictions which He now is laying on Job, from all eternity. Even while great favor and lovingkindness was being shown to him, these were hidden away for him. (2) Others say that these things are life, mercy, favor and providential care. Then it would be as if Job said, 'This long list of blessings which I have mentioned, these tremendous privileges which I have counted up, have been hidden in your heart always — You have had gracious intentions toward me while You have been beating me with Your rod.'

"I know that this is with You"—That is, You remember all of this and have Your record of everything.

Those who make the antecedent to be Job's afflictions are divided, (1) into those who make out a harsh and unbecoming sense, as if Job had said,'I now see that You have had coals of anger raked up in the ashes even while those warm beams of love shone upon me; You held out mercy in Your hand, but something else lay in Your heart.' (2) Those who simply want to keep to the forefront God's sovereign decrees, which would include these which brought severe afflictions upon Job.

As to that harsh interpretation, it is most unworthy of God, it displays an ignorance of His Person and of His dealings with men. Men will wickedly pretend to bless while they hold back plans to blast, but God is not a man that He should do wickedly. Do not allow yourself to believe that God speaks good to those toward whom He intends evil. This is not to say that there are not outward day-to day bequeaths to wicked men, which they misread and call grace (whereas it is not grace or favor which God grants to them, but only common mercy). God does not tell them that He favors them, they merely presume it. Instead God is plain and clear in His message to them in His work, *"Woe to the wicked, It shall go evil with him, for the reward of his hands shall be given to him"* (Isa. 3:11).

It is true, gloriously true, that even while God is ladling out blessed experiences which will leave precious memories He is also treasuring in His heart the forthcoming fulfillment of His decree to splash our lives with afflictions. It is true and it is glorious because it is proof that He loves us, *"If you endure chastening, God deals with you as with sons...But if you are without chastisement, of which all are partakers, then you are bastards and not sons"* (Heb. 12:7,8);

As to the interpretation that Job is speaking of the mercies and favors mentioned in the preceding verses, it appears to be the best interpretation of this place. For then the words will import two things, (1) They would be an argument to move the Lord not to destroy Job, and to assure him that He would not do so. It would be as if he had said, 'Lord, I know that You remember all, and that You know what You have done for me, what it has cost You to make me and then to preserve me — surely, then, You will not pull all of this down in a moment;' (2) The words may import that the Lord in afflicting Job had used only a kind of sacred magic — a magician acts as if he is not even thinking of the thing that He will suddenly do before all — God does not pretend, of course, but He is so far removed from our thinking processes, that when we assume He is doing one thing, He is actually oftentimes doing another, and it suddenly dawns on us that He has been preparing a blessing for us which can hardly be taken in by gross hearts like ours. Job may then be saying to Him,'Lord, I know that You bear favor and good will towards me still. The proof of Your love is not extinct, only covered. You seem to my affliction-dimmed eyes to be an enemy to me at times, but You are my friend — I know that You are my friend! You are drawing clouds between me and the light of Your face, so that dark shadows pass through me and chill me, but I know that Your face is still as full of light toward me as ever. Though I now see nothing but sorrows on every side, yet I know that mercies are hidden in Your heart for me.' These words are an assertion of Job's faith and assurance. He believes sincerely that God loves him, even while His chastenings are becoming heavier and heavier, so heavy that he gasps out bitter complaints which he later wished he could call back.

There is an assumption among men that faith is at its strongest, that the sight of God is at its clearest, when there are no afflictions and discomforts in their lives. Nothing could be further from the truth, as it is written down for us in God's word. Look at that catalog of the faithful in Hebrews 11. When was it that their faith was the strongest? It was when the world was at its bleakest for them, when they were under the sentence of death, faced with hordes of implacable enemies, blinded, tortured, sawn asunder, beaten with cruel whips, etc. Faith does not grow well in the tempid water of prosperity, but it thrives in the chill winds and icy waters of affliction. And when was it that the saints in the Scriptures saw God? Since He is seen by the eye of faith, and since faith is strongest when peril is strong, then they have seen God clearest and best when they were hard put to maintain life and limb!

Job is sliding down toward his lowest level of spiritual activity — he is soon to start his rise toward a faith so strong that it needs nothing but God to convince it that all is well. Satan may still maintain some hope at this point, but the time is now near when he will desperately turn the screws in the hopes of crushing him before his faith gives him the victory. But first we must hear some more bitter complaints from his quivering lips.

"If I sin, then You fix me in Your eye, and You will not acquit me from my iniquity"—Job 10:14.

It is very difficult to connect these words with the former verses, therefore there are a number of conjectures about it. (1) Some say the connection is with the last verse, *"I know this is with You,"* and then these verses explain what it is that he knows is with God, *"If I sin, then You fix me in Your eye,"* etc. (2) Others connect them with the twelfth verse, *"You have granted me life and favor... yet if I sin, then you fix me in Your eye,"* etc. (3) Another goes higher and makes the words depend on the third verse, where Job's last question was, *"Is it good that You should...shine on the wisdom of the wicked?"* And now he adds to that, *"If I sin, then You fix me in Your eye"* etc. Then it would be as if he had said, *"Though You have been pleased to make so many grants of favor to me, all of which were hidden in Your heart so long, yet I know that You will not bear with me if I sin, You will not connive with me in sin. You have not given me all these mercies so that I might grow bold and transgress the rule of Your justice."*

All of these connections give us a good sense.

"If I sin," —Sin is here put in opposition to wickedness, for he goes on in the next verse to say, *" If I am wicked,"* etc. Sin is any transgression against or deviation from the law of God. However small may be the difference in my path and the path marked out for me, it is sin.

"then You fix me in Your eye"—The original has four significations in it, all of them giving us a diversity of interpretations:

1. The word *shamar* has been translated by many words, the major ones being, to keep, to observe, to preserve, to watch, to mark. The basic meaning of the word is this, to watch and to observe so as to keep or preserve that which is being watched. Taking the meaning here as, to keep, or to preserve, then Job's meaning is this, 'When in former times I have sinned, You were pleased to hold back Your severity and instead dealt gently with me. You spared me as a father spares a son that serves him. Then why is the tenor of Your dispensations so much changed from what it was, since You are a God that changes not, and I am no different, I am still a weak, changable and sinful man? If I sin, I know that You will preserve me.'

2. In the sense of the word, to keep, Job is saying, I have maintained such a strict watch over my own heart that I have prevented myself from falling to that sin which I was most subject to commit, then, *"If I am ready to sin, You keep me back from it,"* and that is why I do not understand why You *"will not acquit me from my iniquity."* He knows that he sins, that he has sinned, but he cannot understand why he is being dealt with as if he were a wicked man. It is a valid argument, that if God is pleased to hold us back from sin, then He may very well hold Himself back from destroying us when we sin. This is not to say that those who storm and pout and murmur when they are stopped from sinning will find that God has a mind to spare them, simply because He has stopped them. The restraint of the wicked is a very necessary part of the preservation of the godly. Many are so ungodly that they do not know they have been kept back from sins so heinous that they would vomit if someone told them they were about to do them, as Hazael, who said, *"Am I a dog, that I should do such a thing?"* Yet he did it that next day. These cannot say to God, You have kept us back from such a sin, for they do not even know He did it.

It is the part of grace to rejoice when it finds that God has stopped fleshly lusts from pouring out their corruptions in a godly man's life. Such a man will not go on through the years wickedly remembering what a pleasant life he might have had if God had not stopped him – that is the way the wicked think and remember.

3. When the word is considered in its meaning of keeping safe, or to imprison, then it may well be a sad assertion, *"If I have sinned, You will imprison me and not acquit me from my iniquity."* Certainly, even the best and dearest of God's servants must expect to be shut up and held close until they have repented of their loose behavior. The grace of God will not stand for wantonness, and any David who will take liberties of this sort must expect to not only smart and burn for it, he must expect to be shut up into the prison-house of mourning until he discovers the depths of what he has done.

4. If the meaning accepted is that of observing closely, to fix in a critical and watchful eye, then it will assume somewhat the same meaning as Ps. 130:3, *"If You, Lord, should mark iniquities, who could stand?"* Does the Lord not mark iniquity? Does He not take notice of every sin, especially those committed by His own children? Yes, but when He marks the sin of the faithful, it is not marked down for the purpose of condemnation – it is not that they shall receive greater punishment for the degree of each sin, as it is with the wicked. Job later says, *"For now You number my steps. Do You not watch over my sin?"* (14:6). He does not mean the steps of his outward man, but the steps of his inward man. There is an acting of the soul, as well as of the body. It is God carefully watching over us, keeping us back from committing all the sins that spring up into our minds and out of our hearts, that is our hope of being made fit for the Master's use. Even we can be taught to recognize a lust when it first pecks its way out of the shell of the old man, and if we are given grace to deal with it, we will lop off its head before it becomes enflamed. God sees them before they ever form, before we are formed, in fact. It is His help that we must seek if we are to be preserved from iniquity. If He watches, then shall we not ask Him for a report and His assistance in dealing with those sins which He sees on our horizon? Let us be glad that He fixes us in His eye.

"And You will not acquit me from my iniquity"—If He will not acquit us, why do we have the gospel? Does not the power of Christ's blood cleanse us from all iniquity? The words may be interpreted in three ways, (1) That Job speaks from his unbelief, as if he could not see pardon through the thick cloud of his troubles; as if he could have no evidence that God had mercy in store for him while he endured such plentiful miseries. (2) That he speaks upon a supposition of impenitency, as if he had said, *"If I sin and do not humble myself, then You will not acquit me"* etc. (3) That by iniquity he means his affliction, putting the cause for the effect, so that he is saying, 'You will not take away these afflictions, which are counted as the issue of my iniquity.'

Sin is certainly a debt. If we expect acquital, then we must suppose that we have an obligation. All men as creatures owe a debt of duty to God, and if they fail for even a second to give Him that which is due, then they are sinners and must expect a penalty.

By God's grace, sin may be pardoned. And when it is pardoned, the sinner is acquitted, his debt is taken off and his bonds and penalty are canceled. There can be no further prosecution against a man for any sin that has been once pardoned.

The word which we translated *"acquit"* also bears the meaning of cleansing and purging. Sin defiles the soul, but pardon cleanses it. David prayed that God would purge him, saying, *"Purge me with hyssop and I shall be clean; wash me and I shall be whiter than snow"*(Ps. 51:7). We shall be acquitted, cleansed, and purged if we confess our son, *"If we confess our sins, He is faithful and just to forgive us our sins and to cleanse us from all unrighteousness,"* (1 John 1:9).

While sin remains unpardoned, the soul cannot see any way to get out of its sorrows. The removing of affliction is a sign that sin is forgiven, and the sense of our forgiveness is an argument that affliction shall be removed. On the other hand, a sinner who persists in his sin is an unpardoned sinner – his afflictions shall remain and shall grow, or else they shall be removed and he will grow presumptuous and more ungodly. There is no promise which does not either offer repentance or require repentance. The gospel not only says, *"Believe, and you shall be saved,"* but also *"Repent, and you shall be saved"*–for repentance is the other side of the God-minted coin of faith. It is true that some who are going on in their sins regardless of God are overtaken by grace, but it is not true that grace is promised to any who are determined to go on in their sins. Any man who claims the promises of God must be ready to repent before he lays his hands or heart upon them. However, a sinner is not pardoned for his repentance, it is simply that he cannot be pardoned without it – it is an indispensable means ordained by God.

"If I am wicked, woe to me. And if I am righteous, I will not lift up my head being filled with shame, and looking upon my affliction"–Job 10:15.

In the seventh verse, a large discourse on the differences between the wicked and the righteous was given.

"woe to me"–The word, according to one of the Jewish writers, comes from a root which means to howl (Isa. 13:6; 23:1, etc.). Wicked men howl rather than pray in their distress, because of their extreme worldly woe, *"they have not cried to Me with their hearts when they howled upon their beds"* (Hosea 7:14).

There are legal woes and there are evangelical woes. The law cries, woe! And the gospel also cries, woe! Gospel woes are by far the worst of the two. For the law may say to us, woe! at the same time the gospel is saying to us, mercy! But if the gospel shall say to us, woe! then where shall the hypocrite find mercy? There is no mercy apart from the gospel of Jesus Christ. All kinds of woes may be understood in this place.

Woe is the portion of wicked men. They may laugh, but they shall have woe – the more they laugh, the more misery they shall have. Those who mourn and weep now may be delivered from misery in the life to come, but those who laugh now shall mourn and weep forever (Luke 6:25). Wicked men believe that they can be merry now and have mercy later. They flatter themselves, thinking they are such precious beings that God surely will recognize that they are deserving of special treatment – but their *"iniquity shall be found to be grateful"* (Ps. 36:2). God will not flatter them. Their own consciences will be like a worm that will not die, eating away at them all the while they burn in hell.

Note that a godly man like Job can say, *"If I am wicked, woe to me,"* The Holy Spirit does not hold back from telling the godly, *"If you live according to the flesh, you shall die"* (Rom. 8:13). Let no man promise himself, or others, that they can live according to the flesh and be without the severest of penalties. It is a perversion of the gospel to make it good news to those who presumptuously sin because they presume they are Christ's. It is not the mind of Christ, and no godly man should think it, that we should do evil so that good may come. Let him who claims he is godly read the Scriptures, they shall find a great many threatenings, many terrors promised, to those who persist in pleasing themselves instead of obeying God. But they shall not find one encouragement to sin. If a man promises himself pardon and mercy while he sins, then that man has good reason to doubt that he is in the faith – for it is not a part of faith to presume pardon for persistent sinners. Faith must have a Scripture to hang upon, and there is no Scripture for such a case.

"If I am righteous, I will not lift up my head"–These are in opposition to the foregoing words. Both the persons and the states are opposite, for there are wicked and righteous persons – they cannot be the same. Then there are two states, there is woe, and there is lifting up the head – they cannot be the same either.

Some say that this is a dilemma, or a double argument, by which Job would aggravate the greatness of his affliction. In which case he would be saying, 'Whatever way I look, my case is very sad, for if I am wicked, then woe to me! And if I am righteous, yet I am full of sorrows to the extent that I cannot hold up my head.' However, it rather appears that the latter part of this verse is a picture of Job's humility, not his distress.

"If I am righteous" —It is not that he doubts whether he is righteous or not, for he has many times shown us his assurance that he is righteous already. But he puts the best of his case to show how low he was in his own thoughts even when he was at his best. There is a twofold righteousness, that of justification, and that of sanctification. His meaning is this, *"Suppose I am righteous, as I have said I am, and as God has testified of me, still I cannot lift up my head − or, still I will not lift up my head."*

"I will not lift up my head"—If the righteous cannot lift up the head, then who can? Is Job not degrading righteousness? To answer, the phrase must be opened wider: To lift up the head of another man would be to advance him, as Pharaoh's butler (Gen. 40:13). In this sense, David calls God the lifter of his head (Ps. 3:3). To lift up the head is also to prevail, to get above pressing evils, and to overcome them. The Lord Jesus is promised that He shall lift up His head, after He has gone though the sorrows which must precede His victory (Ps. 110:7).

Again, there is a twofold lifting up of the head, (1) a lifting up of the head with joy and consolation; (2) a lifting up of the head with pride and ostentation (Luke 21:28; Ps. 83:2). It is this last sense, lifting up the head with pride, that Job intends here. However righteous he is, he cannot lift up his head with pride that he is righteous.

Once more, there is a lifting up of our heads in ourselves, and there is a lifting up of our heads in Christ. Job disclaims that he dare lift up his head in himself, but all along he has assumed that he can lift up his head in Christ. If we humbly trust in Him, thinking the thoughts of free grace, we cannot lift up our heads too high − yet, at the same time, we cannot bow our heads low enough when we think of our own works.

Futhermore, Job means less than he speaks when he says that he will not lift up his head. In Scripture, as in other places, there is sometimes more intended than spoken, and sometimes less than spoken. When it is written, *"Your labor shall not be in vain in the Lord, "* there is a far higher meaning than those words can convey. These words of Job are in a sense far below his expression, for his meaning is, I will humble myself before God, I will not and I dare not pride myself and walk with a stretched out neck because I have been declared righteous by God.

To hang down the head in Scripture is to humble oneself, to be sorrowful. The Jews in their formal mourning would hang down the head. Not to lift up the head would, of course, imply the hanging down of the head. If Job will not lift up his head, he will hang it down in humility and sorrow for sin. There is a predictable and constant equation between holiness and humility − the more holiness, that equal amount of humility on the other side. Humility is a great part of our holiness, and holiness is a great part of our humility. God resists the proud, but He exalts the humble. One goes higher in God's sight by going down as low as one can get.

If, then, the righteous have no right or reason for lifting up their heads, they scarcely being saved (1 Pet. 4:18), then how is it that the wicked presume that they can carry their heads high before God. If a man cannot even be proud of his goodness, then how dare a man be proud of his naughtiness? It is the opposite case, for just as holiness and humility go hand in hand, so ungodliness and pride go hand in hand. Pride is the difference between devils and angels, between a pure Adam and an ungodly man.

"being filled with shame and looking upon my affliction"—Job's spirit was seemingly brimful, he had received so much sorrow and grief, he had been driven to blushing, shame and confusion. The word translated *"shame"* can be translated with not only that word, but with blushing and confusion of face. Blushing puts the face into a flame. Confusion carries with it the burning of the ears, and other marks of shame. It was not the reproach of his friends which caused Job to burn with shame, but the reproach of his

afflictions. His superior-acting friends were dead wrong in making his afflictions to be because of his shameful conduct, but nevertheless there is cause to feel confusion and shame when we are sorely afflicted – though then the shame is for the sins we have committed, and the punishment which we know they deserve. Job is not ashamed before his friends, but before his God.

There is also this to what Job says, which may be the fullest meaning of the words, that he is distracted and confused by his many afflictions – he has come to his wit's end. He is not distressed overmuch by his friends' arguments, he finds answers for them even in the midst of his confused situation. But he is distressed to find out that he cannot explain his afflictions on other grounds, and his black circumstances color his mood on the darker side, so that he is confused and distracted by all of it.

"and looking upon my affliction"–There is a discernment of affliction, and there is a looking upon affliction by God, who then will deliver us from it. God always sees us in affliction – did He not just put us in that position? But He will wait, He will watch, He will appear to be looking away as He tends the fires of affliction to make certain that all our dross is burned out of us before He looks upon our affliction and delivers us. It will do Job no good to look upon his affliction, that will but bring him more blushing and confusion. But when God looks, then he shall be delivered. This he much desires.

The word for affliction here is a word which means primarily a weakness, or a casting down – it is the kind of affliction where we are pressed down and at our strength's end.

Some read it imperatively, *"therefore, see my affliction,"* with the meaning then being, Take notice of my sad condition, for I am full of trouble. When we are buried under the sorest afflictions, then we are most desirous of taking our matters before the Lord, for we want Him to see, to look upon our afflictions.

"For it increases! You hunt me like a fierce lion, and again You show Yourself marvelous upon me" –Job 10:16.

Job grows ever more pathetic in his description of his growing and prevailing sorrows. There is a feeling of passionate grief mixed with fear, and he feels he must roll some of it upon the Lord.

'For it increases' – The word sometimes has a good sense, sometimes an ill sense. In a good sense, it means to be lifted up, to be eminent in excellency. In an ill sense, it means to be lifted up with pride. The Vulgate, as ever willing to put comment for translation, has it, *"For pride, You catch me as a lion."* Another gives a sense near that, *"When it lifts up itself, then You hunt me like a fierce lion."* What lifts up? When my head lifts up, in pride and presumption, then God will start to hunt me down and humble me. Another translates with an interrogation, *"I am full of confusion, see my affliction, can it be lifted up?"* Can a man so full of sorrow and shame and confusion lift up his head?

But the word taken as *"increases"* will refer to his afflictions – they increase and multiply at such a rate that he feels like a man that is being hunted down by a fierce lion. A double exposition can be given:

1. It could be Job speaking his wish or desire, 'I am full of confusion, see my affliction. O that my affliction might increase and that I might be weak enough to see an end to my troubles, for I am still too strong to die.' In which case, it would be akin to those other words, *"O that I might have my request and that God would grant me the thing that I long for"* (6:7,8). But Job has spoken this kind of speech too many times before, it is doubtful that it is the meaning of this text.

2. Rather, let the words be declarative, a manifestation of the greatness of his present afflictions. He sees them increasing by leaps and bounds, getting worse and worse, piling

up in heaps upon him. His affliction is growing proud and is pouncing upon him.

Let no man say when he has experienced greater afflictions than he ever knew existed, There cannot be any more, I have experienced all of them. For there are yet afflictions in God's storehouse that you never heard of, and it may be that you are in line for some or all of them, on top of what you have already experienced. Job's furnace of afflictions has been heated and heated, seven times hotter than any mentioned in the Scriptures, perhaps, yet he says that they are increasing, leaping and darting from every direction. As the Lord punishes some seven times more for their sins. (Lev. 26:24), then may He not also decide that a man needs to have seven times more afflictions applied to his corruption in order to purify him, or seven times more in order to increase his grace that much more?

"You hunt me like a fierce lion" —Similitudes do not prove anything, but they illustrate the truth for our weak understandings, The word may be taken for any fierce, cruel and implacable beast that devours. Some render the *"you"* of our text as his afflictions, then Job has it that his afflictions are hunting him down like a fierce lion. Afflictions can tear and rip, pounce suddenly and destroy, like a wild beast.

The comparison laid between the lion and Job, then it would be, *"You hunt me as if I were a lion."* Many of the anceints held to this view, and the Seventy understood it as, *"I am taken like a lion."* So Job would be saying that he was being treated like a beast that was wild and untamable. Lions are hunted either to be imprisoned for the public eye, or for the purpose of destroying them.

However, the comparison is being made between God and the lion; God, like a lion, is hunting Job down. The Scriptures have much of this type of language, picturing God as afflicting His people under the notion of a lion. So the church complains, *"He was to me like a bear lying in wait, like a lion in secret places"* (Lam. 3:10). To Ephraim He was, *"like a lion, and as a young lion...I will tear and go away"* (Hos. 5:14). Hezekiah speaks the same language, *"that as a lion, so He will break all my bones"* (Isa. 38:13).

"You return and show Yourself wonderful upon me"—The sense is the same in both, noting the continued or repeated acts of his affliction. God may be wonderful or marvelous in a fearsome way, as well as in a joyful way. It is as if Job said, Lord, You no sooner cease but You begin again. You no sooner take Your hand off me than I feel it again. If You give over the chase for a while, You pursue it again with assaults more fierce than ever before. I have storm upon storm, grief upon grief, more here and more there. Always and everywhere I am again afflicted, though I am half-dead with affliction already.'

Dawn follows night, but there are false dawns which we promise ourselves while it is still night. Spring follows winter, but there oftentimes much more winter left when we tell ourselves that spring has come. No one can say when God had put a period to his affliction, but all can remain humbled before Him, trusting Him to do that which is best for them.

"marvelous upon me"—That is, You do not afflict me in an ordinary way. Marvels are not performed every day either for us or upon us. There was not, to our knowledge, ever a man who had been tried and afflicted, pounded and pummeled, so much as Job until his day. It was enough to make one marvel, that God should pour out such hot acids upon a good man, that He should continue to erode him even when it appeared that he was at the vanishing point already. Just as Korah, Dathan and Abiram did not die the common or ordinary death, so Job is not suffering the common, ordinary variety of afflictions. The Corinthians had suffered no temptation but that which is common to man, but it appears that Job has at least far more varieties than any that is common to any one man. In fact, his case is so uncommon that there are many who unbelievingly call the story of Job

fictional, a case where an author thought up all the ills that befall mankind and put them all upon one man. But the fiction is not in the story of Job, the storytellers are those who say that Job's story is fictional.

Needless to say, only God can do marvelous things, If it is a marvel, then God did it. As Job is a wonder to those who look on, so God is a wonder to Job. Is it not a wonder to see the patient God angry, the merciful God severe, the compassionate God inexorable? But Job has good company in being made such a spectacle by the marvel-working God, the apostle also speaks of himself and the other apostles, *"For I think that God has set forth us the apostles last as it were appointed to death — for we have been made a spectacle to the world and to angels and to men."* (1 Cor. 4:9) A great God chooses great people to be great wonders to the world, to angels and to men.

"You renew Your witnesses against me and increase Your anger upon me. Changes and war are against me"—Job 10:17.

He is amplifying what has gone before. His afflictions are pictured as witnesses that tell against him.

"renew"—The Hebrew month began with the new moon — it is the word here for *"re - new."* It signifies a change; God renews His witness, He changes His witnesses.

"Your witnesses"—The Seventy say, *Your examinations,* an allusion to the trial of one who is a malefactor. The judge examines him, and if he does not plainly confess, then his examination is renewed. Job, in this sense, would be saying that new examiners come in with new tactics and new pressures to force him. Translating it as *"witnesses"* leaves the sense the same. More evidence and new witnesses being brought against us, we are more likely to break down. But who or what are these new witnesses? One says that they are devils. Satan accused him at first, now he is sending a legion of his devils to witness against Job. Others, not so bizarre of mind, say that the witnesses are Job's three friends. They are lining up to testify against him, as soon as they are able, and with as much vehemence as they can muster. But most say that these witnesses are his afflictions. New troubles on top of old troubles prove and try us far more than if we were allowed to adjust to the old troubles alone. Just as Naomi claimed that the Lord had testified against her in bringing so many believing afflictions upon her (Ruth 1:21), so Job here and elsewhere. *"You have filled me with wrinkles, which is a witness against me. And rising up against me, leanness bears witness to my face"* (Job 16:8).

Afflictions not only witness that we are weak, that we are sinful, that we are ungodly, that we are ignorant, that we are impatient, etc. But they also witness to us and for us, that we are faithful, patient, sincere, submissive, full of the hope and life which the Holy Spirit sheds abroad in the hearts of His saints. To be free of afflictions may witness just the opposite, that we do not have these graces bubbling in our souls.

Afflictions witness the following against us, or for us:

1. They witness that we have sinned and come short of the glory of God. There is no sorrow where there has been no sin. It may be that our afflictions are not tailored exactly to the measure of our sins, compared to the afflictions and sins of other men, but they all witness to our sins. If God hits us with His rod, His bundle of afflictions on our backs, it is certain that there is foolishness and sin bound up in our hearts which He will purge out of us by beating us.

2. They witness especially that there is pride in our lives . If there were no swellings and putrefying sores of pride, then would God take the lance to us? Does the physician lance a healthy patient? Even Paul could say that God had to take measures to keep pride from rising in him, *"lest I should be exalted above measure...there was given to me a thorn in the flesh"* (2 Cor. 12:7). That thorn in his flesh was to keep pricking open the sores of pride which would well up in him. The thorn in the flesh witnesses to the fact that there was pride. That which is sent to remove an evil reveals that there is an evil to

remove

3. They are witnesses to bring to our remembrance sins which we had forgotten. The memory is much activated by affliction. Then we begin to search the archives of our memories in order to find something which may be causing the afflictions to lay upon us so heavily. See how Joseph's brothers have a restoration of memory when they are thrown into prison, *"We are truly guilty concerning our brother"* etc. (Gen. 42:21). Twenty years could not cause that memory to vanish, but buried as it was, it came forth when affliction bore down upon them.

4. Afflictions witness not only of our sins, but of God, that He has an eye on us, and that He cares for us. He will not let us lack anything we need, even if what we need is an affliction. Love is the basis for chastising a child. The rod is to witness that the loving father is displeased with the child's course of action. Though God has an everlasting love for His children, yet He can be and is displeased with them when they disobey Him. He never corrected one when they had done nothing to provoke Him. The provocation may not be as great as that of another one, and the afflictions may be much greater, but this may be an argument for more love, rather than an unequal treatment. God is not unjust to forget our labor of love, so He is not unjust in remembering our transgressions, nor even if He chastises us far more than others who have transgressed in the same way.

5. Of course everyone knows that the world considers afflictions to be witnesses against the godly. They conclude that we are either hypocrites who only pretend to be godly, or that some great ungodliness has caused us to be so severely afflicted. God's precious gems have always been smeared with this proud brush of the world. It is one of Job's greatest afflictions, that these godly friends, who ought to know God better, are smearing him with the worlds filthy brush. It has ever been so. Did not the high priest cry out against Christ, *"What further need do we have of witnesses. You have heard His blasphemy."* Job's friends did not wait for the verdict of the Judge, they heard the testimony of his afflictions, then tried the case themselves, pronounced him guilty, and now they are insisting that he take his punishment according to their judgment. It is this that causes Job to cry out now to God, *"You renew Your witnesses against me!"*

"and increase Your anger upon me"—The word expresses wrath, displeasure, indignation and hot anger. There is a double increase here, an extensive increase of his afflictions, and an intensive increase of his afflictions. Not only were his afflictions coming in greater number, but they were coming in greater weight and magnitude.

The increase of the idea that God was angry was one of the greatest new afflictions upon him. As the love and smiles of God comfort the saints and give them renewed strength to bear afflictions, so the anger of God discomforts the saints and dissipates their strength to bear them. Nebuchadnezzar's seven-times-hotter furnace did not dismay the Hebrew children so long as the Son of God would meet with them there. But let it be known that an angry Father will meet with us in the midst of our afflictions, and we will be cast down exceedingly.

"changes and army after army are against me" new ones and old ones, are like armies flooding in upon him — he had no sooner warded off one than another came pouring upon him, each one leaving their grievous wounds. The changes indicate a cutting off, a destruction, and the army indicate a warfare that has been declared against him. For Job, it is certain, there is a warfare on earth.

"Why then have You brought me forth out of the womb? O that I had given up the spirit and no eye had seen me!" —Job 10:18.

The following verses conclude Job's reply to Bildad, in which there are four remarkable things: (1) He complains that he ever lived a day; (2) He wishes that he had died speedily, (3) He could not have those options, but he notes that he will not live long, in any case, (4) He asks that those few days might be good days.

He returns to a theme which he worked hard in the third chapter. He wishes that he had never been born, that he had been strangled as he came from the womb. He exceeds his place again, for he ought not to cry out to God, *"Why have You brought me forth out of the womb."* Who is he to demand an account from God? There are three sorts of questions, (1) Those that come from a desire to have information – these we ask that we may learn; (2) Those that arise from needless curiosity – these we had better not ask at all; and, (3) Those that arise from pure passion, muddled questions which come out of perturbed minds, which do not seek information or even an answer – these are intended to act as a vent to our passions. Of course, it is wrong to ask when we do not care to get an answer. The fumes and vapors of Job's distempered mind have overwhelmed him here, and his troubled complaint takes on the appearance of a wicked man's blasphemy.

All of us are apt to grow angry with the mercies which we have had when God fails to give us the mercies which we desire. David was glad that God took him out of his mother's womb, but Job was unhappy about it at this moment. Another human trait is the desire for death if one cannot have what he desires, such as Rachel saying that if she could not have children, then she wanted to die. So the common expressions, She was dying to get this or that – she wants it bad enough to die for it. Few are willing to go through with it, but many get the idea.

Job, however, may be due a further sense from the word, which will dilute the acidity of his words (we must remember that Job and his friends were completely in the dark as to the benefits of suffering – it is mostly a New Testament revelation). We may charitably suppose that Job was troubled that he was in a condition of life which hindered the main end of his life, the glorifying of God. He has been careful that God should get glory from everything he did, now it appears to him that God is being despised because of what is happening to him – therefore he would rather die than to have it so, and he could wish that he had never been born than to have it so. Just as the apostle could wish that he were accursed that his brothers might be saved, in the same sense, not in actuality a prayer that it should be so, so Job here, that God may have the glory due to His name.

"Oh that I had given up the spirit, and no eye had seen me"—There is a gentle, an easy kind of death pictured here, and Job wishes that he had had such a death. Some connect it with the former, making it to read declaratively, *"Why have You brought me out of the womb? For then I would quickly have given up the spirit."*

"and no eye had seen me" —He wishes that he had died so speedily that no eye would have seen him, except those of his mother and the midwife.

We may see by Job's case here that unreasonable questions are apt to be followed by unreasonable and undue wishes. It was unreasonable to demand God's answer to his former question, and it is unreasonable to wish here that he had speedily died at birth.

Men had rather not be seen at all than to be seen in misery. When afflictions make them miserable, they look for places to hide from the gaze of men. To be seen is the great desire when all is well. To be hidden is the great desire when all is not well. Men have altogether too much regard for the regard of men. Christ gave His marred face to be spit upon and slapped. As servants, let us be willing to be a spectacle of misery, for by it He may get more glory than we can give to him when we are in all our glory.

"I should have been as though I had not been. I would have been carried from the womb to the grave" —Job 10:19.

Some read it as,*"O that I had been as though I had never been."* Job is confirming what he had said, further declaring his condition, wishing that he had not seen any of this life. The words are plain and need no exposition more than has been given above and in the third chapter;

"Are not my days few? Cease then and let me alone, that I may take comfort a little"—Job 10:20.

Many translators join the verb cease to days, *"Will not my few days cease?"* Others put the days with the latter part, as follows, *"Will He not leave off a little in my days;"*

Let the first clause be a question, then the next words are an inference or use which he makes from it.

"Are not my days few"—Yes, they are few! There are three senses to be made from this: (1) It is a justification of his former wishes and desires to die — have I not a good reason to wish that I had never lived, since my life is to be so short and troubled anyhow? (2) He could be answering those who objected to his wish that he had not lived, saying, 'I know very well that life is a precious jewel. I know that if I had died when I was born that I would have lost much. But what is the life of a few days compared with the life in eternity that is waiting?' (3) The clearest sense of these words is this, that they are the ground of a petition for the mitigation of his troubles. Then he would be saying, 'Lord, I have but a while to live in this world, my days are few, therefore do not think ill of me if I desire a little comfort and refreshing in these few days that are left to me. O that You would slack Your hand and yield to me some ease and comfort!'

"Are not my days few?"—The Hebrew is, *"Is not fewness of days mine?"*—Yes! Abstracts often increase the sense, but sometimes they diminish it. Here the sense is diminutive. It is as if he had said, 'My days are so far from many, they are fewness itself.'

"cease then and let me alone"—He looks upon himself as one that is beseiged with afflictions. So He is praying God to lift the siege, to draw off His force from him, to make peace, or at least to declare an armistice. Just a little rest, he craves, so that I can bear these burdens. It is an argument to move the Lord to forbear sending any more trials, as well as to take off some that he has. David used the same argument (Ps. 89:47; 39:13).

If the Lord will not withdraw His hand, then nothing in the world can give us ease. If we desire cessation of trouble it is to him that we must address ourselves.

Our days are few, but our sins are many. If we had the years of Methuselah, would we not be crying with Job that our lives might be ended early, lest we continue to multiply these sins over our heads? The more spiritual a man becomes, the more educated he is in spiritual matters, and he learns to discern, then to count his sins. O what a swarm of uncounted sins are in the most of us! Yet when we learn to count them, how weighty they become!

"That I may take a little comfort"—The word which we translated to take comfort is one which means such comfort as comes on the heels of extreme discomfort, as if one were to come out of extreme heat with a gasping thirst and find a fountain of sweet waters to drink from, Or, another translation reads, not improperly, *"Set me alone that I may mourn a little."* There are times when moderate mourning serves to revive the mind.

But rather, take it in the general meaning, Job asks that he be let alone long enough to comfort himself, so that his sorrows might abate just a little. If he could but rally and recollect his scattered thoughts a while, he thinks that he might achieve a sweetness of mind again before he dies. From which it may be observed that man desires his own good, he is not satisfied with being, he must have also well-being. It is also observable that though he had great suffering, Job asked only a modest amount of comfort, They who are low make low demands. Those who are swimming in rivers of pleasure, who enjoy much comfort of the body, shall they not magnify their blessings by remembering the mighty God and Master who gave them?

We see again that Job is in earnest, he is convinced that he has but few days to live, and he desires to get into a frame of mind which is commensurate with the profession of faith which he had made and lived.

"before I go where I shall not return, even to the land of darkness and the shadow of death"—Job 10:21.

Death is a going out of the world. Christ intimates His death under this same notion of going, *"If I go, the Comforter will come"* (16:7). Dying is a journey, going from one region to another. In death we change our place, but, alas! for those who go to hell, there is no change of company.

"where I shall not return"—In our earthly journeys, we are pleased much with the thought that we shall return to our homes again. But when we die, we take a journey from which there is no returning. Death is an everlasting departure, we shall never return to this life or to this world after we die. Job believed in a resurrection, a returning from the grave by the power of God, and he knew there was no returning by the power of nature or by the help of any creature. However, when God returns us to earth, it will be the new earth which He will create for the resurrected saints. It will be a happy, blessed earth which we inhabit then, there shall be no tears, no sin, no sorrow. For those who have no better place than this world to go to, there is sadness in thinking of a departure from this world. The saints arm themselves against death with this argument from God's word, *"We know that if our earthly house of this tabernacle was dissolved, we have a building from God, a house not made with hands, eternal in the heavens"* (2 Cor. 5:1). Death can have no victory except over those who put their trust in the false or unfaithful mammon of this world.

"even to the land of darkness and the shadow of death"—It is Job's description of the grave. This is the place where death dwells, a place that defies the imagination of poets and the rhetoric of orators. The Spirit of God rises to the height of eloquence in exposing for us that unpleasant region – it is a land of darkness – it is a land of the shadow of death. It is not an ordinary darkness, but a darkness of the deepest blackness. Likewise, it is not an ordinary shadow of death, but the shadow of death in its most fearsome aspect.

"the land of darkness"—a land that abounds with darkness, a land where darkness is the staple, the only commodity to be had. Darkness is the hangings and the decorations of the house of death. The grave is a *"land of forgetfulness,"* because there all things are forgotten. A land of peace is a land where all is peaceful. So a land of darkness is a land where all is darkness. The description has meaning for us only because there is a natural fear in man in regard to the unknown, which carries over into darkness. Joy is thought of in terms of light, but sorrow in terms of darkness. Darkness is always afflictive, whether it is natural or spiritual. Death is black and grim, only hell shall be more dark than the grave – and the pains of hell are chains of darkness.

"and of the shadow of death "—There is more than the shadow of death in the grave, for death itself dwells there. The words sound as if they would diminish the sense of fear in death, but instead they heighten it. The shadow of death implies thick darkness, the very strength of darkness.

"a land of thick darkness, as darkness itself, a land of the shadow of death, without any order, and where the light is as darkness"—Job 10:22.

Job doubles it for emphasis, adding more descriptive words to what he had said just before.

"as darkness itself"—The word carries with it the meaning of weariness, restlessness and vexation of spirit. To be in a dark condition, to be restless and tormented, in a land of misery, is the utmost opposite to what a man desires. Some darkness has a degree of light mingled with it, but that described here is unmixed darkness, darkness itself. Just as sinful sin is the height of sin (Rom. 7:13), so dark darkness is the height of darkness.

"a land of the shadow of death, without any order"—The lack of order in the grave, or in the state of death, may be understood in two ways, (1) It is without order because it has no changes, no ups and downs, no night and day, winter and summer, etc.; (2) There is no order in going to the grave. Men do not keep to a rule in dying. The old go, but not always before the young. The great ones go, oftentimes first before those of low degree. Death has no master of ceremonies who begins at the least esteemed and works upward. Once there, the grave mingles the dust and bones of one with another. The rich man's dust cannot be distinguished from the dust of the poor – through they may be buried in eminent places and marked under stately monuments, yet their bones do not differ from any other bones around them.

Order has an excellency, there is a beauty in it. The less order there is in a place, the worse it is. Where there is no order, it is the worst place of all to be. It is a kind of death to see any disorder, and a very hell to see all in disorder.

"And where the light is as darkness"—There are some who translate differently, by the verb, *"where it shines like darkness"* And again the Vulgate lays down a paraphrase instead of a translation, *"where there is everlasting horror."* Job said before that it was a land of darkness, a darkness like darkness itself. Yet now he seems to say that there is light in the grave. But his meaning is this, that even that which looks light in the grave is in fact darkness. When the apostle would invincibly argue the infinite wisdom and strength of God, he says, *"the foolishness of God is wiser than men and the weakness of God is stronger than men"* (1 Cor. 1:25). If God is the only wise One and the only strong One, then how can the apostle speak of the foolishness or weakness of God? His meaning is this, that however an act of God appears to man, perhaps he thinks it is foolish or weak, even that act is wiser and/or stronger than whatever wisdom or strength a man may credit to himself or to other men. Job is using this kind of comparison. Even if one were to think there were some bit of light in the grave, that very light would be darkness. It falls in with the statement of the Lord Jesus, *"If, then, the light that is in you is darkness, how great it that darkness!"* (Matt. 6:23).

There are some who understand Job to be describing hell, rather than the grave. The same original word is translated either hell or the grave. Death looks like hell and bears much of its image. Hell is a continued death, being an eternal separation from God. The miserable unbeliever in hell dies continually. The darkness of the grave becomes such a darkness as cannot be described, it must be experienced before one can know what utter darkness it is. Whatever Job says of the grave could be said of hell, only it would be greatly multiplied. But Job is not talking of hell, for he has not such a future awaiting him—he will be going to the grave, but never to hell, for he has nothing to suffer beyond the grave

Death in itself is not in any way desirable. There is no beauty in death, in darkness, in a place where there is no order, in a place where there is no light. Let those who know the Lord Jesus Christ lift up their hearts in thankfulness that He has taken the sting out of death, He has robbed it of its victory over all those who are at one with Him. He has stripped death of all its terror, He has turned what would have been a door into the grave so that it is now to us a door into His bosom. He first entered that dark region Himself, and there He left some beams of light by which we may see Him as we journey through the land of darkness, that land of the shadow of death, on into the land of joy and peace and bliss forevermore.

Job now ends his answer to Bildad, and his complaints to God, having made good answers to the one and ill complaints to the other. God still has him under much darkness, and he is still beset with many disorders of the spirit. His afflictions continue to accelerate and his weaknesses of the flesh grow more and more evident. Yet in all this any honest observer must admit that Job's graces break through many, many times, shining like the jewels of God that they are. None can say that there are no evidences of corruption, but much less could any say that Job did not show the strongest and most glorifying evidence of faith that could possibly be given to us. Make a comparison, as an example, of the words and actions of Job and those of each of his three friends: Job's faith grows stronger by leaps and bounds, and his corruption grows weaker and weaker; whereas there is such a fleshy outbreak of unwarranted and obviously biased charges flowing from the three friends that one must wonder if they are men of faith themselves. If the reader is inclined to side with Job's friends, it would be best to immediately turn to chapter forty-two and see how God sees these charges and countercharges.

END OF VOLUME I OF THIS EDITION
(Volumes I, II and III of Caryl's exposition)